A Modern
Philosophy of Religion

A MODERN PHILOSOPHY OF RELIGION

by

SAMUEL M. THOMPSON

PROFESSOR OF PHILOSOPHY
MONMOUTH COLLEGE

HENRY REGNERY COMPANY
Chicago *1955*

Copyright 1955 by HENRY REGNERY COMPANY, Chicago, Illinois. Copyright under International Copyright Union. Manufactured in the United States of America.

To
GRACE

PREFACE

THERE are a number of different approaches to the philosophy of religion. One approach is to compare different philosophies. Another is to explore various attempts which have been made to solve the important problems. Each of these approaches has its merits, but they both seem to me to suffer from a serious handicap: instead of leading the reader into philosophy they only tell him about it.

This book is written in the conviction that the most effective approach to philosophy is not to collect information about philosophers and their philosophies but to participate actively in the process of philosophical reflection and inquiry. So this is *a* philosophy of religion, not *the* philosophy of religion. My aim is not to explore various philosophies of religion, or to provide a guidebook to the maze of religious thought, but to lead the reader through the development of a positive argument.

So I make no apology for my support of a definite point of view in this book. No book of philosophy can avoid commitment; only a book about philosophy, which is not itself a search for true answers to philosophy's questions, can be neutral. Nor do I make any apology for the fact that the position I take is theism; for theism is not the unacknowledged premise of the argument but, so far as the argument is sound, the conclusion required by the facts.

This is a *philosophy* of religion. It is not theology, save in the sense of what once was called natural theology, nor is it apologetics. My concern here with religion is precisely the concern a philosophy of art has with art, a philosophy of history with history, a philosophy of science with science. My purpose is to try to understand religion, to evaluate it as a source of insight into real existence, and to discover some of its important implications both for philosophy and for life. I believe that a philosophy of religion, to the extent that it is true, is a contribution to religion, for I am

vii

persuaded that any significant religious experience and faith will be enriched and deepened by whatever the understanding can contribute. But a philosophy of religion is primarily a contribution to philosophy. Modern philosophy's neglect of religion is a scandal, as is its neglect of art; and in its neglect it may have missed a most significant avenue to truth.

This is a *modern* philosophy of religion. By this I mean first that it is thought out and formulated in the context of modern knowledge, with no concessions to the obscurantism which so often clouds the thinking of those who try to defend and justify an affirmative religious interpretation of life and existence. Although the position developed here has close affiliations with the oldest philosophical tradition of Western thought, with what has been called so aptly the perennial philosophy, yet this is not a return to the past; it is rather an attempt to recognize and appropriate to our modern needs the continuity of past and present.

One of the significant intellectual developments since the war is a new appreciation of the wisdom embedded in our own long tradition. Nineteenth century positivism and nihilism tried their best to cut the present loose from the past, but it is more and more evident that these anti-intellectual movements succeeded only in poisoning the wells of knowledge and understanding. Much of today's most vigorous intellectual activity is in its attempt to restore access to the sources of our civilization's intellectual and spiritual power.

Our generation has chosen to learn its philosophy the hard way, and the lesson is indeed dear. The first world war saw the collapse of the moral structure of Western culture. There was never a time, of course, when men did not lie and cheat and sell their honor for immediate gain. But in our century men of high position and responsibility have embraced dishonor shamelessly and by deliberate choice. The first world war's public parades of calculated preference for evil prepared the way—leading through the glib inanities of the twenties and the grim insanities of the thirties—for the most terrible and inhuman of all the campaigns of slaughter in man's history. If it seems too much to attribute to nineteenth century anti-intellectualism and nihilism some responsibility for this debacle, let us ask ourselves how men willingly can abandon conscience and honor unless they doubt that there is any real difference between the true and the false and between good and evil. The very corruption of the words "idealism" and "realism" in the popular usage of our day is eloquent testimony to the disastrous effects of the anti-philosophy of the past century.

It is time to recover our heritage. We cannot go back to the past, and would not wish to if we could. (Perhaps the one solid benefit from nihilism's scourge has been to expose and destroy the pretense with which earlier generations so often tried to support their intellectual and spiritual affirmations.) We can, however, re-discover truth once lost, and restate it for our own time and its needs. There are signs of powerful currents moving in that direction, and it is in its cooperation with that movement that this is a modern philosophy of religion.

This is a modern philosophy of religion also in the sense that it takes account of the implications of the twentieth century revolution in physical science. Recent advances in physics have freed that science from the false metaphysical absolutes it had carried on its back since Newton. For the first time since its birth modern physics has become aware of its limitations; and it is finding that its power as a science comes by virtue of those limitations, not in spite of them.

Physics has handed metaphysics back to philosophy, and has come to recognize its own proper role as the study of the basic structures of matter and energy. It no longer tries to specify what are the real and ultimate qualities of things in nature; it concerns itself rather with their dynamic patterns. Cut loose from metaphysics, physics is at last able to develop its abstractions freely, to the limits permitted by its mathematical instruments, with no self-imposed metaphysical limitations to block inquiry away from new and unconventional hypotheses. Once we understand that physics does not define reality we realize that it leaves room for any positive metaphysics not in conflict with physics' own presuppositions. The proper influence of physics on metaphysics is not positive but negative; it does not prescribe what metaphysics shall find, but merely proscribes what is inconsistent with its own possibility.

I am deeply indebted to Mr. Sidney R. Gair, College Editor of Henry Regnery Company, for his countless helpful suggestions, his sustaining encouragement, and his searching criticisms. I am grateful for the time and effort given for friendship's sake by Professor W. E. Schlaretzki and Professor Charles J. Speel II, who read parts of the manuscript and saved me from many errors and the reader from much misunderstanding. I wish also to thank the many publishers and copyright owners who have given permission for the use of quotations. Specific acknowledgment is made in each instance in the notes to the text.

S. M. T.

Monmouth
October 26, 1954

CONTENTS

CHAPTER   PAGE

PREFACE vii

Part One. Religion and Philosophy

1. RELIGION 3
   Why Concern Ourselves with Religion? 3
   What Is Religion? 5
   Can an Atheist Be Religious? 12
   Higher and Lower Religions 16
   True and False Religions 19
2. THE PHILOSOPHY OF RELIGION 24
   Can Religion Establish Its Own Truth? 24
   Can Theology Establish the Truth of Religion? . 27
   The Unique Position of Philosophy as a Mode
      of Inquiry 31
   The Aim of a Philosophy of Religion 35
   The Difference between Philosophy and Religion . 38

Part Two. Faith and Knowledge

3. SENSORY KNOWLEDGE 43
   Belief and Knowledge 43
   The Burden of Proof 48
   The Foundations of Knowledge:
      1. Sense Perception 50
   Sense Perception and Modern Science 55
4. RATIONAL KNOWLEDGE 61
   The Foundations of Knowledge:
      2. Rational Insight 61

xi

CHAPTER   PAGE

    The Relation of Sensory and Rational Knowledge   67
    The Foundations of Knowledge:
        3. Practical Reason   69
5. FAITH AND KNOWLEDGE   73
    Belief and Faith   73
    Knowledge and Faith in Separation   76
    Faith beyond Knowledge   79
    The Guidance of Faith   85

Part Three. Truth

6. THE NATURE OF TRUTH   89
    Religion and the Problem of Truth   89
    The Distinction between True and False . . .   93
    Difference without Conflict   96
    The Whole Truth and All the Truth   98
7. PERSPECTIVES AND DIMENSIONS OF TRUTH   102
    Perspectives of Truth   102
    Appearance and Reality   105
    Two Dimensions of Truth   107
    Essential Truth   109
    Existential Truth   109
    The Extension, Supposition, and Designation
        of Terms   110
    The Priority of Existential Truth   114
8. RELIGIOUS TRUTH   118
    Philosophy's Concern with Religious Truth . .   118
    Religious Truth   121
    Religious and Aesthetic Truth   128
    What Does Religion Tell Us?   130
    Who Is to Judge?   133
9. THE TEST OF RELIGIOUS TRUTH   137
    Religion's Own Test of Truth   137
    The Special Problem of Religious Truth . . .   140

CHAPTER   PAGE

    The Rational Test of Religious Truth 145
    Radical Doubt 150

Part Four. *The Nature of Man*

10. TRADITIONAL AND MODERN IDEAS OF MAN 157
    Traditional and Modern Ideas of Man 157
    The Religious and the Secular 158
    The Conflict between Traditional and Modern
      Ideas of Man 164
    Weakness of the Traditional View of Man . . . 167
    Weakness of the Modern View of Man 170
11. MAN'S EXISTENCE 175
    Man's Dual Existence 175
    Man's Freedom 178
    The Distinction of Occasion from Cause . . . 181
    How Can Man Discover Himself? 185
12. MAN AS PERSON 190
    The Discovery of Man as Person 190
    The Moral Nature of Man 196
    A Religious Answer to the Problem of Man . . 200
    The Dependence of Faith on Knowledge . . . 207

Part Five. *The Idea of God*

13. THE IDEA OF GOD AND NATURALISM 211
    What We Mean by God 211
    Man's Need of the Idea of God 212
    Intelligibility and Unity 216
    Naturalism 219
14. PANTHEISM 227
    The Ambiguity of Pantheism 227
    The Argument for Acosmic Pantheism 231
    The Destruction of Thought 234

CHAPTER		PAGE
	The Dilemma of Pantheism	235
	Monism's Fallacy	237
15.	DEISM AND THEISM	241
	"Rationalistic" Deism	241
	Anti-Rationalistic Deism	244
	The Relation of Theism to Pantheism and Deism	247
	Theism and the Analogy of Being	251
	The Opposition of Theism and Naturalism	253

Part Six. The Existence of God

16.	PROOF IN PHILOSOPHY	257
	A Look Ahead	257
	The Nature of Proof	259
	Philosophy and Its Premises	263
	The Method of Dialectic	268
17.	GOD IN IDEA AND IN EXISTENCE	273
	Kinds of Proofs	273
	From the Idea of God to the Existence of God	274
	Concept and Existence	275
	The Failure of the Ontological Argument	278
	From the Existence of the Idea of God to the Existence of God	280
	From the Existence of the World to the Existence of God	284
	The Steps of the Argument	285
18.	THE EXISTENCE OF THE WORLD	287
	Three Ways to Deny the Existence of the World	287
	Acosmism	288
	Subjectivism	290
	The Failure of Subjectivism	293
	Phenomenalism	301
19.	THE CONTINGENCY OF THE WORLD	303
	The Second Step of the Proof	303

CHAPTER   PAGE

   Contingency 305
   The Mark of the Contingent 306
   Everything in Nature Changes 307
   Everything Which Changes Is Contingent . . . 312
   The Contingency of the World as a Whole . . 318
   The Present State of Our Argument 322

20. THE CAUSE OF NATURE 323
   The Next Step of the Argument 323
   The Bridge from the Contingent to the
      Non-Contingent 326
   Two Levels of Causality 326
   Our Knowledge of Causes 328
   Causality and the Natural Sciences 332
   The Self-Existence of the Cause of Nature . . . 334
   The Cause of Nature Not Self-Caused 336

21. THE EXISTENCE OF GOD 341
   The Cause of Nature and Theism 341
   The Unity of God 342
   The Immanence of God 345
   The World Order and Its Contingency 351
   The World Order and Existence 353
   The World Order and Purpose 356

Part Seven. Our Knowledge about God

22. THE LIKENESS OF GOD 361
   The New Phase of Our Argument 361
   The Problem of Our Knowledge about God . . 361
   How We Think Existence 363
   Our Knowledge of Other Selves 368
   How We Can Know the Nature of God . . . 370

23. KNOWLEDGE BY ANALOGY 375
   How We Can Use Concepts to Think about God 375
   The Relation of Concepts and Judgments . . . 376

CHAPTER   PAGE

Univocal, Equivocal, and Analogous Use
   of Concepts 381
Analogy and Similarity 382
Analogy's Presuppositions 385
Negative and Positive Knowledge by Analogy . 389

24. THE REVELATION OF GOD 392
   The Idea of Revelation 392
   Revelation and Reason 394
   Truth in Thought and Truth in Being 398
   Truth as Revelation 400
   Degrees of Revelation 403

25. THE REALITY OF VALUE 411
   Existence and Value 411
   Existence and Time 415
   The Nature of Value 418
   Value and Potentiality 423
   The Standard of Good 425
   The Infinity of God 426
   The Analogy of Perfection 428
   The Moral Argument for the Existence of God . 431

Part Eight. God and the World

26. CREATION AND TIME 435
   The Idea of Creation 435
   Greek and Hebrew Concepts of Creation . . . 437
   Creation *ex nihilo* 439
   Actual and Potential in Creation 442
   One-Way Dependence 445
   Creation and Modern Ideas of Time 448
   Creation and Evolution 451
   Creation and Authorship 452
   God and Time 455

CHAPTER   PAGE

27. HISTORY AND HUMAN DESTINY 460
    What Is History? 460
    The Continuity of History 462
    Does History Have Meaning for Man? 465
    History and Fate 466
    Destiny without Necessity 470
    Destiny with Necessity and Freedom 472
    History and Progress 475
    God's Purpose and Man's Freedom 479
    The Drama of Human History 482

28. THE PROBLEM OF EVIL 488
    The Problem 488
    Does Evil Exist? 488
    How Does Evil Exist? 492
    Natural and Moral Evil 494
    The Inevitability of Evil 497
    Evil and the Infinity of God 498
    Human Freedom and God 501
    Evil and God's Goodness 504
    The Justification of Evil 507

29. HUMAN BLESSEDNESS 515
    The Idea of Immortality 515
    Levels of Life 517
    The Presence of God in Man 523
    The Presence of Man to God 526
    In Conclusion 528

    NOTES 533

    QUESTIONS AND TOPICS FOR STUDY, WITH
    SUGGESTED READINGS 557

    INDEX 593

A Modern
Philosophy of Religion

Part One

RELIGION AND PHILOSOPHY

CHAPTER I

Religion

WHY CONCERN OURSELVES WITH RELIGION?

THERE is a conversation in Disraeli's *Endymion*, in which the following exchange occurs:

" 'As for that,' said Waldershare, 'sensible men are all of the same religion.'

" 'And pray what is that?' inquired the prince.

" 'Sensible men never tell.' "[1]

It is quite possible the reason why some who consider themselves "sensible men" never tell is that they have nothing to tell. There are many who think they cannot be sensible and religious at the same time. They associate religion with emotional extravagance, sentimentality, and superstition; and it is possible for them to find enough of these things in religion to reassure them in their judgment. On the other hand there have been, and are, men of the greatest good sense, neither sentimental nor extravagantly emotional in their attitudes, men who are contemptuous of superstition and who honor human reason and its work, and yet who are most sincerely and deeply religious. It must be that for these men religion does make sense, and important sense.

If religion does not make sense then it is one of the great mysteries of human history that so many men and women of deep wisdom and wide knowledge have been fooled by it. For these, of all people, are those who have the opportunities which knowledge and wisdom provide to uncover the false and the pretentious. It is not hard to see how it is possible for silly and shallow people to make a silly and shallow thing of religion. What would be really hard to understand is how so many wise, cultivated, and critical minds could take religion seriously if it did not, at its best, make very important sense.

The primary purpose of this study is to try to discover what kind of sense religion makes. We wish to find the kind of truth it has, and the import of that truth. We shall look at the basic ideas of religion to see what help they can give us in our attempt to understand man's nature, his world, and his destiny. We wish to find what religion can contribute as a source of insight into the meaning of life and existence.

The method of our study will be an uncompromising acceptance of the absolute validity of reason. No other course is open to us, for if we took any other course it would not be the study of the *philosophy* of religion in which we should now engage. In our dependence on reason, however, we must not for a moment forget reason's limitations. Reason is not itself sufficient for a knowledge of existence. Yet without reason no knowledge is possible, either of what is or of what may be; although reason is not a sufficient means of knowledge it is a necessary one, and nothing can stand against it. It may well be that religion puts us in touch with what our reason cannot comprehend; but our failure to comprehend comes from our own limitations, it is not because anything real is itself irrational. And if religion does provide contact with a reality which our reason does not understand, we may understand perhaps by means of reason how it is possible for religion to bring us into contact with something we do not understand.

This distinction may seem at first a little difficult to grasp but in one form or another it is familiar to us all. I may not know what is in a letter before I open it, but I understand well enough why I do not know. It seems quite reasonable to me that I should not know. I may not understand the chemical structure of a certain substance, but my awareness of my neglect of chemistry makes me understand perfectly why I do not understand. I may find the chemical structure of the material to be a mystery, but there is no mystery about the fact that I find it to be a mystery. If I am sensi-

4

ble and reasonably modest I do not conclude that because I lack this knowledge the science of chemistry is unintelligible.

I could be guilty of no greater presumption than to make my knowledge and what I happen to understand the measure of reason itself; it would be to assume that I myself am the source of reason and of the intelligibility which belongs to things. "The worst snob in the world," Sydney Harris points out, "is the uncultivated man who smugly believes that whatever he does not understand is meaningless, or else he could understand it."[2] Yet it is precisely this fallacy of measuring the reasonable by what one understands which is involved in any attack upon reason and in any attempt to place limits on its validity. It is not reason which errs when we go wrong; it is ourselves who err in our use of reason. Any appeal to the irrational, any attempt to indict existence because of our own ignorance, is something which cuts its own ground from beneath itself. For any claim of truth is a claim of rational truth. Reason may not be able by itself to show us truth but there is no truth which is not rational truth.

What Is Religion?

Religion is one of the more flexible words of our language. Different people use it with different meanings and for different purposes, and the same person often uses it differently on different occasions. Its popular meaning is so loose that few would think of using the word in a serious discussion without trying to specify the meaning intended. So at the beginning of our discussion of religion and the philosophy of religion we shall have to look carefully into the question of what *religion* means.

It may be well first to try to clear up a common misunderstanding. People who seek precision and clarity in their thinking are likely to distrust such words as *religion*. They prefer, so far as possible, to use clearly defined technical terms. The ideal, some of them think, is a separate word for each distinguishable meaning. This, however, has a serious drawback. It ignores the fact that although different meanings may be distinguishable they need not be separate. We may say of a man, for example, that "business is his religion." This use of *religion* is so different from its usual or primary meaning that we recognize the word here to be a metaphor. Yet for the metaphor to be effective there must be some relation between the meaning of the term in this statement and its primary meaning. If we think about what we mean when we say of a man that "business is his religion" we may have some new light on the meaning of *religion.*

The fact is that any word which takes us close to real things and events is almost sure to acquire variations in its meanings. For the things it takes us to are not experienced in isolation; they are experienced in relation to other things, and each different relation may add something new to the sense of the word. A word acquires fixity of meaning only as it becomes a technical or abstract term, only as we learn to think its meaning in isolation from other things. Abstraction is necessary and useful for certain purposes; but abstractions are products of thinking and inquiry, not the material with which thinking begins.

In our attempt to come to some understanding of what we mean by *religion* it may be well to look first at what seems to be common to all its various meanings. In other words, what do we mean by *religion* in its most general sense? If we reflect for a moment we shall see that in its broadest sense *to be religious is to be serious.* This does not mean *serious* in any negative way, such as *unhappy.* It means rather that we have a concern about something, we are not fooling, we are not flippant, we are not jesting. It means, further, a concern with something we consider important; we attend to it because of its importance and we give to it the degree of consideration its importance deserves.

It is difficult to imagine a person who is serious about nothing. We should suspect one who took the trouble to proclaim such an attitude to be serious at least about not being serious. Just as ordinary waking attention requires that we concentrate our awareness on some things to the exclusion of others so, in order to live and act, we have to be selective. If we live and act with any awareness of what we are doing we judge that some things are more important than others, and we willingly sacrifice the less important to the more important.

Either a man has a serious purpose or he does not act. His purposes may change, and they may be inconsistent with each other; but when he acts he has some purpose at that time. Without purpose a man does not act; he is only acted upon. He does not act; he only reacts. Professor Ralph Barton Perry's discussion of this as it applies to morals is pertinent also to religion. In his discussion of the puritan as "the moral athlete," Professor Perry examines the contention that the puritan overemphasizes moral discipline, that he "takes his game of morality too seriously," so that "he 'exaggerates' morality, as some colleges are said to exaggerate football." Critics of the puritan "who cannot compete with him, because they have only their odd hours to devote to morality, feel that the pace should be slackened. They are advocates of 'morality for all,' 'intramural' morality, morality of a more sportive and spontaneous sort."[3]

> But [says Professor Perry] the force of this plea for the amateur spirit in morality is somewhat weakened by the fact that most of those who utter it believe in being professional *somewhere*. They may be professionals in athletics, and although they think that the puritan's perpetual examination of the state of his soul is in bad taste, they have no hesitation in keeping a similar diary of the state of their muscles. Or they may be men of affairs, and want morality tempered to the tired businessman, who, however, is tired because he is so exceedingly businesslike about his business. These critics also think it morbid to balance one's spiritual account, but feel an irresistible urge to balance their bank accounts. And so with the artist, who is perhaps the most contemptuous critic of the puritan. He objects strongly to moral discipline, but devotes himself with infinite patience to the mastery of his own technique.[4]

It is not a question of whether we shall be serious about something, but a question of what we shall be serious about. In Professor Perry's words, "it is not so much a question of *whether* one shall be strict, as *where* one shall be strict. One will be strict, presumably, about the more important and central things: the athlete about high hurdles, the businessman about profits, the artist about music, painting, or poetry. The difference is over the question of what is important and central."[5]

Every religious statement expresses an evaluation, and every sincere commitment to value is a religious expression. The two go together; we cannot assume a religious attitude toward something we consider inferior or worthless. But recognition of value is not enough, for there must be devotion to it. When we find religious sentiment in its maturity, Professor Allport says, we find a "disposition, built up through experience, to respond favorably, and in certain habitual ways, to conceptual objects and principles that the individual regards as of ultimate importance in his own life, and as having to do with what he regards as permanent or central in the nature of things."[6]

In its broadest sense to be religious is to take toward something we regard important the attitude which is appropriate to the nature of the thing itself. In this sense are included all the meanings of *religious* from the narrowest literal meaning to all the effective metaphorical uses of the term. To be more specific than this we shall have to narrow the meaning by a more definite specification of the objects of religion's interest.

In the more specific sense, to be religious is to have the appropriate attitude toward not just anything of importance but, as Professor Allport suggests, toward something we consider to be of primary importance. A religious person, in the more specific meaning of the term, is one who has an attitude of acceptance and commitment to whatever he takes to be of ultimate value in existence. In so far as this which he takes to be of ultimate value *is* of ultimate value, and his attitude toward it is appropriate to it, then to that extent his religion is true. In so far as he is mistaken in his idea of what is of final worth his religion is false. It is still a religious attitude, else it could not be a false one. But if it is a religious attitude toward what does not merit such an attitude, then the religion it expresses is a false religion.

Many men, for example, have worshipped the state. They have

given to the state a devotion which could be merited only by something of ultimate and final worth. In so far as this is not true of the state we must regard the religion of these men as a false religion.

Although religion concerns man's relation to man, as well as man's relation to God or to whatever it is which he considers as of ultimate importance, yet religion is an intensely personal thing. Its social expression is the expression of the individual's own internal attitudes or else, as religion, it is nothing. The individual's religion is not the internalizing of a social fact; this inverts the true relation between the individual and society in religion; or, in those cases in which this seems to be the case, it is not the individual's own religion he expresses but something he has merely borrowed. The social fabric in which religion expresses itself is woven from the attitudes and evaluations of individual persons.

On this point Professor Allport says that "the place of religion in the personal life is basically different from its place in society. The social scientist argues that the function of religion is to produce social stability. Yet no individual, I venture to assert, is religious for any such reason. Indeed, most people would discard their religion if they thought it was merely a device to keep them out of the hands of the police and out of their neighbor's hair."[7] "Machiavelli saw in the Church an instrument for maintaining civil peace, while his contemporary, St. Catherine of Genoa, found in it the motive and meaning for a life of exceptional charity and devotion. There is a world of difference between the ruler's view and the participant's view."[8]

The same distinction is clearly drawn by Whitehead. "Religion is the art and the theory of the internal life of man, so far as it depends on the man himself and on what is permanent in the nature of things." He goes on to say, "This doctrine is the direct negation of the theory that religion is primarily a social fact. Social facts are of great importance to religion, because there is no such thing as absolutely independent existence. . . . But all collective emotions leave untouched the awful ultimate fact, which is the human being, consciously alone with itself, for its own sake."[9] It is in the light of this that we should understand Whitehead's oft-quoted statement: "Religion is what the individual does with his own solitariness."[10]

Religion is more than merely an attitude, if we think of an attitude simply as a state of mind. Properly understood, of course, an attitude is never a mere state of mind in complete separation from action. Attitudes are incomplete except as they are expressed in thought and action. This shows the close connection of attitude and value, for an attitude may be described as an evaluation in action. The evaluations we act out are the ones we really mean.

Religion is policy; a person's religion is that person's high policy. To the extent that he lives his religion, and does not merely talk about it, he lives in a definitely recognizable way. He deals with things in ways that fit his conception of their importance. He deals with matters of immediate moment not only as they happen to concern him at the moment but with a recognition of their final importance. If they have no such importance he treats them with the triviality they deserve, no matter how seriously others may regard them. But if they do have a bearing on things of final importance he sees this in them and does not permit himself to ignore it. To be religious is to see in the proximate a reflection of the ultimate.

Religion cannot be dismissed as a mere escape, as has so often been attempted. It is true that a religion directs attention to what it considers the basic and final factors in life and existence, but this need not mean that attention is wholly removed from our immediate concerns. Rather it leads us to view the immediate in the light of the ultimate. The fact is that irreligion is more likely than religion to be an escape, an escape from the ultimate to the immediate.

Even less than as an escape from life can religion be dismissed as mere wishful thinking. There is wishful thinking in the name of religion, to be sure, but there is wishful thinking in every activity in which man has a stake. The concerns of religion, Professor Allport points out, are far removed from those of fantasy. "What is demanded by the great religions is self-abnegation, dis-

cipline, surrender. To find one's life one must lose it. Such a trans-
position of values is too extensive to be covered by the formula of
autism that is applied appropriately only to daydreams and to the
rationalizations of daily life that are transparent in their self-cen-
teredness. Only occasionally, I think, do we find individuals in
whom religion runs its course on the level of wish-fulfilling fantasy. When this occurs we are dealing with a merely abortive religious sentiment in the individual."[11] Professor Allport insists that
"it is unsound to trace the origin of the religious quest to the desire for escape from reality. It is true that religion tends to define
reality as congenial to the powers and aspirations of the individual, but so too does any working principle that sustains human
endeavor. Those who find the religious principle of life illusory
would do well not to scrutinize their own working principles too
closely."[12]

Religion, in the sense we have given to it, is the way in which a
life comes to a focus. It reminds us, as we practice it, where we
stand with all our interests and personal concerns. We see these
matters in their context, in the widest and most nearly final context available to our awareness. Whatever else it may be, religious
experience is at least the illumination which is given to the immediate situation by our discovery of its place in the whole range
of being. This of course affects our attitude toward the immediate situation and enables us to deal with it as it truly is rather than
merely as it appears at the moment—it enables us to do this, that
is, in so far as our religion is true.

For example, a religious person who believes in the intrinsic
value of human beings cannot treat a man or a woman or a child
as a mere means to an end. However casual his dealings with them
may be—the clerk at the cigar counter, the waitress in the restau-
rant, the boy who delivers his paper—he will show to each of them
the respect due a person. He will not try to dominate or to hurt or
to demonstrate any fancied superiority. In his attitude and in all
his dealings with them he will show his recognition of the dignity
of their existence as persons.

For those who profess belief in God there is only one true final object of religious devotion because they believe that only in God can ultimate value be found. For those who profess belief in God, religion is the service of God. Since belief in God involves the belief that the source of all existence far exceeds in value anything we can know or imagine, for those who profess such a belief the highest service to God of which they are capable is to serve the best they can imagine. "A man's religion is the audacious bid he makes to bind himself to creation and to the Creator. It is his ultimate attempt to enlarge and to complete his own personality by finding the supreme context in which he rightly belongs."[13]

CAN AN ATHEIST BE RELIGIOUS?

We ended our discussion of the meaning of *religion* with a reference to God. Many would take the connection for granted; indeed they would see no meaning in religion apart from God. Yet we must recognize that there are those who deny the existence of God, who profess atheism, and yet who actually have attitudes which correspond in other respects to what we have called *religion*.

To ask whether an atheist can be religious may seem like asking whether a person can be religiously non-religious. Paradoxical as it may appear this is precisely the impression some people give. An expression of hostility to religion such as we find in the "anti-God crusade" of Soviet Russia shows all the intensity and devotedness of a religious movement. In fact any serious and sincere attack upon religion is likely itself to be a religious expression. In our general conception of the meaning of *religion* we found it to consist primarily of a commitment to values. A crusading atheist certainly behaves as if he considered it worth his while to promote atheism. His case, as he presents it, is that it is better to be an atheist than to believe in God. Unless he thought this, and unless his argument tacitly assumed it, the only appropriate attitude for him to take would be one of indifference.

It may be remarked in passing that even if he is wrong, and the existence of God is a fact, the crusading atheist may still be closer to the truth than the merely indifferent. For he who fights against the truth does, at least, make contact with it; and there is always the chance that in his contact he will come to see the truth for what it is. Clive Bell goes so far as to say: "All uncompromising belief is religious. A man who so cares for truth that he will go to prison, or death, rather than acknowledge a God in whose existence he does not believe, is as religious, and as much a martyr in the cause of religion, as Socrates or Jesus. He has set his criterion of values outside the physical universe."[14]

Students of primitive societies recognize various forms of nature worship as varieties of religion. In some of these there are no "gods" in the usual sense of the term. To consider another and very different example, the Humanism of Auguste Comte was intended to be a religion as well as a philosophy. For the saints of the church it substituted the great men of literature and philosophy and science, and for God it substituted Humanity, the "Great Being" to which it gave adoration and devotion in its forms of worship.

A more recent version of humanism is expressed in the words of a contemporary biologist, Joseph Needham. "Many . . . see that the essence of religion is the sense of the holy (Julian Huxley, J. M. Murry, Canon J. M. Wilson and others). Religion thus becomes no more and no less than the reaction of the human spirit to the facts of human destiny and the forces by which it is influenced; and natural piety, or a divination of sacredness in heroic goodness, becomes the primary religious activity."[15]

One of the most powerful political and cultural forces in the world today is a religion without God. Marxist Communism has its sacred writings and its inspired leaders who can do no wrong; it has rituals corresponding to confirmation, confession, repentance, and absolution. It has its paradise and its hell, its saved and its damned. It demands of its devotees the utmost loyalty and limitless sacrifice. It appeals not to reason and science for its conception of existence—although it does adopt these words for its own use; it demands instead trust in dogma and subjection to authority. Inconsistently it denies all values except economic values and at the same time assumes, without acknowledging the assumption, that it is good to be a Marxist. And it is explicitly and vociferously atheistic.[16]

From these examples it would appear that some exceedingly religious persons are also atheists; and, indeed, that atheism may itself be a form of religion. It is quite possible, however, that many who call themselves *atheists* are not atheists after all; or it may be that *atheism* is yet another ambiguous word which carries different meanings for different people and in different contexts.

We must recognize also that *atheist* is often used more for the purpose of arousing an attitude than for the purpose of clarifying meanings and conveying truth. Where it carries an imputation of evil, where the avowal of atheism is in disrepute, the word is often used as a club to clout an enemy. Many use it, as they use *radical* or *communist* or *red* or *fascist* or *reactionary*, with no concern for its meaning; they are concerned only with the emotional attitudes they can guide, by its use, toward the targets of their animosity.

Atheist may have a merely relative meaning in some of its uses. Those who hold to a certain conception of God may believe that any other supposed idea of God is not an idea of God at all. He who is confident that his idea of God is the only correct and adequate one, and that any idea which differs from his is false, may easily believe that he who uses *God* with a different meaning is not referring to God at all. Relative atheism is the denial of this or that conception of God. It is in this sense that the ancient Romans called the early Christians "atheists," for the Christians did not believe in the existence of the gods recognized and worshipped in the state religion of Rome.

Absolute atheism denies that there is anything real to which the term *God* may appropriately be applied. This of course raises the question of just what usages of *God* are appropriate, and if we wish to see clearly what absolute atheism involves we must keep in mind the widest and most general meaning we can give this word. We need to consider what we must *at least* admit in our conception of God if we are to use the term so that our meaning is in any way consistent with ordinary usage. More than this we shall not attempt at this point.

Any conception of God, whatever else it may include, must regard God as really existing. A non-existing God is a contradiction in terms. A conception of God must consider God to be the primary or ultimate existent; that is to say we cannot apply the word *God* to anything which depends on something else for its existence. Finally, we mean by *God* the source of good and the final reality of value.

If God is at least this, and if by *absolute atheism* we mean the denial of this, then the absolute atheist must hold that there is no final and ultimate reality which depends solely upon itself for its own being and which is also the source of good and the reality of value. Yet, oddly enough, if the absolute atheist considers it worth while to be an atheist he admits value; and at the same time, as an atheist, he seems to deny to value any place in the final structure of being and so in effect he seems to deny the reality of value. The only way he can avoid this inconsistency is to point out some other basis upon which the genuineness of value can be asserted. Otherwise he is advocating nihilism, and in the act of advocating it assumes that what he is doing is worth doing. He fails to see that if no basis for value remains then there is no point even in saying so. If nothing is good it cannot be good to know that nothing is good. If nothing makes any difference then it can make no difference to know that nothing makes any difference.

The atheist may object that there is no connection whatever between the admission of value and the existence of God. There are few problems in the history of thought more fundamental than this, and there have been widely different views concerning it. Nevertheless it seems that an atheist who asserts that values are real (and to regard anything as worth asserting is to assume this) is dangerously close to inconsistency. The problem which faces him is to tell us how values are real, to point out to us the position they occupy in the final structure of existence; he has to explain how they can have any place at all in the kind of real world he is willing to admit. The theist has his answer to this question, and the atheist must not be permitted to evade it.

HIGHER AND LOWER RELIGIONS

It is common to distinguish some religions as "higher" and others as "lower." The religions of primitive peoples, for example, we should likely regard as lower religions while the great monotheistic religions such as Judaism, Christianity, and Islam are higher religions.

In many cases our distinction of religions into higher and lower actually expresses our attitudes toward the cultures to which they belong. The more advanced the culture of a people the more prone we are to consider their religion to be one of the higher religions. This is to be expected, and since it would be nonsense to deny that there is a significant relation between a religion and its culture there is a real foundation for it.

However it is not entirely satisfactory to distinguish religions solely by a cultural index. So far as we are concerned with the intrinsic significance of religion, as distinguished from a concern with religion merely as a cultural expression, we need to find some basis in the content of the religions themselves for the distinction between higher and lower.

If we consider it one of the important functions of religion, whatever else a religion may be, to put us in contact with values and to enable us to realize in our own persons and communities the value possibilities open to us then we have in this the basis for a comparison of religions. A primary difference between religions lies in the differences in the values upon which they are centered. The Old Testament accounts of the victories and the defeats of the Hebrews in their attempts to establish themselves in the Land of Promise contain the constantly recurring theme of the conflict between the religion of Israel and the religion of Baal. The reason for the conflict, and its recurrence, is in the fact that the two religions were centered upon different and incompatible sets of values. The religion of Israel professed allegiance to ideals of racial purity, community responsibility for the weak and unfortunate, the denial of any ultimate power or authority except the power and authority of the Lord of Israel, the primacy of character values over property and possessions, and the supremacy of mercy and love. The religion of Baal, in contrast, accepted as primary the values of sensual gratification and the exercise of physical power. These two basic attitudes toward life could not be reconciled; they could not merge, and as long as both existed side by side they had to be in conflict. The issue between them was the issue of value. If the values of the religion of Israel are superior to the values of the religion of Baal then the religion of Israel was a higher religion than the religion of Baal.

This distinction may help us understand how it is that religion has brought out both the best and the worst in human nature. Since religion is devotion to whatever is believed to be of highest value, it follows that if the value beliefs embodied in a religion are distorted and false, the lowest may receive the devotion which is appropriate only to the highest. It is plain also that man does not always see clearly the true relationships between different kinds and levels of values. In his attempt to serve the best he may use methods which tend to destroy the very thing he prizes most. It is this kind of confusion to which Ernest Barker refers in his vivid and moving portrayal of the medieval crusader: "He might butcher all day, till he waded ankle-deep in blood, and then at nightfall kneel, sobbing for very joy, at the altar of the Sepulchre —for was he not red from the winepress of the Lord?"[17]

Ernst Jünger's celebration of the sickening horror of modern war is an almost religious expression of an inversion of values.

Are not the landscapes which await us, then impossible and fabulous? No poet in his dreams has looked upon these burning fields. They are iron fields of craters, deserts with fiery islands of palm-trees, rolling walls made of fire and steel and plains of the dead, over which red storms drive. Flocks of steel birds swarm through the sky, and armoured machines plunge over the fields. And everything which causes feeling, from appalling physical pain to the uttermost joy of victory, is melted together here in a burning unity, to a picture of life itself blazing like lightning. Song, prayer, rejoicing, cursing and weeping—what more can we wish?[18]

At the other end of the emotional scale we may look at an example of cheapness in religion, as noted by Ralph Waldo Emerson in his *Journal*. "Miss B—, a mantuamaker in Concord, became a 'Medium,' and gave up her old trade for this new one; and is to charge a pistareen a spasm, and nine dollars for a fit. This is the Rat-revelation, the gospel that comes by taps in the wall, and thumps in the table-drawer."[19]

A religion is a lower religion because it sacrifices higher values, the more preferable, to lower values. The higher religion expresses its preferences in accordance with the true positions of the values with which it is concerned. At its best and highest level religion provides for the realization of all varieties and ranks of value with each in its proper place in relation to the others. To seek the pleasures of the senses, for example, as if they were the most important things in life is to crowd out of life other things of far greater importance. It is to lose friendship and love, and it excludes even from the pleasures of sense all those aspects of experience which require intellectual activity and the more discriminating emotional responses. Music becomes nothing but physical stimulation; human contacts may be significant only as occasions contributing directly or indirectly to sexual stimulation and excitement; literature and drama are nothing but experiences of emotional tension and release. This is a degradation of man's nature, not because these pleasures are not themselves positive values but because they are sought in such a way as to exclude more important ones. When we discover what music really has to give us, for example, we find that it does include physical stimulation but it includes it as merely a part of an experience much more significant.

From the highest religion we expect the satisfaction of the deepest and highest needs of human nature; with this everything else will find its proper place. So far as we miss this our religious attitudes and experiences are inadequate and incomplete.

TRUE AND FALSE RELIGIONS

Not only do we distinguish between higher and lower religions, we often distinguish between true and false religions. Of course what people sometimes mean by their distinction between true and false religions might better be called a distinction between "my religion" and "your religion." However the distinction between true and false religions is a genuine one in spite of its frequent corruption into an expression of partisanship, and like the distinction between higher and lower religions it may be understood in terms of the different values expressed in different religions.

If we distinguish between true and false religions on the basis of the values they accept as primary then any religion is true in so far as it is a devotion to genuine values. An absolutely false religion would have to substitute disvalues for values. It would have to be a kind of Satanism which says, "Evil, be thou my good." The attempt to substitute disvalue for value, however, must always fail; it is impossible because it is an attempt to do something inconsistent with itself. To try to put evil in the place of good assumes that it is good to do this, that it is good to substitute evil for good. So the attempt fails, for if the inconsistency is to be avoided there will be no point in making the attempt. The alternative to the search for good is not the search for evil; the alternative is indifference and apathy. In this sense, then, we must conclude that no religion based on positive values, no matter how poor and inadequate those values may be, is completely false. The worship of power and physical strength and sexual potency, upon which some of the more primitive religions are centered, is still devotion to positive value.

There is a sense, however, in which a religion based on inferior values does include in itself something absolutely false. Even if its values are positive and genuine yet it may be absolutely and completely wrong in its assertion that its values are the highest values. The things it values may be desirable, yet it may err in its contention that they are the most desirable and so deserve man's full devotion.

The test of the truth of a religion is, in part at least, the test of its values. This involves questions we cannot examine adequately at this point in our study, but we can call attention here to one of the main principles of value testing. The test of values requires the comparison of competing values within a single consciousness. A person who can appreciate only one of two or more sets of competing values is in no position to decide the justice of their claims.

There are two opposed attitudes with respect to the relation of truth and value in religion. We may rest the case for our evaluations on religious authority, and believe that since that religion makes certain value claims those claims are therefore sound. In other words, we may believe that what our religion says is true because it says it. This is the attitude expressed by Sophocles: "Nothing is wrong which gods command." Or, as opposed to this, we may test a religion by its values, in the spirit of Euripides: "If gods do evil, then they are not gods."[20] It is plain that the second of these is the reasonable attitude, for the first can maintain itself only so long as the truth claims of a religion are not questioned. On the other hand, we have it in our power to compare competing values, and if we insist on judging religious claims by value then we can go behind dogma to a criterion accessible to our own experience. Every great religious advance has come by subjecting dogma to the test of value.

Even those who do assert intelligently the primacy of dogma and of submission to authority may yet admit that value is the test of religious truth. For they do not accept dogma merely because it is dogma, else all dogmas would be on the same footing with them. They accept dogma because they believe it is true, and when they accept it in submission to authority it is because they believe that authority competent to distinguish between true and false dogma. So they accept dogma because they believe it is good to live in the light of truth. However they may have arrived at their beliefs, and however inadequate their beliefs may be, their willingness to put those beliefs into practice in their lives may well spring from devotion to the good and the conviction of the goodness of devotion to the true. Without this a person's religious belief is only an expression of his passive conformity to the social and cultural patterns of his surroundings, or else a channel for the discharge of blind passions and a means of self-justification.

This does not mean that it is safe for us simply to accept or reject religious dogma on the basis of our feelings and the impressions it makes upon us. We need to treat with great respect the judgments of those of wide range of experience and demonstrated sensitivity to values. Still, only our own experience is decisive for ourselves. Recognizing this we must also face the great danger which it holds for us. This is the danger that we shall fail to find or, if we do encounter it, close our hearts to what is of greatest importance; that we shall be content with the common and shoddy attitudes of those who have no vision and who have accepted the role in life of passive conformity with the "accepted" way to live.

If there is a difference between lower and higher values it is quite plain that one who has experienced only the lower values is in no position to appreciate the superiority of the higher. "You would expect, then," Arnold Isenberg tells us, "that people who preen themselves on trivial accomplishments (as the boarding-house keeper on her 'respectability') should also worship false gods and make heroes out of crooners and prize-fighters."[21] It is too seldom recognized, however, that this works the other way as well. One who has never appreciated the appeal and strength of lower values cannot know what it is in which the higher are superior. Experience of the lower values, such as physical pleasure and relief from pain, the joy of defeating a rival in a test of strength or skill, and the pleasures of revenge and retaliation, are experiences open to all. But not all have fully experienced them, for many of us are afraid of anything inferior. We fear it will conquer us, and so we avoid and deny it and refuse to let it have its way with us. Yet one who fails to appreciate the appeal of the inferior, and to see the positive good which it possesses, cannot really grasp the superiority of the higher values. Thus for the timid soul, who lives in constant fear of contamination by what is inferior and does not see that all that exists is in its own way good, the higher values will not be appreciated for what they are; they will seem to him pallid substitutes for something he is missing. Those whose only goodness is innocence often envy, in their ignorance, the ones they consider evil.

It is no accident that so many religious saints and so many of those who have given us our best insight into the highest levels of existence have themselves known at first hand the cheap and poor pleasures of indulgence. Really to appreciate the love of God may require a vivid awareness of the attractiveness of the alternatives. In the words of William Blake, "The road of excess leads to the palace of wisdom," and "If the fool would persist in his folly he would become wise."[22]

This is not to say, as did even some early Christians, that in order to reach the height of religious experience we must indulge ourselves in physical debauchery. Every normal person has within his experience the taste of the pleasures and satisfactions which have the strongest immediate appeal. If he is wise and capable of self control he will moderate his pleasures in the light of their true relation to more important matters. It is in his understanding of their appeal and in his recognition of the hollowness of their promises that he is able to keep the inferior in its proper place in his life. This does not mean absence of experience or a blind denial of one's nature. It is rather the profit derived from strength of character and quickness to learn. From these souls too, the strong and wise and self-controlled, have come insights and revelations of the good.

People often ignore the significance of value experience for religion because of the utter inadequacy of their ideas about religion. Too many who pay lip-service to religion fail to develop any adequate appreciation of what it means. A person who takes religion seriously, and who reflects on the great themes of life under its inspiration, finds that his understanding and interpretation of these ideas develop far beyond the puerile notions he once had. But since much the same language is used by all to refer to religious matters the person whose religious understanding has remained what it was at the age of six or sixteen assumes that others use these terms with the same poverty of meaning they have for him. "Brethren," advises Paul, "do not be children in your thinking; be babes in evil, but in thinking be mature."[23]

The distinction between true and false religions, as well as between higher and lower, turns upon value. These two ways of comparing religions seem much the same. This will not be surprising when we reflect that a religion is an attitude toward what it takes to be of ultimate worth. A religion is an answer to the question of what gives final meaning to life. The distinction between higher and lower religions rests squarely on the fact that values fit together in some kind of a scale, the fact that it makes sense to prefer one to another.[24] Religions are true and false because there is a value scale which belongs to real existence. A false religion is false because it mistakes the nature of our world; it takes the world to be something which it is not. A religion is true in so far as it sees the qualities of life and existence as they really are.

CHAPTER 2

The Philosophy of Religion

CAN RELIGION ESTABLISH ITS OWN TRUTH?

THE QUESTION of whether a religion is true or false is not likely to arise directly from religious experience and practice. It is in our reflective moments, when we look back upon the religious attitudes and actions of ourselves and others, that the question comes. We discover that different people have different religious practices and ideas and that they seem as sincere and as sure they are right as we do ourselves.

Doubts of the truth of religion come also from the seeming conflicts between what we have been taught in the name of religion and what we learn from other sources about ourselves and our world. The whole range of modern culture in the western world has been marked in recent centuries by a persistent conflict between science and religion. There are conflicts also between religion and politics, religion and education, and between certain religious conceptions of man and the uses which modern industry makes of him. We could extend our catalogue to cover the whole range of modern life. For modern life, in those of its aspects which are distinctively modern, is fundamentally secular. Rather than something which permeates life and society and their institutions, religion in the modern world tends to be only one compartment among many. It is expected to keep its proper place and not to intrude beyond its established boundary lines. As Professor Allport says, some people "take over the ancestral religion much as they take over the family jewels. It would be awkward to bring it into too close a relationship with science, with suffering, and with criticism."[1]

It is quite possible that the question of the truth of religion, as it appears in modern thought, is not so much a question of truth in its specific philosophical or logical sense as it is an expression of conflicting loyalties. For where a life is divided into different compartments there is bound to be some degree of rivalry among the various interests involved. Each attempts to capture more of the self and, in so far as the self is a divided self, the more the self is taken by one interest the less is left for the others. We have carried this so far in modern life that we live by the clock and divide ourselves into parts which we measure by hours, minutes, and even by seconds.

If religion is, as we have suggested, an expression of basic evaluations and ultimate loyalties then to try to confine religion to a separate compartment of life as one activity among many is simply incompatible with its nature. As the human self is single and indivisible so the basic attitudes and values of a life must be all of one piece. A man cannot adopt one policy for one part of his activity and another and incompatible policy for another area of activity without destroying his own integrity. For when he is engaged in the one he must at times be aware of the other, and of the fact that the other is his; and so he must in some way or another be perplexed as to which man he is, whether he is one who follows now a policy of kindness and consideration or whether he is a man of ruthless selfishness and cruelty and disregard for the concerns of other people. He may think up excuses for his inconsistencies, or he may not permit himself to think of the matter at all; but he cannot remain in a condition of actual internal, or spiritual, disruption, whether it is conscious or unconscious, and find any real peace and satisfaction. For what brings peace to one part of him will be at odds with the other part. So long as he is aware of himself as the same self which thinks and acts at different times he remains one single self, and he cannot act fully as a self unless the principles on which he acts are compatible with each other. This is the real conflict between the religious and secular aspects of modern life.

Although religious doubt may express a conflict of loyalties yet once it comes out into the open it is a challenge to religion's claim to be true. It makes little difference what is responsible for raising the question, once the truth of a religion is challenged that religion can meet the challenge only by justifying its claim to truth. I may be accused of lying or of dishonesty by someone whose only motive is malice or jealousy and who has no ground for his charge. But I cannot meet the charge by attacking his sincerity or his motives. To attempt to do so is to commit a logical fallacy, the fallacy of argument *ad hominem*. My only defense *against the charge*, if I feel it necessary to defend myself against it, is to show that it is false.

Charles A. Bennett insists that the

metaphysical pretensions of religion [by which he means its claim to be true] are the most important thing about it. We cannot reduce the drama of the religious life to a mere record of mental conflict, to so much natural history of the mind. Unless the issues of destiny are at stake, there is no genuine conflict and no drama. Thus I reject all attempts to hand over religion and its problems to anthropology or sociology or psychology, as though these sciences, separately or together, could provide us with a sufficient explanation or interpretation. The problems of religion are philosophical, and there is no substitute for a philosophy of religion.[2]

It is one thing to understand how it happens that we raise the question of the truth of religion; it is quite another thing to determine how that question is to be answered. Once it is raised, however, either we must find some way of answering it or find some way in which we can live with the question without destroying the basis of our life.

When we look at the question directly it seems quite evident that a religion cannot examine its own truth. If it tries to do this in its own terms, as a part of the expression of the attitudes and practices of which it is composed, it would of course beg the question. It would be trying to answer a question in terms of what has itself been brought into question.

This is the reason religious dispute is so seldom convincing. To be convinced by an argument, in so far as the conviction is to be a logical one, we must accept the argument's premises. If the argument is about the truth of a religion then the premises themselves are in question. To argue from these premises in favor of them can convince only those who are unaware of what is happening. When we concern ourselves with the doctrines of a religion, and deal with them from the standpoint of that religion itself, then those doctrines are simply accepted. A religion proclaims what it takes to be true, and the hearer accepts or rejects. He is convinced or he is not convinced. To try to justify or establish the truth of what a religion proclaims it is necessary to go beyond what it contains within itself.

Can Theology Establish the Truth of Religion?

One of the facts of life today is that few except theologians take theology seriously. It is not true, at least to the same extent, that only scientists take science seriously or that only artists take art seriously or that only philosophers take philosophy seriously. Even philosophy and science, areas of thought we should expect to find somewhat interested in its truth or falsity, pay little attention to theology. They do not listen to theology; at most they notice only that she has spoken and reply to her only to silence her.

Some explanation of the present-day indifference to theology may be found in the tendency for modern interests to separate themselves from each other, and in the relation of this tendency to certain distinctive features of theology itself. A theology is in one respect a rational system and in another respect it is not; its internal structure of ideas is a rational structure but its foundation is faith. It is composed of a set of doctrines concerning God, man, the world, history, and destiny. These doctrines may be organized in a thoroughly logical order. So far as this is the case a theology is a rational system. But the more complete is its logical order the more evident is the dependence of the whole system upon its basic premises. This is true of any logical system, but it is of special importance in the case of theology because theology admittedly obtains its premises from faith. So although theology is a rational system in its inner structure it is a system which rests on faith, and it neither questions nor inquires into the truth of its premises.

As was pointed out before, with his tendency to divide up life into separate compartments the modern man is unlikely to have any single set of basic principles. Jumping from one set to another as he moves from one activity to another, he feels no need to reconcile his various policies with each other in terms of something fundamental to them all. Even a system of philosophy may be built out of a cluster of hypotheses and inferences which have sprung from a thinker's preoccupation with some technical problem of quite limited scope. Whole philosophies have come out of attempts to deal with such problems as the nature of perception, the status of colors and sounds in the physical world, or the nature of verification and of symbolic utterance. Sometimes we find the philosophizing so quaintly naive that the resulting philosophy describes the kind of a world in which the process of constructing a world view could not possibly take place. It is not surprising that schizophrenia, the splitting up of a mind, is today one of the commonest and most characteristic mental disorders.

Modern inquiry and thinking is so specialized it has become provincial, not in a geographic sense but with respect to its subject matter. There are advantages in this, as there are advantages in many other kinds of specializations; but the disadvantages are precisely those which interfere with the achievement of a unified and integrated point of view.

Each specialized interest has its own assumptions which it does not examine, and the less contact there is between these different areas the easier it is to forget the fact that assumptions are made. So some of the attitudes typical of thought today contain the bland assumption that no assumptions are being made. This is one important reason why other fields of inquiry pay no attention to theology, for theology is a field which never ignores its assumptions; or, if it does now and then ignore some of its assumptions, it never ignores the fact that it makes assumptions. Its very admission that it rests upon faith makes theology seem out of step with the rest of modern thought, and so it is left out of the picture.

When theology does try to ignore its assumptions it gives up its claim to be true, and some theologians have been willing to pay even this price in order to feel at home in our splintered society. These theologians, as Arnold S. Nash points out, "vainly seek to make theology 'scientific' by cutting it free from metaphysics and history and resting it on religious experience. Theology then becomes thinking about our nice feelings rather than thinking about God and His relation to man and the world."[3] President Nathan M. Pusey, of Harvard University, reminds us of the consequences of the neglect of metaphysics when he says "it has now become frighteningly clear that if you try to ignore metaphysical considerations (I would say considerations of ultimate things) or cover them up in bursts of energy, they will rise up in perverted and distorted forms to mock one's thus too-circumscribed efforts."[4]

It is not reason, however, which opens the door to theology, it is faith; and unless the door is opened we cannot enter the structure. Some have insisted, in opposition to this, that a person might become an expert in theology without accepting the truth of its principal tenets, even as an anthropologist might become an expert on some primitive system of magic without himself believing in the effectiveness of the magic he studies. It is true we may come to know a great deal about a theology without a belief in its truth, but there is serious question whether we could think ourselves into it and grasp the full meaning of its doctrines without actually entering through the door of faith. The chief importance of theology, to a greater extent perhaps than in any other field of inquiry, lies in the truth or falsity of its premises. Its premises are of such a nature that adequate understanding of what they mean may require a belief in their truth, just as adequate understanding of another's expression of love may depend upon belief in the truth of the expression. Tremendous consequences hinge upon the truth or falsity of the premises of theology, consequences which completely overshadow its merely historical or cultural or psychological significance. The issues are the issues of man's destiny.

Thus far we have found that theology is important if true, and we have found some of the reasons why it is ignored by other fields of inquiry. Our question now is whether theology itself is competent to determine its own truth or falsity. It is likely that a theology originates in the attempt to defend a religious doctrine which has been challenged. But its defense is confined to showing that the doctrine is implied by the basic beliefs of the religion concerned. In other words theology originates in connection with challenges and objections which arise from within a religion; it is not concerned with attacks which come from outside the religion, except in so far as it may serve to protect from heresy those who would reject heresy solely because it is heresy.

As a religion comes into closer contact with ideas and influences alien or antagonistic to itself, more and more questions arise concerning its basic doctrines. As an answer to these questions theology finds itself inadequate. This, however, has not always prevented theologians from making the attempt, and in making the attempt they are not always clear as to their own purpose and function. They sometimes attempt to defend their theological premises by an appeal to theology. From such confusion was born the discipline known as "apologetics." The fate which the various systems of apologetics have met is the appropriate consequence of the confusion upon which they rest. Apologetics is an illegitimate discipline; for if it assumes its premises it is special pleading or else a mere restatement of the theology it purports to defend, while if it examines its premises it is philosophy and so can plead no case but that of truth itself. Apologetics can disguise its dilemma only by a sleight of hand substitution of rationalizing for reason.

Theology is important, but its importance is in the service it renders to those who accept the religious position to which it gives logical and systematic expression. It is important to him who professes a faith to know what is and what is not consistent with his profession. A little theology quickly cools the overheated religious imagination.

Theology helps prevent extravagance and inconsistency; and

it uncovers the less obvious consequences of religious belief. As soon as a religious idea becomes definite enough to pass for a concept it is subject to examination by theology. Thus reason is brought to bear upon it, and only an enemy of reason would venture to say that the long run results of the work of reason can be anything but good.

When we have gone as far as truth will take us in emphasizing the importance of theology we find still echoing in our minds the statement of its limitations. A theology assumes the truth of its own premises; it obtains them from faith and for it their truth is not in question. When question is raised concerning their truth theology has nothing to say. If it is a mistake for other fields of inquiry to ignore theology, it is every bit as serious an error for theology to ignore other fields. This is what happens when theology attempts to assume a position independent of science and philosophy, and attempts to find within itself the warrant of its own truth. In every attempt it may make to insulate itself from other fields, and protect itself from the implications of their discoveries, theology by its own act accepts the very separation from the rest of life and thought to which the modern temper has condemned it. Theology has life in itself only as it permeates all life.

THE UNIQUE POSITION OF PHILOSOPHY AS A MODE OF INQUIRY

In one important respect philosophy differs from all other methods of seeking knowledge. This difference does not necessarily denote superiority, except with respect to matters to which it is relevant. Nor is philosophy warranted, because of this difference between it and other modes of inquiry, in making any claim of infallibility. Its unique position does not protect philosophy from error.

The distinguishing character of philosophy, to which it owes its special position, is found in the fact that it accepts no assumptions as inaccessible to examination. In this respect philosophy differs from theology; for, as we have seen, theology does not subject its basic premises to rational examination. A theology is constructed because of a conviction that certain primary religious beliefs are true and because it seems important to discover what these beliefs imply and what is inconsistent with their truth.

The difference we have mentioned not only distinguishes philosophy from theology, it also marks it off clearly from the natural sciences, from history, and from the social studies. No science can use its own methods to examine the soundness of those methods. When a scientist finds it necessary to appraise the methods of his science he must shift his position, at least temporarily, from the field of his science to the fields of logic and epistemology, both of which belong to philosophy. Nor can a science examine the truth of its basic assumptions about the objects of its inquiry. It assumes, for example, that knowledge is possible, that there is a world of objects to be known, that the acquisition of knowledge is of value, and that the world it inquires into is a rational order to which the laws of logic and mathematics apply. Similar assumptions are made by history and the social studies, with additional assumptions which apply more directly to their special fields.

To point this out is not to suggest that these assumptions are false. On the contrary we have exceedingly strong reasons to consider them true. The point rather is simply that these modes of inquiry do make assumptions which they themselves are incapable of examining, and if it becomes necessary to attack or to defend any of these assumptions the methods used cannot be the methods of the field of inquiry in which the assumption is made. To pretend to avoid metaphysical assumptions is only to confess failure to recognize them.

Why, then, is not philosophy in the same predicament? How is it possible to justify the assumptions of philosophy except from a standpoint outside philosophy itself? This may seem, at first thought, to rest philosophy on dogma or on arbitrary assertion. But such is not the case. The special position of philosophy results from the special character of its assumptions. The key to the puzzle is the fact that philosophy itself is synonymous with the assertion that in its final nature all actual and possible existence is intelligible.

To deny that existence is intelligible cuts us off from any knowledge of it. Such a denial is the assertion of philosophical skepticism, the assertion that real existence cannot be known. But how can we make such an assertion, and pretend that it is known to be true? As Professor DeWolf says, "It has often been pointed out by the critics of complete philosophical skepticism that to establish skepticism a man would have to be omniscient. How can a thinker know that nothing can ever be known, unless he knows so much about everything there is as to be sure that all is of such character as to be unknowable?"[5]

But suppose, it may be proposed, that someone questions the intelligibility of existence. How can philosophy assume that which is brought into question and at the same time justify what it assumes? The answer is that the question itself assumes the very thing it questions, and the role of philosophy in such a dispute is simply to point out that fact. Try as we may to bring reason into question it is only by the use of reason that we can do so. To one who says he rejects reason philosophy's only reply is that the objection cannot be stated without resting the statement upon the very thing it attempts to reject. The act of stating the rejection of reason is one which requires the validity of reason to give it meaning. With the rejection of reason meaning disappears. Existence makes sense, or else it makes sense to say that existence does not make sense; therefore, in not making sense existence does make sense. The intelligibility of existence is the condition which makes it possible for us to make meaningful statements about it.

This becomes clear as soon as we recognize that any statement which claims truth is a statement which rests its claim on such principles of reason as identity and non-contradiction. Unless we admit that what we talk about is what it is, and is not what it is not, our attempt to talk fails. It fails to mean anything. If, then, I try to say that "the rational is false" either I mean it is true that the rational is false, and it is false that the rational is not false, or else my statement means nothing at all. Whatever else it means it has to mean this; and it has to mean this or it means nothing. But the relations by which this minimum meaning operates are logical and rational relationships. So I rest my claim that my denial of reason is true and meaningful upon a relation of reason. If I am at the same time both denying and asserting the same thing, anyone is entitled to ask which I mean. If I answer that I mean both together even though the two are mutually incompatible, then the only remaining course is to reject the statement as meaningless—or perhaps to call in a psychiatrist. With one who attempts to deny the validity of reason we are in the same position we should be with someone who said, "I am going to tell you something important and true but don't believe anything I say." We cannot refute a theory that does not make sense; we can only expose it. But a theory that does not make sense does us this great service, *it* exposes those who think it may be true.

In order that an assertion shall mean any one thing definitely it has to exclude from itself other meanings. Suppose I should utter the sounds appropriate to, "Bladso gellux infism." When I am asked what this means suppose I reply, "Oh, it means everything; there is nothing at all that it does not mean." It would be shorter, and as revealing, simply to say, "It is meaningless; I am merely making up sound combinations." Every meaningful affirmation is also a negation, and every meaningful negation is also an affirmation. Even my assertion that " 'Bladso gellux infism' means everything" is itself meaningless unless this assertion involves the denial that "Bladso gellux infism" has a restricted meaning which excludes other meanings. If, when I say "grass is green," I do not mean "grass is not that which is not green" then I mean nothing at all. But the relation between the two is a logical relation, apprehended by reason, and the one involves the other by virtue of this relation.

Every inquiry has its own assumptions, assumptions bound up with its distinctive methods. Philosophy differs from other inquiries in the fact that its assumptions are the assumptions of any inquiry whatsoever. You accept them or you do not inquire; you do not even inquire about whether you can inquire. Either you accept these assumptions or you do not speak; you accept them or you do not even think, and that includes thinking about not accepting them.

We have here a fundamental principle of our inquiry, and we shall return to this frequently. It is the principle of intelligibility— that whatever is presupposed by the possibility of knowledge cannot itself be brought into question. The furthest we can go is to question the contention that this or that proposition is presupposed by the possibility of knowledge. In so far as the presuppositions of inquiry itself are the presuppositions of philosophy then it follows that no attempt to discredit philosophy as such can be successful. For the attempt to discredit philosophy *is* philosophy in so far as it claims to be true and rests its case on reason and fact; in so far as it does not claim to be true, or does not rest its case on reason and fact, it is senseless and deserves only to be ignored or to have its senselessness pointed out. As Professor Urban says, "Philosophy not only buries its undertakers; it also, by its own inherent logic or dialectic, refutes and reduces to futility those forms of philosophizing which violate the conditions of philosophical intelligibility as such."[6]

THE AIM OF A PHILOSOPHY OF RELIGION

The aim of philosophy is understanding, the discovery of truth, the satisfaction of reason. In the philosophy of religion this aim is directed toward religion. It may be interpreted in two ways, not in conflict with each other but supplementing each other.

There is first the attempt to understand religion, to discover what it is and to uncover the rational meanings which belong to its ideas. Religious ideas are to some degree conceptual; they have logical significance, and by this we mean that it makes sense to raise the question of whether they are true or false. In this aspect of the philosophy of religion we seek to find the rational truth which is contained in religion. This does not mean that all the truth in religion is contained in the rational content we discover, nor does it mean even that we make our chief contact with religious truth by the use of reason. The philosophy of religion is an effort to discover so far as we can what there is in religion which is accessible to our reason.

There is another aspect of the philosophy of religion not adequately expressed in what has been said so far. All knowledge must, in the end, be of a single piece because truth has unity. So far as our knowledge is incomplete the unity of truth may escape us; but when we do not see the unity of truth it is because our knowledge is incomplete, it is not because of any final disruption of any part of truth from any other part. We are like one who has been a short way through a few of the entrances to an enormously complex building. He may know that all the parts he has seen belong to the same building but he may not have gone far enough to see how they fit together.

So far as religion adds to our rational understanding of anything it contributes something to our grasp of the whole pattern of truth. Religion throws light not only on its own objects but on the whole realm of existence, for the objects of religion are related to other things and these relations make a difference to our understanding of the other things. So far as religion has any truth accessible to human reason the philosophy of religion is an essential part of any comprehensive philosophical view. It may well be that religion provides contacts with reality which thought itself cannot give, which are more intimate and more immediate than reason provides. Although we cannot achieve these contacts in philosophy yet a philosophy of religion may help us understand what they are and help us recognize them for what they are. Whatever direct contact with reality religion may provide a comprehensive philosophy must reckon with it, just as a philosophy must take account of our perceptual and aesthetic experience.

When we say that the aim of a philosophy of religion is to try to reach a rational understanding of the truth which religion contains, we do not mean we are primarily concerned with understanding the origins and the varieties of religion, and the phases of its development. Those are matters for historians, anthropologists, and psychologists. The kind of understanding which the philosophy of religion seeks is the discovery of what rational grounds there may be for considering its beliefs to be true or false.

Although philosophy is concerned with the rational aspect of religious ideas and beliefs this does not mean that the rational content which philosophy is able to discover is the only content, or even that it is the most important. Nor are we entitled to assume that the only justification of a religious belief is to show rationally that it is true. There may be other and possibly even superior ways of justifying the claim of religious beliefs to be true. Even this, however, does not put religion out of contact with philosophy. For if there is any other than a rational justification of the truth claim of a religious belief the contention that this kind of justification is itself sound must be subjected to rational examination. Otherwise the claim is sheer assertion.[7]

I may be warranted in believing that my sense perception is a reliable guide in my attempt to discover some of the characteristics of physical objects. It is also quite clear that sense perception is not wholly an act of reason, for it includes sensation as well. Yet my claim that perception provides reliable information is itself subject to rational examination. So even though there may be in religion processes beyond our rational acts and though these may bring us into contact with something real in a way which is not the way of rational thought, yet the claim that these processes are effective needs rational justification.

There are religions and religious sects which attempt to deny all contact between religious faith and reason. Even if they were right they could not consistently give any reasons why they were right. So far as they reject reason they renounce any claim of truth which is entitled to the respect of anyone else. If they should happen to have any truth it is an entirely private truth for which they can make no case.

THE DIFFERENCE BETWEEN PHILOSOPHY AND RELIGION

Philosophy seeks a rational understanding of things and events, of relationships and patterns, in terms of the most general concepts which pertain to knowledge and being. Lack of philosophy is absence of understanding; to lack philosophy is to be naive and provincially minded, to be gullible with respect to current fads of thought, and to be the victim of random associations of ideas and of suggestions planted by those who wish to control the thought of others. It is a kind of ignorance, but it is a special kind of ignorance. It is not like ignorance of chemistry, for example; for although ignorance of chemistry may be a misfortune and on occasion may even have serious consequences, it is not the kind of ignorance which infects the whole outlook and basic judgments of a mind. "No man can live without any basis of philosophy, however primitive, naive, childish or unconscious," Berdyaev tells us. "Every man thinks and speaks, makes use of notions, categories, symbols, myths, and gives vent to appreciations. There is always a childish philosophy at the foundation of a childish faith."[8]

Religion has a certain underlying similarity with philosophy in spite of the very important differences between them. It is similar in the fact that it colors a person's whole outlook. So far as it is genuine it is reflected to some degree in a man's every act and every judgment. It is not one compartment of a self, but rather the design of the whole.

Religion, however, is quite different from philosophy; it is a different kind of activity. There is philosophy of religion but there is no such thing as religious philosophy. Where philosophy's activity is rational inquiry and understanding, religion is an appreciation and appropriation of values by means of contact with the ultimate ground of existence. In philosophy we think about things in terms of concepts; in religion we feel ourselves into a scheme of life and perform the acts which express our devotion to its object. Religion does not explain, or perhaps we should say that its explanations are not conceptual explanations; it does not minister primarily to the needs of reason. Quite the contrary, religion claims to put us in touch with existence in a special way; and in so far as religion's claim is just, philosophy can no more take religion's place than it can take the place of eating and loving.[9]

Even though philosophy cannot take the place of religion it is still not necessary for philosophy to depart in order to permit religion to enter. For the contact with existence which religion provides is one of those matters which philosophy most desires to understand. Where religion is the living out of a value scheme, philosophy is the examination and analysis of it. "In the conflict between religion and philosophy, truth is on the side of religion when philosophy claims to replace it in the sphere of salvation and eternal life; but truth is on the side of philosophy when it claims to attain a higher degree of knowledge than that allowed by the elements of naive knowledge incorporated in religion."[10]

Nothing we have said about the difference between philosophy and religion is intended to deny that understanding, as an activity and as a goal, has its own value. But the value of understanding, the highest of all the intellectual virtues, is not a substitute for religion. The value of religion in its highest forms lies in something which understanding alone does not give, it lies in the special contact with reality which it provides and in the transformation of the self which that contact brings about. It may well be that we are all the better for understanding this work of religion as adequately as we can, but it is something which does not need to be understood in order that it shall take place. Still, the greater the importance we see in religion the more intensely we desire to understand it as well as to experience it. It is this desire that the philosophy of religion attempts to satisfy.

In philosophy, so far as it is true, we come to know and understand reality, but in religion we make contact with it. If reality is the kind which answers our needs and rewards our search for fulfilment, then it is only in *contact* with it that we can find these supports. "And surely," says Professor Bennett, "the most striking historic function of religion has been to lift men from doubt and perplexity to a region of assurance and serenity. If there is any anchorage for human emotions, any one goal for human ambition, any solid foundation for courage to build on, it is religion that has supplied these things. If anywhere we break through from illusion into reality it is in religion that we do so, and any interpretation of faith which ignores or denies this is frankly preposterous."[11]

Part Two

FAITH AND KNOWLEDGE

CHAPTER 3

Sensory Knowledge

BELIEF AND KNOWLEDGE

Belief, *knowledge*, and *faith* are words with closely related meanings. Because the meanings are so closely related it is all the more important to understand clearly where the differences lie.

Belief has the widest meaning of the three. Everything we know we also believe, and every case of faith is also belief. But it is not true that everything we believe we also know, nor is every case of belief also a case of faith; in fact belief includes even more than knowledge and faith together, for there are beliefs which are neither knowledge nor faith.

We believe whatever we judge to be true. The word pertains to assertions and denials. Any assertion or denial we consider true is one we believe; any assertion or denial we consider false is one we disbelieve. "To believe" and "to consider true" are equivalent, and "to disbelieve" and "to consider false" are equivalent.

To state a belief as a belief says nothing, strictly speaking, about the truth or falsity of that which is said to be believed. To state a belief as a belief says only that the speaker judges something to be true. If I say, "I believe there will not be a third world war in the twentieth century," I am speaking directly about myself, not about the state of the world and the prospects of war. I am giving information about my judgment concerning the prospects of war. I am not saying that there will be no third world war in this century, and whether the future brings such an event or does not bring it has nothing to do with the truth or falsity of my statement. The only circumstance under which my statement might

43

be false is that I am lying, that I do not believe what I say I believe.

If, however, I say, "There will be no third world war in the twentieth century," then I am speaking about a state of affairs which apparently depends in no way whatever upon what I believe or disbelieve. Whether my statement is true depends upon the events of the rest of the century. The statement, if made sincerely as a judgment, *is* a belief, but the statement does not include in itself any reference to the fact that it is a belief. It does not depend for its truth or falsity upon my veracity. I may even believe that I am lying and the statement still could be true. On the other hand no lie can be true *if it is stated as a belief*.

When we say that we know we assert more than simply that we accept a statement to be true. Of course we are committing ourselves to the acceptance of it as true, for what we know we also believe. But when we say we know a statement is true we mean we have evidence of such a nature that we cannot in good sense deny the statement in the face of that evidence. (This, of course, is a somewhat loose and imprecise way of putting the matter; greater precision will come later.)

This introduces another concept, *evidence*. By *evidence* we mean what the term literally suggests, that which "shows" or "exhibits" or "brings into view." The evidence shows or brings into view the basis upon which the claim of truth rests. If I say, "Smith is in town, for I saw him with my own eyes," I am offering my own visual perception, together with the fact of my acquaintance with Smith, as evidence of the truth of the statement, "Smith is in town." My claim that the statement, "Smith is in town," is true rests upon my confidence in my own perception.

Evidence may consist of other statements which imply the statement in question. Implication is a logical relation, and its presentation in an argument is called "proof." If we can show that a statement is implied by other statements (called "premises"), and these other statements are known to be true, then the statement which the premises imply (called the "conclusion") is also known to be true. The relation of implication is such that the assertion of the premises together with the denial of the conclusion is a contradiction. The statements, "All graduates of this college can read at least one foreign language," and "All the persons attending the anniversary dinner are graduates of this college," together imply the third statement, "All the persons attending the anniversary dinner can read at least one foreign language." To assert the first two and deny the third is a contradiction.

If I am playing Contract Bridge and know that ten trumps have been played and that I still have three cards of the trump suit in my hand, then I know that no other player can trump a suit in which he is void. Of course I may not have counted the play correctly and so I may only believe and not know that ten trumps have been played. Or I may mistake a card of another suit in my hand for a trump and so believe that I have more trumps than is the case. But if ten trumps have been played and I have only three in my hand then it is impossible for any other player to play a trump. If it happens that another player does lay a trump on a trick then either I have miscounted, or the deck of cards is defective, or a player has reneged, or is cheating, or it is not Bridge that we are playing.

The distinction between belief and knowledge, as we have developed it thus far, may suggest that if it is possible for a belief to be false then no matter how strong the evidence for it we cannot regard that belief to be genuine knowledge. It is this attitude which is expressed in the occasional demand, in the history of philosophy, that we restrict "knowledge" to "certain and necessary truth." The difficulty is that the area of certain and necessary truth will have to be defined in terms of the method of knowing or else there is nothing to certify the correctness of a claim of certainty. Do we judge the soundness of our conclusions by the methods by which we arrive at them, or do we judge the soundness of our methods by the kind of conclusions they lead us to? If the latter, how do we distinguish right from wrong conclusions? Rational and scientific knowledge became possible only as the criteria of truth were found in the methods of inquiry rather than in antecedent beliefs concerning what was true and false.

Of course we do not simply ignore the beliefs we hold prior to the beginning of an inquiry. When I say I know something I assert that a belief is true and I rest the assertion of its truth on evidence and logic. What I mean is that the evidence compels me to accept the truth of what rests upon it. In this I do not often feel it essential to go behind the evidence; usually it is to the relation between the evidence and my belief that I appeal. If I were to express myself fully I should say that *if* this evidence is sound *then* the conclusion I have drawn from it is true. The justification of my position, as thus narrowed, consists in showing the logical relation of the evidence to the conclusion. In the vernacular use of *knowledge* we accept the term as applicable to anything based on evidence which seems obviously true—"obviously true" in the sense that no serious question is raised about it. This, of course, is not a strict use, for what seems true not always is true.

Suppose I am mistaken in what I accept as evidence. I say, "I know that Smith is in town because I saw him on the street a moment ago." Now if I saw Smith on the street a moment ago, and if he has not had time enough since I saw him to get out of town, then it must be that he is still in town. The evidence would require the conclusion. But suppose I am wrong about the evidence, and actually saw someone else whom I mistook for Smith. Is my statement still something I know? The answer is that the statement, "Smith is in town," is not something I know; for it is false, whether I am aware of that fact or not. But suppose I recast my statement and say, "If it was Smith I saw on the street a moment ago then Smith is in town." If this is true it is true whether Smith is in town or not.

No statement of evidence and conclusions contains all the factors involved in the question of truth. There are always some taken for granted; for to try to state them all, except in the form of some blanket assertion, would be an impossibly complex task. The above statement, for example, could be expanded: "If it was Smith I saw on the street, and if he has not had time to get out of town since, then Smith is in town." But this is little more than a tautology, to the effect that if Smith is not out of town, and if by "not out of town" we mean "in town," then Smith is in town. The closer we get to abstract or formal necessity in any statement concerning fact the closer it comes to a loss of contact with fact entirely, so that its truth or falsity does not depend on what the facts are. To state all the factual conditions which the statement assumes we should have to include such provisions as that I am in my right mind, that I am not dreaming or hallucinating, that no unknown method of leaving town more rapidly exists, that no one can be in two places at once, and so on.

A claim of knowledge based on sense perception, for example, always assumes that what was taken to be perception actually was perception. Hallucinations always *seem* to be perceptions, and dreams almost always do; so there is the possibility of our mistaking one of these for perception. Yet we all recognize the tacit condition underlying an appeal to perception as evidence, that the experience was perception and not a dream or an hallucination. Sometimes this comes into the open, especially when we encounter something quite unexpected, and a comment is prefaced with the qualification, "If my eyes do not deceive me . . ." In some borderline cases, for example where sensory or mental abnormalities are involved, the question of the genuineness of the supposed perception may take priority. But, as we shall see later, the fact that we can mistake something else for perception does not disqualify perception as a way of knowing.

Knowledge about existence has an aspect of certainty and an aspect of uncertainty. The certainty, in the sense of formal logical necessity, is in the relation between the evidence and what is inferred from it. However even here we can make mistakes in reasoning. On the other hand even the strictest reasoning guarantees the truth of its conclusions about existence only if the evidence for the conclusions is true. Our confidence in what we take to be knowledge reflects our confidence in our methods of testing the correctness of our reasoning and the soundness of our evidence. We are confident that we can know because we are confident that these methods are sound and that they are adequate to expose false claims to knowledge. The mistakes we make in the use of the methods can be discovered by further use of the same methods. But in so far as we are not competent to use these methods we are not able to acquire genuine knowledge.

Perhaps the most frequent cause of error in our claims to knowledge is our failure to apply the tests we have. Thus we confuse belief with knowledge. On the other hand, in so far as we have applied correctly our methods of testing reasoning and evidence, we do have some knowledge. If we are careful we often can disentangle what we know from what we merely believe or guess or hope to be true. Sometimes this is a matter merely of recognizing which is which. More frequently we need to introduce qualifications to narrow the range of the knowledge claim.

All that we believe because of sound evidence and correct reasoning is knowledge. These have to be the causes of our belief, else our belief is not knowledge no matter how true it may be. Since we may be in error concerning the soundness of our evidence or the correctness of our reasoning we may be in error in our claim to know. Yet in so far as we base our claim to know on reason and evidence there is some genuine knowledge contained within what we think we know. We may not be able precisely to differentiate it from the error with which it is mixed, but it is there nevertheless. This is the reason why, as we shall see presently, the mere possibility of error is not sufficient to invalidate a knowledge claim. It is well to recognize such possibilities where they are significant, for this will lead us to scrutinize carefully our reasoning and evidence. But the outcome of this is no clear-cut alternative of either all right or else all wrong; it is rather the more adequate differentiation of knowledge from insufficiently supported belief. From this we can obtain a principle of method and a basis for a general policy to follow in our present inquiry.

THE BURDEN OF PROOF

Inquiry can never have an absolute starting point. The very undertaking assumes that something is known. Such assumption may be suspect in this or that particular respect, but it cannot be considered altogether false if inquiry is to get started. Furthermore, the natural bent of the mind is to accept its judgments and inferences as true of real things. Doubt does not arise spontaneously concerning any of the generally recognized ways of knowing; doubt comes from conflict.

This has an important bearing on the question of where lies the burden of proof. It appears reasonable to put the burden of proof upon those theories which deny the competence of any of the generally recognized ways of knowing. Since inquiry begins with our common sense ideas about the world we need positive and conclusive evidence to compel us to reject any of the supposed ways of knowing which we ordinarily use. Certainly our uncritical judgments often turn out to be wrong, else we should be aware of few problems. But it is more plausible to believe that they are wrong because of the limitations of our experience and the errors we make in our thinking than to believe that our mental processes are, by their very nature, adapted to error. It is one thing to indict the results of an inquiry; it is quite another thing to indict the very processes of inquiry. For if we doubt the competence of the processes of inquiry how can we trust the processes by which we conclude we should doubt their competence?

A theory which rests on positive evidence can be opposed significantly only by another theory which does better what the original theory attempted. The fact that a theory *might* be false is never sufficient ground for its denial. To show that it is false we must show that it is inconsistent with the facts or incorrectly reasoned. The mere fact that we can doubt its truth is not sufficient reason to do so except as an exercise in speculation.

Even the most fantastic assertions of supposed fact, if they are sincere and responsible assertions, have some basis in reality. The person who hears voices that are not there still has a basis in experience for his assertion. He has an auditory experience but has misinterpreted its import. We cannot dispose of his claim by saying that he did not have the experience; we can only show that what he hears is not what he thinks it is. If we do this successfully then not only shall we take account of facts which he has overlooked but we shall also do justice to the positive facts on which his own interpretation is based.

Just as it is good policy to look on every positive assertion as in some way significant, and to regard every theory based on positive evidence and competently reasoned as expressing some truth, so it is poor policy to accept readily the finality of a negation. On the whole a philosophy is likely to be nearer right in what it affirms than in what it denies. Our positive and carefully formulated theories are likely to be based on positive evidence, but our theoretical negations are more likely to rest on the absence of evidence. There are too many "nothing but" philosophies: reality is *nothing but* matter, or reality is *nothing but* mind, or knowledge is *nothing but* sensations, or values are *nothing but* preferences. To create a limbo of non-being or of illusion or of subjectivity, and to dispose of troublesome facts by sending them there, is to evade philosophy's task—not to accomplish it. Surely we should be modest about the extent and the finality of our positive knowledge; it is so limited and so incomplete. But the only negations we are justified in making under the claim of knowledge are those which rest on conflict with our positive knowledge. How can we know so surely what is not when we know so little of what is?

This is no mere wishful thinking; there is good reason to look with more favor upon affirmations than upon negations. The errors we commit in what we affirm are the result of our misinterpretation of the evidence, and they are open to correction by further evidence as it becomes available. On the other hand, the errors we commit in what we deny are less likely to be the result of inquiry into the evidence as of assumptions and presuppositions we bring to the evidence. So far as this is the case, the discovery of further evidence is not likely to correct them, for their influence upon us is to close our minds to evidence.

The Foundations of Knowledge: 1. Sense Perception

The first foundation of knowledge is sense perception, in which we see and hear and in other ways have our most direct contact with physical things and events. Sense perception, however, is not solely a matter of sensing, else it would not provide knowledge. It includes sensing, but it also includes awareness of the meaning of the sense experience. When I look at a red rose the color is sensed but the sense experience itself may be a part of the wider experience of perceiving the rose. In perception there is recognition and interpretation as well as sensation. Because it includes the intellectual act of knowing, my perception of the rose is not merely an impression upon me or merely something which happens *to* me. It is rather a way in which my mind takes to itself those aspects of the nature of the rose which are made available to my mind by the sensory process. The rose itself of course is not taken into my mind, for the rose is a bloom on a plant growing in my garden; but *what* the rose is my mind in some way takes to itself.

If we are to discover in sense perception something of the nature of the things we perceive, as those things really are, then it cannot be that the things we know are changed by the process of knowing them; nor can it be that the process of knowing them contributes anything to their nature as known, for if knowing something adds in any way to what we take it to be then we have confused what the thing really is with a modified appearance of what it is. The mind does not act on the thing known; rather the thing known must act on the knower in such a way that the mind accommodates itself to the nature of the thing. The thing makes of the knowing mind a version of its own nature. Marble may do this at the hands of a sculptor, to a degree; but marble does not do this of itself. It is the nature of mind, however, to yield itself to the nature of what it apprehends. It takes into itself the very nature of the object.

We often make mistakes in sense perception but this does not destroy its soundness as a basis of knowledge. It is a source of knowledge because it brings to our awareness something of the nature of actual existence, and it is reliable on the whole because we have various methods of checking upon it and of distinguishing genuine perception from such experiences as dreams and hallucinations. The standards that enable us to make this distinction are not arbitrary standards, nor are they subject to our whims and fancies. When correctly applied they give us adequate assurance; when they fail to give adequate assurance either they have not been correctly applied or else we lack adequate knowledge, in this particular case, for their successful application. They may be used incorrectly, but the kind of error which occurs in sense perception is the kind which leaves itself open to correction.

It is unsound in principle to indict sense perception as untrustworthy simply because we are capable of making mistakes in our use of it. We may as well attack the validity of arithmetic when our accounts are out of balance. It is not because sense perception is an inherent falsifier that we make mistakes, but rather because of the carelessness and confusion in our interpretations and inferences. Only because it is essentially sound can we talk about errors in sense perception. We do not, for example, speak of erroneous hallucinations.

If there were no differences between perception and hallucination there would be no point in trying to differentiate one from the other. There are hallucinations, and there are apparently authentic reports of group hallucinations, but the fact that we know this to be the case shows that we have standards by which to distinguish between hallucinations and perceptions. If we did not have such standards, how could we know that there are hallucinations?

Mascall points out that "if a man persists in saying that he is seeing pink snakes with green spots we do not content ourselves with asking the man carefully to examine the snakes; we ourselves proceed carefully to examine the man."[1] With reference to this he observes, "When we examine the man to discover why it is that he is seeing snakes which no one else can see, we have to assume that we are not in error in our perceptions of the man."[2]

Some may object that our reasoning here would apply equally well to the fancies of astrology or numerology or palmistry. If we consider any findings of astrology to be false then do we not presume a standard of truth in astrology and imply that some astrological findings are true? The answer to this is that the parallel does not hold. What is required, if we are to judge the claims of astrology to be false, is that we admit that we possess some kind of knowledge with which those claims are inconsistent. There simply is no such thing as true astrology, and we reject the distinction between true and false astrology. The actual distinction is between astrology as such and whatever is included within the range of truth. We indict the whole system of ideas, but we can do this only because we possess knowledge with which the whole system of astrology is in conflict.

Why then can we not throw doubt on the whole field of sense perception on the ground that we have a body of knowledge with which sense perception is in conflict? We should then no longer distinguish between true and false sense perception; we should instead distinguish between true and false claims to knowledge, and we should include all of sense perception under the head of false claims to knowledge.

The fact is that this is our only alternative if we refuse to accept sense perception as a source of knowledge. We must either accept it as sound in principle, and explain erroneous judgments of perception as errors we make in our use of a sound instrument, or else we must reject it wholly and completely. But if anyone were to make out a case for the complete rejection of sense perception he could do so only by showing that we had a body of knowledge with which sense perception in its entirety was in conflict. We have no such body of knowledge.

A difficulty still remains, for we need to understand how sense perception can be the source of knowledge and of error as well. The answer to this question has already been suggested, that the difference lies in the interpretations we make of our sense experiences. Strictly speaking, of course, sense perception is not a source of error; we should say rather that it is open to misinterpretation. We can be in error also in what we take to be sensation itself, and it is such error as this which leads to hallucination and the confusion of dreaming with perceiving. A true perception does not always carry with it the knowledge that it is a true perception. We obtain knowledge by sense perception, and we know we obtain knowledge by sense perception; we also are led by sense experience into erroneous judgments, and we know that we sometimes err in our perceptual judgments; we have tests of truth which we apply to sense perception, and we know that these standards are sound. We may make mistakes in this or that particular instance of perception and in our application of the standards of truth, for there are circumstances in which our use of these standards is in greater than ordinary danger of error and in which judgment tends to suffer distortion. We make mistakes in perception and we cannot always know which are the true and which are the false perceptions. We do not always, when we know something, know that we know; and we do not always, when we err, know that we err. But we know that even if we err the further use of perception and the further application of the tests of truth will lead eventually to the correction of the error, if its correction lies within the range of our ability and if we do not give up too soon.

Our confidence that perception is a sound source of knowledge concerning physical existence rests to a significant degree on the absence of satisfactory alternative theories of the import of sense experience. The attempt to reject it totally may be an interesting experiment with ideas but it is not the kind of hypothesis we can use as a basis of life and action. It may be amusing, for example, to play with the idea that the whole order of nature, including ourselves together with what we call our memories, came into existence suddenly just five minutes ago. One who has a vivid imagination may think of such things but is not likely to advance it as a serious possibility. Even if it is not inherently self-contradictory or in conflict with other things we know to be true, it has nothing to commend it as an alternative to our belief in the basic soundness of memory. So far as sense perception is concerned, few if any serious thinkers since some of the early Greeks have proposed its total rejection as a basis of knowledge. There have been many different conceptions of the nature of the world about which sense perception informs us, and different ideas of the place of perception in relation to other modes of knowing, but only those who reject all knowledge whatever will deny that some of our knowledge has its roots here.

Sense Perception and Modern Science

What shall we say about the concepts of modern physical science? There certainly seems to be nothing in the formulas and equations of physics to remind us of the mountain or the rose which we perceive. The physicist's instruments and concepts seem to dissolve the world of ordinary experience into unimaginable processes involving strange entities and events never known by man outside the laboratory or the scientific imagination. In this respect modern physics may seem to differ not at all from ancient atomism which purported to explain the experienced properties of things in terms of hidden and unperceived processes and structures, with the result that the perceived features of things were explained away. There is, however, a most important difference between the two theories. Modern physics does have perceptual confirmation of the real existence of the processes and entities it employs in its explanations, while the Greek atomists had no evidence whatever of the real existence of their atoms. There is also an important implication of this difference: if we interpret modern physics so as to undermine the truthfulness of the perceptual confirmation itself then we destroy the only difference between genuine science and imaginative speculation.

> The existence of given facts [Professor Joad reminds us] is . . . a presupposition of the difference between perception and imagination. But, if they do exist, then the only way to discover what manner of facts they are is to go and look, to adopt, in other words, the method of physical science. . . . The method of "going to look," as the empirical philosophers of the seventeenth and eighteenth centuries successfully established against the rationalists, is the only method by means of which certain aspects of the universe can be known. There is, in other words, if you want to know what these aspects of the universe are like, no alternative to sense perception supplemented by scientific method.[3]

We need not doubt that the actual world can be described correctly in terms of the concepts of modern physics, and that such description of the real world is true in so far as it has adequate evidence to support it. The only judge of truth in physics is the physicist. But physics is not philosophy, and the fact that physics is true does not in any way imply that the physicist supplies us with the distinction between the real and the unreal. Unless this distinction is already established he cannot perform the observations and operations which compose his work as a physicist.

It is unfortunate that so many who hear of the startling findings and inferences of the physical sciences think that these discoveries discredit our perceptual experiences. This table on which I write, they say, is not a flat, hard, colored surface. The real table is that complex system of atomic and sub-atomic processes which the physicist's formulas specify. The table I think I see, they tell me, is only an idea formed in my mind by the interaction of light rays and other physical processes involving the real table with the atomic and sub-atomic processes which are my *real* sense organs and my *real* nervous system.

This conception is certainly not physics; it is philosophy—and poor philosophy at that. It is poor philosophy because instead of explaining perception it explains it away, and the very theory which explains perception away has explained away also the test of truth of the physics from which it purports to be derived. If we destroy the truth claim of sense perception we discredit the criterion by which we discover whether or not our concepts apply to real existence.

There is a basic principle here which is of utmost importance for the philosophical interpretation of scientific knowledge. The principle rests on the fact that in so far as perception is the test of existence for scientific method, and thus the test of the *truth* of its conclusions, no use of scientific method can call into question the truthfulness of perception. Scientific investigation may raise doubts about this or that specific experience and its perceptual interpretation; but the only way by which it can expose false claims of perception is by reference to genuine perception. This carries a momentous implication: no discovery in natural science can invalidate any judgment of the nature of existing things obtained through sense perception, except in so far as that judgment involves assumptions concerning properties which are not open to direct inspection or is based on a mistaken understanding of the conditions under which the perception occurred. When psychologists or biologists or physicists draw such conclusions as that colors and sounds are subjective and exist only in the mind of the perceiver and do not belong to the object perceived, they are dabbling in epistemology. They may or may not be competent to speak concerning matters of epistemology; if they are, it is not by virtue of their competence as psychologists or biologists or physicists.

Professor Joad points out that physics "has developed out of common-sense knowledge by a gradual transition which can be historically traced. It is in essence an extension and refinement of common-sense knowledge. This being so, it cannot, it is obvious, be used to impugn the validity of the knowledge upon which it is based and from which it springs without thereby impugning itself. In other words, unless perceptual knowledge be in the main veridical in the sense of giving us true information about an independent and external world, physics cannot itself be true; therefore physics cannot be used to show that perceptual knowledge is not veridical."[4]

But, we may ask, how can a thing be both what we perceive it to be and what physical science says that it is? There is no difference in principle between this and the question of how a thing can be both what it appears to be to the naked eye and what we see it to be when we look at it through a microscope. We discover in things, by perception alone, only those qualities and properties which our instruments and modes of knowing are capable of disclosing. Certainly we see the same thing differently from different perspectives or under different light conditions. But every perception takes place under some set of conditions, and we err when we misunderstand the conditions under which a given disclosure occurs. Atmospheric pressure changes and the sounds we hear seem closer to us, and for a moment we may be confused. Yet the sounds inform us concerning the thing itself, and our information is the more revealing the more adequately we correlate it with the special conditions under which it comes to us. A book is dark blue in the white light of day and seems to be black under a certain artificial light at night. Is the book *really* blue or black? If we understand that the color we see at night is not alone the color reflected by the book but a mixture of that color and the color of the light emitted by the source of illumination, then we have no difficulty answering the question.

Suppose we are told that the real book is colorless, and that it appears colored only because it absorbs certain frequencies of radiation and reflects others to our eyes; the nerve impulse thus activated reaches the appropriate brain centers and then somehow produces a blue or black color-sensum in consciousness. Thus the color we think we see in the thing is only an effect of causes operating on us from the outside; it is not a disclosure of the real nature of the thing which causes the supposed perceptual state. But if we are to know the truth of this causal theory of perception we shall have to verify the existence of the causes it refers to. How can we do this, if our experience is itself only the end-effects of causes? If we say we infer the cause from the effect, then reason and not perception is our contact with real existence; and we shall have to repudiate the whole corpus of modern science. Shall we say we imagine a cause which, if it existed, would produce our experience as its effects; therefore the cause exists? This is sheer speculation concerning fact, and it commits the very same error as that of the Greek atomists. It is contrary to the whole spirit and method of modern science, because modern science verifies existence not by inference alone nor by possibility but by sense perception. If sense perception is nothing but the effect of things upon us, so that the color we see in a rose has the very same cognitive significance as a sunburn, then the significance of science itself as a way of knowing has been destroyed.

In sense perception the physical processes which link our senses to the things we perceive are processes which communicate something of the nature of the thing perceived. When I see fire burning or see a coin lying on a table, the light rays emitted or reflected by the physical thing carry its color to my sense organs of vision. They do not change the color of the retina, but the changes they induce in the retina enable me to sense the color communicated by the light. The light itself is colored, and the color the light carries is abstracted from it in the process of sensing; it is precisely this in which sensory cognition consists, and of course the act of sensing is not physical but mental. In this it is the color I am aware of, not the physical processes which communicate it; and in so far as it is the color communicated from the thing itself, my awareness of the color is an awareness of a quality of the thing.

It is no simple matter to understand the nature of sensory knowledge and the processes by which it takes place, and this is not the place or occasion to explore the problem. But we must recognize at this point the need to hold fast to our assurance that genuine sensory knowledge occurs and that it is our one means of contact with external existence. The things we perceive must exist; they must have qualities which can be transmitted to our sense organs; there must be a medium by which their qualities are transmitted to our sense organs; there must be the appropriation by the sense organs of the qualities thus transmitted; and finally, we must be aware of the thing itself by means of the quality transmitted from it by the appropriate medium to our sense organs and abstracted by them.[5]

It certainly is true that real things show themselves to us from many perspectives and under many varieties of conditions. As we come to understand better the conditions under which perception occurs we understand better the real natures of the things themselves. But the fact that a thing shows us different aspects under different circumstances does not mean that the thing perceived is relative to, or constituted by, our modes of perception and thought. The nature of the thing is what it is. The method of knowing may determine just what qualities and aspects of the thing we may discover, but it does not bestow on the thing itself those qualities we do find. We do not fish for minnows with a coarse net; nor, if we are so foolish as to attempt it, does our failure to find minnows in our net establish their non-existence. Yet the fish we do catch in our net do not derive their size and possibility of being caught from the structure and operations of the net which catches them.

Physical science is a search into the structure of things, not a catalogue of the properties we find in our direct experience. It is an attempt to understand how it is that things have the properties they have, and to uncover other properties which direct experience does not disclose. The difference between sense perception and a scientific account of a thing's nature is the difference between immediate, superficial, and incomplete knowledge on the one hand and, on the other, a fund of knowledge more adequate to the intrinsic structure of the thing itself. But superficial knowledge, in so far as it is knowledge, is not in conflict with more extended knowledge; we do not replace our first and incomplete sensory knowledge with our more extended knowledge, we only supplement it. Scientific inquiry builds upon perception; it carries our knowledge of things beyond the direct reach of perception; but it must always return to perception for verification if it is to support its claim to be knowledge of what really exists.

The significance of perceptual confirmation is shown by the different fates of two important hypotheses in physics. The hypothesis of an ether seemed, for a time, a useful tool in modern physics. In spite of the fact that there was no perceptual confirmation of the existence of an ether as the medium of light, it became one of the basic concepts of physical theory. But the experiments of Michelson and Morley, which were intended to establish the fact of the real existence of an ether, unexpectedly failed to do so; they showed that no such medium for the transmission of light exists. In contrast with the fate of the ether hypothesis we may consider the theory of relativity. Originally it too served as a useful hypothesis for the explanation of certain observations which seemed inconsistent with traditional ideas of space and time. Eventually, however, the theory of relativity was shown to be true of real existence when predictions which were formulated as implications of the theory were confirmed by direct observation.

CHAPTER 4

Rational Knowledge

THE FOUNDATIONS OF KNOWLEDGE: 2. RATIONAL INSIGHT

RATIONAL insight is the direct awareness of forms and relations as such. It is of two kinds, or has two fields of operation; one of these is recognized almost without exception but the other is not so universally acknowledged.

The first of these two operations of rational insight is the awareness of logical relations. I recognize, for example, without any further consideration than my understanding of what the statements mean, that it cannot be true both that "all Christians love their neighbors" and that "some Christians do not love their neighbors." It cannot be true that the number I am thinking of is a prime number and also that its last digit is 4, such as 4 itself, or 14, or 324, or 6974. There are very many of these relations, and we are so familiar with them that we constantly make use of our ability to apprehend them in all phases of our waking life. The lack of such an ability would be a mental defect or a sign of extreme immaturity. All logical reasoning is based on this, and without it even meaningful assertion is impossible.

The awareness of logical relations is knowledge of being. The notion that reason is merely the awareness of ideas, of relations which hold within our thought, is to deny its claim to know the objects to which it refers. The relations *by means of which I think* are logical relations, but what I think about by means of logical relations is being. Even my thought about logical relations is not itself those relations; it is a mental act. Suppose I think the proposition, "All men are mortal." My thought of this makes use of the logical identity by which the subject and predicate are united in the proposition. Now I can think something about this relation, for example that the predicate is affirmed of the subject universally. But I can apprehend this property of the proposition because of the logical relation between the proposition itself and *what I think about it*. Rational insight is a discovery of the nature of being. It is a source of knowledge only because it *refers to* or *intends* something other than itself. It is not a play of ideas or a mental construction; it is the disclosure of the nature of something—something actual or possible or imagined. In so far as what we think is true or false it is so because it is *true to* or *false to* something to which it refers. If it refers to nothing, then it only is. It does not disclose. To use G. H. Hardy's example from mathematics, "317 is a prime, not because we think so, or because our minds are shaped in one way rather than another, but *because it is so*, because mathematical reality is built that way."[1]

The obvious example of rational knowledge of possibility is mathematics. In mathematics we have knowledge *of something;* its meaning is not in itself but in its reference to possible existence. The use of mathematical marks and devices without reference to being would be, at best, nothing more than their combinations in various patterns. Such patterns may deserve our aesthetic appreciation, but they would not, merely as such, be mathematics. Morris R. Cohen makes this plain:

> The operations of mathematics are in fact significant because they apply not only to the marks actually used but to all possible objects. Just as the particular diagrams in Euclid are not the true objects of the demonstration but only aids to our imagination to help us envisage the possible entities to which they can be applied, so do the various letters and other marks enter logic and mathematics, not in their status as specific physical objects, but rather as representatives of all possible entities. A mathematical statement has in this way reference beyond the immediate sounds or marks that enter it.[2]

Our awareness of logical relations is not cut off entirely from actual existence in spite of the fact that such relations hold good of all possible being. In fact if we recognize that logical relations and mathematics are true of any possible world then we also have admitted their application to the actual world. If one set of propositions, the premises, implies certain other propositions, the conclusions, then if the premises are true of the actual world the conclusions also must be true of it. This applies to the actual world as it applies to all worlds we can think about, and of course it is silly to try to think of worlds we cannot think about. To deny that two mutually contradictory propositions can both be true of the real world is to say something about the real world. Whatever its nature may be, and however ignorant of its nature we may be, we may be sure that the real world rejects contradiction. Either this is the case or else logic is only a game we play according to a set of arbitrary conventions we accept as rules of the game.

We have a moral responsibility toward our reasoning. For if we claim to establish certain conclusions by reasoning and then refuse to accept them as true in our belief and action, the best that we can say for ourselves is that we are insincere. If we are sincere we have to accept the consequences of our thinking, and if we refuse to do this our claim that our thinking is true is belied by our own repudiation of its consequences. "At this point," says Bertrand Russell,

> as at many others, I am brought up against a distinction, not always clear-cut, between argumentation as a game and philosophy as a serious attempt to decide what to think. Hume, as a professional, affected to doubt many things which, in fact, he did not doubt; I have done the same thing myself. What is objective in such scepticism is the discovery that from A it is impossible to deduce B, although, hitherto, it has been thought possible, and although it has been held that this was the only good ground for believing B. But if, in fact, a man is going to go on believing B just as firmly as before, his scepticism is insincere. As a general rule, the effect of logical analysis is to show the mutual independence of propositions which had been thought to be logically connected. Hegel, who deduced from pure logic the whole nature of the world, including the non-existence of the asteroids, was only enabled to do so by his logical incompetence. As logic improves, less and less can be proved. The result, if we regard logical analysis as a game, is an insincere scepticism. But if we are unwilling to profess disbeliefs that we are in

fact incapable of entertaining, the result of logical analysis is to increase the number of independent premisses that we accept in our analysis of knowledge.[3]

If we try to assert seriously that logic is only a game we find we have to recognize that either logic is a game or it is not, and that it cannot both be a game and in the same sense not be a game. If this is not so then for me to say that logic is only a game is meaningless. I can say, at most, that I am playing that logic is only a game. This, in turn, can mean, at most, that I am playing that I am playing that logic is only a game—and so on. But each of the statements which takes us into this endless series is meaningless except in so far as its truth involves the falsity of its denial, and this is the case only if logical relations hold good of all that is possible. If logic is a game it is an odd kind of game. It is a game we have to play, for even in the act of choosing whether we shall play it we have to perform the act of choice in accordance with the rules of that game.

The second kind of rational insight is the direct recognition of the presence of certain forms and relations in actual existence itself. We know from our study of geometry the properties of triangles, and what we know applies to all actual and possible triangles. But we do not know from geometry that this particular physical object, this piece of sawed board, is triangular in shape. Geometry may tell us what criteria to apply to recognize the triangular, but it does not tell us that we shall find here and now this particular instance of the triangular. To recognize a particular thing as an instance of general law is a kind of rational insight. We sense the color of the wood, and in a certain way we may be said to sense its shape; that is, we see where the limits of its extension are and we see these limits in a certain pattern. But there is rational insight in the recognition that this is a pattern and in our awareness of what kind of a pattern it is. There is more here than a mere response to a pattern which, as the Gestalt psychologists have shown, occurs at the sensory level. There is the act of understanding *this* to be *an instance of* some kind of thing. Without this kind of rational insight the first kind would be of little use to us, for we should be unable to detect the occasions to which it applies.

The second kind of rational insight does not, as does the first, involve us in contradiction if we deny it. I can imagine without contradiction, for example, a world in which there are no things with the shape of a plane triangle. It is apparent that the latter kind of rational insight occurs only as we make contact with actual existence. It is not the same as sense perception, for it is not the way by which we discover qualities; it concerns rather the patterns and relations of the qualities we discover in perception. We do not sense these patterns, but we discover them involved in what we do sense. We can construct abstract geometries which apply, so far as we know, only to imaginary worlds, but the actual world which confronts us in real existence is one in which there are certain very definite and restricted space relations. We can discover these relations, and relations of relations. Sequences of sounds which man finds significant, such as melodies and harmonies, are not constructed by rule. They are discovered, noted, improvised by impulse and under the guidance of feeling and attitude. Yet we discover in them extremely complex patterns of sound and rhythm. Out of this come the music disciplines, all based on forms and relations which, although contained in sensory and perceptual experience, nothing less than reason could discover and recognize.

Rational insight into existence, as distinguished from rational insight into possibility, depends on sense perception of external things or our direct awareness of our own mental acts. But what comes to us in perception does not make itself intelligible without the cooperation of reason. There are spatial patterns in what I see, but only by rational insight can I *discern* those patterns as such and discover their features. A flaming match is thrust into water and its flame is extinguished. I perceive the sequence of events but only by my understanding can I recognize a cause and effect relation in the sequence. The *what* which comes by perception is understood, so far as it is understood at all, by the use of concepts.

To be sure [says Professor Veatch] there is no denying that all that we see with our eyes are mere colors, or that all that we hear with our ears are mere sounds, etc. And yet, does it follow from this that nothing more is given or presented in sense experience than colors, sounds, odors, etc? Quite the contrary; it is quite possible that a great deal more might be given in sensation than the senses themselves are able to discern. In such a case, while what would be presented to us through the senses would really be so presented, it would still not be through the senses alone that we would come to apprehend what was so presented. In other words, as Gilson has put it, "the senses would be the bearer of a message which they themselves would be incapable of reading and which only the intellect could decipher."[4]

The usual objection to admitting that we have rational insight into existence is the fact that we are sometimes mistaken in the judgments we base on these insights. The objection itself, however, assumes that knowledge is confined to that which excludes error, that we must not consider we have knowledge unless it is impossible that we can ever call anything by the name of "knowledge" and be wrong.

The difficulty here is that again, as in the attacks on sense perception, two things are confused. It is confusion between knowledge of something and the knowledge that we have knowledge of something. This confusion is the basis of every attempt to equate knowledge and absolute certainty. The fact is that knowledge is always incomplete; our knowledge of existence is never final and finished, for it is always in the making. The various bits we find all pertain to one world and they all fit together, but we do not have enough knowledge to grasp all the relationships within our one world. We go wrong not in claiming to know something; we go wrong in failing to recognize the limitations of our knowledge and its conditional character. Any attempt to start with absolute and final certainty, such as Descartes' attempt in the early years of modern thought, leads directly to the conclusion that the area of such knowledge is a zero quantity. It leads inexorably to skepticism, as inexorably as Descartes' starting point led to Hume's conclusions.

Does this mean that we can have knowledge which is not true? Of course not. False assertions do not constitute knowledge, and if we believe them to be true we are in error. But it is the case that we can be mistaken about whether we have this or that knowledge. I may believe I know something and yet not know it; or I may not realize that I know something I do know. In each case I fail to know whether I know.

Is knowledge, then, equivalent to true belief? Suppose a fortune teller informs me that the New York team will win the American League baseball pennant, suppose I believe the fortune teller, and suppose it turns out that New York does win the pennant. Was my belief a case of knowledge? The answer is clearly negative. For the basis of my belief was entirely irrelevant to the truth or falsity of the belief. True beliefs make up knowledge in so far as the basis for accepting the belief as true is the reason why the belief is true. If we follow this guide we may make mistakes, and we may think we know many things we do not. But we shall open the way to obtain some of the knowledge available to us and we shall be on the road which leads to the discovery of error and to its correction.

The alternatives are not, as much of contemporary thought implies, those of knowing everything or knowing nothing. The belief that knowledge is impossible is intellectual suicide, and the belief that error is impossible is insanity. In so far as modern thought tortures itself into this dilemma it shows it has failed to learn its lesson from Plato and Aristotle, the master teachers of all Western thought. For it was likely this very dilemma, emerging from Socrates' inquiries into knowledge, which launched Plato upon his own independent search as a philosopher; and it was on the foundations laid by Plato that Aristotle built.

THE RELATION OF SENSORY AND RATIONAL KNOWLEDGE

Sense and reason are different, but they are not in opposition; they are not mutually exclusive, but complementary. Sense does not provide knowledge from itself alone. It provides the materials of knowledge. Reason does not provide knowledge from itself alone, for unless we have something to think *about* we do not think. Of course we can think about thinking, but only after we have engaged in thinking. Even when we think about thinking, the thinking we think about is not our thought about it.

What this all means is that the object of awareness is being, and what we know is always the nature of some being. It may be a mental being, or a logical entity, or a fiction, or a word, or it may be a real existent. We discover the nature of the being we know by whatever processes of knowing we are able to use. The mutual relevance of sensory and rational knowledge is not to be found in the relationship of sense and reason, as activities, but in the unity of the being to which they both refer. Sense and reason are mutually relevant because the things we know are accessible to our senses and because what we thus have sensory access to involves the relations and forms which reason apprehends.

As Professor Wild points out, if we "intellectualize sense" or "sensationalize reason," we either lose the really existing individual thing which sensory knowledge discloses, and dissolve it into a cluster of universals, or else we lose the cognitive significance of reason and reduce it to "unverifiable assumptions and guesses about the individual, material objects which sense alone apprehends."[5]

The basic fallacy lies in a failure to see that sense and reason are *distinct* faculties, each with a *distinct object of its own*. Rational cognition cannot be explained unless it actually apprehends some object distinct from that of sense. But if we are not to construct an artificial world of separate Platonic universals apart from the material things of sense, how are we to answer the crucial question as to *where* this object is and *what* it is? . . . The object of reason is precisely *where* the object of sense is. It is precisely something implicit in the material thing, either its essence or the essence of one of its accidents. . . . Reason apprehends the very same thing (materially) which sense apprehends, but it grasps something in this thing (formally) which sense cannot grasp. . . .[6]

THE FOUNDATIONS OF KNOWLEDGE: 3. PRACTICAL REASON

Reason is not only theoretical, it is also practical. By this we mean it is concerned with and manifested in practice and action. As *practical* reason it is not concerned with action in the sense that it formulates plans and designs, for plans and designs are themselves the work of theory. A plan, even the best, remains only a plan until it is implemented. It does not provide for its own execution. We may distinguish between plans as practicable and impracticable, but this is not the same as the distinction between the practical and the theoretical.

By *practical reason* we refer to the fact that action and practice has its own rational pattern. It is reason embodied in action as distinguished from reason explicit in concepts. Practical reason is the way in which action and practice make sense; it is the guidance of action by the rational pattern inherent in the situation.

If, for example, I wish to go from where I am to a place a mile away, I do not proceed by facing in the right direction and attempting to jump the whole distance. Such an attempt would not make sense, for it does not fit the circumstances. I do not have the kind of equipment which enables me to jump a mile in one leap. To expect that kind of action of myself is to demand something which contradicts my nature. If, however, I set out to walk the distance then under ordinary circumstances my action makes sense. The action fits the situation. So far as it is guided in terms of what makes sense the act is an instance of practical reason. If, in addition, I think out my plan of action before I act then theoretical reason as well is involved. Practical reason provides us with knowledge because our action reveals our grasp of certain properties and characteristics of the world in which we act.

I cannot be certain, in theory, that my house will be habitable tomorrow; a windstorm, an earthquake, a fire may destroy it. But I do not act as if I anticipated the occurrence of such things. They are possibilities, and I may take reasonable precautions, for example, to prevent loss from fire, and I may carry insurance protection against this or other contingencies. But if I were to act as if I expected these things to happen I should now be moving my goods to a safer place and arranging for other accommodations for my family. Instead I find myself sitting in a lawn chair, shaded by a tree from the summer sun, engaged in writing about the practical reason.

What kind of knowledge does this embody? It is not knowledge that disaster will not come to my property; I well know it is possible, for I have seen some homes destroyed by fire and others by wind. The knowledge which is expressed in this action and attitude is that such events occur so suddenly and from causes so impossible for me to control, and they are relatively so infrequent, it would be foolish for me to spend my time and money preparing each day to meet such contingencies directly. It is because of the nature of these events and because of their relation to other events that the reasonable policy is to take the ordinary precautions to protect myself from severe financial loss.

I have no certain knowledge that when I take my next step the earth will not open at my feet and swallow me up. But I cannot therefore remain the rest of my life rooted to the spot where I stand. My physical needs require me to move from this spot if I am to attend to them, and if I am to continue to live I must attend to them. I am forced, by practical necessity, to act as if the ground I walk on will hold me up; I am forced to act as if the buildings I enter will remain intact and will not come down upon my head. To live I must act, and every act commits me to assumptions concerning myself and the things which the action concerns.

I do not know that the assumptions I make in action will hold good in every instance. Earthquakes do occur; buildings do collapse. But my action shows my confidence in the reasonableness of my assumptions. Even when such an assumption turns out in one instance to be mistaken it still may have been reasonable to have made it. When I set out on an automobile trip I assume that I shall not have a serious accident or breakdown. Should I actually have an accident the fact of its occurrence does not mean that I was unreasonable to expect to arrive at my destination without trouble.

My action, of course, may be based on faith, and not be an expression of practical reason at all. If I assume a building will not collapse because that assumption is the reasonable one to make under the circumstances, because it is rationally appropriate, then my action is guided by reason. But if it is based on faith then it rests solely on my willingness to trust the building's stability; there is here no awareness of the appropriateness or reasonableness of the assumption to the circumstances.

If it is reasonable for me to act on certain expectations even if I do not know for sure that they will be fulfilled then my practice embodies in action certain ideas about the kind of world I am in, and these ideas are expressed in my action whether I am aware of them or not. So far as these ideas fit the real nature of the world they are true, and my action reflects something of the intrinsic structure of the world and of the laws of its operation. My action is an expression of reason, not alone of the reason in me but also of the reason in things.

The test of truth in the operation of practical reason is, as we should expect, a test we find in practice. It is the test of success or failure. If my practical assumptions repeatedly interfere with action, or make action impossible, that fact is an indication of their falsity. If I blithely set out on a long and hard automobile trip, with no time to spare in reaching my destination, and if the car I propose to drive is a broken-down wreck I shall likely learn some of the facts of life and make a closer contact than I had made before with the reason that is in things.

Here again we have knowledge, and its possession is compatible with the possibility of our being in error. We may know from the evidence available that certain localities are in less danger from floods or earthquakes than others. On this knowledge we act, in spite of the fact that specific events may be contrary to the general tendencies. This is the kind of a world in which there are discoverable tendencies and probabilities, and in which exceptions to these general tendencies do occasionally happen. If anyone objects that we do not know it is this kind of world the reply is that neither he nor anyone else can act in this world on the basis of any contrary conception of it. The discovery of our inability to act on other terms may well be called a *working knowledge* of the nature of our world. It does not need to be formulated in concepts, for such would be a theoretical act of reason; for practical reason it is enough that this knowledge is implicit in attitude and act.

CHAPTER 5

Faith and Knowledge

I MAY SAY of a person, "I believe what he says; I have faith in him." I may believe what he says because I have faith in him, but it is unlikely that I have faith in him because I believe what he says. This expresses something of the distinction between belief and faith.

Belief refers primarily to the acceptance of statements as true. We believe or disbelieve a claim of truth. When I say that I believe a man, as distinguished from the statement that I believe *in* him, I mean I believe that what he says is true.

Faith is a kind of belief, but it is not merely belief. It is belief in a different dimension, on a different level, performing a different function, and having a different object. Faith is not merely belief, it is belief *in* something. It is not merely belief in the truth of an assertion or denial, it is belief in a person or a people or a cause or a policy or a destiny.

Although the exposure of its falsehood may destroy a faith yet faith is not concerned primarily with truth. Its primary concern is with value. It is concerned with truth, with rational and logical truth, but its concern with this is secondary—secondary in the sense that this concern follows from its primary concern with value.

We believe in our friends, for example. We believe, let us say, in their integrity and trustworthiness and in their essential goodness. We believe they feel toward us the attitudes they express in word and deed. It does not occur to us that they are performing calculated acts intended to create in us a false confidence so that they can the more easily destroy us. It is not that we have had them shadowed by detectives and have searched their rooms and read their mail and tapped their telephones and recorded their private conversations and then, having found nothing to warrant distrust, we give them our confidence. Such action would destroy faith, not establish it. We have a phrase which fits it precisely,—to act in that way would be to act "in bad faith."

Faith requires belief, in the sense of intellectual assent, but it is more than this. It is first of all a way of life, or a part of a way of life. Without intellectual assent a way of life would lack integrity; it would be the living of a lie. But intellectual assent is not primary. A man who acts as if he loves a woman even when he is convinced he does not acts with duplicity. But a man's love for a woman is not primarily a matter of intellectual conviction.

The distinctive feature of faith, in contrast with mere belief, is the element in it of will and action. Belief is an act of the intellect, and faith has been described as "an act of the intellect commanded by the will."[1] But faith is more than an act of the intellect, and the will does more than command. Faith is not merely the assent that something is true, it is our readiness to act on what we believe true. Faith is will lured by value into action.

Faith is decision. It expresses in action what otherwise would be merely a conclusion, a judgment, an intellectual affirmation. Thus faith is true or false not only as a belief or judgment is true or false but in the correspondence of action to judgment. What I know does not constitute faith, nor does what I believe. My faith is my action in accordance with what I accept as true. This is faith's truth—a kind of truth that concerns its existence rather than its significance as mere cognition. Knowledge cannot take the place of faith, for wide knowledge and high erudition may well be in company with a paralysis of the will. We have to give ourselves to what we know before knowledge and faith come together; and this bridge is never built from the side of knowledge.

When I have faith in something I believe it has a certain character, that it is of a certain nature. My faith in a man involves a belief about what kind of man he is. If my faith leads me to trust

74

him it is likely I believe he is trustworthy, although, as we shall see, there may be exceptions to this. But to believe a man trustworthy and to show that I have trust in him are different acts, one is of the intellect and the other is of the will; and I do not show trust in him until I act on my belief that he is trustworthy.

Sometimes, however, the kind of belief which faith involves is of a different order. I may have serious doubts about a man's ability to carry out an important task and yet I may entrust it to him in spite of my doubts. I may believe, for example, that my act of trust in him will give him confidence and help him rise to the occasion. My faith is not based on a positive and confident belief that he will succeed; I have faith in him as one who has the essential ability and I hope that my act of trust may help him make successful use of that ability. A man's gifts may be like a seed which lies dormant in the soil until warmed by the sun.

In like manner it is possible for religious faith to be present in the face of doubt. I may have intellectual doubts concerning the existence of God and yet have faith in God's existence. It may occur to me, for example, that there may be a basis for belief in God which I cannot reach except by an act of faith. The act of faith in this case is not simply the removal of doubt by sheer strength of will. I do not say, "I refuse to doubt," and so come to a belief in the truth of the proposition, "God exists." I ask myself rather what difference it would make in my policy and action if I did believe that God exists, and I then adopt for myself by an act of will the policy I should follow if I did believe. I may find then that belief follows the act. Faith here does not rest on a prior belief in the existence of God, but it does rest on belief. I could not thus act if I did not believe in the possibility of God's existence and if I did not believe that our intellectual assents and dissents may be influenced by our actions and that in action I may discover grounds for belief which are not available to me in mere reflection and abstract thought.

In the same way a man may express faith in a cause even though he believes it to be a hopeless cause. He may throw himself into a struggle against tyranny even though he believes, in his moments of cool reflective analysis of the facts, that the struggle cannot succeed. Yet faith does not operate here without belief. He does believe it is right for him to engage in the struggle, and he may discover sources of strength in his cause which he could not have known if he had remained aloof. As we shall see later, something of this same relation is to be found between belief and knowledge.

We still must say, as before, that faith requires belief; but we see now that the relation between faith and belief is not always so simple as it may appear at first sight. The belief essential to faith may be a belief in the possibilities, in the resources and hidden strength or in the undisclosed worth of a person or a cause or of the basis of existence itself. Faith is the willingness to be led by the best and highest possibilities. I show my fullest measure of faith in a man when I act as if he were actually the best he could possibly be. I reach the height of religious faith when I act as if existence is actually, in its final and ultimate nature, the absolute perfection of being I can think it to be.

KNOWLEDGE AND FAITH IN SEPARATION

Knowledge and faith are commonly thought to be different, mutually exclusive, and even antagonistic to each other. They are different, as we have seen, and it is true they do not always go together. But in their true character they are complementary, and where they are antagonistic there is something wrong with what we take to be knowledge or with faith or with both. For knowledge and faith are both concerned with truth, although not in the same way, and truth is single and absolute in its self-consistency. No other possibility can be discussed intelligibly, for any attempt to divide truth or to state a doctrine of double truth cries out for an answer to the question of which kind of truth is claimed for the doctrine of double truth.[2]

Men have long taken sides on the matter of knowledge and faith, and indeed this is inevitable if they are thought to be in opposition. Those who align themselves with knowledge, in opposition to faith, are inclined to assume that when faith comes in conflict with what they themselves take to be knowledge the error lies with the claims of faith. Those who side with faith, in opposition to knowledge, tend to regard as spurious any claim of knowledge which does not fit their own scheme of faith. As Professor J. Harry Cotton points out, the repudiation of knowledge in the interests of faith is self-defeating.

> The exponents of faith sometimes glory in the irrational as such. *Credo quia absurdum.* They seem to believe that the defects of our human reason are inevitable and incurable; that theoretic interest is by its very nature hostile to the attitude of faith. When, therefore, such theologians insist on writing books in which they profess to despise reason and set forth their profession in pages and pages of reasoned argument, they are guilty of pretense. When these writers present conclusions which they insist belong to the realm of fact, meanwhile denying the ability of human thought to grasp what they say, they are in a very awkward position.[3]

He who takes the side of knowledge against faith judges the claims of faith by what he thinks he knows, and so attributes finality to his own version of knowledge; the other judges the claims of knowledge by faith, and so attributes finality to that faith. The appropriate reply to both parties is that we do not know as much as the one thinks we know and that in none of us is faith so pure and free of distorting influences that we can permit the faith we have to supplant or block the processes of inquiry.

Each party, as a matter of fact, is untrue to its own professed cause. To pretend that our present knowledge is final is contrary to the very spirit of rational inquiry. Its result is not to advance the search for knowledge and encourage the correction of error; it is rather to shut off inquiry at its source. For our motives in seeking knowledge are curiosity and need, and neither of these can show itself in the presence of final judgments. Similarly, to presume that faith can take the place of search and investigation is contrary to the spirit of faith—and it would seem contrary most of all to the spirit of religious faith. The humility of genuine faith, which is intensely aware of its own ignorance, cannot endure along with the assertion of an exclusive ownership of truth. The stronger a man's faith the more vividly aware is he of the possibility that he may be wrong. It is the awareness of this possibility which calls out the resources of his faith, and it is in the light of his awareness of this possibility that the strength of his faith shows itself. The weakest faith can stand so long as it is sure it is right. Only doubt can provide a real test of faith's strength. The saint does not feel his own sainthood; rather it is he who shows us doubt doing its worst with faith at its strongest. Christians who believe that God became man are taught that the man whom He became did not escape doubt, and that more than any physical pain His agony was the agony of despair.

Doubt does not destroy faith; doubt tests faith. But the relation of doubt and faith is dynamic, not passive. Faith has its own response to doubt, for doubt is the occasion for faith to examine itself and its cause. As ignorance is overcome by knowledge, faith may find a new direction and a more adequate awareness of its purpose. On the other hand, when faith survives doubt and persists in spite of a disbelief which threatens its integrity, we may well re-examine our beliefs and our supposed knowledge. That a conviction of value survives the opposition of what we believe and what we think we know does not guarantee the soundness of the conviction; it is, however, an occasion for the reappraisal of knowledge's claims. The only basis for harmony of faith and knowledge, if neither is to be made the tool of the other, is that both shall remain alive and active and flexible. Knowledge must always be ready to learn, and faith must always be ready to submit to what it discovers to be better than what it had seen before.

If knowledge and faith should not be separated it must be because there is in each a relevance to the other. This means that intellect and will are, in their essential nature, complementary and not opposed. "There is no mind without interest and no will which is completely blind,"[4] Father D'Arcy reminds us. The attempt to separate knowledge and faith is the perversion of both. As President Pusey says, "We need to know, but we need also to believe, and what we want especially to do is to believe knowingly and to know with conviction."[5]

The willingness to put our faith to the test is what preserves it as faith. An unwillingness to venture is the negation of faith; it is the will's denial of what is affirmed in faith's name. When faith takes the place of knowledge, and tries to assume the role of knowledge, it becomes fanaticism. In an essay on Pascal, Charles Morgan points this out in commenting that "Pascal's faith is never isolated from its intellectual context or from the promptings of the heart. It is neither sentimental nor cold. Fanaticism, like fear, arises from a split in the human personality; faith, and Pascal's conspicuously, from an integration of it."[6]

Thus we see the results of the separation of knowledge and faith. Such separation leads, on the one hand, to paralysis of will, and, on the other, to fanaticism. In his comment on Pascal's attitude to what he calls "indifferentism," Morgan remarks the close relationship of these two consequences of the separation of knowledge and faith.

> What Pascal thinks of as indifferentism has, then, precisely what we should not expect it to have—a link in motive with totalitarianism: the link being a refusal to ask questions, a desire to suspend criticism, an incapacity to supplement reason with faith, and faith with reason, a slave's willingness to separate them, a fanatic's longing to keep them apart. This particular complex of motive, this black despair of which the negative expression is indifferentism and the positive totalitarianism, is the sin that Pascal does not forgive.[7]

Faith beyond Knowledge

In spite of its relation to knowledge, faith cannot confine itself within the limits of knowledge. Where knowledge can guide action it is the proper guide for action to follow, and the willingness to act on what we know is still faith. But we cannot avoid the need to act beyond the range of our knowledge. Not only in religion but in all those causes which inspire devotion and sacrifice we see faith leave the security of knowledge behind.

Leaders of the Greek resistance to Persia and leaders of the American Revolution had faith in their causes. Their action was based not on knowledge but on will. They were determined to make their cause prevail and to this end they pledged all they had —property, life, and honor. They did not know that success would come. In both these great wars, each of which meant so much to posterity, there were times when no disinterested observer could have given any kind of encouragement based on a sober evaluation of the available evidence. But in neither case was strength of faith proportioned to the apparent probability of success. A similar and no doubt as strong a faith led the American Indians of the western plains in their resistance to the white man's ruthless and conscienceless violation of his sacred word, the word he had given in solemn treaty to those weaker than himself. Their cause seemed hopeless, and it was; but in some of them this only intensified the determination to resist to the end.

We find in such instances the essential character of faith as an act of will. It is not confidence in success, rather it is determination to serve the cause with utter devotion no matter what the outcome. Faith such as this expresses a fundamental evaluation; it is not a theory about values, but evaluation in act.

Even the success of the cause is not always the primary consideration, for, where success is all that counts, a man is a fool to continue to fight when the odds against him seem hopeless. When he has done all he can to win and when success finally becomes impossible there is nothing more he can do to bring success. But men do continue to fight against hopeless odds, and it is not always because they have lost their judgment and balance in the intensity of the struggle. Sometimes their faithfulness to the cause is itself more important than any consequence. They have a commitment, and they must keep it. They judge it better to die for a faith than to abandon it and live. And yet this is not the whole story, else what we call "faith" might be only desperation and the abandonment of everything to the defeat of hopelessness.

The willingness to give up even life itself for a faith may express a confidence that the present defeat is only temporary and that finally the cause itself will triumph. It is not my victory, as my own, but the victory of the cause which counts. So long as man has been man there have been those who have seen the need to devote themselves to ends they could not hope to see realized. As Moses looked upon the promised land which he himself could not enter he surely felt personal disappointment, but his personal disappointment was not a denial of the success of his mission.

Even the hope of ultimate success for a cause, however, is not essential for faithful service in its behalf. Where good is defeated and loss seems final, the witness of devotion to the good is most precious and itself is another good which rises out of defeat. Out of defeat and out of the demonstration of devotion to the defeated cause can come transformations of life and of society beyond anticipation. Remote as they were from one another, different as their backgrounds were, Aeschylus and Isaiah and Shakespeare and Milton speak the same truth: The tragedies of the human spirit are the sources of its greatest creations, and in its tragedies it discloses and discovers what it itself most truly is.

This does not imply that faith is always sound, for men have shown courageous and sacrificial devotion to mean causes—to the extension of brutal tyranny and the preservation of human slavery. But in sincerity and devotion there is genuine faith, though it may be misplaced and misguided.

The attitude of faith in a cause, at its highest stretch, is the attitude that the attempt to make this cause prevail must take precedence over all else; it is a willingness to sacrifice to it everything subordinate, even the sacrifice of going down to destruction in defeat. It is not merely desperation's cry that either this cause must prevail or life will not be worth living. It is rather that my witness to the cause justifies any loss I may have to suffer. Where faithfulness is worth the price paid for it then that faith is a true faith; where it is not, faith becomes fanaticism.

The same relation of faith and knowledge is seen in personal relations. When I say I have faith in the integrity of a friend I do not claim to know that he has the integrity I attribute to him. I take instead a position which does not rest on knowledge. I may learn something about him which destroys my faith in him, but so long as my faith remains it determines my interpretation of the facts I learn concerning him. If I am wrong then my faith is misplaced, but it is none the less genuine faith. A man gullible about his own interests is a fool, and a proper object of derision; but a gullibility which expresses faith in a friend is, at worst, misfortune, and it arouses sympathy and pity.

Faith in a friend's integrity is quite different from the kind of faith which is the will to act in the light of knowledge. If I employ a stranger in a position of trust I base my judgment of his reliability and honesty on the information I can secure about his character and past performance. This is not faith except as it is faith in the sources and reliability of my information. My decision about the man is an inference from the facts, and the facts and logic control the inference. From these I construct my judgment of the man, of his character and of his likely actions. The faith I express in this is not faith in him but faith in my own judgment. As I come to know him as a person, however, my attitude toward him may shift from its basis in knowledge to a genuine faith.

The fact that faith takes us beyond knowledge sometimes leads to the attempt to separate them. We see this in some interpretations of religious faith; we see it especially on the part of those who are concerned about modern man's over-confidence in his own powers, about his complacent acceptance of his own knowledge as adequate for all his needs. Reinhold Niebuhr writes:

> Though the religious faith through which God is apprehended cannot be in contradiction to reason in the sense that the ultimate principle of meaning cannot be in contradiction to the subordinate principle of meaning which is found in rational coherence yet, on the other hand religious faith cannot be simply subordinated to reason or made to stand under its judgment. When this is done the reason which asks the question whether the God of religious faith is plausible has already implied a negative answer in the question because it has made itself God and naturally cannot tolerate another.

The usual procedure in purely rational and intellectual judgments upon religion is to find the God of religious faith essentially identical with the god of reason, with the distinction that religious faith is regarded as a somewhat crude form of apprehending what reason apprehends more purely.[8]

Here reason is accused of claiming for itself what, in its proper role, it cannot claim and does not claim. Faith, Niebuhr admits, cannot be in contradiction to reason. Thus reason does exercise a control over faith. Faith and knowledge cannot conflict, for where they are in contradiction faith must give way to knowledge or else show that the knowledge claimed is false. But this does not mean that reason shall prescribe the content of faith where faith carries the will beyond the range of knowledge. Unless faith or reason is in error, the God of religious faith is the same God as the God of reason. But our rational knowledge of God is not the same as the content of faith. To recognize the poverty of our rational knowledge does not require us to repudiate what little we may have; and it may be that this knowledge, instead of dictating to faith and prescribing its content, provides a sound foundation from which faith may reach beyond the range of knowledge itself. The same reason that finds God's existence, as we shall see later, discovers also its own inability to compass God's essence. It is this which justifies faith's venture beyond the limits of knowledge and at the same time justifies our demand that faith observe the negative control which reason exercises when it forbids contradiction. In the words of Benjamin Whichcote, "If Reason may not *command*, it will *condemn*," and "Reason *discovers* what is Natural; and Reason *receives* what is Supernatural."[9]

To rest in an opposition of faith and reason is fatal. Professor Blanshard warns us of the consequences:

Start with the assumption that what God says must at least make human sense, and we know what to think when some dervish from the desert or from Berchtesgaden raises his voice to claim guidance from above. Start from the assumption of Kierkegaard, Barth and

Brunner that revelation must needs be an offense to our understanding, and what is to prevent us also from becoming blind followers of the blind?[10]

Faith is in conflict only with our delusions of grandeur, of omniscience, of finality. Its enemies are the children of pride. Where there is charity and humility, there philosophy and science and art and faith are all allies. No one prescribes to the others, for each sees the others as supplementing itself. Each has its own place to fill and its own function to perform, but none is complete or adequate by itself.

If we look again at the way in which we express our faith in persons, and the circumstances in which we have such faith in them, we may see more clearly the relation of faith to knowledge. Few of us are ready to give our confidence and trust at random. We trust those who seem trustworthy, and the initial judgment about a person's trustworthiness is usually the outcome of contact with him and knowledge about him. Once confidence is established, and we believe *in* him, we have a new basis for our relationship with him.

How can I be sure of those whose loyalty and good will I trust? Knowledge is inadequate. Is the remedy to refuse to trust? It is possible that the real need here is not the need to be sure but rather the need to act on the presumption that the best I can think of those I trust is true—the best I can think, that is, within the limits of what I know about them. If I am wrong I shall discover my error; but I am likely to discover it only if I have the faith which is positive action in terms of what I believe. The misplaced beliefs of romantic love, for example, are not likely ever to be discovered as long as that love is expressed only in imagination.

But faith is the source also of positive knowledge. Just as genuine love discloses in its objects qualities which cannot be seen through any other eyes, so faith in a man may be the essential condition of some of the knowledge we have about him. Some of a man's traits and attitudes remain hidden in his superficial contacts and find expression only in response to another's faith in him.

84

It is sometimes by trusting a man that we discover his trustworthiness; it is by belief in him that we discover him to be the kind of man who deserves, more than we had imagined, our belief in him.

THE GUIDANCE OF FAITH

If faith is the willingness to act, and if we have to act where knowledge does not guide us, then what is our guide? Action does not guide itself; without guidance, action is senseless and random, or else it is perfectly arbitrary. We need to see now how faith can find a guide when knowledge is not sufficient.

What distinguishes our action in faith from action at random, from blind impulse? It is the guidance of action by value. So far as my knowledge and reason take me, I desire that what I believe I shall believe because I know it to be true; and so far as my judgment of value is sound I desire that what I *believe in* I shall believe in because it is good. These two attitudes are in harmony in so far as I do not mistake the false for the true and evil for good, provided that truth and goodness are ultimately one being. Since my knowledge of truth is limited and my appreciation of value is incomplete, I cannot know truth and goodness *as* one being; I do not grasp them in their true unity. Although I cannot know them in their final unity, yet I may know *that* they are one. How else could I act and still make sense in my action?

It is sometimes reasonable to trust what we do not know is trustworthy; we can justify rationally a course of action which is not guided by reason; we know that we must act at times without knowledge to guide us. When we have gone as far as knowledge can take us and cannot stop where it stops, we have to follow our sense of value; the willingness to act on this is faith. Although this is faith and not reason, it is reasonable that in some of our actions value and not knowledge shall guide us.

To act in faith is to risk being wrong for a stake greater than the mere avoidance of error. The basis of faith's commitment is not limited to what we can prove, it reaches also to what gives meaning to life and action. If existence has meaning then this is also a kind of a test of truth. Is it conceivable that what appears to be the dedication of a life to God is always sheer pretense or pathetic delusion? If it is, then what sweet fruits may sometimes be grown of duplicity and falsehood! That our deepest needs can be satisfied by what is false is surely a contradiction; for either the fiction is not merely a fiction or else the needs it satisfies are only apparent and not real. Can we say that existence and value are in ultimate opposition? The answer is that if real being is not at least the best I can imagine then my beliefs cannot both be true and satisfy the best in me.

If our evaluations are twisted, our feelings deceptive, our natures corrupted, then faith may take us away from the good in the direction of evil. It is a question of what we are. As Aristotle tells us, the man of strong and good character acts rightly by habit; he does not have to force himself to do what he ought to do. He chooses the good by preference. So also to a man of false prejudice the truth seems strange and unbelievable. Thus it is that what we believe in, our basic faith, is the expression of what we are; and if our faith is false there is something false in us, and if it is cheap there is something cheap in us. So far as our basic faith is true we are conformed in our nature to that pattern of good which is the final meaning of all existence.

So far as our faith is true, what we believe in is what we should know, in the light of a more adequate knowledge than we now have, to be that which truly deserves our trust. Without this knowledge we can only test value against value, and create in the testing our capacity to recognize and to prefer the greater to the lesser.

Part Three
TRUTH

CHAPTER 6

The Nature of Truth

RELIGION AND THE PROBLEM OF TRUTH

WE BEGAN our study of the philosophy of religion with an attempt to understand something of the essential nature of religion. This led us to inquire into the nature of belief and knowledge and faith and to try to clarify their relations with each other. We are now ready to look at some questions our earlier reflections have prepared us to consider. In this and the following three chapters we shall concern ourselves directly with the nature of truth and the kind of contact with truth which religion can provide.

The question of truth is of great concern for any serious attempt to understand religion. The possibility that it is true is one of the most important reasons why we are interested in religion; and for a philosophy of religion this concern outweighs all others.

There are many people who would hesitate to admit that religion is true but who yet are perfectly willing to grant that it is a desirable thing to have. They admit the value of religion to society, and recognize that it helps to strengthen and support men and women in the difficult trials of life. The impression these people give, however, is sometimes most disturbing, in their support of religion as an instrument in the service of society and a builder of morale for the individual. They remind us of those who advocate teaching children there is a Santa Claus because it is an interesting and happy belief for children to have. These are the people who would support with enthusiasm a "Go to Church Sunday" or a "Remember God Week." They look on churches and other religions institutions as perhaps they look upon the armed forces, the police, and the fire department—as another source of strength and protection for society.

Religion, they think, helps also to maintain a higher level of morality; religious people generally pay their bills, are usually faithful to their husbands and wives, and seldom become intoxicated or disturb the peace. So people are urged to go to church or temple, and to observe the customs and abide by the rules of their religious communities. They are encouraged to think that in doing these things they will be better citizens and help build a better society; and sometimes the impression is given that they should do these things in order to be better citizens and to build a better society.

These benefits which are said to flow from religion are quite often among its effects. True religion is a source of strength, and its practice does often promote social unity and loyalty to the good. A society composed largely of sincerely religious persons, whose religion has the dignity of truth, is sure to be a better society than one whose people are devoted to nothing, where the hand of each is raised against the other, and where goodness and truth are lost in deception and distortion. But this fact alone is not a sound basis for advocating religion. With as good reason we might advocate the dissemination of any falsehood calculated to promote unity and loyalty within a society.

Although religion requires sincerity, sincerity is not enough; for belief needs also to be true. The sincerity with which a person holds a belief may be some indication of its truth, provided he who holds it is a person of knowledge and integrity. On the other hand, sincerity in false belief may equally well expose the frailty of the mind which holds it.

The only sound reason to advocate that a religious doctrine be accepted is to be found in its truth. If there is truth in religion then in addition to sincerity there must be the desire for truth, a desire strong enough to compel belief to change wherever it is found to be false. If there is truth in religion then one opinion is not as good as another; and although we respect a man's right to hold a false opinion it is because we respect his manhood and not because we respect his opinion or because we honor error.

Belief is spontaneous. We tend to accept as true anything not in conflict with another and stronger belief. One result of this is that we are often duped; we make mistakes; we act on beliefs that are false and their falsity brings tragedy upon us. Yet no matter how exposed to error we may be it is still the case that we are made for truth. Our bent is in truth's direction and it is only by deception that we can be made satisfied with anything else.

We believe what we find credible, but we cannot always be sure that what is credible is also true; for by itself credibility is not a trustworthy guide. Yet credibility does have some significance in the search for true belief. In so far as my nature conforms to and responds to truth then I shall find the true to be credible and the false to be incredible. But in so far as my nature is twisted and perverse then to me the false may seem true. The discovery of truth is a gift of our nature so far as our discovery of truth depends on our fitness to apprehend it. To the extent that a sincere belief is false the presence of that belief in us is an expression of the deficiency or perversion of our nature and experience. To advocate the propagation of false belief for some ulterior purpose, no matter how noble the purpose may appear to be, is to advocate the distortion or the destruction of man's nature.

Kimball Young tells us, for example, that "the mores consist of the codes of social conduct which grow up in any community or society. The mores are the generally accepted and expected forms of conduct which are assumed to be necessary for group welfare."[1] As a consequence, they frequently acquire a religious sanction. Dr. Young is inclined to be tolerant of this trimming because of its psychological usefulness. "Aside from stimulating individual participation in various group situations, religious experience, at least in our Western culture, acts as an important balancing factor in personality. Such experience gives the person faced with difficulties, crises, or conflicts, surcease from worry and considerable faith in himself."[2] This, however, seems to be the whole significance of religion, and we must not confuse it with those things which pertain to the real objective order. "In contrast . . . to the common-sense material world, we find a world based on fantasy or wishful thinking, particularly in religion, art, and play. This world helps to fulfil life, gives it a richer, more pleasing, and more personally satisfying meaning."[3]

To put religion and art in a class with play, as belonging to "a world based on fantasy or wishful thinking," and then to consider that this "world" of fantasy "helps to fulfil life," and gives it a "richer" meaning, is an astounding combination of ideas. A life which can find genuine fulfilment in a world of fantasy seems out of place in the world of real existence. Such a life would be more at home in one of Leibniz's possible worlds which, falling short of being the best of all possible worlds, did not have real existence bestowed upon it.[4]

Psychological satisfaction from false belief is possible to most of us only on condition we do not know the belief is false. Children whose differentiation between the true and false is not yet clear and those neurotics who fail to differentiate between what they wish were true and what is true may find satisfaction and fulfilment in fantasy. But most of us would agree with Plato: "To be deceived about the truth of things and so to be in ignorance and error and to harbour untruth in the soul is a thing no one would consent to. Falsehood in that quarter is abhorred above everything."[5]

As soon as we begin to justify religion as a means to an end we then justify any substitute or alternative which may serve as well the end we seek. Only our lack of knowledge of how to do it will prevent us then from taking our children, as soon as they are born, and subjecting them to the kind of psychological manipulations which will give us the product we want. Indeed it is this very thing which every society attempts to do as soon as the recognition of the sanctity of the person begins to weaken. Only by means of religion does the conception of the ultimate worth of the individual ever permeate a society and filter into its customs and attitudes. As religion loses its strength the individual loses his protection against those who would make him their tool.

The fundamental question about religion is not whether it is socially useful, or whether it contributes to the peace of mind of those who practice it. The question about religion is whether it is true, whether it does actually put us into that relation with ultimate being in which we find most completely what we are and what is our final destiny. It is from its truth that the benefits of religion flow. Because religion claims first of all to be true and to bring us to truth, this is the claim we must examine first. If religion is not a way to truth then it is a hollow thing, a puffed-up emptiness, and its supposed benefits are illusions of value in a meaningless world.

The difficulties which many of us meet in our attempts to discover and recognize the truth in religion are often the result of inadequate and superficial conceptions of truth. So to understand how and in what way religion is true we need first to pay some attention to the nature of truth.

The Distinction between True and False

"The investigation of truth," says Aristotle,

> is in one way hard, in another easy. An indication of this is found in the fact that no one is able to attain the truth adequately, while, on the other hand, we do not collectively fail, but every one says something true about the nature of things, and while individually we contribute little or nothing to the truth, by the union of all a considerable amount is amassed. Therefore, since the truth seems to be like the proverbial door, which no one can fail to hit, in this respect it must be easy, but the fact that we can have a whole truth and not the particular part we aim at shows the difficulty of it.[6]

It seems a simple matter to recognize the difference between the true and the false. It seems so simple that to ask what we mean when we say a statement is true is likely to arouse suspicion. What we do mean is usually so apparent we are likely to think either that the questioner expresses the cynicism (if such it was) of Pilate's "What is truth?" or that the question prepares the way for the introduction of bewildering and disturbing subtleties. To hear the question asked puts us on our guard and may even arouse our resentment.

93

Suppose I am telling what a good time I had at a party last night, how delightful was the food and drink and conversation, when someone interrupts to ask, "Just what do you mean by a 'good time'?" I feel only irritation at this intrusion. It is the same kind of irritation we may feel at the question, "What is truth?" I may feel like saying to the one, "Anyone knows what I mean by a 'good time'; and if, by some defect in your nature or by your lack of experience, you do not know, there is nothing I can do with words to remedy the matter." To the other we may feel like saying, "Everyone knows what we mean by 'truth,' and the difference between true and false statements; and if by chance you do not know then it is pointless to try to tell you, for you would not know what we were trying to do in answering your question truthfully. The fact that you can ask the question, moreover, shows that you have some awareness of the difference between true and false."

In the main the objection is sound. Truth is a simple matter, and the awareness of the distinction between true and false statements is a condition without which any discussion of the question is pointless. It is the case, also, that the question, "What is truth?" can be a device to distract attention from an issue or to hide an evasion. There certainly are occasions where the question is irrelevant and where to raise it is a stupid intrusion. But when we have said all this we have not told the whole story; for truth, like love and honor, is both simple and complex—both easy and hard. There are clear and unmistakable outlines where failure of recognition is almost surely a failure of intelligence or of character. But within the broad outlines there are distinctions which become important to us as soon as we turn our attention to the matters to which they are relevant. It is because some of these distinctions are overlooked that there is so much confusion and misunderstanding about truth in religion.

The plain and obvious sense of *true* is "conformity with what is." Truth, in this obvious sense, pertains to judgments and their expression in propositions. It does not pertain to concepts or to terms alone. We do not say, in this sense of *true*, that "*man* is true."

For merely to utter the word *man* is not to claim truth; it does not raise the question of true and false unless something more is understood besides what is spoken. But to say, "Man is animal," is to say something which may be true or false; and its utterance, unless qualified to the contrary, is its assertion *as true*. Even to say, " 'Man is animal' is false," is to assert something as true about the proposition, "Man is animal." Even when we lie we still express a *claim* of truth for our statements although we know ourselves that they are false.

Aristotle defines *true* and *false* in this way: "To say of what is that it is not, or of what is not that it is, is false, while to say of what is that it is, and of what is not that it is not, is true."[7] A judgment is true, then, if *what we judge something to be* is *what the thing is*. The nature we attribute to a thing in judgment is the very nature of the thing itself. A judgment is false if *what we judge something to be* is not *what the thing is*. The nature we attribute to it is not the nature of the thing to which we attribute it. *What we say* (or think) *about it* is not *what it is*.

In true judgment there is identity of thought and being, in the sense that what we think something to be is what that something is. What we think is not all of what the thing is, but there is some identity or else the thought does not grasp the real nature of the thing it thinks about, or perception does not discover the real nature of the thing perceived. A frequent misunderstanding is to look at this relation of identity as one of copying. But if thought were only a copy of what it thinks about, and if in perception we only had a copy of what we suppose we perceive, how could we know the copy to be a copy? And how might we verify its correctness? A tracing or a picture, which are examples of actual copies, do not themselves proclaim their character as copies. To know them to be copies is to know them in relation to what they copy; we have to know the things they copy in order to know that these are copies. A picture is a picture; to know that it is also a picture of something actual I have to know more than the picture, and more of the original than the picture tells me itself. So if our thoughts were true only as copies of things we should have to know them in relation to the things, that is, *as* copies. But if we had in thought only copies, and not the very nature of the things we know or think about, how could we know our thoughts to be copies?

When we say that such and such a thing is—for example, that there is a platypus—our statement is true if *what we assert to be* is *something which is.* If platypuses exist, then what they are has being not only in idea but it has its own existence in reality. Such a statement does not say anything true about the nature of the platypus, for it does not pretend to tell us *what* it is. So also when we say, "Unicorns exist," the statement is false because the *what* of the unicorn which we have in idea is not a *what* which has its own existence in reality; in other words, there are no real unicorns. There is nothing real, the nature of which we think when we think "unicorn."

This brings us to another sense of *true* and *false,* the sense they have as pertaining to being rather than to thought. This is well stated by Erich Frank:

> There is truth and falsity not only in thought but also in being, as Aristotle remarked. A being is true in so far as in its existence it adequately expresses what it is. Whatever exists, however, exists not only in itself but also in relation to other things. Thus it also may be said that a being is true so far as, in its relations to others and to itself, it exhibits its real nature. With regard to thought itself, modern thinkers including sceptics are inclined to recognize only cognitive truth—as if our knowledge had no existence of its own. Granted by reasoning we understand our knowledge as different from its object and thus as relative and subjective, the relation of knowledge and object cannot be relative also.[8] Thus as a kind of being, as a mode of human existence, our knowledge is true to the extent in which it adequately expresses its essential relation to its objects—a relation by which knowledge itself is determined.[9]

DIFFERENCE WITHOUT CONFLICT

All truth is one; there is no disruption or failure of harmony within it. The failure, as we have said before, is in us and not in it. But truth is not always expressed in identical terms, or in the same way, or through the same medium. Two people describing something they observed together may describe the same event in different ways. The fact that they differ does not mean that the two descriptions cannot both be true. If one description is true and the other is false they certainly will differ, but the fact that descriptions differ in no way implies that one at least is false.

One person may include in his description what the other leaves out, and yet what he does include may still be true, and it may well be that he has included all he needs to include to make his account both true and adequate. Difference is not contradiction; the confusion of difference with contradiction is at the root both of the relativism which denies that anything is "really true" at all and of absolutisms such as Hegel's which deny final truth to anything short of all the truth.

Suppose I am a guest at a meeting of a club where most of the members are strangers to me. Someone points out the man who is president of the club. Later in the evening my host introduces me to a man I recognize to be the same, and calls him Mr. Baker. These, then, are different designations which refer to the same person. It happens that the president of the club is Mr. Baker; but there is nothing about the office of president which requires it to be filled by someone named "Baker," nor will Baker cease to be Baker when his term of office expires. Although these are two different truths about the man—he is president of the club and his name is Baker, each is completely and finally and separately true. Each can be known to be true without knowledge of the other, and whether or not the other is known does not affect the finality with which the one is known.

When we say that each may be known to be true without knowledge of the other we do not mean to deny that the two are related. We mean to assert that they can be different and logically independent and yet refer to the same object. We are not asserting, either, that to know a man's name to be "Baker" is to know all there is to know about the man, nor is it to know all there is to know about the fact that this is his name. The point is that we can know this fact, and know the truth of the statement of this fact, without knowing certain other facts about the man. To repeat, different truths can be known about the same thing and the knowledge of one truth may be quite independent of the knowledge of others. We have emphasized and repeated this apparently simple and obvious point because a failure to recognize it may have grave results. Such failure is involved, for example, in many of the attempts to argue that since science is true religion is false. For there is often the tacit assumption that since what science says and what religion says are different they are therefore in conflict, and so if one is true the other is false.

One may say of a lump of sugar, "This is white," and another may say of the same, "This is sweet." But it hardly makes sense for the other to say, "You are wrong, it is not white; for I have tasted it and it is sweet." White and sweet are not mutually exclusive properties. Each one pertains to the sugar, each in its own way and in its own right. The same lump of sugar is both white and sweet. Yet, silly as it would be to treat these properties as mutually exclusive because they are different, we find this very kind of confusion in many of the controversies which arouse in people the strongest feelings. Because an investigator finds something to be true of physical things, of human nature, or of society, he may repudiate indignantly—as if it were an attack upon his veracity or his knowledge—the assertion that there are other things true of nature or man or society.

People discover that they have different ideas about something and so they are tempted to assume that they are thinking about different things. In this they are perilously close to the assumption that their thought creates what they think about.[10]

THE WHOLE TRUTH AND ALL THE TRUTH

A statement is true if what it says to be the case is the case, and it is false if what it says to be the case is not the case. Its truth is complete if a statement omits nothing essential to the sense which it purports to have; in other words, its truth is complete if its performance meets the demands of its promise.

If you ask me where I was last night I may tell you I attended a concert. If the intent of your question was to inquire what affair, if any, took me away from home, and if it is the case that I attended the concert, then my reply is true and it is the complete truth. But if I understand that the intent of your statement is to find out all the places I stopped while away from home then I have not told the whole truth if it is the case that after the concert I stopped at a store to buy a magazine.

The wording of a question alone seldom reveals its whole intent. We infer the intent, or guess it, from the circumstances of the question and from what we know of the questioner's interests and concerns. Suppose I have a friend with whom I occasionally discuss the novels we have read, and our references to reading are to fiction or general literature. If he asks me casually whether I have read anything recently I am not telling a falsehood when I say "No," even if it is the case that I have been reading a number of books and essays in technical philosophy. For I understand what he means, in this instance, by "anything."

Sometimes we misunderstand each other on such points and have to clear up the confusion. Yet the very fact that we recognize the trouble to be a misunderstanding implies that the statement is unsatisfactory not because it is false but because in some respect it lacks relevance or appropriateness. Usually we have no difficulty in telling what a statement must include if it is to be true and the whole truth. It is when we miss the intent of a question that trouble arises; and the trouble in such a case is that one question is asked while a different one is answered.

Some have contended that no statement can be fully true because no statement can have all the truth—and by "all the truth" these persons seem to mean "everything that is true." If you ask me to tell you everything that is true about what I did last night I shall have to reply by describing every contraction of every muscle fiber of my body, every alteration in potential of every neuron of my nervous system, and I shall have to identify every spot my

feet touched and every particle of air I breathed, give a report on every droplet of vapor I exhaled, and an account of the ultimate effects of the stresses my weight exerted on the path I walked. This would be the merest beginning, and no life could be long enough nor any man's knowledge full enough to complete the answer. For every item is connected with others; causes and effects reach into the present from a largely unknown past and stretch into a future of mystery.

To contend that no answer to a question is fully true unless it tells all the truth leaves out of consideration the fact that a question was asked. Unless we presuppose some limits of relevance we cannot ask a question that makes sense. Even when friends meet after a long separation and one exclaims, "Tell me everything!" it is well understood what "everything" refers to.

The intent of a question governs the amount of detail necessary to answer the question with the whole truth. If you ask me what I did last evening I do not as a rule suppose I must tell you about changing my clothes, how many minutes it took me to go from one place to another together with the exact route I followed, and other such details. However if you were a police officer investigating a crime and wished a statement which would account for all my time between certain hours, then I should have to include such details to make my statement the whole truth. If you are asked whether you own any land your affirmative answer is true and the whole truth provided you have title to the land and provided this information meets the intent of the question. But if the intent of the question is to determine your financial condition then your answer is not the whole truth if it is the case that your land carries a mortgage. The whole truth is not all that is true; it is all the truth that is relevant.

In order to be true or false a statement must be relevant to something, else there is nothing for it to be true of and its meaning is indeterminate. Is it true, for example, that "they have wings"? The question cannot be answered until we specify the reference of "they." If "they" refers to goats then the statement is false; if it refers to sparrows it is true.

It should now be plain that if we ask what kind of a world this is, or what man's nature is, a scientific answer may be the whole truth if the question is a scientific question. If the question is a scientific question then a philosophical or religious answer is not so much false as irrelevant, for such an answer is not to the question asked but to some other question. It should be every bit as plain that if the question is a religious question, if for example we are concerned to know what it is in life and existence which deserves our final devotion, then a scientific answer is irrelevant.

CHAPTER 7

Perspectives and Dimensions of Truth

PERSPECTIVES OF TRUTH

THERE is only one real world but there are many different accounts of it. Even if truth is absolute yet every expression of truth is limited. No account of the real world can possibly tell us everything about the world, for the account itself is something which occurs in the real world and it cannot tell us about itself. Since however there is only one real world it follows that all true statements refer to the same world, and so all different expressions of truth are complementary.

So, too, if there are different statements about the same thing within the one world the different statements are complementary in so far as they are true. They may tell us different things about the same object, as do the statements "sugar is white" and "sugar is sweet." Or two different statements may describe the same thing from different points of reference or different perspectives.

We think of *perspective* in its proper sense as the spatial proportions of a physical arrangement, as the parts are ordered with reference to some specific position. Suppose there are two trees, a maple and an elm, some twenty feet apart, and that the maple is due north of the elm. If I view these trees from a point some distance south the elm will be closer than the maple. Their arrangement with reference to my position is one perspective, and it is this arrangement which would appear in a photograph taken from my position. From other points the two may be approximately the same distance away, and from still other points the maple will be closer than the elm.

Spatial perspective gives us a clue to other differences. In fact we carry over quite directly the idea of perspective into the broader meaning we give to the phrase "point of view." A spatial perspective is literally a point of view, but there are also differences in points of view which are not limited to differences of spatial perspective. We view things not alone from different positions in space but also from different positions in time and from different personal and cultural backgrounds. We understand things in terms of different concepts and categories; even the structure of our language predisposes us to notice some aspects of the things we encounter and to overlook other aspects.

Two witnesses may report the same event in quite different terms but without conflict with each other. A member of the crew of an ocean liner and a passenger on the same ship may give quite different but also quite true accounts of the same voyage. We know how different are the accounts which different historians sometimes give of the same events. One may organize his account about one aspect of the events he describes, and another about another aspect. One account of the American War of Independence may place its chief emphasis on the military operations. Another account may concern itself mainly with the economic or social or political issues of the war. The accounts may both be true, and each may be a valuable supplement to the other. The difference may well be called a *difference of perspective*, and we shall use *perspective* in this more inclusive sense. Accounts of the same thing from different perspectives may be called *versions*.

A version of truth informs us of the nature of the one real world as it appears from a certain perspective. For although the world is one yet every awareness of the world which arises within the world is limited. For the awareness is itself an event which belongs to the one real world, and it has its own time and place and relationships within that world; so it does not exhibit to us the world in its oneness and completeness.

Any awareness of existence available to us must be from some perspective and cannot be from all. No description of existence can be complete, for it has to be in terms of some set of concepts and categories. I may describe a house in terms of its architecture or in terms of its materials or in terms of its legal title. Each of these is a separate description, and no one of these can include any of the others. Truth is a modest maiden, never seen unclothed. But truth is a wealthy maiden with a great variety of costumes. She can wear anything which fits her. Some costumes, of course, are more becoming than others, and some may be more like masquerade than sober dress. In any case, however, if we recognize the nature of the costume the lady wears we are in little danger of deception. To reject religious truth because it is different from scientific truth is to say that the same lady cannot wear different costumes.

A version of truth is only one among many. There is always more to be said than can be said in any one account of existence. But a version of truth, although only one among many versions, is still a version of truth and not of error. It is a partial and limited account of real existence, and we find its faults and limitations not in what it contains but in what it lacks. Thus because a version of truth is not everything, we must not rashly conclude it is nothing. No perspective gives all truth yet any perspective may give some truth. But the possible perspectives of the real cannot be exhausted in any set of actual perspectives. Every perspective of existence is itself a position within existence, and since existence is a real unity it is no mere sum of parts. So we cannot reach complete truth by adding together the partial truths we obtain from different perspectives.

We must be careful to remember also that although a version of truth is not complete truth it still may well be completely true. It is the confusion of these two assertions which infects with error the common and naive relativist theories of truth. The relativist forgets that although the appearance of something is relative to its point of reference yet the fact that the thing appears as it does from that point of reference is not relative but absolute.

Any serious and sincere affirmation for which there are reasons or which is based on experience is a version of truth. If its denial is the sincere expression of how existence appears from another perspective, and is no mere arbitrary negation, then the denial also is a version of truth. But truth itself is not split, and in so far as the denial has positive grounds the apparent conflict indicates a hidden difference of perspective. To that extent the denial really supplements what it purports to deny. One, at least, of the two statements needs revision if the apparent conflict is not to be misleading. But the aim of a revision should be to save the truth the statement contains, not to lose it. The first step in overcoming apparent conflicts among different versions of truth is to recognize the differences of perspective.

Do we differ fundamentally? Then you or I or both of us must be wrong, or we are both right and our difference is a difference of perspective. Too often we assume that if we differ then one of us at least is wrong, and each of us is sure it is the other. We fail to consider with enough care the possibility that our difference is not between the true and the false but between two versions of the true. To discover this, when it is the case, each of us must see not only from his own perspective but must come as near as he can to the other's perspective, so that the two may approach each other in each mind and in each one's experience. So each of us discovers that there is more he must see before he can find the truth in what he has already seen.

We must ask ourselves what it is we really want. Is what I want simply to make my view prevail? Is my aim to establish my version against other versions? Or is it to find the object and to find out all I can about it, to enrich and extend my understanding of it? If it is this, then the apparent differences and conflicts which other points of view have with my own will serve as clues which I can follow to fresh perspectives and new understanding of the object.

Appearance and Reality

Knowledge involves perspective because the knower and the known are two different things. Knowing is an activity of the knower, not of the thing known, and the situation and circumstances of the knowing occasion make a difference to the knowing activity. I see the same physical object differently from different physical positions. This can be a source of error and confusion, but it need not be. It is only in our ignorance that we fall into error because of differences of perspective. For if I have an adequate understanding of the object itself, and if I take account of the circumstances of the perception, I understand that the appearance of the object is precisely the way in which a thing of its real nature should appear under those conditions of distance and lighting, etc., in which the perception occurs. A child may be puzzled by the fact that a stick which before looked to be straight appears bent when half submerged in water. But anyone who understands the physical facts involved would be much more puzzled if the stick did not appear bent under those conditions.

Our knowledge of external things begins with appearances. From these appearances, and from our knowledge of the conditions under which we have them, we build up an understanding of the object which accounts for the appearances we have of it. Thus from its appearances we discover the real essence of the thing itself. To deny this would require us to deny that we have different appearances of the same object, or else to deny that the appearances from which we form our concept of a thing are genuine appearances of the thing itself.

The distinction between appearance and reality has caused considerable difficulty in those modern theories of knowledge which have developed under the influence of Descartes' approach. For any attempt to work out a theory of knowledge by beginning with something exclusively mental, as that which is known, leads to subjectivism and skepticism, or else to the view that the mind makes what it "knows." The key to the difficulty, and the primary error to avoid, is the separation of appearance and reality. Once we look on the appearance of something as numerically distinct from the reality of which it is the appearance, we have severed the appearance from reality and the two cannot be brought together again. We find ourselves in communication with a world of appearances only, while reality is composed of unknown and unknowable things-in-themselves; or else the appearances take the place of reality. If knowledge is knowledge of reality, and if the appearances of reality to us are the way in which we obtain knowledge of it, then we cannot permit our theory to separate the appearances from the reality which appears.

"An appearance is never a separate entity," Professor Wild points out, "numerically distinct from that which appears. It is always the reality itself which appears in different ways to different cognitive apprehensions. The difference can be explained by the different *cognitive acts*. There is no need to multiply *a different object* for each divergent mode of apprehension."[1] A thing is precisely what it appears to be in so far as its appearance is understood in the light of the conditions under which it is obtained. The appearance of a thing is a manifestation of *what* the thing really is. It does not show us *all* of what the thing is, but what it does show us of the thing is what the thing really is.

Two Dimensions of Truth

Many of the more serious misunderstandings about religion are the result of misunderstandings about truth. In spite of all the technical elaborations of method, our scientists and our students of society often have superficial notions of truth; those who study man and his world from the approach of literature and the arts may have different ideas of truth, but their ideas may also be one-sided and inadequate. Just as the inhabitants of an isolated community may believe that their ways of doing things are the only right ways, so those who isolate themselves within a special field of study, and confine their serious inquiry and reflection to that single field, are not likely to appreciate the importance of unfamiliar problems and methods. What differs from the familiar seems strange, somewhat unreal, and perhaps even menacing. Often an extension of knowledge has been met with fear and dismay, not alone by the ignorant but by the learned as well. All too readily we interpret difference as conflict.

We have already seen, however, that difference does not always mean conflict, and it is now our purpose to see how this applies to claims of truth in areas which so long have seemed hostile to each other. Truth is conformity of perception or thought with being, and there are as many ways of securing truth as there are ways in which we can reach being. Among the dependable ways to truth, the choice of which to take is governed by relevance. The poet and the historian and the scientist, for example, do not use the same methods. But this is not, as so often it is thought to be, a sign of imperfection in poetry or history or science. It is only because they do use different methods that each can discover what escapes the others. But if the historian tries to ape the scientist or the poet he succeeds only in demonstrating his incompetence in all fields; and the same principle applies to the others as well.

A statement may be true because it gives us information about the nature of something, about *what* something is. If I say, for example, that this sealed tin contains coffee, roasted dark and ground fine, and if my statement is true, it provides information about the contents of the tin. The information may be complete, so far as it pretends to go, and if my statement is true you do not have to open the tin to find out something of the nature of its contents.

Let us call this a *dimension* of truth, for we have here a useful metaphor to distinguish some of the ways in which truth is found. We may call this dimension of truth *descriptive* truth, or *essential* truth, for it gives us information about *what* the object is. A second dimension of truth we may call *existential* truth, for it informs us not *what* something is but of the fact *that* something is. This is an important distinction, one which is necessary for the later stages of our study. However, we must emphasize, here at the very start of our discussion of this distinction, that essential and existential truth have close relations with each other; the distinction is not one of mutual opposition but, as soon we shall see more fully, of complementary aspects. That they are complementary and not mutually opposed does not lessen in any way the need to differentiate them clearly, for one does not take the place of the other and the failure to differentiate them is responsible for much confusion in our thinking.

ESSENTIAL TRUTH

When we speak of *essential truth* we refer to truth concerning the *essence* of something. The term *essence* is an old word in philosophy, and it is also one of those technical words which have been taken over into non-technical language. Its use in philosophy is certainly not free from ambiguity and its popular use is quite equivocal and vague. In popular use, for example, there are such variations as the "essence of poetry" and "essential oils" and "essential foods." For the strict meaning of *essence* in traditional philosophy we may use Professor Wild's definition: "The various determining traits that a thing must have to be at all, and without which it cannot be, make up its *essence* or possibility."[2] This definition differentiates *essence* from *accidents*, or those traits which are not involved in its essence. For example, to be rational is a part of the essence of man, but the fact that a man has blue rather than brown eyes is an accident, for he is no less a man if he has one eye-color rather than another.

We are not concerned here, however, with the differentiation of essence from accident. We are concerned rather with a broader, and perhaps less precise, sense of *essence*, the sense given to it when we wish to distinguish *what* a thing is from the fact *that* it is.[3] It is in this sense that we propose to use *essence*, unless indication to the contrary is given. So when we speak of *essential truth* we shall mean the kind of truth a statement has if it tells us faithfully and correctly something of the nature of the thing to which it refers. The statement, "Baseballs are spherical," has essential truth. This does not tell us whether there are any baseballs, or where to find them, but it does tell us something of what baseballs are like. It is a partial answer to the question, "What *kind* of thing is a baseball?"

EXISTENTIAL TRUTH

If we go back now to our example of the tin of coffee we may use it also to illustrate, very superficially, the other dimension of truth. Suppose we have no descriptive label to tell us what is in the tin, but instead we find only a set of instructions telling us how to open it. If by following these instructions we are able to open it then we may say that the directions are correct or true. This kind of truth we may call *existential truth* to distinguish it from descriptive or essential truth.

A statement which has existential truth puts us in contact with something which exists but it need tell us nothing of what the thing is like. If a statement purports to put us in contact with something and does not, then it is false or else we have failed to interpret it correctly. An obvious illustration is the combination of a safe. If I open the safe when I follow the combination correctly then we may say the combination is true. If the safe does not open then either the purported combination is false or I have failed to follow it properly. But a combination to a safe tells us nothing about what is in the safe, and in this respect it has no essential truth. Of course an expert on safes may be able to tell from the combination itself something about the kind of lock the safe has, but this means only that something which has existential truth in one reference (with reference to the contents of the safe) may have essential truth in another reference (with reference to the nature of the lock).

In recent years the idea of existential truth has been associated with the movement in philosophy known as "Existentialism." Our use here of the term *existential truth* is much broader, however, and comes out of the long tradition of classical philosophy. It is based on the distinction between essence and existence which goes back to Aristotle, and it is intended to express the existential references of propositions.

The Extension, Supposition, and Designation of Terms

Existential reference may be understood more easily, perhaps, if we approach it by easy stages. Let us look first at the distinction of the denotation from the connotation of terms, or, as some logicians prefer to call it, the distinction of the *extension* from the *comprehension* of terms. As Joseph points out, "terms have two functions, both of which may be called meaning. They direct our thought to some subject, and they suggest what that subject is, to which our thought is directed."[4] "A word," he says in another place, "denotes anything of which it can be predicated as a name; *man* denotes Socrates and Caesar, *artist* Beethoven and Giotto, *triangle* this and that triangular figure."[5] All the things denoted by a term constitute its extension.

Shall we say that the proper use of a term with respect to its extension gives it existential truth? Although our distinction between extension and comprehension may suggest that this is the case, we must be careful to avoid such an identification. The extension of a term, as we have noted, is composed of all the instances to which it may properly refer. But a term does not of itself *say* anything. What does the term "man" say? By itself, nothing. It has meaning in that it can be used to refer to things, but it does not accomplish that reference of thought to things when it stands by itself. Its extension is the sum-total of those things to which it can meaningfully refer when used in propositions or statements. Until we use it in a proposition we do not specify which of the things included in its extension we might be thinking about. If I say, "A man is to give a violin recital here tonight," the word "man" in this case refers to a definite and specific person. Because this reference is included within the extension of "man" we can use the word to refer meaningfully to this person. But the term's extension is not its reference to this man, for this is only a part of its extension. Only from the complete proposition can we discover which of the things that "man" might refer to it actually does refer to here. Even if the term itself is so stated that it narrows down the possible references to one individual only, without the use of the term in a statement, we still do not have an actual reference of the term to that thing until it is used in a statement. "The man who is to give a violin recital here tonight" may be capable of referring correctly to only one man in the world. Yet the term by itself does not actually perform the reference it is capable of performing when used in a proposition, for it does not *say* anything.

The traditional name for the actual reference of a term to something is *supposition*. Professor McCall defines *supposition* as "*the mode of existence for which the term stands.*" He adds that "supposition is never a property of a term taken *in itself* but only *of a term taken in relation to another term in a proposition.*" The reason for this is that "a term *in itself* (e.g., 'man') does not stand for *existence*, it stands simply for a meaning or essence, which may or may not exist."[6]

The supposition of a term is defined as the *mode* of existence for which it stands. For example, in the sentence, "Man is a noun," the term "man" refers here to the word itself. The mode of existence it refers to is the kind of existence which words have, or verbal existence. If we say, "Man is an animal species," the term "man" refers not to something which really exists but to a way in which we conceive certain things. Only individual men exist, and we think of them as constituting a species. This mode of existence is conceptual or mental. If, however, we say, "Man is animal," we refer to the actually existing instances of man (including, of course, those which have existed in the past and those which will exist in the future). The test by which a supposition of real existence can be distinguished from one of mental existence is the possibility of asserting the same thing of an individual instance. We can say truly, "This man is an animal," but if we say, "This man is an animal species," we say something false.[7]

The supposition of a term is the *mode* of existence for which it stands. But when terms are used in propositions their reference to existence may be much more specific. If I say, "My brown coat is at the cleaners," I may be understood, by one familiar with my wardrobe, to refer to a certain really existing individual coat. "My brown coat" is a term with real supposition, but it refers also to a certain individual real thing. We shall call this reference to a certain specific existence the "designation" of a term.[8] In "The words I am thinking of now are in the French language," the phrase (or term) "the words I am thinking of now" has verbal supposition. Its designation is composed of those very French words I refer to in the sentence. Anyone who heard me speak the sentence and understood what I said would be able to identify the supposition of the term; but no one but myself would know the designation unless I gave him additional information identifying the specific words themselves.

Our doctrine of existential truth concerns the way in which, when understood, a proposition makes known or discloses a fact of existence. As we shall see later, all propositions have designation—else the claim of truth would be pointless. But not all propositions have as their *primary function* to designate existence. "What a concept means or signifies is primarily a 'what' (i.e., a nature or essence) and secondarily the individuals that might be such a 'what' or have such a nature or essence."[9] In so far as propositions inform us truly of *what* something is, they have essential truth. In so far as propositions inform us *that* something is, they have existential truth in the sense in which we are using it here.

Existential truth, however, is not merely logical designation, for the disclosure of existence concerns the meanings of statements in addition to their strictly logical functions. Existential truth pertains to that which discloses existence and places the knower in such a relation to the object that the object's existence becomes known to him. We may discover our own existence, for example, or catch ourselves in the act of existing, when we are aware of making decisions. A set of directions for reaching a destination, or a set of plans for building a house, may have existential truth. So too may that which opens our hearts and prepares our minds for the awareness of the presence of God—and in this, of course, we see the special importance of existential truth for religion.

Because we so often ignore the distinction between essential and existential truth, and assume that "truth" always means *essential truth*, we are in danger of missing the most significant of all the truth accessible to us. We miss most of the truth in art and literature and in our closest human relations as well as nearly all the truth accessible to us in religion.

THE PRIORITY OF EXISTENTIAL TRUTH

Up to this point we have considered only some of the more obvious instances of existential truth. These have been open and explicit cases of existential truth, direct pointers toward actually existing situations; and they have been superficial and unimportant instances. There are other cases of existential truth in which the function of disclosing existence is not explicit but tacit and inferential. In fact it is the case that any statement must involve some kind of existential truth. We can never begin with truth which is solely essential and somehow derive from it knowledge of actual existence.

Before we look into this and some of its examples we should understand its relevance to our discussion at this point. One of the most serious confusions in the history of thought is the recurring failure to recognize the dependence of essential truth on existential truth. Repeatedly in medieval and modern thought we find attempts to construct a logical demonstration that there is something which really exists. What this amounts to is the attempt to begin with a conception of the nature of something which might possibly exist, and to infer from the nature it would have if it did exist the fact that it does exist. It is as if I knew enough about an acquaintance to be confident about what kind of garden he would have if he had a garden, and then to infer from this that he has a garden. The sober fact is that we can demonstrate existence only by other existence.

One result of this confusion is to narrow unnecessarily our conception of the range and variety of existence, and consequently to narrow the area of knowledge. It would seem to be the sensible thing to begin inquiry by examining existences as we encounter them and to try to discover the nature of these things. But too often we make the mistake by beginning with some prior conception of the properties or traits which must be present before we shall accept any candidate for the role of existent, and then conclude from *what* something must be if it is to be at all the *fact* that it is. It is as if someone should construct a container with a narrow opening and propose to store his possessions in that container. As he puts them in one by one he occasionally finds an article too large for the opening, so he throws it aside with the comment that it cannot be his.

Suppose a person sets out to prove from what its nature would be if it existed that something does exist. He must assume, whether he is aware of it or not, that we can know the nature of something before we can know the existence of anything. He assumes that we can have some essential truth before we have any existential truth, and that we can know something about what is possible before we know anything actual.

We need only uncover this assumption and make it explicit to see that it is false. It is false, and plainly false, because any statement not only expresses its meaning but the expression of the statement is itself a fact. If I say, "It is raining," my statement is true or false. If rain is falling at the time and place the statement refers to then the statement is true, and if not then the statement is false. But this is not the whole story. My statement, or even my thought, "It is raining," is itself something which occurs. I say something or I think something, and no matter *what* it is I say or think an event of thinking or speaking has taken place.

Not only is a thought or an expression an occurrence, but the fact of its existence compels us to admit also any other facts which its existence discloses. There is a context of fact within which assertion takes place, and in so far as one actual event depends on other actual events for its occurrence the fact that an assertion occurs requires us to recognize other facts as well. To try to deny this places us in an impossible situation. It puts us in a position where we make a statement which has such a meaning that if the statement were true it could not be asserted. In such a case the meaning of the statement and the fact that it is asserted are in mutual conflict. To say this in terms of the technical phrases we have used above, the essential and the existential meanings of the statement are incompatible with each other.[10]

For example, if I say, "I cannot speak a single sentence in English," the fact that I make the statement belies the truth of the statement I make. For this statement is itself an English sentence, and my assertion shows that I can speak at least one English sentence. So it is utterly impossible for the statement to be true if it is a fact that I utter it. If, however, I say, "This assertion I am now making is the only sentence in English I am able to speak," then there is no conflict between what the statement means and the fact that I have made it.

The statement, "Nothing exists," shows the same conflict between what it says and the fact that it is said. For if I can say that nothing exists then the statement itself is expressed and its expression is something which actually happens. If I deny this I have to deny that I made the assertion.

It is because so much of religious truth is either explicitly or tacitly existential that we have had to pay such close attention to the distinction between essential and existential truth. It is because so much of modern thought has ignored existential truth that it has been able to ignore, as completely as it has, the truth we encounter in religion.

This distinction is important to us for another reason. A frequent tactic in the attempt to discredit religion is to argue that the objects with which religion is concerned, such as the human soul and God and value, are objects whose existence has not been demonstrated. This can be a psychologically powerful and convincing argument if he who uses it is permitted to single out some specific kind of demonstration as the only acceptable kind. Such is the very device often used. If religious experience does not provide us with full knowledge of the nature of its objects this failure is offered as evidence against the existence of those objects. Because religious truth, which is primarily existential truth, is incomplete and inadequate as essential truth the enemies of religion deny that it is any kind of truth at all. This is either a trick or, where sincere, it is confusion. In so far as religion offers existential truth, to indict it for failure to provide essential truth is to attack it for failing to do what it did not set out to do. This is as sensible as to attack a man who sets a record for the mile run for his failure to break the record for the hundred yard dash.

The fault, however, is not all on one side. For in so far as we claim for religion a kind and degree of essential truth which it does not possess, and so try to make it do the work not alone of religion but also the work of history and science, we expose religion to attacks it cannot possibly meet. Religious obscurantism which rejects most or all of modern scientific and historical knowledge because it thinks it sees a conflict between such knowledge and religion is guilty of just this confusion. It is ironic that these misguided defenders of religion and the enemies of religion are in such close agreement.

CHAPTER 8

Religious Truth

PHILOSOPHY'S CONCERN WITH RELIGIOUS TRUTH

IN THIS chapter we shall try to find what kind of truth religion may have, and in the next, what tests we may use to determine the truth or falsity of religious beliefs. What is truth in religion, and how do we recognize it and distinguish it from what is false?

A philosophy of religion cannot recognize and apply just any kind of truth test which may seem to commend itself. A philosophy of religion, because it is philosophy, is limited to rational tests, or to tests which can be shown to have rational justification. Of course there are religious beliefs which can find no defense in a philosophy, for there are beliefs which are held with no reference to evidence or to any kind of rational justification. Many people hold such beliefs with complete confidence in their truth; they are matters of faith, and of faith alone. Such beliefs do not rest on evidence; faith does not follow evidence, for when faith finds evidence it becomes knowledge. Absence of evidence, however, does not prevent belief. It is quite possible to hold a belief as a matter of faith and still be quite clearly aware that we do not know the belief to be true. This occurs not only in religion but in politics as well, and in many areas of personal relations.

Although a philosophy of religion has nothing to say directly about the truth or falsity of beliefs which do not rest on evidence, it does have something to say indirectly about such beliefs. We cannot appraise these beliefs rationally yet we may quite well find sometimes that there is a rational justification for holding a belief even if we cannot establish its truth. This does not mean that we are thereby warranted in claiming that we know the belief to be true; it means rather that it is reasonable, in such case, to hold the belief in spite of the fact that we do not know it to be true.

It is important to understand this distinction, as well as to explore the special conditions under which truth is available and testable in religion. It is important because some of the influential philosophies of the present day seem deliberately to seek a standpoint which excludes all such uses of reason. For example, naturalism and positivism, which are still fashionable in some quarters, attempt to set limits upon the subject-matter of philosophy. The limits which they try to set are not limits which reason provides but limits based on a willingness or unwillingness to apply rational inquiry to certain areas of investigation. As one contemporary naturalist explains, "there is no distinction between the naturalist and the proponents of other philosophies in respect to method, but only in respect to their selection of terms for treatment by the philosophic method . . . the terms selected by the naturalist for philosophic treatment are exclusively those which can be incorporated within scientific method and its conclusions."[1]

This is nothing more or less than an attempt to fix the limits of the field of philosophy by fiat and to use the natural sciences as the basis of a new authoritarian orthodoxy. As the orthodoxy of another day used its prestige and authority in the attempt to discredit the new sciences, so today there are some who attempt to erect a new orthodoxy on the basis of nineteenth century naturalism and positivism. Like theology this new dogma refuses to try to make a rational case for its premises; and yet it has no foundation of faith, as does theology, to serve as the source of its premises—unless, indeed, we may speak of faith in the doctrine of unfaith. Philosophy cannot thus arbitrarily choose its own limits. Even such lofty purpose as the attempt to exclude what is temperamentally distasteful to some philosophers will not justify such a course. For either philosophy's limitation to those matters which "can be incorporated within scientific method and its conclusions" is rationally justified or it is not. If it is, then on this view of philosophy the rational justification of such a limitation cannot itself be a part of philosophy. If it cannot be justified rationally then it is a purely arbitrary restriction. Such a restriction can rest only on some practical concern or on an agreement among those of the same tastes; and in fact this matter of taste or preference seems to be the requirement for admittance to the naturalistic fold. Those who confine their thinking to the area included within scientific method and its conclusions do so because they prefer to do so, or because of a restriction of their interest in rational inquiry. If, however, a naturalist insists that there is cogent reason for this restriction of the field of philosophy then according to his own theory that argument belongs not to philosophy but to something we should have to call a theory about philosophy, or meta-philosophy. But the theory about philosophy obviously could not be naturalistic, for naturalism would be its conclusion.

At best, naturalism is a philosophy of science and positivism is a philosophy of scientific method. Each has made important contributions to its restricted field, and each should be respected for its contributions. But in so far as they are restricted in their fields neither one has anything to say about what lies beyond those restrictions. It is quite proper for naturalism to insist that religion and its claims of truth are not appropriate subject-matter for a philosophy of science. It is quite another thing to declare that religion is not an appropriate subject-matter for philosophy.

The distinction between proof of the truth of a belief and rational justification for holding a belief is a distinction which only philosophy can establish. For this distinction itself is either a rational distinction or else it is arbitrary and has no warrant for a claim to be true. Unless it is a rational distinction it is, at best, a matter of convenience or of taste, and so commands no respect for any truth-claim which may be made in its behalf. However, even though the question of the soundness of this distinction is a proper subject of philosophical inquiry, it does not follow that philosophy can provide the content of beliefs which it may show we are rationally justified in holding without proof.

A somewhat parallel distinction is found in philosophy's role with respect to essential and existential truth. Philosophy is not itself a rich source of existential truth. Its main contribution, in this connection, is to make us aware of the distinction between essential and existential truth, and to give us some indication of how existential truth may be obtained. Philosophy's concern is a concern *about* existential truth, to understand its nature and how it differs from essential truth. But our understanding of the *nature* of existential truth is itself an instance of essential truth. So although religious truth is existential yet knowledge about religious truth has essential truth. This is the concern of a philosophy of religion; and since this is its concern, we must not expect a philosophy of religion to supply us with religious truth. It may provide rational justification for the belief that there is existential truth in religion but it cannot tell us what that truth is. If religious truth is existential then it is a truth which can be reached only by the practice of the religion which offers it.

Religious Truth

The use of such terms as "religious truth," "scientific truth," and "historical truth" suggests perhaps that we have as many different kinds of truth. Of course there is only one truth, in the sense that all limited and specific expressions of truth refer to the one world of real being. Our so-called "many truths" are partial versions and limited expressions of the one truth. We make contact with existence in many different ways. We are creatures of intellect, but not of intellect alone, for we feel and sense and imagine and appreciate and these are all links with existence. In all of them we discover something of what it means to be. In his many-sided nature man is like a prism which breaks the white light of truth into different hues.

The contrast between what we know and what we feel is often made too sharp and pushed too far. In our feelings and emotions we have significant links with the world beyond us. Emotions show the effect upon us of the situations out of which those emotions arise, and they may be clues to the nature of the total situation. A visitor in a home, for example, may be puzzled when one of the family shows irritation at what another has said. The visitor may see nothing to resent, yet the mere fact that emotion was aroused shows him that there are tensions within that family which are not obvious to an outsider. Feelings and emotions are not only symptomatic of some of the less obvious aspects of a human situation, they also show something of a person's total attitude and evaluation. They are the most frequently used of all of our various ways of showing how we, as existing and active selves, stand with respect to the other persons and situations which confront us.

Many believe that religion is one of the contacts we have with real existence, and that it is not merely one contact among many but is of primary importance. It takes us, they think, further along the way to significant truth than does any other way we can follow, and provides in its own terms final answers to life's mysteries and puzzles. We shall examine some aspects of these claims in this chapter. They surely deserve examination, for if they are sound they plainly are important and if they are not sound their falsity should be exposed.

It is not likely that the answer to religion's claims of truth can be a simple "yes" or "no." For one thing the claims are not always consistent with each other, and the same claims may be made for incompatible religious beliefs. We must remember also that religion is often expected to do things which are not within its nature to do, and even the strongest supporter of religion should not wish to make claims for it which do not fit its character. Such misunderstandings do occur, however, and many of the common criticisms of religion and excuses for ignoring it are in fact attacks upon religion for failing to do what it is not competent to do. Religion is not philosophy, and it cannot take the place of philosophy; it is not science, nor is it history. But because religion fails to take the place of philosophy or science or history it is rejected by some as of no significance.

There is an important distinction between the truth available in religion and that available in such fields as science or history or philosophy. The distinction concerns the conditions under which we find truth. To discover or apprehend truth in philosophy or science or history requires a fairly high order of intelligence together with disciplined and methodical investigation. But to take hold of religious truth we need only an open spirit and the willingness to receive it.

When we obtain truth in the sciences or in the formal disciplines we are like one who seeks a treasure, who learns the methods of search and studies the prospective areas to find the more favorable spots to investigate. When we secure religious truth we are like a person who receives a precious thing as a gift, a prize of such worth that it makes the products of his own search seem like cheap baubles. This gift is ours not because we deserve it; it comes to us because he who gives it loves us. Its value is not alone its own worth, for it bears in itself the image of the giver's love.

This we may say of religious truth at its best if the claims which are made for it are warranted. Of course we do not always find it at its best, and some of the claims made in behalf of its shabbier versions are certainly spurious. Here as elsewhere we often try to identify the prize by its wrappings, and sometimes we reject the gold for the tinsel.

If the sober claims in behalf of honest religion are true then like many other gifts which life holds for us the value of this one does not depend on the understanding of him who receives it. He may or may not be aware of the value of what he receives, but the benefits it brings do not wait on understanding. It is thus that religious truth is available to the simple as well as to the wise, to the children along with their fathers. There are many levels of understanding of truth, but the efficacy of truth does not always depend upon the level at which it is understood. In fact there is room for the surmise that the truth we can best understand may not be the truth which means the most to us; sometimes it seems even that there may be an inverse relation between ease of understanding and the importance of what is known.

I may have singular understanding of many abstruse and recondite matters and yet find myself bewildered when I try to understand the things which make my life most worth living. How do we explain, for example, the devotion of loved ones who give without thought of return; and this despite the fact that they may know us better than we know ourselves, and see our weaknesses and our meannesses in sharp detail without the mist with which our own self-love obscures them? When music has its way with us and when poetry lets us see through the veil of language, do we understand what has happened and how it has come about?

Much of the truth religion brings us is the truth it dramatizes. But to receive truth is to have it, and some truth is as much received when we take it in dramatic form as when we understand it conceptually. It is the truth which does the work in us, not our understanding of it; just as it is the love a mother gives her child which molds the young life, not the child's understanding of that love.

Why are the conditions for the reception of religious truth so different from the conditions for the discovery of some of the other kinds of truth? A partial answer to this question appears in the distinction between existential and essential truth. The formal studies of nature and man are concerned with essential truth; they attempt to discover the true character of those things and processes which they study. Religious truth, however, is mainly existential. Its aim is not to understand its objects but rather to find them and to make effective contact with them. It is like the difference between a man who studies the psychology and sociology of marriage, seeking perhaps to understand the cultural origins of marriage customs or to discover the conditions which make for a successful marriage, and a man who is not looking for information about marriage but who is looking for a wife.

Scientists and philosophers seek descriptive and conceptual truth. They look for general laws and principles, and so they think in terms of concepts and abstract systems. What we seek in religion, however, is not a conceptual understanding of general principles but contact with existence. It is proper to the nature of some truth that it should come to man more directly, and with greater effect, in act and deed than in formulas and statements of general principles. We need not so much to comprehend as to appropriate. So we find truth expressed in religion not in the form of principles but in specific cases. Its effective expression stirs the heart and arouses the imagination. Story, poetry, parable, ritual and ceremony, physical symbols—all these are channels through which it flows. This is so for the same reason that a child learns of the love which others have for him not by scientific analysis or philosophic discourse but in his experience of that love's manifestations. Even the words he comes to use when he tries to talk about it make no pretense of descriptive accuracy or logical refinement of meaning. So, too, in religion it is by contact that we find truth if there is truth there to find. In religion at its best we take the bread of life not to study its chemistry but to eat it.

We need no longer make the mistake of looking to religion for factual information about the natural world. This is not to deny that religion can contribute to our insight into nature, but only to point out that religion is not the place to go for factual information about nature or understanding of its laws. Religion may help us understand how it is that there are laws of nature, but it can tell us nothing of what those laws are. Before the discovery of the methods of scientific inquiry men went to religion and to the nature-lore which had formed a deposit about the ideas of religion.[2] They went there because they had no other place to go. But now we understand better the differences between various kinds of inquiry, and we know much more about the methods which are appropriate to each. We do not find answers to scientific questions in religion, and as we come to understand this we no longer look for them there. But it is just as important to understand also that we do not find answers to religious questions in science.

Religion is concerned more with what the facts mean than with what they are. It is concerned with man's ultimate significance, with his place in the cosmos; it has to do not with his space and time location in the physical universe but with his proper role with respect to final things. Religion communicates its message in terms of feeling and attitude, not by concepts. Religion is concerned with what attitudes are appropriate to existence, and of course it is true that what is appropriate to existence depends on what existence is; so a religion does assume that the real world is the kind of world in which its beliefs and attitudes are significant and true. But religion does not formulate and communicate its assumptions in concepts or in abstract theory. It communicates in narrative, myth, poetry, and ceremony; and when beliefs about existence are told us as a story we find that the story does not itself tell us what it means.

Many religious people are quite disturbed by the suggestion that religion communicates its truth by means of myth. To speak of myth, they think, is to speak of untruth. Is not a myth the story of something that never happened, an account of an imaginary event, and so is it not false by definition? This confusion is, perhaps, a part of the price paid for a communication of truth which does not require understanding in order to be effective. To deny myth a place in religion does not in any way protect religion's claim to truth. On the contrary, it narrows the capacity to receive religious truth and it impoverishes the appreciation of what little is received. It may seem incredible to us that intelligent and learned men should deny, for the protection of religious faith, the sphericity and motion of the earth. But they have, as they have denied man's animal descent and the geological history of the earth. In this their error is two-fold: they retain a false conception of nature, and they miss the real significance of religious truth.

"It is the genius of true myth," says Reinhold Niebuhr, "to suggest the dimension of depth in reality and to point to a realm of essence which transcends the surface of history, on which the cause-effect sequences, discovered and analyzed by science, occur. . . . But since myth cannot speak of the trans-historical without using symbols and events in history as its forms of expression, it invariably falsifies the facts of history, as seen by science, to state its truth."[3] Canon Streeter reminds us where we must look if we are to find the truth which a religion possesses. "It is not surprising, then, to find that Religion in the past has had recourse to myth, ritual (which is a form of drama), hymn, parable, epigram and paradox—all of them methods of Art."[4] "A religion is true if, and in proportion as, the quality which it expresses is actually existent in, and characteristic of, Reality. It follows that to test the element of truth in any religion we must direct our attention first of all, not to the intellectual constructions of the theologian, but to myth and rite, to hymn and prayer, to parable and proverb, to the mystic's meditation and the prophet's trumpet call."[5]

The language of religion must never be confused with the language of theory. As soon as a religious term is used for a concept it shifts its reference from religion to theology or philosophy. When religion speaks she speaks in order to turn our attention to what is important, not to inform us concerning its nature or even to explain rationally why it is important. But as religion shows its object to us and we turn our view toward it we find it for ourselves. Religion does not argue, it exhibits; it is not theory, but disclosure.

Religion is not an exercise of reason, but this in no way compromises its rationality. Eating is not a way in which we use reason either, for we eat with our hands and teeth and jaws and organs of digestion. But it is reasonable and rational for us to eat, and to eat as we do. Building a bridge is not an exercise in mathematics; it is a construction job. But this fact in no way compromises, or makes any less valid, the mathematics used in the design of the bridge. As religion is not an exercise of reason so the language of religion differs from the language of reason; it differs in precisely the way in which the expression of attitude and evaluation differs from the expression of conceptual analysis.

If religion does have its own truth, is there any way in which its truth might come to us which would be more effective than the way which religion actually follows to do its work in us? Tragedy, suffering and loss, awareness of sin and contrition, thankfulness for the gifts which come to us in spite of our lack of desert, the glow of love in which we put ourselves in another's place and feel something of what he feels and see things the way he sees them—men have long thought that these are the experiences and attitudes which open the mind and heart to hear and do the will of God. Religious worship rehearses these things and reflects, in its forms and associations, their universal and cosmic setting. This is not theory at work, nor is it essential truth we find here. If it is true at all its truth *is* the renewal of our relation to God, the reestablishment of our true orientation. It is *not* knowledge about God we secure here; if it is anything at all it is contact with Him.

RELIGIOUS AND AESTHETIC TRUTH

Aesthetic truth has similarities with religious truth, and if we look at some of these we may get a clearer view of religious truth. Aesthetic truth differs in much the same way as does religious truth from essential truth. In music or poetry or painting we seem at times to establish a direct contact with a level of organization of existence to which there is no other way of access. Aesthetic experience is a communication of what cannot be communicated in any other way. What we find there cannot be described or reported; it can only be experienced. As Charles Morgan says, "Art is news of reality not to be expressed in other terms."[6]

The close relation of religion and art is obvious in religion's extensive use of art for its own purposes. But religion and art are not aspects of each other, or two words for the same thing. Art puts us in contact with inherently significant form, and in doing this it opens up to us aspects of nature and life and mind we could encounter in no other way. Religion, in so far as it is true and effective, puts us in contact with ultimate being, with the source of all existence and value. In spite of this basic difference, religion and art have much in common, and we shall find that careful attention to aesthetic experience will help us see better what happens in religious experience.

We all know, for example, the powerful impact of poetry and drama upon our attitudes and emotions. We cannot explain this solely in terms of some power they have, as stimuli, to arouse emotion—as if this were something which takes place all by itself, a mere response to stimulation. In fact, poetry which merely arouses emotion is nothing but a superficial manipulation of the feelings we already have formed. Great poetry and great drama, however, put us into new perspectives toward the things that matter. They reveal to us unsuspected relations and meanings. The emotions they seem to arouse are not aroused directly by them, by playing on our feelings. For it is what the poem or play has led us to see, it is existence from this new perspective, which is the immediate occasion of the emotion. When it is real existence that we see from this perspective, we have poetic or dramatic truth.

Poetic truth works in us without requiring any understanding on our part of how it works. Our ideas and attitudes are altered; we do not know by what process the alteration takes place; we know only that it has taken place. In the childhood of the race as in the childhood of the man poetry is the only effective means of communication. By this kind of contact with existence man first discovers his world.

The parallel at this point between religious and poetic truth is close. To point this out is not, as some may object, to "reduce" religion to poetry. For one thing the charge that we are "reducing" religion to poetry rests on a misconception of poetry. We somehow have got our conception of "truth" these days much too narrow—the result perhaps of the recently acquired prestige of the natural sciences. But important as scientific truth is, and too few of us even yet fully understand how important it is, it still is not the truth of primary importance. The truth of primary importance is the truth by which we live and in which we find our moral and spiritual destiny. Before a man is a scientist he is a man; and if his scientific knowledge is to have a place in his way of life, a place which is reasonable and which is the place where it belongs, then he must have a way of life and a basic attitude toward existence. This, of course, will likely be influenced by his scientific knowledge, but it can not be composed of it.

Still, we may ask, why talk about truth at all in connection with poetry and religion? Are we not concerned here with causes and effects rather than with truth? We read a poem, or see a play, and the experience influences us. Its effect may be far reaching, in fact it may change our plans or even our whole outlook. It is not improbable that many a young man's choice of profession has turned upon the influence of a novel or a play or a religious experience. It is a matter of influence, not of truth. When we reflect on this, do we not have to admit that the effects of religion may be quite independent of its truth or falsity?

The reply to this objection is to accept what it affirms and to reject what it denies. These things do influence us, and so are causes which act upon us. They affect our attitudes and our relations with our world. But it is also the case that a purported revelation of the world in poetry or religion may be a falsification. The falsity of a picture does not destroy its power to influence any more than a lie carries in itself a guarantee against deception. Unless the basis of our action is sound, unless the view by which we chart our course is true, our action will be appropriate and successful only by accident.[7]

What Does Religion Tell Us?

We have emphasized the importance of religious truth and in this we have tried to express the attitude of those who believe they have found in religion a way to truth. But not everyone has this high opinion of the claims of religion. Many are hostile or contemptuous, and many others simply ignore religion and its claims. If religion is true and if its truth is important how can intelligent, sincere, and experienced people ignore or despise it?

So we may be asked to spell out, so all can see and understand, the nature of this thing for which such sweeping claims are made. "You talk," we are told, "about something of supreme value to which religion takes us. But you never tell us what it is. For all we know it may be a sham or a delusion. It is as if you offered to sell us something, and yet in all your assurances of its great value you fail to tell us what it is. How, then, can you expect us to pay serious attention to your claims?" This objection deserves careful study. We have to try to answer it or else show that it is based on misunderstanding.

What we are asked to do here is to formulate in words a description of the objects which religion claims to unveil to us, and by use of these words to communicate this information to those who have not found these objects in religious practice and experience. Once we understand what we are asked to do we see how impossible it is to comply. It is like asking someone to describe to us a painting he has seen and to communicate his experience to us in words. The trouble with such a request is the fact that the painter says what he has to say in color and composition, not in words. If this were not the case we could print the painting in type. What the composer says he says in music, not in words. If he had something to say in words he would write a letter or an essay. Even the novelist, whose medium is language, speaks in narrative and plot and depiction of character, not in concepts and abstract formulas.

One weakness of the rationalist is his desire to verbalize everything. This desire is so strong, and words seem so important to him, that he often appears to think that the essential nature of the thing he talks about is to be found in the words of the talk rather than in what the words refer to. What he cannot reduce to formula, or express in terms of concepts, he is tempted to reject as unreal. Parmenides held that the real is the thinkable, and Plato taught that the real is the knowable; but the modern intellectual seems inclined to believe that the real is the speakable.

James Fitzjames Stephen protests against this when he says:

> It is surely clear that our words, the sounds which we make with our lips, are but very imperfect symbols, that they all presuppose matter and sensation, and are thus unequal to the task of expressing that which, to use poor but necessary metaphors, lies behind and above matter and sensation. Most words are metaphors from sensible objects. "Spirit" means breathing, but I think no one will ever use words to much purpose unless he can feel and see that eloquence is eloquence and logic logic only if and in so far as the skin of language covers firm bone and hard muscle. It seems to me that we are spirits in prison, able only to make signals to each other, but with a world of things to think and to say which our signals cannot describe at all.[8]

So we reply to our questioner, and tell him that if he wishes to find out what religion is like he cannot find this out by having someone tell him in the right words. He needs rather to have the experience of religion. There is only one answer to the question, "What is it like?" and that answer is, "Try it and find out."

Does this not place us, and our discussion itself, in an impossible position? We advise the inquirer to find out for himself what it is he asks about. If he does so we need not tell him about it; and if he does not then there is no point in our talking about it, for he will have no idea of what we mean.

This position would be indeed an impossible one if it were not for another alternative, the very alternative which our whole discussion has followed from its start. We cannot communicate in words what religion says, yet we may be able to say something about the significance of religion and so justify the importance we give to it provided its claim of truth is sound. If, for example, a person says he has a device for heating houses which cuts the cost of fuel in half he need not describe the device, nor tell us how it works, to convince us of its importance. Of course we may not be convinced that he has any such device, and we likely would not wish to buy it without some information about it, but most of us would agree that if it is what he says it is then he has something important and useful.

What, then, does religion claim to do to us and for us? If we look at the more serious and persistent of these claims they seem to involve one basic assertion. This is the assertion that true religion places us in the most effective direct contact we can have with whatever is ultimate and final in real being. In doing this, so it is said, religion shows us to ourselves as we are; it shows us in our proper relations to others and to the whole order of existence; it provides the perspective from which alone we can distinguish the important from the trivial; and it gives us a hint of our final destiny, of a destiny beyond anything else we can imagine or dream.

This is what we are told by those whose religious experience has taken its place in the center of their lives. This is what they tell us, that is, when we can persuade them to speak. Those who ignore or dismiss religion tell us nothing like this about it. But when we look at what they do say we often find one of two things to be the case. Either they speak without the experience, or else it is apparent from what they do say about it that the religious experience on which they base their judgment is only the immature and confused emotional agitation—or the escape into the fabulous —of early childhood.

Who Is to Judge?

In our consideration of religion's claims to truth we must keep in mind always the importance of going behind the various attitudes toward religion which we encounter in order to evaluate their significance. The opinions of one who has not discovered for himself something of the best of what religion can mean to man is not likely to be of much significance. Such opinions have about as much meaning as the discourses of a color-blind person on the aesthetic qualities of a painting, or of a tone-deaf critic of music. For unless he speaks of what he knows in his own experience he literally does not know what he is talking about. We cannot observe religion or religious activity from the outside. We can observe the behavior of people while they are engaged in the performance of religious ceremony and ritual, but this does not tell us what their acts mean to them. At best we can infer that an act of ritual does seem to be of profound significance to him who performs it, but we cannot tell by observation what its significance is. Nor are we much better off when the worshipper tries to explain what the act means to him. He can tell no more than can a man who tries to tell what it means for him to love his wife and children. Such things are expressed in words only by poets, and the poets cannot talk to us unless we have something in our own experience to give their words meaning.

When we say that only those who have some personal experience and appreciation of religion are in a position to evaluate its

claims, do we not define competence to decide between conflicting claims in terms of adherence to one side of the conflict? Is this
not like saying to a prospective juror, "The defendant is innocent;
I am sure of that; so unless you believe he is innocent you are not
competent to sit on the jury"? Are we not in the same position as
a Marxist who insists that only the disciplined and indoctrinated
Marxist is capable of understanding what Marxism means and of
seeing its truth? In other words, do we not here beg the question?
Few would insist that only those who have had tuberculosis or
cancer are qualified to diagnose those diseases. If religion is false,
if it is only a way in which men delude themselves, then religious
experience might itself pervert men's judgment.

We must keep one thing clearly before us if we are to deal with
this difficulty, and that is the distinction between a man's judgment about something and the evidence of his competence to
judge. If we say that only those who agree with us in their political opinions are competent to judge concerning political issues,
we beg the question. The evidence in support of a man's competence to judge in a specific instance must be independent of the
judgment in that instance. What a man's judgment is, never by
itself demonstrates his competence to judge. For he may be merely
echoing the opinions of another; his mind and voice may be nothing more than a relay station for the ideas of someone else.

On the other hand, a man's opinions may themselves be sufficient evidence of his incompetence to form significant opinions
in that field. We should need no further evidence of a man's ignorance of astronomy, and of his utter incompetence as a judge in
that field, than to discover that he believes the earth is flat. We
need no further evidence of a man's incompetence to evaluate a
serious musical composition than his complaint that it does not
"have a tune." A critic may have been steeped in the classics and
may be an expert in musicology, but unless he has given modern
composers a prolonged and careful and sympathetic hearing, and
tried to find for himself what they have intended to do in their
compositions, his opinions about modern music are not significant.
So, too, a critic of the claims of religion who shows, in what he

says about it, that he has observed it only from the outside or that he identifies it with something in his own childhood or that he confuses the letter with the spirit, merely proclaims his own incompetence. For example, no one is in a position to pass judgment on the great religious faiths of Western civilization, Judaism and Christianity, who has not immersed himself sympathetically in the stream of literature which is the life-blood of these religions. He needs to understand from the inside and to feel in his own experience the inner meaning of at least some of their forms of worship.

The hostile critic who shows that he knows whereof he speaks, and knows in this intimate and personal sense, must be listened to with respect. The problem is to find him. Almost invariably the hostile critics of religion show no comprehension of what they are talking about. Either their encounter with religion has been external and superficial or else their attitude is a reaction against the grotesque and silly interpretations of their own childhood. This does not mean that there is nothing to criticize in the practice of religion; occasionally religion can benefit even from its hostile critics. Many of the things which Sigmund Freud had to say about religion were true enough. He had unusual insight into some of the psychological uses of religious belief, and he saw the frequent close relation of religious ideas with neurotic syndromes. But nowhere in Freud's principal writings is there the slightest indication that he ever dreamed of what religion at its best means to men and women whose religious faith feels itself completely at home and entirely secure in the company of their own highly developed critical intelligence.

Among the more widely publicized philosophers of recent years who have been hostile or indifferent to religion are Bertrand Russell and John Dewey. There is nothing in Russell's writings to show that he has the slightest inkling of what it is that men and women of high intelligence and broad learning and stable personality have seen in religion. What he says about the religious attitudes and practices he attacks may be true enough, but the things he attacks are a caricature of religious faith.[9] John Dewey's only attempt to give a sympathetic hearing to religion, in *A Com-*

mon Faith, shows an almost complete lack of awareness of what has happened in serious religious thought since the period of his own childhood. His book seems, at best, an attempt to salvage something from the ideas current in the more naive of the religiously toned "uplift" tracts of the late nineteenth century.[10]

No informed person who takes religion seriously will give much weight to the objections of Lord Russell and Mr. Dewey. But if he is serious he will give careful attention to such men as Alfred North Whitehead and William Ernest Hocking, Charles Hartshorne, and Erich Frank, to mention but a few. He may not agree with them; but he will recognize that they are not nineteenth century, that what they have to say about religion is no silly and puerile misconception of it. Their credentials are in what they write, in the evidence they give of their own wide acquaintance with and profound understanding of even those religious ideas they oppose.

The long line of the great interpreters of religious faith is not composed of simpletons and fools. We cannot read them with a feeling of pity for their gullibility and innocence. Among them are the most powerful, subtle, and perceptive minds in history. If we do not see what they see, if we are puzzled by what seems plain to them, we wonder whether we have not missed something. We cannot help noting that this is not the case with those who find no place for faith. This line, too, has its geniuses. But these are not the ones who carry us beyond what we understand. We understand their premises and their evidence, and we see how they reach their conclusions. In Lucretius and in Hume, for example, we do not feel that they are appealing to something beyond our grasp. What we do feel is that they have omitted something. They make us uneasy because of what they seem to overlook. Some of the men of faith also make us uneasy, but they make us uneasy because of what they make us feel *we* have overlooked.

CHAPTER 9

The Test of Religious Truth

RELIGION'S OWN TEST OF TRUTH

CLAIMS of religious truth may be examined at two levels. They may be tested within the limits of a particular religious faith, and by criteria which that religion specifies. Such tests assume the truth of the religion within which they are used, and so this level of test is a matter of inner consistency. A religion is bound to reject what is inconsistent with its own principles in so far as the inconsistency is recognized and its principles are adhered to, unless the conflicts are considered non-essential. If there were only one true religion it would contain in itself the tests of truth for all religions, but it seems quite plain that a claim to be the only true religion cannot be warranted by any test of truth within that religion itself.

This suggests the other level at which a claim of religious truth may be tested. It is the test of the primary principles of the religion itself. We refer here not to particular beliefs within a religion, to be examined in the light of the standards which that religion sets up; we refer rather to the truth of those standards themselves. This presents a special problem which we shall return to later in the chapter; it is, in fact, the central problem for a philosophy of religion. At this point, however, we shall look at some of the internal tests of truth which are used by actual religions. One reason for this is to see something of the great differences there can be in tests of religious truth.

If the beliefs of a religion are fantastic so also are likely to be its tests of truth. There is a religious sect, active recently in this country, which uses as a test the bite of poisonous snakes. To survive the bite of such a creature, presumably while under the spell of some strong religious emotion, is supposed to be the way in which God identifies those who are to be His authentic spokesmen. This, of course, is sheer savagery. Again, some piteous creatures so interpret the written oracles of their faith that they allow their own children to die rather than permit blood-transfusions. Here ignorance and arrogance go hand in hand.

Sometimese striking qualities of physique and personality are accepted as true signs of religious authority. Where people expect that a message from God, or from their gods, will be distinctive and will carry something of the mystery of its source in its content and in its mode of transmission, pathological behavior and unrestrained emotional frenzy may be looked upon as indications of religious truth. In religions with well established traditions and a highly organized priesthood, the very occupancy of a religious office will carry authority with it, especially if it is supposed that the occupant is in some way chosen by God.

Some of these tests have been used in the two higher religions of our own culture, Judaism and Christianity. But in both of these the supreme test of truth is moral and spiritual. It is in certain qualities of attitude, attitudes reflected in thought and practice, that the difference between the true and false is to be found. When we say that a religion, such as one of these, is true, we mean that he who has the faith to perform the acts which it prescribes in the attitudes which it enjoins will find the presence of God and will do the will of God. Truth here is existential truth, and its standards are existential standards. An attitude is an existing fact, it is the fusion of motive and feeling and expectation and evaluation in which action takes place. Mood alone is not enough, nor is feeling alone.

It is true that feeling alone is often taken to be the true test. Much of conventional religious worship seems intended to produce certain states of feeling. The presence of the desired feeling is taken to be the test of the success of the religious act. Anything which can be done in the presence of the feeling induced by the religious exercise is thought to be warranted by it. But since people are able to have intense and vivid religious feelings together with hate for others, and since few persecutions can match the vicious cruelty of some which have been blessed in the name of God under the guidance of such feelings, this test seems defective. It is the other way, in the teachings of the higher religions: the test of a religious feeling or emotion is the attitude it evokes. Religious feeling may be dangerous if it is not subjected to this test.

Micah, the prophet, saw the fundamental importance of attitude, and he set it forth in vivid contrast to conventional ideas of man's relation to God—and in contrast to traditional ceremonies which evoked intense emotions of awe and adoration.

> With what shall I come before the LORD,
>   and bow myself before God on high?
> Shall I come before him with burnt offerings,
>   with calves a year old?
> Will the Lord be pleased with thousands of rams,
>   with ten thousands of rivers of oil?
> Shall I give my first-born for my transgression,
>   the fruit of my body for the sin of my soul?"
> He has showed you, O man, what is good;
>   and what does the LORD require of you
> But to do justice, and to love kindness,
>   and to walk humbly with your God?[1]

It is in our desire to do justice and in our love of kindness and in our humility before God that we find God.

What brings human blessedness? One answer is given in the Sermon on the Mount. It is to be poor in spirit, to accept suffering and persecution, to be meek and merciful, to hunger and thirst for righteousness, to be pure in heart (that is, sincere), and to be peacemakers.[2] Over and over again Paul echoes this theme. "Put on then, as God's chosen ones, holy and beloved, compassion, kindness, lowliness, meekness, and patience, forbearing one another and, if one has a complaint against another, forgiving each other; as the Lord has forgiven you, so you also must forgive. And above all these put on love, which binds everything together in perfect harmony. . . . And be thankful."[3] Paul's supreme expression of this attitude is in his incomparable celebration of love. To speak in the tongues of angels, to have prophetic powers, to understand all mysteries and have all knowledge, to have all faith—even faith that will remove mountains—these are nothing without love. What are the signs of love? They are patience and kindness, absence of jealousy and boasting and arrogance and rudeness; they are the refusal to insist on one's rights, freedom from irritableness and resentment, the refusal to rejoice at wrong and the willingness to rejoice in the right.[4]

In Christianity the supreme test of truth is not agreement with dogma or theological correctness. Doctrine does not test belief; rather the tests of doctrine are in the fruits of belief as they are found in attitude and deed. What does your religious belief lead you to do and what are the attitudes it induces in you? What leads, says Paul, to "immorality, impurity, licentiousness, idolatry, sorcery, enmity, strife, jealousy, anger, selfishness, dissension, party spirit, envy, drunkenness, carousing, and the like" is false.[5] These are the "works of the flesh," the consequences of man's attempt to live without God and of his pretense to self-sufficiency. How can we tell that it is God's presence in us which guides us, and that "our sufficiency is from God"?[6] Paul's answer is, by the "fruit of the Spirit." The "fruit of the Spirit is love, joy, peace, patience, kindness, goodness, faithfulness, gentleness, self-control."[7] And Paul adds, "If we live by the Spirit, let us also walk by the Spirit. Let us have no self-conceit, no provoking of one another, no envy of one another."[8]

THE SPECIAL PROBLEM OF RELIGIOUS TRUTH

Religious truth is existential. If religion is true it brings us into the appropriate relationship with its object. Its object, by whatever name it is called, is thought to be in some sense the final reality or at least it is that to which man owes his final devotion. If the object of religion is God, as the higher theistic religions assert, then a true religion opens our awareness to the presence of God and so makes accessible to us the fruits of that awareness. But religion does not bring us an understanding of the nature of its object. If its object is God then we must go to theology and philosophy if we seek some understanding of God's nature, and if it has some other object then we must go to the science which studies the nature of that object. Yet the study of theology or the philosophy of religion or a special science is not a religious exercise; it is no more a religious act than the study of nutrition is nutritious.

The religions which center upon God, especially the higher of the monotheistic religions, are faced with a special difficulty. One aspect of the difficulty is found in the fact that although such a religion does not provide any adequate understanding of the nature of God, the people who profess that religion do engage in acts and ceremonies which express some definite ideas about God. These ceremonies may include, for example, such acts as adoration, petition, confession and repentance, and the services of love. They could not be performed meaningfully in the absence of some ideas about God, ideas which enable the worshipper to think of God as the appropriate object of such acts. Yet we could not expect those ideas about God to be at all adequate, for no theistic religion restricts these acts to those who have demonstrated their theological or philosophical competence.

The ideas about God involved in the practice of religion do not provide, by themselves, a conceptual understanding of God's nature. They apply to God, as we shall see later, as metaphors or analogies. They express something about the nature of God, but they do not express it directly; they express it in terms of other things, of things which come within the range of man's direct experience. God is described, for example, as a father, and this familiar human relationship of father and child is thought to tell us something of what God is like. If an analogy does succeed in expressing the nature of God in terms of something else then it is true, but it is true as an analogy and not as a concept adequate to its object.[9] So the problem of existence is especially acute when we are concerned with the existence of God. Not only are we unable to verify the existence of God directly, we are unable even to say what it is whose existence we cannot verify directly except as we refer to it in analogy with something else.

A religion like some varieties of Humanism, or like the religion of Marxist Communism, does not have the same difficulty which confronts theism. For a religion which worships Humanity worships something whose specific instances, at least, can be examined directly. A religion which finds its ultimates in a social goal, such as the classless society of Marxism, is not troubled by the possible disparity between its ideas about that society and reality; for its society is not actual, it is not yet in existence, so its nature can be dictated by dogma. In neither of these religions is the existence of the object or the nature of the object a problem. The only basic problem of the one is whether its object is worthy of worship, and of the other whether the attainment of its ideal is the ultimate fulfilment of existence. The special problem of religious truth which concerns us here is one which presses hardest upon the theistic religions, and we shall discuss it with reference to them.

Religious forms and creeds do not themselves guarantee truth. They are like the labels on packages, for whether a package is full or empty does not show on the label, and sometimes the label's description of the contents is misleading. So religious forms may be used without effect, just as one may read a label and fail to use what is in the package.

If we are going to apply the test of truth which one of the higher theistic religions provides then we need some assurance that the religion which supplies this test is itself true. Suppose that what Paul calls the "fruit of the Spirit" is in truth the fruit of weakness. How can we tell? What are the credentials of the criterion Paul offers us. Paul himself would insist, perhaps, that this criterion is the obvious implication of the nature of God as He shows Himself to us. We may well grant that the values implicit in this criterion will show their superiority on comparison with any rival set, but how can we trust them to take us to God unless we know there is a God for them to take us to? If we *believe* that God exists, and if our belief is true, well and good; but not even

Paul asks us to accept the existence of God on faith. "Ever since the creation of the world his invisible nature, namely, his eternal power and deity, has been clearly perceived in the things that have been made."[10]

It would be a simple matter to test the truth of religion if we could use the common tests of existential truth. For the usual tests are simply the presence or absence of the objects to which the statements apply. We are seldom left in uncertainty about the existence of something we see with our own eyes or hear with our own ears or touch with our own hands. But the problem is a more difficult one if the existence in question cannot be confirmed in this straightforward way. Of course we can be fooled by our senses, but still we have ways of avoiding this which work quite well in most cases. But when we are concerned with a supposed existent with which, even if it does exist, we cannot make direct and unequivocal contact our problem is exceedingly difficult. This is the special problem of religious truth. Religion requires the existence of its object, unless it is a kind of religion which does not claim existence for its object. But the existence to which religion promises to take us cannot be found in the direct experience which provides the ordinary tests of existential truth. How, then, is religious truth to be tested?

In raising this problem we do not mean to say that even if God exists we can have no direct contacts with God. We mean rather that if the existence of God is problematical then it is also problematical that our contacts are contacts with God. There may be no question about our having the experience which we interpret as contact with God; the question concerns our interpretation of the experience. Perhaps I have a most complete confidence in the existence of God because I have experiences which seem to me to make sense only if I understand them as contacts with God. But I may be mistaken, not about having the experiences but about the kind of interpretation which makes sense.

At one time, for example, physicists thought that the transfer of heat from a hot to a cold body could be understood only as the passage of some invisible material fluid, which they called "caloric" or "phlogiston," from the hot to the cold body. So when I conclude that God is present, and conclude this on the ground that my experience makes sense only on that supposition, I may be quite mistaken. Perhaps I rule out too quickly and too uncritically other plausible explanations. Or perhaps I am simply ignorant and do not know of the other explanations.

We well know how prone man is to give a religious interpretation to the things he does not understand and which yet seem important to him. Thus has man long interpreted matters of chance and mystery. Before the causes of disease were known disease was thought to be an act of God. Storms, earthquakes, and all kinds of natural disasters were understood in the same way. No doubt there is much today in the beliefs of even the more advanced religions which mistakes mystery for value and takes ignorance to be a sign of religious truth. It is this fact which puts us on our guard against a too easy acceptance of claims which are made in the name of religion.

So it is that when we try to apply the ordinary tests of existential truth to the special case of religious truth we find ourselves in trouble. For the object of religious belief does not confront us in the unequivocable fashion of the more familiar physical objects. The strongest and most persistent of all religious doubts are those which question the existence of the objects of religion. Religion claims truth, and the truth it claims is existential truth; but the very objects to which religion claims to take us are those things whose existence is questioned. How then can we apply the test of existential truth to religious truth?

It is no answer to our problem to appeal to the assurance of faith. It is the case that faith's sureness of the presence of God is sometimes stronger than our ordinary confidence in our senses, but such assurance is not itself a test of truth. If strength of belief alone were a test of truth then the truest beliefs would be those of delusion, for nowhere is belief held more strongly or more implacably or more fiercely in the face of contrary evidence than in the delusions of paranoia.

THE RATIONAL TEST OF RELIGIOUS TRUTH

If we cannot test religious truth directly then our test must be indirect. Of course if it is a test of existential truth the test must involve some direct reference to existence; but in the test of religious truth the existence which primarily concerns us, such as the existence of God, may not be something to which we can refer directly. Even so, our difficulty may seem easy to resolve, for I may establish indirectly the existence of one thing (A) by confirming directly the existence of something else (B), provided B could not exist if it were not for the existence of A. My argument, then, would be:

(1) The existence of B requires the existence of A.
(2) B does exist (a fact which I verify directly).
(3) Therefore, A exists.

We follow here in principle the same line of reasoning which a farmer may use in reaching the conclusion that a fox robbed his hen roost. He did not see the fox there, but he has reason to think that there are foxes in the area. He knows that they take chickens. He knows that his chickens have been taken by an animal rather than by a human thief, for he finds telltale signs. Among these are prints which he is sure can be made only by a fox, and these prints lead to and from the chicken house. The inference is plain; all the signs point to a fact which, although not verified directly, is the only plausible explanation of the signs themselves.

We have here the application of a general principle of verification which applies to claims of existential truth. When we find changes in existing things, and we can account plausibly for those changes only by reference to the existence of something else which is not directly present to us, then those changes we observe are signs of the existence of something else.

This kind of inference is so common and familiar that we apply it often without any clear awareness of our mode of thinking. Robinson Crusoe's sight of the footprint in the sand led directly to his awareness of the existence of another person on his island. For here he found a physical fact, something in actual existence, and he knew without question that the existence of this fact required the existence of another fact. He knew it because he knew that human footprints in the sand do not form themselves, and because he knew that in those circumstances the print could have been made only by another human foot. He assumed, of course, that everything which happens makes sense; and this we must assume in any inquiry.

Perhaps the test of religious truth is the same in principle. We have certain experiences in which we encounter actual existence. If the only plausible explanation of the existence of these things we find is the existence of the object of religious belief, and if the rule of inference we apply in the ordinary affairs of life is sound, we can hardly avoid the conclusion that the object of religious belief does exist. The matter seems to be quite obvious. The test of existence in the case of religious truth is the same in principle as the test we use in our everyday encounters with existence. It is the same principle by which a letter implies a writer, a sonata a composer, a house a builder, and so on throughout the whole range of our contacts with our world. This applies not alone to human contacts either; for coal deposits, oil pools, certain arrangements of geological strata, growth rings of trees—all are signs of certain definite existing situations in the past.

But is the matter so simple after all? We have neglected one important difference between the examples we have used and the use of the same indirect method in establishing, say, the existence of God. The difference is in the fact that when we infer that a fox has been in the hen house we already know that foxes exist, and it is only the recent presence here of *a* fox which our argument establishes. Robinson Crusoe already knew that other human beings existed, it was only the recent presence of one at that place which the footprint showed. We might very well use this same kind of argument to establish that God was present and acting in some specific situation if we already knew the existence of God. But how can we use this argument to establish God's existence itself?

The indirect argument, as we ordinarily use it, enables us to infer existence from existence. But in these familiar uses of it we go from one existence in our world to some other existence in that same world. Our inference rests on what we know of things in this world, and of the conditions under which they occur. But how can we use such a principle of inference to go from the existence of something in our world to the existence of God?

One thing we must recognize. The encounter with some unexplained natural fact does not itself justify an inference of the existence of something beyond the natural world, *in so far as it is possible that this so far unexplained fact has an explanation in terms of other facts of nature.* In so far as that possibility, as a possibility, is intelligible we must content ourselves to wait for our explanation until we have a more adequate understanding of our own world. So far as this is the case, any interpretation we may make of the fact which attributes to it anything but a natural significance is an interpretation which rests on faith and not on reason. Such interpretations may be justified in certain circumstances; we must not pre-judge them. But their justification does not furnish rational evidence of religious truth.

There are only two circumstances which justify our use of the indirect argument to establish the existence of something which is not itself a part of our world of nature. One circumstance is our discovery of something in our world which nothing else in our world could possibly account for. The other circumstance would be the discovery that this world of nature itself requires something else to account for its existence. Within these restrictions the test of existential truth may be used as a test of religious truth, provided the basic principle of the test is sound. If we can infer soundly from existence to existence in the natural order then the use of the same principle to establish religious truth is sound provided its use is limited by the restrictions we have pointed out.

The restrictions which hedge our use of the argument from

existence to existence when we apply it to religion can be seen also from a different approach. For somewhat similar restrictions apply to any sound use of the principle. Suppose we admit that the indirect argument is sound in principle, how can we be sure we have applied it correctly? The assurance it gives is not absolute, for many errors can arise in our use of the principle. If I argue: "B exists, and if B exists then A exists, therefore A exists" there are several points at which I may be in error. The argument itself is logically valid, but this means only that if the premises are true the conclusion is true. But are the premises true? Suppose we grant that B does exist, still the second premise, that if B exists then A exists, may be false.

The problem this raises is important enough to merit our careful attention, for it is misunderstanding on this point which has led some to dismiss religion's claims of truth and has led others to offer a faulty justification of those claims. When we say that if B exists (e.g., the footprint in the sand) then A exists (the earlier presence of another human being at that place), we argue that A was the cause of B. But we go further than this, for we rest our case on the conviction that *only* A could cause B. In Robinson Crusoe's case the argument was quite convincing. He had been confident that he was the only person on the island, and he knew of no way a footprint could get into the sand except by the pressure of a human foot, and he knew it was not his own foot that made it. His assurance rested on these two foundations: footprints do not bring themselves into existence, and this footprint in this set of circumstances could have been made only by a human being and by someone other than himself.

The argument from the existence of B to the existence of A is inconclusive just to the extent that there are other possible causes of B. Before the argument is conclusive we have to narrow down the possibilities to A alone. Crusoe did this by means of the positive knowledge he had of footprints, the island he was on, and other physical facts. We must also narrow down the possibilities, and as successfully, when we use this principle to test claims of religious truth.

It is not enough, as a test of religious truth, that we encounter something in existence for which we can find no explanation in the world of nature. We are not warranted in carrying our inference from natural fact to God for the reason merely that there is something in nature which we do not understand. If we were justified in such a course then the greater our ignorance the greater our evidence of God's existence and action; and it is just this kind of error which religious obscurantism so often makes when it discourages and even actively opposes the study of nature for fear something will be taken away from God. We cannot argue from ignorance; our argument needs a positive basis in evidence if it is to have any rational strength. Its positive basis, the only sound positive basis, is not the existence of something we are unable to account for in terms of nature, it is rather the positive evidence we have that the existence in question is one for which no process of nature or natural cause could possibly account. Our evidence must show that no matter how much more complete man's knowledge of nature may become he still will never be able to find in nature the explanation of some of the existence he actually encounters.

We must not assume that there is general agreement on this method of solving our problem. For many reasons men have often hesitated to apply this principle to the objects of religious faith. Their objections we shall consider when we come to examine more directly the way in which this principle applies to the existence of God. At this present point in our discussion, however, we may note one peculiar fact, that most of those who attempt to discredit the indirect test when it is applied to the existence of God find themselves forced finally to reject its application to all other things as well. For often their criticism turns from a special application of the principle to the principle itself, and they find themselves drawing the somewhat disturbing conclusion that nothing which exists testifies to the existence of anything else. Although many have announced that this is their conclusion no one yet has provided a demonstation of how it can be put into practice.

RADICAL DOUBT

The rational test of religious truth is not itself a part of religion. As we have already suggested, it turns out to be the question of the real existence of the object of religion, that is, of God. The practice of a religion rarely, if ever, includes examination of the evidence for the existence of God. This problem concerns rather the very foundation of such a religion, for example, as a theistic one. Confidence in the existence of God, whether a matter of faith or the result of a supposed rational demonstration, is the door through which we enter a theistic religion. Doubts of the existence of God are possible, of course, without compromising the religion based upon the existence of God, but only those doubts which can be overcome by acts of worship and practice which belong to the religion itself. Such doubts are fears lest the tabernacle of God be empty; they are overcome by entering the tabernacle and finding Him there. The more radical doubt, however, is doubt of the existence of a God to be there. To look for an answer to this doubt within the religion which it has undermined is hopeless, for this radical doubt has brought into question the significance of the very thing to which we should be looking if we followed such a course.

By a *radical doubt* of the existence of God we mean a doubt which attacks the very roots of such a belief. A radical doubt, in so far as it is not merely arbitrary and wilful, is the outcome of an apparent conflict between belief in the existence of God and other beliefs about the real world. This is the doubt which is characteristic of the present secular age. It comes from the acquisition of a conception of the world which logically excludes belief in the existence of God, or at least makes such belief seem irrelevant to our positive knowledge. This is not the kind of disbelief which arises within the practice of religion, and it is not to be overcome by intensification of religious devotion. A disbelief so overcome is plainly not the radical doubt we refer to here. For radical doubt would make the acts of devotion seem a sham and a mockery.

THE TEST OF RELIGIOUS TRUTH

Only pretense could sustain a man in his performance of those acts when his disbelief has made them meaningless.

If God does exist, and if the best in religion is the appropriate response by man to God, then the only remedy for radical doubt is an examination of the rational evidence for God's existence. If the results of this examination are positive then belief in the existence of God will be an intellectual conviction. We hear much from the side of religious faith which is in disparagement of intellectual inquiry in matters of religion. We are told that faith alone, as an act of will, is the remedy for doubt. Too often those who say this seem themselves never to have been aware of the basic intellectual issues which have perplexed our present ways of thinking. They wave such things away as nothing but weakness of faith or as evidence of the doubter's own disobedience to God. They seem not to understand that it is the object of faith itself and it is the very God to whom the doubter is accused of disobedience which is brought in question. No man of integrity will worship a God in whose existence he does not believe; for to him this would be to live and act a lie. The doubter is told to accept the pretended God as real and his doubts will vanish. If he did this, of course his doubts would vanish; but what he is advised to do is the very thing his doubts prevent him from doing.

Radical doubt is based on what is taken to be genuine and authenticated knowledge. If I hold what I take to be a positive and rational conception of the real world, and if belief in the existence of God is logically incompatible with this conception, I cannot arrive at a belief in the existence of God by an act of faith or by an exercise of will. I must first replace or doubt my philosophy, or else compromise my intellectual integrity. Exhortation to believe is the expression of an utter misconception of the nature of my disbelief, and he who utters it, knowing the nature of my disbelief, is an ignoramus or a fool. If what I do believe on what I take to be positive evidence and a rational interpretation of that evidence does leave room to affirm the existence of God, without contradiction, then there may be some point to the advice to try the affirmation before the belief is established. Or if I do arrive at an intellectual conviction of the existence of God, it may well be good advice to trust God beyond the reach of my own understanding. Certainly it is good advice if the God whose existence I am convinced I know is understood by me to be trustworthy beyond the reach of my own understanding. But the doubt which this method meets is not radical doubt. In radical doubt we have positive reasons, which we are unable intellectually to abandon, for the denial of the existence of God. If God does exist, then we are mistaken in our reasons. For radical doubt the only remedy is to discover that we are mistaken.

Only a philosophy of religion can meet such doubts on their own ground. The existence of God, the very condition without which theistic religion makes no sense at all, must be established by rational argument directed to conclusive evidence. The currently fashionable air of snobbish superiority to such a philosophy of religion, on the part of many leaders in the field of religious thought itself, is hardly in place in this secular age. In a way, perhaps, those are fortunate whose doubts have never reached very deep—if what they believe is indeed the truth. But the very foundation on which they stand disqualifies them from meeting the position of radical doubt. If they are to do so, they must leave the protection of their own faith and face the fundamental issue in the arena of reason and evidence.

The central question for a philosophy of religion which attempts to go to the foundation of the case for religion is the question of the existence of God. Only this kind of approach can hope to neutralize what Walter Lippmann long ago called "the acids of modernity."[11] If theism is true, it is a true philosophy. We can no longer effectively state its case by exhortation to seek God or in terms of a theistic theology. The case for theism can be stated for the modern mind only as sound and true philosophy, based on and defended by philosophical considerations alone. It is no answer to a philosophy which excludes God to accuse the philosophers of sinful pride in reason; they may as well be accused of sinful pride in their own intellectual integrity. The only way we can meet such philosophies is to show that they are false philosophies, that they misunderstand and misinterpret the evidence from which they draw their conclusions concerning knowledge and existence. Our study, in Part Four, of the nature of man will prepare us for this central problem of a modern philosophy of religion—the problem of the existence of God.

Part Four

THE NATURE OF MAN

CHAPTER 10

Traditional and Modern Ideas of Man

TRADITIONAL AND MODERN IDEAS OF MAN

I F THERE is anything we encounter directly in our world that no processes or events in nature can possibly account for we should expect it to be something in the nature of man. In order to consider this possibility we must look carefully at the nature of man, and the most convenient approach is to examine some of the changes which have taken place in man's conception of his own nature. We shall look particularly at some of the differences between the traditional and contemporary views of man.

In certain respects these two outlooks are directly opposed to each other, and their opposition involves some of the basic problems which any religious conception of man must face. When we speak here of the "traditional" and "contemporary" ideas of man we do not mean, of course, that there is one single theory of man's nature which we call the "traditional" one and another single theory which we call the "contemporary." What we mean is that there are certain common features of the various views of man which were accepted before the modern era and there are other common features of the views of man which express the modern attitude. The separation in time is not complete, for many in the modern world have been little touched by modern thought, while in ancient and medieval thought there were those whose conceptions of man's nature had some of the characteristics of contemporary views.

The change from the traditional to the contemporary view was slow, but it gained headway in the seventeenth century and was firmly rooted in European thought by the close of the eighteenth century. The traditional view of man was primarily a religious view while the modern conception is distinctively secular. The change from the one to the other was a part of the general secularization of life which is characteristic of the modern age. Philosophy, the sciences, the arts, and the economic life of society became independent of religious control and, to a considerable extent, independent of religious influence. The centers of interest shifted and so also shifted the areas of distinctive achievement. Theology gave up its place as the integration of knowledge and thought; and with this, thought lost its integration. Philosophy, mathematics and the special sciences went their own ways without much reference to each other. The church gave up its place as the integrating institution of society; and with this, society lost its integration. The place of the church was taken partly by the state, and with the development of the modern nation-states the political unity of the western world was broken. With the loss of integration of life and thought there came, as it seems there always come under such circumstances, widespread attacks upon the competence of human reason. Reason yearns for unity, and where unity seems lost, confidence in reason weakens.

The Religious and the Secular

We need first to understand the transition from the religious to the secular society, for, as we shall see, there is good reason to think that the secularization of modern life is itself an important step in the development of religious ideas. This phase of the modern development of religion is emphasized by Professor A. A. Bowman.

There was a time when the whole business of living, whether in its normal aspect as a daily routine, or in its periodic crises, was accompanied by a brooding sense of demonic presences, to which man was fain to address himself for succour and protection. Every contingency was an occasion for religious ceremonial. The religious attitude was habitual. In the course of centuries, during which man has learned to relate himself as a person to nature as a set of impersonal forces, this attitude has undergone a striking reversal. So far at least as the western world is concerned, it would not be too much to say that on the whole man hardly knows what to do with his religion, or where to find a place for it in the circle of his interests. It has very largely ceased to be the *normal*—it is probably seldom the *paramount*—business of life. In most cases religion has become little better than an obscure background, with episodic incursions upon the steady march of our secular preoccupations.[1]

There are many ways of accounting for this. "One is that the day of religion is virtually over, that the growth of knowledge and the mechanical mastery of nature have superseded what was really no better than a primitive misunderstanding, and that the time will in all probability come when science and social organization between them will quietly take over whatever still remains within the doubtful and hesitating jurisdiction of religion."[2] At the opposite extreme is the insistence that "the secularist tendency represents a fundamental blunder, a loss of insight into the deeper truth, and a growing blindness to the essential values."[3] The view which attempts to find a compromise between these extremes is "the attitude of those who, acknowledging the validity of the secular standpoint as embodied in science and in the economic and political organization of human life, still seek to find a place for religion in those fields of experience—for example, in creative artistic endeavour, friendship and moral feeling—which seem to them to evade the categories of science and the regimentation of life along official lines."[4]

All these explanations are likely too simple to account for a highly complex process of cultural change. Fundamental changes in society are no mere parade through time of different interests and activities. Man's nature is the same today as it was five centuries ago, even if his concept of it is not. It is reasonable to look for some very intimate connection between the religious and secular eras of our civilization's history rather than to regard the change as nothing more than the happy victory of knowledge over superstition, or as merely the defeat of truth by submergence in the trivialities of modern life, or as a division of the territory between two enemies.

When we look more carefully at the relation of the religious and the secular we find that the very concept of the secular is formed from a religious perspective. It may well be that the emergence of the secular age, instead of being the defeat of religion in our culture, is itself an important positive advance in the development of religion. This is Professor Bowman's conception of the matter. It is his position that "the *development of a secular standpoint can be understood only from the religious point of view. It is a phenomenon of the process by which . . . religion advances beyond its own animistic beginnings.*"[5]

Primitive religion is nature worship, and as individualized gods emerge they are endowed with the powers to do those things which man sees happening in nature. His gods are the active principles in nature, the real causes of all that takes place. In the first attempts to explain the actions of things in terms of things themselves it was said, as in the words attributed to Thales, that all things are "full of gods."[6] But such gods are not God, as the theist thinks of God. They are as remote from God as are the forces of nature themselves, for they are in truth nothing but the forces of nature personified. "If God is to be treated as God," Bowman points out, "Nature must be treated as Nature."[7]

The development is from natural forces to moral relationship.

As time goes on, the nature of deity defines itself less and less in terms of any merely external relationship to nature, and more and more in terms of an inner moral relationship with man. To the deeper consciousness of the prophet, in the hour of his spiritual crisis, the death-dealing terrors of nature, in which the primitive mind would have seen the very type of divine action, lose all religious significance. They have no message to convey to the spirit that calamity has crushed.[8] Neither the "great and strong wind" that "rent the mountains, and brake in pieces the rocks before Jehovah," nor yet the earthquake that followed the wind, nor the fire that succeeded the earthquake could inspire the sense of a divine presence. Jehovah was not in these, but in the still small voice that came when nature's voice was hushed. For the fierce and disappointed prophet nature had become opaque to godhead, her most impressive forms impervious to the meanings with which in an earlier age they had been saturated.[9]

So the gods of the heathen are not gods at all. "There are things in the world which are not gods and are not haunted by them: there is an aspect of things which is not divine."[10]

We too often think of our modern age as an age of light which emerged, a few centuries back, from an age of darkness. We think of our own time as the very negation of the one it has followed. If pressed to try to account for the change we likely will explain it as the result of the influence of science. It was the discovery of scientific method and the development of techniques based on the sciences which created and built the modern world. According to Bowman this reverses the true causal order. "It would be a fundamental error to explain the origin of the secular standpoint by attributing it to the development of physical science in modern times. The secular standpoint is not the product of science; science is *its* product."[11]

The scientific outlook, which the modern mind so proudly claims as its distinctive achievement, was made possible by medieval theology. Whitehead tells us that "the greatest contribution of medievalism to the formation of the scientific movement" was "the inexpugnable belief that every detailed occurrence can be correlated with its antecedents in a perfectly definite manner, exemplifying general principles. Without this belief the incredible labours of scientists would be without hope. It is this instinctive conviction, vividly poised before the imagination, which is the motive power of research:—that there is a secret, a secret which can be unveiled." This conviction can have had only one source. "It must come from the medieval insistence on the rationality of God." Thus, Whitehead contends, "the faith in the possibility of science, generated antecedently to the development of modern scientific theory, is an unconscious derivative from medieval theology."[12]

Just as mistaken as the idea that modern secularism is the product of modern science is the idea that the medieval age was one of faith while our own is an age of reason. "Science," says Whitehead, "has never shaken off the impress of its origin in the historical revolt of the later Renaissance. It has remained predominantly an anti-rationalistic movement, based on a naïve faith. What reasoning it has wanted, has been borrowed from mathematics which is a surviving relic of Greek rationalism, following the deductive method. Science repudiates philosophy. In other words, it has never cared to justify its faith or to explain its meanings; and has remained blandly indifferent to its refutation by Hume."[13] He points out that Hume's attack on reason was felt by the church but ignored by scientists: ". . . it illustrates the anti-rationalism of the scientific public that, when Hume did appear, it was only the religious implications of his philosophy which attracted attention. This was because the clergy were in principle rationalists, whereas the men of science were content with a simple faith in the order of nature."[14]

Science is possible because of faith in the order of nature, a belief which has come to the modern mind from medieval theology and which could not possibly be shown to be true by means of the methods of science. Not only do scientists act on this faith in the order of nature, but in our modern world the non-scientist lives by his faith in science. In our advanced technological society we depend on machines and devices which few of us understand. The knowledge and skills which make our mode of life possible are the exclusive possession of specialists; the rest of us, with hardly a thought of what we do, give ourselves into the trust of men we do not know and whose knowledge is only a mystery to us. Did any tribal medicine-man ever command greater confidence?

It is not strange that we should give our faith to those who know and who can apply their knowledge successfully. We ourselves do not need expert knowledge in order to recognize the success of scientific technology. A man does not have to be able even to read and write in order to use the telephone or to drive an automobile. The advances in scientific knowledge and their technological applications have shown evidence of their soundness in their very success. The discovery of how to release atomic energy under controlled conditions, for example, could have been no accident except with respect to this or that detail. It was not something waiting to be seen, as were most of the early modern scientific discoveries. The whole project of atomic investigation required the elaborate processing of materials in accordance with a complex theoretical scheme, and the success of the project would be incredible if the theory on which it proceeded were false.

One consequence of the secular disintegration of society is that we give our trust not only to those who know but also to those who merely claim to know. We follow prophets and soothsayers as readily as we accept scientific discoveries and inventions. The very success of science and technology has made us gullible in the presence of all such claims. When self-appointed prophets borrow for themselves the prestige of the scientist they become irresistible. Our trouble is that we have lost touch with the standards by which such claims can be judged. Political and educational and moral swindles can be perpetrated because they present themselves in the name of science. The vermin that infest our modern world crawl into the white walled laboratories of science for protection. Our ignorance of what science is, of where its limits lie and of what subjects of inquiry are appropriate to it, prevents us from distinguishing the invaders from those who rightfully belong there. A picture of a man in a white coat, for example, is all that is needed to make plausible the most fantastic and silly claims ever brewed in the brain of an advertising copy-writer.

An understanding of the nature of the conflict between traditional and modern ideas of man will help us see where religion belongs in a secularized society. In order for religion to do its own work and to occupy the place where it properly belongs, it was necessary to drive it out of those places where it does not belong and to take away from it the functions it attempted to perform in spite of its utter unfitness to do so. As Professor Bowman says, "the first step in the process of finding the divine presence everywhere in the world of men and things is to distinguish the world of men and things from the divine being."[15] We cannot recognize the presence of God in nature unless we distinguish nature from God, for without this distinction nature would *be* God. We cannot see the relevance of God's will to our own decision and action unless we distinguish ourselves from God, for without this distinction the decision and action would not be our own but God's. It is only because theism cannot accept the divinity of nature and of man that it can recognize the presence of God in nature and in man.

THE CONFLICT BETWEEN TRADITIONAL AND MODERN IDEAS OF MAN

The opposition between the traditional and modern ideas of man is a complex one. Not only are they mutually inconsistent at many points, in the sense that if one is true in some of its conceptions the other must be false in some of its views, but their opposition is itself an important part of the structure of each of the two attitudes. There are certain areas in which there is a kind of agreement between the two conceptions of man, but the two differ strikingly in their interpretations of their areas of agreement. Each includes in itself something which belongs to the other, but they give to these common elements contrary interpretations.

The traditional attitude gives to man the position of chief importance in nature. It sees him as the crown of the natural order. It is for him and in his interest that the world of nature exists. Sun and moon and stars give him light; the air is for him to breathe; plant and animal life provide his food, and in the animal world he finds helpers for his daily tasks. When nature destroys him and his own it is because of man's sin; and when nature prospers him it is man's reward for righteousness and submission to the divine order.

In this conception of man, the significance of his position in the natural world is to be found in his high responsibility and in his subordination to divinity. Although supreme in nature man is not supreme in existence. His very awareness of his pre-eminence and power in the world of nature increases his humility as he compares himself with his maker. He sees that it is not his purpose which governs nature but the divine purpose; and he himself, together with his purposes, is an instrument for the purposes of God.

The modern view of man has a certain limited agreement with the traditional view of man's subordinate position in the order of being. The modern attitude, however, does not see man in subordination to a divine order; it sees rather his insignificance in contrast with the unimaginable extent of the physical universe. The few miles, even the hundreds and thousands, which measure his distances and movements on the surface of this modest satellite of a minor star of one of the galaxies seem nearly nothing in contrast with the distances which astronomers measure in light-years. Not only do the enormous distances in space humble man's conception of himself and of his little corner of the world, but the thousands of millions of years our universe has endured make man's history seem but a moment. Man is indeed a lowly thing, and his very habitation is but a speck of dust in the great cosmos which is nature.

The insignificance of man, however, is not the last word. Modern man's awareness of his lowly position in nature is itself turned into a mark of his potentialities. For lowly man has increased enormously his knowledge and understanding of the universe. In his knowledge there is power. One of the weaker of the animals, slow and awkward in his movements, defenseless against cold and heat, man applies his knowledge of the forces of nature and harnesses these neutral and brutal energies to his own purpose. The world was not made for man, as the traditional view so mistakenly supposed, but man is in the process of turning it to his own uses. Modern man is determined to bring it to pass that the world shall be turned to man's use.

[Modern man] maintains that the true aim of human life is to bring about a constant development of man's natural and rational faculties, to contribute to the advancement of culture and civiliza-tion—which are to lead to an ever more complete rule over nature and thus to even greater happiness and general welfare. The mod-ern individual feels sure that he can be master over his own destiny, and for this reason he is so busy in this world that he cannot con-cern himself with the Beyond. It would indeed seem to be true that the faith in this world, in man and his earthly life, has really brought about greater happiness, a wider range of freedom and justice. Modern man trusts in himself and is certain that the future of the race can be determined by himself.[16]

Man was not placed in a position of supremacy in nature, but he is now on the way to making himself supreme. He is not con-tent with the prospect of finding greater happiness and increasing the range of freedom and justice. His purpose is limited only by his imagination. He looks forward to the time when he will bring other planets of our sun under his sway, as he makes swifter and swifter progress in mastering the energies of this planet. Then will come dreams of the conquest of other sun systems, and even other galaxies. For there is nothing in the modern attitude to prevent such dreams. Man's weaknesses and limitations are nothing but functions of his ignorance, and their cure is in the extension of his knowledge. The extension of his knowledge, he conceives of as nothing else than more of what he already has. He sees no limits to his potential power. Already some enthusiasts imagine that after conquering the problems of interplanetary travel man will learn even to control time, and with time space, so that distances which we measure in light years may be shrunk at will to manageable size. The mite of nature will become the master.

So the modern view accepts, in its own interpretation, the fact of man's subordination. But it turns the discovery of this into the foundation of an almost limitless power which he will use to bring the universe itself under his control. The traditional view, on the other hand, begins with man's original supremacy in the world of nature. But the basis of this, and its final significance, is in man's subordination to another order of existence and to purposes which are not his own. From his immediate and obvious preeminence the traditional view infers his ultimate subordination; while from his immediate and obvious subordination, obvious in the light of man's new knowledge, the modern view looks to his ultimate supremacy.

As man depends more and more on his own power he pays less and less attention to religion. It no longer is the center of his life, the source of meaning and the way to salvation. In the words of Erich Frank:

> The attitude of the average person towards religion is one of detached scepticism, and modern philosophy has been determined by a similar mode of thinking. Both the philosophic and the ordinary points of view reflect a feeling of intellectual prowess. Descartes, flung by doubt into the abyss of desperation, found the Archimedean point in the certainty of his own Ego and in the evidence of his ideas. It is precisely in his sceptical doubt that he found the proof for the sovereignty of his reason, and this proof gave him the strength to defy the world. This sovereign feeling of the intellect, which considers itself capable of understanding everything outside itself in the categories of its own thinking and acting, has remained the basic principle of modern philosophy.[17]

Weakness of the Traditional View of Man

The traditional view of man in European thought was composed of Hebrew-Christian religious ideas interpreted in terms of the Platonic-Aristotelian metaphysics and placed in an order of nature described in terms of Aristotle's physics and the Ptolemaic astronomy. The chief concern of the traditional view centered upon its conception of the welfare and destiny of the human soul. The supposed facts about nature, provided by the Aristotelian-Ptolemaic cosmology, were of little importance excepts as the background of man's existence. It was man and God who played the principal parts in the drama of existence; the natural world was merely the stage upon which some of the scenes of that drama were played. In spite of the fact that the cosmology was not important in itself, it became so closely associated with the traditional religious ideas of man that attempts to examine it critically were resisted and led to repressive measures.

Giordano Bruno, for example, was one of the first philosophers to take the new Copernican cosmology seriously. Because of the conclusions he drew from it he was seized by the Inquisition, and after some seven years of imprisonment was burned at the stake in 1600. His younger contemporary, Galileo, was brought before the Inquisition and forced to recant his heresy concerning the revolution of the earth about the sun. Even when the new science could no longer be resisted, it was never entirely assimiliated into the religious view.[18]

The fatal defect of the traditional conception of man and the order of nature is that the supposed facts which provide the framework of that conception are wrong. In a sense, we may say, the religious conception of man and his destiny had come to be an interpretation of the significance of the natural world. Nature existed, it was thought, for the sake of a divine plan. The facts which were understood in the light of this interpretation were so wrongly conceived that it may be difficult to understand how any part of the traditional view survived the influence of the new cosmology. Yet, on second thought, it may occur to us that the survival of any part of the traditional view of man indicates that there are elements of truth in it which are independent of its pre-scientific cosmology.

The traditional conception of man may still have some force if we should find, for example, that it rests more significantly on certain moral and religious insights than upon the pre-scientific cosmology. In so far as this is the case the pre-scientific cosmology was only an accidental ingredient of the traditional conception of man, not an essential part. Yet it remains every bit as true that the cosmology of that view is false, and the supposed facts concerning the physical world which that view includes are in most respects wrong. The presence of such error easily leads to misunderstandings; and where some of the alleged facts interpreted are not facts at all, the interpretations are always in danger. If there is truth in the traditional view of man, and if it is to be available to an age which has discovered the falsity of the traditional cosmology, then that truth must be dissociated from the world view of ancient times and it must be shown to be consistent with the facts of nature as we know them.

With its lack of firmly established information about the world of nature, pre-scientific thinking went to religion for much of its explanation of what happens in that world. It *did* go to religion because it had no other place to go. It *could* go to religion because there was then no clear distinction between religious and scientific ideas. Religious ideas had collected about themselves the lore and legend, the superstitions and the hearsays, of tradition. Divinities and supernatural agencies thus were used to explain all those events in nature for which natural causes were not known. Since the explanations were in terms of supernatural agencies those explanations themselves acquired religious sanction. So the traditional view of man and nature was largely a religious view, and whatever parts of it were religiously irrelevant were seldom so recognized.

To the extent that a religious view of man and the world rests merely on ignorance, or on uncontrolled imaginative speculation, its area is invaded and its authority threatened by every advance of scientific knowledge. For the scientific account of the facts rests on positive evidence and controlled inference. If the religious view of man is to avoid fatal confusion it must leave to the natural sciences the determination of the facts which come within the proper fields of those sciences, and it must distinguish carefully from those facts the positive evidence on which it rests its own case. From what we know of pre-scientific thinking it seems reasonable to conclude that the traditional religious view of man was derived mainly from sources independent of the cosmologies of the time, and that those cosmologies were used merely as a framework for the religious interpretation. If this is the case then it is quite possible that we may be able to separate the parts of the religious conception of man which are of primary importance from the cosmological speculations associated with it.

Such a separation seems the more plausible the more apparent it becomes that the real source of the traditional view of man was his insights into his own spiritual and moral nature. This, in fact, is the case. The Hebrew conception of man was not derived from speculations about nature. It came from prophets and poets. The Greek ideas of man came not from the nature philosophers but, first, from the poets and dramatists, and then from philosophers who were primarily concerned with man's soul. Such insights may still be true in spite of the collapse of the stage which was built for them. They are not themselves scientific facts. They transcend all scientific facts, and they cannot be in conflict with any scientific facts; for the two levels of understanding are different and the methods of inquiry used in one do not apply to the other. When scientific findings are so interpreted as to have a moral or religious significance then we may be quite sure that the interpretation is not itself a part of scientific inquiry. The truth of the interpretation is in no way guaranteed or even supported by the truth of the scientific reports themselves. When, on the other hand, religious or moral ideas are "explained" in terms of certain beliefs concerning the facts of nature then only the appropriate natural sciences are competent to decide whether those beliefs are true.

> It is obvious [Erich Frank points out] that religious documents necessarily reflect . . . the intellectual background of the time and sphere in which they were written. But such connotations are of no consequence for the understanding of the quintessence of their truth. It is not the aim of religion to prove scientific propositions, but only to reveal religious truths. These revelations, therefore, for the modern philosopher become truly understandable only if he shows regard for their essence rather than for their accidental connotations. Interpreted in this way, they will divulge to him their full philosophical meaning, which remains valid even for the modern intellect. And this, in my opinion, is the task which religion imposes upon the philosopher.[19]

WEAKNESS OF THE MODERN VIEW OF MAN

In so far as the traditional view of man is true, it is true in spite of its errors concerning man's natural history and the order of nature which he inhabits; it is true of man, if it is true of him at all, only in what it reveals of his moral and spiritual nature. The weakness of the modern view is the strength of the traditional view, and the strength of the modern is the weakness of the traditional. The strength of the modern conception of man and the natural world is in the factual knowledge which is the fruit of modern scientific inquiry. This knowledge is neither final nor complete, yet within the range of its application it is the best we have. The scientific method of inquiry is a method which invites error to expose itself, and so to bring its mistakes into the open for correction.

The weakness of the modern view of man is its neglect or denial of a different order of facts about man's nature. When modern man discovered something of the power of this new tool of investigation, the method of science, his enthusiasm led him to seek by it the answers to all his questions. The answers which had come to man by other ways of inquiry seemed, by contrast, so insecure that he lost whatever respect he had had for them. So we find some recent thinkers, for example Comte in the middle of the nineteenth century, proposing that the field of knowledge be restricted to the positive sciences. Where existing sciences did not provide information concerning important areas of fact, the remedy was to institute new fields of scientific investigation. So Comte proposed a new science of sociology, the scientific study of society. In much the same spirit, although not according to Comte's own suggestion, the new science of psychology appeared.

Modern scientific knowledge provides the factual basis of a radically different conception of the natural world. Astronomy and physics, the two sciences which developed most rapidly in the earlier part of the modern period, provide the framework of the new cosmology. Into this framework the sciences which study the earth and its inhabitants together with the long and complex evolution of their present forms, such as geology and the biological sciences, fit their new knowledge.

The new cosmology is not complete, for the sciences which contribute to it are themselves rapidly advancing in their own fields. In little more than a half century the very foundations of the new cosmology have shifted as a result of the influence of the principle of relativity in physics and astronomy, while our conceptions of matter and energy have had to be revised drastically with the application of the relativity principle and the quantum theory to the study of the structure of the atom.

Our scientific knowledge, and so our conceptions of the cosmos which we develop under the guidance of this knowledge, is incomplete in the sense that there is more to be discovered and new discoveries may alter the ideas which developed from earlier investigation. But this is not a fault of the new conception of the world; it is in its very spirit, for the scientific attitude toward any set of conclusions is an attitude of tentative acceptance in the light of evidence presently available. The scientific attitude does not resist the changes which new evidence makes necessary; it welcomes those changes.

There is, however, a quite different kind of incompleteness which limits the scope of scientific knowledge. The scope of scientific knowledge is limited to those things to which the scientific method is applicable. Since the distinctive feature of scientific method is found in its requirement that perceptual confirmation shall be included, directly or indirectly, in its test of truth, it is plain that this method is applicable only to those things and events which can be observed or indirectly confirmed in sense perception. But we cannot assume, with any rational justification, that the total range of real being is subject to this same limitation. If there are other facts, if there are facts which scientific inquiry cannot disclose because of the inherent limitation of its method, then an adequate world view and an adequate view of man must read these other facts correctly and rightly evaluate them. The scientific account of man and of the world may be quite true, but it may also fall quite short of giving us the whole truth.

We shall see, as we look at the nature of man, that this is most certainly the case. There are aspects of the nature of man which no natural history of man can include; and because of this, man is more than the order of nature can either produce from itself or contain within itself. Man is a fact of nature, but man is not only a fact of nature. The weakness of the modern view is its attempt to understand man, and to reckon with him, solely as a product and function of the world of nature. As Sullivan says:

> Even should science be able to progress without importing values into its scheme, that fact would afford no presumption against the existence of values. For one major result of recent physical speculation has been to show the precise nature of the limitations to scientific knowledge. Science gives us knowledge of structure, but not of substance. It may be assumed that this is the only kind of knowledge possible to us, but there seem to be no good reasons for such an assumption. Science, indeed, tells us a very great deal less about the universe than we have been accustomed to suppose, and there is no reason to believe that all we can ever know must be couched in terms of its thin and largely arbitrary abstractions.[20]

A philosophy which attempts to secure all its data from science can never be adequate, for such a restriction cuts it off forever from value. Science cannot even justify its own existence scientifically, for the value of science, whatever it may be, is not a scientific fact. A philosophy which denies the reality of value denies the reality of its own worth. Such a world view may have certain advantages, but its defects are fatal. With reference to the system of ideas of early modern science, for example, Whitehead remarks that "we must note its astounding efficiency as a system of concepts for the organisation of scientific research. In this respect, it is fully worthy of the genius of the century which produced it. It has held its own as the guiding principle of scientific studies ever since. It is still reigning. Every university in the world organises itself in accordance with it. No alternative system of organising the pursuit of scientific truth has been suggested. It is not only reigning, but it is without a rival." To this Whitehead adds: "And yet—it is quite unbelievable."[21] It is unbelievable because of what it leaves out. Composed of "high abstractions," it confuses these with concrete realities.

Science and religion are concerned with different perspectives of truth. They come into conflict in so far as either regards its own part as the whole of truth or considers its own perspective the only correct one. Again, conflict is nothing but a misinterpretation of difference. "On the one side," says Whitehead, "there is the law of gravitation, and on the other the contemplation of the beauty of holiness. What one side sees, the other misses; and vice versa."[22]

> Consider, for example, [he continues] the lives of John Wesley and of Saint Francis of Assisi. For physical science you have in these lives merely ordinary examples of the operation of the principles of physiological chemistry, and of the dynamics of nervous reactions: for religion you have lives of the most profound significance in the history of the world. Can you be surprised that, in the absence of a perfect and complete phrasing of the principles of science and of the principles of religion which apply to these specific cases, the accounts of these lives from these divergent standpoints should involve discrepancies? It would be a miracle if it were not so.[23]

Scientism, or the doctrine that all knowledge is scientific knowledge, insists that since science tells us something it must tell us everything, while religious obscurantism contends that since science does not tell us everything it cannot tell us anything. Both are wrong. The positive power of science comes from its method, and it is by virtue of its own exclusion of any consideration of ultimates that it can use the method it does.

If we had to choose, and fortunately we do not, which would it be more important for us to choose, religious and moral truth without scientific truth or scientific truth without religious and moral truth? If anything in the physical universe seems established, it is the sphericity of the earth. Kruger, the Boer leader, was fanatically certain that the earth is flat; but this belief did not prevent him from being an extremely formidable soldier. On the other hand, what William James called medical materialism is just as demonstrably false as is belief that the earth is flat; but there is this crucial difference, that a consistent materialism will paralyze completely a human being's psychic energies. We do not have to make such a choice, but to reflect on the alternatives may help us recognize the importance of what the modern view of man overlooks.

CHAPTER II

Man's Existence

MAN'S DUAL EXISTENCE

LIKE other things in the natural world, man exists and he has his own nature. But unlike other things he knows he has a nature and he knows something about that nature. He is aware of other things as well; there is in him the awareness of things which themselves do not exist in him, and he is aware also that this is so. So man is not only an existing fact, he is also the existence of an awareness of existence.

But is not man's awareness of existence just another item in the sum of facts which make up the whole of existence? Let us suppose, for a moment, that man and all which his nature includes are but the product of a series of events in nature. Man knows something of his antecedents, of the long and tortuous process by which he evolved from a world which was once without life or awareness. As life evolves it takes on this and that new feature; and as this process continues it takes on eventually a very special feature, self-awareness. But this new stage is surely like nothing which has gone before. For now life is aware of itself, and it includes in its awareness a knowledge of the long process by which that awareness has come to be.

When we try to consider the fact of awareness as merely one among other facts, differing perhaps only in complexity from other facts, we fail to recognize that the occurrence of an act of awareness is the occurrence of a special kind of fact. Suppose we think we have two facts: (A) an occurrence and (B) the awareness of A. If B is the awareness of A, then we cannot understand B simply as something which takes place and, like A or any other occurrence, has its own nature. For if B is the awareness of A then it is the nature of B to contain somehow in itself the nature of A. If B is awareness of A, then B has to grasp the nature of A and still be distinct from it. Whatever the relation of A and B, it surely is not the relation merely of two items which are added together to make a sum. If man's existence is composed partly of his own knowledge of his existence, or of his knowledge of other existences, then he is not merely a sum of facts and his make-up is not confined to what his history, as a series of events in nature, discloses.

It is difficult to find as clear and at the same time as concise a statement of this principle as Thomas Hill Green's:

> No one and no number of a series of related events can be the consciousness of the series as related. Nor can any product of the series be so either. Even if this product could be anything else than a further event, it could at any rate only be something that super-venes at a certain stage upon such of the events as have so far elapsed. But a consciousness of certain events cannot be anything that thus succeeds them. It must be equally present to all the events of which it is the consciousness. For this reason an intelligent experience, or experience as the source of knowledge, can neither be constituted by events of which it is the experience, nor be a product of them.[1]

The knower of nature cannot be wholly the product of nature.

> Nature, with all that belongs to it, is a process of change: change on a uniform method, no doubt, but change still. All the relations under which we know it are relations in the way of change or by which change is determined. But neither can any process of change yield a consciousness of itself, which, in order to be a consciousness of the change, must be equally present to all stages of the change; nor can any consciousness of change, since the whole of it must be present at once, be itself a process of change. There may be a change into a state of consciousness of change, and a change out of it, on the part of this man or that; but within the consciousness itself there can be no change, because no relation of before and after, of here and there, between its constituent members—between the pres-entation, for instance, of point A and that of point B in the process which forms the object of consciousness.[2]

The consciousness of change does not change; the change of which it is aware is not in it but in the thing or event it is aware of. If the consciousness of change itself changes, then it is *another* awareness.

We have made progress in explaining man's nature and existence as natural fact. Why cannot we look forward to the completion of this task in the future? Is it not simply a matter of pushing our studies of man further? Biology, psychology, anthropology, sociology, economics, and history all help to illuminate man's nature. We have made progress, and the progress we have made encourages us to think that all we need is more of the same thing.

We begin to think that we have solved the enigma, that we have explained man, at least in principle. Then we are pulled up short. It occurs to us that if we really are to explain man completely we must include an explanation of the power to explain. For we are men, we who do the explaining, and the power to explain is a fact. But how can we explain the power to explain? How can we explain the fact that such events as explanations take place? Surely the explanation of explanation would have to include itself, and yet it plainly cannot include itself. Here we find ourselves in the same difficulty we should encounter if we should demand a rational demonstration of the validity of reason, or a logical proof of the soundness of logical proof.

A fact is one thing but the understanding of that fact is another. Yet the understanding of a fact is not merely another fact, of the same order as the fact which it understands. We may understand how we happen to understand this or that particular fact, but can we understand how we happen to be something which can understand? Even if we can, it is difficult to see how we can understand this in terms of the other things we understand; or how we can explain the power to explain, and explain it by reference to the things we have explained by means of it. As Green says, "We may decide all the questions that have been debated between materialists and spiritualists as to the explanation of particular facts in favour of the former, but the possibility of explaining them at all will still remain to be explained."[3] Man is not only fact, explained or explainable fact; he is also explaining fact. He has another kind of existence than the kind of existence a fact has. Whatever this kind of existence is, it is not a mere collection of facts. It is another order of existence.

Physically man is a frail and insignificant creature crawling about the surface of a minor satellite of a minor star. Physical forces may easily annihilate him. But he alone in this vast panoply of nature is able to lift all these things, as well as himself, into that immaterial presence before the mind which we call consciousness or awareness. Noetically or intentionally man is all things—a microcosm, including everything from the stellar galaxies to the atomic nuclei, within the range of his immaterial awareness. This is the ultimate source of human freedom and dignity, and it is in this sense alone, as St. Augustine pointed out, that we can understand the Christian dogma that man is made in the image of God.[4]

MAN'S FREEDOM

What other order of existence can there be except actual fact? There is one approach to this which may be of special significance for our problem. Existence as fact is existence which is brought to be and made to be what it is by something else. But the "something else" also exists, and if it exists as fact—on the same level— then it in turn is existence which depends for what it is on something else. This suggests how we may understand existence of a different order; this is the concept of existence which makes fact. This other dimension or order of existence is free and creative existence. Man is not only fact, made what he is by other things; he is to some degree free and creative. He not only is brought to be, but in some sense and to some degree he also brings to be. If this is the case then we can see how it is that the natural sciences can tell us much about man's nature and yet be incapable of explaining, in their own terms, all that man is.

That man is free we may be confident, as confident as we are that man is capable of knowing. For unless man is free, capable of some kind of genuine creative act, then he cannot know. He can only react, and his supposed awareness that he can react is only another reaction, and so on endlessly. If all he is and all he does are determined by facts outside himself, so that he is only another fact, then what he says and what he thinks he cannot help saying and thinking. Even if he says and thinks this, and if what he thinks and says is true, then he thinks and speaks as he does because he is forced to think and speak as he does; that what he says happens to be true is sheer accident, or chance coincidence. But it is our usual judgment that when a man thinks and speaks without control he has become a patient, and his speech and thought are merely the symptoms of the causes which affect him.

In William Aylott Orton's words, "determinism is not, and never was, a working philosophy of life. One can conceivably die by it; no one ever consistently lived by it. If people would reflect more simply and sincerely on their actual experience of living they would be less vulnerable to a great deal of academic nonsense, and philosophy would be the gainer. In essence determinism is one of those theories which, as Professor Broad said of behaviorism, 'are so preposterously silly that only very learned men could have thought of them.' "[5] Whether or not we are in fact free is a question only for those who wish to play games with concepts. Once we see what the question is we see that the very possibility of considering it *as a question to which true or false answers may be given* presupposes the fact of freedom. Of course if our thinking were only a game, then there would be no question of true and false; the only issue would be between correct and incorrect moves. But if our thinking were only a game we could not raise the question of whether the statement, "This move is correct," is a true statement.

If, when I say that such and such is the case, I am not free to say that such and such is not the case, then my statement cannot be accepted as a significant report of truth. For in so far as I can be considered to tell the truth about a situation, it must be recognized that what I do say or do not say is said in accordance with what I find that situation to be. If what I say is only a function of internal changes taking place within me, or merely a function of a complex of internal and external fact, then my statement has no significant reference to the situation it purports to refer to. I must be able so to control what I say that I can conform it to the nature of the situation to which it refers, as I apprehend the nature of that situation. In order that I may be able to do this, I must be free of any compulsion to say one thing rather than another. Unless I am free to affirm or deny as I judge the nature of the object to which my affirmations or denials refer, then my affirmations and denials are mere oddities of behavior—mere responses to stimuli. But then so too is this affirmation, and this, and so on. Without freedom the very "if . . . then" of the first sentence of this paragraph is meaningless. Where the argument against freedom uses that relation it renders itself meaningless, for it can use it only by presupposing the fact of freedom. And if it does not use the "if . . . then" relation it is no argument.

If man is something which knows, then he is free; and if he is free, then he must be capable to some degree to determine his own nature. He must be able, in some measure, to make himself what he is to be. He cannot be a mere collection of effects of other causes. If this is the case, then in the world of nature man is unique, and it is difficult to see how this in which he is unique can have come to him from nature.

Capable of free creative act, man exists as a person. In so far as he exists as a person he exists as free act, and the limitations upon his freedom are the limitations upon his existence as a person. For in spite of this which distinguishes him from other things in nature, we must remember that he does not exist only as a person; he is also a part of nature.

The problem of man's nature is the problem of the mutual relations of these two ways of existence. "What is man?" is the question of what are the limits upon his creativity and freedom, and of how he exercises his freedom within those limits. At what points does he reach these limits, and what does he do with respect to them?

The Distinction of Occasion from Cause

Philosophers sometimes deny that our ability to know presupposes our freedom. The following is Professor Lucius Garvin's exceptionally clear statement of the view that the possibility of knowledge is consistent with determinism.

The contention that determinism reduces reflective thinking to a mechanical response to outer stimuli, making genuine evaluation of arguments (including those in support of determinism) impossible, is superficially neat, but in reality erroneous. The chief point to be made here is that the validity or invalidity of an argument depends upon the nature of the argument, upon the connection of conclusion and premises, not upon the caused or uncaused character of John Doe's mental processes as he examines the argument for its validity. If, on examining an argument—say the one in favor of determinism—he perceives its soundness, his perception of that soundness is not nullified by the fact that it had causes (or even by the fact, if it were a fact, that it did not have causes). There is nothing about determinism that requires the denial that the processes of selective attention, discrimination, sifting of evidence, and drawing of conclusions take place; all that is affirmed is that they take place according to deterministically operative laws of cause and effect. We may or may not err in the conclusions we draw. If we do err, the *source* of that error is explicable in terms of causes; but its *nature* is explicable in terms of a failure correctly to analyze the argument.[6]

This statement of the case for determinism fails to take account of the distinctive nature of knowledge. The only cause we could recognize as the cause of our judgment that an argument is sound, if it were a cause, would be the soundness of the argument itself. This would be the only cause we could recognize, that is, if our recognition that the argument is sound were truly knowledge of its soundness and if what we call a "cause" here were actually a cause. Of course, we may be taught to say the argument is sound whether we see its soundness or not. We may even be taught to use certain logical signs in a mechanical fashion, as tags to identify sound and unsound arguments; but this would not be to *know* the soundness of the argument unless we recognize why the logical patterns themselves are signs of soundness or unsoundness.

Anything which influences our judgment concerning the soundness of an argument, except the soundness of the argument itself, introduces irrelevant considerations. Our likes and dislikes have no place here, although they may well have helped to cause us to attend to the argument. Mental associations cannot be allowed to influence our judgment, no matter how important they may be in helping us to understand the meaning of the argument we judge. Previous education may be a necessary condition for the proper evaluation of the argument. It enables us to understand what we are to judge and even provides us with the logical techniques which we use. But given all the conditions and qualifications, the only cause we could admit (if it were a cause) which makes the whole difference between the judgment, "The argument *is* valid," and the judgment, "The argument *is not* valid," is the validity or invalidity of the argument itself.

This brings us to the difficulty with the determinist's position. The only cause we could admit, if it were a cause, simply is not a cause at all. The logical soundness of the argument cannot be a cause, for causes are real beings and this supposed cause is not. The soundness of the argument is the logical relation of premises and conclusion, and this is not a real existent. Logical relations are not real beings; they are the means by which we know real beings.[7] If they are not real beings they cannot be real causes. What we know cannot, merely as a *known what*, be a cause; what we know can be a cause only as it acts for itself in its own existence.

This distinction is no mere sophistry introduced to protect a dogma from attack; it is a distinction necessary to protect knowledge from attempts to reduce it to behavior. Man is cognizing existence as well as physical fact. He is acted upon, it is true, and his actions are influenced by the causes which work on him. It is true also that to judge and to think are acts. But *what* is judged and *what* is thought are not, as essences apprehended in cognitive act, themselves acts of the mind. To read a book, for example, is an act; but the meaning grasped in the reading is not an act. The book is about something, and what I obtain from reading the book is an awareness of the things the book is written about. My act of knowing grasps the nature of those things. But the act of grasping and what is grasped are not the same, else every act of knowing would be the knowing of itself only—but it could not even know itself unless it knew itself by *another* act.

Awareness may guide action, for in our freedom our will can submit itself to what we know. Does not our knowledge, then, influence our action, and so is it not a cause? It may influence our action in a sense, in the sense that it is a factor in our action, but it cannot play the role of a real cause. Our knowledge is available for use in action, for we can plan our action and make our decisions in the light of our knowledge. But we may also disregard our knowledge; in fact we can act in defiance of our knowledge, and to our sorrow we sometimes do. *That* we know is a fact, but *what* we know is present to us mentally and not really. In knowing the thing we grasp its essence, but we do not take to ourselves its existence. If it does not exist in us, it cannot act in us. It may act *on* us, of course, in its own right as a real existent; but in such case the real thing is the cause, not its essence grasped by us mentally.

A message may influence my action, in a loose sense of "influence." But actually the meaning of the message is not a cause. If the message does affect my action it is by virtue of something other than the meaning which I apprehend. But may not a message cause an emotional shock, for example? I do not feel the shock until I read and understand the message, so is it not the meaning of the message which causes the shock? A friend dies, let us say, but I do not know about it at the time. Later I receive a message telling me of his death and I grieve for him. Is not the discovery of his death the cause of my grief? The answer, as will be plain if we reflect carefully, is "No." Receipt of the message may be the *occasion* of my grief, but it is not the cause. The loss of my friend is the cause. I do not grieve because I received the message; I grieve because my friend has died. But if I had not known of his death, some one may suggest, I should not have grieved, so does not the discovery of his death cause me to grieve? If I agree to this then I am saying that I sorrow because I learned of his death, not because of his death. I am saying that it would make no difference to me whether he lived or died provided only that, if he died, I should not learn of it.

Knowledge is a guide but not, in its role as knowledge, a cause. I say, "The guide brought me here." But actually he did not, unless he was more than a guide. I brought myself, or I was transported; I walked or I rode. I followed the guide, but I did not have to follow him; if I had to follow him then what was happening to me was something more than being guided. He did not cause my action; he only provided a pattern by which I acted. A music score may guide the artist's performance, but the score does not cause his performance. He may follow it or not, as his ability permits and as he pleases. It makes no difference to the score whether he plays the music or not, and it makes no difference to the musical meaning of the score. The score is not itself a part of the performance. It is only a guide which the player may follow. If a music score caused the player to follow it then to learn to play a musical instrument would be an easy matter.

Only a free agent can respond to occasions as well as to causes. An occasion is a situation in the light of which an agent acts. But the causes of his action are in himself and in the real beings which influence him. In so far as he is free he can act in a way which is appropriate to the occasion or in a way which is not. The presence of food may not be a cause of my eating, although it is the case that I cannot eat food which is not present. The presence of the food may be the occasion of my eating. If I am hungry and if food is available, then it is likely that the cause is my hunger, not the food. The presence of food may stimulate hunger, but this is a different situation. For here the food plays a double role; it is both cause and occasion. But the respect in which it is cause is not the respect in which it is occasion. I may feel hungry at the sight of food, for example, and yet not eat it because its presence happens not to be the appropriate occasion to eat. A man stands ready to throw a switch when he gets a signal; a railroad engineer is ready to pull out of the station when he gets the sign. But the signal does not cause the man to throw the switch or the engineer to start the train.

Because is an ambiguous word. We use it to refer to real causes and we use it to refer to reasons, and in popular speech we often confuse real causes and reasons. "The car skidded because the road was icy," we say. Here the ice on the road is the cause of the skid. But it is not the reason for the skid. To say that the ice on the road is the reason for the skid means, on any careful interpretation of the language, that the driver saw the ice and decided to skid the car. The statement, "He went to bed because he was tired," may leave us in doubt as to its meaning. Does it mean that he was tired and for this reason decided to go to bed? Or does it mean that a great weariness overcame him and he found himself, as it were, put through the actions of retiring?

The confusion concerning causes and occasions is a part of the same misunderstanding which enables some philosophers to consider cognition as itself only one among man's many reactions to stimuli. Knowledge, on this view, is just another effect of causes operating on the organism, and it in turn is the cause of other effects. Knowledge, in short, is considered simply one of the connecting links in the causal chain of human behavior. This is only one more way in which philosophical naturalism commits its characteristic fallacy, the fallacy of mistaking essence for existence. It considers essences themselves as real things, and permits them to act as causes and to be effects in the same way that real things— that is, essences which have their own existence—can act as causes and as effects.

How Can Man Discover Himself?

It is not by impersonal observation, or by classifying or theorizing or conducting control experiments, that man can discover himself. These methods will give him information about himself, important information he can obtain in no other way, but they will not disclose what is distinctive in him. How could they? Do they not deal with man, in all of their applications to him, solely as natural fact? If there is anything distinctive in man, if there is anything in him which is not natural fact, then the methods appropriate to the discovery and examination of natural facts will fail to find it no matter how thoroughly they are applied.

Philosophy has never succeeded in defining the nature of man, and never will [says Professor Orton]. Obviously, if my dog could define the nature of dog she would be more than dog to begin with; yet, being very elderly and wise, she not only knows a great deal about dog, she knows a good deal about me. This sort of knowing, of course, is the oldest and deepest kind: knowing in experience; it is what is referred to by that etymological root of immemorial antiquity, the k-n or g-n root that survives in words like cunning, *connaître*, king; it is what the English Bible means when it says "Adam knew Eve his wife," and again when it says, "Ye shall know the truth, and the truth shall make you free." This kind of knowing, which modern education systematically ignores, is not a matter of making sentences and syllogisms, it is all along a species of doing and experiencing; and what its exponents say (the Church is not the only one) is that by living according to a certain pattern, a man may attain practical wisdom and spiritual freedom.[8]

In a way, perhaps, philosophy can define the nature of man, but the truth about man which we grasp by means of such definition is only essential truth, and Professor Orton here refers to existential truth. Our knowledge of man's essence is formal and abstract, for example, that man is a rational animal. This is true enough, as essential truth, but it is a poor and thin truth to know about man. It does not give us man in his existence. Definition can only add details and spell out further implications; it cannot take us closer to man. Philosophy cannot give us man in his existence, but the very distinctions which philosophy makes between essential and existential tuth may show us where to look to find him.[9]

Man can discover himself best, perhaps, in his intense awareness of his own existence, in those moments when he is directly conscious of what it is for him to be. He discovers himself only as he consciously lives through the process of being a self. He is most a self in the act of free decision, especially in the act of deciding and thus determining the kind of self he shall be. To be a self is to act, to act freely, and to act freely in creating fact.

But man is not sheer creative act; he is also natural fact, and he is subject to the limitations of those aspects of his nature which come to him not by his own act as a self but which are given to him by other things. Man discovers what he is by discovering what he is not.[10] He aims at something and finds he cannot reach it. So he discovers a limit, and this limit is one of the boundary lines of his nature. In this he is more than an animal, for no mere animal is conscious of its aim.

As Frank tells us, man discovers two kinds of limits: the limits of special situations and the limits on man as man. Man discovers what he distinctively is when he finds the limits on man as such. These are death, moral failure, his relative position in time and history, the blind and irrational impulses of his nature which break him apart from himself, and the conflicts with others which reflect and project the conflict within himself.

These limits, however, are negative. How can the discovery of limits make us aware of what lies within? The answer is that our distinctive nature, in its positive aspect, is the need and the struggle to transcend these limits. This, it is plain, is what constitutes free creative act. This is the distinctive existence of man. If we look at the facts we can see this mode of man's being expressed and embodied in all he has done that is characteristically human. It is in his art, his literature, his religion, his science, his social and political organization. These activities are no mere instinctive functions, or mechanical consequences of pre-existing causes, or adjustments to environment. Every one is an attempt by man to transcend his limits as man.

Why should not man simply accept his limits and make no effort to get beyond them? Here it is that man differs from animal life. For him to submit to the conditions of his existence as he finds them would be for him to cease to be a self, to abdicate his nature as a self. And yet to say that man can abdicate his nature as a self and accept his limits is a manifest contradiction; for to accept limits can be the act only of a self, and for man to attempt to abdicate his nature as a self is only a disguised attempt to overcome by evasion the limits he recognizes.

So whatever man does, as man, he is in fact trying to make over the conditions of his life in accordance with his concepts and the models he invents or discovers. For man to be, as man, is for him to bring to be. For other things in nature, to be is to have been brought into being by something else. Man, it has been said, is a tool-making animal. But when this is said there is too often little understanding that in so far as man is tool-making he is different from animal life. To make tools, as tools, is to set out to make existence over. It occurs only in response to the intention to bring into actual existence what so far is only a possibility. This is not as a bird builds a nest or a beaver builds a dam, driven by instinctual needs which perhaps are aroused by sensory patterns and associated neural engrams. The animal has no preview of the goal as a possibility. Of course man, like other animals, has his drives and organic needs; but unlike the animals that are only animals, man's actions are controlled partly by the meaning of his experience and the content of his consciousness, by what he knows and what he thinks.

Man's nature is a paradox. It is a tension between tendencies which attempt to negate each other. The incongruity of man's nature is found in the fact that he can exist as man only as he is a creator and yet his nature, including that in his nature by virtue of which he is creative, is given to him from outside himself. He is only in small part his own creation. The means of creative activity, of changing the possible to the actual, he can find only in what is already actual. Each man depends on factors, biological and social and cultural, which he had no part in making. His greatest delusion, born of his awareness of himself and of his freedom, is the delusion that his existence and destiny depend only on himself, that his freedom is unconditioned. This is the delusion that he is himself the principle of being, that he is God. Yet if he is free, man's existence and destiny surely must depend to some degree upon something within himself. He is not himself the ultimate principle of being, yet how can we escape the conclusion that this final principle of being—which religion calls "God"—is in some sense within man? If this is true it explains what nothing else has been able to explain.

Has man learned anything more important than the things he has learned in suffering and defeat? Our own failures force us to see ourselves as we are, and human tragedy forces us to see man as he is. As Miss Hamilton says, "where great souls suffer inexplicably, there tragedy is, never to be easily concealed or ignored. It has in it that which startles the mind to attention and brings the spirit up sharp against the enigma of human life."[11] Our victories come out of our defeats, for in defeat our limits are most plainly shown to us. We find what we truly are in humiliation, in being torn and broken apart, in finding ourselves cast down, by having our very successes turn to ashes in our mouths. For what is humiliated is our pretense, and what is broken apart is what we have put together artificially and in defiance of our own nature, the success which turns to ashes in our mouth is the success we achieve in being false to ourselves. In despair we may give up, and cease to be anything ourselves; or we may turn ourselves into mere reflections of other things, collections of mirror images of others; or we may build ourselves an unreal world, and in delusion see ourselves to be what we are not and stake the value of life on what is nothing. Our only hope is to discover ourselves in our defeat, and to discover the kind of victory which is truly within our grasp.

CHAPTER 12

Man as Person

THE DISCOVERY OF MAN AS PERSON

As we hurry about from one place to another we are in almost constant contact with people. But most of the contacts we have with people are not with them *as people;*
that is, in their true existence as persons. We call them people and
persons, and of course we are dimly aware most of the time that
each is a self; but we do not often meet them and deal with them
as selves. They are human, members of the human race, and so
certain attitudes and responses are appropriate. Yet these are seldom more than surface contacts; change the cast, and the relationships would change little.[1]

At the more superficial levels of contact other people are only
bodies, moving about or fixed in position. As bodies they are little more than occupiers of space. I step aside to avoid a collision
with another on the sidewalk, and I step aside much in the same
way for one as for another. I enter a train or bus and the people
already there I see only as seat-occupiers. A person may be only
the consumer of a plate of food, a ticket-buyer, or appear in any
of the many functions people perform without their nature as
selves entering very far into the situation.

In some of our encounters with people, however, we find the
persons, or selves, which they are. Some of the things a person
does are genuine personal expressions, and his existence as a person is discovered in the act. We catch him in his true role. The
act expresses an attitude which involves an awareness of himself
and his relation to other people, and also his recognition of their
awareness of him as a self whose action is controlled to some de-

gree by what he knows and wills; it expresses the fundamental beliefs by which he lives and the values which shape his choices. We see him, so far as we understand him, as he is within himself— not all of what he is, but what we see is truly what he is.

The differences between things, animals, and persons or selves is brought out in Father D'Arcy's comparison:

> In distinguishing living things from non-living we are aware of what may be called an embryonic selfhood in them. That is to say, we realize that they are growing of themselves and by their own effort. There is the beginning of a new unity and inner life, for which the word growth is often used. Most on reflection would say that there is no need to postulate anything beyond the life of the bodily organism to explain what happens. The bodily metabolism, the reflex actions, the instincts and impulses, the formation of habits, the life of the senses, all proceed within a determined end, which is specific and limited and transitory. We can speak of an organic unity and even of individual characteristics, but only by metaphor, of a person. That is to say, the self of an animal has not come into its own kingdom; it cannot take charge of its own being and appoint its own objectives, weigh them, reckon its own powers by reference to its past and its future hopes, retire behind its desires and activities to a deeper self, which has its scouts and patrols in thought and conscience, and suffers loss or gain in all experience. Selfhood, at least, means this, and in the world we know it is the prerogative of human beings alone. Man has been called a tool-bearing animal, but he is far more than this; he has a power to mirror himself and to mirror within himself the length and breadth of reality, and he can stand off from his impulses and thoughts and guide them in a direction which he himself chooses. Moreover, one part of himself, and that the most intimate, does not belong to any thing, being or power in the world. There he knows himself morally, and not physically, subject to an absolute, a subjection which is first discerned in the duty of keeping his word, saying what is true and choosing what is right. It is on these grounds he claims to be regarded as a moral person with rights and duties, a self in the full and proper sense of the word.[2]

We all are familiar with the difference between a person who gives us his confidence and one who holds back. Both acts, of course, are the acts of persons; but the one shows himself in the act while the other conceals himself. He who conceals himself holds back not mere information, or his opinion; he holds back himself. Of course an act of concealment or of dissembling may be quite revealing of the person, for it shows him to be a person who conceals himself. But the view it gives us is partial; most of what we learn from it we learn by inference. When a man gives his confidence he shows himself, and the fuller his confidence the more he shows himself. The man who holds back refuses to open the curtain upon his true feelings and attitudes and judgment. His act is his own act, but it comes from the surface or else it is calculated, contrived, artificial, insincere.

We often have seen the change from an impersonal, conventional, restrained expression of feeling and ideas to an intensely personal expression. Here is a man in a group which is carrying on idle conversation. He may be on the edge of the group, listening perhaps with half an ear but not participating actively. Suppose the conversation touches one of his deep and intimate interests. His whole attitude changes. He may become the dominant figure, the center of the group's activity. He now puts himself into the situation, where before he had put only a few of his words—perhaps noncommittal and impersonal—and his physical presence. Now his whole mind, his feelings, his deepest personal convictions find expression in what he says. The presence of the person has become manifest.

The act of a person is the more personal the more of himself it expresses. In so far as it is a personal act, and to the degree that it is a personal act, it brings the whole self to a focus upon this situation. If we were to sustain ourselves unremittingly as persons we should have to involve ourselves completely in every conscious moment of our lives. Of course we cannot do this, for we are not complete as persons. Nor are we persons only, for we are also animals, and we are so many pounds of flesh and bones, and we are occupiers of space and time. It is true that our animal functions are transformed by the fact that we also are persons, our flesh and bones are differently regarded by those who recognize us as persons, and our physical presence does not have the same meaning as that of any equivalent mass; yet these things do limit us in our role as selves.

Relations among persons are different from relations among things. Even if sometimes we treat people as things, or as animals, we do this with reservations. We remember that there are limits which derive from the fact that they are not only things or animals but persons as well. If we forget this we are in for trouble— trouble with them and perhaps with society. We are in for trouble, that is, unless we are clever at disguising our actions. To forget this sinks man deep into evil. The evil of human slavery, for example, is its degradation of people into animals and things, and most other wrongs in a society are degrees of the same.

Rebecca West considers this so important that she calls it the sin against the Holy Ghost. "What is the sin against the Holy Ghost? It is perhaps to deal with people as if they were things: to pick them up and set them down, without respect for their uniqueness, for their own wills."[3] It is possible that even this is not the sin at its worst. The sin against the Holy Ghost does not appear in its full depravity when I commit it for the sake of my own mean and selfish ends. The sin plumbs its darkest depths when I treat people as things for the sake of their own welfare. For then I set myself up as the source and creator of good, and so usurp the place of God. As there is no greater possible presumption so there is no greater possible evil.

The distinctive character of personal relations comes from the mutual recognition that all parties to the relation are free, rational, volitional, evaluating agents, willing and able to assume responsibility for their actions. Each acknowledges that others are capable of forming their own conceptions of what they shall be and what they shall do, of forming those conceptions under the guidance of knowledge and reason, and able to initiate and carry through the actions necessary to attain the ends they set for themselves. Even to use a person requires that we recognize him to be more than what we use him for. A person has this peculiarity: unless he is something of value in himself he cannot be of use, as a person, to anything beyond himself. The limitations upon the acts of a person are the limitations in his existence as a person. They do not flow from his positive nature as a person, from reason or will or from the ability to act on a decision; they arise from the sub-personal aspects of his nature.

We find the personal not alone in the actual presence of living and acting persons. We find it also in some of the products of their personal action. In literature and the arts we encounter levels of meaning which are personal, and even in more routine and superficial actions we often see the stamp of a personal style.

To recognize the personal for what it is requires a personal response. Sometimes the recognition is dim and partial, so much so that it is almost as nothing. I may see vaguely that something I hear or read is a deep personal expression. Certainly I see this immediately when I compare, say, a serious poem with a witty jingle. But even so I may not look carefully enough to see the personal in the expression; I see that there is the personal, but I do not catch what it is. It is as if I have a glimpse from the corner of my eye of a moving object, and am aware that something is there but fail to look at it closely enough to identify it. If my recognition of a personal expression is to be adequate for communication then my response to that expression must also be personal. The response to the creative act of a person is, too, a response to that person, indirect as it may be and ignorant as we may be of his personality and character. To recognize a creation for what it is, is to recognize a creator and to see something of the creator in the creation.

To recognize another as a person requires a personal response on my part. The personal response involves the recognition that it is not only the response *of* a person but the response *to* a person. We do not make personal responses except to persons, or to something we falsely take to be a person; or, if we do so consciously, as a man may talk to his dog, we are quite aware that we are engaged in make-believe. If the other is judged to be a person, but is not, then our response is inappropriate and involves assumptions which are false.

All of this may seem somewhat trivial, but it has a sober side. For if my personal response is one which changes me in any im-

portant respect, and if I make that response to something which
is not personal but which I falsely judge to be so, then the change
in me is based on something false. To that extent it makes of me
something false. This is the true weakness, for example, of attempts to teach morality by holding up unreal models; for it is
not morality which is taught thus, but some sort of sentimentality.
As we shall see later, this is also the weakness of attempts to preserve the morale-supporting qualities of religion while denying
the reality of the object of religion.

Perhaps the most familiar and illuminating example of the personal is found in love and affection. The love of a man and a
woman is discovered by one of them perhaps when he comes to
see the difference which the other's existence makes to his own.
Here are two people of separate lives, and now their paths have
crossed. But it is more than a change of paths; the changes are in
the persons. Each now lives a different life, different hopes and
fears move him, different values are now seen to belong to familiar
things. The whole meaning of life changes.

All this, of course, may be illusion. People do deceive one another. But in so far as the judgment one makes about the other is
false, he is mistaken not only about the other's feelings but about
the other's mode of existence. It is not as if he had mistaken salt
for sugar. It is rather a mistake about a personal-moral character.
It is a mistake about the process of personal act and decision which
constitutes that person's existence as a person. The real fact of
the other's life, of the other's very existence as a person, is not the
apparent one. The error does not concern a human body, or even
a set of physical actions. He has erred in thinking that the person
he imagined is the one which exists; and he has found that the one
which does exist is not the person he thought to exist.

To be a person is not to be a property—or a set of properties—of
a human body. To be a person is to exist at a different level from
that on which any physical body exists. It is to exist at the level
of self-aware, purposeful, evaluative, choice-making act. It is desire and reason and will united in one act. We are wrong, and
create unending confusion, when we treat "person" as some kind

of pervasive substratum in which the distinctive properties of individual persons somehow "inhere." Each person is individual in his existence; he is a unique individual and an unalienable existence. For a person fully exists, in so far as he exists as a person, in act alone. Still, we must remind ourselves and our fellows, that in our role as persons we do not exist wholly as persons.

Although we do not exist solely as persons our nature is not broken into separate and irreconcilable parts. The personal and sub-personal aspects of our nature are not mutually irrelevant. It is by means of our enforced recognition of our limitations as persons that we become most vividly aware of our powers as persons. Perhaps the modern conception of man is able to ignore, even to doubt, man's freedom and creativity because it sees no limitation upon him as mere natural fact; and this may be its fatal weakness, the weakness by which man may destroy himself. Only as we recognize and act through our limitations rather than attempt to defy them can our real powers as persons express themselves. The artist is limited by his material, but the more artist he is the greater is his success in speaking through his medium.

The Moral Nature of Man

Man's nature is mixed. A man exists as a physical process, as one of the space-time events of the physical world; he is an animal, and differs no more from many other animals in his animal nature than they differ from each other; and he is a self, and as a self he is unique among all the beings of the earth.

Because man's nature is mixed it is easy to understand why his policy and his acts are so often defective, for a mixed nature can operate effectively only so far as its various components maintain their proper relations with each other. Man's knowledge is sadly limited, and even the knowledge he has he does not always use. His thinking is influenced by his emotions, the remote is hidden from his view by the familiar and immediate, and irrelevant circumstances weaken his will and deflect his action. Man does not do as he would, sometimes because he cannot and sometimes because he will not, for will which initiates action sometimes weakens and sickens before the action is complete. He has disappointments, he has regrets, and he has remorse. In the fact that he holds himself responsible for some of his failures we see at least a part of man's moral nature.

Men pass judgment upon themselves. They are aware of their failure to fulfil the obligations they accept. They judge themselves, what they are, in the light of a conception of what they ought to be. In so far as they are not actually what they believe they ought to be, and in so far as they guide their actions not by what they are but by what they believe they ought to be, they live not as mere natural facts but in terms of something which goes beyond natural fact. A man is, and so is a fact; but he demands of himself that he be what he ought to be, and he judges himself by that standard. By virtue of his moral nature he denies his complete submergence in natural fact. He is fact, it is true; but he sees himself also as under a moral necessity to make fact, and to make it in accordance with models which are not themselves mere facts of nature.

Human nature contains within itself the power to act for the sake of what it understands its own end to be. This is will; it is genuine action, not merely reaction. Man is a moral agent because it is good to be and because man has to decide to some degree the manner in which he shall be. "Men and women, except the scum, live and die for what they are, not for what they possess or may acquire."[4] In free action man is able to act in terms of the possible, and so his action is not confined to a mere response to the actual. He can transform the possible into the actual in accordance with his own desire and foresight.

Man has ideas of what he should be and he acknowledges his obligation to act in accordance with those ideas. But on what does this obligation rest? What justifies the judgment he passes upon himself when he fails to do what he thinks he should do? If the judgment a man passes upon himself is a true judgment then his idea of what he ought to be and do must be true and binding upon him. Of what is it true, and what is it which binds him? Unless his idea of what he ought to be is an idea of something real then the judgment he passes upon himself is not a true judgment. If persons exist as persons, and if their self-judgment is true, then there must be something real in terms of which they judge themselves.

But this is nonsense, our critics may say. The standard by which you judge yourself need have no being except in your own mind. It is at best only an ideal which your mind creates, influenced perhaps by the opinions and attitudes of others and by your social tradition. You find yourself wanting in something when you compare what you are with the picture you have in your mind. Your ideal sums up for you what you desire to be. The standard exists only in your mind; it is your own psychological creation, the projection of your wishes and desires. Or perhaps you judge yourself by comparison with others. They exist, to be sure, and only in this way does any standard have any real existence; but of course they exist as actualities, not as ideals.

The issue here turns on one point. Are the imperfections I seem to discover in myself genuine imperfections or are they only pseudo-imperfections? If I am imperfect only in comparison with an idea I have, and if this is only a subjective construction of my own, then my supposed imperfection is only a subjective construction. It, in turn, is only an idea in my mind. Such standards have no authority over me. There is not the slightest reason why I should submit to them except my own preference of the moment. If this is the case, then perhaps I ought to rid myself of such morbid ideas as those of obligation and right, and accept myself as I am.

Unless the standard by which we differentiate good from evil is founded in real being, in real being to which we owe conformity by our very nature, the distinction between good and evil deserves not the slightest respect. Even the statement of the preceding paragraph, that "if this is the case, then perhaps I ought to rid myself of such morbid ideas . . . and accept myself as I am," turns out to be absurd. For "if this is the case" then there is no "ought." There is no reason why I should not be morbid if I please to be morbid. There is no reason why I should not be cruel if I please to be cruel, or should not wantonly murder if I please to murder, or should not live a lie if I prefer to live a lie. For these things are wrong, "if this is the case," only in comparison with an idea in my mind; so, to abolish their wrongness, I need only change my ideas. Why not, then, use words which do not mislead? Why not describe these things for what they are, not "wrong" but "displeasing"? And if only displeasing, then what of it? Who cares? And if anyone does care, what if he does? It concerns me only as his caring pleases or displeases me. The "concern" itself is only a vanishing feeling, a fact of the psychological order, another idea, which when gone is as if it had not been.

When I say I like something, I mean that it is in harmony with my tastes and preferences, but when I say something is good I mean that it fits a standard of excellence. It would be bold and over-weening for me to regard my tastes and preferences as the standards of excellence. I may hope that they fit those standards, but if they do it is because they conform to those standards, not because the standards conform to my tastes and preferences.

Unless we can deal with men as genuine moral agents, as men who are under real obligation and do not act merely by present impulse and preference, we have to deal with them as things. A man who feels no obligation is unaware of himself as a self. He cannot resent slights, for there is nothing he recognizes in himself capable of being slighted; he does not understand contempt, but confuses it with dislike; ridicule is only an occasion for laughter, hatred is mere frustration, and love is a feeling of desire and an anticipation of pleasure. When a man gives me his promise, and I have reason to think that he acknowledges no obligation to keep his promises, I cannot treat it as a promise. It is an expression of his present intention, perhaps, but it throws no light on his future intentions—the intentions he will have when the time for the fulfilment of his promise arrives. His present intention is only a psychological fact of the moment. If I am to deal with him I shall have to try to calculate or predict what his state of mind will be at the later time. I shall have to estimate the likely influences on his conduct between now and then and, as a weather forecaster plots the probable path of a storm, I shall have to guess what he will be wishing in the future. But if a man acts under obligation, and understands himself to be bound by it, then I am not concerned with the influences and preferences which may intervene. I deal with him as one who is responsible for his own actions.

If man has a moral nature then he is under the rule of values which belong to reality itself. But to what reality do they belong? They are not real in the way that natural fact is real, for then they would only be. Values not only are; they determine what *ought to be*. They must belong to an order of being beyond nature, but one which yet shows itself in nature and in man himself—else it would not be accessible to man. In short, if persons exist as persons, and if their moral self-judgments are true, they must be in contact with real being which is not itself a part of nature and to which they are beholden. In their efforts to understand this, men have returned again and again to the religious answers. If, among the religious answers, the theistic conception of God should be true, it would have the advantage of making intelligible man's moral nature and hence his very existence as a person.

A Religious Answer to the Problem of Man

It is in those moments of clear insight into ourselves, when we see ourselves for what we are and in contrast with what we ought to be, that certain of the religious interpretations of man's nature and of his position in the order of real being seem most convincing. We have a conception of God, let us say, in which we suppose ourselves to be seen by God as we truly are. We imagine ourselves naked before Him, without the disguises and make-believe with which we show ourselves to the world and, more often than not, to ourselves as well. We cannot conceal or run away or dissemble; our motives are laid bare, and we appear as we are.

There appears from time to time in the history of religion [says Professor Bennett], the idea of God as the adversary of man. You find it in the concept of the wrath of God, in the "consuming flame of divine love" of which the mystics speak. It is eloquent in the speech of the Lord to Job from the whirlwind. It has received memorable treatment in Francis Thompson's poem "The Hound of Heaven." What is finally valid in this conception is the thought that the divine scrutiny is inescapable and that there is no salvation for the soul that will not stand and turn and face that scrutiny. In the presence of God the soul stands stripped of all pretension, of all artificial merit, of all self-respect that is derived from merely human approval. God is the final judge, the ultimate test: before him one is thrown back upon whatever literal substance one has. Here is the means for the self to discover what it ultimately *amounts to.*[5]

Perhaps my awareness of God leads me to see something about myself which I can accept only if I have to accept it. For I see something about myself which wounds my pride and exposes my pretense. Yet I cannot deny that what I see is truly myself. I try to shrug it off, but I cannot shake my recognition of myself in what I see. For even as I deny it I know the denial is only an evasion. Yet the verdict I cannot deny is empty unless that which shows me what I am, the measure by which I discover my lack, is grounded in reality. "This fundamental need for a self-respect which rests upon self-knowledge," says Professor Bennett, "is something that is frustrated by any subjectivist philosophy. Subjectivism forgets that man needs some Ultimate Other-than-Man against which he may measure himself; it fails to see that only the most outer can satisfy the most inner."[6] The standard by which I judge myself must be so grounded in reality that it is more than just another fact, for as it works in me it evaluates fact.

> I had heard of thee by the hearing of the ear,
>   but now my eye sees thee;
> therefore I despise myself,
>   and repent in dust and ashes.[7]

Of course there are many experiences in which, as we say, a person discovers or finds himself. In some the disclosure is less adequate than in others. Perhaps I overhear a conversation about my-self, and what I hear is far from complimentary. My first emotion may be anger and resentment, and I am ready with my protest or an act of retaliation. But something holds me back, and what holds me back is the sudden and overwhelming recognition of myself in what I have heard. I see myself in a new light. I am amazed and humiliated by what I see and by the fact that it is myself; yet I cannot reject it, for now that it is said I recognize its application to myself.

I may find myself in a play, or in a piece of fiction. What I read about is not myself, but what I find puts me in a perspective from which I seem to see in myself what before I had overlooked. So I say that the play or novel is true; it gives us man in his true exist-ence, and I see myself in its light.

Neither of these experiences, to see myself from another per-son's perspective or to see myself by the light of an artist's picture of man, is sufficient to reveal the truth about myself. Friends and acquaintances can be mistaken, and an artist's idea of man can be false. With nothing else to guide me I discover, in the first of these experiences, that some people find fault with me. I recognize that there is in me that with which they find fault. *But is what they find fault with, really a fault?* So far there is nothing which pro-vides the slightest clue to the answer to this question. For the sup-posed fault, the character or personality trait which they disclose to me, cannot be recognized by me as a fault except by reference to a standard. Is the artist's idea of man true? The work of the artist does not carry the answer to this question.

Where do we find the standard by which to judge other stan-dards? Is it an authoritarian deliverance? Even those who submit to an external authority for decision in these things must find that the external authority has also an inner authority in their own hearts and minds. No act of submission is done under submission; for if it seems so it is only a pretended act, not a genuine act of submission. So the question of an external authority is not the fundamental question in religion or in politics or in ethics or in matters of taste or in any other area of decision. The fundamental question is the question of internal authority. "There comes a time," Gilson tells us, "when a man simply cannot refuse to accept certain conclusions without refusing to trust his own understanding, whereby he is a man; and just as he himself accepts a truth, he states it, together with his reasons for so doing, so that other men may accept it too, in the light, not of his own mind, but of theirs."[8]

What is this internal authority to which we submit in so far as we become aware of its decisions, and in so far as we act as rational and free agents? There seems only one credible answer, although this one answer is said in many different ways. The authority within us to which we yield is the spirit of truth. It is truth, in so far as it can enter into us, which judges us. Truth does not judge itself; only falsehood and error can pretend to judge truth. The perfection of man's nature and his whole duty is to know the best he can know, to understand as best he can understand, to make his decisions in the light of that knowledge and understanding with complete sincerity and good will, and to act in accordance with those decisions. This is for him to live in free submission to the spirit of truth.

In so far as truth judges the self, truth surely is not the self it judges. Behind myself, behind every facet of myself, there is an awareness of myself. It catches my errors, my twistings and turnings, my rationalizing and self-justification, and sees them for what they are. But it is not a part of what it catches or of what it sees. Men have called it the image of God, and others have called it the presence of God. What else can it be? "There is a life," says Aristotle, "which is higher than the measure of humanity. Men live it not by virtue of their humanity, but by virtue of something in them that is divine."[9] The Apostle Paul, distinguishing more definitely between the human and the divine, says: "God has revealed to us through the Spirit. For the Spirit searches everything, even the depths of God. For what person knows a man's thoughts except the spirit of the man which is in him? So also no one comprehends the thoughts of God except the Spirit of God. Now we have received not the spirit of the world, but the Spirit which is from God, that we may understand the gifts bestowed on us by God."[10]

Professor A. Campbell Garnett sees the presence of God in us as a *will* to pursue the greatest good:

> If this will to the greatest good, which is the source and ultimate guide of our lives, our Alpha and Omega, is rightly called "God," then we see God face to face. We know him more intimately than we know any other person. For we only look on the external face of another man; we merely guess at the life within him. But we look upon the actual will of God in operation (his inner soul) as we do upon our own. We see the essential nature of his will more clearly and simply than we do the complex nature of our own. For God is in us. He is a part of us. We are products of his activity, outgrowths of his life. And he is active still within us, guiding us, admonishing us, using us, cheering us with the sense of inner peace and strength when we are in harmony with him.[11]

Man is weak, but it is not because he is weak that he fails. He fails because he neglects to reckon with his weakness and tries to play a role in which he would have no weakness. And if he discovers his pretense, what reveals it to him? If he reveals it to himself then it was not *his* pretense, it was the pretense of only a part of him. We are impatient and hateful and cruel, and in our impatience and hate and cruelty we destroy what we set out to build. We can do this only as we are deceived; we confuse impatience and ill-temper with strength, hatefulness with a consciousness of superiority, cruelty with justice. If we discover these deceptions, what shows them to us? If we say that one part of us passes judgment upon another part of us, then how can we tell which part of us is the rightful judge of the others? But suppose there is present to our spirit another Spirit which allows us, if we wish, to see ourselves—at least dimly—through His awareness. If this is so, it explains much; if it is not so, there is much to be explained.

The objection, however, will recur that this is nothing more than psychology. We discover new things about our motives, and this discovery changes our attitudes and our personal policies. So we become, in part at least, new persons. This, it may be argued, is found in the results of every successful psychoanalysis. The patient gains insight into himself; he sees himself as he really is and not in the images he has carried over from infancy and early childhood. This new insight into himself leads to a reorganization of his personality and character.

This is not the place to discuss the merits of psychoanalysis. There seems little doubt that it has had its successes as a method of treating personality disorders. It has brought many into working relations with themselves and with other people. There is still the question whether these results are accomplished by bringing to the patient an insight into himself, so that he sees himself as he is, or whether they are accomplished by helping the patient to construct a more stable and satisfying image of himself in relation to others.

The religious believer is convinced that the changes in himself are in some sense the work of God. Are they, or are they nothing more than the psychological effects of seeing himself from a new perspective? A part of the answer to this question is to recognize that we must avoid a false exclusion. The changes may be, in part at least, psychological changes, and yet they may require that he see himself from a perspective which it is not in his own power to achieve. But could not the role he ascribes to God be filled by the analyst, or even by the poets and dramatists and novelists who hold the mirror of life before his eyes?

One approach to an answer to this question is to compare the consequences. Are the results of psychological treatment, of social conditioning, and of religious belief the same? We must admit there are similarities. But suppose we try to look at each at its best. To do this we need to ask of each, "What values, and what conception of the highest purpose open to human life, give the new content and the new direction to the lives you touch? What can you accomplish in your greatest successes?" Psychological treatment, at its best, brings a man back to a satisfactory basis of life. Religion, at its best, seems to lift man to new levels of life; it is not merely remedial, it is positive transformation. When has a man's mastery of his superego led him into a life of sacrificial devotion which has forced tribute even from those who cannot share his beliefs?

If religion is only an illusion then we find ourselves in a sad and disturbing situation. For we now have to admit that the highest reaches of human nature, the nature of man at his best and noblest, the purest expressions of sacrificial love and devotion, all these are the product of illusion and deception. If we say that religion is an illusion we shall have to accept the implication of this, that our world is ultimately the kind of world in which the highest levels are reached by believing what is not true and by acting on what is false.

Religion offers an answer to man's problem. It is a significant answer; if it is true it is an adequate answer, and if its truth is grasped it is a satisfying answer. The truth which is present to us as the awareness of ourselves, the truth which judges us, can be no abstract and impersonal truth. It performs the acts of a person, and so we can think of it in no other way than as Truth in Person. God is not *a* person, because God is more than person; but the most adequate manifestation of God we can grasp is the personal. So God present to us is God as Person. If in Him we find the perfection of Person, not as an ideal but as real existence, then we have our standard by which to find the truth about ourselves.

This is precisely the answer of the higher religions, and it is spelled out most explicitly in the Christian faith. As was mentioned earlier in this chapter, we find the personal not only in the actual presence of persons but also in their work. Yet we must recognize now that what we find in the work and in the products of personal activity is a poor and inadequate expression of the person. So we may find God in His work in nature; but if we are to find God in the most adequate expression of Himself which we are able to recognize, an expression of God to which we can respond with the whole self, then we must find God as Person. It is this which Christianity offers in explicit terms, not as allegory or suggestion but spelled out in two ways, as a fact of history and as the believer's ever-present experience.

Archbishop Temple puts the matter in these terms:

When I read Shakespeare's plays, I find there the thoughts of Shakespeare, not Shakespeare the "thinking, living, acting man." When I hear my friend speak, or watch his action, I find there his living self. . . . Personality can only reveal itself in persons. Consequently it is specially in Human Nature—in men and women—that we see God.[12]

J. E. Turner comments:

The fullest revelation of any individual consists in his revelation of himself, *as a person*, to his intimate friends. For intellectual and artistic brilliance often conceals a man's true personality because it tends to sever him from his fellows, and so to distort their estimate of him; his great abilities, therefore, are no more than aspects of his complete selfhood which may conflict to some extent with other aspects, so that to consider them alone is to falsify his actual character. It is true that anyone who could properly appreciate all these diverse aspects alike and together would thereby gain an almost exhaustive insight into his personality—"almost," because some modicum possibly remains ever concealed; but such insight is very rarely obtained. The same principle . . . holds true of the revelation of Deity.[13]

The Dependence of Faith on Knowledge

Is the religious answer true, or is it only speculation and myth? Perhaps each of us has to answer this for himself. We may be sure that unless God does really exist, the religious answer to man's problems is only myth. No force of belief can give it more than psychological and cultural existence. When we see how much depends on the fact of God's existence we begin to be aware of the tremendous importance of that problem. We shall recognize, too, that for inquiring man, for men who so highly respect reason and truth that they are unsatisfied with a faith which is not grounded in knowledge, the problem of the existence of God is also the fundamental intellectual problem. Faith is indispensable, not alone in religion but everywhere in life. But to ask that faith have its roots in knowledge is not to substitute knowledge for faith; it is the roots of faith, not the growth and flower of the plant, which we want to be firmly established in knowledge.

We shall therefore approach the problems of the idea of God and the existence of God as philosophical problems. This is no denial of their religious significance. Modern man at his best is not content with conjecture or with agreeable possibilities. He demands to know. Where his knowledge is plainly inadequate to guide him, where he has to walk by faith, he wants his faith to be grounded in knowledge. The complaint that the God of the philosophers is not the God of faith is, at best, a play on words. If God is one, and if the God of the philosophers is God and if the God of faith is God, then it is the same God. What the philosophers find may be poor and empty in comparison with what faith finds. But if what philosophy finds in its proof of God's existence is not true, then faith has no defense against the danger that what it finds is only illusion, rich and satisfying illusion perhaps, but still illusion. But if faith complements knowledge, if we can *know* that God exists and if we can know that the God who exists is nothing less than the best that faith can desire, then faith's mistakes are only the errors of its own inadequacy. If we know that God exists then we know that faith has its own truth. But this does not assimilate faith to knowledge, for we do not know *what* that truth is. Only in faith can we find it.[14]

We know by reason based on experience; we act by faith. The faith by which we act is not alone faith in reason's interpretation, for this would take us no further than reason lights the way. Faith in God, although it may be based on the intellect's perception of God's existence, takes us further than knowledge can go. It lets us hear His Spirit within us as He speaks to our innermost selves, and it lets us follow Him wherever He leads. But if we do not know that God exists we have no assurance that there is a God to speak to us. If, in spite of this, we believe that it is God who does speak to us, then our faith is not alone faith in God, it is also faith in the essential rightness of our own propensities for belief. It is in this, and not in his respect for reason and knowledge, that man shows spiritual pride.[15]

Part Five

THE IDEA OF GOD

CHAPTER 13

The Idea of God and Naturalism

WHAT WE MEAN BY GOD

THUS FAR in our discussion of religion we have used the word "God" with little or no explanation, as if everyone who reads this may be expected to know its meaning. There is, of course, a meaning which anyone who is acquainted with the language does understand, just as any literate person understands such words as "society," "history," "cause," "knowledge," "family," "corporation," "person," and "friend." Yet these words, like "God," do not carry all their meaning within the obvious and familiar senses which we immediately recognize. They have levels of meaning that go much deeper, that raise serious questions and involve differences of opinion. When we inquire as to what precisely is the nature of the situation to which the word refers we encounter difficulties. Misunderstandings and confusions in our conceptions begin to appear, and we find we have to try to answer questions which we had not dreamed of before.

We know in a general way, for example, what "society" refers to. But when we try to work out a precise and comprehensive concept of society we find ourselves involved eventually in problems that have been at the bottom of some of the most acute political conflicts in history. Yet people who have different conceptions of the nature of society agree fairly well concerning what actual situations are instances of society. In other words, the problem is not, as some would try to show, a merely verbal problem. The remedy for our differences here is not semantics; it is rather a more complete understanding of the nature of society.

Lawyers and legislators and judges may dispute concerning the nature of corporations, but they usually know that those on one side of the dispute are talking about the same things that those on the other side are talking about. If this were not true their disputes would be nothing but misunderstandings about the meanings of words. So it is with the word "God." We have a common understanding of the obvious and accepted meaning of the word if we are acquainted with our own language. Our problems arise, and our disputes become more than merely verbal, when we push our inquiry into the more obscure aspects of the things to which our words refer.

Everyone who is at home in the English language understands the word "God" in its common meaning. "God" means "the supreme and ultimate being." Those who use the term ordinarily think of the supreme and ultimate being as one which is also supreme and ultimate value; if they dissociate value from being they are not likely to find the word "God" significant or pertinent. Some would not hesitate to use the term to refer to an impersonal being or principle, as in Spinoza's meaning, while others would reserve the term for a being which is in some sense personal. There are a few who wish to retain the word even though they recognize no being or real existence to which it applies; they use it to refer to some abstract principle or relationship. As we shall see later, it is difficult to defend such usage. Plato, for whom the ultimate is the Form of the Good, differentiates God from the Forms; for him God is a being with soul and reason. He is supremely good. "So, being without jealousy, he desired that all things should come as near as possible to being like himself. . . . In virtue of this reasoning, when he framed the universe, he fashioned reason within soul and soul within body, to the end that the work he accomplished might be by nature as excellent and perfect as possible."[1] Most of those who use the word "God" at all would agree that it refers to a level of being which is ultimate, not dependent on anything else for its own existence, and is that on which other things do depend.

Man's Need of the Idea of God

The idea of God, in man's belief and practice, appears in response to a problem. As soon as man becomes aware of the problem he finds that the idea of God, in some form or other, comes to him. It would not be too much to say that this is one of the inevitabilities of human thought. A man may dismiss the idea, or scorn it, or attack it; but he can avoid thinking it only so far as he avoids thinking about the problem which suggests it. Even if the problem were a pseudo-problem, as the positivist says it is, it would be a pseudo-problem which man would have to think about. He would have to think about it at least to the point where he became convinced that it should be dismissed. For even if the positivist were correct in his contention that this is a pseudo-problem and that the word "God" is meaningless, each man who became aware of the supposed problem which leads to the idea of God would have to take some position with respect to it or else simply quit thinking.

The problem which man cannot escape, and which in turn compels him to think about God, is the problem of understanding himself and the things which make up his world. In his first groping attempts to understand his world man tries to explain some things in terms of others. His methods of finding and formulating explanations may be crude and primitive, but this does not lessen the significance of the fact that he makes the attempt. For if he did not he would not be man. The human mind is inherently restless when puzzled; it has either to evade the puzzle or try to probe its mystery. There are puzzles for the plain reason that the things which man encounters in his world do not account for themselves. He finds them, but he does not find with them their title to existence nor a schedule of their hidden properties and their future operations. Why does this or that, rather than something else, exist? There are so many possibilities man can think of, but which he does not find in existence and which yet seem to him to be so much more worthy of existence. It is this particular being —this tree, this mountain, this river, this son or daughter—which is here, and not another. Why this and not something else? For everything that happens a cause must be found or the mind remains unsatisfied.

When we say that the problem of understanding himself and

his world is what leads man to the idea of God we do not mean that the idea of God comes to man from his abstract and theoretical preoccupations. The need to understand and explain is the most practical of all needs, for on its satisfaction depends man's power to control the conditions of his life. The attempt to satisfy this need is made first of all for the sake of immediate and pressing ends. They are such ends as the satisfaction of hunger, the avoidance of destruction, and the continuation of the community life.

Although the lower animals live their lives as mere pawns of their own instincts and the forces of nature, man does not and never has. So long as he has been man he has confronted his world as something over against himself toward which *he* acts, whether his act be one of submission or rebellion or manipulation. He is not himself merely one of the channels which the energies of nature follow, for he differentiates himself from what is other than himself—perhaps not with accuracy, but at all events with some notion of what he is, whether it be true or false, adequate or inadequate. The animal reacts to stimuli: he attacks, devours, mates, seeks protection, and flees from danger. But in this there is no awareness of himself as one who performs these acts. Man also responds to stimuli, but his response is controlled to some degree by his recognition of himself as an agent with certain continuing needs and interests. He knows himself as the same self he 'was yesterday and the days before. He sees himself who he hopes will have at some future time the satisfactions which he now anticipates. He has a continuing existence of his own in the unity of his awareness, in the fact that both he and the things he knows come together in the same awareness. He may not clearly differentiate his own person from his community or tribe or clan, but still his participation in the communal life is *his own* life; it does not dissolve him into a mere part of the community. His pleasures and pains, joys and sorrows, are *his*.

The world which confronts man, and which he confronts in his awareness of his own existence, is one of mystery. The things which belong to that world have their own ways of being and of acting. They are both intimate and strange, friendly and hostile, amenable and resistant to his desires. He sees himself dependent upon these things and yet they are not within his power to control. It is true that he finds ways of influencing them, or thinks he does, but the successful use even of those methods he is most sure of requires vigilance lest he unwittingly commit some error. When magic fails, for example, those who believe in the efficacy of magic are not thereby made skeptical; it has failed because he who tried to use it was not entitled or qualified to use it or because he made some mistake in procedure.

Even at the most primitive level the origin of the idea of the divine seems to be in man's response to the mysteries of nature and life. His awareness of need and the recognition of his own helplessness are its roots, just as these are the roots in man's nature of all his religious consciousness. He who lacks religious consciousness either does not feel needs or else he is entirely confident of his own power to satisfy them. Perhaps he takes for granted an automatic provision for all his wants, as may, for example, a member of a privileged class who never for a moment doubts that his special situation is guaranteed forever by the nature of things. Perhaps he lives in a time, as in our own age, when man can imagine himself to be potentially omnipotent, so that all failure is temporary, all error is inadvertent, and the remedy for every lack is a more extensive and more carefully controlled application of methods already known and mastered. For him who has no religious awareness the mysteries are either in final subjugation to his interests or else they have been abolished—in principle at least. Such confidence, however, can hardly survive scrutiny, whether it is the confidence we find in the modern attitude of self-sufficiency or in the complacent acceptance of privilege and superiority.

Man's response to mystery is a practical response. He looks for help in the ordinary and extraordinary affairs of life: help to secure food, to defeat his enemies, to protect himself from the powers and agencies which show themselves in the forces of nature. His response is also a psychological response; he feels awe and fear, and he needs reassurance. In this context, practical and psychological, he performs his rituals and makes his sacrifices in petition and for the appeasement of the gods and their agents.

The development of religion is interwoven with the development of human society and human knowledge. In some areas mystery does give way to knowledge, and as cultural and political organization changes so does also man's conception of his needs. This is not to say that the development of man's religious ideas is merely the product of other changes, for religion did not stand apart as a separate activity until secularism split it from other human concerns. But as life changed so religion changed with it. Even where traditional forms and rituals are preserved, their earlier meanings sometimes may be forgotten and they may take on new significance.

One of the most important and far-reaching changes in man's conception of his needs came with his discovery of his moral nature. The idea of the divine as the force in control of physical forces and life energies changed into the conception of a God who is primarily moral in His nature. This discovery of God as moral comes only as man discovers that his own moral needs are more important than all others, and it did not come all at once. The development from polytheism to monotheism reflects a conception of nature and existence which sees in them some kind of basic and ultimate unity. If God is conceived as one, it seems inevitable that He will be thought of in terms of the highest kind of unity man can think. Monotheism seems to be the inevitable consequence of man's attempt to establish the effective and true relation between himself and the divine. It is inevitable, that is, provided experience and thought are allowed to take their natural development and are not frozen by custom and form, or by intellectual stagnation, at a less advanced stage. We shall try to see the underlying logic of this advance to monotheism.

INTELLIGIBILITY AND UNITY

As man tries to understand himself and the things and events in his world, and as he begins to explain some things in terms of other things, he comes inevitably to the idea that behind all these causes there is one fundamental and ultimate cause or principle of explanation. The suggestion is irresistible; he cannot possibly miss thinking of it except as he misses thinking. For the need to explain is not satisfied merely by finding explanations; it turns upon the explanations themselves, and demands that they be explained. So there is no stopping place for thought short of some one ultimate cause or principle, for only if thought arrives at one single final principle can it ever arrive at an explanation which does not itself demand to be explained.

Even when men arrive at a final dualistic conception of existence, when they find for example a final good principle and a final evil principle or a final spiritual principle and a final material principle, neither side of the dualism is ultimate in itself. In such a theory it is the principle of duality which is ultimate, and everything else is explained in terms of this duality. In like manner a radical pluralism does not have as many ultimate principles as it has different kinds of irreducible entities; it has only one basic principle, the plurality of existing entities.

This demand of the mind is one of the strong driving forces of human thinking, no matter what may be the level upon which that thinking takes place. In the childhood of human culture man's thinking is in the form of story and myth. He explains by personifying his principles and causes. But unless his thinking is halted by some paralysis, by some culturally induced inhibition, he inevitably turns to one of his gods or nature-personifications as the chief one; or he finds his final explanations in some fundamental relationship among his gods or in some principle to which they are subject. He thinks in terms of something supreme and in terms of the dependence of other things upon it.

With the appearance of philosophy, and the attempt to discover rational explanations, personified causes give way to natural causes. Natural causes, in turn, are understood in terms of some single principle. It was Plato who seems first to have carried this to its furthest point and attributed to his first principle a unique mode of being. If there is one principle of explanation which accounts for all other things and yet needs nothing to account for itself, then, Plato thought, this one principle must differ from all other things not only in its nature but also in its mode of being. He calls it the "Form of the Good," and he means by this the first principle upon which depends the structure and pattern of all real being. To put this in our own terms, the Form of the Good is that which accounts for the fact that the laws of nature are what they are and are not other than what they are. As has been already mentioned, Plato did not call the Form of the Good "God," since he thought of God as a spiritual being or soul. Yet in what he says about the Form of the Good we find suggestions of some of the most important and distinctive points of later concepts of God.

This, then, which gives to the objects of knowledge their truth and to him who knows them his power of knowing, is the Form or essential nature of Goodness. It is the cause of knowledge and truth; and so, while you may think of it as an object of knowledge, you will do well to regard it as something beyond truth and knowledge and, precious as these both are, of still higher worth. And, just as in our analogy light and vision were to be thought of as like the Sun, but not identical with it, so here both knowledge and truth are to be regarded as like the Good, but to identify either with the Good is wrong. The Good must hold a yet higher place of honour. . . . But I want to follow up our analogy still further. You will agree that the Sun not only makes the things we see visible, but also brings them into existence and gives them growth and nourishment; yet he is not the same thing as existence.[2] And so with the objects of knowledge: these derive from the Good not only their power of being known, but their very being and reality; and Goodness is not the same thing as being, but even beyond being, surpassing it in dignity and power.[3]

In so far as a religion has the slightest intellectual significance, we may rightly expect to find in it powerful tendencies in the direction either of monism or monotheism. In monism all being is conceived as one absolute unity, while plurality and difference and change are indications of unreality. Monism appears in religious thought as pantheism, the identification of *the all* with God.

Monotheism, in so far as we understand it in distinction from monism, is either deistic or theistic. These, then, are the three ideas of God which we may expect to find in intellectually significant religious thought, and of course a philosophy of religion has little concern with ideas which are not intellectually significant. As a preliminary to our examination of pantheism and deism and theism, however, we shall consider naturalism. The reason for this is that some proponents of naturalism attempt, as it were, to "naturalize" God, that is, to identify God with some part or aspect of the natural order.

NATURALISM

It may seem strange, at first thought, to include naturalism as one of the four basic ideas of God. For naturalism derives its distinctive character from the doctrine that nature alone is real and that there is neither need nor justification for us to appeal to any being or principle beyond nature. Naturalism, in the words of one of its adherents, "means a philosophical position, empirical in method, that regards everything that exists or occurs to be conditioned in its existence or occurrence by causal factors within one all-encompassing system of nature, however 'spiritual' or purposeful or rational some of these things and events may in their functions and values prove to be."[4]

It is apparent that naturalism is limited to three alternatives so far as its position concerning God is concerned. It may deny the existence of God, in all acceptable senses of the term, on the ground that there is nothing within the system of nature to which the word "God" properly applies. The second possibility is to identify God with something within the system of nature. The third possibility is to identify God with the system of nature as a whole. Since the latter alternative merges naturalism with pantheism we shall not consider it at this point. The first alternative, atheistic naturalism, may also be dismissed here with little comment. It is true, of course, that a professedly atheistic naturalism must formulate some conception of God, else it would not know what it attempts to deny. But the force of its argument is directed against the view that God exists "beyond" or "above" nature, as a being which in some sense transcends nature. We shall consider the merits of this contention when we come to examine the arguments in support of the doctrine that God does exist as a being which transcends nature.

Our present problem, therefore, is to look at the attempt to formulate a significant concept of God which identifies God with something within nature. In an earlier chapter we referred to Auguste Comte's conception of God as Humanity, and this could provide us with an interesting illustration of a naturalistic conception of God. There is, however, a more recent attempt to formulate a strictly naturalistic concept of God. Because it is closer to us, and because of its present wide influence, we shall use it as a sample of the naturalistic concept. This is the view developed by John Dewey in *A Common Faith*.

Dewey rejects the conception of God as "some kind of Being having prior and therefore non-ideal existence."[5] Such a concept he considers false, unnecessary, and harmful. He thus eliminates from consideration both the deistic and theistic concepts of God. He is willing to use the term "God" to refer to something within the order of nature, although he seems somewhat reluctant to admit the term even in this sense and prefers to speak of "the divine" rather than of "God."[6]

Dewey's specific statement of what he means by "God" is that "it denotes the unity of all ideal ends arousing us to desire and actions."[7] The word "God," he says, "means the ideal ends that at a given time and place one acknowledges as having authority over his volition and emotion, the values to which one is supremely devoted, as far as these ends, through imagination, take on unity."[8] " 'God' represents a unification of ideal values that is essentially imaginative in origin when the imagination supervenes in conduct."[9] The idea of God, he says again, is "one of ideal possibilities unified through imaginative realization and projection."[10] Thus "God" means, for Dewey, something which exists in our imagination and, since imagination is a natural process, God is something which is entirely natural.

Dewey takes some pains to protect his concept of God from the criticism that it refers to something fanciful and unreal. The misunderstanding, he says, arises from

> our frequent use of the word "imagination" to denote fantasy and doubtful reality. But the reality of ideal ends as ideals is vouched for by their undeniable power in action. An ideal is not an illusion because imagination is the organ through which it is apprehended. For *all* possibilities reach us through the imagination. In a definite sense the only meaning that can be assigned the term "imagination" is that things unrealized in fact come home to us and have power to stir us. The unification effected through imagination is not fanciful, for it is the reflex of the unification of practical and emotional attitudes. The unity signifies not a single Being, but the unity of loyalty and effort evoked by the fact that many ends are one in the power of their ideal, or imaginative, quality to stir and hold us.[11]

A little later Dewey returns to answer again the same criticism:

> The view I have advanced is sometimes treated as if the identification of the divine with ideal ends left the ideal wholly without roots in existence and without support from existence. The objection implies that my view commits one to such a separation of the ideal and the existent that the ideal has no chance to find lodgment even as a seed that might grow and bear fruit. On the contrary, what I have been criticizing is the *identification* of the ideal with a particular Being, especially when that identification makes necessary the conclusion that this Being is outside of nature, and what I have tried to show is that the ideal itself has its roots in natural conditions; it emerges when the imagination idealizes existence by laying hold of the possibilities offered to thought and action. There are values, goods, actually realized upon a natural basis—the goods of human association, of art and knowledge. The idealizing imagination seizes upon the most precious things found in the climacteric moments of experience and projects them. We need no external criterion and guarantee for their goodness. They are had, they exist as good, and out of them we frame our ideal ends.[12]

When we try to find precisely what Dewey's concern with the

idea of God actually is, we find it hard to decide whether he is telling us of what might be left in the traditional concept of God when we deny that God is a real "single Being," or whether he considers the idea of God to be a significant and useful concept when understood and used in his terms. Dewey, at times, sounds somewhat like a loving parent who feels it is time to tell a child that there is no Santa Claus. He may tell the child that there is no Santa Claus as a real person, but that Santa really is the imaginary expression of the love which parents have for their children—the Christmas Spirit. "Now that you are growing up," the parent may say, "You no longer need believe in Santa as a person. But we ought to keep the spirit of Santa Claus in our hearts and participate in the love and joy of the holiday season." When we understand what Dewey means in his own use of "God" or "the divine" it becomes quite clear that he has no real need of it in his philosophy. Like Santa Claus, the God-myth has served a purpose in making us aware of certain values; but now that we are aware of those values we no longer need the myth by which this awareness was transmitted to us. If this is the case then such a conception of God requires little attention from a philosophy of religion. The proper field of its study is anthropology or folklore, or perhaps the history of ideas.

If, however, we suppose that Dewey intends this concept to serve a serious purpose in our thought and action then we must ask just what mode of existence this God of naturalism has. It is, Dewey tells us, "the unity of all ideal ends arousing us to desire and actions."[13] By "ends" he means the goals which, when reached, terminate a course of action in some kind of satisfaction. An end is that part of an act which is not yet actual but which will become actualized with the completion of the act. It seems to be the latter stages, or perhaps the completion, of the act as we are aware of that completion from a perspective within the course of the act itself. In other words, it is the idea we have, before the act is completed, of the completion we intend it to have. Ideal ends are the goals which are present to us in idea before they are realized in action and which are accepted by us as the goals by reference to which we shall direct our action. We see ourselves as incomplete, our desires are only partially fulfilled and our needs remain unsatisfied. We imagine various changes from our present condition which, we think, would bring satisfaction, and these changes which we imagine we adopt as the goals of our action. These are our "ideal ends"; they are rooted in our actual condition but they refer directly to situations not yet actual.

In these ideal ends, however, we do not yet have what Dewey calls "God" or "the divine." God is, specifically, the *unity* of ideal ends. It is here that we find the only clue to a distinction between ends which ought to be realized and ends which do not deserve realization. It seems that the ends that ought to be realized are the ends that can be unified, that is, ends that are coherent and provide mutual support and are not in conflict. Since the basic reference of Dewey's philosophy is social rather than individual, he conceives the harmony or unity of ideal ends as a social unity.

If this is what Dewey means then he appears to provide a distinction between acceptable and unacceptable ends of action. But the appearance is deceptive, for not the slightest justification is given for the contention that these ends which he considers desirable for man to realize are truly desirable. Why are unified goals "better" than goals in conflict? Shall we say they are better because harmonized goals are capable of realization while conflicting goals cannot be realized? If so, then why is it "good" to realize any goals? Why is it good to live at all? Because Dewey ignores these questions he repeatedly confuses the desirable with the desired, the preferable with what in fact is preferred. Although he insists that the ends in question are not just any ends, yet even here he confuses what ought to be desired with what in fact is desired. The idea of God "involves no miscellaneous worship of everything in general. It selects those factors in existence that generate and support our idea of good as an end to be striven for. It excludes a multitude of forces that at any given time are irrelevant to this function. Nature produces whatever gives reinforcement and direction but also what occasions discord and confusion. The 'divine' is thus a term of human choice and aspiration."[14] It is, we should note, "our idea of good" to which the "divine" refers, not that which is good independently of our judgment and choice.

What then is the point, in Dewey's view, of any reference at all to God, since God is an imaginary construction and so exists only in idea? Dewey says in answer to this:

> In a distracted age the need for such an idea is urgent. It can unify interests and energies now dispersed; it can direct action and generate the heat of emotion and the light of intelligence. Whether one gives the name "God" to this union, operative in thought and action, is a matter for individual decision. But the *function* of such a working union of the ideal and actual seems to me to be identical with the force that has in fact been attached to the conception of God in all the religions that have a spiritual content; and a clear idea of that function seems to me urgently needed at the present time.[15]

This attempt by Dewey to justify the inclusion of the concept of God in his philosophy is surely a failure. For the distinctive usefulness of the idea is in the associations it brings from other religions. In Dewey's religious view God is nothing but the "union of interests and energies," so how can the idea of God as conceived in Dewey's terms "generate the heat of emotion and the light of intelligence"? It can generate nothing more than the idea of "the unity of ideal ends" can generate *unless we carry over into this new idea of God some of the meanings which belonged to it in the context of the very religions which Dewey repudiates.* Would Dewey propose that we continue to teach what he considers false religious beliefs in order that we may employ the heat and light which these false beliefs generate? Surely not, for he considers such beliefs to be harmful as well as false. Yet if God is nothing but the imaginative unity of ideal ends what else can be gained by referring to this unity as "God"? Professor Gordon W. Allport's comment concerning the attitude of the mature mind toward humanism as a religion has a most pertinent application to Dewey's proposed "common faith." "But humanism, he suspects [that is, the person of mature mind], is something like science— acceptable so far as it goes, but quite uncurious regarding its own presuppositions. He doubts that the motive power for humanism is more than the lingering breeze of the powerful dynamic of Christian faith."[16]

Whatever may be the use of such a conception of God it contributes nothing in itself except the name. Its significance for a philosophy of religion is precisely the significance of "the unity of ideal ends." Even Dewey's own phrases betray him, for it is quite apparent that the unity of ends has no significance apart from the ends themselves. What possible *religious* attitude can we take toward the *unity* of ideal ends? When we consider what is, in fact, the highest level of life and value which Dewey can conceive we find in it no place for religion or for any of those qualities of character and personality which constitute man's true greatness. On Dewey's view *the high point of human nobility of character is found in man's most shrewdly calculated manipulation of tools and instruments in an intensely emotional drive to get what he wants and to prevent one desire from interfering with others.* Whatever this may amount to as a prescription for human action and for some kinds of human progress, it is not worth discussing as religion.

In so far as religion involves worship and dedication, the kind of religious conception Dewey finds acceptable is plainly absurd. How can man worship an idea, a God which has being only in our thought, unless man mistakenly believes his imaginary God to be real? When we look at this in the context of Dewey's philosophy the absurdity is even more obvious. For Dewey regards all values as instrumental. The final ends of human action are the satisfaction of the biological (including the psycho-social) drives inherent in the complex protoplasmic process we call life. "Ideal ends" can mean, in such a context, only those possible situations which enhance the satisfaction of our original biological drives. To promote the unity of ideal ends can be only to serve the more complete satisfaction of those drives: it can have no other meaning. The fact is that Dewey's interpretation of the religious, if it means anything, is a throw-back to some sort of primitive nature-worship whose deities are personifications of biological and physical forces, except that Dewey's version omits the personification process.[17]

Naturalistic religion is found most frequently in the form of humanism. In some cases humanism is a lineal descendent of Comte's Religion of Humanity. Others have become humanists because they feel the need to express a religious attitude and know nothing better, for its object, than man. Still others have given up an earlier theistic or, more likely, deistic view and have embraced humanism as containing the maximum religious meaning they can accept. Thus a few have been born and reared in the humanist tradition; some want to be rescued from the bleak nihilism of naturalism without going so far as to examine the premises of naturalism itself; and some are dissatisfied theists or deists who have turned to the worship of man and have accepted human progress as the ultimate goal of existence—an anthropomorphism, by the way, of the most extreme form.

Whatever the motive which leads to the worship of humanity as God, and the acceptance of human welfare as the ultimate test of value, humanism seems to be an attempt to preserve some of the attitudes of religion without the realities which make sense of those attitudes. As Charles A. Bennett says, "One does not need to be pessimist or cynic to feel that man is one of the poorest substitutes for God that ingenuity can propose. It is better to repudiate religion and all its works than to chatter about worshipping or adoring humanity."[18]

Sir James Fitzjames Stephen's characterization of the Religion of Humanity applies as well to all naturalistic versions of religion. "The human race is an enormous agglomeration of bubbles which are continually bursting and ceasing to be. No one made it or knows anything worth knowing about it. Love it dearly, oh ye bubbles." He comments: "This is a sort of religion, no doubt, but it seems to me a very silly one."[19]

CHAPTER 14

Pantheism

THE AMBIGUITY OF PANTHEISM

PANTHEISM is the concept of God which identifies God with the world and the world with God. The world and God are one. Any naturalism that considers the world of nature to be a unity and regards the world in its unity as divine is a version of pantheism.

In spite of the apparently plain meaning of "pantheism," there are two distinct interpretations of the term and these lead to different concepts of God. Which interpretation appears depends upon where we start in our attempt to think of God and the world as one. If we start with God then we tend to absorb the world into God, and to deny that the world has any existence in its own right. If we start with the world we tend to absorb God into the world and to interpret "God" to mean nothing but the unity of the world; so that God exists, on this view, not as God but as the world unified.

This basic ambiguity of pantheism is well expressed by A. E. Garvie. Pantheism, he says,

is the view that all is God, and that God is all, but, since thought may move either from God to all or from all to God, it can assume two forms. If it begins with the religious belief or the philosophic faith in God as infinite and eternal reality, then the finite and temporal world is swallowed up in God, and pantheism becomes acosmism, *i.e.* the world is an illusion in comparison with God as reality. If it begins with the scientific conception or the poetic vision of the world as unity, then God is lost in the world, and pantheism becomes pancosmism.[1]

"Cosmic Pantheism" is the term used by John Oman for what Garvie calls "pancosmism."[2] It is very closely related to the religion of nature, including all primitive religion. Such religions seek "the abiding in the Natural through faith in an animistic force indefinitely many and vaguely one."[3] This version of pantheism denies all meaning to the idea of God which may point beyond the world. God "becomes but a name for the unity of the world, the multiplicity of which alone is real for observation and imagination."[4] We have here a view which can be of little concern to a philosophy of religion. For the unity of the world is not a real being; on this view the only reality is the world itself. Its unity, considered simply as such, is an abstraction; so the God of this kind of pantheism is only an abstraction. God's only existence here is conceptual; God is not a real being but a being of reason, that is, God exists as such only in our concept of the unity of the world. The only difference between this and other varieties of naturalism is its attitude that the world is in some sense divine.

"Cosmic Pantheism," says Oman, "differs from the Religion of Nature more in dialectic than in faith. Its unity is the old diffused power [of animism and polytheism]; its way of dealing with life magical; its oneness of all things a sack to hold primitive animisms and every other kind of belief." Acosmic pantheism, on the other hand, denies the reality of nature, "excluding the Natural wholly from the Supernatural, as illusion." The supernatural is a self-enclosed unity.[5]

Oman points out that cosmic pantheism always tends to give way to the acosmic or mystical variety. "Pantheism, from its earliest Indian to the latest Hegelian manifestation, starts by imposing the idea of unity upon experience: and the peace of mind it offers, which for struggling humanity is its chief attraction, is the finality thereby assured from the start." This, however, is not sufficient. If the source of human misery is in the plurality and unceasing change of the things of the world, we do not change the condition of things by thinking of them as a unity. For "to impose unity upon all things is not to bring all things into unity." The things from which come our woes are still real, though conceived as one—"if the all in any way includes the real, it is not less distressing for being called God." If we are to escape evil, we have to see that what distresses us is not real; so we must understand the world of change and plurality as not real. "Hence the pantheism of 'all is God' changes constantly into the mysticism of 'God is all.' "[6]

It would seem that acosmic pantheism, by turning all human striving and failure into unreality or illusion, should be a most optimistic religion. As Oman says, "logically, it seems difficult to pass to pessimism, because, if all things are Brahma are they not good, and if our soul or *atman* is all Brahma is it not also good? But . . . the passage from pantheistic optimism to the sense that all is unreality and all misery has always been both certain and rapid."[8] The reason for this shift from optimism to pessimism seems plain, for if the striving which leads to failure and misery is unreal simply because it is striving, and because it involves change, then for the same reason the striving which leads to apparent success and triumph is unreal. "When all is given by process," Oman points out, "there is no real room for human achievement."[9]

Acosmic pantheism includes the world in God. But the world is in God not as the world, but as God. God's infinity cannot be exhausted in identification with any limited kind or kinds of being. God is beyond knowledge and beyond thought, and beyond understanding in terms of anything which belongs to the world. Pantheism of this variety is associated with many religious mysticisms. Garvie calls this form "theistic," because, as he says, in it, "if inconsistently, there still survives as a rule a vague apprehension of God as theism conceives Him."[10]

When we try to distinguish theistic pantheism from theism proper we often find views which shift from one to the other. Theistic pantheism is, of course, a religious interpretation of reality, and almost inevitably it involves religious mysticism. Yet religious mysticism certainly does not either presuppose or imply pantheism. In fact, the greater the emphasis upon the practice of mysticism within a pantheistic framework of thought the greater the likelihood of a shift of emphasis toward theism, in which a definite distinction is maintained between God and the world. For the practice of mysticism would seem to require an initial recognition of the distinction between man and God and a sense of man's distance, as man, from God. It is for this reason that some of the great religious mysticisms, such as the religion of Vishnu and the philosophy of Plotinus, seem to shift back and forth between pantheism and theism.

John R. Everett brings out the unstable position of the religion of Vishnu with respect to its pantheistic and theistic tendencies.

> The Gītā conceives of Vishnu as the all-pervading first principle of the universe. "There is nothing else that is outside of Me; on Me this All is strung like beads of pearls on a string. . . . Also the seed of all beings, that I am. There is no being, moving or motionless, that is without Me." Such statements seem to indicate a close connection between the theism of the Gītā and the Brahman of the Upanishads. In many places the concept of Vishnu as a kind of pantheistic deity is strong and overt, yet the burden of the poem indicates the belief that Vishnu is a separate deity who creates, sustains and "makes the wheels of the universe go around." He is at the same time in all natural processes and all human beings and above them. As the transcendent god he is the object of all knowledge and the creator of all things. As the immanent god he is the "soul of all" and the reality of all things. The Gītā is never consistent in its emphasis upon either of these aspects: at one point Vishnu is "both immortality and death, both existence and non-existence . . . the beginning and the middle and the end of being"; while in another place Vishnu says, "I am the strength of the strong, free from lust and passion; I am desire in all being but not such desire as is opposed to righteousness."[11]

The unstable relation of pantheism and theism in such instances as this is not surprising, for until the concept of creation was developed under the influence of Hebrew-Christian thought, philosophy possessed no adequate means of conceiving the relation of God and the world without the danger of one absorbing the other. Either God (or the gods) was conceived as a part of the world-order or else the world, where distinguished from God at all, was understood as an overflow or "emanation" from God.

This latter conception involved a falling away from the original One, and a consequent degradation to lower and lower levels the further the emanation proceeds from its original source. It was only when the concept of creation was clearly defined in contrast to emanation that a steady distinction could be maintained between pantheism and theism. For it was only with the idea of creation that religious thought came into possession of a way of thinking both the existence of God and the existence of the world without confusing the two or reducing one to the other or considering one to be only a function or an aspect of the other.

The Argument for Acosmic Pantheism

Acosmic pantheism begins with the idea of God as the ultimate, as the one unconditioned Unity. If the word "real" has been associated with the world, with temporal and plural being, then the One is referred to as beyond reality and beyond being. This is what Plato says of the Form of the Good in the passage quoted earlier from his *Republic*.[12] If, however, the One is conceived as real then the world must be designated as unreal. It is reasonable to suppose that the first of these usages would be found in those versions of pantheism which have a strong theistic tendency, where there is still an inclination to assert some mode of real existence of the world, while the latter is more likely to be found in those versions of pantheism which have an originally negative attitude toward the world. Be this as it may, only confusion can come from the attempt to move back and forth from one of these terminologies to the other. Since we wish to discuss pantheism in an unequivocal form we shall refer to God, the One, as the Real, while the world will be considered unreal. This is what an acosmic pantheism should assert about the world, if the term "acosmic" is to be applied to it appropriately.

The argument for acosmic pantheism asserts that the Real, as ultimate, cannot be plural, for then there would be at least two realities. If two, then each would have to be different from the other, since obviously if they were identical they would not be

231

two but one. If the first of these two realities differs from the second *with respect to what constitutes the reality of the second,* then in that respect the first would have to be unreal. The second would have a reality which the first did not have. Likewise if the second differs from the first with respect to that in the first which constitutes its reality, then the second must lack that reality and so be unreal with respect to it. This is the basic argument in support of the doctrine that the Real must be One.

Let us see how it might be applied in criticism of a frankly dualistic theory. Suppose we say that there are two kinds of reality, matter and mind. Matter, let us say, is extended mass, occupying space and enduring in time. Mind, on the other hand, is unextended, and does not occupy space. Although we may understand it as enduring in time, it is able to transcend time separations in its awareness, and its characteristic activity is to know or to be aware. Now if matter is real, there are certain properties of the real which mind lacks, for example, extension and mass. If mind is real, there are certain properties of the real which matter lacks, for example, awareness and knowledge. So neither matter nor mind can be *the real as such.* Each, with respect to something which belongs to the real, is deficient; and so each is deficiently real. What is this but to be in certain respects unreal?

We cannot meet this argument by saying that mind and matter are both real, but are different kinds of reality. For if there are two kinds of reality there must be something to distinguish them. That in the one which distinguishes it from the other is either real or unreal. If it is real, then the second lacks this characteristic of reality and is deficiently real. If, however, the mark of distinction between the two is not real, then the difference is not real and there is only one reality instead of two. So if there is anything fully real, it is the One. Since it is one it must be unconditioned, that is, absolute. For if the Real is one there is nothing distinct from it, or other than it, to limit or condition it. If anything real lay behind or beyond the Real, the Real would be other than what lay beyond it and so in this respect unreal. But this is a contradiction.

What, then, is the one absolute unconditioned reality to which this argument takes us? We cannot say anything of what it is, for once we say that it has this or that character, x, we imply that it excludes all that is not that character, or not-x. If not-x is real, then we have destroyed the unity of the Real, for now the Real is composed of both x and not-x, and these are mutually exclusive. So not-x must be illusion or mere appearance. But if so, then x, in so far as its nature as x is defined by differentiating it from not-x, is a function of illusion and unreality. In short, to say that the Real is this or that is to exclude from the Real whatever is not included in our "this or that." So the statement that the Real is this or that is meaningless or false.

Can we then say anything at all about the Real? We seem to be able to say only what it is not. We can approach it only by negation, by excluding from it all that is unreal and that has the characteristics of unreality, such as plurality and change and limitation and difference. So all the things which appear to make up our world, and all the things we can think (since to think requires that we differentiate the object of our thought from what it is not), must be excluded from the One. Excluded from the Real, the things of the world can be only illusion.

We still have not yet reached the end. For to attribute even unity and reality to the One is false. What can we mean by "one" except the meaning we secure as we contrast it with the many: what does "real" mean, except as we differentiate it from unreal; and how can we think anything absolute or unconditioned except in contrast with the relative and conditioned? So thought itself turns out to be incapable of grasping the Real. The Real is not rational; it is suprarational, above thought and above reason.

Any pantheism which follows the logic of its argument to this point must find some way of reaching the One, or God, which does not require thinking or reason. Its contact with God may be in a mystical experience of identification, in which is lost all appearance of separate existence. In such an experience the finite self loses itself in God—as a raindrop which falls into a stream that flows into the great river is finally lost in the mighty ocean.

Or perhaps it will be Spinoza's "third kind of knowledge" in which the separations and relations of ordinary thinking all merge into a single intuitive act.

THE DESTRUCTION OF THOUGHT

In a philosophy such as this, thought proceeds to its own destruction. We find ourselves enmeshed in the hopeless snarl of advancing reasons why reason is incompetent. If the One is beyond all thought it is beyond the thought that it is beyond all thought. And it is beyond this thought as well, and also the thought that this is so. To this there is no end—not even the fact that there is no end. If we are to avoid this drop into the abyss of the meaningless we must stand firm on the recognition that we cannot give an intelligible account of that which is absolutely unintelligible, for then its unintelligibility would be intelligible and it would not be absolutely unintelligible.

Even if we carry our pantheism only so far as to say that the Real is one and absolute and yet affirm that its unity and absoluteness are intelligible, we still meet difficulties. For example, Spinoza's "third kind of knowledge" is an intuitive grasp of the one Substance in its unity, and so carries us beyond the level of discursive thinking. But Spinoza attempts to preserve its rationality. It is, he thinks, the fulfilment of reason, the completion of that of which ordinary reasoning is a limited and special form. According to this interpretation the world of plurality and change is destined to be understood as illusion, so far as it is viewed in its plurality and separateness. But this cannot stand when we consider it in the light of Spinoza's doctrine of an all-inclusive necessity.

Let us consider for a moment the consequences of admitting, in the context of a philosophy such as Spinoza's, that illusions do occur.[13] If the illusion is an actual occurrence then it must have its place in God, which is the all-inclusive reality. But in so far as we understand it in God, that is in its true nature, then it is no longer illusion in the sense of error. On the level of ordinary perception, if we may use this as an analogy, a straight stick partly submerged in water appears bent. If I judge that the stick is really bent then my judgment is erroneous. But if I understand something of the principles of light refraction and see how those principles apply to this situation then I can understand why a stick which is actually straight must appear bent under these conditions. I recognize that it would be impossible for a stick really straight not to appear bent when partially submerged in water at this angle. So the illusion does not lead me into an erroneous judgment. Thus it is with him who thinks that men and trees and mountains and rivers and all the other things which seem to make up the actual world, really exist. These things appear separate and independent and to be in some sense things which exist by themselves; and this appearance is false, according to Spinoza. But he who understands that these things are not substances but are only modes of the one Substance is no longer deceived, and his judgment is not in error on this point.

But what of the person who does not understand the true situation? Shall we say, as Spinoza surely would say, that if *we* understand all the conditions involved in that person's failure to understand then we should see how it is necessary that he fails to understand? And if we fail to see this? Then of course we fail because we have to fail. Our failure is a function of all the conditions which, taken together in their true unity, are the one Substance. So illusion turns out to be not illusion at all; and error turns out to be impossible. What we call "illusion" and "error" are but aspects of the real unity which is Spinoza's God. So nothing can be said significantly of any appearance or of any finite mode of existence except that it is God, and the world of nature collapses into nothingness so far as any distinction between it and God is concerned. But so does our awareness of this, and our attempts to assert that this is the case.

THE DILEMMA OF PANTHEISM

Every philosophy claims to be true, and its claim is asserted against opposing philosophies. But if the opposing philosophies are inevitable, and they must be for a philosophy which asserts universal necessity, they are modes of thought which have to occur as they do under the conditions which generated them. Under those conditions they could be no other than what they are. If this is the case then those supposedly opposing philosophies are in truth but exemplifications of the very philosophy which they oppose. It is in this way that Hegel, whose pantheism is more elaborately developed than Spinoza's, explained the existence of philosophies other than his own and apparently opposed to his. Each philosophy, even in its opposition to truth, discloses some truth. So its opposition is not the ultimate thing about it. When we reach this point, however, we cannot stop. Every thought occurs by necessity, and even he who denies this denies it with an inexorable necessity. Our thinking then is simply the expression of the inevitable. The issue raised by pantheism comes to this: either all so-called error is hidden truth, or else error is possible; on the first alternative, all meaning collapses into the absolute unity of the one Real, and so is unutterable; on the second alternative, Reality is not an all-inclusive One.

The practicing pantheist tries to avoid this difficulty, but his attempt involves him in inconsistency. When the question is raised as to how we can account for the fact that there are unreal appearances, the pantheist (and this applies particularly to those who have been influenced by neo-Platonism) excludes them from God. He relegates appearances to a realm of non-being which somehow stands over against the one true Being. This results in a strong dualistic tendency, a tendency to ascribe to non-being some kind of positive actuality. The world is described as an emanation of God, the over-flow of Being into non-being, which shows itself in an infinite series of degrees of falling away from Being. But once we admit degrees of being we shatter pantheism's primary principle of the all-inclusive unity of Being. The proposition, "Outside God nothing is," becomes, "Outside God there is something which we call 'nothing.'" If the pantheist should reply that he admits no degrees of being but only degrees of non-being, his reply would be only a rephrasing of the position we have to reject. Either the lower grades of being are real in their distinction from God or they are sheer illusion which can have no being even as illusion. If the first is the case, then the One gives way to the many; if the second, then even the occurrence of illusion cannot actually happen. From all this we must draw the important conclusion that being can be mixed with non-being only if there are more beings than one.

MONISM'S FALLACY

Pantheism, absolute idealism (such as the philosophy of Hegel), in fact any kind of genuine and thorough-going monism—all these result from a basic logical error. It is because pantheism is based on a fundamental misunderstanding of the nature of thought and the relation of thought to its objects that it involves itself in so serious a logical tangle. Furthermore, we can find here also the explanation of the fact that pantheism breaks into two different and conflicting doctrines, the version which absorbs the world into God and the version which absorbs God into the world.

Like any kind of thinking, the thinking which leads to pantheism must employ logical operations and forms. The basic confusion of the pantheist's thinking is his radical misunderstanding of the logical relations which must be employed in any act of thinking. To be specific, the basic and fatal confusion in the pantheist's thinking is to be found in his distinctive doctrine that God and the world are identical. Any attempt to identify God and the world is bound to fail just so far as it recognizes the slightest distinction between the world as such and God as such; for any distinction whatever is enough to destroy the identity. On the other hand, if there is no distinction then we do not have two things to identify with each other, and so again the basic pantheistic doctrine fails.

The source of the difficulty is the pantheist's failure to understand that *no two real beings are or can be identical*. The reason for his failure to understand this is his failure to understand logic; for identity is a logical relation, not a relation among really existing things. Identity is found not in the relations of real things to one another but in the relation of our concepts to the things we think about.[14] Two real beings cannot be identical because in so far as they are two they are different, and so not the same. On the other hand, what is contained in a concept may be identical with the nature of the really existing thing to which the concept refers, for in this case the identity is not the identity of the concept *as a real being* with the existing thing.

My concept of man, for example, is not itself a man; it is a concept, and it exists as an idea. But my concept of man may refer to a real being, i.e., to a really existing man. When I say, "This man is wise," my statement, if true, refers to a real man and attributes to him a character which belongs to his real nature. That we can do this is possible only because we can differentiate in our thinking between *what* something is and the fact *that* it is, between the nature of a thing as the nature of this or that kind of thing, without considering its existence or non-existence, and that same nature as actually existent in this particular thing. We can assert in a logical proposition that this nature (the character of being wise) which we have separated in thought from the real thing is identical with the nature which does exist in the real thing. We can do this because we are not trying to identify two real existences. When I say, "This man is wise," I do not mean, "This man is the concept of wisdom"; nor do I mean that there are two real things, *this man* and *wisdom as such* (or some supposed state of *being wise*), which are identical. This man is not wisdom, for there are other men, in addition to him, who also are wise. What I do mean when I say, "This man is wise," is that the content of the concept *wise*, that is, what I think when I think of something as being wise, is of the very nature of this actually existing man.

There is a parallel between this and the identity which a photograph has with its subject. I have here a picture of a man, but the picture is not the man nor is the man the picture. As real beings they are two distinct and very different things. The identity is not between the man and *what the picture is*; the identity is between the man and *what the picture shows*. What is the picture?

238

It is a piece of paper which has been treated with certain chemicals. The man, on the other hand, is a living, thinking, acting organism and person. He has a certain appearance of facial features, and the picture *shows* something of *what* these features are. But the features which the picture *shows* are not the features of the chemically processed paper which the picture *is;* they are the features of the man himself.

We can use identity as a logical relation for the reason that in an assertion, or in any employment of concepts in judgment, the being or existence of the concept is not a factor in the judgment itself (except, of course, in those cases in which we think or judge concerning concepts; and even here the concept as employed is not the concept as judged). The identity of a logical judgment is the fact that the nature I think is the nature which actually exists in this instance. "This man is wise," is a true judgment in so far as the really existing nature of the man is the same nature I think in the concept *wise.* The character of *being wise*, which I think in my concept, is the very same character of *being wise* which exists in "this man."

When we consider the world in its manifold differences and in the apparent plurality of existences which compose it, we can think these as constituting a unity of some kind. But when we express this in the statement, "The real world in all its variety and difference is one," the identity which is present here is the identity of the content of the concept of *one* and of *the really existing nature of the world.* In other words, we think the real world in terms of the concept of *unity.* We cannot make logical sense out of this statement if we take it to mean that we have *the real world,* on the one hand, and *a really existing unity,* on the other hand, and that these two real beings are one being. But this is precisely what pantheism attempts to do.

The same difficulty arises no matter whether we begin with God or with the world. When we say, "God is the world," we think *the world* in concept and attribute its content to the real being we call "God." When we say, "The world is God," we think *God* in concept and attribute the content of that concept to the real being we call "the world." Either way we go we can find logical sense in our statement only if we recognize that the identity we assert is logical identity and not an identity of real beings, and that we use this relation of logical identity because its use is what enables us to refer to the very nature of the thing we think or speak about. Our judgment is not *about* a relation of identity; rather, it is the use of identity in our judgment which enables us to make judgments *about* the thing itself. The error of the pantheist is his notion that he is thinking about a relation of identity when he thinks about the relation of God and the world. The fact is that we think *with* the relation of identity; that is we think *by means of it,* when we think about things. When we think *about* the relation of identity we are thinking about thinking, that is, about logic.

CHAPTER 15

Deism and Theism

"Rationalistic" Deism

Deism, in contrast to pantheism, denies the unity of God and the world. According to the deist, God brought the world into existence and established its nature and laws; but God and the world are not only distinct, they are separate. God completely transcends the world; He is not present in the world nor is anything in the world also in God. When we consider deism in terms of this bald statement it is plain that such a conception of God and the world can have little religious significance.

This judgment finds support in the fact that deism, in its fully explicit and acknowledged form, flared up briefly in the eighteenth century and then quickly died. This short burst of admittedly deistic thought left behind only the tacit assumptions of a pale and unreflective religious sentiment. Eighteenth century deism was the corpse of a living religion. Of this corpse only the skeleton survives, in the dry bones of polite lip-service paid to the forms and symbols of conventional religion.

> The doctrine of transcendence in its extreme form [says Mascall], results in the view that God has no real concern with the universe. He must presumably have created it, or it would not be here, but it would be ridiculous to suppose that he can have any present dealings with it. Historically this view was embodied in the Deism of the eighteenth century, to which it was particularly congenial. For, since it believed nature to be God's handiwork and therefore to manifest his character in the same way in which a sculptor or an author is made known to us in his works, it provided the basis for a sincere, if restrained and chilly, religious reverence,

while at the same time involving no untidy interference with the orderly course of natural law as expounded by Newton and his successors. . . . Whatever God might have done in the past when the world first came into being, his present relation to it is simply that of an artist to his work; . . . and the attitude to God which the contemplation of nature is expected to produce in us is presumably not unlike the attitude to Sir Christopher Wren that is induced by walking around St. Paul's Cathedral.[1] . . . A religion of unbalanced transcendence allows no place for intimate communion between man and God. In eighteenth-century Deism, worship becomes the orderly admiration by man of the divine perfection; there is more than a suggestion of the notion that worship is not so much something that man does for the glory of God as something that he does for his own good; it becomes what has been aptly called "the art of spiritual cosmetics."[2]

The doctrines of eighteenth century deism are few and simple, and they set deism off in direct opposition to pantheism, both as a conception of God and the world and as a basis of religious practice. On its face, deism is an abstractly rationalistic natural religion. It purports to infer the existence of God from nature, and it is composed of three basic doctrines: the doctrine that God is the maker of the world; the doctrine of providence, that God exercises a benevolent management of the world in which He makes specific adjustments when things go wrong; and the doctrine of immortality, in which each man receives the reward or punishment he has earned by his moral conduct on earth.

In its doctrine that God is the maker of the world, deism maintains a sharp separation of God from the world. The deist thinks of God on the analogy of an artisan who designs and fabricates a machine. In the doctrine of providence God is the repairman who puts things right when the machine breaks down. In the doctrine of immortality, God is the record-keeper and the distributor of the rewards and punishments which the record calls for. The chief significance of the doctrine of immortality is that it provides opportunity to insure the just distribution of rewards and punishments, in proportion to merit and offense. Since things do not come out even on earth, since the good on earth often suffer and the evil prosper, there must be an after life in which the score is evened and the books are brought into balance. For its assumption that such an after life is immortal, deism offers not the slightest justification; it gives no reason why, after the books are balanced, the account should not be closed. Finally, man's only relation to God which deism recognized is the worship of praise, which consists almost entirely of a recognition of the authority of God, and the acts of prayer in which man petitions for the redress of wrongs and to be forgiven the debt of punishment he has incurred by his sin.

Dryden, in his *Religio Laici,* describes these basic doctrines of deism and manages to include in his brief description a summary of the rationalizations, or pseudo-reasonings, by which they are constructed. Although Dryden's account of deism is not sympathetic, neither is it malicious. He formulates it in preparation for his criticism; and although his statement is short and naked, it is fair. His characterization is worth quoting in full because it communicates so effectively not only the doctrine and arguments of deism but its mood as well.

> God is that spring of good, supreme and best,
> We made to serve, and in that service blest;
> If so, some rules of worship must be given,
> Distributed alike to all by Heaven;
> Else God were partial, and to some denied
> The means His justice should for all provide.
> This general worship is to PRAISE and PRAY;
> One part to borrow blessings, one to pay;
> And when frail nature slides into offence,
> The sacrifice for crime is penitence.
> Yet since the effects of Providence, we find,
> Are variously dispensed to human kind;
> That vice triumphs and virtue suffers here,
> (A brand that sovereign justice cannot bear:)
> Our Reason prompts us to a future state,
> The last appeal from Fortune and from Fate,
> Where God's all-righteous ways will be declared,
> The bad meet punishment, the good reward.[3]

A somewhat ironic characterization of deism is found in the summary by Principal Oman. Deism's three doctrines are, he says,

"(1) God as the creator or rather manufacturer of the world, and moral governor or rather Lord Chief Justice; (2) providence as a very skilful designer of a benevolent mind, who, the better he had done his work at the beginning, the less he had to interfere with it—all his dealings after creation being interference; (3) immortality as the necessary court of assize, of which a morality depending on reward and punishment stood very much in need, but by which it was only made less moral."[4]

It is easy to see how Gilson can call deism "one of the most delectable objects of contemplation for the connoisseurs of human silliness."[5] For the religion based on such a conception surely deserves no serious consideration, and a philosophy of religion in support of this version of deism would not be worth writing. The significance of such a philosophy of religion would differ only in degree from, let us say, that of a "philosophy" of the designing, manufacture, and upkeep of motor cars.

If we ask what led men to such a preposterous conception of God and the world we may find that the answer lies in no special religious impulse. It was rather a short and quick flight away from religion. It was the expression, appropriate to its age, of modern man's growing illusion of self-sufficiency. At the same time it promised to remove the supposed obstacles which religion seemed to place in the way of the advancing scientific conception of nature. To those who could not bring themselves to deny outright all the basic beliefs of theistic religion, deism seemed to provide an opportunity to affirm some of the more fundamental of these in such manner that they would not interfere with other concerns. Unfortunately, however, "God" and "providence" and "immortality" lose their meaning when deism takes them over from theism. When taken out of their proper context they are as worthless as the contents of a stolen checkbook.

ANTI-RATIONALISTIC DEISM

If this were the whole story of deism our present purposes would be better served by its omission. Unfortunately not all deism is recognized for what it is. There have been, and there are today, concepts of God and of the relation of God and the world which reflect the primary characteristiç of deism. That is to say, they are views which separate the world from God. The chief difference between these unacknowledged versions of deism and the deism of the eighteenth century is that these do not pretend to be rationalistic. On the contrary, they are explicitly and emphatically anti-rational.

Yet this apparent difference is less real than it seems, for the "rationalism" of deism proper was no true work of reason. It was an artificial scheme produced by somewhat the same kind of thinking that constructs legal fictions, that rationalizes myths, and that builds stick-and-ball models of atoms and molecules. The effect of such schemes is not to disclose rational connections but to remove the need for further thought. So although outwardly rationalistic, the deism of the eighteenth century was as different from the proper work of reason as is the most outspoken anti-rationalism. The only plausible explanation for such a deception is the philosophical innocence and superficiality of the age which produced it.

There is, however, a tacit deism which is one of the strong contemporary influences in religious thought. It has some important similarities with religious ideas which appeared, under the influence of extreme nominalism,[6] during the last part of the medieval period. This current version of deism emphasizes the absolute transcendence, or "otherness," of God. It establishes religion upon a principle of radical irrationality, and demands a kind of faith which has no living contact with knowledge or with reason. It contends that we who belong to the world are, by that fact, cut off from God. Our nature is utterly different from God's, and God is utterly beyond us. Neither by act nor by thought can we reach Him. Man and God can come together only by the act of God, and that act is completely and absolutely arbitrary.

The religious significance of such a view of God and the world is well expressed by a contemporary theologian. "Deity thus becomes synonymous with sheer mystery, with the unknowable and 'numinous,' from which every recognizable feature has been systematically erased; and quite apart from the purely theoretical aspects of the problem, it is surely obvious that so far as its practical issues are concerned, any such standpoint completely destroys the foundation of all the highest forms of religion, and thereby reduces them to the level of irrational savagery."[7]

Such religion can have no philosophy, for it can neither appeal to reason nor provide justification for what it asserts. You believe or you do not. *What* you believe makes no sense; *that* you believe makes no sense; the illusion that your belief does make sense is but the manifestation of sinful human pride. So even if deism in this version were true, whatever "true" may mean in such a context, it is a concept of God for which a philosophy of religion can have no concern. Its devotees are wisely advised to flee from philosophy, and from all human pretensions to knowledge. Only a dogmatic theology which has severed its connections with human thought and has reduced itself to a series or oracular pronouncements can speak of such a God. Since what it does say when it speaks can make no rational sense, we must suppose that its language is the language of a mystery cult, and that only the initiated can know its esoteric meaning.

It is no insult to say that this variety of deism is absurd, for it prides itself upon its absurdity. In this it is like its forerunners, the extravagant anti-rationalism and nominalism which grew from the ruins of medieval thought and which found truth in contradiction and looked upon reason as evil. Reason was sacrificed to will; God was nothing but will, and all that counted in man was will. The essence of truth was its arbitrariness. In such a view God is not only unknowable, He is unthinkable.[8]

Out of this came such fruits as positivism and relativism; and it is significant that some contemporary versions of tacit deism support the same tendencies. Political states become corrupt, the inverted religion of communism threatens civilization and society; but none of this concerns those contemporary deists who have nothing to say except to talk again of the absolute otherness of God and to commend the utter absurdity of their faith as the mark of its truth. Our concern for human affairs, they tell us, is but the Devil tempting us to use our knowledge and our rational powers instead of abandoning ourselves to blind and arbitrary and senseless faith.

We shall now dismiss from our discussion both pantheism and deism. In all their varieties they either are demonstrably false or else their possible truth provides nothing of significance for a philosophy of religion. Pantheism's basic tenet is the consequence of logical confusion. In its concept of God it is either a variety of naturalism or, at its higher levels, it passes into mysticism. In so far as the God of mysticism is of interest to rational inquiry it is because of what it has in common with the God of theism. Deism, in its explicit form, is silly and trivial; in its tacit versions it is the shameless embrace of anti-rationalism and absurdity. Of all the views we have thus far considered we are left only atheistic naturalism; and against it stands only theism. The issue of the existence of God lies between these two. Before we face that issue we have only to consider briefly the theistic conception of God. Our concern at this point is not so much to understand it in its full nature as to differentiate it from pantheism and deism and to determine its true relation to these other conceptions of God.

The Relation of Theism to Pantheism and Deism

One way to approach the theistic idea of God is to compare it with pantheism and deism. Pantheism affirms the immanence of God in the world and denies that God and the world are distinct. Deism affirms the transcendence of God and denies God's immanence. Theism accepts the affirmations of both theism and deism, and in this of course rejects their denials.

> For theism [says Warren Nelson Nevius], God is an infinite spiritual Being, personal in the fullest sense of the word, and he is at once the First Cause and the immanent principle by which the universe is sustained. . . . God is immanent, but he is also transcendent. He is transcendent, but not apart from his immanence. . . . It is he

who upholds all things "by the word of his power." He is within the processes of nature, himself their directing and activating force. But he is also transcendent, a Being not limited by his universe.[9]

For pantheism, man and nature are swallowed up in God; for deism, man and nature are excluded from God; for theism, God enters into what He has made to exist. The problem of the relation of God and the world is not, for theism, the question of transcendence *versus* immanence; it is rather the problem of understanding how God can be both transcendent and immanent.

Theism is sometimes described as a compromise of pantheism and deism, or as an intermediate view which lies between the extremes of the other two. But theism cannot be a compromise of pantheism and deism, for each of the two is the negation of the other. Theism is, it is true, a third alternative; but it is not a compromise. It purports to bring together what, in both pantheism and deism, are directly opposed to each other; and it can do this only if it finds new ground on which to stand. For the same reason we cannot consider theism a middle point of a line joining the extremes of pantheism and deism. For there are no quantitative gradations between the two. Theism involves a different basic conception; it is no mere additional variation upon an old theme.

Pantheism and deism both are products of the kind of thinking which finds itself compelled to decide whether God and the world are the same or whether they are different. These two alternatives are exhaustive for such thinking; there is no third possibility, for to say that God and the world are both the same and different is to say that they are both the same and not the same. It is of no help to qualify "same" and "different" and to speak of "same in some respects" and "different in other respects." For the issue arises again, at each level of such differentiation. In this kind of thinking, the respects in which two things are the same are respects in which they are absolutely the same, and the respects in which they are different are respects in which they are absolutely different. When the problem is understood in these terms one or the other of the alternative conceptions must be

chosen. The only way to find a further alternative is to understand the problem in other terms.

The kind of thinking which finds itself caught between pantheism and deism can be described and analyzed from several different approaches. We may, perhaps, best approach it by saying
that it is the kind of thinking which confuses abstractions and
real existence. We note, for example, that certain things are alike
in certain respects and we form the idea of a class to which these
things belong. Such a class may be a natural species, as in plant
or animal life, or it may be a classification based on some single
common character. Then we form ideas of still more general
classes, and this continues until we think we reach the class of
all that is, or the class of being-in-general. From this point it is
but a step to the inference that *being-in-general* exists somehow
as *a real being* in its own right, and that the real existence of anything else is simply the extent to which it has within itself this
being-in-general. From this comes the pantheistic conception that
all being is one and that all that is is one being. The difficulty, of
course, is that there is no such real entity as being-in-general.

In technical terms we may say that pantheism is the result of
treating the concept of being as a "univocal concept." That is, we
assume that "being" means precisely the same in every instance
to which it may be applied. On this view anything which has
being has precisely the same kind of being, and has being in precisely the same sense, as anything else which has being. It is no
wonder that this line of thought cannot avoid the conclusion that,
so far as their being is concerned (and of course in every other
respect they simply would not be), all things are the same and
there is only one being.

Deism, in contrast with theism but employing essentially the
same kind of thinking, insists upon the complete separation of
God and the world. Deism also asserts that they both exist. But
since they are separate, and since one is in no respect what the
other is, deism is forced—wherever it carries its theme far enough
—to assert that "being" has utterly different meanings in its reference to the existence of God and in its reference to the existence

of the world. Thus, for deism, the concept of being is what we call an "equivocal concept." The *being* of God and the *being* of the world have no more to do with each other than the *lock* of a door has to do with a *lock* of hair. This is why, when deism abandons the artificial rationalism of its eighteenth century version, the separation of God and the world is made so complete that whatever relation they may have is a logical absurdity. For this doctrine is the product of a logic in which distinction can mean only absolute separation and absolute otherness, and which has no stopping point short of absolute skepticism. Concepts, in pantheistic and deistic thinking, are either univocal or equivocal. Sameness is absolute sameness, and difference is absolute difference. So the assertion of any sameness is the assertion of absolute sameness, and the assertion of any difference is the assertion of absolute difference.

Theism did not wait to come into existence as a conception of God until this logical problem was solved. The origin of theism was religious, not logical or philosophical. It was in man's religious experience that he felt most strongly the need to affirm both the immediate presence and the transcendence of God. All that is most profound and irresistible in religious experience testified to the presence of God in man, in nature, and in history. But this same God which is present in the world is not a part of the world. He is a God infinitely beyond man and the world. Only thus could the God which man finds present to himself be also the God of his worship and adoration.

Theism as a religious attitude may be affirmed in spite of all the difficulties which are encountered in the attempt to understand how it can be that God is both immanent and transcendent. For many a man the overwhelming personal assurance that this is so is sufficient. Many neither can nor desire to understand. Yet there are others whose desire to understand increases as they feel increasingly the tremendous import of such a conception of the relation of God and the world. The means by which an understanding of this may be approached is the recognition that we are not confined to univocal and equivocal concepts, but that there is a third manner of thought which is based on *the analogy of being*.

THEISM AND THE ANALOGY OF BEING

Theism becomes accessible to thought when we see that we are not confined to the disjunction between *no difference*, on one hand, and *nothing but difference* on the other. Things can be understood as both alike and different when we find their similarity to be a similarity of relationship. This requires us to understand properly the function of our own minds in the processes of knowing, and particularly their ability to abstract in thought the forms and relations which hold good of things and to think these as universals. Two things thus may be thought in terms of the same essence, because the essence of the one thing *as abstracted and held in thought* is the very same as the essences of the other thing *as it is abstracted and held in thought*. It is because thought can thus abstract, and in abstracting form universal concepts, that the awareness of things is possible. Because in thought we can hold essence apart from existence, and in judgment re-unite them, we can think about the relation of the essence of a thing to its existence. When we speak of the analogy of being we mean that although each individual real thing has the existence which is appropriate to its essence (or nature), and which is specifically the existence of just that essence and of no other, yet the *relation* between the essence (or *what* it is) and the existence (or the fact *that* it is) of one real thing is similar to the relation between the essence and the existence of another real thing.

The pen I hold in my hand has a certain nature. I could describe its shape, color, functions, relations to other things including spatial and temporal relations, and so on. This set of characteristics in this combination is peculiar to a pen, and not only to *a* pen but, if we make our description complete enough, to *this* pen. The difference between this pen and an imaginary pen with just the same set of characteristics is the fact that the properties and qualities of this pen have actual existence. But the *existence* of this pen is not an *additional property*, nor is it something completely cut off from this pen's real nature. The existence of this pen is not the addition of being-in-general to other properties, nor is the real pen a mysterious, hidden x to which the supposedly known properties cannot actually belong: a thing-in-itself which is unknown and unknowable. The case is rather that the existence of this pen is the kind of existence which is appropriate to its own real nature. Of course the nature of an imaginary pen may also be one to which an existence would be appropriate, but no real causes have operated to bring its nature into actual existence as there have in the case of my real pen. The real pen exists as a pen exists, not as a dog exists nor as a rose exists nor as a man exists. But just as this pen exists in the pen's way of existing so does a man exist in a man's way of existing. In this respect the pen's existence and the man's existence are similar; the essence of the pen is related to the existence of the pen as the essence of the man is related to the existence of the man.

The concept of analogy is a difficult one, but it is so important that the attempt to understand it is well worth the effort. We shall not attempt to provide at this point an adequate explanation of analogy, for this belongs to our discussion of the nature of God.[10] But it is important here to recognize that there is this additional alternative way of thinking, and to have some general idea of what the difference is, for it is in terms of analogy that some small degree of rational understanding of the theistic concept of God has been secured. If this way of thinking is sound we have this hope: that no matter how far removed is the nature of God from our own nature, yet in so far as we have some understanding of how our own nature is related to its existence we have also some awareness of how the nature of God is related to God's existence. We can think God in analogy with ourselves and the world, and our thinking will not be entirely futile. With this basis it makes rational sense to attribute to God the attributes which religious experience has used in its attempt to express the nature of God; and this is something which cannot make sense if we must confine our thinking to univocal concepts at the risk of falling into equivocation.

The great benefit of this mode of thinking is that it enables us to come much closer to a rational and intelligible account of the God of the highest and deepest religious faith. We have in analogy a certain justification for our religious impulse to attribute to God not only absolute being but also such attributes as wisdom, holiness, goodness, power, and truth by virtue of which we conceive the God of religion to be a living God. We have by this approach some justification for thinking of God as both the creative source of all other being and also its ultimate good and goal. We can understand something of how man has his being in God, and yet how it is truly man's own being (and not God's being) which man has in God—how man has his own being and not some mere illusory shadow of God's being. We can begin to understand how finite existence can have its source in infinite being; and we can understand something of how there can be suffering and evil in a world created by omnipotent goodness.

It is in theism that the concept of God comes alive, that rational thought can echo something of what religion finds God to be. It is in theism that the ultimates of existence and value are more than mere abstractions. It is in theism that religious thought can, for the first time, advance beyond myth and symbol and make rational contact with the objects of religion. No philosophical theism, however, can do justice to the objects of faith. It is true only so far as it can go, and it cannot go far. Yet it can go far enough to underwrite faith's affirmation that Goodness and Truth are one Being.

THE OPPOSITION OF THEISM AND NATURALISM

As we have already said, the issue now lies between atheistic naturalism and theism. Pantheism is either an inadequate theism, or else it is naturalism disguised by a name. Deism at best is but a distorted and grotesque shadow of theism; it is a rationalizing attempt to avoid theism, and at the same time to lull intelligence to sleep, by appearing to eject God from the world. The important issue is between naturalism and theism, and it is the issue between an ultimate reality which is an IT IS and an ultimate reality which is an I AM. This is a difference of great import, for on it hinges not only our destiny but the significance of our very existence from day to day.

Theism, however, is no bare denial of naturalism. When the theist denies what the naturalist asserts, when he overlooks the evidence for naturalism's positive concept, he weakens his case for theism. For he denies that there is a real natural order with an existence of its own and acting in accord with its own laws. But, as we shall see later, when the naturalist denies the distinctive positive principle of the theist he turns every fact into a miracle and brings into question the real existence of nature itself; or, at best, he finds himself committed to an ultimate reality the existence of which is an ultimate irrationality. Naturalism opposes theism by means of its negations, but theism opposes naturalism by means of its affirmations. We shall find our evidence for theism's affirmations in that very world of nature which naturalism and theism both call the real world.

A theism which asserts the existence of the world of nature may be called *realistic theism*. We shall find in realistic theism something more than merely a plausible framework for religion. It is itself a philosophy, a philosophy which has its roots in the most elemental facts of existence and knowledge. It does as full justice to religion as philosophy can do, but its claim to significance does not rest on this alone; it rests rather on its merits as philosophy. The adequacy of a philosophy of religion is its adequacy as a philosophy. To appreciate the strength of the case for theism as a philosophy it is necessary to think about God, in philosophical terms, more carefully and more persistently than has been the usual practice in recent philosophy. The neglect of theism in technical philosophy is not surprising when we see how little effort is made there even to try to understand what men have meant, in their serious and responsible thinking, by "God." How can a thinker evaluate the case for theism if his own idea of God is only an echo of the dark and weird fantasies of infancy's first gropings in its twisting and squirming world, or if it is but a synthesis of the tag-ends of childhood impressions dressed up in the garb of a technical vocabulary?

Part Six

THE EXISTENCE OF GOD

CHAPTER 16

Proof in Philosophy

A Look Ahead

E NOW begin our account of the journey of the human
intellect to God. It is a long and hazardous road, with
many false starts, wrong turns, and blind alleys. Some
of these we must explore, in order to see which ways not to go.
Thus we shall examine the attempt to go from the idea of God
to the existence of God, and then we shall look at the attempt to
go from the existence of the idea of God to the existence of God.
From our inspection of these false starts we shall learn how to
recognize the right one (Chapter 17). The road which takes us
to our destination is the one which begins with the real existence of the world, and leads from that starting place to the existence of God. We shall construct a logical map of the course
to follow (Chapter 17), but before we set out on the actual
journey we must first test our starting place and justify our confidence that there is a real world from which our thought can
start. This will require an examination of the attempts to deny
the existence of the world (Chapter 18).

It has long been the fashion in some quarters in philosophy to
regard lightly the attempts to prove the existence of God. The
proofs are often merely waved away as unworthy of serious consideration. This attitude, however, is by no means characteristic
of philosophers as such. It is found mainly among those whose
thinking has been influenced by one or more of the now old-fash-
ioned varieties of irrationalism. If the experience of philosophers
themselves has any bearing on the matter it seems to support the
observation that, in general, those who accept the rule of reason

find their thought bound by some of the rational arguments for the existence of God.

Thus there has grown up a division among philosophers concerning this matter. The ones who distrust or repudiate the intellect give no evidence of a willingness to think through these demonstrations with patient attention to the whole range of issues involved in them. Those who think it possible to prove the existence of God are too often content merely to repeat the standard formulas and see no occasion to carry the statement of the proofs back to basic principles. For they are already pretty well agreed among themselves on the soundness of some at least of the traditional arguments. So there is a failure of minds to meet. One side takes very much for granted what the other side denies. As a result the student who is looking for light on the problem often gets the impression that the issue is a matter to be decided by the relative prestige of the opposing parties, or by the smartness or cleverness of a writer's manner.

The nihilist knows that he can attract—or, more accurately, that until recently he could attract—more followers, and more quickly acquire a reputation, by making fun of his opponents than by a serious examination of their case. The rational theist seems too often to feel it is hopeless to try to get a hearing from the nihilist or atheist, so, with a few harsh observations concerning their gullibility or prejudice, he gives up trying to convince his opponents and writes for those who already share his basic position. Consequently, he starts in the middle, not at the beginning, for there is little point in repeating what he and his readers already agree to. The present discussion of the problem of the existence of God is written in the belief that the rational arguments need to be restated, from the ground up, for the benefit primarily of those who are seeking a solution of the problem and not for those whose minds are already made up.

The intellect's case for the existence of God, once it is examined, is amazingly strong. Indeed, it can now be sneered out of consideration only by those who are unaware that the entire cult of irrationalism is, in its turn, as we have just said, discredited as one kind of 19th century anti-intellectualism. To call the roll of those who have seen this would call up many of the giants in the history of philosophy. But the argument cannot be seen in its full strength, especially by those who are not familiar with its historical development, unless it is carried back to its foundations. This is what we now propose to do.

Since for some time now we shall be concerned with attempts to demonstrate the existence of God it will be well to consider carefully just what a *proof* is. We need to understand what we can justifiably claim for a proof, and we need to understand also what lies beyond its reach. We must have some idea of the difference between sound and unsound proof, and although we cannot here explore the field of logic we can formulate the outline of a demonstration so that its logical cogency is plain.

The Nature of Proof

In our earlier discussion of the idea of God we narrowed down the alternatives to atheistic naturalism and theism. The issue between these two views can be resolved in one of three ways. We may prove that God exists, we may prove that God does not exist, or we may establish a genuine skepticism by proof that neither of these other proofs is possible. The first and second of these ways of solving the problem are in opposition to each other, and each of these is in opposition to the third; so the three are mutually exclusive.

These three alternatives are also exhaustive, so far as any genuine solution of the problem is concerned; for the issue here is between the true and the false, not merely between belief and disbelief. Of course there are other attitudes which we may take toward the matter. We may consider that all attempted proofs are so far unsuccessful, without ruling out the possibility of other proofs as yet unknown. This would be an attitude of *agnosticism.* Or we may refuse to deal with the matter on the basis of knowledge, and treat it solely as a matter of faith (*fideism*), or even as a matter of taste or preference (*estheticism*). We may affirm or deny arbitrarily and without reason (*irrationalism*, including some versions of *existentialism*), we may limit the meaning of "knowledge" by arbitrary definition (*positivism*), or we may simply ignore the question (*indifferentism*). It is obvious that none of these approaches provides a rational solution of the problem; and so, if such a solution is to be had at this stage of our knowledge it will involve *proof*. Any disposal of the problem which does not solve it by means of proof is at best a temporary settlement, not a solution.

For this reason we must consider what is and what is not proof, and turn our attention briefly to some of the conditions which genuine proof must satisfy. There is much confusion concerning this, and sometimes it leads to preposterous demands. Some insist that a proof of the existence of God shall have a finality and certainty they require of nothing else. In this area of thought, and in this alone, they insist that soundness of proof is equivalent to absolute certainty. This is an unwarranted demand upon proof, a demand never justified with respect to other areas of thought which directly concern existence and fact. These people may be willing to send a man to the electric chair if there is a degree of evidence which excludes *reasonable* doubt, but they refuse to consider seriously the evidence for the existence of God unless it excludes *all possible* doubt.

There are others who judge the soundness of a proof by its success in convincing them that its conclusion is true. Yet it is plain that an argument may be sound without being convincing to all who attempt to follow it; some may not understand that particular argument, and others may not understand what an argument, as such, is and what it tries to do. On the other hand, an argument may be convincing and yet unsound, else logical fallacies would not occur in our thinking. One of the reasons for the discussion of proof at this point is to help the reader judge the force of the arguments in accordance with their logical and evidential value.

Proof is first of all an intellectual operation. To prove the truth of a statement we offer reasons in the form of factual evidence or premises, and then we show that our statement is so related logically to these reasons that if they are true it is true. *Their* truth carries *its* truth with them. Logical proof, as such, is the exhibition of the logical relations between reasons and conclusion so as to show that the assertion of the reasons together with the denial of the conclusion involves us in an inconsistency. To establish the truth of a conclusion by proof, then, requires the satisfaction of two conditions: (1) The premises, or statements of reasons, must be true, and (2) the conclusion must follow by logical necessity from its premises.

These two conditions reveal the strength and the limitation of proof. Its strength lies in the finality with which we can judge the logical relations of premises and their conclusions. Formal logic provides us with tests to apply to assertions of such logical relations, and our tests are conclusive in so far as we apply them properly. The limitation of proof is in the fact that no single proof can establish the truth of its own premises. If we are to prove that they are true we must construct an additional proof for each premise, in which the premise of the first proof now becomes the conclusion of another proof. This, in turn, requires more premises, and if we are to prove them true we must show that each follows as the conclusion of still another set of premises.

It is clear from this that we cannot show the truth of any statement merely by showing that it is a valid conclusion. For, as we shall see, a conclusion may be valid but not true. It is valid if it follows logically from its premises, but to know it is true we must know also that its premises are true. In so far as we consider proof in an exclusively formal sense, as an abstract logical relation between premises and conclusion, we shall be faced with this difficulty. For if formal proof has to precede knowledge then we can never capture a set of premises which are known to be true; the truth of each will always depend in the truth of *its* premises, and so on without end.

So unless we have some knowledge to begin with proof is useless, in so far as any contribution to our knowledge of real existence is concerned. The net effect of proof is to lift the conclusion to the same level of knowledge as the premises. Proof goes from the better known to the lesser known, when it is used to extend our knowledge, and its effect is to transfer to the conclusion—or what before the proof was the lesser known—all the assurance of truth possessed by the premises. If we do not already have some knowledge, there is nothing for proof to transfer.

If the premises of a logically valid argument are false, proof gives us no help in showing whether the conclusion is true or false. A conclusion may be true, as in the argument: "All horses are rational, and all men are horses, therefore all men are rational." Or it may be false, as in the argument: "All horses are divine, and all men are horses, therefore all men are divine." Both arguments are *valid*, by which we mean that *if* the premises *were true* the conclusion *would have to be true*. But in neither case here is the condition satisfied, the condition, namely, that the premises be true. If any one premise is false the conclusion may be either true or false in spite of the logical validity of the argument.

If the conclusion of a valid argument is false then we know that one at least of the premises is false, and possibly both. This is plain from the fact that if the premises are true the conclusion must be true. When we discover that a conclusion is false we know that the condition which guarantees the truth of the conclusion of a valid argument has not been met. In the argument, "All liquid is boiling hot, and all water is liquid, therefore all water is boiling hot," the falsity of the conclusion requires that at least one premise be false. For the argument is valid, and if the premises were both true the conclusion would have to be true. But suppose I argue, "Anything boiling is a liquid, and all water is liquid, therefore all water is boiling." Here we have a false conclusion together with true premises, and it may seem that our rule fails. The rule does not fail, however, for the argument is not logically valid. The parts of the argument are not in such relations with each other that if the premises are true the conclusion has to be true. If an argument in this form has true premises and a true conclusion it is only by accident or coincidence.

The import of logical proof with respect to its application to arguments concerning the existence of God should now be clear. If our proofs are correctly constructed, that is to say, if they meet the requirements of logic, then we shall have as great assurance of the truth of our conclusion as we have of the truth of our premises. Or, to state the matter differently, if we insist upon denying the conclusion we shall be required to deny the truth of at least one premise, and we shall have to accept all the logical consequences of that denial. If we find, for example, that to deny the existence of God requires us to deny the existence of the world, then if we are willing to accept the non-existence of the world in order to avoid accepting the existence of God we must regard the world as non-existent for all our purposes and in all our thought.

Our important task in this examination of the case for the existence of God is to consider the basic premises of the argument. If we are to demonstrate the existence of God we shall have to have true premises, and we need now to consider how we can obtain true premises without finding ourselves caught in an endless regression.

PHILOSOPHY AND ITS PREMISES

As we have already noted, the truth of a conclusion cannot be established by formal proof alone. Proof proceeds from its premises to its conclusions. If the premises are in question then either they must undergo proof or else their truth must be established in some other way. In the empirical sciences the final appeal, in the test of truth, is to sense perception. It is by this that the sciences make contact with real existence. Scientific data come from perception, and it is to perception that the scientist returns for verification of his hypotheses.

Philosophy cannot limit itself to sense perception, for the justification of such limitation would be itself a philosophical problem. On the other hand, the method of philosophy cannot be restricted to formal reasoning from premises to conclusion. The truth of the conclusion reached by such reasoning is not guaranteed by the validity of the reasoning process; in addition to valid reasoning we need true premises. Thus it is that the method of philosophy must include some way of obtaining premises which are true and some method of showing they are true. Philosophy does appeal to experience, not only to sense perception but to the whole range of human experience. But its interpretation of what is experienced requires more than experience itself; it requires the work of the intellect.

It is difficult to give an appropriate name to the method of philosophical inquiry without inviting misunderstanding. For one thing, the method of philosophy is itself a philosophical problem. Thus it is quite difficult to define philosophy in terms of a specific methodology. It seems safer to formulate our definition, as we have done earlier,[1] in broad and inclusive terms. Philosophy, we said there, is distinguished from other modes of inquiry in that it accepts no assumptions as inaccessible to examination. This means it accepts no assumptions which are not accessible to examination by its own methods, and this includes assumptions concerning method. This is philosophy's uniqueness, as well as the reason for its fundamental importance in human inquiry. Philosophy not only accepts no assumptions which are not open to examination by philosophy itself, but it is the only discipline which can concern itself with the examination and justification of its own assumptions. In all other kinds of inquiry, the basic assumptions of the inquiry itself are presumed to be true if the distinctive methods of that mode of inquiry are to be used at all. Since the methods of inquiry of other disciplines can be used only if the assumptions basic to those fields of inquiry are accepted, it is plain that the assumptions cannot be investigated by the very methods which presuppose them.

The sciences which use empirical observation, for example, could not very well observe unless they assumed that there is something to observe. I cannot set out to observe a specimen or to note the properties of a substance or to measure changes of weight unless I assume there is a specimen to observe or a substance with properties to note or that there is something weighable. If, for some reason, I come to think that the specimen I suppose I am observing does not exist, I either try to find out what it was that I was observing or else I must conclude that I was not observing at all.

When a historian investigates past events he assumes that there were past events and that some knowledge about them is now possible. The records of the past he assumes to be real. Although the historian is careful to establish the reliability of what he takes to be a record of the past, and so is not willing merely to assume that this or that is a dependable record, yet he does assume that there are records of the past. If he did not, he would not be studying and writing history; he would be engaged, perhaps, in the study of whether the study of history is possible, and this is a question of the philosophy of history or of metaphysics rather than of history itself. As with the sciences and history, so it is with theology. A theologian who did not believe that there was anything for theology to study would have chosen an odd way to spend his time.

This does not mean that the non-philosophical studies are never concerned with questions of existence; the point is rather that they can investigate a question of existence only by the study of other existence which is not in question or by checking against certain marks of existence which are taken for granted. The historian, for example, has his tests by which he judges the authenticity of a document. But he cannot use these tests unless he can assume the existence of the materials to which he applies his tests, and the tests would be meaningless unless he believed that past events had actually occurred. The existence of the planet Neptune was discovered in 1846 by Johann Galle of Berlin who looked for it at the place and time implied by the independent calculations of two other astronomers, U. J. J. Leverrier in France and John Couch Adams in England. In all this it was assumed that there was something in existence to account for observations of apparent irregularities in the motion of the planet Uranus. Basic to this was the assumption that whatever the heavens may contain they contain nothing which does not conform to the laws of motion and of gravitation.

When questions are raised about the existence of what the sciences assume to exist, those questions are philosophical and not scientific. For example, early in modern physics the real existence of such qualities as colors and sounds was attacked. It was argued that these qualities belong rather to the mind of the one who observes than to the real nature of the thing observed. Such was the contention of Galileo.

> Nevertheless I say, that indeed I feel myself impelled by the necessity, as soon as I conceive a piece of matter or corporeal substance, of conceiving that in its own nature it is bounded and figured in such and such a figure, that in relation to others it is large or small, that it is in this or that place, in this or that time, that it is in motion or remains at rest, that it touches or does not touch another body, that it is single, few, or many; in short by no imagination can a body be separated from such conditions: but that it must be white or red, bitter or sweet, sounding or mute, of a pleasant or unpleasant odour, I do not perceive my mind forced to acknowledge it necessarily accompanied by such conditions; so if the senses were not the escorts, perhaps the reason or the imagination by itself would never have arrived at them. Hence I think that those tastes, odours, colours, etc., on the side of the object in which they seem to exist, are nothing else than mere names, but hold their residence solely in the sensitive body; so that if the animal were removed, every such quality would be abolished and annihilated.[2]

Whatever may be the merits of this view, it is not science. It is a theory of what is real and what is not. The purpose of the theory is to provide a conception of real existence such that the results of scientific inquiry, by the methods Galileo used, would constitute genuine knowledge. Whether the theory of primary and secondary qualities is true or not is itself a problem which cannot be investigated by the methods of science. Galileo's own reason for accepting it is that "I do not perceive my mind forced to acknowledge it [i.e. a piece of matter or corporeal substance] necessarily accompanied by such conditions" [i.e., "white or red, bitter or sweet, sounding or mute, of a pleasant or unpleasant odour"]. Thus the justification offered is metaphysical and epistemological, not scientific. So far as his own scientific investigation is concerned, Galileo's doctrine of primary and secondary qualities is sheer assumption. Even the positivists and naturalists who define the real in terms of the results of scientific investigation cannot support the truth of this doctrine by scientific evidence. It is in this respect that philosophy differs from the sciences and from the other disciplines, in the fact that it and it alone can examine its own assumptions. When the primary assumptions of any other field of inquiry are examined, the problem no longer belongs to that field; the inquiry shifts to philosophy.

Whether electrons exist or not is a problem of physics. But if we are to ask whether physics gives us knowledge of the real world or is concerned only with the correlation of pointer-readings, the question is philosophical and physics is incompetent to provide an answer. The *physicist* may be competent, but only because he has competence in philosophy as well as in physics. His knowledge of physics may provide him with information essential for a competent consideration of the problem, but he cannot use the methods of physics in solving the problem. Likewise the problem of the causes of cancer is one for the medical sciences to solve, but no science can solve the problem of whether there are relations of cause and effect in reality.

Philosophy alone is in a position to examine its own assumptions, and thus to examine the truth of its premises, because philosophy is concerned with ultimates. Philosophy as an enterprise is synonymous with the intelligibility of all that is actual and possible, and this is itself the ultimate assumption of any inquiry whatever. For to deny intelligibility is to destroy the possibility of inquiry. Such a denial would render meaningless the very process by which it had been reached. It would, in fact, destroy its own meaning; for if nothing is intelligible then the fact that nothing is intelligible is not intelligible and the statement that nothing is intelligible is meaningless. This is one principle which cannot be successfully challenged: Whatever is presupposed by the possibility of knowledge cannot itself be meaningfully denied.

When we say that something is intelligible we mean, speaking loosely, that whatever it may be it makes sense. More precisely, to be intelligible means to be capable of being understood. This does not refer merely to what *is* understood or even to what *can be* understood by us or by any finite mind; it includes also what could be understood only by an infinite mind. Furthermore, when we speak here of what can be understood, we are not using the word "understand" to refer to a psychological clarification. To understand, as an intellectual act, means rather to apprehend or grasp the real nature of something; it is for the intellect to see into the real essence of something and to free itself from confusion and error concerning *what* the thing really is.

THE METHOD OF DIALECTIC

Philosophy must have a way to reach its ultimate principles, to justify its basic premises. Its method is to uncover hidden assumptions and to examine them in the light of their logical consequences. The traditional and appropriate name for this method of inquiry is *dialectic*. Unfortunately the term is sometimes used with other or more restricted meanings, but if we keep to the basic meaning it has had in the tradition of philosophy which began with Socrates and Plato we shall find it useful in distinguishing the method of philosophy from methods used in other fields of inquiry.

Wilbur Marshall Urban describes the three stages which are generally recognized as belonging to dialectic.

It consists in the first instance in developing the "underivable first principles" upon which an opinion or belief rests and forcing the one who holds them to acknowledge them explicitly. In this procedure the method of self refutation is the outstanding feature. . . . It consists, secondly, in comparing antithetical, i.e. apparently mutually contradictory doctrines, for the sake of determining whether they are really contradictory, and thus leading through initial, and perhaps inevitable exclusive theories, to some truth which includes them both. Finally, it consists in exhibiting a complex truth, by looking at one side and then at the other, in order to obtain a combined view of the whole. This insight which follows upon the transcendence of antithetical positions is called the dialectical synthesis.[3]

We find the roots of dialectic in the very earliest philosophies which were concerned not only with what is true but with the problem of how we arrive at truth and distinguish it from what is false. Parmenides and Zeno of Elea prepared the way for dialectic, but it was in the philosophy of Plato that dialectic was worked out explicitly as the method of philosophy. Plato doubtless was much influenced by Socrates' use of question and answer, but the formulation of the method we owe to Plato.[4]

Although Plato's account of dialectic and his own practice of the method are not always in harmony,[5] yet he does attempt a description of dialectic as the distinctive method of philosophy. The problem is how we reach basic principles which are not themselves derived from other principles but are those on which other knowledge rests. Professor Robinson explains how Plato understood this, as follows:

> He thought that you took an hypothesis and deduced its consequences, trying your hardest to discover some contradiction in those consequences. When you did discover one, the hypothesis was thereby refuted. You then took another hypothesis, usually a modification of the first one designed to avoid the contradiction which had refuted that. You then deduced the consequences of this second hypothesis, and again tried your hardest to make it lead to a contradiction. You continued this process for a long time, making a great effort to be patient and thorough. Some day, after months or years of labor, you reflected that you had now been attempting to refute the same hypothesis for many weeks, that this last hypothesis had endured every test and stood consistent in all its consequences, which you had deduced on every side as far as it seemed possible to go. With this reflection (if you ever got so far) it dawned upon you that this hypothesis was certainly true, that it was no longer an hypothesis but an anhypotheton.[6]

The method, thus described, seems singularly incomplete; the positive basis for accepting the hypothesis as true seems to be nothing more than failure to refute it. But this is only part of the story, the negative part. The positive side of this, in Plato's own words, is found in

> all that unaided reasoning apprehends by the power of dialectic, when it treats its assumptions, not as first principles, but as *hypotheses* in the literal sense, things "laid down" like a flight of steps up which it may mount all the way to something that is not hypothetical, the first principle of all; and having grasped this, may turn back and, holding on to the consequences which depend upon it, descend at last to a conclusion.[7]

Dialectic is thus the preparation for and culminates in rational insight.[8]

So if we ask how we can identify a "first principle," how we know when to trust and when not to trust what seem to be intuitions of primary truths, Plato's apparently negative answer—our inability to refute them—does in fact have a positive basis. If he himself did not make this as explicit as we might wish, it is likely he saw no need to; for he supposed that those who submit to the dialectic will see the truth and will discover what it means to have the mind compelled by the nature of being itself.

If we wish to spell out more explicitly the kind of assurance that dialectic provides we may do so in our own terms. What dialectic leads to is the discovery that certain premises are true by virtue of the fact that their denial has implications which we know are false. This, of course, is the way in which dialectic operates at every stage. But its culmination is reached when the mind discovers that to deny a principle implies the unintelligibility of the denial itself. That principle is established as true because its denial is self-refuting.[9]

Although dialectic, in its original meaning, involved conversation and discussion and thus was a cooperative process of inquiry, yet this may be more incidental than essential. What is essential to dialectic is the confrontation of one view with contrary views, and the exploration of the consequences of each view considered. Plato represents Socrates, for example in the *Protagoras* and in the early part of the *Republic,* as emphasizing the difference between his method of question and answer and the method of the Sophists who preferred to make long speeches and to secure agreement by persuasion. The fault of the Sophist method, however, is perhaps not so much that one person does all the talking as the fact that he is not compelled to face and answer the objections which might be raised against the view which he presents. Since the Sophist's method of persuasion was primarily rhetorical, he sought first of all to make his case appeal to his listeners rather than to examine the truth of his thesis by meeting the objections to it. Quite naturally he did not welcome interruption or objection. When the Sophist method was used to present conflicting points of view, it turned into debate. Each speaker in turn presented his case and perhaps replied to his opponent. The result was that the issue was decided on the basis of the effectiveness and skill of presentation rather than by evidence and logic.

The method of conversation was an effective protection against this. Yet the essential features of dialectic can be preserved without the use of group discussion. Aristotle provides abundant illustration of this in his persistent exploration of alternative solutions of the problems he is discussing. His own conclusions often emerge from his discussion of the views of others, and he seems always intent upon doing justice to the truth contained in different points of view. A formalized version of dialectic was developed in the middle ages. This grew out of the use of discussion, and as written down it seems to be a guide to the kind of discussion the author wishes the reader to conduct in his own mind. The question is put, alternative views are considered, the position to be defended is stated, the reasons in support of it are given, and finally the conflicting views are re-examined in the light of the solution offered and either reconciled partially with it or else their specific divergence is pointed out. The most extensive and highly developed example of this is found in the writing of St. Thomas Aquinas.

The essential feature of dialectic seems to be to advance from one hypothesis to a more adequate one by a process of thought which uncovers and makes explicit the implications of the hypothesis under examination. Any hypothesis which is seriously entertained as the answer to a question has some plausibility. If it did not, it would not be considered. If it is false, or inadequate, its weakness is not likely to show on the surface, else it would have been rejected as soon as proposed. How can we find out whether it has a weakness? The answer is to bring out into the open its unexpressed assumptions and its implicit consequences. In other words, we cross-examine it.

There are two aspects of the cross-examination which we need to note and distinguish with care. One is to spell out the implications of the hypothesis and show that either these implications must be accepted or else the hypothesis abandoned. This is used at every level of dialectical thinking as well as in the hypothetico-deductive method of scientific investigation. The other aspect is primarily the method of philosophy, and in its final stages belongs to philosophy alone. This is to demand the reasons which support a claim of truth, and to follow these back through their reasons, in turn, until we come to reasons which show their own truth. As we have said before, we arrive at this stage when we reach principles which cannot be denied except at the sacrifice of intelligibility.

CHAPTER 17

God in Idea and in Existence

KINDS OF PROOFS

THERE have been many different kinds of attempts to demonstrate the existence of God, and these vary greatly in significance. We shall attempt no systematic survey of these proofs, and yet in our study of the problems of the existence of God and our knowledge of God (Parts Six and Seven) we shall have occasion to consider all of the chief types of such argument.

The present chapter is concerned with the *ontological* argument for the existence of God, the contention that the idea of God implies His existence. We shall examine this in its classic form, as stated by Anselm, and we shall consider also a modification of this argument as it is found in Descartes.

The premise of the *cosmological* argument is the real existence of the world, and the argument tries to show that the existence of God is the necessary condition for the existence of the world. As we shall see later in the chapter, this is the argument we propose to develop in the remainder of Part Six.

One of the most popular of the arguments for the existence of God has as its premise the fact of order and the indications of design in nature, the *teleological* argument. We shall consider this not as an independent argument but as an aspect of the cosmological argument (Chapter 21, "The Existence of God").

Since the time of Immanuel Kant considerable attention has been given to the *moral* argument. The premise of this argument is the reality of values—especially moral values, and the contention is that the reality of values implies the existence of God. We shall consider this argument in Chapter 25, "The Reality of Value."

FROM THE IDEA OF GOD TO THE EXISTENCE OF GOD

One of the most ingenious and, at the same time, most puzzling and tantalizing of the arguments which have been offered to prove the existence of God goes by the technical name of the "ontological argument." Its distinctive character is its attempt to go from the idea of God to the existence of God. According to this argument the very concept of God is such that we cannot consistently deny God's existence. Its classical formulation is by Anselm (1033–1109).

Anselm begins by reminding us that God is, we believe, "a being than which nothing greater can be conceived." From this, he argues, it follows that God exists. Although "the fool hath said in his heart, there is no God . . . this very fool, when he hears of this being of which I speak—a being than which nothing greater can be conceived—understands what he hears, and what he understands is in his understanding; although he does not understand it to exist." Since the fool understands this then even he must see that "that, than which nothing greater can be conceived, cannot exist in the understanding alone. For, suppose it exists in the understanding alone: then it can be conceived to exist in reality; which is greater."[1]

We may restate this argument as a disjunction. The very idea of God is of a being greater than which nothing can be conceived. This is what we mean when we use the word. Both the theist and the atheist agree on the meaning, but the atheist contends that no such "greatest being" actually exists. Anselm's reply narrows down the issue to two mutually exclusive and exhaustive alternatives; and in any case of such alternatives, if one is false the other must be true. Either it is true that God exists, or it is false; there is no middle ground. If it is false that God exists then our conception of God is not the conception of "a being than which nothing greater can be conceived." It is rather the conception of a being than which something greater *can* be conceived, namely, a being which *does exist*. A being which does exist is greater than a being which does not, and so if the God we conceive does not exist then it is not God we conceive. This, Anselm thinks, puts the atheist in an impossible position. In order to deny the existence of God he must have a concept of God, else he would not know what he is denying. But if he has a concept of God then he has to admit the existence of God, the very thing he set out to deny.

This much we can say for Anselm's argument: it is true that *if* God exists and *if* we can form a concept adequate to God's nature, then we have to think of God's nature as necessarily existent. But this is no proof that God does exist; it does not remove the initial *if*. The reason we cannot remove the initial *if* is the fact that we cannot satisfy the second *if*. For we cannot form a concept adequate to God's nature. If *we* are to infer the existence of God from the essence of God we must infer God's existence from *our* concept of God, that is, not from the essence of God as such but from only so much of God's essence as we can contain in our own limited understandings. Anselm is right in this respect, that if God does exist and if we could grasp the nature of God as God is, then the existence of God would be evident. But his argument shifts from the essence of God, as God is, to our limited grasp of God's essence. This basic ambiguity will appear more clearly, perhaps, when we consider the attempt to prove the existence of God from the existence of the idea of God.

Concept and Existence

The weakness of the ontological argument is its assumption that we can form a concept of existence, or that we can include the existence of something within our concept of it—as a part of that concept. The fact is rather that we form concepts of *what exists;* and a concept of what exists contains in itself only the *what* of what exists. The *existence* of what exists is not a part of the concept.

I can think now of a rose I saw in my garden last evening. If my thought of the rose is true then *what I think* is the same as *what the rose is*. In the rose and in my mind is the same *what* (although, of course, I do not grasp in concept all of what the rose is). It is convenient to call the *what* the "essence," and so we may say that when I think about the rose as it really is, the essence which I think in concept is the very essence of the rose itself.

This immediately suggests a question. My idea of the rose is surely not the rose itself. How, then, can we say that the essence which I hold in concept is the very same as the essence of the rose itself? The answer is that the very same essence can be in the rose and in my thought only if it has at least two ways of existing: it has its own existence in the rose and it exists in concept in my mind. Its own existence is the rose itself; in my mind the essence of the rose exists in idea.

In my thinking I can make no contact with any real existence except the real existence of my thought itself. My thought about something is not in direct contact with the real existence I think about, for I think the essence in abstraction from *its* existence. When the essence of something comes into my thought it does not bring its own existence along with it; its own existence is not in my thought but in itself. I can think of it as something which does exist, but when I try to clarify the meaning of the clause "which does exist" I can do this only by referring to an instance of existence. *Mere* existence, *bare* existence, existence *in general* simply lack all content. Or, to put the matter positively, every real existent is the existence of a specific *what*, of its very own essence. We discover existence beyond ourselves directly only in sense perception, and any sound inference to such an existence must be an inference from the existence of the things we perceive or from our own existence. Our only direct contact with real existence is experience; and although we can think *about* experience, that is, understand something of *what* it is, we cannot think experience into existence.

When we try to form a concept of the existence of something without including any of its essence in the concept, we find there is nothing left for thought to grasp. I cannot take into my thought the existence of the rose, for this would be to have the rose actually growing in my thought instead of in the garden. When we speak of the existence of the rose, or of anything else, our speech has meaning only in so far as it brings to mind an idea of *what* is said to exist. If I say, "Durlock really exists," what can you understand me to mean here by "exists"? Only if you speculate about *what* I mean can the assertion that Durlock exists have any meaning at all. That is to say, only if you think some essence do you have anything in mind to attribute existence to.

You may wonder what I mean when I say, "Durlock exists," and say to yourself, "That word *Durlock* sounds as if it may be a proper name. Is it the name of a person, or a town, or perhaps the trade-mark of a manufactured article?" Such speculations will provide possible interpretations of the statement that Durlock exists. But this is the case only because these guesses provide essences which can have some mode of existence.[2]

In the emphatic words of Gilson, "It is not enough to say that *being* is conceivable apart from existence; in a certain sense it must be said that *being* is always *conceived* by us apart from existence, for the very simple reason that existence itself cannot possibly be *conceived*."[3] Thus, he says, conceptual knowledge has the character of "existential neutrality."[4] It makes no difference to the concept of something whether that thing exists or not. This is not to say that the assertion of existence is meaningless, but rather that the idea of existence is meaningless when we try to think of existence by itself apart from any consideration of *what* exists. It is the *what* which we think in concept; when we assert existence in judgment or proposition we do not express *what* the thing is apart from the fact *that* it is, but we assert the existence of the *what*. Although we have no concept of existence as such we do have concepts of existents, but the existence of an existent is not included in our concept of what it is.

It is only because our concepts do have "existential neutrality" that we can use them to think the nature of really existing things. For suppose we were able to have a concept of existence, then no concept of anything real could hold true of that real thing unless the fact *that* the thing is were included in the concept of *what* it is. Then if my concept were to be true of real existence there would have to exist really a *what that exists*. If I conceive truly of this existent, then there would have to exist the *existence of a what that exists*. Suppose I think of a tree outside my window, and insist that my concept of the tree includes the real existence of the tree. Then *what* is it that I judge does exist? In this circumstance I can say only that I judge that the *existing tree* exists. But this is not in fact what I do judge, for it is plain that I judge that the *tree* exists. The very tree that I think in idea is the very tree that exists. To say that the existing tree exists is either mere repetition, and so in itself meaningless, or else it takes us in the direction of subjectivism and suggests that the only real existence of things is the existence they have in our minds. In the first instance, the word *existing* in the statement, "The existing tree exists," is superfluous; in the second instance, the word *exists* is superfluous.

I can think of an airplane now directly overhead but flying at such an altitude that I cannot see or hear it. I can form a detailed concept of such a plane, but I do not know whether this plane which I conceive actually exists or not. Suppose it does exist; then what exists in reality is in some respect the very nature which I think in my idea of the plane. Suppose only that I believe that it exists; then *what* I believe exists is the nature of a possible existent, and I happen to believe that such possible existent is actual. Suppose it does not exist, and yet I believe that it does; then the very nature which would have its own existence if my belief were true is a nature which does not have its own existence. Unless the concept is existentially neutral I cannot assert possible existence, real existence, and nonexistence of the same thing in the same way. If I should assert that something exists and you should deny it, we would not be talking about the same thing unless our concepts were existentially neutral, and so your denial would not be a denial of what I affirm.[5]

THE FAILURE OF THE ONTOLOGICAL ARGUMENT

The crucial point, on which the force of Anselm's argument depends, is his contention that existence is an added perfection, that in addition to what a possible thing is, there is—if it really exists—the added property of existence. A God which exists, he contends, is a more perfect God than one which does not exist. But we can see now that the difference here is not the difference between a more perfect and a less perfect God; rather it is the difference between a God which is and a God which is not, between an existing God and a mere idea of God, between a God which exists in reality and a God which exists only in our concept of Him.

The attempt to include existence as a part of the nature of a thing condemns us to the copy theory of truth, to the theory that our ideas are true only by virtue of the fact that they are copies of real things. Suppose I say that among the attributes of God are those of unity, wisdom, holiness, goodness, and existence. Now does this God which I conceive as a God of wisdom, holiness, goodness, and existence, really exist? If so, then there must be in reality something of which my idea is a copy. There must be a *real* existence which my *idea* of existence copies, or else my concept of God is not of a God which exists. But if this is what truth means how can we ever discover whether our ideas are true or false? Can I compare my idea of God with God apart from my idea, to see whether the idea truly copies the reality? This will not do; for one thing the very comparison would itself be in idea, and I should have to compare my idea of the comparison with the real relation between my idea of God and God. But, anyway, if I am restricted to my ideas I cannot compare those ideas with what are not ideas to see if the idea copies the real thing itself. If my contact with existence is only in idea then I am shut up within my own consciousness and have no sound reason to assert the existence of anything but my own ideas. The existence of God, we must conclude, is not included in our concept of God. The existence of the God we conceive is the very actuality of that nature or essence, not a part of it.

Finally, the ontological argument obtains a specious logical force from a hidden shift of meanings. The fact that this is the case, and that it is not immediately obvious, is perhaps the reason why the argument is so puzzling. The equivocation is between the *real existence of the concept of God*, the actual fact that I form the idea of God in my mind, and the supposed *concept of the real existence of God*. Only if the *real existence of the concept of God* were the *concept of the real existence of God* would this argument be sound. The crucial error, again, is in the supposition that we can have a concept of existence. Existence is fact, not concept. When we conceive fact, it is its *nature*, or *what* the fact is, which we conceive, not *that* the fact is. *That the fact is* belongs to the fact, not to our concepts. Our concepts have their own being as concepts, but they do not have or contain the being of the facts they conceive. We may know whether a supposed fact is or is not, but we do not know this by means of concepts alone; our knowledge of it requires contact with existence.[6]

The ontological argument fails, but this does not mean it is simply false. It fails as a demonstration of the existence of God. We cannot use it to establish God's existence. On the other hand, as we shall see later, this does not mean that its basic principle—that God necessarily exists—is false. The difficulty is rather in the fact that we cannot grasp in concept the nature of God so that we can see, from the idea alone, His necessary existence. If, however, we should discover a cogent proof of God's existence, then what the ontological argument says about God could have great significance. But the argument itself does not furnish proof of existence.

From the Existence of the Idea of God to the Existence of God

We may be able to see more clearly one of the weaknesses of the ontological argument if we look at another approach which, in spite of important differences, retains some elements of the ontological argument. This is the argument that since we do, in fact, have an idea of God it must be true that God exists. We find this approach in one of Descartes' attempts to demonstrate the existence of God.

Descartes concludes and summarizes this part of his argument as follows:

> By the name God, I understand a substance infinite [eternal, immutable], independent, all-knowing, all-powerful, and by which I myself, and every other thing that exists, if any such there be, were created. But these properties are so great and excellent, that the more attentively I consider them the less I feel persuaded that the idea I have of them owes its origin to myself alone. And thus it is absolutely necessary to conclude, from all that I have before said, that God exists: for though the idea of substance be in my mind owing to this, that I myself am a substance, I should not, however, have the idea of an infinite substance, seeing I am a finite being, unless it were given me by some substance in reality infinite.[7]

This differs from the ontological argument, since it argues not from the content of the concept of God to the existence of God but from effect to cause, from the existence of the concept of God to the existence of God. Yet it is of special interest at this point because Descartes commits openly the same fallacy which is hidden in Anselm's thought. Descartes argues that I have an idea of God and my idea is the idea of an infinite being. But since I am finite I myself cannot be the cause of my idea, since a cause must be adequate to its effect. Therefore God exists, for only an existing infinite being can be an adequate cause of my idea. Here the fallacy is so obvious that the real problem may appear to be how so keen a mind as his could miss it. For Descartes actually equivocates between the *idea of an infinite being* and an *idea which itself is something infinite*. Only if the *idea* is infinite does it require a *cause* which is infinite. The idea of an infinite being no more needs itself to be infinite than the idea of a square figure needs itself to be a square figure. Of course a finite being's idea of the infinite may not encompass in idea all that the infinite is, but the sole alternatives are not all or nothing. It is not hard to see that Descartes' equivocation here is related directly to one of the difficulties we found in Anselm's argument, and this would be a convenient point at which to give further consideration to this aspect of Anselm's argument.

In his discussion and defence of the ontological argument Anselm quite properly recognizes that in God there is a unique involvement of existence and essence. For if God is necessary being then the essence of God is, precisely, His existence. It is the very nature of God to exist. This may seem, at first thought, to be contrary to our earlier contention that the existence of something is not a part of its essence, and that our concepts include only essences and are existentially neutral. But there is no conflict here. For since our concepts are existentially neutral and since it is of the very nature of God to exist—His essence *is* His existence and His existence *is* His essence, it follows that we cannot have in concept the real nature of God as He is in Himself. In the case of every other existent the essence can be thought apart from existence, but in the case of God essence and existence cannot be separated even in our thought. Anselm recognized that the existence of God is not the same existence as the existence of other things, and he was right in this. He was wrong in his assumption that we can conceive God in His real nature.

If God is necessary being then it is plain that if we could grasp, in our understandings, the real nature of God as He is in Himself then in apprehending God's essence we should also apprehend His existence. But we cannot grasp such an essence, the essence of being whose very essence it is to exist, in our concepts. For our thinking takes place as a process of abstraction; what we do in thinking is to abstract the essences of things from their existence and to hold the essences, in abstraction from their existences, in our concepts. It is the very nature of a concept to be the awareness of the nature of something else. *Conceptual thought is impossible except with reference to things whose essences can be abstracted from their existence.* But if God is necessary being, whose essence is His existence, then God is the one real being to which this process of conceptual thought cannot apply. We cannot abstract the essence of God from His existence so that we can think *what* God truly is; for to *think* the *what* we have to get it apart from its own existence, and in the case of God this is impossible. So the very feature of our thought which fits it for the true knowledge of other things makes it incapable of grasping the nature of God.

At this point some may object that we are doing here the very thing we argue cannot be done. How can we know that God's essence is His existence unless we have a true concept of God's essence? The answer is that our knowledge here is partly negative. If God is necessary being then His essence and existence cannot be separated; we cannot have the one without the other. What, positively, this involves concerning the nature of God we can understand only indirectly and by analogy. Our concepts may apply to God, not univocally but by analogy; we cannot think the nature of God as such, but in thinking the natures of other things, and in our experience of the existence of other things, our thinking and experience show us indirectly something of God. This we shall consider in a later chapter.

The fact that Anselm and Descartes committed the fallacy of equivocation in their arguments for the existence of God should be reason for caution in simply dismissing the matter as another of the mistakes of the philosophers. Minds of their caliber do not fall into the traps of schoolboy logic exercises. There is something very silly in the attitudes of those who today would sweep away all the work of the past as childishly naive. For these were powerful intelligences; and those who dismiss them so abruptly, and refute them so easily, seldom show much evidence of more than a superficial and second-hand acquaintance with what they attack.

Although the ontological argument does not accomplish what Anselm hoped it would, yet it may still be a significant contribution to the problem. As Gilson points out, Anselm's proof

comes essentially to this: that there exists a being whose intrinsic necessity is such as to be reflected in the very idea we form of Him. God exists so necessarily in Himself that even in our thought He cannot not exist. . . . Where St. Anselm went wrong, as his successors very well saw, was in failing to notice that the necessity of affirming God, instead of constituting in itself a deductive proof of His existence, is really no more than the basis for an induction. In other words, the analytical process, by which from the idea of God is drawn the necessity of His existence, is not in fact the proof that God exists, but might very well become the initial datum of this proof, for we might try to show that the very necessity of affirming God postulates God's existence as its sole sufficient reason.[8]

It is, perhaps, this aspect of the matter which Descartes attempted to express in his contention that only the existence of God is sufficient to account for the fact that we have the idea of God. We may better understand the point which Descartes tries to formulate, and which Gilson makes explicit in his appraisal of the ontological argument, if we restate it in a quite different manner: The argument expresses, in its own way, the fact that if we grasp the true significance of our knowledge of being, and if we permit our minds to follow out the implications of the assertion of being, we are driven irresistibly to the affirmation of being which exists in and of itself. Our attempt to show this in terms of the basic principles involved in any assertion of existence and in any attempt to understand the existence of our world will be our major concern in the next four chapters.

FROM THE EXISTENCE OF THE WORLD TO THE EXISTENCE OF GOD

The best evidence of the existence of God, and the basis of the most compelling proof, is the existence of the world. *The world exists, therefore God exists.* This is the argument. It can be challenged in only two ways. If we are to deny the conclusion then we must either deny the premise, that the world exists, or deny that the conclusion follows from the premise.

If thought is to advance from the existence of the world to the existence of God its advance must rest upon the need to go beyond the world in order to account for the fact that the world really exists. The world does exist, it cannot account for its own existence, therefore there is something other than the world which does account for the world's existence. It is plain that this other is self-existent, else it would not provide a complete account of the world's existence; and the self-existent cause of the world is God.

We shall now draw up a formal statement of the course of argument we propose to follow. From this formal statement of the basic argument it will be possible to note our progress as the discussion advances.

The Steps of the Argument

Proposition 1: *The world of nature is an actually existing world which includes within itself the real things and events we find by means of our experience.* In the next chapter we shall show that this proposition is true by showing the failure of its only significant alternative, subjectivism.

Proposition 2: *Any such world of actually existing things and events is a world which is neither self-existent nor contains anything self-existent as a part of itself.* We shall consider this in Chapter 19, "The Contingency of the World."

Proposition 3: *The world of nature is a world which neither exists by itself nor contains anything self-existent as a part of itself.* This is the conclusion which follows from the first two propositions as premises. If they **are** true then this one also must be true.

Proposition 4: *Whatever neither exists by itself nor contains anything self-existent as a part of itself depends for its existence upon something which does exist in and of itself and does not in turn depend on anything else.* This will be the subject of Chapter 20, "The Cause of Nature."

Proposition 5: *Anything which depends for its existence on something which is self-existent depends for its existence upon a really existing God.* This proposition completes the ground work of the argument for the existence of God. Proposition 6 follows as the conclusion from 4 and 5, while Proposition 7 is the conclusion which follows from 3 and 6 as premises. These two conclusions complete the argument:

Proposition 6: *Anything which is not self-existent depends for its existence upon a really existing God.*

Proposition 7: *The world of nature depends for its existence upon a really existing God.*

It will be seen from the relations of these seven propositions that 1, 2, 4, and 5 are the basic premises. Propositions 3 and 6 follow from these, and Proposition 7 follows from 3 and 6. So the crucial part of the proof is that which concerns the basic premises. One of the following four chapters will be devoted to each of these four basic premises.

CHAPTER 18

The Existence of the World

THREE WAYS TO DENY THE EXISTENCE OF THE WORLD

Our first proposition asserts that the world of nature is an actually existing world which includes within itself the real things and events we find by means of our experience. There are, in principle, only three ways to deny this. One is to assert that the so-called world of nature, including the supposed things and events which constitute it, is simply nothing. What we take to be our awareness of real existence is illusion, an illusion which is the awareness of what is not. This view is called "acosmism."

A second way to deny the existence of the world as something which is real in its own right is to assert that the supposed real things and events that we seem to find in that world are nothing but functions of something else. This takes two forms, subjectivism and phenomenalism. For subjectivism the supposed things and events of nature are but ideas, either ideas in our own minds or ideas in a cosmic mind. Thus nature evaporates into ideas, and the world is a function of mind.

For phenomenalism the world as it appears to be is not the real world; the appearances of existence are but functions of a reality that is unknown and unknowable in its true nature, or else they are functions of a reality quite unlike its appearances to us. Schopenhauer's philosophy of will and various materialisms are examples of the latter, while the philosophies of Kant and of Herbert Spencer illustrate the former. It is our purpose in this chapter to show that all three of these attempts to deny the real existence of our world fail to stand up under criticism. Each shows its falsity in its own implications.

Acosmism

We have already seen, in an earlier chapter,[1] what happens when we try to assert that reality is an absolute unity which excludes all variety and change. When first we try to distinguish the real from the unreal we are tempted to dispose of the unreal by relegating it to a realm of its own. But if there is any place (to speak metaphorically) where we can send the unreal, to rid the real of its presence, that place itself and its contents must have some kind of being. If what is thought to be real in its own right turns out to be only an idea, then of course it is still real—as an idea, even if it does not exist in its own right. If we are to explain apparent realities in terms of ideas, there have to be ideas. Simply to relegate an appearance to a realm of unreality is to turn the unreality into a kind of reality. "If any man thinks," says Jonathan Edwards, "that he can conceive well enough how there should be Nothing, I will engage, that what he means by Nothing, is as much Something, as anything that he ever thought of in his life."[2] Or, to paraphrase Professor Veatch, the realm of being "leaves nothing out, save nothing."[3]

When we try to assert sheer nonbeing of anything we involve ourselves in an inconsistency. We cannot say of anything of which we can think, that it is absolute nothingness. The very idea of absolute nothingness is itself something. When we ask what it is the idea *of* we discover that the only nothingness we can find any meaning for is a relative nothingness. A thing is nothing with respect to this or that order of being, and we mean that it is excluded from this or that order. But what is excluded from one order of being must belong to another order if we are to have anything to refer to when we speak of "nothing." At the very least, it exists in idea.

It is in perception that we find what we take to be the world of nature. To try to dispose of perception as mere illusion leaves unaccounted for the fact that we do have such illusions. For whatever we may do with our so-called sense perceptions, they do occur—else acosmism would have nothing to dispose of. To declare a judgment false does not negate the fact of the judgment itself, and if we are to understand the situation adequately we need to know how the false judgment happened to be made. Illusions occur, even for acosmism, and any true account of reality which asserts this must have some place in its scheme of things for the real occurrence of illusions. Once we see we must admit the occurrence of illusions in order even to state the position of acosmism, we see how short a step it is from acosmism to subjectivism. In fact, there is not much of any other place for acosmism to go. Either it leaves its illusions as facts dangling in a positive nothingness, a naive and unrecognized nonsense excusable only in the very initial attempts to think philosophically, or it shifts to subjectivism.

The cardinal principle of philosophy is that everything exists. We simply cannot assert sheer nonexistence. The attempt to do so destroys its own meaning, for it is the attempt to refer to a realm or class or instance of a nonexisting something. Every awareness, every thought, no matter how fantastic or how impossible is its content, is an existent. To deny this of a supposed thought about nothing is to deny the very occurrence of a thought about nothing; and this, of course, requires us to think about a thought about nothing. "In spite of . . . difficulties in apprehending it," Professor Wild reminds us, "existence is a peculiarly distinctive and indubitable datum of experience. As a matter of fact, it pervades all the other more restricted data, for a nonexistent datum is impossible."[4]

Everything exists, but not everything is real. The distinction between what is real and what is unreal is the distinction between what has its own existence and what exists only in something else. If I imagine a fire-breathing dragon, for example, *what* I imagine does not have its own existence, but my image of it does. Of course the essence of the image and the essence of the dragon are two different essences. When I think of the dragon I am not thinking of my image of the dragon; I am thinking of *what* a dragon would *be* if such things existed. The essence of an image of a dragon is not composed of the characteristics of dragons, for such would constitute the essence of a dragon. The essence of the image of a dragon is the essence of a certain mental state, and like the essences of all acts of awareness its essence includes the property of presenting the nature of something other than itself. In this case the essence presented in the image is of something fictive, which exists only in such imaginary construction and not of itself. Since in the case of an image "not even the very principle on which it has come into being belongs to the image itself," says Plato, referring to the content of the image, ". . . it is proper that it should come to be *in* something else, clinging in some sort to existence on pain of being nothing at all."[5] Subjectivism, which we shall now examine, is the doctrine that all existence is mental; real things are either ideas in the mind or are the minds which have ideas.

SUBJECTIVISM

One of the more familiar statements of subjectivism is by Bishop Berkeley:

> Some truths there are so near and obvious to the mind, that a man need only open his eyes to see them. Such I take this important one to be, to wit, that all the choir of heaven and furniture of the earth, in a word all those bodies which compose the mighty frame of the world, have not any subsistence without a mind, that their *being (esse)* is to be perceived or known; that consequently so long as they are not actually perceived by me, or do not exist in my mind or that of any other *created spirit*, they must either have no existence at all, *or else subsist in the mind of some eternal spirit:* it being perfectly unintelligible and involving all the absurdity of abstraction, to attribute to any single part of them an existence independent of a spirit. To be convinced of which, the reader need only reflect and try to separate in his own thoughts the being of a sensible thing from its being perceived.[6]

Although this does not deny outright the existence of the world, it does deny that the things of the world exist in their own right.

They have none but a mental existence. Their being is not in their own act, but merely in being perceived.

Subjectivism has a long history and has had stout defenders. It would be presumptuous to try to do justice to its motives and manifold forms in a few brief paragraphs. Some of the great philosophers of all times have been subjectivists; it is only because they have done their work so well—in exploring the far reaches of the implications of their common basic position—that we are able to see the difficulties implicit in their first principles.

The crucial issue between subjectivism and the view that the things of the world have their own existence concerns the nature of ideas, the mental states or acts by which awareness takes place.[7] Subjectivism arises out of a misconception of the nature of ideas. It understands *idea* to be that of which the mind is directly aware; awareness is awareness *of* ideas. Realism, in contrast with subjectivism, regards the idea as an awareness of something other than itself. Subjectivism is forced to consider everything capable of being known to be in some sense mental, of the nature of ideas. Realism, however, escapes any such limitation upon the range of knowledge, for it considers ideas to be not the things known but the acts by which other things are known.

The plausibility of subjectivism comes from the fact that ideas are, in some circumstances, the very things of which we are aware. Realism's case, however, rests on the fact that even when ideas are the things of which we are aware, our awareness of this or that particular idea is itself another idea. The idea of which we are aware is never the awareness of the idea. Realism also finds that in certain crucial instances, such as in sense perception, what we are aware of is simply not of the nature of ideas. We can see this when we compare carefully our actual experience in sense perception with memory and imagination.

If I say, for example, that I have an idea of the Statue of Liberty I may mean that I am thinking of the statue as a real physical thing, located in a certain place and describable in certain specific terms. The idea here is my thought of the thing. On the other hand, I may mean that I have a mental picture of the Statue of

Liberty and that it is the mental picture I am aware of. I recognize it to be an image of the real statue because of the points of similarity between the two, and because I use the image to intend or mean the statue. In attending to the image I may ignore its reference to the real statue, and examine the image for its vividness, detail, and other psychological characteristics. The situation is ambiguous. I may think of the statue itself, and my images of the statue assist me in thinking of it. Or I may have an image of the statue and direct my attention to the image, so that it is the image I am thinking about and not the statue. We need to clarify this ambiguity if we are to understand the role of ideas in our knowledge of objects.

It happens that I am, at this moment, many hundreds of miles away from the Statue of Liberty. It is impossible that I should now be looking at that statue directly; I have only my image of it. So it is when I think of something in the past. I cannot bring back the past as a now present event and view that event directly. I can think of it only as I have memories or images, and these memories and images are within my mind—they do not belong to the event.

Suppose now I look at the clock which faces me from a few feet away. Is not this the same kind of awareness as the other instances? I have an image of the clock in my mind, and it is the image of the clock I am directly aware of. It may be that the only difference between this and a memory, or the thought of something which is at a distance, is the process by which the image arises. I now remember looking last night at another clock in another room of the house. Is not the only difference the fact that my present image is caused by present sensory stimulation while the memory image is aroused by some process of association?

When we reach this point we see how the subjectivist can take the next step and declare that since each of these instances of awareness is an awareness of an image we do not need to assume the existence of anything non-mental. My perception of the clock, he contends, is just as much an awareness of something mental as my awareness of a memory image of another clock previously perceived. The only difference between perception, memory, and imagination is in some of the properties of the images. When the images have a certain steadiness and do not come and go at will, the experience is perception; but even in perception it is the images the mind is aware of. So we need assume only the existence of the mind and its own states.

The Failure of Subjectivism

The subjectivist interpretation of the processes of awareness contains enough truth to give the whole theory an initial plausibility. For we are now aware of events in our past by means of memories, and our memories are heavily loaded with images. If I wish to recall the specific features of any particular object I have seen in the past I do try to form as vivid an image of it as possible and I inspect that image with care. Even when I perceive the clock that is now within my range of vision there are images of other things which enter into my present awareness. But where the subjectivist is wrong is in his contention that what I really see as I look at this clock now is an image of the clock and not the clock itself.

When I look at the clock and perceive it there is, of course, something mental taking place. Perception is an act of the mind, not of the clock. We may admit also that perception involves the formation of images, for if it did not we should have serious trouble in explaining how we can confuse dreams and hallucinations with perceptions. Although the images formed in the process of perception provide the materials or contents of our later memories and imaginings, still we must recognize that in perception itself it is not the image of which we are aware. Even one so close to positivism as Hans Reichenbach says, "I cannot admit that impressions [i.e. sensations] have the character of observable facts. What I observe are things, not impressions . . . I do not say that I doubt the existence of my impressions. I believe that there are impressions; but I have never *sensed* them."[8]

If, in the course of an act of perception, attention shifts to the image the process becomes one of memory or imagination or introspection; it is no longer perception. The mental act of perception is the act by which we are aware of the real thing. The process of perception lets us see or hear or feel what the thing itself is. When the nature of the thing itself is communicated to our senses, and our attention is upon it, then we are aware of the thing—not of an awareness. If the thing itself is not present in sensation then the best we can do is to direct our attention to an image in place of the thing.

There is one fact which seems to settle this matter conclusively. This is the fact that our minds simply do not have within themselves the power to produce images, or anything else which might intrude itself between our awareness and the object we perceive. A person who has never seen colors is unable to form images of colors. If such were possible then a baby born blind as a result of some malformation of the eyes should be able, in later life, provided the visual centers of the brain are normal, to form images of all visible colors and forms. But a person blind from birth is incapable of visual imagery. The possibility of any specific kind of imagery requires previous perception, and so it seems highly improbable—indeed, it approaches the fantastic—to suppose that perception itself is the awareness of ideas in the mind, or of any mental content as such, whatever it may be called. In perception we see, hear, feel, smell, and taste the real things with which we are in contact by means of our senses.

Suppose the subjectivist replies that the only difference between perception and other modes of imagery is that sensory stimulation is necessary for the first occasion of an image, and that perception is only imagery under the control of sensory stimuli. One reason why this answer will not stand up is that the subjectivist has no place in his scheme for the senses or the nervous system or for what we call physical stimuli except in so far as they are understood to be nothing but ideas in the mind. So the most he can say is that the difference between perception and other forms of imagery is a difference which lies in the images themselves or in the other images accompanying the ones we identify. But the difference between perception and imagery can hardly lie in the images themselves, else we should have no basis for the distinction of perception from dreams and hallucinations. If it lies in the accompanying images, images we specify as images of sensory processes for example, then anyone capable of having the appropriate accessory or accompanying images should be able to generate the so-called percepts.

If we are challenged to explain how perception, as the realist understands it, is possible, and if this means we are expected to explain it in terms of other mental processes, then the challenge cannot be met. But it is itself based on a misconception of where the explaining belongs. We are not in a position to explain perception in terms of, or by reduction to, other processes—whether imagery or whatever they may be. Rather it is by reference to perception that we account for our knowledge, for our memory and imagery, and for the control of our thinking by the nature of reality. So far as the process of perception itself is concerned, we need only recognize that our minds are so constituted that they are able to appropriate to themselves certain characteristics of the things with which they are linked by means of our senses. Perception *is* this process of appropriation. The mind takes something of the *what* of the thing perceived, and this essence becomes now a part of the mind's own possessions. In this the thing perceived is not robbed of its own essence, for we do not take the *thing itself* into the mind; rather the mind takes to itself the *nature* of the thing.

> Every sensation [Professor Wild points out], is *of* something; every concept *of* something; every proposition *about* something. All cognition, at every level, has this relational or intentional structure. In this structure, the cognitive act-relation is existentially private, and belongs to the knowing agent. But *the object* is not necessarily private. The act is thus distinct from the object, and yet united with it in a peculiar way. This relation is absolutely *sui generis*, and cannot be confused with any other known type of relation. In particular, the presence of an object before a knowing

faculty must not be confused, as it so often is, with the physical presence of some property or impression *within* a physical or "mental" container.[9]

It is of the very nature of mind to take to itself the natures of other things. Originally the mind has, in and of itself, no nature but the various acts and processes by which it is able to take to itself the natures of other things. Once the mind has done this, attention can then be directed toward the essence which has become a part of its furnishings. But in the act of doing this, the act of appropriation in perception, attention must be directed by sensation to the thing perceived. If our attention in perception wanders to contents already in possession of the mind, we confuse what we see or hear with what we imagine.

The images we use in remembering and imagining have a role somewhat like our use of a photograph to help us remember the details of something. But when we use a photograph we *perceive* the picture, not our image of it. Even in our awareness of our own ideas the awareness of an idea is never the idea of which we are, in that instance, aware. I am aware of being aware, but only in reflection, and the reflective awareness is not itself the original experience of which I am aware. What we do in reflecting, explains Harmon M. Chapman, is this:

> Without completely taking leave of the natural attitude [of ordinary experience], we yet transcend it, stepping back, so to speak, as though upon higher ground so as to survey not only (as formerly) the world but also our experience of it. Thus, whereas in the natural attitude we are concerned with the world simply, in the reflective attitude we are concerned with both world and experience.[10]

Perhaps the most serious error the subjectivist makes is his neglect of experience itself, his failure to take account of our direct and immediate differentiation of perception from imagery. We do distinguish the two, and usually we make the distinction so easily and unmistakably that we are largely unaware of making it at all. Our perceptions are plainly what they are, perceptions; and our images are equally obvious in their character as images, just as our processes of inference and of calculation and anticipation are recognizable for what they are when we turn our attention to them. We are able to make these distinctions for the very good reason that we can attend to what we are doing and can recognize some of the features of the intellectual act itself. Of course children have to learn to make these distinctions with clarity, and any one of us is liable to error and confusion in some circumstances. But perceiving is an act which is different from attending to images, and as a rule we make the distinction with no trouble at all. To the contention that since we are sometimes mistaken it may be that we are always mistaken, we may reply that only if there are times when we are not mistaken can we recognize that there are times when we are mistaken.

Not only do we perceive and remember and imagine and think, but what clinches the case against the subjectivist is that we are aware that we perceive and remember and imagine and think. Such awareness is not infallible, for people do mistake imagining for remembering and for perceiving, and, if they are uninstructed, even for thinking. But the acts of the mind are accessible to awareness, and this fact is one of the necessary conditions for knowledge; its absence in animals makes knowledge impossible for them in spite of keenness of sensation and associative abilities. Until a child learns to recognize the difference between perceiving and imagining he cannot come to an *understanding* of *what* things are; he can only react to stimuli and accumulate experiences.

The subjectivist may insist that what we call perception is still only a special kind of imagery, and, just as it takes a child some years to learn to distinguish between different kinds of mental acts, so it takes some special reflection and critical analysis before the common sense mind can recognize that what it calls perception is actually a form of imagery. We recognize images for what they are, and common sense attitudes assume that we recognize percepts as radically different from images; so, says the subjectivist, we need to apply the critical analysis of philosophic reflection before we can discover that this supposed recognition of perception as different from imagery is false, and that the two are basically the same.

What can we reply to this? Perhaps the best reply is that our recognition of the difference between image and percept, once we have reached the level of development at which the difference becomes clear, is so obvious and so fundamental to all our judgment that we cannot make sense of the attempt to deny it. But some philosophers do deny it. What of them? The answer is that the philosopher seldom denies that we do *seem* to distinguish radically between what we call perception and what we call imagery. He denies only that it is the kind of a difference which a realist, along with the common sense interpretation of perception, thinks it is. Those who go so far as to deny, as did David Hume, that there is any difference at all except a difference of degree of vividness and steadiness, also find it impossible, as did Hume, to put their theory into practice.

The weakness of the subjectivist's position is that he says, in effect, that we have to distrust and nullify a certain basic kind of experience which all men seem to have and all men seem ready to trust until they are convinced it is false. It is a basic judgment of experience that perception is the direct awareness of some real thing which exists in its own right, independent of our awareness of it. We are directly aware that knowing is an awareness of something other than itself. It is our confidence in our awareness of what we are doing, when we perceive or imagine or reason, which is the basis of realism—the solid empirical basis. The subjectivist must destroy that confidence in order to be believed; he must convince us that one of these basic activities is false in principle and radically deceptive by its very nature. But if one, why not the others as well? And if we cannot trust our seeming awareness that we are perceiving, then how can we trust our seeming awareness that we are imagining or remembering or thinking—or even our awareness that we are aware?

The answer to subjectivism is that any theory which impeaches any basic mental act impeaches in principle the whole range of mental activity. It impeaches eventually reason itself, and thus it

impeaches its own impeachment. It leads, as it has led some philosophers, even to the denial of images, and, incredible as it may
seem, to the denial of any awareness of any mental process and
finally to the denial of all awareness. We cannot permit theory to
invalidate experience and to destroy the basic conceptions upon
which alone we are able to act and to maintain ourselves. Any
theory which does imply such consequences only demonstrates
its own falsity. Either we trust our basic mental processes, including our recognition of the nature of perception, or else the whole
range of the work of mind is called into question. If mind is incompetent, by what process do we know this? We cannot know
it by virtue of what our minds tell us, for on such a view they
themselves would be suspect.

Still, we may be told, it is only reason we must trust. All other
processes are subject to it and must justify themselves before it
if we are to accept anything from them as true or significant. It
surely is true that we must trust reason; but reason alone is not
enough. Reason alone does not give truth; it gives only validity.
Reason gives us no *existence* except its own, and truth concerns the
relation of thought to existence—not only the relation of thought
to its own existence but the relation of thought to the existence it
means or intends. Perception, memory, imagination, reason—all
are essential to the proper and fruitful use of the mind. Perception
puts us in contact with real existence beyond ourselves; memory
enables us to attend to what we have experienced in the past; imagination is the way to the new and the original, and it is the
mental process by which we are aware of possible individual
things; reason shows us the necessities which govern our inference, and includes in its action insight into rational relations.

One of the best taught of all the lessons of philosophy, taught
to those who have attended to it, is the lesson of what happens
when we try to make ideas the sole objects of mind, and then
seek to justify the claim of knowledge of real existence by virtue
of a similarity between our ideas and real things. It was this which
John Locke attempted late in the seventeenth century, and only
the original ambiguity of his conception of *idea* kept him from see-

ing for himself the subjectivist and skeptical consequences of such an approach. Bishop Berkeley, whom we quoted above, brought out the inherent subjectivism which was one aspect of Locke's philosophy. David Hume, whose honest clarity of thought and willingness to tell what he saw gives him a special position among philosophers, demonstrated the skeptical consequences of Locke's theory of ideas. In Hume's hands both the real world of nature and the minds which pretend to know it dissolve into series of bits of awareness which mean nothing beyond themselves except other bits and which have no relations among themselves except psychological relations. Hume's honesty extended to the admission that he could not believe his own philosophy, by which he meant that philosophy fails in its attempt to make experience intelligible. What Hume did not understand is that the real failure lay in the basic presuppositions of the whole line of thought which he had brought to its conclusion.

The attempt to interpret *idea* as that of which we are aware brings itself to its own destruction. Suppose we grant that we are aware of ideas. What is the awareness of the idea? Is it another idea? If so, then this other idea is not itself something of which we are aware but an act of awareness of something other than itself. But the idea of which it is the awareness is quite a different sort of thing. *It* is not here the awareness of something else; it is solely and exclusively something of which we are aware. So to be aware of this kind of idea requires another kind of idea. Suppose I say that in my perception of the clock what I am aware of is my idea of the clock. Then what about my awareness of my idea of the clock, that is, what about my own recognition that I am aware of the idea of the clock? Is that another idea? If so, and if an idea is what we are aware of rather than the awareness of something other than itself, then I need still another idea, namely, an idea of the idea of the clock. There is no end to this road once we begin to travel it; the remedy is not to get on it. Surely the difficulty we find here must warn us that even if some ideas were what we are aware of, still there would have to be acts of the mind which are themselves the awareness of something other than themselves.

Once we recognize that awareness is always awareness of something other than itself, we can avoid the misunderstanding that leads to subjectivism. Professor Chapman puts it in this way:

> It pertains, then, to the cognitive nature of consciousness that in every act it have an object or that it possess an intrinsic reference to an object which is other than the act itself. Being intrinsic to the act, this "objective reference" is such that no act can properly be described without specifying also what object it is "of." Thus it is not sufficient to say of an act that it is a visual perception of something. I must, in order to identify the act and to distinguish it from others of the same kind, say also what this something is. I must state, for example, not merely that "I see something," but also that "I see the ink bottle," or "I see the pencil," and so forth. Otherwise I could not significantly distinguish between two acts of seeing. In describing an act, therefore, two things *at least* must be specified: One, we must state its *mode*, that is, that it is a perception (visual, auditory, and so forth) or a recollection or an anticipation or a conception, and so on; and two, we must carefully state its specific objective reference, for this no less than the former *is an essential part of the act and not a part of the object.*[11]

We have now reached the end of our argument that the existence of the natural world can neither be denied outright nor reduced to something mental. We must now consider phenomenalism, the view that we are aware only of the appearances of things and not of things as they really are.

PHENOMENALISM

Phenomenalism asserts that we are aware of appearances only, not of what things themselves really are. In a sense it is true that we are aware of appearances; in this realism agrees with phenomenalism. Our awareness of an object is the object's appearance to us. But realism insists that the appearance reveals the nature of the object as that object really is while phenomenalism contends that the appearances do not show us what the object really is.

Phenomenalism is always an unstable position. Either it goes beyond itself into realism by admitting that things really are what they appear to be, or else it shrinks into subjectivism by cutting away all connection between the appearance of something and that of which it is the appearance. The explanation for this, and the fatal flaw of phenomenalism, lies in its attempt to construct out of appearances a kind of half-real and half-unreal world, a "twilight existence" between the mind that knows and the reality it seeks to know.[12] The difficulty is that the difference between real and unreal is not subject to compromise; there is no middle ground.

If appearances of reality are not fully real, how can we make sense of the assertion that there are such appearances? C. E. M. Joad points out that, on this view, they are

> quasi-real appearances of a reality which must somehow be credited with the power of generating what is less real, or becoming what is less real than itself. Assuming such a feat to be possible, it follows that we must qualify the unity of the real with the capacity for generating, or expressing itself in, or appearing as—the difficulty remains unaffected whatever terminology we use—the world or worlds of appearance. And not merely with the capacity for generating *any* world or worlds of appearance, but just those particular worlds with all their richness of qualitative differentiation which do in fact appear. Reality must, to use an expression of Professor Whitehead's, be patient of the fact that water is H_2O, that a substance with the specific gravity of gold should be yellow, and that white ant queens lay eggs at the rate of about one every three seconds. But if the potentiality for all the distinctions and characters that do in fact appear must be conceived to be latent in reality in order to account for the fact that the world or worlds of appearance appear to be just as it is or as they are, it is difficult to see in what sense it or they can be *merely* appearance.[13]

This takes us to realism, to the real existence of our world of things as what we perceive them to be. If our argument is sound we have established our first basic premise.

CHAPTER 19

The Contingency of the World

THE SECOND STEP OF THE PROOF

W E HAVE found that every attempt to deny the existence
of the world of nature fails. There are only three ways
to attempt this: to assert that the world is nothing but
illusion, to reduce it to ideas, or to regard it as the appearance of
something other than itself. When we examine the first we find
that it leads to the second; the second is based on a misunderstanding concerning the nature of ideas and their role in knowing. Furthermore, it requires us to repudiate sense perception, one of our
fundamental ways of knowing, and this would impeach the whole
range of the knowing processes. The very possibility of inquiry
rests on the integrity of the basic acts of knowing. Any theory
of knowledge or conception of existence which implies the inherent unsoundness of a basic knowing process, as distinguished
from its erroneous use, refutes itself by virtue of that implication.
Such an outcome is evidence either of an error of reasoning or of
the presence of a false assumption. To accept such a consequence,
and to rest with it, is an act of intellectual suicide which leaves
behind only the verbal corpse of a theory.

We found phenomenalism to be a position of unstable equilibrium between subjectivism and realism. Phenomenalism tries
to unite a realistic doctrine of existence with a subjectivist theory
of knowledge, a union which can lead only to divorce. We cannot long pretend to know the existence of a reality that is beyond
the reach of our knowledge. Either appearances disclose the nature of what appears or else we have no reason to suppose that
they are appearances of anything but themselves; these are the

alternatives of realism and subjectivism. With the failure of sub-jectivism we find no remaining alternative to realism, and out first premise is established.

The next step of our proof is to establish the truth of our sec-ond basic premise, that *the world of real things which we discover in sense perception is a world that neither exists by itself nor con-tains anything self-existent as a part of itself.* There are two ways by which this can be denied. We may assert that the real world does contain something self-existent which accounts for the exist-ence of the other things we find in the world, or we may contend that even if nothing *in* the world is self-existent yet the world *as a whole* is self-existent. Our first concern in this chapter is to see whether it is possible to defend successfully the view that the real world of nature contains something self-existent as a part of itself.

Before we begin to develop this step of our argument we need to take careful note of one important point. We have found that the world we are in contact with in sense perception is the real world, and that it really has the qualities which sense perception discloses. In so far as we have established this we have shown the falsity of all theories which deny that things really are what we perceive them to be. On the other hand, we must be careful not to assume that ordinary sense perception shows us *all* of the na-ture of these things we perceive. In connection with a discussion of certain problems of visual perception, Professor Wild gives us a clear expression of this distinction.

> No genuine realist has ever claimed . . . that true apprehension must mean an *exhaustive* apprehension of *everything that is there.* If the sensory faculty can identify itself with some real formal structure as it really is *outside the eye*, this is sufficient. . . . If this occurs, we shall not attain a knowledge of physical existence that is comprehensive and exhaustive. We shall not know the very com-plex physical situation as God might know it, but we shall really know something outside us as it really is in itself, not some sub-jective construction. . . . In this case . . . we shall be justified in *identifying* the appearance as an imperfectly cognized aspect of the reality—the thing as it is in itself.[1]

The natural sciences take us far beyond the limits of direct perception, but the sciences supplement rather than invalidate perception. Sense perception is the criterion by which the truth of scientific hypotheses is tested, so the conclusions of scientific inquiry cannot very well invalidate their own criterion of truth.[2]

Contingency

When we say that neither the world itself nor anything within the world can account for its own existence we say that the world is *contingent*. As contingent we say that its very existence, the fact that it is, depends on something else; that this holds true of everything in the world and of the world itself. The real things of nature have their own existence, but in so far as they are contingent each depends for its existence upon something else.

Nothing contingent exists of necessity. It is such that it might have not existed. This house, for example, is a contingent thing. It exists not solely because of what *it* is but because of the acts of other things. It exists because the material of which it was built existed, because a plan or design for such a house was conceived, because people and machines arranged the materials in accordance with the design. Someone, sometime, made the decision to build this house. Until that decision was made and carried out in act it was still possible for him to decide to build a different kind of house or even not to build at all. The house has a definite nature but the fact that this nature is the nature of something actual, and not merely imaginary or merely possible, depends upon something other than the nature of the house. It depends on the acts and potentialities of really existing things, the human agents and physical materials and mechanical devices which brought the house into being. That the house continues to exist depends, among other things, on the relative stability of the ground on which it rests, of the atmosphere which surrounds it, and of the temperature. An earthquake, a tornado, or a fire can bring its existence to an end.

Here is a plant which actually exists. But it exists only because somehow, by some cause which was not itself a part of the plant, the seed was dropped at this place; it exists because the soil here contained elements the seed needed in order to sprout and to grow; it exists because the sun warmed the earth and later, by its direct effects on the plant, enabled it to appropriate and modify chemically the energy which came to it. The plant is real, and its existence is its own; the existence here is the existence of the plant, not of something else. But its existence, although truly its own, was given to it by the agency of other things.

As we look about us at the multitude of things which make up our world we find that every one of them seems to depend on other things for its own existence. In all the variety of the things we find there is nothing which seems to exist wholly by its own act. But, of course, we may be mistaken about this. Perhaps there is something in nature which is an exception to the apparent rule of contingency. Our first problem is to consider this possibility.

The Mark of the Contingent

If we are trying to find something self-existent in the world it will not do simply to begin to look around us in the hope of encountering what we seek. For even if we were lucky enough to hit upon something which seemed self-existent we still would need a standard by which we could recognize its status as non-contingent. If, on the other hand, we already have such a standard then perhaps we shall not have to apply it separately to every distinct thing we find. If we should find that the difference between self-existence and contingency is revealed by some feature which all things of the natural world share then our search is over. This is precisely what we should expect to be the case if all the things in nature are contingent, for it is reasonable to suppose that they are contingent for the same reason. This method of solving our problem is not scientific, in the narrower sense of the word; what we seek here is rather a dialectical solution to a philosophical problem. What, we ask, is presupposed by the observed qualities and characteristics of things with respect to their status in reality?

The one characteristic of all the things in nature by virtue of which they are contingent appears to be *change*. It is because they all change, without interruption and without exception, that they are all contingent. If this is true then we may be sure that if there is something self-existent in nature it must be changeless.

We now have two questions to consider. The first question is whether everything that exists in nature is something that changes. The other question concerns the relation of change and contingency: Is everything that changes necessarily contingent?

Everything in Nature Changes

The first of these questions must be answered in the affirmative provided we recognize that all natural existence is temporal. Nothing can exist in time—that is, have duration—except as it undergoes change. It is an inconsistency to say that a thing endures and also to say that it is identically the same at any two moments of its duration. In so far as it becomes different from one moment to another it changes. We need now to see why this is true, and then we shall look more carefully at the statement that all natural existence is temporal.

Let there be no mistake concerning the principle we are discussing here: endurance necessarily involves change. A grain of sand, a plant, a star, a continent—no such things remain absolutely the same throughout any amount of duration, no matter how small. It makes no difference whether we are talking about an individual thing or about something collective. In asserting that *it* endures, that we have *the same thing* at *different times*, we have to accept the fact of its change or else we contradict ourselves.

At first thought it may seem that we contradict ourselves when we say we have the same thing at different times and yet that this thing has changed. How can something which has changed be the same as it was before it changed? This difficulty, however, is the result of a misunderstanding. We do not mean that we have the *same thing* in the sense that it has not changed, if the thing itself exists as a changing thing. A thing that changes has different states or different characteristics at different times, and the thing which had the earlier states is the thing which now has the later ones. We do not have first the thing apart from change and then subject it to change; rather the thing we have is itself a process of change. To be a natural existent is to be a process; real metaphysical substance is being in act; existence is dynamic, not static.

Only in its potentialities can an existing thing remain unchanged, and its potentialities are not themselves existents. Their presence means that the process which constitutes the actual existent is not yet complete. So, though a potentiality may remain unchanged through a period of time, it is not something which *exists* unchanged through time.

In Whitehead's words, *"The process is itself the actuality."* "It took a long while, centuries in fact, for philosophers to get beyond the idea of static matter," he explained in conversation with Lucien Price.

> Certain substances, like water or fire, could be seen to be changing rapidly; others, like rock, looked immutable. We now know that a piece of granite is a raging mass of activity, that it is changing at a terrific rate; but until we did know it, a rock seemed to possess little or no life, though it looked immensely permanent. . . . Our human bodies change from day to day; certain external appearances of them are the same, but change is constant and sometimes visible. The constellations do not appear to change at all, though we know that they do, as we know that the nebulae have come into their present form but are also passing into another. Whether the change occurs in a minute or in billions of years, is merely a matter of human measurement; the fact of change is not affected by our using, as human beings, the only standards of measurement we have, which are necessarily affected by the limitations of our own lives. . . . This little table by my side [as he said this, Price reports, he tapped the table with his fingers] is in process of change. If you were to shut it up somewhere for ten thousand years and then went back to look at it, the change might be so pronounced that you would hardly know it had been a table; yet the process which

would produce that so visible change is going on in it right now, although for all practical human purposes it is the same table you saw the last time you were here and the same one I have seen around for forty years.[3]

At another time, referring to the two wine glasses they were holding, Whitehead remarked to Price that

the glasses are also raging with molecular activity, and, if we were not in the habit of measuring time by the ridiculously inadequate yardsticks of our consciousness in this human life span, we should remember that those glasses are disintegrating before our very eyes.[4]

We can see the reason for asserting that endurance implies change if we ask ourselves what it means *to be in time, to be temporal, to endure*. It means, first of all, that the enduring thing's existence does not happen all at once. It exists at one time, t_1, and it also exists at another time, t_2. *What* it is at t_2 cannot be identical with *what* it was at t_1, or else it was already at t_1 what it now is at t_2. Its states at t_2 and t_1 would be identical, and so there would be no difference between t_2 and t_1, and so we could not differentiate them. We could have only one t for this thing. This thing would have to be all it is at one instant, and so it would have to be outside of time altogether. For no matter how small a duration may be it is still duration, and some change is necessary if a thing may truly be said to endure at all.

To say that a thing endures but does not change is to deny that it has a history, that anything happens to it, that it does anything. It is to make the thing independent of the temporal. If we say that it simply persists absolutely unaltered from moment to moment then we are saying that there is nothing in it, or pertaining to it, which constitutes a transition from one moment to another. It cannot act during its supposed unchanging existence, for such an act would have to be without beginning and without end and without differentiation of stages; in other words, its whole existence would have to be included in one act that is entirely outside of time. Time would be irrelevant to its nature and to its existence.

What can we mean if we try to say that a changeless thing is "in time"? If it does not change then *what* it is at one moment is identical with *what* it is at any other moment. There is nothing in the thing itself to differentiate one of its moments from another. What, then, does differentiate the two moments from each other? Is it something else? If so, it is the duration in time of something else we are talking about rather than the duration of our supposed unchanging thing. Or is the difference between one moment and another moment to be found in time itself rather than in the things which exist in time? Perhaps time itself is like a moving stream which carries us on its crest past the things which make up the real world; the stream moves, the things it passes remain still.

Something like this idea seems our only hope if we are to be able to think of things existing unchanged in time. The change cannot be in the things, so it must be in time. But this involves us in even greater trouble, for it requires us to think of time as something real in itself, as something which has its own existence apart from the things we say exist in time. Now if the differences between before and after are differences which happen to time itself, rather than to things in time, then time itself must be something which changes. To note and date the changes which happen to time we need another time; and so on, without end. Our error, of course, is in the attempt to think of time as a real existent in its own right.

Time is not itself a reality. It is rather the measure of change.[5] Without change existence has no temporal aspect. Without change there is no way in which we can distinguish between *before* and *after;* without change a thing has no *before* and *after.*

If we say that a thing endures unchanged not in its own time but throughout the time of something else, then the time we refer to has nothing to do with the thing which does not change. There is a sense in which we can say that the *sum of two plus two* remains the same through all time. But we do not mean "remains" in the sense of a continuing existence, for the *sum of two plus two* is a mathematical relation which applies to every possible and actual existent but it is not something which has its own existence.

Each temporal thing has its own time. Its own time is the measure of its own duration. One thing's duration is measured against the duration of another thing; there is no single all-inclusive time which exists somehow in independence of all individual durations, against which they can be measured. So a thing which does not have its own time is not "in time" at all. There is no point in saying that it endures through the time of something else, for if it does not have its own time there is nothing about it to measure against the time of something else.

Everything that exists in such a way that we can apply to it the distinction between *before* and *after* is in process of change. For this distinction applies to a thing only if what it *was* is not identical with what it *is*. If what it *is* differs from what it *was*, then either it has changed or we have two things instead of one. The same consideration applies to each of these two, and so on without end.

All that is temporal is in process of change. We have now only to ask whether there is anything in nature which is not temporal. If we wish to find something in nature which is not temporal, where shall we look? It can be nothing we perceive, for perception requires sensation and sensation is of the temporal. It would have to be something we conceive. Is it number? Is it a geometric entity? Is it a ratio, a formula, a pattern? But these do not have their own existence. Their being is in the essences of actual and possible existents and in the concepts by which these essences are known. They pertain to essences, and they have existence only in and through the existence of essences to which they pertain. They have their being in the being of something else, and we discover them only by abstraction.

Perhaps there are really existing non-temporal things in nature which are beyond the reach of our sense perception. Since such things would be out of the reach of our experience we cannot exclude the possibility of their existence by an appeal to experience. So we shall have to examine the case for their possible existence by reason alone.

If there were really existing non-temporal things in nature we should have to find out about their existence by inference. The only kind of inference which would establish their existence would be to show that their existence is necessary to account for the existence of the things we do experience. To show this we should have to show that the things we do experience depend on these inferred non-temporal things. Thus the Greek atomists supposed they had demonstrated the existence of unchanging atoms as the ultimate realities which account for the appearances of change in nature. But any such attempt fails, for its inevitable result is to identify real existence with these unchanging entities and to deny real existence of the objects of sense perception. The objects of sense perception could no longer be considered to exist in their own right; we should have to understand them as unreal appearances of the real. Any such speculation requires us to reject sense perception as a mode of knowing real existence, and thus it destroys the very criterion by which we distinguish between what does and what does not exist.

Everything Which Changes Is Contingent

If everything which exists in nature changes the "everything" which exists in nature is contingent, for change implies contingency. It is this relation of change and contingency which we now have to examine. We need to understand why every changing thing is contingent.

The reason, in brief, is this. A changing thing, such as a plant or an animal, includes in every stage of its development potentialities which are not yet actual. It is not yet all that it can come to be, and yet in acquiring its new characteristics it will not lose its original nature as a plant or an animal. Of course if it does lose its nature the change which occurs in this instance is not a stage of its own development; it is a change from the kind of thing it was to something of another kind, as when the plant or animal dies. Change itself is the process by which the potential becomes

actual. This process, however, requires more than merely the potentialities of the thing which is changing; it requires something
to bring about their fulfilment. For in that respect in which a thing
is potential only, the thing itself cannot bring the potential into
actuality. If it could bring about the change from within itself
then in that respect it would be not potential but actual.

An infant, for example, has potentialities of growth and maturation which, if realized, will make of him an adult person. Pup-
pies and kittens do not have these potentialities. They have their
own, but not those of a human infant. There is nothing we can
do to a puppy or a kitten, there is no influence we can bring to
bear, to bring out the nature of an adult person. Yet the infant,
who does have this potentiality, cannot of himself, with the acts
he is already capable of performing, become what he is capable of
becoming. He depends on things and persons other than himself,
and what he receives from these other things enables him to grow
and to mature.

When something changes it passes from one state or condition
to another. Water boils, and changes from liquid to vapor. It does
not do this of itself, however. A certain relation between the temperature of the water and the pressure of the atmosphere must be
established before the change from liquid to vapor occurs. It is
impossible for the water itself to establish this relationship. In
other words, the conditions under which the change occurs do
not lie wholly within the thing which changes.

If we were to have change without contingency it is plain that
the changing thing would have to be in complete isolation. It is
also plain, from our scientific knowledge of nature, that no physical thing or system of things in nature is isolated. We can isolate
certain processes in certain respects, but never absolutely. We
cannot remove a physical system from gravitational fields, or insulate it from all forms of energy exchange with its environment.
But even if we try to conceive of a process of change in isolation,
so that every state through which a thing passes comes wholly
from within itself, we find that we have compromised the reality
of the supposed change. A thing which seemed to pass through a

succession of states, each of which was necessitated entirely by what the thing was before, can hardly be said to change. Could something completely self-determined pass through a succession of states? Can there be an unfolding in time of the nature of something which is not dependent in any way on anything else for what emerges during the unfolding? The totality of the states through which we might suppose such a thing to pass could not occur in any temporal sequence. For if what is potential in a thing, such as an expected future state, is not dependent on anything else for its realization then it is not potential but actual.

Suppose we try to conceive the growth of a plant as something not dependent on anything outside the plant. We might observe that the seed would sprout, the leaves would form, and the plant would live its life with no help from sun or earth or moisture. But if we reflect a moment it becomes plain that if the seed exists with these potentialities within it, and if nothing further is required for their actualization, then they are already actual. The seed is already sprouted, the leaves already formed, the life processes actual all at once.

If something happens *to* a thing then that thing was to some extent indeterminate and incomplete, and this is true even if what happens to it is its destruction. What it was did not include all that it comes to be. Anything capable of change is open to influence from outside itself. In other words, it is both actual and potential. It is incompletely actual, for it has potentialities which so far are unrealized. This brings us face to face with the necessary connection between change and contingency. It rests upon the fact that everything for which change is possible has alternative possibilities within its own nature, and so it cannot from its own nature determine which of those alternative possibilities will be realized. Water, for example, is of such a nature that it can either boil or freeze. It cannot do both together. Consequently the nature of water itself is not enough to account for its actual boiling or its actual freezing. What happens to it depends on what it is, but not alone on what it is; what happens to it depends also on what influences it is subjected to from outside itself.

In order to be able to say truly of something that *it* changes, that which changes must be incompletely actual at each moment or in each phase of its change. On the other hand, if the so-called changes which a thing is said to undergo should come wholly and entirely from itself then every stage of the supposed change would be a change from one thing to another or, if we insist that we have only one thing here, then every stage of the thing's existence would already contain everything yet to come.

It is apparent from this that no real being whose changes come wholly from within itself can be understood to act under the limitations of time. For if the supposed future stages are to be actual at every moment of the thing's existence, they turn out not to be really future at all. They are already actual. So if the thing which acts has nothing potential in it, and this must be the case if all which is to come comes from it alone, and if it is to be one being and not as many different beings as there are distinguishable moments of its existence, then it cannot exist spread out in time.

The only way we can think of a changing thing, and preserve for it the continuity it must have if we are to think of it as one thing, is to recognize that at each stage it is incompletely actual and partly potential. In so far as a thing is potential it is open to influences from outside itself. Its own nature does not account completely for what it becomes in the course of the changes it undergoes. Its own nature does limit its potentialities. I cannot plant a stone and from it grow a tree. But if what is potential is to become actual then other things must act upon it.

Suppose we had a clock which did not have to be wound and which existed and acted in absolute isolation from everything else (assuming we can mean something intelligible by such a supposition). The minute-hand is now at *2*, and I say that in five minutes it will point at *3*. What can I mean here by "it"? What justifies my supposition that the hand now at *2* is the same hand which will be at *3*? What is there about it now which has anything to do with a clock-hand pointing at *3* unless the later position is now potential and not actual? So far as we consider the hand as something itself, its later positions are potential, for they depend on the action of the clock mechanism. But suppose we think of the position of the hand in terms of the clock mechanism as a whole. The change from one stage to another would be already completely determined from within the clock itself. The action of the clock would be a predetermined sequence of events. Even so, we cannot escape potentiality, for the fact that the action is a *sequence* and does not happen all at once depends on the mutual interaction of the parts of the mechanism. Even if the mechanism as a whole were isolated, the parts would not be isolated from each other. To have the kind of isolation which would exclude potentiality we should have to have something not composed of parts. It would have to be a simple rather than a composite being, and its act would not be in time.

If we try to deny potentiality and still assert motion and duration then we have to say that motion is from point to point and no point has extension, and that duration is from instant to instant and no instant has duration. If duration is dissolved into instants we lose the distinction of before and after unless we introduce duration somehow *between* the instants. If we introduce duration between the instants, then each instant is a separate existent, for the duration does not belong to it.

It needs hardly to be said that on such a view as this the world of nature, as we experience it, does not exist. For this means that there is no more real motion or real duration or real continuity among the things in nature than there is among the separate still pictures which flash on the cinema screen at a rate which produces the illusion of movement. The only continuity is in the film, the projector, and the screen; there is no continuity among the pictures on the screen. The only motion is in the projector and the film, not in the pictures on the screen. A world without potentiality is like the pictures on the screen without the screen or the projector or the film.

Real things both change and endure. To say that a thing changes is to assume that there is some sense in which it is the same thing before and after the change. Otherwise we should say not that a thing changes but that one thing gives way to another. So there must be something about a thing by virtue of which it *endures* through the changes which constitute its temporal existence. The unity of the existence of a thing is to be found in its original potentialities, which in turn are based on the actual nature it has to begin with. Its actual nature, so far as it is actual at any moment, is incomplete. Its potentialities are not exhausted. Exhaust or destroy the potentialities of an existing thing and its existence is at an end; it has given way to something else.

A normal infant has, at birth, the potentialities of development through childhood and adolescence into adult maturity. His potentialities of becoming a human adult are the same in infancy and childhood and adolescence. Events may occur which destroy these potentialities; the child may die, or injury may limit his development. But we know that whatever he is able actually to be at any stage of his development is something for which he had the potentiality from the beginning of his existence. A man who becomes a musician was born an infant capable of developing into a man who is a musician. This is not to say that he was capable of becoming an infant musician; it is to say rather that he was an infant capable of becoming an adult musician in the fullness of his development. That capability persisted unchanged until it was realized. Whatever changes occurred in the person's actual state from time to time, there was at no time the kind of change which destroyed this potentiality. At any moment of its existence a thing is more potentially than it is actually; as soon as it loses the potentialities it has by virtue of its special nature it ceases to be what it was and has been changed into something else. The living man becomes a corpse, the plant has died, the iron has rusted away.

If everything which exists in nature is temporal, and if everything temporal contains within itself the distinction between before and after, and if this distinction holds good only of things that change (as a distinction *within* the thing), and if anything that changes combines in itself both the actual and potential at any moment of its existence, and if the potential as such is incapable of bringing itself into actuality and so depends for this on something else, then everything which exists in nature is contingent. With this we have established one part of our second premise.

THE CONTINGENCY OF THE WORLD AS A WHOLE

Sometimes we find the argument offered, in defense of naturalism, that even if everything in nature is contingent it does not follow that nature as a whole is contingent. Nature may be a non-contingent whole of contingent things. In a recent textbook for courses in the introduction to philosophy the argument from the contingency of the world to the existence of God is thus quite casually dismissed.

It may be admitted [the author says], that nothing in Nature contains its own reason for being, and that therefore things and events are indeed contingent. But to infer from the contingency of things and events, taken individually, that Nature as a whole is contingent, and thus dependent upon another being, is to commit the fallacy of composition. This fallacy consists in arguing from the properties of the parts, taken separately, to a property of the whole, taken together. Because sodium and chlorine are poisonous, it does not follow that table salt, which is composed of these elements, is equally poisonous. Although any part of Nature, taken singly, may be contingent or dependent for its existence on something else, it does not follow that Nature, taken as a whole, is also contingent. In other words, there is no reason why Nature cannot be considered to be the ultimate ground of all existence, even though its parts depend for their existence on other parts.[6]

If this criticism is sound then it turns out that the more than two thousand years of concern with this matter is all the result of a school-boy mistake. It was Aristotle who called attention explicitly to the fallacy of composition, and it now appears that neither he nor those who learned from him had the wit to see that the argument from contingency is nothing more than the elaboration of one of the most elementary and obvious of fallacies.

This criticism of the argument from contingency is based on a confusion of thought, a confusion so intimately tied in with the very statement of the criticism itself that our author spells it out for us in his own words. "This fallacy consists," the author says in the passage just quoted, "in arguing from the *properties* of the parts, taken separately, to a *property* of the whole, taken together." Then in the next sentence but one he adds, "Although any part of Nature, taken singly, may be contingent or *dependent for its existence on something else*, it does not follow that Nature, taken as a whole, is also contingent." The words and phrases here in italics identify the confusion. It is plain that the author means by "contingent" the dependence of something upon something else for its *existence;* and yet in his statement of the fallacy of composition he refers not to existence but to properties.

The fallacy of composition is committed only with respect to the essences or natures of things, not with respect to their existence. We commit the fallacy of composition when we ascribe to a collection or group *as a whole* properties which belong only to the individual things themselves. But existence is not a property, and to be contingent is not to have contingency as a property. The contingency of a thing is simply the fact that the thing in question, *with its properties*, depends on something else for its *existence*.

In so far as nature is composed of really existing individual things this is the only kind of real existence it has. It does not also really exist as a whole in distinction from the existence of its parts. Nature exists bit by bit in time; the *whole* of nature includes not only what is, but what was and no longer is and what will be but not yet is. At no time in its history is the whole of nature in existence. How then could a partially non-existent whole confer existence upon the contingent parts of that whole? The parts of nature which now exist are all contingent; the parts of nature which do not now exist are now inoperative. Some may try to avoid this by saying that the sum total of what exists in nature must be non-contingent because that is all there is; but *all there is* at any time is not the whole of nature, for the whole of nature includes also what has been and what will be.

There is one further way of trying to avoid the theistic consequences of recognizing the contingency of things in nature. This is to admit that everything in nature is contingent, that each depends on other things as its causes, and that these in turn depend on other things, and yet to insist that we do not need to go beyond nature to account for the existence of things in nature because this series of causes is infinite. The point is that if there is no limit to the series of causes then the supply of contingent causes is inexhaustible, and so we do not need anything non-contingent.

Here again we have one of the recurring confusions, characteristic of the strategems of naturalism, which have served to obscure the essential weaknesses of such philosophies. But this desperate attempt to save naturalism and avoid theism fails because there can be no infinite series of actually existing things or events. Any sum of actual entities, whether past and future existents are included or not, must be a finite number. To designate a series or sum as infinite is to deny that it is a series or sum of real existents.

Our previously quoted author offers us an excellent example of this very confusion. In commenting on Aristotle's proof of the existence of an "unmoved mover," i.e. of an uncaused cause, our author makes this observation. "Further, Aristotle's argument assumes that an infinite series of movers is impossible. But there is nothing about an infinite series, as such, which is self-contradictory. It is possible to construct such a series in arithmetic."[7]

It *is* possible to construct an infinite series in arithmetic. Furthermore, we can apply the concept of infinite series to any real continuum. But this is possible only because a continuum is not something put together out of the items which constitute the series; the items of such a series are obtained by abstraction from the continuum. If, on the other hand, the parts of a whole are themselves really existing things, and the whole is constructed from them, then the sum of parts is finite. The unity of such a whole is something imposed upon the parts, or is a set of relations they have with each other, as the unity of a wall built of bricks or the unity of a family composed of individual people. If the whole is the really existing thing, and it is a continuum, such as the surface of a physical object, then the parts are obtained by abstraction from the whole or by division of it. Since there are no limits to this process of division there is no limit to the number of parts which might be marked off within the whole. But in this case the parts themselves do not exist as individual things. If we break up the continuum into physically separate parts so that the parts do exist as individual things, then we destroy its continuity; and we shall never, at any stage in the process of physical division, have other than a finite number of parts.

The same principle applies in mathematics itself, wherever the distinction between the discrete and the continuous is recognized. A line, for example, is a continuum, and we say that the line contains an infinite series of points. But we can say this only as we understand the points to be limits of segments of the line rather than parts of which the line is composed, and we can say it only because nothing in the nature of the line limits the number of possible divisions of it into segments. There is no limit to the ways in which the line may be divided. But the points we determine in any division of the line are not themselves parts of the line. Any part of the line is a segment, and a point belongs to the line only as a limit of a segment.

That we can construct an infinite series in arithmetic has no bearing on the question of whether there can have existed an infinite series of real causes. The series of real causes in nature is not itself a mathematical series, however applicable to it any mathematical series may be. The concept of infinite series is applicable to real existence only as we do, in concept, analyze and differentiate within a real continuum. But the parts we obtain by such analysis are not parts of which the continuum is constructed; they exist, when considered by themselves, only as conceptual constructs. For the limits which differentiate a part from the rest of the continuum to which it belongs are conceptually determined; they are not real distinctions which exist apart from each other in the thing itself. Here again we have one of the oldest of philosophy's lessons, as old as Zeno and his puzzles concerning space and time and motion.

THE PRESENT STATE OF OUR ARGUMENT

We have now found that the real world of actually existing things and events is neither self-existent nor contains anything self-existent as a part of itself. We found in Chapter 18 that the world of nature is an actually existing world which contains the real things and events we find by means of our experience. These two basic premises imply the third proposition as their conclusion, that the world of nature is contingent, that is, that it contains nothing self-existent nor is a self-existent whole. In the next chapter we shall try to see whether the real existence of a world of contingent beings presupposes the existence of something which is not contingent.

CHAPTER 20

The Cause of Nature

THE NEXT STEP OF THE ARGUMENT

W E NOW HAVE two premises of our proof yet to establish, the fourth and the fifth propositions. The fourth states that *anything which neither exists of itself nor contains anything self-existent as a part of itself depends for its existence upon something which exists in and of itself and does not in turn depend on anything else.*

We have seen already that nature is through and through contingent. Why then should we have to take this further step in our proof? Does not the contingency of nature simply mean that there is something beyond nature on which nature depends? Is it not obvious that, in the long run, we cannot rest here with something contingent, since the same arguments would compel us to push further and further until we found something not contingent? But this is not sufficient. Our argument for contingency has been largely negative, in the sense that we have shown that there is nothing in nature the essence of which necessarily involves existence. We have not yet shown the actual existence of something beyond nature upon which nature depends.

The importance of this next step lies in the fact that we are not entitled simply to assume existence where we need it in order to make our answers come out right. We may be told, for example, that although nature and the things in nature are not self-existent we still have no reason to assert the positive existence of something else on which they depend. Perhaps they simply are, and their failure to account for their own existence means only that their existence is not to be accounted for. It is a mystery. Perhaps at this point we are up against a dead end, and intelligence can carry us no further. And, in truth, we have reached the end unless there is something to take us further. Our direct contact with existence is limited to our sensory experience and our self-awareness, and even if our experience includes in some way a contact with existence beyond nature we shall have to discover this fact by rational examination of the conditions of the existence we find presented to us directly in experience. These are the reasons why we must continue our argument with an examination of the evidence for the actual existence of something on which nature depends.

This is necessary in order to meet the kind of objection which Professor Lamprecht raises in discussing the argument from the contingency of the world to the existence of God. Professor Lamprecht is quite willing to grant that all things which exist in nature are contingent.

> Every existence [he says] is contingent for its production upon both the materials that lend themselves to its production and also the efficient causes capable of so treating those materials as to bring about its production. Every event, as well as every existence, is contingent; for, however necessary it may be for us to accept events after they have occurred and to face them frankly for what they are as they are occurring, they are still, in advance of their occurrence, only among the possibilities that might happen contingently upon the prior occurrence of other requisite events.[1]

He then argues that even if no objection is raised to the inference from this to the contingency of the world as a whole we still should not be entitled to assert necessary existence as that on which the existence of the world depends:

> . . . the necessary ground of the contingent world (whatever that phrase may mean) can hardly be said to exist. There may be some totality of truth of which the world is the expression, or some set of first principles of which the world is the development, or some system of "universals" of which the world, in Plato's language, is the "imitation" or in which the world "participates." But to identify God with such entities is hardly to have an existent God, and

surely it is not to have a God of the qualities and character which religious men are prone to attribute to God.[2]

If we follow this phase of Professor Lamprecht's discussion a step further we shall find an illustration of the method of solving problems by the arbitrary definition of terms—a method often used in defense of philosophical naturalism:

> God as a Platonic form or set of moral ideals is real as all ideal possibilities are real and can hardly be denied in that sense by those who understand what is meant. But, if the point be granted, the language used . . . seems undesirable. God in this sense does not "exist"; that is, God in this sense is not meant to be taken as anything within the spatial-temporal world of which alone "existence" can be affirmed. And just as it is linguistically undesirable to speak of existence in this way, so it may well be urged that it is undesirable to speak of God in this way.[3]

It is apparent that we need to spell out the connection between the fact of contingency and the real existence of something, not itself contingent, on which contingent existence depends. This is not a problem to be solved by making rules about the use of language. The only appropriate method is careful analysis of what we actually find in experience in order to discover what it forces us to conclude concerning the conditions of its own existence. We need also to look very carefully at what is involved in assertions of existence. The identification of existence with the spatio-temporal world cannot be supported by mere assertion; nor does linguistic usage justify such a restriction, unless we can be persuaded to legislate concerning language on the basis of some set of metaphysical or anti-metaphysical prejudices. We have already seen some of the difficulties involved in statements of existence and we have explored some of the issues concerning the existence of God which hang on this problem. We shall now consider the positive grounds for asserting that the contingent world depends for its existence upon the existence of something that is not contingent.

THE BRIDGE FROM THE CONTINGENT TO THE NON-CONTINGENT

The bridge which carries intelligence from a contingent natural world to a real existence beyond nature is the principle of causality. The causal principle applies to every contingent existence, and because of this we do not reach the end when we discover that nothing in nature can account for its own existence. As we shall see later, the penalty for denying the principle of causality is to be compelled, so far as logic governs our inferences, to deny the real existence of the things we find in the world of nature.

TWO LEVELS OF CAUSALITY

Our direct acquaintance with causality is, of course, with its operation in nature. Wherever we find change we understand it in terms of causes. Changes are brought about; they do not happen of themselves. As we saw earlier, if a thing seemed to go through a process of change and yet if the later stages of the process came wholly from within itself we should not say that the thing itself really had changed. If the growth of a plant depended on nothing outside itself, if it were only the unfolding of what was there in the plant all the time, we should not say that change had occurred. For the plant would have been, all along, what it gradually showed itself to be—like the artificial Japanese flowers which bring out their hidden blooms when dropped into water. But of course there are no plants which unfold themselves in isolation. We know of no things in nature which exist in isolation, and if there were such, their existence would not be temporal. Even the Japanese paper flower needs contact with water before it opens, and so there has to be a cause which accounts at least for the *emergence* of what was there before in secret.

Things in nature depend on other things for *what* they are; we may even say they depend on other things, but only in a limited sense, for the fact *that* they are. Natural causes bring things into existence in the sense that they bring it to pass that this individual thing and that individual thing come to exist. In doing this, however, natural causes must make use of something that already exists. Everything which comes to be in nature has a material cause, and in every case its material cause is something that exists. But what is brought to be does not have the same existence as its material cause; else it would simply *be* its material cause, and no change would have occurred. So it is only in a restricted and relative sense that we may say that natural causes bring things into existence. The existence into which a natural cause brings something is an existence which comes from other things, from things which already exist. Natural causes bring something new into existence by changing things which already exist. No natural cause initiates existence. As we shall see later in this chapter, not only is this a fact which we discover in our experience of things but when we examine the causal process more closely we see that it is *impossible* for any contingent thing to be a cause of existence. Contingent causes are causes of change alone.

Contingent causes, however, are not enough. For the existence which contingent causes use to produce their effects still needs to be accounted for. Natural causation presupposes existence. If we are to find the cause of the existence which natural causes presuppose we must look beyond nature. We have to explain the existence of a world in which it is possible for natural causes to bring about real changes, if we are to explain it at all, in terms of a cause beyond that world itself. We require not only *causes in nature*, we need a *Cause of Nature*. Natural causes are causes of change, but the Cause of Nature is a cause of existence.

Before we undertake to cross the bridge from the contingent world of nature to the Cause of Nature we must look more directly at the causal principle itself. We need to understand the basis of our confidence in the genuineness of this principle. So much depends upon it that we cannot afford to take it for granted, especially in the light of the attempts which have been made to discredit it.

OUR KNOWLEDGE OF CAUSES

The causal principle has been challenged many times in the history of philosophy. It is said, for example, that we cannot sense or perceive causation and therefore we are not justified in claiming real existence for it. The perceptual criterion of existence fails in this case, and our belief in real causation is sheer assumption. But this is an obvious misapplication of the perceptual test of existence; for the test applies to real beings, and causation is not a real being. Real beings are causes, just as they are material. We do not perceive their materiality directly, as we perceive their color. We perceive the things and *understand* them to be material. We do not sense or perceive the causal efficacy of a thing. We perceive the thing in its action and we *understand* it to be a cause. The basis of our understanding is our inability otherwise to make rational sense of its real existence as what we find it to be. Every attempt in the history of philosophy to deny the causal principle has resulted in the cleavage of reason from experience. It has rendered real existence unintelligible, or else it has denied the real existence of what we experience; it has led, in the latter case, to skepticism or, in the former case, to an apriorism which tries to spin real existence out of mere essence. The philosophical significance of these consequences lies in the fact that each is an effective refutation of the premise from which it follows.

I strike a match and touch it to a piece of paper, and the paper goes up in flame. Even if I ignore the causal relation temporarily it is still the case that what I perceive requires, for its perception, some conceptual understanding. I recognize these things; I am aware of the sequence of events; I link together in my awareness the early and the late stages of the occurrence as belonging to a single action. If we are to understand the connections within this occurrence, the time relation of the parts to each other, we have to understand them in terms of cause and effect.

Suppose, for a moment, that the flame of the match actually had nothing to do with the burning of the paper. These then would not be parts of one event, but would be quite independent.

The fact that the flame of the match is followed by the flame of the paper would be coincidence. The paper would have burned, just as it did, even if the match had not been lighted. Now this, of course, could well be true. But if we came to believe that it is true we should likely wonder what actually did cause the paper to burn. If we found that someone had focussed the rays of the sun, by means of a burning-glass, to cause the paper to burn then our understanding would be satisfied, and we could accept the relation of the flame of the match and the burning of the paper as mere coincidence.

But suppose that somehow we were led to believe that nothing caused the paper to burst into flame. Then we should have to revise drastically our concept of paper. For there is nothing in the physical properties of paper, as we understand its nature from our knowledge of the materials of which it is made and of the processes of its manufacture, to account for its self-ignition. So we should have to develop some other conception of the nature of paper, a conception moreover which would find no support from our ordinary methods of investigation. This would require us to abandon our confidence in our knowledge of the nature of things, the knowledge which has developed out of experience and scientific investigation. Or else we should have to conclude that this was not ordinary paper, after all.

Our knowledge of causes is rational knowledge. If we are to know the existence of a thing which we consider to be a cause we need direct or indirect perceptual confirmation. We perceive *that* it is, we discover in perception much of *what* it is, and our understanding of its action and relations in terms of the causal principle makes the facts of perception intelligible to us. As D. J. B. Hawkins says, "The apprehension of causation is not given in immediate experience but is the fruit of an analysis of that experience."[4] It is for the sake of intelligibility that we appeal to causes and refuse to accept the given situation without further explanation.

This is brought out quite clearly by Hawkins' illustrations:

> Now, on the plane of our common-sense thinking [he asks], when do we ask for an explanation of a state of fact? We say, for instance: Why did he go to France? How is it that this book came

to be here? Why did those weeds come up again? We ask these questions because we do not know what there is about him and the circumstances of his life from which it would follow that he went to France, because there is nothing in the nature of this book which necessitates its being in this place rather than that, because we think that the precautions which we have taken preclude any necessary conjunction between the weeds and their coming up again. It is therefore apparent that we feel the need of explanation when we find a conjunction of factors in which the relatively given is not a sufficient ground of the relatively not-given. . . . Hence we see what kind of thing must of its nature exist and what kind of thing requires a cause. A cause is required by a thing in which there is internal incoherence, in the sense that its abstract elements in the order of the structure of the thing do not imply one another. Only a perfect unity, which, considered abstractly at any level, implies all that it is, exists of itself as absolutely given.[5]

We have already seen that no temporal thing exists of itself. *What* it *is* in any moment of its existence does not imply what it will be in another moment of its existence, else it would have the whole of its nature included within every moment of its existence, and it would exist not as something temporal but all at once. To challenge the causal principle is to challenge the intelligibility of existence in time. Such challenges have occurred; but they always lead to, or arise from, subjectivism or positivism or skepticism concerning real existence. So it is not merely that we need the idea of causation as some sort of pattern for the arrangement of our perceptions, as in a phenomenalism such as Kant's, but causation must really take place. Real things have to *be* causes, not just *appear* to be. For if causation does not really happen then change is not real and the world of nature does not exist.

The existence or non-existence of the things we perceive is the issue which hangs on the truth or falsity of the causal principle. Either there is real causation or there is no difference between the actual and the possible. Real being, as Gilson says, "is that being which belongs to an essence when, once a mere possible, it has become actual owing to the efficacy of its causes."[6] The truth of sense perception presupposes the truth of the causal principle.

But this is not all. The fact that there is a world in which natural causes act also requires the causal principle for its explanation. For if the world exists, from what does it obtain its existence? Not from itself, else it would not be contingent. Nor can anything real have drawn itself from the limbo of mere possibility, because *the merely possible does not act.* If there is nothing from which the world has obtained its existence, then it has not obtained it. The world does not exist unless there is something which has brought it into existence. Our knowledge that the world has a cause is our discovery that to assert of the world the kind of existence we find that it has and to deny that the world has a cause is to contradict ourselves.

The foundation of our confidence in the truth of the causal principle is not preference, nor is it merely a part of our psychology that we believe it, nor is it scientific evidence. The foundation of our confidence in its truth rests on our discovery of the distinction between essence and existence and our recognition that there is nothing in the essence of anything contingent to tie existence to it. If existence is to come to an essence it must come from something that exists. Causality is the link of existence with existence. To deny it is to deny that existence is linked. It is to assert that there are nothing but little plops of sheer evanescence which come from nothing, become nothing, are utterly discontinuous and irrelevant to each other, and among which the distinction between before and after loses its meaning. It is to assert, in other words, the complete and absolute collapse of the attempt to mean anything by assertion.

In linking existence with existence the causal principle expresses the intelligibility of existence. For to discover the cause of something which exists enables us to understand the fact of its existence. If we know, for example, that the cause of the increase of the number of mosquitoes in a certain area is the presence of pools of stagnant water then we understand how it happens that there are more mosquitoes. The fact makes sense. If the mosquitoes simply appeared, with nothing to account for their appearance, we should be puzzled. If we cared enough we should look for a cause. If we were told that there was no reason for such a thing to happen, that mosquitoes simply begin to be with nothing to bring them into existence, we should consider such a statement nonsense—unless, of course, we were positivists or skeptics withdrawn from the real world in order to philosophize about a world in which, if it were real, no philosophizing could take place. In short, the real question involved in the application of the causal principle to nature and to things in nature is the question of whether their existence makes sense or whether it is an ultimate irrationality. If it should make sense for their existence to be an ultimate irrationality then it would not be irrational; if it does not make sense for their existence to be an ultimate irrationality then to assert that it is such is to indulge in utterly groundless dogmatizing.

When we see the issue in this light then our proper course is plain. We cannot accept, here or elsewhere, the finality of the irrational. Whatever we may think about existence, whatever it may be and however feeble our understanding of it may be, it must be intelligible if our thinking is to be relevant to it. This includes our thinking about its supposed possible unintelligibility. There may be, and surely are, many matters we do not understand about the things that exist; but to conclude from this that existence is unintelligible is possible only for those who have the effrontery to confuse their own powers of understanding with intelligibility itself, and who assume that what they do not understand they could fail to understand only because it is in itself irrational.

CAUSALITY AND THE NATURAL SCIENCES

If we are told that there is no scientific evidence which supports the view that there are causes operative in nature we must reply that the question of whether or not there are causes is not a scientific problem. The causal principle can be neither established nor shown to be false by any special science. The findings of the special sciences may support or refute the belief that this or that cause is operative in a given situation, but the question of whether there are causes or not is beyond their reach. This is not in question; it is presupposed by the sciences. We do not expect the sciences to establish the existence of the things they investigate; they assume the existence of those things, and their investigations could not get under way unless they did make such assumptions. In so far as the special sciences assume the existence of the things they investigate they assume also that the causal principle applies to those things.

This does not mean that a scientific report needs to make explicit reference to the existence of its objects and to the causal principle. No explicit reference to the existence of anything is necessary unless the fact of such existence happens to be questioned in the course of inquiry. If it is questioned in a scientific inquiry, the question is answered by reference to something that does exist and the existence of which is not in question. Thus even a scientific answer to a question concerning existence assumes the existence of other things, it does not itself establish the fact that there are real existents.

As we have said, the same thing is true of the causal principle. As Mascall puts it,

> the method of investigation of the world which physical science adopts—observation of measurable phenomena and their correlation and prediction by general statements—is such as to exclude efficient causality from its purview, and hence renders it quite incompetent to decide whether there is efficient causality or not. Efficient causality is not a physical concept but a metaphysical one, and it is only because the physical scientists of the eighteenth and nineteenth centuries insisted on illicitly talking physics in terms of efficient causality that their successors, having discovered that efficient causality is not what physics is as a matter of fact concerned with, have only too often assumed that it is nonexistent.[7]

The further a science goes in the direction of a mathematical formulation the less explicit reference there is to causality, for the causal relation cannot be expressed in mathematical terms. But this does not mean that the success of physics in reaching a more

333

completely mathematical formulation is evidence of the falsity or the meaninglessness of causality. In this connection it is most significant that as soon as the mathematical formulas of physics are applied to real existence, for example in engineering and technology, the causal principle takes control. Physics' susceptibility to technological application under the control of the causal principle should be proof enough that the truth of physics' formulas is not in any way in conflict with the causal principle.

The world that the sciences investigate is an intelligible world and it is a world of contingency. As Mascall says, in another place:

> The type of universe whose investigation requires the methods of modern science must, I would suggest, have two characteristics: contingency and rationality. If rationality were absent, there would be no laws for science to discover; if contingency were absent, there would be no need for empirical observation and experiment, for every truth about the world could be deduced from first principles. The combination of the two characteristics is precisely correlative to a technique which believes that there are uniformities in nature and yet that these uniformities need to be discovered.[8]

Since a contingent world can be an intelligible world—that, is a rational order of existence—only if it is a causal order, it is apparent that the truth of the causal principle is presupposed by the very possibility of scientific inquiry.

The Self-Existence of the Cause of Nature

It remains now only to understand the reasons why the Cause of Nature is something which exists in and of itself and does not depend on anything else. The Cause of Nature is not contingent, as are the causes which operate within nature. If it were contingent then it would not be the Cause *of* Nature, but only another cause within nature. What differentiates the Cause of Nature from causes in nature is the fact that it is a cause of existence while natural causes are causes of change. In order to bring something new into existence, natural causes must work on something which already exists. But the Cause of Nature brings nature into existence in the act of bestowing existence upon what is, without existence, only a possibility.

Natural causes, as we have already seen, operate upon existence; what they do is to alter existing things. This is not the case with the Cause of Nature. The Cause of Nature does not bring nature into existence by changing into, or being changed into, nature. For if this were so then the so-called "Cause of Nature" would itself have been only a preceding state of nature. Nor does the Cause of Nature bring nature into existence by changing something else into nature, as Plato's Demiurge made the world out of unformed matter. For if there had been something which really existed and which was changed into nature, then this something else was itself only a preceding state of nature and not something "else" at all. Whatever material the Cause of Nature might use in the fashioning of the world would be itself a preceding state of that very world, and so we are not in this way able to account for the existence of the world. At best we should account only for some particular state of the world.

The conclusion we are forced to draw from this is that the Cause of Nature brought the world into existence simply by bestowing existence upon it. The act by which this Cause brings the world to be is an act which requires no already existing material with which to work. It requires only that the world which is to exist shall be a possible world. A possible world is made to exist in reality by a Cause which itself is not brought into existence nor dependent in any way on anything else for its existence.

Existence which is capable of bestowing existence, and is not limited to bringing about changes in what already exists, cannot itself have received its existence from something else. For then its own existence would be contingent upon something else, and a contingent cause can only change what already exists, it cannot give existence. Here is the nerve of our argument for the existence of a non-contingent Cause of Nature: *any cause able to bestow existence must be a self-existing being*.

It is impossible for a contingent cause to give existence to what does not exist. The reason for this lies in the general principle that *no thing can act except in accordance with its own nature.* A man, for example, is by nature rational, sentient, capable of speech, capable of locomotion, equipped with very complex manipulative organs in his hands. He has a limited range of muscular strength and of physical endurance, and so on. Whatever act a man performs he performs in accordance with his nature. It is by virtue of *what* he is, of his essence, that he is able to perform the acts he does perform and to cause the effects he does cause. But a man is contingent. It is not by virtue of his own nature that he exists. As is the case with every contingent thing, and as we have already seen in an earlier stage of our argument, a man's essence does not include his existence. The act of existing is not a part of his essence. *It is his essence which does exist, but it is not his essence to exist.* That his essence is an essence which exists he owes to something else. Since it is not his essence to exist, and since he can act only in accordance with his own nature, a man cannot by his own act bestow existence upon anything else. He does not possess existence *in* his nature; he is rather the existence *of* his nature.

Since anything which acts must act by its own nature, else the act would not be *its* act, it follows that something which so acts as to bestow existence must itself be something whose very essence is the act of existence. So the essence of the Cause of Nature must be existence itself. The essence of a contingent thing can only *receive* existence. Once it exists it can give of its essence to something else which exists; but it cannot give existence, for existence is not in its nature. The Cause of Nature also gives of its essence in its act, but since *its essence is existence* it gives existence.

The Cause of Nature Not Self-Caused

We must be careful at this point not to confuse the idea of a self-existing being with that of a self-caused being. The distinction may seem unnecessarily subtle, yet to ignore it would have serious consequences. This can be illustrated by reference to a somewhat typical example of the attempt to refute the argument from contingency by confusing the self-existent with the self-caused.

"The argument from causality," says a critic we have quoted before, "does not answer the child's question 'Who made God?' Those who defend this argument deny self-causing power to Nature but attribute it without hesitation to God. But, when we make God, rather than Nature, the exception to causality as ordinarily experienced, we evade rather than solve the difficulty of accounting for the world. What we have done is simply to set the difficulty back one stage, by postulating a cause outside of Nature which is unlike other causes."[9]

Assuming for the moment what we intend to show in the next chapter, that the Cause of Nature is God, let us try to clarify the distinction which this criticism confuses. If we were to say that God causes Himself to exist then we should be back in the same difficulties we found with the attempts to find ultimate existence in nature. Perhaps we do not find our thought saddled with an infinite series of gods, but we have something just as troublesome. For with the idea of a self-caused God we have a divine *nature* or *essence* which somehow generates its own existence out of itself. Thus there would have to be some kind of being logically prior to existence from which existence follows, such as, for example, Plato's *Form of the Good*, or Plotinus' *One*. Consequently ultimate reality would be beyond existence, and existence would not be real. If we are content merely to say that God has "self-causing power" in contrast with nature, then we shall find ourselves caught in this difficulty.

The question "Who made God?" and the notion that God is self-caused both rest on a profound misconception of the point of the argument from contingency. Certainly if this argument is used to establish a reality which is the source of existence in the sense that it causes itself and everything else to be, the argument fails. It fails because it would assume the priority of the essence of God to the existence of God, and it would assume that this essence somehow generates its own existence. This would make God both contingent and not contingent, contingent in that essence is in some sense distinct from existence, as that from which existence flows, and non-contingent in that existence flows from God's essence and not from anything else. This makes the existence of God unintelligible; for no essence, as essence in distinction from existence, can be understood to have from itself any kind of being except the kind of being which pertains to essence alone. If our idea of God is one in which essence is prior to existence then God exists only as, say, an ideal exists, or God is contingent and must have received His *real* existence from something else—and so is not God, or else being is ultimately unintelligible.

If we argue from the existence of the world to the existence of God as Being Who causes Himself to be, then Kant's criticism of the cosmological argument is sound. In fact, all the attacks upon the cosmological argument that seem plausible obtain their plausibility by giving this essentialist interpretation to the argument. It is in this way that we can see and expose the error of Kant's attempt to refute the causal argument for the existence of God.

The whole point of Kant's criticism rests squarely on the central theme of his critical philosophy: that we have genuine knowledge of phenomena alone, and not of any real existent. When we come to his attempt to refute the causal argument for the existence of God by reducing it to a version of the ontological argument, we find that his criticism rests on the supposition that the existence of God is somehow to be guaranteed by His essence.

Even if the causal argument begins with an empirical premise, with the fact of finite existence, Kant insists, that empirical premise cannot tell us what properties this being (God) must have. So reason cuts loose from experience entirely,

and endeavours to discover from mere concepts what properties an absolutely necessary being must have, that is, which among all possible things contains in itself the conditions *(requisita)* essential to absolute necessity. Now these, it is supposed, are nowhere to be found save in the concept of an *ens realissimum;* and the conclusion is therefore drawn, that the *ens realissimum* is the absolutely necessary being. But it is evident that we are here presupposing that the concept of the highest reality is completely adequate to the concept of absolute necessity of existence; that is, that the latter can be inferred from the former. Now this is the proposition maintained by the ontological proof; it is here being assumed in the cosmological proof, and indeed made the basis of the proof; and yet it is an assumption with which this latter proof has professed to dispense.[10]

Kant's criticism of the causal argument thus lies in his denial that the concept of God can justify the conclusion that God exists. His criticism does not apply to any argument from contingency which actually goes from the existence of the world to the existence of God. The connection of the world and God here is not by concept; it is rather through the real existence of the world that the existence of God is known. We do not go from a knowledge of *what* the world is to a knowledge of *what* God must be if He exists, and then find that our concept of God's essence forces us to assert His existence. We go rather from our knowledge *that* the world is to our conclusion *that* God is. We do not argue from the essence of the world, but from the fact that the essences of things in the world have real existence. It would make no difference what *kind* of world did exist, it would make no difference which essences might have existence, the same consideration would apply. It is from the contingency of their existence, not from the implications of their essence, that we conclude the dependence of the things in the world upon a self-existent cause.

"To posit essence or supreme essentiality as the supreme degree of reality is therefore the most disastrous of all metaphysical mistakes," says Gilson, "because it is to substitute *essentia* for *esse* as the ultimate root of all being."[11] As he says in another place, "once removed from being, existence can never be pushed back into it, and, once deprived of its existence, being is unable to give an intelligible account of itself."[12]

It is precisely because in Kant's philosophy reason has lost all contact with existence that Kant can understand the argument from contingency only as a special form of the ontological argument. For Kant, existence has become a category, it is a way in which we think things rather than that things are. Although Kant does not make the mistake of the ontological argument, and include existence as a *part of* essence, yet for him existence—along with possibility and necessity—is a *mode* of essence.[13] It is true that a mode of essence pertains to an essence without modifying it; I may think, for example, the same essence—such as the essence of a house—as possible or actual or necessary. Yet this is still only a way of thinking; it is not *how the essence is*. Modality is how we think *about* essences, whether we think them as possible or actual or necessary; it is not their existence or non-existence.

The question is how we shall understand the existence of God and the relation of God's existence to His nature. There is only one answer to this if the existence of God is to make intelligible to us the existence of the world we know. This answer is that God's existence *is* His nature; it is the very nature of God to exist. Existence is not a part of His nature, nor is it something which happens to His nature; existence *is* His nature. God is not self-caused, for He needs no cause, not even Himself. *That* God is does not flow from *what* He is. *What* He is, is *that* He is.

The very point of the argument from contingency, the point that natural things are contingent in their *existence*, should warn us away from any conception of God which makes essence prior to existence or even differentiates them in their application to God. It is true that the child who asks "Who made God?" can scarcely be expected to see the real thrust of the argument from contingency; but a philosopher should, especially if he represents himself to be in a position to judge its cogency. For this emphasis on God's *existence* and denial of the priority of His *essence* over His *existence* is no novelty, contrived in desperation to meet the present-day critics of theism. Nor is it something for which a philosopher who comments on theism may be forgiven for overlooking. For God has been known by the name "Existence" longer than there have been philosophers. His name is as old as the story of Moses, and it has played a part in every conception of God which has known the Moses story.

CHAPTER 21

The Existence of God

THE CAUSE OF NATURE AND THEISM

WE COME now to the consideration of our fifth proposition, and with it we complete our argument in support of the basic premises of the proof of the existence of God. This premise asserts that anything which depends for its existence upon something self-existent depends upon a really existing God. In other words, the self-existing Cause of Nature is God.

In our earlier discussion of the idea of God we found that the common meaning of "God" is "supreme and ultimate being," and that the word refers to "a level of being which is ultimate, not dependent on anything else for its own existence, and is that on which other things do depend."[1] It may seem that our argument in support of the fourth proposition has already established the fifth. For there we found that the Cause of Nature fits the idea of God; it is self-existent, and so not dependent on anything else for its own existence, and it is that on which other things depend.

We have yet to show, however, that the Cause of Nature fits the *theistic* idea of God. Of course we have done this in a formal fashion; for if the alternatives are correctly narrowed down to atheistic naturalism and theism, and if we have excluded naturalism, then theism is the only remaining possibility. On the other hand, if we are to find positive evidence in support of theism we need to go further. This is important because there is a positive case for theism; we should not be content merely to establish theism by default.

We have already discussed in somewhat abstract terms the theistic idea of God, with special reference to its differentiation from deism and pantheism.[2] Our problem now is to consider the God of theism as the self-existent Cause of Nature whose reality we have found to be implicated in the existence of a real world of contingent beings. We are concerned here with what are called the *attributes* of God as these are understood to pertain to the God of theism.

We do not intend to anticipate any more than necessary the subjects of Parts Seven and Eight. The infinity of God, for example, we shall consider in connection with Chapter 25, "The Reality of Value." God as creator and the goodness of God we shall consider in Part Eight, on the relation of God and the world. In the present chapter we want primarily to find the minimum requirements of a theistic idea of God, and to see whether these follow from our conclusions concerning the self-existence of the Cause of Nature.

It will be sufficient at this point to show that the Cause of Nature is one and not many, is present in nature—that is, immanent as well as transcendent, and is a Being who acts purposively. We shall find that the unity of God is no mere abstract unity, that the immanence of God is active and not passive, and that it is the purpose of God which makes the difference between the existence of one kind of a world rather than another. At this stage of our discussion, however, we must keep in mind constantly that our statements about God may be in need of further interpretation. This is not to say that they are not true, but that we need further understanding of the ways in which we know God before we can know in what respects and in what senses our statements about God are true. We found it necessary in our earlier consideration of theism as an idea of God to pay some attention to analogy.[3] We shall return to this in a later chapter, Chapter 23, "Knowledge by Analogy."

The Unity of God

There can be only one self-existing being. If there were two or more they would have to differ. The only way in which another being can differ from one self-existing being is to be other than self-existing. So there can be only one which is self-existent.

Suppose we say that we have two self-existing beings which are identical in their self-existence but which differ in some other respects. But this leads directly to the denial of the self-existence of at least one of the two. For either the attributes or characteristics which differentiate these two beings from each other follow by necessity from their self-existence or they do not. If they do, then the two will have precisely the same attributes and, since there remains nothing to differentiate them, they will be one and not two. If the differentiating characteristics do not follow by necessity from their self-existence then one of these beings must derive a part, at least, of what it is from other things, and so it is not self-existent. In other words, if two beings exist one must be contingent.

For the same reasons we are forced to deny that God is in any way composite, or made up of parts. The one God is one, in being and act.

The oneness and unity of ultimate existence, or ultimate reality, is one of the early discoveries of philosophy. The reason why some of the philosophies which embody this insight in their teaching are unable to avoid monism, and thus unable to admit the existence of other things than the One, is their failure to recognize the possibility that contingent existence may be also real existence.

Thus far we have stated the principle of the unity of God in quite abstract terms. This is essential, for it shows us certain theoretical requirements which our thinking must satisfy if we are to avoid confusion and error. But the unity of God means something much more significant to us than shows on the surface of these abstractions, and when we see what this further meaning is we shall see our abstractions as the framework of a religious faith which lives in man's communion with God.

The significance of the unity of God is, in brief, this: The only kind of self-existent unity we can imagine in a God who is the Cause of Nature is the kind of unity we see most plainly in self-awareness. God's awareness of Himself and thus of His own act of existence is far beyond anything we can find in our own experience; but what we ourselves do experience as self-conscious and self-determined agents gives us a glimpse of what the unity of God must be like. Although with us the unity of awareness is incomplete, yet we are quite conscious that each particular act is the focus upon a present situation of much that comes from our past experience and of much of what we anticipate for the future. The finite self, so far as it can, acts as a whole when it acts at its fullest stretch. So far as possible, every part of the self is present now, and the action performed is determined to some degree by the knowledge and purpose and judgment of the self that acts.

The unity of self-conscious choice and action is the highest unity we know. It is a unity which holds in one mind the wide variety of experience, which takes to itself in idea the essences of many things which have their own existence in wide separation from each other. The distinctions of space and time keep things apart, but they need not keep apart the mind's awareness of those things. It is only as things come together in our minds, and thus in a way in which they could not possibly *be* together in their own existence, that we can discover some of the relations they have with each other. The significance of one event in history, for example, may not appear for decades or even for centuries. So the truth about that event can be known only by a mind capable of bringing its *what* into a present relation with the *whats* of later events.

The final ultimate unity we can imagine is one in which all things, actual and possible, are present together and at once to an infinite mind. This is inadequate as a statement, of course; but it is the least we may say. Anything less than this would be a broken unity. The fullest awareness of existence is in its presence to one single act of absolute knowledge.

It is one thing simply to say that God is omniscient; it is much more to understand what this means to us as persons. For if this is true, then how little aware we may be of God we have to recognize that God is fully aware of us. Our every thought and feeling is present to Him; not only are they present to Him, they are present to Him more fully and more vividly than to ourselves. For He sees each one in the context not only of our own past and our own future but of all that is.

All this may be too much to draw out of mere unity. But the unity of God is not "mere unity." It is the unity of Him who is self-existence, whose nature it is to exist. It is the unity of pure act, of act not dependent or contingent but self-existent act. How can we think this except in terms of absolute freedom under absolute knowledge, of omnipotence in omniscience? Anything less conflicts with the self-existence of God.

The Immanence of God

God gives existence to the world. We found this presupposed by the real existence of the things which make up our world. Although these things which exist do have their own existence, so that they are not in fact the existence of something else, yet the existence they have does not come from themselves. As natural beings they obtain their existence from natural causes, but the existence they obtain from their natural causes is only passed on to them by those causes. That there is a natural order in which those causes act depends on God.

What this means is that although God gives existence He cannot give it away. He cannot alienate existence from Himself; for, since His existence is His essence, to alienate existence from Himself would be to negate His own essence. A created being such as man may, perhaps, by his own act alienate himself from God; but he cannot remove his existence from its dependence on God. God can exclude a possible existent from real existence, and can end the existence of something actual; but God cannot give existence away. For to say that He can is to say that God can create something to be self-existent, that He can make a contingent being to be noncontingent. This cannot be, for it is a contradiction.

We see here again the fallacy of deism. The deist supposes that God makes the world and then the world maintains itself in existence. Only thus can the deist deny the immanence of God. But what the deist asserts is absurd; for he attributes to God an act which contradicts His nature. This is one reason why any deism that is allowed to develop its own consequences leads to irrationalism and embraces absurdity as the test of truth. For the deist supposes that God creates that which is to exist without God, and this is to say that God creates a world to be an uncreated world.

Someone may ask, "Can God not create a world and then decree that the world should exist in and of itself apart from God from that point on?" This would mean that after the world is created God then acts further to render the created order self-existent. But this is to say that the self-existence of such a world would be contingent, and so that the world has a contingent non-contingency. This is nonsense. It is like my saying, "I shall give you a gift, and along with it I give you also a way of possessing this gift so that it is not a gift." If I do provide a way for you to possess this thing so that it is not a gift, if I provide a way for you to earn it, for example, then of course it is not a gift at all.

There is one possible confusion lurking here which we must be careful to avoid. The fact that God sustains the existence of contingent things does not mean that those things are His existence. He has really given to them an existence of their own. In giving them existence He provides the ground of their action. But their acts are their own, not the acts of God. God's act is to bring them to be real agents in their own right. God is present in things as a giver is present in his gift. The gift expresses the nature of the giver; so the gift of existence expresses the nature of God, whose nature it is to exist. But the recipient can do what he pleases with the gift, within the range of possibility. If he could not, it would not be a gift; it would be, at best, only a loan. So a contingent being acts in accordance with its own nature; and if this being is a person who possesses freedom he can act as he pleases, within the limits of his nature. For his existence is really *his*, and his action is really his own. If it were not, then existence would not have been given to him; it would have been only a loan.

There is a difficulty which arises at this point. It is truly a *dif-*

ficult difficulty, but because of the misunderstanding it has caused we must pay some attention to it here. The question is this: If things in nature depend ultimately on God for their existence, and if they cannot escape this dependence, does it follow that God creates each thing anew in each instant of its existence? This has been a problem both to philosophers and to theologians. If we say "No" to this question, it would seem that things are independent of God, and we have displaced theism with deism. If we say "Yes," it would seem that we deny real existence to things, and we have displaced theism with pantheism. The theistic answer requires, as do the theistic answers to so many problems, that we re-think the problem and try to see whether the alternatives so far recognized are not incomplete. Before we do this we must look briefly at some of the implications of our assertion of the real existence of things in time.

When we ask whether God does not create each thing anew in each instant of its existence, the question itself assumes that things exist by instants. This can mean only that they exist through successive durationless points of time. This must be implied by the question, for if God should create a thing so that it existed by virtue of that creative act through any duration, however short, that thing would not be created anew each instant. For an instant is a durationless unit while the smallest part of duration is still duration, if indeed we can speak intelligibly of a *smallest* part. If we say that things in time exist by instants we contradict ourselves, for instants are not themselves parts of time. As a geometric point is the limit of a line and not part of a line so an instant is a limit of duration and not a part of duration. If we divide an actual duration into parts we approach but never reach a durationless instant. The instant is the limit, but it is a limit external to the series of divisions and not a member of that series. Even Bertrand Russell, in his attempt to interpret physical things not as each a "single persistent entity, but as a series of entities succeeding each other in time," was unable to carry this to the place where duration is dissolved into instants. Somewhat reluctantly, one feels, and with a wistful hope that a little of something may be closer

347

to nothing than a lot, Russell has to retain some duration in these entities which succeed each other—"each lasting," he says, "for a very brief period, though probably not for a mere mathematical instant."[4]

If things existed by instants then this tree I suppose I see now would not be one tree but a succession of trees, each existing at a timeless instant and giving place to its successor. But this involves a contradiction in so far as it attempts to reduce succession to a series of instants, for if we dissolve duration into instants there is nothing in the instants themselves on which we can base a distinction between before and after. On such a conception time is nothing but the scanning of a series of instants; yet to *scan* the series requires a duration which is other than that of a series of instants.

To say that one of any two items of a series comes *before* the other while the other comes *after* the one, it is necessary for those two items to belong to a single duration. If they do not they have no time relation at all. Just as we can locate one geometric point to the right or left of another only if we understand both points to be on the same continuous surface so we can think of one instant as after another only as we think of those instants with reference to a continuous duration. Otherwise there is nothing to link the two. They certainly contain nothing in themselves to provide a time link, for each is gone as soon as it is. We may relate them by locating them in terms of our own time, but that is our time— not their time.

Any attempt to interpret a duration as a series of instants requires us to understand it as composed of infinitesimals. But, as we have already seen,[5] nothing exists as a sum of infinite parts. We may analyze a continuum mathematically by application of an infinite series to it, but no real continuum is put together out of the items which constitute such a series. Concerning the doctrine that time is made up of elements without duration, Maïmonides says, "time would be an object of position and order," and adds— as Gilson says, "scornfully"—"what can be expected of those who do not regard the nature of things?"[6] Whitehead puts the matter bluntly enough: "there are no infinitesimals."[7]

Let us look now at another problem which arises when we try to grasp something of what the immanence of God means. Perhaps there are real things but perhaps they do not really act. Perhaps they only transmit the action of God. But this is plainly wrong. For if things only transmit the acts of God they still *do* something: they transmit those acts. If we say that this is not to act but is to be acted upon, we say that to transmit the act of God is nothing, and so these things are nothing. Their existence is the same as their non-existence. If, however, they contribute even to the transmitting of God's act then it is by *their* nature, and in accordance with it, that they act. Their participation in God's act, no matter how slight, would be their own act.

All such difficulties may be avoided if we keep two things clear in our minds. In the first place, the things which really exist really act. Their acts are their own in every sense, for each thing acts in accordance with its own nature. In the second place, nothing can act unless it really exists. In none of the actions of contingent things upon each other is there the act of giving existence. But the things which act do have a *given* existence, and no matter how long they continue to exist their existence is still a given existence. Their dependence upon God never ceases. Yet their *existence* is not *their act;* their acts are the acts of the existing essence of which they are constituted.

Perhaps a simple analogy may help to make this clear. Suppose I am playing with a small child who wants to get a toy from a shelf too high for him to reach. I lift him, and he picks up what he wants from the shelf. My act of lifting him is not his act of picking up the toy. It is true that if I do not hold him he cannot reach what he wants, but my support does not free him from the need to reach and pick up the toy for himself. So long as he is supported he is able thus to act at this height, but the support I give him is not his act. Nor does the fact that he is supported in such a way that he can reach the toy require him actually to do so.

A better analogy may be found in the relation of parents and their children. Parents maintain the home. In a sense, we may say, they enable the home to exist. It is because the home exists that the children can do the things they do and live the lives they live.

But their acts as children in the home are not the acts by which their parents maintain the home. Furthermore, the parental maintenance of the home is, in certain respects, a continued action. If it ceases, even for a short time, the conditions under which the children live will be different, and they no longer will have opportunity to do all of the same things they did before. Unless they are maintained and provided for they will soon cease to live.

A still closer analogy may be found in the relation of a legal corporation to the state. A corporation receives legal existence by virtue of the act of the legislature of the state which charters it. All the acts of the corporation depend for their legal validity, and thus for their occurrence as corporate actions, upon the authority of the state. Yet an act performed by the corporation, such as the act of entering into a contract with another corporation, is not an act of the state or of its government. Neither does the property of a corporation belong to the state. On the other hand, the corporation, although it is capable of legal action of its own, can act only in accordance with the powers bestowed upon it by the state; and the state may dissolve it at any time, and may expropriate its possessions. The legal existence of the corporation and its power to act legally in its own right are analogous to the real existence of a natural being and its own real action. The dependence of the corporation on the state, a dependence which continues so long as the corporation retains legal existence, and the fact that its existence as a corporation is a continuing expression of the chartering power and authority of the state, are analogous to the immanence of God in nature and in man.

The nature of God is reflected by every existing thing; each thing shows by its very existence something of the nature of God, for *to exist* is the nature of God. Each thing depends ultimately on God for its existence; but in no case is the existence of a contingent thing the existence of God, nor is an act of a contingent thing an act of God. But the existence of the order of nature to which every contingent thing belongs is the act of God. Some of the implications of this we shall see as we look at the reasons for attributing purposive action to God.

The World Order and Its Contingency

The theistic conception of God and of His relation to the world requires that in some sense the existence of the world is a purposive act. This means, of course, that the existence of the world is in some sense a personal act. The God of theism, in other words, is a personal God who acts in accordance with His own purpose.[8] As we shall see later, such statements as this need careful interpretation and qualification. "Purposive" and "personal" do not pertain to God in the same sense that they pertain to ourselves. We are concerned here primarily to deny that God acts by necessity and that God is a being which excludes the personal. There is a likeness of God's act to our own purposive action, and a likeness of God's agency to our own nature as persons.

The reason we have to understand God in these terms is the fact that the things which really exist in the world constitute, in their relations with each other, a world order. The things that exist maintain a definite *structured* relationship with each other. They act in accordance with law. Causal agency is specific and determinate, not indefinite and capable of every conceivable kind of action. Oak trees do not bear apples, and rivers do not flow uphill.

> The causal relation [D. J. B. Hawkins points out] depends on the nature of the cause and the nature of the effect; causation takes place in accordance with causal laws. Anything does not produce anything but a thing is such that it produces an effect of a certain kind. Hence, not only is the effect determined by the cause, but from another point of view the cause is determined to its effect. Even in a case of relative indetermination, it would be determined at any rate to a possible range of effects. And this is a predetermination, or rather a timeless determination, because it depends upon the natures of the cause and of the effect. . . . It is the conception of the effect as that towards which the cause is of its nature directed even before it acts which earns for the effect the name of final cause and provides the basis for the classical affirmation of universal teleology. For in this sense it is obviously true to say that every agent acts for an end—*omne agens agit propter finem.*[9]

351

The recognition that the world is an ordered world brings us face to face with two basic philosophical considerations. The first of these is that the actual world order is not the only possible one. We can conceive of different possible world orders. Although our imaginations may not be able to picture such a world yet we can understand what would be some of the properties of things in a world of five or six space dimensions. We have no reason to think that all the non-actual world orders we can conceive are inherently inconsistent, and so not really possible. The second fact we must face is that the real things which make up our actual world order are capable, so far as their essential natures are concerned, of maintaining other systems of relations with each other. In other words, the actual world order is not the only system of relations which could hold among the things which really exist. Their actual relations do not exhaust their potentialities, for if they did the work of human artifice would be impossible.

The existence of the actual world order is not self-explanatory. There is nothing about it which accounts for the fact of its existence. There could have been a different actual world than there is. Nor is the actual world order the only possible world order in which the things which do exist could exist. The real things of our world could also exist, so far as their own natures are concerned, in some different world order. Some features of our world order are necessary features of any world order; it cannot be self-contradictory, for example. But many of its specific features are contingent. In other words, the order of nature is neither inherently necessary nor is it a necessary consequence of the nature of the things which really exist. The situation is somewhat like the existence of a factory which produces, say, washing machines. The factory has a certain definite organization and certain definite operations which are performed upon the raw materials. But the existence of such a factory is not self-explanatory. There might have been here a plant to make automobiles, or no factory at all. Furthermore, the specific internal organization of the factory is not the only organization in which the very same people and things might manufacture washing machines. The office organization, the relations of the various departments, the production line itself are all specific arrangements of personnel and equipment which might have been different even with the use of the very same people and the same equipment.

To deny this is to assert that the actual things which exist, being what they are, could stand in no other relations to each other than they do. It would be like saying that if we have a set of checkers and a checkerboard the only game we can play with this equipment is checkers. This could be true only if nature were a closed system. There are no closed systems in nature, and this is true of nature itself in so far as nature is contingent.

The World Order and Existence

The relation of the world order to the things which it contains requires further examination. We may be in danger here of thinking along some such analogy as that of marbles in a bag, where the marbles stand for the things in nature and the bag for the order of nature which contains these things. Such an analogy is seriously misleading, and one of the important reasons why it is misleading is its suggestion that the world order, like the bag which holds the marbles, is itself a real being. On such a view we should have the things in the world plus another real thing, namely, the order of the things in the world. But if the order of things were itself a real thing it could not be the order of things. It would be just one more thing which then would have to stand in some ordered relation with the other things. So we should have to have another order of things, and so on indefinitely.

The world order is not itself an existent, except as we take it to refer to the totality of real existents in their relations with each other. When we consider the world order itself, in distinction from the things which exemplify it in their relationships, then we must remember that it is an *order of things* and not itself one of the things. It is a system of real relations of real things, but it is not itself a real thing. Real things have the properties and the interrelations which our concepts of the world order specify, in so far as those concepts are true. What we call "scientific laws" are specific aspects of the world order, and these laws are all contingent. We cannot discover them from the nature of being as such; metaphysics or ontology can never take the place of the natural sciences. Scientific laws can be discovered only by empirical inquiry. The necessary laws of nature, however, are those which hold of any possible existence. These are not discovered by scientific investigation but are what we find to be presupposed by the real existence or possible existence of the objects which experience discloses.

Once we understand that the world order is not itself a thing but is the system of relations of real things we are tempted to infer that the world order is nothing more than a consequence of the nature and actions of the things which exist. We form our ideas of the world order by abstraction, by thinking the relations of things apart from the things themselves. Thus we may assume that we need not account for the fact that the actual world order is not different; we may take it to be only the network of relations of things. To account for the world order we need only account for the things which constitute it. To say that there is a world order is to say only that there are the real things of which the world is composed, just as to say that a family lives in this house is to say only that two or three or more people, who sustain a certain set of relations with each other, live here. The existence of the family is the existence of the people who comprise it.

Yet if our analogy holds we can see that this way of handling the problem is wrong. For the existence of the members of the family does not account for the existence of the family; that is, it does not account for the fact that these persons have just this set of relations with each other. It would do so only if these people could exist as people only in this family relationship. The family may break up and some, at least, of its members continue to live as real people. Certainly they would be affected by such a change in their circumstances, but their existence as persons would not have to be in jeopardy. So it is with the order of nature. Things which exist in nature are capable of many possible systems of interrelationship, and their actual relations do not exhaust the possibilities. As we have already said, nothing we know about real things justifies the inference that there are closed systems in nature. The only basis for considering the whole of nature to be a closed system is the naturalistic dogma that nature is all there is; and for this there is, and can be, no positive evidence. In so far as the constituents of a system or order of existence could have been different or are actually open to influences from outside that system then that system does not provide the only possible set of relations which those things can have with respect to each other. This is the situation if real existence is individual existence and if individuals are not mere functions of the system to which they belong.

The real potentialities of the things which actually exist are not exhausted by any specific order of relations which they sustain with each other. This holds true of systems within nature; it is true of systems of systems; it is true of the order of nature itself. The order of nature, then, is not what it is solely by virtue of the properties and potential interrelations of the individual things which it contains. These same things might have been ordered with respect to each other in many other different ways. In other words, the order of nature to which things belong is not entirely their own doing. So if we are to account for the fact that there is actually this order rather than another, we can do so only by reference to a cause outside nature and, as we shall see, by reference to a cause capable of purposeful act.

The same automobiles traveling intersecting highways may be four streams of smoothly flowing traffic, so that the movement on one road synchronizes with a halt of the movement on the other, or they may be in a hopeless snarl which brings all movement to a stop. The difference does not lie in the make up and potentialities of the automobiles, nor, necessarily, even in the character and attitudes of the drivers. The difference lies in the presence or absence of a system of traffic control. There is no one necessary system, nor only one possible successful system. The traffic may

be regulated by stop-and-go lights, by stop signs, by a traffic po-
liceman, or by custom and tradition. The requirement is that some
specific orderly mode of procedure be observed, but this or that
specific system is not necessitated by the nature of the individual
things to which it applies.

What happens to this or that individual thing within a determinate order of existing things may not be the same as what would
happen to it within a different arrangement of the same things.
Our problem is to account for this, in principle, without attributing real causal efficacy to the order apart from the things themselves; for to attribute causal efficacy to the world order as such
would be to assume that it is a real existent in its own right. We
shall be able to avoid this difficulty if we recognize that events
in nature are the products of joint causes. The juncture of causes,
in its broadest and most fundamental aspects, is the order of nature. The real causes are the actually existing things in nature, but
they do not work separately to produce their effects; they act in
orderly relationship with each other. The fact that they act together in accordance with the order of nature actually in effect,
and not in accordance with some other possible order, can be explained only by a cause from outside nature itself.

THE WORLD ORDER AND PURPOSE

When we ask what kind of cause can account for the fact that
we have this world order and not another, we find it necessary
to consider what kind of cause can give effect to one among many
genuine possibilities. If the selection of one possibility among
many alternatives is not merely the working out of a pre-determined necessity there remains, within the range of our experience
and acquaintance, only one plausible conception of such a cause.
This is the kind of cause which selects one possibility from among
many by means of adequate knowledge of what the alternatives
are together with intelligent decision for the sake of some end.
In other words we have only one clue to the problem of explain-

ing why there is this order of nature rather than another, and that clue is our own experience of purposeful choice. The cause which brings this world to be and which gives to it the order it has may not be an intelligence like our own, or form purposes in the manner of ourselves; but of one thing we may be sure, it is nothing less than our intelligence and our capacity for purposeful act.

Perhaps it is with something of a shock that we find ourselves thinking of the world order in terms of a purpose which it fulfils. For generations now, this kind of thinking has been suspect; the idea of purpose in nature violates one of the strongest of modern intellectual taboos. This, we are told, is anthropomorphic thinking; it is a fanciful projection into nature of our own psychological traits. To clinch the matter we are assured that there is not the slightest scientific evidence of purpose in nature, at least below the level of human action.

It is true that the natural sciences, developed in accordance with the modern conception of scientific method, do not themselves provide us with evidence of purpose in nature. But the reason they do not give us evidence of purpose is not that nature lacks purpose; it is that the fact that even if nature is the expression of purpose the methods of natural science are not competent to discover and establish it. The scientist may bring to his investigation an understanding of the purposive character of nature, knowledge which he obtains perhaps from philosophy and not from science, and this may greatly influence his scientific investigations. Many such investigations would not take place at all in the absence of such an understanding of nature. The scientific investigation may, indeed, be the attempt to discover the facts that will fit into a teleological pattern. But the pattern is not discovered by the scientific study; it is presupposed by it. William Harvey's epochal treatise, *The Motion of the Heart and Blood*, is a report of studies made under the guidance of a conception of a purposeful relationship in the operation of the body. It seems to him true because, as he remarks at the close, "it would be very difficult to explain in any other way to what purpose all is constructed and arranged as we have seen it to be."[10] The structure and arrangement is what

357

he discovered; the purpose is what makes these facts intelligible.

The test of truth in natural science is sense perception, and the presence of purpose in nature cannot be verified by sense perception; for purpose is not what we *see* in nature, but how we *understand* what we see. We are concerned here with something more fundamental than anything which belongs within the range of inquiry of the natural sciences. Our concern here is with the conditions of the very existence of the world which science investigates. *Our concern here is not with the physical properties of things; it is with the conditions which account for the fact that there are things with physical properties to investigate.* The purpose for which the order of nature exists is not a physical property, nor a pattern of physical properties. It is not a possession of the world at all; it is rather the purpose expressed in the act of the world's cause. If that cause is God, then it is God's purpose which concerns us.

The real existence of the things which make up the order of nature, and their existence in that order in which they are, is intelligible only on the supposition that this world has been brought into existence by one self-existent, intelligent, and purposeful God. *If God exists, the existence of the world makes sense.*

Part Seven

OUR KNOWLEDGE ABOUT GOD

The Likeness of God

THE NEW PHASE OF OUR ARGUMENT

No MATTER how compelling may be the reasons which lead us to affirm the existence of God, the conclusion we reach seems more important in what it points to than in what it says. If our knowledge of God is confined to the knowledge that He exists, we know little more than that we live our lives in a world which God has brought into existence for His own purpose. We have no inkling, so far, of what that purpose is nor of the meaning of our own existence. Our knowledge that God exists may protect us from some serious errors, but this is mainly a negative import. Such knowledge by itself gives no positive guidance to our lives. It is of little religious significance by itself; it assures us that some kind of religious attitude is possible, but it tells us little of what attitudes and actions are appropriate to us in our relation to God. So we need to press immediately our inquiry concerning the nature of God. This falls quite naturally into two parts. What kind of knowledge may we obtain concerning the nature of God, and what do we find out about God and our relation to Him when we seek to discover His nature? The first of these questions we shall consider in this part; the second will concern us in our study of the relation of God to the world and to man.

THE PROBLEM OF OUR KNOWLEDGE ABOUT GOD

When we begin to ask what we can know about God, and how we can obtain such knowledge, we are faced with a special problem. We recall that in connection with our discussion and criticism of subjectivism we found that it is impossible to form a *concept* of existence as such.[1] Concepts concern essence, not existence. To form a concept we have to abstract essence from existence. But the very heart of our argument for the existence of God is the discovery that the nature or essence of God is existence. It seems, then, that we can form no concept of God, for if the essence of God is existence then the essence of God cannot be distinguished from His existence, even in thought. If we can form no concept of God then it is a puzzle to understand how we can know anything of the nature of God except the bare fact that God is existence.

There is, indeed, a sense in which this is true. We can know nothing of the nature of God except that He is existence. But perhaps the fact of God's existence is not a "bare" fact. Since there is no such thing as "bare" existence, or existence "in general," our knowledge that God is existence may be a far richer knowledge than we suspect.

Our knowledge about things is by concepts. In an earlier discussion of knowledge we found that our knowledge about real things depends on our power to abstract their essences and to hold these before us in thought.[2] We discover their essences first in perception, and it is our ability to think them apart from their real existence, to possess in our thought the *what* without the *that*, which makes conceptual knowledge possible. But since the essence of God is His existence we cannot think His essence apart from His existence. It is apparent that whatever the knowledge we may obtain about God, it cannot be conceptual knowledge in the ordinary sense. Every true statement we make about God is a statement about His existence, not about His essence in distinction from His existence.

So long as we are talking about finite beings [Mascall points out] we can make statements about their natures or essences without any assertion about their existence. I can say that a unicorn has a horn on its nose and that a rhinoceros has a horn on its nose without suggesting that any animals with horns on their noses exist; that rhinoceroses do exist and that unicorns do not is a purely empirical fact. But I cannot say that God is good without asserting the existence of a good being; for since God is by definition self-existent being, to affirm that God is good is to speak of self-existent goodness, that is to say of goodness that cannot but exist.[3]

Since our knowledge of existence is not conceptual, how are we to know about God? The assertion that God is good can be understood only as the assertion that God is the real existence of good. But how do we come to know this? It is the existence of good we assert here. How do we come to discover this existence? We shall have to consider our way of coming to know existence and see how this applies to our attempt to know about God. Our knowledge that God exists comes by way of demonstration. But it is one thing to know that God exists; it is another thing to know the God who does exist. Unless we can *find* the existence of God, as well as infer it from the evidence, our knowledge that God exists has only theoretical significance.

How We Think Existence

Our knowledge of the existence of things in nature is, without exception, sensory knowledge. In perception we *find* the existence of the things we perceive. The act of perception is the discovery of their existence. Their existence is given; we do not think it, or construct it.[4]

This may suggest that when we are not actually perceiving a thing we cannot think its existence. It is true that we cannot, if we mean the thought of its existence apart from its essence; for the existence of a thing apart from its essence has no content. What is true *about* a thing is contained or grounded in its essence, and if we exclude its essence from our thought then there is nothing about it for us to think. Existence without essence is utterly empty, for the only existence a thing has is the existence of its essence. So when we try to do without its essence in our thought, and attend to its existence alone, we find that we have nothing

363

our minds can grasp in thought, for there is nothing left for them to grasp. In this respect it is true that we cannot think the existence of anything. Existence by itself, bare existence, is nothing; for it is the existence of nothing. It is not enough to say that it is the emptiest of all concepts, for it is not a concept at all.

If I try to think the existence of something, say this pen I hold in my hand, I can think it only as the existence of *what* I see and feel. If I try to seize its existence in thought by thinking the difference between its actual existence and its possible non-existence, I find that I grasp in thought only its essence. If I say to myself, "Suppose this pen were not here; suppose my hand were empty," it is the existence *of the pen*, not some indeterminate existence, which is the difference between its *being* here or somewhere and its not being here or anywhere. In whatever way I think this the idea of existence which I form is of a specific existence, specified in terms of *what* the existent is. What I think is the presence or absence of the *pen*. If I ask what it would mean to say that there is an existent but it has no nature, I can find meaning in such a question only as I understand that the essence is unknown. For if I take it to mean that the essence is lacking then I can understand it only as a reference to the existence of nothing. This is either a simple denial of existence, or else it is an attempt to give positive meaning to "nothing." The latter is possible only as an equivocation, well illustrated by the logic textbook example: "Nothing is hotter than the sun; anything is hotter than nothing; therefore, anything is hotter than the sun."

It is in this sense that when we are not actually perceiving a thing we cannot think its existence. For that matter, we cannot *think* its *existence*, merely as such, even when we perceive it. We can think what it is, but we perceive that it is. This is not to say that perception excludes conceptual thought, for it clearly does not. It is to say rather that the aspect of perception by means of which we discover the existence of something is its sensory aspect.

Even if we cannot think the existence of something, however, we yet can think about it; but our thought about its existence is not conceptual thought. We need, says Gilson, "to grasp again

Being as the existence of essence, not as the essence of existence; to touch it as an act, not to conceive it as a thing."[5] I can think about the existence of a tree I do not now perceive, in the sense that my thought which takes place now refers to, and is intended to refer to, the actual tree which exists where I cannot see it now. But how do I think about its existence? I do not separate the essence and the existence of the tree and try to think about the existence without the essence; for, as we have seen, without the essence there is nothing to think about. When I say that I think about the existence of the tree I mean that I think about a certain existing tree as distinguished from a purely imaginary or a merely possible tree. To think about the tree *as existing* does not consist in taking a concept of the tree and a concept of existence and then combining them in my thought. This would be to try to think *tree-ness* and *existence-ness* in combination. But there is no *existence-ness* to think. I can never derive the existence of anything from concepts, that is from essence alone. To think about the tree *as existing* is rather a way of thinking about the tree which involves in some manner my memory or awareness of having perceived it.

It is in a similar way that I think about the possible existence of things. I can think about owning a dog, and I can think about a dog I might own without referring in my thought to any actual dog. I do this by imagining a dog. The imaginary dog may have quite distinct and specific characteristics of breed, color, size, and so on. I may be able even to paint a picture of the dog I imagine. When I think about this dog's possible *existence* I do so by imagining the dog to be real and imagining that I actually perceive it.

Of course everything that goes into my image of the dog comes from my own perceptual experience. But I use this material, in forming images, without restricting it to an awareness of the actual perceptual experiences from which I obtained it. In fact I may have forgotten most of my actual experiences which gave me my ideas of what dogs are like. I am aware that this idea of this particular dog is one I have constructed in my imagination. I am aware also that this dog does not exist. No matter how closely some real dog happens to match the characteristics of my imaginary dog, it is not the real dog I am thinking about but the imaginary dog. I can imagine a dog without thinking of its possible existence, for I may simply ignore the matter of its existence or non-existence. If I think about the possible existence of the imaginary dog then I have to have in imagination not only the dog-image but also the image of myself perceiving the dog. I have to imagine a situation which includes the dog and the perception of the dog.

This is in no way intended to suggest that the existence of a thing consists in its being perceived, or that the possible existence of something consists in its being imagined. The question we are discussing here concerns our awareness of existence, not *what* existence is *as existence*. To try to specify the latter would be to try to form a concept of bare existence, and so it would reduce existence to essence. This is the very confusion on which subjectivism rests. We find actual existence in perception, we think of possible existence by the use of imagination; but the existence we find in perception is not itself a percept, and the possible existence we imagine is not itself an image.

If our account of this is true then we have found that the act of thinking about the existence of something is never an exclusively conceptual act. To think about the existence of something, as distinguished from the experience of its existence, requires memory and imagination. Memory and imagination always refer to specific individual things and situations. I can imagine a particular dog, but I cannot form an image of *dogness*. I can use an image to aid my conceptual thinking, but the image itself will not exhibit all the properties of *dogness* which my concept refers to. In so far as I use the image only to aid my conceptual thinking, the image is not an image of what I am thinking about; for I am thinking about the general nature of dogs, not about any particular actual or imaginary dog. The image is an image only of an instance of what I am thinking about. It is true my conceptual thinking may concern any actual or possible dog, but as conceptual it concerns dogs without reference to their existence or non-existence.

What goes into my concept of *man* I have to get from my experience. But when I think about man as such the question of the existence or non-existence of this or that actual or legendary or imaginary man may not arise at all. The essence of man is abstracted from all its instances, and my thought concerns the essence exclusively. But as soon as I begin to wonder, for example, whether Ulysses ever really lived then I have to use imagination. If I try to imagine his existence as a man I imagine him with a human body, moving and acting and performing the mental and physical functions of a man. I imagine him in such a way that if what I imagine had been real then what I imagine could have been perceived as actual by anyone present and capable of perception.

There are some things we can think about, and yet in spite of the fact that we can think about them we cannot imagine their real existence. We can think about a number or a triangle, for example, but we cannot imagine the real existence of either. Numbers and triangles cannot have their own real existence, for they are universals. They are not real beings, but beings of reason. We discover them in our experience of things, but they are not themselves things which we experience. We discover them only as we abstract from what we experience. We can think of the real existence of something triangular or of something numbered, but we cannot think of the real existence of a triangle or of a number itself. No actual existent can be *the number six*, although it may be six of something or *the sixth*. No actual existent can be *the equilateral triangle*.

It is true there have been many attempts in the history of philosophy to identify ultimate reality with universals or forms. The most familiar of these is in the philosophy of Plato. But, as we have already seen in another connection, all such attempts to find the real in the universal or formal involve the priority of essence to existence. This leads to the view that reality is somehow beyond existence, and consequently that existence is not real. The world of experience vanishes into illusion, into illusion that reality itself cannot account for.

If perception were our only contact with existence then we

could not even think about the existence of anything non-physical. But perception is not our only contact with existence. We can prove that this is so, and the proof once and for all excludes from serious consideration any variety of philosophy which attempts to restrict real existence to the physical. The proof lies in the fact that we could not use perception as a test of real existence unless we were directly aware of the actual occurrence of the perception. A possible perception, a perception which only *might* have happened, is no test of real existence. Unless we can be aware of the actual occurrence of the perceptual act as it occurs we cannot identify this or that experience as perceptual; and if we cannot identify an act of perception as truly perception, then we cannot use perception as a test of existence.

But how are we aware that we perceive? We do not *perceive* that we perceive (except as we use "perceive" in the first instance to refer to a kind of awareness which is not itself *sense* perception). We are *directly* aware that we perceive. No sensation is necessary for this awareness, for it is not an awareness of something distinct from ourselves which consequently requires a physical medium with which our bodies are in contact. Our awareness is of ourselves and of our own mental acts.

These then are our contacts with existence, our sense experience of other things and our direct experience of ourselves. From this limitation upon our contact with existence, together with the fact that the nature of God is existence and we can have no concept of existence, comes the problem of how we can have any knowledge about God.

OUR KNOWLEDGE OF OTHER SELVES

We know the existence of the things we discover in sense perception and we know our own existence. But how can we know the existence of any other thing? I can perceive another human body, and thus discover its existence, but how can I know the existence of another human mind? I am not directly aware of

the other mind's awareness, and of course I have no sense perception of the other mind's awareness. I can imagine the existence of
the other mind, but how can I know that what I imagine it to be
is what it is?

If this presents a problem then how much more acute is the
problem of our knowledge of the nature of God, for the essence
of God is existence. I can imagine what it would be like to be another person, but even my imagination seems incapable of giving
me any idea of the nature of God. My imagination, for one thing,
is time-bound while the God it would catch in its net is beyond
time. To know the nature of God is to know God's existence. It
is not enough to demonstrate *that* God exists, we have to know
in some way what it is like for God to exist. We know God's existence in one way when we know *that* God exists. We now have
to know God's existence in another way, we have to know it as
what God is. It may help us with this problem if we look a little
further into our knowledge of other minds. We may find some
connection between the two, and the answer to one may contribute to the answer to the other.

Our knowledge that other minds exist is not direct but inferential. The inference is sound if it satisfies the conditions under
which inference gives us knowledge of existence. If we know the
existence of something (or the occurrence of something) which
does not account for itself, then we know indirectly the existence
of whatever is necessary to account for it. We perceive the existence of human bodies and we are aware of much of their action.
We discover them engaging in activities which they can perform
only if they are *minded* bodies, only if those actions express the
purposes and the experiences and the powers of perceiving and
imagining and thinking which can be performed by nothing but
really existing minds. He who denies the real existence of other
minds accepts as true something which he contradicts in action
in every personal contact he has. But this knowledge is like our
knowledge that the contingency of the world implies the existence of God. It does not bring us into contact with other minds
so that we discover from it what it is like for other minds to exist.

When I try to think what the experience and life of another person is like I can only imagine myself in his place. I think of what it would be like for me to do the things he does and to have the experiences he seems to have. This is the only material I have from which to construct a plausible picture of what he is like. Of course I recognize that he does not have his experiences just as I imagine them; and along with my imagining is the continuing awareness that it is not his actual experience I am conscious of, but my own imagined version of it. What I imagine can be true of him just so far as his experience and my experience are similar. What I imagine about him shows me what he is like in himself to the extent that it contains something in which his experience and my experience are alike.

When I look at something green and I see another person in such a position that I infer he is looking at the same thing, I usually suppose that he sees the same green and sees it much as I do. If I know he is color-blind then I make an exception, although if I believe that he sees at all I suppose that *what* he sees is in some respects the same as *what* I see, and so that his experience in seeing this thing is in some respects like my own experience. The foundation of my inference is that we are both persons and selves, and that since I know my own experience, its structure and qualities, I know in this instance at least something of the true nature of a personal self. *In so far as what I know of myself is knowledge of what it is like to be a self, and in so far as this other is a self, then what I know from myself of what it is like to be a self is true also of this other self.* But this principle would not justify my inference if I did not know the other to be a self, for such knowledge is one of the essential premises on which the conclusion depends.

How We Can Know the Nature of God

We now are in reach of part of the answer, in principle at least, to the question of how we can come to know something of the

370

nature of God. In principle it is by the same kind of inference by which we come to know something of the nature of the experience of another self. In my awareness of myself I am aware of something which pertains also to God. There is a likeness of God to myself, so that in my awareness of myself I am aware of something to which the nature of God has a likeness.

What can this be in me to which God has a likeness? To answer this we need only recall that the essence of God is existence. So it is quite apparent that it is my existence, which I find directly in my awareness of myself, to which the nature of God has a likeness. But the nature of God has a likeness not alone to my existence; there is a likeness of God to every real existent. Perhaps one likeness is closer than another, but even the most remote is still a likeness. We may point to the likeness of the nature of God to every real existent by pointing to the difference between a thing's merely possible existence and its actual real existence. In its difference from what does not exist every real thing shows us something of the nature of God.

So we know something about the nature of God in every discovery and experience of real existence. The more vivid our impression of the actuality of something, in contrast with its mere possibility, the closer we are to an awareness of the nature of God. No doubt there are many for whom a consciousness of God is difficult or seemingly absent. In some cases this may be only a failure to recognize it for what it is. "The plain man," Mascall points out, "need not be able to analyse systematically the apprehension of God and the creature in the cosmological relation; he need not indeed necessarily know that the apprehension of God and the creature in the cosmological relation is what he is in fact having. What *is* important is that he should have it."[6] Some simply do not know God by the name "Existence," but they may know existence. What they do not know is that the experience of existence is a disclosure of the nature of God. Others, however, seem to lack the very awareness of existence. Perhaps their experience is not vivid, or is too limited and empty for them to become aware of alternative possibilities; or perhaps they are tem-

371

peramentally so passive and acquiescent that they live without purpose or drive or interest. They have lost entirely childhood's wonder at what it finds. Some seem almost to repudiate their very nature as selves. They are not so much self-conscious and self-directing agents as they are mere functions of other things; instead of acting they react.

The impact of the actual, the sense of the uniqueness of everything that is actual, the sense of its inability to account for itself, the immeasurable distance between what is and what is not, comes to us in these verses by Chesterton:

> When all my days are ending
>   And I have no song to sing,
> I think I shall not be too old
>   To stare at everything;
> As I stared once at a nursery door
>   Or a tall tree and a swing.
>
> Wherein God's ponderous mercy hangs
>   On all my sins and me,
> Because He does not take away
>   The terror from the tree
> And stones still shine along the road
>   That are and cannot be.[7]

Mascall comments, with reference to this, "It is this recognition that things 'are which cannot be'—that is, which cannot account for their own occurrence—that is the necessary basis of the cosmological or existential approach to theism. We shall never become theists if we take the world for granted; but so long as we do *not* take it for granted we are within measurable distance of taking it as granted to us by God."[8] And Whitehead tells us, "The concept of 'God' is the way in which we understand this incredible fact—that what cannot be, yet is."[9]

Our awareness of real existence is strong in those moments when we are most conscious of the final and unalterable exclusion of earlier possibilities. "Customarily it is in the critical periods of life, when desire is more intense," Professor Allport points out, "that religious consciousness is acute. Many people are religious only in moments of crisis; the rest of the time they rub along comfortably and godlessly, content to let their religious sentiment lie dormant."[10] The death of someone we care for comes as a finality. We cannot bring back a life that has ended. We may have been well aware of the likelihood of imminent death, but so long as life remained we held to the hope that needs only possibility to feed on. Once the fact is accomplished, we have to accept it. But the closer in our memory are those hopes of a day or even of minutes ago, the stronger is the impact on our awareness of the difference between what is and what might have been, between what did come to pass and what we had hoped would come to pass.

No people in history have surpassed the Hebrew people in the vividness of their consciousness of God. They saw God reflected in all that happened, a factor in all their action. The reason for this we may not know completely, but one thing stands out in Hebrew life and history—and that is the incessant insecurity of their existence. They had dreams of power and glory, and their dreams repeatedly were shattered by events. Even the brief taste they had, now and then, of political stability and respite from attack only whetted their appetites and intensified their longing. Disaster after disaster brought again and again the discovery of God. It was not Job in his prosperity and honor who became aware of God. It was Job in tribulation, in suffering which carried him to the point where death was the sweetest relief he could imagine, who became truly aware of God. It was when the prophets saw the darkness ahead that they felt full of the message of God.

We learn partly by contrast what it is to exist. When we see before our eyes the destruction of something we love or value we find a void in our lives. It is the non-existence of what we cared for which brings home to us what existence really is. It is the shock of discovery of the difference between what we dreamed would be and what we find really is which makes us see existence. As we live and learn, as we mature in judgment and wisdom, we discover the precariousness of all things. If a speeding car had swerved a few inches further last night as I stepped into a dark street I would not be alive today. I cannot remember that and rest in my continuing life as something which goes on only because it has been. So we discover the absolute difference between real existence and mere possibility, a difference which cannot be expressed in terms of degree or quantity. With this there must be some inkling, by contrast if by no other way, of what it means for an existence to have nothing about it that is precarious or merely possible or contingent.

In Mascall's words, again:

> the apprehension of God as the cause of finite beings upon which the whole existential approach is based, is not a mere apprehension of God's existence; it is a recognition of his nature as well. Strange as it may seem to anyone who has never made the experiment, the contemplation of finite beings does reveal that they both declare by their finitude that God in his self-existence is altogether other than they and at the same time that in their genuine but limited perfection they are like him.[11]

The fact that contingent existence shows us the likeness of God enables us to have an awareness of God in our awareness of ourselves and of the things of our world. It also provides a basis for a more direct inquiry into the nature of God. We see the sun, to use Plato's image, reflected in the things which it has brought into existence. Their light and color is the sun's light and color. But we see this not as it is in the sun; we see it as it is reflected in things. We cannot look at the sun directly and see what it is in itself; yet from what we see reflected in other things we can draw some knowledge of the sun itself. So the likeness of God in the things of the world may provide a basis of some knowledge of God Himself.

CHAPTER 23

Knowledge by Analogy

How We Can Use Concepts to Think about God

WE HAVE found that the essence of God is existence, and that we cannot form a concept of existence because in this instance the process of concept formation cannot take place. To think conceptually about a thing is to abstract its essence from its existence. We cannot hold its existence in our thought; the only existence in our thought is the existence of the thought itself. The existence of the thing we think about belongs to it, to the thing itself, and its existence is not the same as the occurrence of a thought about it. But unless the essence I hold in thought is the very essence which exists as the thing I think about then my thinking does not reveal to me the nature of that thing as it is in itself. So if I am to know the nature of a thing my thought must capture for itself the essence of that thing without its existence. This is what we call abstraction, and of course it can be performed only upon essences which can be held by the mind apart from their own existence. It is obvious that if the essence of God is existence then the essence of God cannot be held in thought. The process of abstraction cannot be performed upon it, for to try to take the essence of God without His existence is to lose His essence. The mind which tries to grasp the essence of God is like a child who tries to grasp a soap bubble and opens his hands only to find them empty.

In spite of all this we do find ourselves engaged in thinking about God. We have seen already that we can think about existence in ways which are not exclusively conceptual, by use of memory and imagery. Every encounter with existence is an encounter with God's likeness, and to recognize this is—in a way—to think about God. But we think about God in a way more direct than this. The field of theology is composed of the results of man's attempts to think systematically and conceptually about God. Now if we cannot think about God, what is it that men are doing when they construct their theologies? If we cannot think about God in terms of theory and by the use of concepts then how can we even think truly that we cannot think about God? Only the mind's silence can meet the mystery of the unthinkable. We cannot think about the absolutely unthinkable; not even that it is unthinkable. God is inconceivable, and yet we conceive Him to be inconceivable. Is this a contradiction, or nonsense, or are we missing something?

What we have missed is the possibility of thinking about something by means of concepts but in a way which does not require us to abstract the nature of the thing from its existence and to hold that nature in our thought apart from its existence. How is this possible? The answer, once we see it, is surprisingly simple. In order to use concepts in our thinking about that of which we cannot form concepts, all we have to do is to use concepts of other things. We simply use the concept of one thing to think about another thing. We have to see now how this can be done.

The Relation of Concepts and Judgments

What makes this possible is the fact that concepts themselves are only essences held in thought. They do not, as concepts alone, involve existence. So far as I think in concepts alone the whole matter of existence or non-existence, or of what kind of being is involved, is in suspension. As I think *man*, or *dog*, or *molecule*, or *pleasure* in concept I simply do not include in my thought anything of the *being* of these things. I neither affirm nor deny that what I think has this or that or any kind of being. In order that my thought may connect the concept with being I have to use the concept in an affirmation or a denial, as in "this *is* a dog" or "pleasure *is* a feeling," and so on. The concept must enter into a judgment; and the connection with being which the conceived essence is thought to have is shown by the proposition in which the judgment is expressed. We can get the essence of something in thought only if we abstract that essence from its existence. We can reunite that essence with existence, in thought, only if we include it in a direct reference to existence; and this is the function of judgment.

We do not mean by this that concepts float around in a realm of their own waiting for some mind to attach them to existence. We obtain our concepts by abstracting essence from existence, but this does not mean that our minds remove the essence and leave the existence bare. Abstraction is not removal. The essences we conceive are still essences of existence; the abstraction is logical, not real. So the essences we conceive do still, even as conceived, have a concern with real existence. As Professor Veatch says:

> Whatever may be true of the concept of an essence, the essence itself is ordered to existence; the "what," in short, is what *is*, or at least what is supposed to *be*. What could an essence *be*, if it could not be said to be at all, at least in some sense of being? Without being, indeed, an essence is just nothing. . . . Accordingly . . . the only place where human beings can attain and apprehend essences is where they *are*, and where they are, at least for human beings, is in the changing, evolving world roundabout us. In other words, it is by abstracting them from sensory experience that we attain our concepts of essences, it being in such experiences that we are presented with things that are.[1]

This is stated as emphatically by Mascall.

> What is given to us in the finite world is not a realm of essences, some of which exist, but a realm of existent acts, each of which, in view of its determinate character, gives rise to a particular essence. To ask what a being is, therefore, is simply to ask how it exists, for its essence is nothing but the mode of its existence.[2]

The essence of a thing is *what it is*, and each of these three words is important. The essence of a thing is its *what;* it is *its* what, and not the "what" of something else; and it is what that thing *is.*

Although concepts are ordered to existence and are obtained by thought from existence, yet the existence of the essence conceived is not itself shown by the concept. Every man has had a mother, but to know the man is not to know his mother. Every scene caught in a photograph has its own definite location in space and time, but the photograph does not have to include an identification of the locale, nor does it contain any assurance of the present existence of what it pictures. When a man dies the pictures of him which are left behind do not fade out. Every concept is derived from our experience of real existence, but it does not carry that real existence with it nor does it contain the marks that tell us of its source. "As is obvious," says Professor Veatch, "the mere concept of an essence gives no indication of the existence or non-existence of that essence. That is to say, a concept is, as such, merely of the 'what' and not of the 'that.'" He points out that "the concept of an essence is as such never the concept of an existing essence. True, it may have been derived from existents, and it may be used to describe existents; still, it itself presents only the 'what' and never the 'that.'"[3]

Perhaps now we begin to see how we can use the concept of one thing to think about another thing. The significant point about the relation of concept and judgment, so far as our problem is concerned, is that *the essence conceived does not control its own use in judgment.* The act of judging is under the control of the mind which judges. To think "animal" and to judge "animals are living creatures" are different acts, and the first does not control the second. One reason we may be confident that the concept does not control the judgment is the fact that we can make false judgments. The same essence held in concept can be affirmed or denied truly or falsely of this or that real existent. Some people say there are flying saucers and others say there are not; some people say there are disembodied spirits and others say there are not. Unless a mode of being, such as existence, can be both affirmed and denied of the very same essence then these affirmations and denials which we actually make would be impossible. This is not to say that an essence can be both affirmed and denied of the same thing *truly;* for what we here refer to is our power to judge, and this includes our power to judge falsely as well as truly.

The act of judging adds something not found in the concept alone. It adds a reference to being. The reference to being is not a part of the concept, for the same concept may be linked in judgment either in affirmation or negation with this or that being. When a concept enters into a judgment we say it *intends* something; and the expression of the judgment, that is of the intention, we call a *proposition.* The proposition expresses *what* is intended, and it expresses this *as intended.* It includes what we wish to say concerning being, and it also says it about being.

Professor Veatch points out that

> while concepts do acquaint us with what things are, they seem always to stop short of disclosing the fact that these "whats" are indeed the "whats" of real existing beings, the very "whats" that things actually *are.* In other words, it is the intention of essences *in their very existence* and as actually existing that concepts would seem not to suffice for. Moreover, since it is only insofar as intentions are directed toward things as they really are, that they can be said to be true or false, it is understandable why only propositions and not concepts should be susceptible of truth or falsity.[4]

A concept, as concept alone, is held in abstraction from all specific intentions. Its only intentionality, as a concept alone, is its availability for use in some specific judgment. Having been obtained by abstraction from being, the concept is always ready to intend, or to refer to something; but it does not actually accomplish this by itself. Because the intention of a concept is not itself a part of the concept, the same concept may therefore intend different things in different judgments. This is plainly so in the reference of concepts to actual existence. The concept *man,* for example, may intend or refer to *this man* or *that man,* or any other, when it is used in judgment. But this is not all; the freedom of intention of concepts is still wider. The intention of the essence conceived is not restricted to its own existence, for it may also intend the existence of something else if such is the import of the proposition which expresses the intention. Whether a concept intends its own existence or some other existence is not governed by the concept as such; it is disclosed only in a proposition which expresses the judgment.

Perhaps the most familiar example of such a shift of intention is the metaphor. If I say, "This man was a solid rock in the face of attack," I do not assert the real existence of the essence conceived as a "solid rock." There are solid rocks, to be sure, and my conception of a solid rock is derived from my experience of such things. But here the concept of a solid rock is used to refer to something else; it is used to indicate indirectly the nature of this man. Sometimes we cannot avoid using a shift of intention if we are to communicate our meaning. This is plainly so when we try to describe to a person the appearance of something he has never seen. It is likewise the only way in which a poet can communicate those subtle nuances in the nature of things which have not already been caught and fixed in familiar concepts.

We have now answered in principle the question of how it is possible for us to use concepts to think about something of which we cannot form concepts. The concept of one thing can be made to intend something else, and the "something else" it is made to intend may itself be something we are incapable of conceiving. As we shall see presently, there are ways of thinking which carry the same principle a step further. Not only may we use a concept to think about something other than the real existence of its essence, but we may use our awareness of the relation of an essence to its existence to think the relation of another essence to *its* existence. This is what we call *knowing by analogy*.

Throughout our discussion of analogy it will be important to remember that this way of knowing is, as we have shown, based solidly on our experience of real existence, and is made possible by the very properties of concepts and propositions which enable us to use them as instruments of any knowledge we can obtain. To deny the propriety of their use to obtain knowledge by analogy, when that use is guarded by an understanding of what we are doing and of its import, is to challenge the propriety of any cognitive use of concepts and propositions. For that in their logical nature which enables us to use them in the one case is what enables us to use them in the other. It is quite significant that philosophical attacks upon knowledge by analogy come, as a rule, from quarters where any claim of genuine knowledge of real existence as it is in itself is considered doubtful or is denied outright.

Univocal, Equivocal, and Analogous Use of Concepts

We have already referred to the distinction between univocal, equivocal, and analogous uses of concepts.[5] A concept is used univocally when it attributes the same essence to different things in the same sense. I say that Mr. Smith is a "man" and I say that Mr. Jones is a "man." I mean that in this respect they have the same essence; they are both human, in the same sense and in the same way. Suppose, however, that someone replies that Miss Brown then is not human, for she is a woman and not a man. The use of "man" in this latter statement obviously does not have the same meaning as it had in the statements about Mr. Smith and Mr. Jones, for in the denial that Miss Brown is a man the word refers to a difference of sex. "Man" may also refer to a difference of maturity, as when we use "man" to distinguish an adult male from a child. When we say of a child that he is not yet a man we do not mean that he is not yet human; we mean that he is not yet an adult. If we use "man" in any two of these senses indiscriminately, as if the meanings were the same, we are in fact using two concepts as if they were the same when they are not the same at all. This is equivocation.

Suppose, however, that we say to a youngster, "Be a man!" We surely do not mean by this, "Change yourself now from a child to an adult," in the sense of actually becoming older. Nor does our injunction presuppose that the child is now subhuman and that we wish him to become human. We do not mean quite anything which we should mean if we were using "man" univocally with any of the three meanings of the paragraph before this one. Our use of "man" in this exhortation is an example of analogy. We know that the child is not a man, in the sense of being an adult, and we do not wish him to change now into an adult. What we mean to enjoin upon him is a mode of action by which he will show, even as a child, something of the qualities and attitudes of maturity. We do not wish him to imitate an adult, or to be a miniature adult. It is not the behavior of an adult human dwarf that we desire for him. On the contrary, we wish him to show those qualities and attitudes of maturity in the guise in which they are appropriate to childhood.

Fortitude and patience, for example, are virtues of manhood; but, in his own way, a child may show these qualities also. As we see them in a child we see them in modes appropriate to the nature of a child rather than in the mode appropriate to an adult. Trembling lips do not mean the same in a man as in a child who is trying to be brave. So a child, in showing such qualities, has not become literally (univocally) an adult; but in his fortitude and patience he is something like an adult. It is false to say that he is a man, if we are using "man" univocally with its meaning as "adult"; but still it is not an equivocation. It lies between the two, and is an analogy. The fortitude and patience we hope the child may show is a manifestation of human excellence in manhood's youth just as the adult's very different way of showing his fortitude and patience is an expression of a human excellence appropriate to man's maturity. The acts and attitudes of the youth have here the same significance with respect to the nature and character of man in his youth that the adult acts and attitudes have with respect to human nature in its maturity. But no explanation in univocal terms can quite contain the wealth of meaning which analogy gives to these three short words, "Be a man!"

ANALOGY AND SIMILARITY

When we first try to clarify the relation of analogy perhaps we tend to think of it as nothing more than similarity. It is, in fact, a kind of similarity; but to leave it at this is quite unsatisfactory and misleading. For similarity, in our usual notion of it, is a relation in which two or more different things have some quality or character in common. When we say, for example, that one house is similar to another we mean, ordinarily, that there are certain features of design or of appearance or of construction in which the two are the same. The houses are not the same, but a part of the nature of one is the same as a part of the nature of the other. They may be of the same design, built from the same plans, but differently located and painted in different colors. So when we direct our attention to the design as such we find that whatever characterization of design applies to one house is true also of the other. Similarity is a partial identity of essence, and in this respect it differs from analogy.

On the other hand, even though analogy is not partial identity, at least in the obvious way of ordinary similarity, it would seem that there must be something which things have in common if we are to think of them in terms of analogy. The plan of one of the houses mentioned above is not related by analogy to the plan of the other; in certain respects, at least, the plan of one house is identical with the plan of the other. But suppose we consider two very different houses, radically different in design and specifications. Although we may find that the idea of *house* as applied to the two is univocal, yet they do not in any respect have the same plan. Still the plans are not utterly different as would be the plan for a house in which to live and, say, Napoleon's plan to found a *House,* in the sense of a dynasty, or the plan which the Old Testament attributes to Israel's Yahweh for the *House of David.* Two dwellings, built from different plans, may nevertheless be said to be built from analogous plans. It is the differentiating feature of analogy we wish to find.

When we say that two sets of house plans are analogous in spite of no similarity between them, in the ordinary sense of "similarity," what is their relation? Do we not find it in the way in which the plan of each house is related to the structure which is built in accordance with it? The identity is not identity of plan, but an identity of the relation of the plan to the house. In this respect, of course, the analogy is much broader than one of house plans alone. For any plan of any structure, built to plan in the same sense as is a house, is analogous in this way to any other. We can limit the analogy to house plans if we relate the plan not merely to the structure but to the kind of structure which fulfils the functions of a family dwelling.

Of course we do not use analogy as the means of knowing about such things as house plans where we can examine the plans themselves. But different house plans are analogous, and because this is the case we can know something by analogy about dwellings of which we have no direct knowledge at all. We may know by analogy something of how a certain pre-historic people lived even though we have no trace of their actual dwellings. It is our knowledge by analogy which guides us in our search for the relics of their actual dwellings. We know that their dwellings, whatever their design, were made for living. In so far as those people had life functions like our own there would be something of the same relation in the two cases between the design of the dwelling and the ends served by the structure itself. To deny this would be, in effect, to suppose that those early people, if they had dwellings, did not use them. Although this knowledge would not help us in the least in an attempt to draw a true picture of such a dwelling before we had seen one, yet our knowledge by analogy would help us recognize the dwellings if we happened to uncover them in our explorations.

Knowledge requires identity; identity is itself the logical relation upon which knowledge rests. So knowledge by analogy cannot occur in the absence of identity. Univocal conceptual knowledge of a real existent requires that the essence conceived shall be the identical essence that exists. Analogy is not identity of essence in concept with essence in existence, for the things we know by analogy alone are things of which we cannot form such concepts. Analogy rests, rather, on identity of relation.

At this stage, then, analogy may be understood as a *proportion: A* is to *B* as *C* is to *D*. We do not mean by this that *A* or *B* or *C* or

D is identical with any of the others. If we say "two is to four as six is to twelve," we use four different numbers; no two are the same. The identity holds between the relation of the first two, on the one hand, and the relation of the other two. If we state this as an equation our attention is called immediately to the point of identity: $2/4 = 6/12$.

Analogy's Presuppositions

The question which immediately comes to mind is how this will help us in our attempt to think about the nature of God. Does not an analogy of proportion, assuming for the moment that it does apply in this instance, require that we know more about the terms of the proportion than we are able to know in the application of the analogy to God? Let us examine this problem with respect to the assertion of the goodness of God.

In order to think of God as good we have to use a concept of good obtained from our own experience. Suppose we understand "good," as it refers to ourselves, to mean the realization of those potentialities of our nature which give to it the most complete expression in act of which it is capable. How can we shift the intention of this concept from ourselves to God and thus know something of God's goodness? Of course it is not the *concept* of God's goodness we seek, for we cannot form such a concept. It is the awareness of good in ourselves which somehow has to intend the nature of God if we are to know God by analogy. The analogy holds, provided man's goodness has the same relation to man's nature as God's goodness has to God's nature. But where do we find a bridge from one side of the proportion to the other?

What is the alternative to the admission that our knowledge of human goodness is knowledge of God's goodness by analogy? The alternative can be only that "goodness" in these applications is equivocal; and this would mean that we know nothing whatever of the goodness of God. We may just as well, and better—if we wish to avoid misunderstanding—refer to the x-ness of God.

If we look again at our numerical proportion, two is to four as six is to twelve, we find that knowledge of the relation of two to four is not enough to enable us to find the values of the other side of the proportion. If our problems is to find x, where $2/4 = x/12$ or where $2/4 = 6/x$, the solution is easy. But suppose our problem is to find x and y where $2/4 = x/y$. We know from this that x and y can refer to any two values where $y = 2x$, but this does not tell us what are the specific values of x and y in any actual case. A man who wishes to borrow from me may tell me he has liabilities and assets in the ratio of two to four, and although this does assure me of his present solvency it gives me no information about his ability to repay a loan of a thousand dollars. For the ratio may be true whether his assets are one dollar or a hundred thousand.

The statement, then, that man's goodness has the same relation to man's nature as God's goodness has to God's nature tells us nothing determinate about God unless we already have independent knowledge either of God's goodness or of His nature.[6] Proportion alone is not enough; and so analogy, in the sense of proportion, is not itself a source of knowledge about God. On the other hand, if our prior proof of God's existence is sound then we do have independent knowledge of God's nature. We found that the nature of God is existence, for God is self-existence. Consequently, if we know that God's goodness is related to His nature as our goodness is related to our nature, our understanding of goodness as it is in man provides a basis for our knowledge of God's goodness by analogy.

Even this, however, is not enough. There are two conditions which must be satisfied if we are to be able to attribute goodness to God by analogy. Up to this point we have taken account of only one of these. We have found that we have to have prior and independent knowledge of God's nature. This we have in our knowledge that God is self-existent being, and so this condition has been met. But in addition to this we have to know that the relation between man's goodness and man's nature is the same as the relation between God's goodness and His nature. In other words we have to know that the analogy of proportion actually applies as between man and God.

We know that, so far as goodness is concerned, the analogy of proportion holds as between man and God because we know that it holds as between any two real existents. The reason for this is apparent once we see the difference between such predicates as *being, goodness,* and *truth,* on the one hand, and ordinary concepts on the other. I may say that a man is trustworthy, and anyone who knows the meanings of the terms knows what I intend by this statement. If someone is doubtful about my meaning he may ask me to define "trustworthy," and my definition then shows what I mean by it. The way in which such predicates as *being* and *goodness* and *truth* differ from this is that they are logically indefinable. Since they are indefinable they cannot be attributed univocally to different subjects. If they cannot be attributed univocally then they either cannot be attributed at all to different subjects, without equivocation, or else they have to be attributed analogously.

"Being" is not a class concept, nor can the term be given formal definition. If we were to define "being" we should have to differentiate it from those things which lack being. If we define "man," for example, as "rational animal" we differentiate man as *rational* animal from those animals which are not rational, and by implication from those beings which are not animal. But we cannot differentiate *beings* from those things that are not beings, for all things have being. There is no non-being. This is why we cannot treat of being as a class concept or as a category. The reference to being transcends all distinctions of categories and all differences of predication, and for this reason it has been called traditionally a "transcendental."[7]

Good is also a transcendental, for the same reason, provided we understand "good" to mean "excellence in existence," or "existential excellence"—the realization of potentiality. There is nothing which is non-good, for there is nothing which is non-being. Absence of good is absence of being. Absence of truth is likewise absence of being, for truth is the real existence of the essence referred to being in judgment. No two beings are identical in their being, or have the self-same identical good; nor are any two beings the actual being of the very same essence, and so no two beings are the truth of the same essence. Each individual being is itself only; it has its own good, and it is its own truth. But each individual being is identical with every other in these respects, in the fact that it is itself only, in the fact that its own real existence is its own good, and in the fact that its own essence is true to its own existence.

This is the foundation for the application of the analogy of proportion to all real beings. It is founded on the radically individual nature of real being, which is implied by our finding that real being is existence. Universals and classes have being, but their being is not real existence; they do not have their own existence. They have being only in and through some real existence, the existence of the thought by which we are aware of them or the existence of those individual realities which exemplify them and from the natures of which we abstract them. No two realities have the same existence. The universals we attribute to them univocally in concept have, as universals in abstraction from real existence, mental existence only. The universal has being, that is, only in the existence of the real things from which the mind abstracts it and in the existence of the act of thought by which the mind apprehends it. There is no such real being as *man*. There are *men*, but *man* is not real; by this we mean there is *a* man, but not *the* man. Our concept of *man* we form by abstraction, and we attribute it truly to individual men. But the more complete our knowledge of a particular man's nature the closer we come to the awareness of a nature which we can attribute truly to him alone. Since his existence is the existence of the very nature he is, it is plain that we cannot truly attribute his existence to any other nature. So we cannot think the existence of things univocally; nor their goodness or truth, since these express the principle that real being is actual existence.

NEGATIVE AND POSITIVE KNOWLEDGE BY ANALOGY

Our knowledge of God's goodness is, in one respect, negative knowledge. We, as contingent beings, do not know self-existence in ourselves. So we do not and cannot know self-existence as it is. But we do know goodness as it is in a contingent being, and we know something of the limits which the contingency of a contingent being places upon its goodness. Man's goodness, for example, cannot endow the non-existent with existence; and, as we have already seen, it is because of man's contingency that this is true. But man's knowledge of goodness in a finite being enables him to know by analogy the goodness of God.

To know the goodness of God by analogy is not to know goodness as it is in God. We know goodness as it is in man, and this is knowledge by analogy of the goodness of God. We can know nothing except what is negative of what it is like *to be goodness*, as God is goodness. But, by analogy, we can know something positive *about* God's goodness; for by analogy we know that as man's goodness is the goodness appropriate to man's nature so the goodness of God is goodness appropriate to self-existence. God's goodness is infinite and unconditioned goodness, as God's existence is infinite and unconditioned existence. This is negative knowledge still, but it has positive implications *for us*. It means that the goodness of God is beyond anything we can conceive or imagine, and it means that nothing short of the best we can conceive or imagine is appropriate for us to attribute by analogy to God. Even our best is not appropriate in itself; it does not apply univocally to God. But it is appropriate for us to attribute to God by analogy the best we can conceive or imagine.

A small child expresses his love for his mother in a gift of service or with something he has made or something he values. His service is not needed for its practical results, nor is his gift useful or beautiful in its own right or by the standards of her to whom he gives it. The child's very idea of his mother is an idea he forms almost wholly in terms of what she does for him and with him.

He has no conception of his mother's own life, of her interests and activities as a woman. He cannot know her thoughts, at best he knows only in terms of his own narrow experience what she means when she speaks to him. What it means to her, when she speaks, he has not the slightest conception. So his service to her, his efforts to "help," and the pieces of paper he colors and pastes for her happiness, are appropriate gifts. But they are appropriate in the sense that they are appropriate for him to give; they are appropriate to the nature, to the needs and the welfare, of his mother only as his love and affection are valued by her *for his sake* and not for the improvement of her circumstances or the growth of her popularity or the increase of her property. She values these things for his sake because she loves him.

In this we have some indication of the significance of our knowledge by analogy of the goodness of God. Our own greatest good, the most complete realization open to us of our highest potentialities, is appropriate to our nature as the self-existent and absolute goodness of God is appropriate to His nature. But we know nothing of what it is to be absolute goodness itself. We know only that there is absolute goodness, and we know this in our knowledge that there is self-existent being. As Mascall says, "Analogy does not enable us to *conceive* God's goodness as identical with his essence but to *affirm* it as identical with his existence."[8]

If we try to think the goodness of God we have to think it in terms of our own knowledge and experience of good. Since our good is conditioned and limited the best we can do is to attribute to God by analogy the least conditioned and least limited good we can conceive. But still we have to remember that all finite goods, although some may be greater good than others, are equally finite and equally contingent in comparison with self-existent good. The gift of our best as our tribute to the goodness of God is not appropriate because of what it adds to God or contributes to His good. For nothing can add to His good. It is appropriate *for us*. To think God in terms of the best we can conceive is the appropriate way for us to think of God; for, relative to us, it is the least false. The principle of knowledge by analogy enables us at this point to go further and to assert that this is true by analogy of God Himself. Our idea of good thus may have, as its logical intention, the nature of God. It is not the concept of God's essence, but of our own nature; yet we can use it to refer to God. We still must remember, however, that analogy does not capture for our minds the goodness of God in terms of what that goodness is; so far as its actual content is concerned, it finds the goodness of God only in terms of what it is not. But it really finds the goodness of God in these terms. Knowledge which is intrinsically negative is transformed by analogy into something positive. Yet once we forget that our assertions about the nature of God are true only by analogy, once we take them to be true univocally (i.e. literally), they collapse into mere negations.

CHAPTER 24

The Revelation of God

W E FIND the likeness of God in existence and we know God by analogy. We have now to consider the possibility that there are circumstances in which the presence and action and will of God are shown to us in special ways. As we shall see, it is not the place of a philosophy of religion to consider what the revelation of God consists of, or to consider the conflicting claims for this or that as a true revelation. But a philosophy of religion is concerned with the question of whether there is a reasonable basis for the belief in the possibility of revelation. We shall expect to find that our experience of revelation is a religious experience, not an experience in which philosophical truth is imparted to us; we should expect it to be a religious experience in which our minds and hearts are lighted by truth and goodness in some way which has particular significance for us in our relation to God.

Although all things that exist proclaim the existence of God, they do so first of all by their existence alone. In this respect all contingent things are on the same level; each is equally contingent, and each equally points to God in its contingency. How, then, can some things show us more of God than do other things? It surely cannot be by means of essence alone, considered apart from existence; for such abstraction leaves out entirely the likeness of God. We seem left with only one alternative, that if God shows Himself more plainly in some things than in others it is because of differences in the relation of essence to existence.

The revelation of God occurs where the veil of finiteness and contingency discloses something of what it conceals. I may look about at field and forest and see not one of the creatures which take part in the teeming life of that place. Yet here and there a movement of the grass, the sudden swaying of a single stalk, the rustle of leaves reveal the presences they hide. The smooth surface of a pond shows nothing of the restless life it covers. But in a movement here, in a ripple there, and in an occasional splash the ceaseless activity below the surface shows its presence. In plot and character a writer tells his story, but his novel need not be autobiographical to tell us also something of the writer. He does not tell us the details of his life but he shows us something of his mind. How little we know of the details of Shakespeare's life and how much we know of the qualities of his spirit! The writer's evaluations, his conception of good and evil, his admirations and his contempts, his ideal of life and his conception of the relations of character and destiny show through the fiction which hides the real events and the real people who have been the author's teachers.

Thus the idea of revelation need not suggest that God simply exhibits Himself to us as He is. For this we know cannot be; we see and know by means of our own ways of seeing and knowing. "Revelation," says one writer, "is the act of God in disclosing or communicating truth to the human soul."[1] But if truth is to be communicated it must be expressed in terms which man can appreciate. God's act is His existence, and we must try to see how the act of existence can be a revelation of God. Yet the truth which comes by revelation is religious truth; it is existential rather than essential truth.

Seldom has the theistic idea of revelation been better expressed than in the key passage of Archbishop Temple's discussion:

> We affirm, then, that unless all existence is a medium of Revelation, no particular Revelation is possible; for the possibility of Revelation depends on the personal quality of that supreme and ultimate Reality which is God. If there is no ultimate Reality, which is the ground of all else, then there is no God to be revealed; if that Reality is not personal, there can be no special revelation, but only

uniform procedure; if there be an ultimate Reality, and this is personal, then all existence is revelation. . . . Only if God is revealed in the rising of the sun in the sky can He be revealed in the rising of a son of man from the dead; only if He is revealed in the history of Syrians and Philistines can He be revealed in the history of Israel; only if He chooses all men for His own can He choose any at all; only if nothing is profane can anything be sacred.[2]

Revelation is not a one-way process. It comes from God to man, but in order to be effective it requires man's response. To be revealed visibly means more than merely to be made visible, in the sense of "able to be seen"; it means also "to be seen." What is made available must be appropriated, else revelation is incomplete; and revelation is incomplete just in so far as it is not appropriated. The world-process, to quote further from Archbishop Temple, "and all occurrences within it—including the intelligences of men—are due to the purposive action of that Person whose reality has been established as the governing fact of existence. *He guides the process; He guides the minds of men; the interaction of the process and the minds which are alike guided by Him is the essence of revelation.*"[3] But whether we think of revelation as general or special, "*the principle of revelation is the same—the coincidence of event and appreciation.*"[4]

REVELATION AND REASON

Rational knowledge and revelation are thought by some to be opposed. Those who set great store by revelation are sometimes antagonistic to reason. Karl Barth, for example, has this to say concerning natural theology, by which he means the attempt to know God by the use of reason:

When a man is occupied with genuine theology, he will always regard the so-called natural theology as an abyss. If he does not want to fall into it he will not go near it. In horror and indignation he will turn his back on it as the great temptation and fountain of errors. He does not meddle with it. . . . In the complete repudiation of natural theology, one does not first stare at a snake, in order to continue to stare, until he is hypnotized and is then really bitten by it. When he first sees it he strikes it with his walking stick and strikes it dead.[5]

Barth recognizes that we cannot escape philosophy. "If we open our mouths, we find ourselves in the province of philosophy."[6] This does not mean, however, that philosophy and theology can be partners, that "there are two sources of revelation, reason and history on the one side, and Holy Scripture on the other."[7] He tries to remove the difficulty by saying that the dogmatic theologian is "at liberty" to use philosophical conceptions but that he is subject to none.[8] He then declares the independence of dogmatic theology from philosophy:

> Further, it is forced down my throat that the Dogmatic theologian is under the obligation to "justify" himself in his utterances before philosophy. To that my answer is likewise, No. Dogmatics has to justify itself only before God in Jesus Christ; concretely, before Holy Scripture within the Church. Certainly it has also the responsibility of speaking so that it can be *understood*, but there is not the slightest chance that any philosophy could here step forth as norm. . . . It cannot be otherwise than that Dogmatics runs counter to every philosophy no matter what form it may have assumed.[9]

Quite properly, for any view which asserts that we have knowledge of God by revelation, Barth here repudiates the claim that reason supplies the content of revealed truth. But in doing this he pushes the difference between reason and revelation beyond its proper limits, and turns difference into opposition. Reason does not tell us what to find in revelation, and in this respect revelation is not dependent on reason. But there is a way in which revelation does depend on reason, and this is in our need to use reason to examine the claims of that which purports to be revelation. No claim of revelation can be self-justifying; for what is claimed to be a revelation is always claimed to be a revelation of something. That it does reveal what it claims to reveal cannot be shown in the supposed revelation itself. The claim has to be examined independently.[10]

To those who assert that the true recognition and authentication of revelation in religion is an act of faith the reply is that this only pushes the matter back a step. Even those who take such a position must have some marks of faith which they accept, and must have some reason for accepting these as the marks of faith. For they surely do not accept at face value every claim of everything which announces itself to be the product of religious faith. Even if what a believer advances as the criterion of true faith is not a rational criterion, still he must have some reason for accepting it as a true criterion. Even those whose attack on reason is most extreme repudiate also all claims of faith which differ from their own. They can do this meaningfully only if they abandon the claim to objective truth and admit that their utterances are but expressions of subjective attitudes, only if they abandon the claim to communicate and recognize their utterances to be nothing but rhapsodic expressions of feeling.

Someone may show me the picture of a man and tell me it is the picture of his brother. If it is a good likeness and if it is a picture of his brother, then it shows me something of what his brother looks like. But the picture does not authenticate itself. Even if it contains in itself evidence of its authenticity it cannot, with any finality, proclaim its own authenticity. What evidence it may contain must be interpreted in terms of other related facts, in terms of facts which are not a part of the picture itself. Perhaps it is true in some sense or other that God "speaks" to man. But what is revealed to man does not establish its own authenticity as a revelation. A man who thinks he hears God "speak" to him may believe most firmly that it was God he heard. But his belief that this is so in no way establishes the truth of the belief. In no human condition is there stronger conviction of the truth of one's beliefs than in psychopathic delusion. As we have pointed out before, if strength of belief is a test of truth then we should look for wisdom behind the walls of our mental hospitals.

It would be uncharitable to assume that the followers of Father

Divine are insincere in their expressed belief that he is God, whatever they may mean by such a fantastic assertion. The devotion and sacrifice of some of them testify to their sincerity. But their belief and action show, in a way which would be almost incredible as an example of human behavior if it had been invented by a novelist, the extremes to which the claims of revelation can go when reason is excluded.

To test the genuineness of a purported revelation we have to look at the evidence, and the knowledge that it is genuine will have a rational basis if it is knowledge at all. This does not mean that what is revealed is revealed in rational terms. What is revealed may be something we could never have reached by our own efforts and our own reason. This distinction is so clear and so familiar it is difficult to understand how it ever can be ignored. It is the distinction between what a purported revelation actually *is*, on the one hand, and what it *shows* to us on the other. The first is a matter of authenticity, and it can be established only by independent evidence. Unless the revelation is authentic then what it says does not have the significance it purports to have. A newly discovered letter, supposed to have been written by some historical figure, may tell us things about past events which, if true, could have been discovered in no other way. But what it tells us is of no historical significance unless the letter is authentic. Although much of the evidence used to judge its authenticity may be internal evidence, yet this evidence has to be interpreted by reference to knowledge which is independent of the letter.

The dependence of revelation on reason for the authentication of its claims is nowhere stated more clearly than by John Locke, the great English philosopher of the seventeenth century, who was himself not only a firm believer in divine revelation but also a believer in the divine inspiration of the writings which make up the Bible.

God when he makes the prophet does not unmake the man. He leaves all his faculties in the natural state, to enable him to judge of his inspirations, whether they be of *divine* original or no. When he

397

illuminates the mind with supernatural light, he does not extinguish that which is natural. If he would have us assent to the truth of any proposition, he either evidences that truth by the usual methods of natural reason, or else makes it known to be a truth which he would have us assent to by his authority, and convinces us that it is from him, by some marks which reason cannot be mistaken in. *Reason must be our last judge and guide in everything.* I do not mean that we must consult reason, and examine whether a proposition revealed from God can be made out by natural principles, and if it cannot, that then we may reject it: but consult it we must, and by it examine whether it be a revelation from God or no: and if reason finds it to be revealed from God, reason then declares for it as much as for any other truth, and makes it one of her dictates. Every conceit that thoroughly warms our fancies must pass for an inspiration, if there be nothing but the strength of our persuasions, whereby to judge of our persuasions: if reason must not examine their truth by something extrinsical to the persuasions themselves, inspirations and delusions, truth and falsehood, will have the same measure, and will not be possible to be distinguished.[11]

The claim to be a revelation is subject to reason's tests; the only way it can escape its debt to reason is to abandon its claim of truth, but with this it gives up also its claim to be a revelation. A faith which does not have its roots in knowledge becomes the creature of the imagination, the disguise of self-interest, the rationalization of prejudice and malice.

TRUTH IN THOUGHT AND TRUTH IN BEING

We may say of someone, "It is true that he is a friend," or we may say, "He is a true friend." The first is a statement about a statement, and we may make this explicit by writing it: " 'He is a friend' is a true statement." In the second case *true* qualifies not a statement but the noun *friend*. So here we assert truth of a thing, not of a statement. Yet in the first example as well, we assert truth of a thing, although indirectly. For if the statement within the statement, i.e. "He is a friend," did not intend to refer to some actual state of affairs there would be no point in the assertion that it is a true statement. In either case we mean that what "he" is, his nature or essence, conforms to the nature of a friend.

As we have already seen,[12] truth is in being as well as in idea. When we speak of the truth of ideas and statements we mean "conformity with fact," "agreement with reality." It may seem, at first thought, that this is the only precise logical meaning of *truth*. Yet we remember that *truth* may mean also "genuineness," "reality," "actual existence." *The truth* is "the facts of the matter," "the actual state of the case," "the matter or circumstance as it really is." It means, too, "agreement with a standard, pattern, or rule"; or "exact, accurate, precise"; or "rightly answering to the description," "properly so called," "not counterfeit, spurious, or imaginary"; or "conforming or approaching to the ideal character of such."[13]

Even when we say a statement is true we cannot confine the reference of *true* to the statement itself. When I say, "The statement, 'He is a friend,' is true," I mean something by "friend." The word intends the nature of him of whom I speak. When I say the statement, "He is a friend," is true, I mean that in this person to whom I refer in the statement we have an instance of being a friend. The essence which I hold in idea when I think *friend* is an essence which has an actual existence of its own in this man to whom I refer.

Truth is in the relation of essence to being. To deny this, to say that truth is in idea but not in being, is to say that it is in essence alone. But why not say this? Suppose we say that true and false pertain to the essences of things as we think them. Truth, let us say, concerns the relation of the essence as we think it to the essence as it exists in fact. It is the conformity of the idea of a thing to the real nature of the thing. The thing itself is simply what it is, and my idea of the thing is true in so far as my idea matches the real nature of the thing itself.

The difficulty with such an interpretation of truth is that it so separates the idea of a thing from the nature of the thing that we could never know whether or not our ideas were true. If the essence I hold in idea is not the very essence which exists as the thing

to which my idea refers, I have no basis for judging truth. If I have only what purports to be a picture of a man I have never seen, I cannot judge by the picture alone how good a likeness it is. If we consider ideas as if they were only pictures of things, we have no basis on which to distinguish the true from the false. An idea is what it is, and it presents what it presents. Unless some of our ideas confront us with the nature of the thing *as it is in the thing*, then we cannot compare any of our ideas with the things which they supposedly intend.

To distinguish a true judgment from a false judgment I must be able somehow to compare the *what* as it is in idea with the *what* as it is in the thing to which my judgment refers. This requires a direct presentation of the nature of the thing, and this, as we have already seen,[14] we have in sense perception. It requires direct presentation because unless the *what* as it is in idea is the very same *what* as it is in the thing I cannot know the thing by means of the idea.

There is a sense in which we may say that a thing simply is what it is. In this respect the search for truth is the attempt to discover *what a thing is*. But even so, the truth we discover when our search is successful is in the thing itself and not in our idea of the thing. The truth we discover is the real existence of the essence we find the thing to be. That Galileo's assertion that the earth moves is true means that what he said about the nature of the earth is *what the earth actually is*. The statement is true because the *what* of which it asserts existence is the *what* which does exist. The truth which the statement discloses is the real existence of the *what*; the intention is fulfilled in existence. But the statement is the assertion of an intention, it is not the *what* intended. The intended *what* is the nature of the thing itself. So truth is in the thing. The statement reaches truth, finds truth; perception and thought disclose truth.

Truth as Revelation

We have found that the nature of God is self-existence, and that self-existence is absolute good and absolute truth. God is ab-

solute good because there is no respect in which His nature is merely potential and not actual. He is absolute truth because His nature is completely and utterly fulfilled by His existence. So we should expect to find God revealed more plainly in some things than in others, that is, in those things which show us more of the meaning of goodness and truth. The revelation of the goodness of God is in the discovery of value; the revelation of the truth of God is in the individual who, in his real existence, fulfils in act the goodness of God. We find God most plainly in that which exhibits the most complete realization in existence of its essence.

Good is value; the good of a thing is what that thing ought to be. Truth is the realization in being of what ought to be. This is existential and substantive truth, not merely essential and abstract truth. It is truth in the sense in which we say that a ship sailed a true course, or that this animal is a true specimen of its species, or that the edge of a board is true. In these, truth pertains not merely to a statement or a proposition but to an existent. It consists of the conformity of the thing to some standard or pattern. To draw a line true is to draw it straight, if it is to be a straight line, or—whatever line it is to be—to draw it accurately in accordance with the intent. The act fits the purpose; the thing fulfils its nature. But truth without value is trivial. The purpose must be good, the nature fulfilled must be worth fulfilling, if truth is to tell us anything significant about God. So, also, it is good in act, not merely in idea or purpose, which points to God.

Every existent is true; it is truly what it is and truly not what it is not. But there is another aspect of the truth of things in which we may see that some things are more true than others. To return to an earlier example, I may say of someone that he is a "false friend." Now what can I mean by this? If he is a friend at all, he is the friend he is and he truly is such a friend. If he is not a friend then he is not a friend at all, not even a "false friend." (The same holds with respect to any degree of friendship one may wish to distinguish.) Is "false friend" merely the equivalent of "not a friend"? If so, then why not simply say, "He is not a friend"?

A teacher watches a pupil as he tries to draw certain figures. The teacher points to something the pupil has drawn and says,

"Your circle is not right." What does the teacher mean? Does he mean that the figure is not a circle? If so, why does he not say, "That is not a circle"? But neither is a straight line, and we should see little point in calling attention to a fact such as that. "He is a false friend" and "Your circle is not right" mean more than merely "He is not a friend" and "That is not a circle."

In each of these instances we have something which, in some sense, purports to be what it is not. There is no point in referring to someone as a "false friend" if he makes no claim to friendship or if we have no reason to think of him as a friend. I surely should not say of a stranger, "He is a false friend," if I mean only to deny that we are friends. A false friend is one who claims to be a friend, or who is taken to be a friend, and who in truth is not a friend. An incorrectly drawn circle is a figure intended to represent a circle which does not fulfil the intention. If the school boy had no intention of drawing a circle it would not be relevant to say, "Your circle is not right."

We are concerned here with more than merely what a thing is. We are concerned with the relation between the thing itself, with the actual nature which it has, and a nature which is claimed for it or which it is intended to be. It is in this sense that one thing may be truer than another. The thing itself, considered only for what it is, is what it is. It is the actually existing instance of its own nature. In this respect it is truly what it is. We can say it is false only with respect to a standard or criterion or intention or expectation. Only in comparison with such an intention or standard can the actual nature of a thing be considered true or false.

It is in this sense that truth may be a revelation of God. If there are standards of comparison and judgment which reflect the nature of God in an especially adequate or significant way, the things which are truer to those standards are fuller revelations of God. The importance of truth as revelation of God lies in the fact that *a standard or criterion or intention alone does not reveal God to us.* For God is not an ideal; He is absolute existence. The ideal does not show God except in its actual existence. *What* it is, is important; but the revelation of God comes only in what the thing *is.*

I might describe in great detail my conception of a God-like man. I might be able to tell much about the motives I think he would have, the attitudes he would show toward others, the conception he would have of his own nature, and the life he would live. But this would be no revelation of God; it would be a revelation of nothing more than my ideas of godliness in man. If I am to have a revelation of God in human nature two conditions must be fulfilled. My ideal of the God-like man must be in actual existence, and my conception of God-likeness must conform to the nature of God. If we are to find a revelation of God we must look for it in actual existence, and we must have some assurance that what it shows us is the nature of God. The latter condition can be satisfied only if we can find real distinctions of value in existence, and only if we can recognize those values which show the nature of God. We have to be able to distinguish genuine values from false and higher values from lower. We are in search of real things and events which show us the value scale in its true arrangement.

Degrees of Revelation

All finite things have their existence in time. They are in process; they undergo change. Not all of the nature of a thing exists at the same time. Its *what* is only incompletely existent at any moment, and this is one aspect of its finiteness. Another aspect of the finiteness of things is their dependence for what they are on what other things are. A finite thing is the prisoner of its surroundings; a change of a few degrees in temperature, perhaps, and it is doomed. Contingent things show their finiteness again in difference and plurality; two things may both exist although each is what the other is not.

In many of these ways of showing the finiteness of things there are differences of degree. All finite things are in process, yet in the changes it undergoes one thing may reflect more plainly than does another what it has been and what it is to be. We recognize this in those things whose present nature we cannot understand without some knowledge of their past; we see this especially in those things which seem to exist more for what they promise to be than for what they are now. Some episodes mean more than others, for in some episodes in the life of a thing there is crowded more of its true nature than in others. This is significant, of course, only with respect to those things which have in their nature much yet to be, which are rich in possibility. A stone is little different at one time from what it is at another. It gradually weathers and wears away, but its act of existence from moment to moment is little else than repetition. A plant, however, has its existence in a life process, in germination, growth, and seasonal changes.

An animal organism and a diamond are both resistent to change, but in very different ways. The diamond is more resistent than the organism, but there is more to preserve in the organism than in the diamond. More is at stake in the continued existence of the organism than in that of the diamond. The diamond will never be much different, no matter what happens to it, except in its destruction. The organism shows, in change and variety and in the maintenance of its own identity through change and variety, so much more of what it means to be. When we compare non-living things, living organisms, and knowing and purposing persons as different levels of existence we find that each higher level includes in itself the lower levels as well. In this respect alone there are differences in the degree to which the possible has become actual; there are differences in the internal richness and complexity of the *what* which has come to exist. The whole sweep of the nature of being is more completely focussed upon, or embodied in, one act of existence than in another.

We all see this principle at work in many different instances. We see it in a single act of a man, in an act which brings out of hiding his real character and basic attitudes. We may see in a single decision the epitome of the training and experience of childhood and youth, and that single act may reveal for the first time, perhaps, the kind of man he is. Even an off-hand comment, incidental to something else, can expose the very depths of a person's character.

For more than fifteen years George Washington had lived the life of a planter at Mount Vernon. Absorbed in the problems of a changing economy, devoted to his dream of wealth and of the position in society which great wealth would make possible, engrossed in speculation in land and in the search for new methods of restoring the productivity of land worn out, Washington never forgot that honor and duty come first. Always ready to serve his friends, he would lend freely while admonishing the borrower of his folly in borrowing. A successful man of affairs, he was always ready to assist in the affairs of others. Aware of his responsibility, he sought and secured public office. But what, in his life and thought, was fundamental? Heart and soul he seemed absorbed in the affairs of his estate, and in his plans for quick and easy wealth by way of speculation in land. His civic duty he did as befitted a man of his position, and we have the impression that it was for him more a duty than a satisfaction and accomplishment.

During the Richmond Convention of March 1775, when the shadow of war was dark, Washington wrote, at the end of a letter to his brother:

> I had like to have forgot to express my entire approbation of the laudable pursuit you are engaged in of training an Independent Company. I have promised to review the Independent Company of Richmond [County] sometime this summer, they having made me a tender of the command of it[.] At the same time I could review yours and shall very cheerfully accept the honor of commanding it if occasion requires it to be drawn out, as it is my full intention to devote my life and fortune in the cause we are engaged in, if need be.[15]

Freeman comments on this: "That was all. The quiet dedication seemed little more than an incidental explanation of his reason for being willing to take command of still another Independent Company."[16] But this short clause, "it is my full intention to devote my life and fortune in the cause we are engaged in," shows in the clearest possible definition what was primary and what was secondary in Washington's life and character. It is a revelation of what was hidden under the routine activities and the immediate concerns of his daily life.

As a single act or a single statement may show the character of a man, so a single being may reveal in a way peculiar to itself something of the nature of God. For in some things more plainly than in others we discover what it means to exist. Some things reflect in their own nature more of the nature of other things; some things bring the past and future into the present as other things do not. In so far as an essence is in existence we find the nature of God as Truth; and this is revealed the more plainly the more of the essence shows itself in existence.

It is in man himself, in his most intimate experience, that we should expect to find the fullest revelation of God as Truth. This is especially the case when we reflect on what man is. He is a self, aware of himself and of his own acts. He is able to choose with some degree of freedom what he shall do and what he shall not do, acting in the light of some knowledge of what has been and what is and what is possible. He is able to judge and to evaluate in accordance with objective principles of universal application, to lift his judgment out of his own individual and private perspective and see things as they are for all men. He is not merely a part of the world he inhabits, nor is he merely an episode in history's stream; for there is a way in which he includes his world and history in himself. In so far as he knows his world and its history they exist conceptually in his own thought. *He is not only his own existence, but in his existence he possesses also the nature of other existents; and in this sense all things which he knows are in him.* Each human mind is a lens which concentrates in one actual existent what does not of itself exist there; each human mind is a discovery from a unique perspective of the unity and coherence of all existence. So man has in himself more of *what being is* than has any other being we know in this world.

Man is not himself the existence of the things he knows, nor does he appropriate their existence into himself. But he does, in a sense, take their essence into his existence. Because he knows things which are not a part of himself, but which have and keep their own existence in becoming known, the essences of these things exist *conceptually in him* as well as *really in the things themselves.*

It is not difficult to recognize different levels in the relation of the nature of a thing to its own existence, but we do not always see clearly just what this difference of level is. It has to do with the way in which a thing depends on other things. All natural things are equally dependent on other things for their existence, and so are equally contingent. But some things are more dependent on other things for what takes place in the course of their existence, while other things control to a greater degree, by the actuality of their own nature, the course of their existence. A living organism, for example, determines by its own make-up just what shall be some of the effects upon it of other things in its environment. It assimilates other things to itself, in nourishment and growth, and in this respect other things give up their own natures and become parts of the organism.

Anything that exists determines partly by its own nature, by *what* it is, what will happen to it. Exposure to moisture, for example, has different effects on limestone, granite, and iron. The moisture need not be different in these different cases in order that the effects shall be different. But none of these things assimilates to its own nature the moisture which affects it. Living organisms are also subject to changes induced by external influences, in the sense that external things can act on an organism to change it. But some things which exist in their own right are acted upon by the organism. The organism assimilates them to itself so that they no longer have their own separate existence but participate in the organism's existence. We have here not merely a matter of joint effects, as moisture affects iron to produce an oxide; we have rather a case in which one thing gives up its own existence to contribute to something which exists in a different way. Iron does not feed on moisture to remain iron; on the contrary, moisture changes the chemical structure of a part of the iron. A living organism, in contrast, assimilates its food to sustain its life, to remain what it is, and to realize the life-process appropriate to its nature.

Not only do sentient organisms assimilate other things as food, but they also take to themselves something of the nature of other things without appropriating the existence of those things. What they see, hear, feel, or taste becomes the occasion for the release of complex activities which originate from within the organism itself. Sensation guides these acts but in no way constitutes them or brings them into existence; it helps to determine which of the possible acts of an organism will occur in a specific situation. The thing which is sensed lends its nature to the organism without modifying or giving up its own nature and without sacrifice of its own existence.

Man is more than living and more than sentient. He is capable of rational knowledge. He appropriates to his own mind the essences of things captured in sensation. They are not merely guides to his responses; they are the awareness of the nature of other things. The awareness he has, he keeps; it becomes a part of him— not of his body, nor is it his food and drink—but a part of his awareness. For as he abstracts what is common to the things he knows by sensation, he assimilates mentally what is the nature also of other things, of all other individual existents which have in *their* nature what he has found in the things he has perceived. For the same reason we can see that man's power to abstract gives him not only knowledge of what things *are*, but also knowledge of what things *may be*.

The more man knows of the actual the more he knows of the possible, and the more he can determine from within himself what shall be. It is the chemist who knows the properties of a material who can find how to break down its structure and to build a new chemical structure which has new properties. Man does not merely react to things under the control of sensation; his conceptual knowledge of things enables him to choose one course of action from among many possible ones. So his knowledge does not compel this or that action; it is rather the guide he can follow in his attempt to compare the possible courses of action with respect to his own purposes. His act thus may be governed by his own purpose, and he is most a man when this is how he acts.

Ideally a man's act focusses upon that one occasion the various

natures of all the things he knows which are relevant to his purpose, the results of all similar acts he knows about from the past,
the possible goals he may adopt for his own action, and the principles of evaluation by which he selects and rejects possible goals
for himself. In his act are focussed the past with the present, the
possible with the actual, and value with fact. In his act are focussed
rays which reflect the whole range of being.

Since a man is one actual existent and since all his action is the
action of the same self, there is continuity in all he does. It is as if
his whole life were one single act. Of course it is not, for his power
comes gradually and his freedom has to be tried and exercised
long before it becomes effective. Man exists in time, and the past
is irrevocable, but it is not hard to see that one single act may be
the ideal limit of man's being. The closer he approaches this the
more he shows in himself the nature of self-existence, and the better we can see the analogy of God to man—of self-existence to
contingent existence. We see the nature of God in the nature of
man, and we see this because, more than anything else we know,
man is the image of God.

To see in man the image of God, and to be able to recognize
those instances of human life and action which show us more of
God, is a revelation of God. But if it is God which thus is revealed
to us it must be truely the image of God which is revealed in man.
Such a revelation is not self-authenticating, and our recognition
of it as a revelation depends on our previously established idea of
God as self-existence. We may agree, too, that the best in man is
our best revelation of God and yet disagree on what is best in man.
If the idea of God is only a projection of man's preferences then
man's God will be made in man's image. Only if the idea of God
is developed under the control of reason and only if we have a
standard by which the best can be identified can we have confidence that our religious attitudes conform to truth in being. For
this reason it is necessary to consider the question of the reality
of value, and this we shall do in the next chapter.

Of this, however, we may be sure, that if there is a revelation of
God which is fully adequate for man it must be a revelation ac-

complished in and through a person. Seldom, of ever, has this been put more clearly than by Archbishop Temple in his Gifford Lectures. His statement of the nature of revelation, his careful and precise location of the limits of what a philosophy of religion (which he refers to here as "Natural Theology") can say concerning revelation, and his statement of the norm by which authentic revelation is to be recognized are an invaluable contribution to a modern philosophy of religion. In his conception of revelation philosophy is not required to make concessions to theology which threaten its own autonomy as philosophy, and yet there is room left, in the view which he presents, for a reach beyond the range of knowledge to the best in Christendom's traditional faith and the theology which has developed within it.

In the words of Temple:

> *Knowledge of God can be fully given to man only in a person, never in a doctrine, still less in a formless faith, whatever that may be. . . . What is offered to man's apprehension in any specific Revelation is not truth concerning God but the living God Himself.*[17]

CHAPTER 25

The Reality of Value

EXISTENCE AND VALUE

ALL WE CAN KNOW about God is His existence. But the existence we know Him to be is self-existence; and so, in knowing His existence we know that He has all the fulness of being which self-existence implies. As self-existence God is self-existent good, and as self-existent good God is the reality of value. So our evaluations, in so far as they are true, reveal the nature of God to us. In other words, where we find good we find God reflected in finite existence. If we consider briefly what we mean by *good* we shall see why this is true.

The many systems of ethics which man has developed show wide differences in their concepts of the good. But in one respect there is considerable agreement. In all but the merely negative concepts, such as we find in positivism and nihilism, there is some recognition that the good is *that which ought to be*. For something to lack good, to be defective, is for it to lack the completeness appropriate to its nature. Even if the good were mere pleasure we should have to recognize an obligation to seek pleasure, and so, for such an ethical theory, the pleasurable is that which ought to be. Any ethics which looks upon the good as the desir*able*, as distinguished from that which is merely desir*ed*, must recognize the good as that which ought to be.

Thus the actual is good in so far as the actual is what it ought to be; the actual falls short of the good in so far as it is not what it ought to be. Yet everything that is is good. It is good by virtue of the fact that it is. In so far as anything lacks good, it lacks good not by virtue of what it is but by virtue of what it is not. "Thus we must reason in two different ways," says Maritain, "according to whether we are considering the line of evil or the line of good. Such a dissymmetry is absolutely necessary from the very fact that the line of good is the line of being, and the line of evil is the line of non-being and of privation."[1] Each being is good as a being; to go beyond this, to recognize imperfection in something which exists, requires us to refer to a standard by which we can determine not only what a thing *is* but what it *ought to be*. But such a standard, as we shall see, must be no mere *ideal* standard, in the sense of an imaginary standard; it must be an existing standard. No mere possibility can have authority over the actual. The principle of value must itself be real existence, or else our submission to it is nothing but preference or taste. If there is no absolute standard of value in real existence then every event is on the same level as every other. To dislodge a stone, to step on a clod of earth, and to kill a man all have the same significance, namely, none at all. Which should happen is a matter of supreme indifference.

Urban calls this the characteristic presupposition of all traditional philosophy. It is the principle

that ultimately being and value are inseparable—that the validity of our values rests upon the fact that they are grounded in being, while the significance of being rests upon the fact that being includes value as part of its nature.

This was technically expressed in the famous doctrine of the "transcendentals." Whatever is, in so far as it is or has being, is at the same time, and for this very reason, also true, good and beautiful. "The humblest form of existence exhibits the inseparable privileges of being, which are truth, goodness and beauty." These transcendentals are not predicates in the ordinary sense that being might have them or have them not; rather are they inseparable from being as such. This is the axiom of intelligibility—the inseparability of being and value—which underlies *philosophia perennis* in all its forms and expressions.[2]

The notion of *what a thing ought to be* may seem paradoxical. Is not a thing simply what it is? When we speak of what a thing ought to be do we not imply that it would be better for it to be what it is not? Yet the fact is that we do so speak of things, and unless there is some sense in our doing so then much of what goes into our ordinary attitudes toward things is entirely out of place. For hardly anything in our commerce with things and persons is free of the influence of attitudes of acceptance and rejection, of approval and disapproval, of differentiation between the better and the worse. Those who say that these are mere states of mind and have no meaning with respect to the things themselves are seldom willing to have their value judgments and preferences so regarded by others. They usually act as if other people *ought* to respect their feelings, and yet on their own view the "ought" which they seem to expect the other person to follow is nothing but a feeling or preference in the other's mind. I may wish another person to have a different state of mind, or I may wish he did prefer what he does not prefer, but how can I expect his state of mind to be normative in his action? It may induce an action, in the sense of causing it, by virtue of some psychological effect which accompanies it, but this is quite different from the claim that he *ought* so to act.

Some who teach that value is subjective, that right and wrong are only expressions of attitudes and do not pertain to the nature of real things, do still insist, for example, that intellectual freedom *ought* to be safeguarded. They insist that other people ought to respect their individual rights which they exercise in our social order. They protest bitterly when these freedoms and rights are infringed, and when they accuse others of wrongdoing we seem to detect in their accusations something more than merely a notification that they do not experience pleasure in what has happened. So their actions and the claims they express belie their theories. It would be difficult indeed for a person to live and act except on the principle that things are not always what they ought to be, that is, on the principle that differences of value do pertain to the real nature of things themselves and are not mere subjective states of mind. The fact that we do take the attitudes toward things that we do is meaningless except as an item in our personal history unless there is some kind of conformity or non-conformity of attitude and thing. An attitude is significant by virtue of its relevance to the nature of the thing toward which it is directed. We need to find what it is in things themselves which make value judgments true and false.

Some try to interpret values as mere states of mind, and thus hope to exclude them from the real nature of things. What they seem to forget is that states of mind are real events themselves, and so they have succeeded, at best, only in restricting the scope of reality to which value belongs. Those who try to reduce values to subjective states of mind either agree that certain states of mind are desirable or else they have to give up any basis for the claim that we should seek to have such states of mind. For if one state of mind, or one kind of feeling, is really preferable to another then value does not lie in the content of the awareness itself but characterizes the state of mind as something which really takes place. States of mind are real events, and if they have value then value pertains to reality itself.

The ethical theory known as "hedonism" illustrates this, for although hedonism attempts to reduce value to a feeling of pleasure it does not succeed in banishing value from real existence. If pleasure really is a good then it must be good for me to have pleasurable feelings. That good can scarcely consist merely of the pleasurableness of the experience of pleasure. It may be the pleasurableness of the experience that makes it good for me to have pleasure, but it is my having the experience, the actual occurrence of the pleasure, which benefits me. Otherwise the pleasure aspect of an experience and good are mere verbal equivalents, and to say that something is good is only to report merely as a fact that it arouses a certain feeling-quality. If this is the case, it is nonsense to say that we *ought* to have pleasure. On this interpretation the hedonist who commends pleasure can mean only that it gives him pleasure to commend pleasure.

The attempt to exclude value from reality by identifying it with feeling is a failure. For feelings are real events. Theories like hedonism succeed only in impoverishing reality by narrowing the range of value to evanescent states of mind. But states of mind, however evanescent they may be, are still real events. Furthermore, it is difficult even to formulate such a theory as hedonism without implying that it is good for the *self* to have pleasure. In so far as this is the case, hedonism is no mere restriction of the good to feeling; it is rather the welfare of the self as such. To avoid this existential aspect of hedonism we should have to deny that feelings are real events, or that they are experiences of selves, or we should have to interpret the good as a mere verbal equivalent for the pleasurable quality of a feeling experience. In the latter case, as we have already seen, we may *prefer* "good" to "evil," but there is no reason why we ought to and there can be no foundation for the assertion that such a "good" is prefer*able* to "evil."

EXISTENCE AND TIME

One reason why it seems paradoxical to speak of "what a thing ought to be" is our tendency to look upon existence as a merely passive and uniform "is-ness," as if it were a special quality which some essences carry, along with color, shape, and sound. Such a conception gives the impression of paradox to any recognition of the dynamic of existence. To exist is not merely to be; it is to act. There are ways of being which are not being in act, even though all being which does not have its own existence depends on something which does exist. Numbers, qualities, and relations, for example, have being but they do not exist of themselves. They are real only by virtue of the real existence to which they belong and in which they have their being.

Real existence itself is activity, but in so far as any act is finite it is temporal. This means it is not fully *in act* in any one moment of its existence. When we say what a thing is, and say it in such a way as to make explicit its temporality, we have to include what it was and what it will be. When I say, "John *is* a man," I may mean, of course, that he is *now* a man. But the man he is does not exist altogether in the now; the man he is transcends the present in its existence and includes the past and the future. We are easily confused on this point because of the ease with which we pass back and forth between those uses of the verb "to be" which include differences of tense and those which do not. "Is" may mean "is now"; as the copula of a logical proposition, however, all import of tense is excluded.

To speak of what a thing ought to be, in contrast with what it is, seems paradoxical because of our uncritical assumption that things have what Whitehead calls "simple location in space and time."[3] The doctrine of simple location in time is the one which concerns us here. This is the doctrine that "if material has existed during any period, it has equally been in existence during any portion of that period. In other words, dividing the time does not divide the material."[4] Whitehead points out the consequences of this:

> Furthermore, this fact that the material is indifferent to the division of time leads to the conclusion that the lapse of time is an accident, rather than of the essence, of the material. The material is fully itself in any sub-period however short. Thus the transition of time has nothing to do with the character of the material. The material is equally itself at an instant of time. Here an instant of time is conceived as in itself without transition, since the temporal transition is the succession of instants.[5]

Such a doctrine is no longer tenable; the progress of physics alone has made it no longer plausible. It persists, however, in many of our unconscious assumptions, and its uncritical acceptance makes it difficult for us to recognize that time is in the thing rather than that the thing is in time.

Although Whitehead's criticism of the fallacy of simple location in space and time leads him to attack the concept of substance,[6] yet it is the idea of substance as a substratum in which qualities inhere which he rejects. It is possible to use Whitehead's criticism of the fallacy of simple location as the basis of a rehabilitation of the concept of substance. For it is substance as a passive "is-ness" to which Whitehead objects. This surely is far removed from the concept of substance, as it appears in the great tradition of philosophy, as being in act. Finite substances do, it is true, include potentiality, but their potentiality is only the incompleteness which they show at any particular stage of their existence.

Any case of energy is a substance, and to speak of it as substance is only to refer to the act which constitutes it. To call an act "substance" is to say that it has its own existence in distinction from an act which is the act *of* something. There is the act of *being* something, and there is the act of *doing* something; but only that which has its own existence can act.

Finite substances are not fully actual at any moment of their existence. At any moment they are incompletely actual, that is, potential as well as actual; and this means that *there is in the act now something which is not fully intelligible apart from what it is to become.* A finite substance exists as a *what becoming actual.* It is an essence in process of realization; it is existence in process. Thus the potentiality of the finite *is* its temporality. The potential exists as the essence not yet actual but which must become actual if what is already actual is to be intelligible.

A finite substance does not have its full existence all together. Its existence is temporal; its nature is realized gradually, bit by bit, stage by stage. The difference between good and not good is the difference between a development appropriate to the nature of a thing and a course of change which interferes with the true development of its essential nature. Its development can go wrong either from the effects of external causes or, in the case of a person, from his own choice. In the former instance we recognize the individual to be a poor specimen of its kind; in the latter case we have moral evil.

We can see now why self-existence is necessarily self-existent good. In self-existence there is nothing potential; all is fully actual. God's nature is existence in its completion; there is in God nothing which is a not-yet-in-existence. So all that God ought to be, the unqualified and absolute perfection of existence, is *what God is.* We can see also why it is that finite things can be judged good or bad. Since a finite thing does not have its nature all at once, and since it is dependent on things outside itself for much which happens to it, the nature it actually comes to have may not be that which properly belongs to it. Unless there is a potential nature which properly belongs to a thing, we have no basis for judgments of better or worse. There is a place only for preferences, and a judgment of better or worse which is only a preference is one for which we can claim no respect. Such a judgment is only a wish.

The Nature of Value

We are all familiar with the distinction between a descriptive statement and an evaluation. "The house is of Early American design," is nothing more than a statement of fact. If, however, we say, "The house is a good example of Early American," we do more than merely state a fact; we express an evaluation. "The music is played by the Civic Orchestra," and, "The music is played well," also illustrate the distinction. So, again, do: "He is a married man," and, "He is a good man."

The theory of value is an abstruse subject, and there is much disagreement among those who have cultivated this field. We cannot pretend here to give an adequate survey of these many and conflicting theories of value, but we can look at what may be said to be the four chief varieties of value theory. Some interpret evaluation as nothing but an attitude, a liking or disliking, an approval or disapproval. Others understand evaluation to be the expression of an exhortation or persuasion and so as neither true nor false. Others consider values to be real beings in their own right, while still others look upon values as attributes of real existents. The first two may be called "subjectivist" theories, and although we already have seen something of the weakness of such views we shall look more closely at them in this part of our discussion. We shall then compare the two concepts of value which admit that it is objective.

If, when I say "It is good to be honest," I mean only, "I approve of being honest," then evaluation has evaporated. I thus state only a fact about my attitude or state of mind. Approval and disapproval are only facts, psychological events, states of mind. Unless I introduce a hidden assumption that what I approve is therefore good, in the sense that my approval confers goodness upon it—that it is good by virtue of the fact that I approve it and not that I approve it because it is good—there is here nothing but a report concerning myself and my attitude. It has no more ethical significance than does the statement, "I like to eat roast beef." If what I mean, however, is that I approve something because it is good, then of course I do not take "good" *to mean* "what I approve." In the latter case good is not a function of approval, but approval is governed by the apprehension of good.

The outcome of subjectivism is the denial of the reality of values. "Values," says John Dewey, "are as unstable as the forms of clouds. The things that possess them are exposed to all the contingencies of existence, and they are indifferent to our likings and tastes."[7] Thus in identifying values with our likings and tastes, Dewey excludes them from the things to which we ordinarily refer them. But to refuse to identify value with feeling does not mean that feeling has nothing to do with value. On the contrary, feeling, which originally is a guide to organismic response and adjustment, becomes in the mature person the clue to values and a medium in which they find fulfilment.

One writer provides us with an example of the subjectivist conception of value carried to its ultimate absurdity: "Man alone is able to engage in symbolic intercommunication with his fellows. He expels air from his lungs, now and again causes a slight disturbance in the atmosphere, and thereby arbitrarily endows a circumambient world with meaning and value."[8]

If an evaluation is only a persuasion or an exhortation, as the second theory of value asserts, then it cannot be said to be true or false, and so the expression of an evaluation is not a proposition. It follows that an attempt to persuade or to exhort can be given no support or justification. If I am to justify my attempt to persuade someone to do something, such justification must rest on the fact that it is better for him to do it than not to do it. Suppose

I say, "To support the Community Chest is good." If I mean by this only, "Let us support the Community Chest campaign," or "Will you not give your support?" then I have destroyed any rational basis for my statement of good. If you ask, "Why should I support the campaign?" I can answer only, "Do support it." If I say I recognize that I ought to support the campaign then, on this interpretation of "ought," I mean only that I recognize the fact that I have been persuaded to support it. To refuse is only to resist persuasion. To kill, lie, cheat, and steal is only to resist persuasion to live at peace with others and to respect their persons and property. There is no ground on which it can be contended that it is *better* for me to submit to persuasion than to resist it. If I am told it is "better" to submit to persuasion then, on this interpretation, such a statement is only an attempt to persuade me to submit to persuasion.

Values are not mere states of mind, nor are values reducible to persuasions. They are objective facts. Yet, although they are objective and although absolute value is self-existent being, finite values are not real beings in their own right. Values are real, but they are not, merely as values, real existents. A value is a *value of* something. It pertains to the nature of real things, but it is not itself something real with its own separate existence. For if good were itself a real existent we could not attribute goodness to anything else. To say, "This man is good," requires a relation of identity between "man" and "good," and if "good" is a real existent then the relation of identity does not hold. As we have already seen,[9] the relation of identity is a logical relation, not a real relation. If we are to predicate "good" of "this man" then "good" must pertain to the essence of this man; but if the good which we predicate is itself a real existent we cannot predicate it. I can say "John is a man," for here I predicate the concept *man* of John by virtue of the identity of this concept with John's nature. But I should not say "John is man," if I mean by "man" something which has its own existence just as John has his own existence.

For reasons such as this we cannot understand values as real beings existing in a realm of their own. Values are genuine attributes of real things, but they are not really existing things in their own right. On the other hand, they are not attributes in the same way that, say, *green* is the color of grass or *sweet* is a quality of sugar. For a thing which is good in itself is good not only by virtue of what it is but also by virtue of its conformity to a standard. Value is a demand to be preferred, a justifiable claim of *rightness to be*. The justification of such demands and claims lies in the fact that to deny them is to diminish and to impoverish being; it is to make real existence less and emptier than it would be if we should accede to these claims and fulfil them in act. The ultimate principle on which this rests, and which can be denied only at the sacrifice of all meaning, is that it is good to be. From this there follows, as a corollary, that the more something is the better it is; the closer it comes to the completion of its essence in existence the more adequately it exhibits good in being.

Some things, and stages in the development of things, exist not for what they are but for the existence beyond themselves which they make possible. If we insist that everything real exists solely for itself, we try to assert in theory what we cannot follow in practice. In so far as a thing is *what it is now* for the sake of *what it may be in the future*, its present nature has potentialities which belong to it in a special way. To fail to realize these potentialities is to negate its earlier nature. Here, then, is an objective standard of good, and one which interprets good as a relation of essence and existence. Those theories of good which do not so link it, as value, with real existence are open to a fatal objection. Of every claim of *good* or of *oughtness* which such theories express we may ask, "What of it?" To this question they have, and can have, no reply. He who says that good is only a feeling cannot tell us why those feelings *should* be preferred. The fact that we do prefer something may explain the fact that we seek it, but the fact that we prefer something in no way justifies the claim that we ought to prefer it.

A human infant is born equipped with nerve structures and organs of response which are not yet ready to perform the functions appropriate to them in their full development. What is the significance of the existence of such actual but, in its present form, unusable equipment? Surely we cannot avoid recognizing that its significance points to a not-yet-realized future state. It is not for what they are but for what they will be that the immature nerve centers and organs of speech exist in the new-born infant. If that infant grows and develops normally these centers and organs undergo the changes which eventually make them usable for speech. This is a fulfilment of what the infant was; it is the realization of potentialities grounded in actual structures. Such development is part of the good of that individual because the failure of such development would negate what before was an actuality. What we mean is this: An embryonic organ cannot perform the functions appropriate to its nature unless it matures. Interference with its maturation renders meaningless and of no effect something which was actual at an earlier stage. Some things, or parts of things, exist for what they promise rather than for the sake of what they are. There may be those who deny this in theory, but it is safe to say that if they practice medicine or teach the young they cannot deny it in act.

This means that real being does set standards to which existing things ought to conform. This, in turn, means that among the possible changes which a finite thing may undergo, some possibilities are those which ought to be realized while others are those which ought not be realized. In other words, there is for a thing a determinate nature which includes potentialities which may or may not be realized or maintained in the course of future events. At any stage of its existence it has potentialities appropriate to it, as distinguished from those inappropriate to it, because no matter how incomplete its nature may be at that stage it is a determinate nature. *What it is* at any stage of its existence is a nature with possibilities which will fulfil it. There is more in the present actual make-up of a thing than is essential to its present functions and activities. This "something more" can become effectively operative only under certain limited sets of conditions, and if those conditions are not satisfied then the thing's earlier nature is denied its full realization. Its natural development has been aborted.

The distinction between the appearance and the reality of value has been expressed often in terms of a contrast between pleasure and happiness. Charles Morgan states this in a manner which emphasizes the relation of value to the real natures of things:

> Distinguish clearly betweeen happiness and pleasure. Pleasure depends upon the immediate satisfaction of desire; happiness is the feeling a man sometimes has that his life has value, that it is moving towards a great purpose, and, above all, that it is working out its own completeness; unhappiness is confusion and division of mind, a sense of being thwarted, of having lost one's way, of living haphazard in obedience to no form. An unhappy life is like a bad book—it runs hither and thither and carries within it no assurance of form. And the chief difficulty of living is the difficulty we all have in perceiving what the form of our life really is or indeed that it has a form.[10]

VALUE AND POTENTIALITY

To attribute real good to something is to admit the distinction between what a thing ought to be and what it ought not to be. Unless we have a standard by which we can evaluate a thing we are unable to make use of such a distinction. The thing is what it is. If it makes sense to say that there is something it ought to be or that there is something it ought not to be, there are potentialities which fit the nature of the thing and there are other potentialities which do not conform to the nature of the thing. It is quite possible, for example, to rear human beings in such a way that they become not much more than beasts of burden. A normal child can be trained and conditioned in a way that will dull his intelligence, keep his wants on a simple animal level, numb his emotions and feelings, and so make of him little more than a living automaton. If we say that to do this is evil we must mean that such treatment destroys or interferes with the development of something which a human being ought to be.

Most of the things we make or use we evaluate as means to ends. There may be intrinsic excellence, however, even in a fabricated thing intended to be used as a means to an end if that thing shows in its own nature an effective use of the materials and an aesthetically good unity of design and function. The article, we may say, is a good specimen of a good design. But we need more than this for intrinsic good. We need some assurance that it is good for a specimen to be, and so the standard itself has to be one which makes demands that ought to be met. In the case of things which contribute to human welfare it is the fact that man's purposes and wants ought to have satisfaction which is the basis of a valid judgment of real value.

Excellence of making, however, belongs also to the maker. As Plato was fond of pointing out, we call a man a "good shoemaker" or a "good pilot" if he performs those functions well. When we extend this to say that a man is a "good man" if he performs well the functions of being a man, *good* begins to acquire a meaning it did not have when used only to distinguish good from poor specimens. Of course we do say that this or that man is a good specimen of a man, but if we include all that really goes into the make-up of a good specimen of mankind we include a kind of excellence we attribute to nothing else in nature. For a man to be a good man, for him to be a success as a man in the most important sense, is something which depends largely on his own choices and his own will. We may say that a good thing is made, by its causes, to be good, but a good man is to some extent the cause of his own goodness. He can view the alternatives and he can decide himself what shall be the standard by which he chooses from among them.

It is not possible to realize all of a person's potentialities, for the realization of some interfere with the realization of others. So we need a standard of what is best for man. This standard must be one which shows what is *really* best, not merely what seems to be best; thus it must be an existent standard and not a merely ideal standard. Where do we find an existential standard by which to choose among the possibilities and to judge the actual in terms of what it ought to be?

THE STANDARD OF GOOD

The highest good for man is the most complete realization of his highest potentialities. This is a formula easy to arrive at and quite plausible. Its fault, as a working standard, is its failure to specify what are the highest of man's potentialities. But this fault may be remedied if what a man *is*, as *man*, determines what he ought to become. Man's actual nature obviously does limit his potentialities. He cannot learn to fly as a bird flies, for his actual physical make-up prevents this; he is not equipped with wings. He cannot subsist on what a horse eats, for man's actual digestive system is unable to handle such a diet. But is there any way in which man's actual nature provides a positive criterion of what he ought to be?

We may look at this question first in the abstract. We may find, for example, some such positive criterion in the relation of man's potentialities to the development of the whole range of his abilities. It is better to realize those potentialities which permit the realization of other potentialities; it is better to develop those abilities which leave room for the development of other abilities congenial to man's nature. It is better for a man, in his fullest and most mature development, to have unity of purpose and integrity of character than to be divided against himself.

That is better for man which contributes the more to, and interferes the less with, his inclusive and unified development. To take a specific example, a man may be capable of both power and love. If power can be subordinated to love without being destroyed and if the attempt to subordinate love to power destroys love, then love is higher than power and power *ought* to be subordinated to love. For if power is not subordinated to love then a man is unable both to exercise power and to love, and to be most fully man he needs to be capable of both.

At this point we find great differences among things with respect to the conditions under which their potentialities are real-

425

ized. Material things, for example, can be used in the construction of something. We use lumber to build a house, and in using lumber for this purpose we take advantage of some of the potentialities inherent in its actual qualities. But once we use a piece of lumber for one purpose it becomes unavailable for other purposes. Even if we take apart the thing we had constructed, the pieces of lumber we salvage are more restricted in their use than they were in their original form. The more we have to process a thing in order to use it for one purpose the less available it is for other purposes. This suggests that those things are of more worth, and are higher in the scale of being, which not only have the wider range of potentialities inherent in their nature but which also are the more capable of realizing some of these without excluding others.

Perhaps by this time the direction of our thought begins to be clear. The final and ultimate level of value is the complete realization in complete unity of the whole potentiality of an existent. So the absolute standard of value is self-existence. What *can belong* to self-existence is what *ought to belong* to existence; and since what *can belong* to self-existence *does belong* to it, we have in God the ultimate standard of value. What this means for man we can see only as it is shown to us in a person.

THE INFINITY OF GOD

To say that God is the absolute standard of value does not mean that all possibility is realized in God. To interpret the relation of value to existence in this way is to involve ourselves in a deterministic pantheism or else is to deny the infinity of God. The first includes the world in God, and so denies its own actual existence. The second destroys the very basis upon which we can admit the contingency of the world and at the same time find a rational explanation of the fact that it does exist; for a finite God cannot be self-existent. It is not all possibility which is realized in God, for

God Himself brings into existence what is not self-existent. The potentialities of finite existence pertain to finite existence, not to God. The potentiality completely realized in God is God's own nature.

"It is no limitation of Omnipotence," Samuel Johnson has the poet say, "to suppose that one thing is not consistent with another, that the same proposition cannot be at once true and false, that the same number cannot be even and odd, that cogitation cannot be conferred on that which is created incapable of cogitation."[11] To admit that there are things which God cannot do does not imply His finitude. God cannot do evil; but this, so far from limiting God, is only a negative expression of His nature as absolute goodness. It is no more a limitation upon Him than the inability of a sensitive and charitable man to wantonly hurt another is a limitation upon that man's nature. A man who is cruel is less of a man than one who cannot bring himself to do an act of cruelty, for he lacks sensitiveness and feeling and appreciation and so he acts in accordance with standards which are inappropriate to human excellence.

Evil is the negation of existence. That is evil which destroys or obstructs what ought to be; it is evil because of this, and not in its own being. Evil is the not-being of what ought to be. The absoluteness and infinity of God is no mere grab-bag all-inclusiveness. It is rather the utter exclusion from God of what is merely potential, and so of all non-being. It is the exclusion from God of all contingent actuality. God is all that self-existence is; and so He is complete, lacking nothing which belongs to self-existence. As creator He does not create to satisfy His own need, for if He had any need unsatisfied He would be not creator but fabricator, containing in Himself something potential as the material with which to work and limited in His work by the nature of that material. To assert the infinity of God is to deny such limitation. But to say, as some have, that the infinity of God is incompatible with the fact of finite existence is to say that in God essence is primary and existence is the consequent. It is to accept subjectivism, or else to find an original, uncreated, unintelligible formless matter or ultimate surd which stands over against God as one of two ultimate beings.[12]

The Analogy of Perfection

The distinction of actual and potential, as we find it reflected in every contingent existent, is an indication of the nature of God. Things that exist in time do not possess their natures completely during any part of the duration of their existence. The life of a plant, for example, is growth and change. It takes on its full nature stage by stage, not all at once. As each stage appears, earlier stages are gone not to return. Yet what is manifested stage by stage in the growth of the plant is a definite nature. The material which the plant assimilates in its growth, which is appropriated by the life process with which the plant begins its individual existence, exhibits a definite pattern of qualities and processes which constitute the real nature of that plant. It is only because a thing has a definite nature to be realized that one part of the thing goes with other parts and one stage of development fits the other stages.

Each actually existing thing has a determinate nature. It is what it is, and not something else. Nothing that exists in time has its complete nature all together; at each stage of its existence it shows, at best, the aspect of its nature appropriate to that stage. But the fact that there is a definite nature to be realized in time means that what will complete the development of a thing is not arbitrarily determined. What key will unlock a door depends on the make-up of the lock in the door, not on the attractiveness or availability of the key. A man has the ability to walk, if he has developed normally and has suffered no injury which interfered with that ability. But during the first months of his life he was not able to walk. Yet to be able to walk is a part of a man's nature; it is a part of his nature even before he can walk, for it is a potentiality which belongs to what he already is actually. The appropriate exercise of the functions already within the power of an infant, together with his normal maturation, brings to him eventually the ability to walk, to speak, and to think. If he grows and develops in such a way that he never becomes able to walk or to speak or to think then he never acquires, in its fulness, the nature which belongs to him as human.

This means that in so far as an actual existent has potentialities, and by virtue of the fact that there is a determinate nature which belongs to each actual existent, there are some possible eventualities which are more appropriate to its nature than are others. Some of the things which can happen to a plant or to an animal in the course of its life promote and assist the development appropriate to it; other things can happen to it which interfere with its development or end its existence. I may plant a bush, for example, and expect it to bloom in a few months. But if it has no water it will not grow; it withers and dies.

"But," we may ask, "is it not every bit as true to the nature of the plant to wither and die if it has no water as to grow and bloom if it has what it needs for growth?" Failure to grow is certainly one of the possibilities which lies ahead of a planted shrub. It may seem, at first thought, that this eventuality is grounded in the plant's actual nature as definitely as its possible growth and maturation. But if we reflect a moment we see that the possibility of withering and dying before it matures is not a part of the nature of the plant *as a plant;* it is a possibility which faces the plant only in the sense that the plant can cease to be a living thing, only in the sense that the life it has can be destroyed. This eventuality comes about only by the negation of the plant's nature *as a plant.* To undergo such changes as will bring about the destruction of the plant is a part of the potentialities of some of the constituent materials which go into the make-up of the plant, but this is not among the potentialities of the plant *as a plant.* "The tendency of every creature to persevere in being is a reality, but this tendency does not come from its own sole power, it comes from the Cause from which it derives its being; as, on the other hand, if we say that it tends to non-being, this is not because of its nature but because of its deficiency."[13]

Perfection is the complete realization of the potentialities inherent in the nature of a thing. We have a hint of perfection, so far as temporal things are concerned, in those individual animals, for example, which exhibit in themselves most adequately the characteristics appropriate to their species and breed. We see something of what perfection means in those plants which have the strength, the color and texture, the quantity and quality of fruit appropriate to the variety to which they belong. Yet to compare things with respect to their perfection can be misleading, for each thing which really exists has its own perfection; it has its own perfection because it has its own existence. Its perfection consists of the actuality of its being; its imperfection is in the fact that not all of its being is actual in its unity and completeness. Yet this is how contingent existence must be if it is to be at all. In so far as its nature does have existence, its good is realized. "From the goodness of the least creature guess we at the excellent goodness of the great Creator."[14]

Finite perfection differs from absolute perfection; nevertheless it is perfection, not imperfection. But it is the perfection of contingent existence. It is the perfection which pertains to what truly exists, but it is the perfection proper to the contingent mode of finite existence. It is perfection which does not exclude potentiality, but that of which potentiality is the complement. Unless the existence of a thing in time is the actualization of a determinate essence, then existence itself would be indeterminate and so would be no more than possibility. But since the existence of a thing in time means that one phase of its existence is not every phase of its existence, then that *it*—a determinate something—should exist in time, it must be potentially more than it is actually at any moment of its existence.

Absolute perfection is unattainable by any temporal thing; for at any stage of its existence there are alternative possibilities open to it which cannot all be realized. They cannot all be realized because the realization of *any* genuine potentiality is dependent on causes which are not themselves part of the thing. These different causes cannot all operate, for the operation of some excludes that of others. A young man decides to prepare for a career in law. His preparation for the practice of law and his career as a lawyer are the realization of potentialities he had from the beginning of his existence. He might have become an engineer, or a physician, or have entered any one of scores of trades and professions. He might even fit himself for two or even three or four professions and trades. But human life is too short for him to fit himself for all the possible occupations which lie within the range of his powers. Some must be denied if others are to be realized. No one can be in two places at the same time, and no one can follow two mutually exclusive courses of action at the same time. If I make a wrong turn on a journey, I can go back and take the right road; but I cannot go back and bring it to pass that I did not take the wrong turn. I live my life not alone under the limitations of my nature but also under the limitations of space and time and history and the culture into which I was born.

In all this we find a clue to the perfection of God, a key which helps us apprehend what it means to be self-existent. Our knowledge here is negative knowledge, it is true, but it is significant nevertheless. For we know what the potential is, and we are able to differentiate it from the actual. So we know what God is not, and we know how those real beings which are not God differ from Him. In Him there is nothing potential, for if there were then God would depend on something beyond Himself to bring the potential to actuality. At the very least, God would depend on something else to endow Him with that potentiality.

The Moral Argument for the Existence of God

If good is objective, if it really belongs to the nature of things, then God must exist. This, in brief, is the heart of what has been called the "moral argument for the existence of God."[15] We may consider this the major premise of the argument. The second premise is that the values which man finds in his moral experience are objective and are not merely ideas in our minds or subjective attitudes or means to ends. If the second premise can be established then the conclusion follows that God exists.

The difficulty with the moral argument appears when we try to establish the second premise independently of the conclusion. The fault of the argument is in its major premise, in which the true order of antecendent and consequent is reversed. Instead of, "If good is real then God exists," the proper statement is, "If God exists then the good is real." In other words, we cannot establish the reality of good from the idea of good. The reality of good can be established only by reference to a real existence which cannot not be good.

> In plain truth [says Professor Cotton] none of our human values can be taken as a fixed point in our thinking about God. Our idea of the true, our conception of the moral good, our feelings of the beautiful—what discerning mind can ever claim finality for them? Our truth—it is perverted by our partial perspective which we brashly erect into a universal. Our goodness—it is at best pretentious and showy. Our vision of the moral good cannot escape some perversion by our practice. Our beautiful—it finds expression by faithfully reflecting in art, music, and drama the chaotic despair of our culture. It is just these values of ours that desperately need redemption and "trans-valuation." How shall we recognize the truth when we encounter it? How shall we be brave enough to confront the really good, when it rebukes our pride and shatters our self-esteem? How shall our eyes become pure so that we can look on the truly beautiful? These are the first questions which a theology of values ought to face. To start with our values and to build a system upon them is simply to reverse the right method and to be condemned to confusion from the start.[16]

How is man to find real value, and to distinguish it from the appearance of value? There is only one way, and that is to find absolute value embodied in real existence. This is the answer of religion, and it is an answer most explicit in the Christian religion. When absolute good comes to man through the channel of his own nature alone its image is so twisted and distorted by the medium through which it passes that he cannot see it as good.

Part Eight

GOD AND THE WORLD

CHAPTER 26

Creation and Time

THE IDEA OF CREATION

WE COME NOW to consider the relation of God and the world. The most fundamental aspect of that relation, the way in which God and the world are related *in their existence*, is expressed in the idea of creation. "To create" is "to make," but in a restricted sense. "To create" is "to bring into existence," but "to make" may mean merely "to change one thing into another." A man builds a house, and we may say that he makes the house. He uses materials of wood and metal and stone, and he puts these together in such a way that the house is constructed. But to make the house in this way is not to bring into existence; it is to transform and change the relations of things already in existence. The materials already exist and are capable of undergoing the changes which are necessary if the house is to be built. If a man were to create a house, in the sense of "create" which distinguishes it from "making," he would have to bring the materials themselves into existence.

There are some human activities which seem closer to creation than building a house. The architect's act of designing the house, for example, may seem more like creation than the work of the builder who constructs the house according to the architect's plan. So does any work of an artist, of the painter and the poet and the composer. They do not, in that part of their work we call "creative," merely take already existing materials and fabricate them into something else; for if their work is only adaptation and the borrowing of others' inventions, we deny that it is creative. The creative artist does get suggestions from others, but in what we call "creative" work what is borrowed is so slight in comparison with what the artist does with it we put the emphasis on the artist's own development of the material. Brahms' "Variations on a Theme by Haydn," for example, is a creative composition, while the adaptation for orchestra of Moussorgsky's "Pictures at an Exhibition" is not creative in the same sense.

Although we can best think of creation by God in analogy with human creation, we must keep in mind that this is only an analogy; *creation* is not used univocally in the two instances. Even if the artist does not obtain his ideas by transformation of pre-existing material, yet his work of art is made and not created. He creates the idea, the plan, the design; but he makes the painting or statue or music out of what already exists. Canvas and pigments, marble and bronze, paper and ink, and the strings and hammers and tubes of metal and wood which are made to sound—none of these are made to be by the artist or composer. So we have this limitation in human creation: In so far as the work of the artist is creative and not the transformation of one thing into another, he does not produce something which has its own existence; what he produces exists only in idea. In so far as he gives existence to what he invents, he has to use pre-existing materials and so the existence of what he makes does not come from him.

To think of God's act of creation in analogy with the human artist we restrict our analogy to the artist's invention of his form or design or idea. The idea of divine creation differs from the work of the artist in that God gives to what He creates its own existence. He acts by giving existence to what He wills to be. Not only does God differ from the human artist in the fact that He gives existence in His creative act, but He also is the sole source of what He creates. The human artist depends on his experience of other things for the ideas he expresses in his work. The forms of nature, the work of other artists, those human experiences in which the meaning of life is found—these are sources of the artist's ideas. So far as human art is concerned, the more it has to work with the greater is the opportunity for artistic genius to show itself.

GREEK AND HEBREW CONCEPTS OF CREATION

The idea of creation as the act of bringing something into existence seems to have been foreign to Greek thinking. Although, as we have already seen,[1] Plato does speak of the Form of the Good as the source of existence, he evidently does not think of the relation of the Good to existence as one of creation. When he discusses the question of how the world of nature came to be he uses the figure of the Demiurge who makes the world out of a pre-existing chaos, using the Forms as the guiding patterns. "Desiring, then, that all things should be good and, so far as might be, nothing imperfect, the god took over all that is visible—not at rest, but in discordant and unordered motion—and brought it from disorder into order, since he judged that order was in every way the better."[2]

The difference between the Old Testament idea of creation and Plato's, says Frank, "is most adequately formulated by Philo, *De Somniis*, 14, 76: 'God, when He gave birth to all things, not only brought them into sight but also made things which before were not, not just handling material as a *demiurge*, an *artificer*, but being Himself its *creator*.' " Frank points out that this is why

the translators of the Septuagint in rendering the corresponding Hebrew word did not choose the Platonic word *demiurge*, which signifies the craftsman who shapes material with his hands, but rather the word *ktistes*, a word which in classical Greek means "the founder," especially the founder of a city. The creation of the world is a spiritual process which may actually be compared with that of a ruler who through his will alone founds a city out of nothing. . . .[3]

It has been a matter of dispute whether the creation story of the first chapter of *Genesis* expresses the idea of creation as giving existence to the world, or whether it means only that God made the world out of a pre-existing chaos by imposing order upon it. Strachan points out that "our interpretation of the opening sentences [of Genesis] is affected by our solution of a difficult and

437

delicate problem of syntax." He gives the following rendering of the passage: "When God began to create the heaven and the earth—the earth being without form and void, and darkness being upon the face of the deep, and the spirit of God brooding upon the face of the waters—God said, Let there be light, and there was light." Strachan comments: "If this exegesis is correct, the writer teaches a dualism. He thinks of a dark watery chaos existing before the creation began, and gives it the mythical name *Těhōm* ('the Deep'), which is evidently the Heb. equivalent of the Bab. *Tiamāt*."[4]

In a very recent commentary, however, the interpretation of this passage is different. The writer of the *Genesis* passage, says Cuthbert A. Simpson, "was endeavoring to present the idea of a creation *ex nihilo*, at least in so far as he could conceive of it." Although this account of creation does include "the idea of an already existing darkness . . . and of an already existing chaos," yet "to counter any suggestion that the chaos did not derive its existence from God, he prefaced his account with the phrase 'in the beginning of God's creating the heavens and the earth.' " By this the writer intended to imply

that the first step in the creation of the organized universe was the creation of chaos . . . which God then proceeded to reduce to order. In this way [the writer] was able to reconcile those features in the myth he was revising which were dualistic in their implications with his conviction, arrived at on religious grounds, that the universe owed its existence to God, a conviction to which, it may be noted, the Second Isaiah had already given utterance, "I [God] form the light, and create darkness." (Isa. 45:7.)[5]

We may not know at what period in Hebrew thought the idea of creation came to be fully developed, but it seems to be Hebrew in origin—or, at least, it has been transmitted to us through Hebrew influences. It is possible that creation was not clearly and sharply differentiated from the process of fabricating something out of a pre-existing material until the attempt was made to express Hebrew ideas in terms of Greek concepts. At this point it became necessary to make the distinction entirely explicit if the Hebrew idea was not to be obscured by the modes of thought in which it obtained theoretical expression. For we must remember that the logical analysis of concepts, which was so important a part of Greek philosophy, is quite foreign to Hebrew thought. There is little trace of philosophy in Hebrew thinking; it announces and celebrates truth, but it does not inquire or openly subject its thought to rational control.

This may be the significance of Philo's formulation of the doctrine of creation *ex nihilo*. In Philo we have the first attempt at a systematic expression of the religious ideas of Judaism in terms of the concepts of Greek philosophy. For, although Philo does not develop this doctrine nor always adhere to it in his presentation of the idea of creation, he does formulate it explicitly.[6] If we ask why Philo should do this, the plausible answer is that he recognized something in the Hebrew idea of creation that the Greek concept of *making* could not do justice to.

CREATION *ex nihilo*

The concept of creation *ex nihilo* needs careful analysis if we are to avoid confusing it, on the one hand, with a kind of making which is nothing more than the transformation of an already existing material and, on the other, with the view that all things have their existence only in God. The first of these we have already considered. The latter confusion leads to some version of pantheism, or else to a view which denies efficacious being to created things.[7] To confuse creation with making is to deny that creation confers existence, for existence is already a fact; the material out of which the world is made has its own existence. The second kind of confusion also denies that creation confers existence, for on this view the supposedly created thing never does exist in its own right. The first denies the "*ex nihilo*" in the phrase "creation *ex nihilo*"; the second denies the "creation."

Creation *ex nihilo* presupposes, of course, the Creator. It is creation *from* nothing, but it is not creation *by* nothing. So here again we have to be careful to avoid confusion. We must not allow the *nihilo* to carry over from the material of creation, to which it properly refers, to the Creator. The Creator is self-existence; in Him is all the fulness of being in act. All possibility has existence in Him.

When we say that all possibility has existence in God we do not mean that God has given to everything possible its own existence. Only to what He has created has He given an existence of its own. Uncreated potentialities, such as the worlds which God could create but does not, do have an existence. We are bound to admit this by our fundamental ontological principle, the principle that all being is existence. But the existence which uncreated possibilities have is not their own existence; it is in God that they have their being. We can think this in analogy with the distinction of possible and actual so familiar to us in our own experience. I plan to make something; but, before I make it, what I plan to make does not yet have its own existence. It exists in idea. The idea, however, does have its own existence; it is an item in my mental life. But *what* the idea is *about* does not have its own existence.

What God creates does have, as created, its own existence. But this is not its only link with existence. As creatable, it exists in God, and we have a partial understanding of this in our own experience of the relation of a prior plan to a completed project. Yet our understanding of this is by analogy, for our experience of making something in accordance with a prior plan involves time. We act in time, and the distinction of before and after applies *to us* as well as to the processes by which we make things and to the things we make. It is here, as presently we shall see more fully, that we find a major difference between our activity and God's act of creation. Still we must not forget that the created order does exist in God as well as in its own right. So *what it is* is also *what can be in self-existence*, as what this actual machine is is also a *what* which can be thought in idea and delineated in the drawings of an engineer.

To say that the created order exists in God as well as in its own right is to say that God knows all things. We think of this in analogy with our own way of knowing, in which the essence of the thing known has its own existence in the thing and also exists in concept in our minds. If the created order exists in God then it cannot be such as to violate the nature of God, which is self-existence. It cannot violate its own nature by conflict with itself. It must act in accordance with its own nature; that is, what it expresses in act is its true essence and not the essence of what it is not.

The impossible to exist cannot be in self-existence. God cannot create, for example, a square circle. It is not only that the created order excludes square circles from itself; it is rather that a square circle cannot be. In so far as a figure is square it is not circular, and in so far as it is circular it is not square. A "square circle" is a contradiction of terms. It is not a concept, for it cannot be thought. It is a verbal phrase which purports to attribute to one kind of figure, a circle, properties which cannot belong to it. When we say that these properties "cannot belong" to a circle, we mean that no geometric figure which has these properties is a circle. We can think "square" and we can think "circle," but when we try to combine these into a concept all we can think is their difference and incompatibility.

Creation *ex nihilo* cannot be understood apart from the nature of God as self-existence. We understand it as the free act of God, for since there is no potentiality in God nothing can constrain Him. But God's creative act is not arbitrary, for He can act only in accordance with His nature—that is, in accordance with self-existence. God cannot do evil; He cannot change His nature; He cannot be a lie. So the existence of God is also the source of creation; the phrase *ex nihilo* refers only to what might be conceived to exist outside God, uncreated and ultimate in its own right.

It is here that our view both agrees with and differs from Whitehead's conception of the Creator and the created. God, says Whitehead, "must include all possibilities of physical value conceptually, thereby holding the ideal forms apart in equal, conceptual realization of knowledge. Thus, as concepts, they are grasped together in the synthesis of omniscience." But he goes on to say: "The limitation of God is his goodness. . . . It is not true that God is in all respects infinite. If He were, He would be evil as well as good. Also this unlimited fusion of evil with good would mean mere nothingness. He is something decided and is thereby limited."[8] At this point there is a failure to see that God is self-existence, and to see that self-existence is self-existent good. The infinity of God thus undergoes a curious transformation into a kind of *all* which includes non-being as a part of its positive content. All being, on the contrary, is good—simply by virtue of the fact that it is being.[9]

ACTUAL AND POTENTIAL IN CREATION

We may distinguish the actual and the possible on two levels. We may think of possible worlds which do not actually exist. In so far as such a world is genuinely possible there is nothing in the conception of it to exclude existence. This means that its nature, as we conceive it, is not inconsistent with itself. If such a world were created it *would* express the nature of God as our actual world *does* express the nature of God. For if such a world were created it would have an existence of its own, as does our world. On the other hand, our distinction between the actual and possible may refer to our actual world. We may think of possibilities which, if they were actual, would belong to our own real world.

We may illustrate this difference by reference to two kinds of works of fiction. One may have the setting and characters of an imaginary world, as, for example, the stories of the Greek gods. The other kind has as its setting the real world, and its characters and action are such as might exist in the real world. The potential, in this second way of thinking the distinction of potential and actual, comes even closer to the actual when it is the distinction between what a really existing thing is and what it can become. Here we attribute potentialities to actual things, and it is this relation of actual and potential we wish to consider at this point.

What is it we know when we recognize that some potentialities really pertain to a thing? We do not know the future of that thing, for its future does not depend solely on itself. What possibilities will be realized, from among all the possibilities inherent in the nature of a thing, depends not only on that thing's nature but also on the causes which will affect it. Nothing inconsistent with its nature can happen to a thing, but this is only a negative determination. What does happen to a thing, within the limits imposed by its nature, depends on other things. The more fully we know the nature of a thing the more fully we know what it will be *if* this or that or some other contingency occurs. To know its nature completely would be to know what it would be in each of every possible set of conditions, and this would require us to know all possible sets of conditions. To each of these possibilities in turn the same considerations apply. So complete knowledge is not within the reach of a finite mind, to which the nature of real existence is disclosed bit by bit in experience.

Still, our finite minds do know something of the potentialities of things. If these potentialities are truly known then what we hold in concept, in our thought concerning the potentialities inherent in a thing, must have being. It cannot have its only being in our ideas, for in such case our ideation would not be knowledge; it would be only the act of entertaining ideas. Does the man exist in the child? If so then the child is not child but man. How does the possible, which not yet is but may be, have being? If it does not have being, our judgments concerning it are neither true nor false. The potential must have some kind of being; it cannot be sheer unreality.

Can a capacity be [asks Professor Demos] unless there is something *actual*, of which the capacity is an attribute; or in which the capacity is lodged? Even as a problem of linguistics, there are difficulties; it seems impossible to make a property-statement without including a substance-word. Take solubility; this expresses an interaction between (say) sugar and water; it is some sort of capacity for action or being acted on. But how can we have action except as the action of a substance; how express the solubility in question except in the phrase: "if water acts on sugar, then etc."? It seems to me that a substance is required as something which *has* properties and so as being not reducible to them.[10]

Even if we grant this (and it seems something necessary to assert whenever existence appears to be in danger of dissolution into mental states or sensations at the hands of subjectivism or positivism), we still have the question of what kind of being which a capacity has as the capacity of something actual. (Of course there is danger of generating a false problem by our way of formulating it. We may seem here close to the use of "capacity" as a substance-word. Yet this confusion can be avoided if we keep clear in our minds the *supposition*[11] of "capacity" in this context. "Capacity" here is a concept, and its use as the subject of a logical proposition in no way implies reference to something which has its own real existence.) The very use of the category of substance with reference to finite things is a denial that *what is* is a *what* which is fully actual all at once. The idea of substance links together, as of one being, transitory stages which succeed one another in time. Our question remains. How does the potentiality which belongs to the nature of an existing thing have being?

It will not do to set up another order of being, over against the actual, which we call the potential. Such an order of being must be real or not; if real, then according to our ontological principle that all real being is existence, it exists. But if it exists, it is actual and not potential. If it is to be non-actual, and if all real being is existence, then it must have its being in something else. This "something else" must be real existence.

That a thing which gradually unfolds its nature in time should have a nature to unfold, implies that the real existence of that nature in time is not the only being it has. Its own real existence in time is not its only link with real existence. That there should be a determinate nature to come into its own existence in time requires that this determinate nature should have also a mode of being which is not in time. It was his clear recognition of this, and his attempt to render intelligible the relation between an essence's existence in time and its connection with timeless existence, which led Plato to his theory of Forms. Once we see the problem we face, once we admit the existence of real things in time, we see that some such doctrine as that of Plato's Forms is inescapable. No matter how incomplete and undefinitive we may consider Plato's doctrine to be—and perhaps no one ever saw better than Plato the inadequacy of his own tentative formulations of it—this much of it is unavoidable. We may disagree with Plato's view that the Forms have their own existence, but we can see why it is necessary to assert that they have some root in existence other than, and more fundamental than, the existence they have in time. This more fundamental existence cannot be itself in time, else the same difficulty would arise concerning it.

If the Forms of things do not have their own existence apart from the temporal order, what is this other and more fundamental root in existence which they do have? Surely by now the analogy of man and God has suggested an answer, the same answer which seems to have been given by all the theistic philosophers who faced Plato's problem and recognized the cogency of his doctrine of Forms. Their answer is that the Forms have being in self-existence, and we may call them by analogy the "ideas" of God.

ONE-WAY DEPENDENCE

Real possibilities, at any stage in the development of a thing, are all consistent with the nature of the thing at that stage. They are not, however, all consistent with each other; they are genuine alternatives, and some are mutually exclusive. This is possible because of the fact that *what* each is does not determine whether it will be realized in fact. The selection from among the possibilities is made by the causes which operate on the thing in its actual existence. God does not cause this or that potentiality to become actual in nature; rather the actually existing things in nature act on each other as real causes. God "sees" all the possibilities of the natural order, and included among these are the ones which will be realized. But God is not the cause which selects one set of possibilities to become actual. He is the Cause of Nature, as we have already seen, and in this sense He brings into actual existence the processes which go on in nature. But God creates things to be real existents and it is their acts which determine, within the range of real possibility, what shall be and what shall not be. Even when we think of God acting directly in nature we have to think of such action, as we shall see presently, as employing the things which exist in nature and as taking place in accordance with *what* they truly are.

Existence in nature is temporal; the existence of God is not. God cannot be limited by time. Yet the development from potential to actual is in time, and so it is not the act of God in the same sense in which it is the act of the causes at work in nature. It is the act of God in the sense that the existence of the created order of nature is the act of God. But God creates the world to have its own existence, and so the things which exist in nature are subject to the causes which work in nature.

There is nothing potential in God because there is no existence other than God which does not have its source in Him. He cannot be dependent upon what He Himself brings into being. It is the nature of God to create, for His proper name is Existence. But what He creates depends on Him; He does not depend on His own creation. We ourselves depend on what we do, and perhaps even on what we make, for our own felicity and happiness; but we are incomplete, and our natures come into existence in temporal activity. God lacks nothing, for He is in His very nature complete and absolute existence.

But does it not seem that God would be different if He had acted differently? God's creative act is not by necessity; for there is nothing in existence to compel Him except what He Himself brings into being, and this is *His* creature. The actual world does not have to be. Well, then, suppose there had been a different world than this. Would this not mean a difference in God? Would not God have had different "purposes" if He had created a different world? Would it not have been because He saw that it was better for that other world to be?

446

These questions acquire their appearance of plausibility from our mistake of thinking of God as acting in time. God does not act in time, even though our apprehension of God's creative act is in time. God is self-existent; only the contingent is temporal. Time, or the duration which time measures, is itself the creature of God. The *act* of God is like our own act only in part, only in this respect, that it makes the possible to be actual. But it is different in this other respect, that the potential which God makes to be actual is not His potentiality. It follows that its actualization is not in any sense or in any respect His own actualization. *Thus what God makes actual must have an existence of its own; it cannot have its own actuality in God.*

The essence of God is existence and, as Professor Wild points out, under this existence "all modes of being and perfection are contained. If we say that such a being would be better with something else in addition, we are denying His unlimited goodness. We are conceiving of Him in an anthropomorphic manner as imperfect and needing something more to be perfected. We are no longer thinking of God but of a finite being seeking to realize itself and requiring to be sustained by an external cause." This notion of a finite God, says Wild, "explains nothing, but itself requires an ultimate explanation. The first cause was under no moral necessity to create a world. Such a world could add no perfection not already contained in the divine infinity. It could add more beings—not more being."[12]

In the words of Mascall:

The fundamental affirmation of traditional Christian theism can thus be stated in the following highly remarkable form: the existence of the world implies the existence of a God, and moreover the existence of a God whose existence does *not* imply the existence of a world. We cannot see *why* God exists or *how* he exists, or even how it is possible that he should exist; we can only see that if he did not exist nothing else could. We cannot see why he creates or how he creates; we can only see that unless he did create, the world would not be here. We can see why we cannot see all this, and that must suffice us.[13]

447

CREATION AND MODERN IDEAS OF TIME

Misunderstanding about time is perhaps the one most important source of confusion in the idea of creation. The traditional concept of creation comes to us in the setting of a false cosmology, and this is one source of the difficulty. For even in those rare cases in which there was some notion of creation as the act of bringing the world into existence, the language used to describe creation suggested that it took place in time. It was assumed that time includes not only the events of nature but also events which occurred "before" nature was. Religious myth always describes its events as happening in both space and time, and it tends to express differences between levels of life and existence by translating them into differences of time periods.

Until after the nineteenth century, modern cosmology was based on the assumptions which furnished the framework of Newtonian physics and astronomy. An infinite, uniform, three-dimensional, rectilinear space, satisfying the postulates of Euclidean geometry, and an infinite, uniform, one-dimensional time provided the setting in which material masses moved about and in certain mysterious ways, as in gravitation, exerted force on each other. In spite of a half-century of relativity physics and astronomy the Newtonian cosmology is the picture of the natural order which is still tacitly accepted by the educated classes of Western society. Even nineteenth century physicists had difficulty in fitting the newly discovered facts concerning electricity and magnetism into the Newtonian scheme. But popular thinking is seldom disturbed by conflicts and incongruities; it can swallow anything with which it is sufficiently familiar, for in popular thinking intelligibility is a function not of logical consistency or of factual evidence but of familiarity.

During the past half-century the new physics of relativity and quantum mechanics has had wide and convincing confirmation. Much of the Newtonian physics remains, for it can be understood in part as a special case of the more general principles developed in the new physics. But the basic assumptions which gave to Newtonian science its cosmological framework are no longer plausible. The space and time absolutes of that cosmology are gone. No longer are space and time the containers in which events transpire; space-time is itself of the structure of the events.

A further complication appeared a century ago with the popularization of the theory of evolution. This seemed to many to be a direct attack upon the doctrine of creation, and bitter warfare raged between those who rejected creation because they accepted evolution and those who rejected evolution because they accepted creation. Since evolution was "science" and creation was "religion," this conflict renewed, on other fronts, the long struggle which had been going on, in the open or under cover, since the beginning of modern science.

The result of all this is that if the idea of creation is to find a place in today's thought its entrance there is bound to cause internal stress. Those who accept what they think of as the "scientific" world picture are disturbed by echoes of a pre-scientific cosmology which seem to accompany the idea of creation. So they are inclined to judge the concept of creation by its ancient setting and to dismiss it as a part of a mythical history. Many who refuse to give up the idea of creation judge modern conceptions by the mythical world views in which the idea of creation originally appeared. Both sides are victims of an unfortunate misunderstanding.

The key to the trouble is the misunderstanding about time. If we are to think clearly about creation we have to think clearly about time, and if we are to think clearly about time we have to understand what kind of thinking we can do about time. We have to understand that we cannot determine the nature of time by intuition and *a priori* assumption; the meaning of time with respect to events in nature must be investigated by the same methods and the same principles of experimental control which are essential to any scientific inquiry. For the basic facts about time have to be found out in experience.

This is not the way in which Newton obtained the concept

449

of time that he used in his physics. The Newtonian concept of time was rather one of the underlying assumptions concerning the physical world upon which scientific inquiry operated. It was not itself the consequence of empirical study; it was rather a part of the assumed framework in terms of which the results of inquiry were interpreted. There was, it is true, a kind of partial verification of the space and time assumptions of Newtonian physics, in so far as those assumptions did not lead to consequences known to be false. But we have since discovered that some of the consequences of these assumptions are false, and we realize now that the reason this was not known earlier was because of the lack of technical facilities to make the necessary observations and experiments. It was not until the assumption of uniform and absolute space and time was found to have consequences with which scientifically controlled observation was in conflict that physicists turned their attention to the empirical investigation of space and time. The implications of the Michelson-Morley experiment include the destruction of the absolutes in the conceptual framework of the Newtonian world.[14]

It is not our purpose here to explore the new space-time concept of relativity physics and astronomy. We need note only that we can no longer accept the Newtonian assumptions concerning space and time without doing violence to the facts established by recent scientific inquiry. The meaning which this has for us here is that it removes at one stroke the chief obstacle, for the modern mind, to the plausibility of the concept of creation. For no longer can we consider space and time to be uniform absolute containers within which all events occur. Real things are not *in* an absolute space and an absolute time; rather space and time, or space-time, are to be understood as characteristics of things within the world of nature. Nature is not in space or in time; space-time is in nature.

We no longer need be concerned with the difficulties which arise from the notion that the creation of the world was an event which took place in time. For if time is *in* the world then the creation of the world is also the creation of time. If time is not a real being but only the measure of change then it belongs to the world of changing contingent things. Professor Wild's statement brings out clearly the way in which time belongs to the real world.

> Time is the measure of change. As such it has something in it which is purely mental and not found outside the mind, as the piece of wood in front of me is not neatly divided into the inches and feet by which I measure it. But time is not a pure construction or fiction. It is founded upon something really existing in the extra-mental change, just as the correct measure of the stick is based upon an extension really in the wood. Time is a certain mode of existence really present in external changes so far as they provide a foundation for the measuring concept in the mind.[15]

The act of creation, as an act of God, cannot be in time. We can only say that with creation duration came to be—or rather that enduring changing things came to be. We can speak only metaphorically or figuratively or by analogy of anything "before creation." It follows that we cannot treat of creation as an event in the history of the world. It was not the first thing which happened to the world that the world was created, for apart from creation there is no world for anything to happen to. So creation is not an event in history at all; it is the presupposition of history.

> To confuse the idea of creation with the metaphysical assumption that the world had a beginning in time [says Frank] means a complete misunderstanding of the significance of creation. . . . Since it is precisely the temporal character of the world that is indicative of its essence,[16] a beginning of the world in time would imply that the world had a beginning within itself. But the fact that the world was created does not mean that it has a limit in time, it rather indicates that the world itself and consequently also time border on something which is beyond time and therefore eternal.[17]

CREATION AND EVOLUTION

We may see now how absurd it is to suppose that there is a conflict between creation and evolution. In order to be in conflict the two theories would have to refer to the same thing, so that the assertion of creation would be a denial of evolution and the assertion of evolution would be a denial of creation. But if creation is the act by which the world of nature receives existence, it is quite plain that creation and evolution are not rival accounts of the same thing. Hence it is impossible for them to be in conflict. Creation concerns the fact that the world exists; evolution refers to processes and patterns of development which go on within the created world.

The same principle applies to the supposed conflict between the doctrine that animal species and man are creations of God and the theory that they are products of evolution. To take the scientific accounts of origins at face value means simply that the world which receives its existence from God and has its existence sustained by God is the kind of world in which living organisms evolve. The forms of life are modified by their environments and become adapted to the conditions of survival and propagation. Life itself may have been synthesized from complex non-living molecular structures. If not thus, we may be sure it started by some process, for we know that there was a time when the earth was without life. Yet when the earth was without life it even then carried the potentiality of life within it. The earth belonged to an order of existence pregnant with life and with the almost inconceivably complex structures, of nervous system and brain, which are used at their highest levels as the means by which reason itself enters into the events of the world. Life and mind are created, and by this we mean that they are the distinctive and significant features of the created order; but they have their own natural history, in their natural antecedents and causes.

CREATION AND AUTHORSHIP

Perhaps we can understand better the relation of creation to the processes within nature if we look at it in analogy with the relation between the author of a novel and the events and characters of the story. Everything which happens in a well written novel has its causes in the personalities and circumstances which make up the plot and setting and action of the story; yet the novel is the literary creation of its author. If the people in a novel are mere puppets, we are justified in the complaint that the author has failed to create his characters. He does not permit his characters to act in terms of their own fictional nature; in fact, they do not even have a fictional nature in terms of which they can act. In so far as the author is successful in his attempt to create a fictional person, the actions attributed to that person in the novel must follow from his character and its relation to the circumstances of the plot and situation. So when a person dies in the course of the story we do not say that the author killed him; we attribute his death to causes which themselves are part of the story. If it is apparent that the author has disposed of a character in order to deal with some plot problem, or if the author introduces the arbitrary manipulations of a *deus ex machina*, then we recognize the author's failure as a creative artist.

On the other hand, it is true that the novel or play which is constructed with artistic skill does show throughout the hand of its author. He does not use his characters as puppets, but this does not mean that they do not express and carry out the author's purposes. Rather it is the case that the characters and situations express by means of their own nature the theme of the work and the mind of the author. The characters of the plot need show no awareness of the theme which their action expresses, for they express it in what they do by virtue of what they are. So we may say by analogy that the purposes of God are carried out in nature and in history by the acts of men who act not as they are compelled to move by God but in accordance with their own nature.

This conception of God and nature does not exclude the possibility of what we may call, by analogy, the *intervention* by God in nature, any more than the structure of a novel excludes intervention by its author. The author of a novel may introduce a character, and for a specific purpose. But the introduction must fit the plot and the character who is introduced must act in accordance with his own nature. It is in his own action for his own ends and by his own motives that he accomplishes the purpose of the author.

God can act on or in the world only in terms of the nature of the world. In a sense this is not an absolute limitation, for if God willed a consequence contrary to what can happen in our real world He could create an order of existence in which, according to the nature of that order, such a consequence would occur. But in another sense the limitation is absolute, in the sense that God cannot create or bring to be the self-contradictory. In no possible world can God bring into existence a square circle or bring it about that the number "2" is a factor of the number "5." In no actual world can God bring into existence anything which does not make actual a real potentiality of that world.

This does not deny the possibility of what we call the "supernatural" in nature. Events may appear within the world of nature in spite of the fact that their appearance cannot be completely accounted for in terms of natural causes. They would thus appear to be, so far as their natural antecedents were concerned, uncaused events. No scientific scheme of explanation could account for them; or, in so far as such an account were possible, it would still be inadequate. To assert that the things in nature act only in accordance with their own essences does not exclude the possibility of the appearance in nature of things not the result of the essences and actions of other natural entities.

The notion of *miracle* as something which happens in nature and is contrary to the laws of nature is a curiously confused concept. In the first place, no such conception can be found in the Biblical sources of the Hebrew-Christian tradition, for those sources did not have the conception of natural law. To call an event a *miracle* is to call it a "marvel," and to say that it evokes wonder and awe. It is to say that the event is inexplicable apart from its supernatural significance. Even if direct intervention by God occurs in nature only our ignorance can make it appear capricious. Whatever it is, it has its explanation and it fits the rational order of being. If we cannot account for it in terms of the natural order it is because the natural order is not the whole of the rational order of being. We have to assume that complete knowledge would show us the absolute harmony of divine and natural causation in every event.

What we have called the "limitations" upon God's act do not in any sense imply that God is finite. For God's limits are the limits of possibility. Short of these limits, the limits of being as such, God is not limited. A genuine limit upon God would have to be a limit of existence rather than of possibility, and in God existence exhausts the possible. To limit God it would be necessary for something else to exist independently of God.

God and Time

God is eternal; God is not in time, nor is His existence temporal in any sense which would imply the distinction between actual and potential. Yet God is not timeless in the empty and negative sense in which a number or the relation between the sides of a triangle are timeless. For God is the source of being which has duration. The question, then, is how we are to think the temporal in relation to God.

In one phase of our experience we have something which may serve as the basis of an analogy. As we live through an event the present is not only distinguished from the past and the future but the three are distinct aspects of the experience itself. But after the event is over, in another "now" which is not itself a part of the time of the event itself, we can look back and recall the event in its totality. We do not recall it as a timeless thing, for it was not, and the process of recall is of course something which happens in time. But the order of our recall is not limited by the time-direction of the original experience; we can traverse the event in memory from earlier to later or from later to earlier. We can start at the beginning and follow the way in which the event took place, or we can start somewhere else and move backward to the beginning. We have, as it were, a view of the totality of the event, and this approaches a view of it all at once.

There is another way in which the recall of an event differs from the original experience. In recall, my awareness of each episode is illumined by my knowledge of what has come before and what came after that part of the event. In the original experience, each episode was known and understood only in the light of what had gone before; but in memory that limitation has been overcome. It is not difficult to see that if the event I recall were my own creative act rather than something which happened *to* me, my awareness of *what* it is would not be limited by the time relationships within the event itself.

We have here some basis for an analogical concept of God's awareness of the temporal order which is His creation. He is aware of the whole event of nature. He knows every episode, but He knows it in its place in the whole event of nature. Thus His knowledge of one episode is, in this sense, the same as His knowledge of every other; yet in knowing the whole event of nature He differentiates every part from every other part.

If we could live a second time through an experience we had lived through once before with this difference, that we should have the experience the second time together with the memory of the first, we would be a step closer to a grasp of God's awareness of the world. We do have almost such an experience in hearing over and over again a familiar musical composition to which we listen with the fullest possible awareness. We can think of God's knowledge of the temporal order on the analogy of a musician's knowledge of a music score. He knows every note, and as he hears the composition played he hears every note and every phrase in terms of what has come before and of what is to come after. The temporal passage from phrase to phrase is not a limitation to which he is subject so much as it is a character of what he hears which lies within the event itself. Stretched to its ultimate limit we might say that he would hear in each sound the whole composition. If his hearing the music did not itself have to take place in time, what is past and future in the composition—relative to any part of it—would all be present.

God's knowledge includes the temporal. How it includes the temporal without itself being temporal is suggested by our own very meager experience of a temporal succession which, at the same time, we know as a whole. For theism, God is living spirit; He is no mere abstract principle. He has life, but the whole of His living existence is present in every part of it. Included within His being is His act of creation and His awareness in its final detail of every part of the event of nature. We ourselves see the event of nature only from a perspective which lies within the event. We can grasp as a whole, and that quite incompletely, only a brief part of the event which is nature. God's perspective lies outside nature and outside time, and He sees all in its completeness. He sees every part in its relation to all else. Of course this does not mean that God is composed of parts, or that His awareness is composed of parts. Every aspect of God is God in His unity of existence.

The best analogy of God's relation to the world is with a human "creator." The writer creates his event of fiction, and his novel or play has its own dramatic time. The novelist is not himself a part of the action of the novel, and the dramatic time of the novel is not a part of the novelist's existence. The novelist happens to exist in time, and here of course the analogy does not hold, but the time in which the novelist exists is not the dramatic time of the novel. When I think an imaginary event it takes time for me to think it. But the time it takes me to think the event and the time of the event I imagine, are different. Neither is a part of the other, and if we were to represent the two times by means of lines they would be tangential lines which would have no common segment.

The relation here of the two times is like my awareness in imagery of a place in space. I can "see" before me in imagery a corner of a room in another part of the house. Here is a chair and a table, and they have their own definite space relations in my image. But the space of the image in no way conflicts with or is a part of the space arrangement I *perceive* before me where I now am. I actually see in front of me a desk and a bookcase. But the perceived and the imaged spaces have no relation to each other in this particular experience. The table does not get in the way of the bookcase. No part of one is anywhere *in* the other. Of course as I think the plan of the house I can relate the two places to each other, but the space I hold in imagery and the space I now perceive do not in any way merge or combine. So it is with a time lapse which I imagine or remember. It does not in any way merge or combine with the time lapse which is occupied by my act of imagining or remembering. God's awareness is not in time, and in this respect our analogy does not apply, but there is time in *what God is aware of*. God can be aware of the temporal in an awareness which is not temporal, for past and future are themselves present in God's awareness.

We do not have three times, present, past and future, says Augustine. The three times are rather "the present of past events, the present of present events, and the present of future events. These three exist in the soul, so to speak, and elsewhere I do not see them: the present of past events is memory; the present of present events, awareness; and the present of future events, expectation."[18]

For many this seems to raise a serious problem. For some, in fact, it is the one insuperable difficulty in traditional theism. If God knows nature in its entirety, and knows each episode in the light of all that is before and after, then it would seem that the whole event of nature must be a completely determined event. Everything that happens would seem thus to happen of necessity and there would be no place for freedom. But we have already seen that freedom is presupposed by the very possibility of knowledge and is a necessary condition of human responsibility. How can we reconcile God's omniscience with man's freedom?

This difficulty is the result of the same misunderstanding we have met before, and here we shall let Mascall show us the answer to the problem.

It has frequently been alleged that a radical omniscience on the part of God is incompatible with human freedom. If God knows today what I shall decide to do tomorrow, how can my choice be free? And if my choice is genuinely free, how can God know now what I am going to do? The controversies around these questions ...

must surely represent one of the most elaborate and unnecessary discussions in the history of philosophy. And if the questions are posed in these terms it seems impossible to give a satisfactory answer, for the simple reason that the very posing of the questions introduces an error into the discussion. For, if God's existence is outside time, it is strictly meaningless to talk about what God knows *today*, since God's "today" is eternity. It is *true today* that God knows what I shall do tomorrow, but it is not true that God *knows it today*. And so the question falls to the ground.[19]

One word, perhaps, should be added. Our knowledge of God, and what we say about God, is true by analogy. When we think of God's knowledge in analogy with our temporal knowledge, it is hardly proper for us to draw implications from that aspect of our knowledge which we specifically deny of God's knowledge, namely, its temporal character. The language of religion will continue to speak of God's knowledge and action as if He knows and acts in time. The justification of this is in its effect in putting us in closer contact with God, that is, in its existential truth. We are not justified in taking religious expressions as univocally true and constructing theories upon them.

CHAPTER 27

History and Human Destiny

What Is History?

WE THINK of history as the past. But history is not merely the fact that there has been a past. A past which only "has been" and is not now could have little significance. A past which only "has been" would be cut off from all contact with the present, for even if it is only remembered it is more than a mere "has been." Here, again, a problem is illumined by the distinction between essence and existence, for to remember the past is to bring it, in essence, into the present. I remember something I did yesterday, and although what I did had its existence yesterday yet the memory of it exists now. The awareness of the past event, the awareness which is the memory, brings the *what* of the past into the present. The past does not itself come into the present, but *what the past was* is present now in my awareness. History is the discovery that there *was* a past, and this discovery brings *what the past was* into the present as an ingredient of itself. Or we may say that history is the way in which the past exists in the present. The things of the past do not have their own past existence in the present, but history saves something of the *what* of the past as the existence of those past events goes out. First, men's memories, with memories of memories and celebrations as reminders, preserve from the past what men will need for present action. Then lasting symbols hold the past for each new present, and our increasing knowledge of what things are helps us understand what they were.

This does not mean merely that past events have consequences which endure into the present; for a present consequence of the past is, as such, present and not past. The irritation I feel today because of something which happened yesterday may linger, after I have forgotten yesterday's trouble, as one of its effects. Present consequences are not enough to give us history unless we discover through them the past of which they are the consequences. Unless they recall to us *what* the past was, they are only a part of the present. If there is to be history, and if it is to have any significance for the present, then the past, *as the past*, has to enter the present. The past has to make a difference to the present not merely as a part of the present, but as a part of the present which comes from the past and which is known to be from the past. Knowledge of the past in the present is not history unless the past is known *as the past*. This means it must be given a position of its own in time in differentiation from the present. The times assigned to past events may be inaccurate, and past events may be placed in a framework of myth and legend; but in one way or another the human mind feels itself compelled to interpret the present in the light of a past just as soon as it recognizes the temporality of its world.

Only in awareness can the past enter the present and influence it. The past cannot have its own existence in the present; it can be in the present only in essence. This means that the past can be present only in cognition and, consequently, that history is possible only for self-conscious awareness. There are two reasons for this. One is the fact that the *what* of the past can be held in the present, and recognized as the *what* of the past, only by a knowing mind which relates its own present awareness to its own past. Unless I am aware of myself as the same self now which also was in the past, there can be no way in which the actuality of the present and the essence of the past can meet in a single conscious awareness. There would be no more connection between my awareness now and my awareness then than there is between my awareness now and some other person's awareness then. Without the union of past and present in one consciousness, an awareness of the past would *seem* to be an awareness of the present; what is in the present only in essence would *seem* to be in the present in

its very existence. In hallucination and dream, where our awareness of self, and so of the mental processes which are in operation
at the time, is very dim or almost entirely absent, we make little
distinction between past and present or between fantasy and perception. Memories seem to be present experiences and fantasies
are not distinguished from actual perceptions.

The other reason why history requires a self-conscious awareness is that an awareness which is taking place now can contain
the *what* of something past, and recognize it as such, only in logical judgment. The present awareness *intends* the past, and in order to do so it has to be referred to the past. The mere presence
of its own content is not enough. A picture, for example, may
present something of the essence of another thing. But, as we saw
earlier, even though a picture is a picture of something other than
itself, of something which has its own existence, yet the relation
of the picture to what it pictures is not a part of the picture. Nor
can the picture itself in any way refer itself to what it represents.
Such reference can be made only by a mind capable of forming
concepts and of using concepts in logical judgment. This requires
the use of logical identity, a relation which cannot belong to real
existence as such but can pertain only to the relation of concepts
to what they intend in judgment. Only a mind aware of its own
activities, *as its own,* can distinguish what it thinks from what
really exists.

THE CONTINUITY OF HISTORY

As finite beings we live and act in the present. The past has been
and is no more; the future is yet to be, and is not yet. Memory and
anticipation are our ways of projecting our own present beyond
its range, or of bringing past and future into our present. In memory and anticipation we strain to burst the bounds of the present, or at least to push them back and forward and so enlarge
the present. Memory is our closest approach to the expansion
of the present to include the past, and history is the supplement of
memory.

From the idea of the expansion of the present to include the past and future it is a short step to the idea of a present which includes within itself all which *we* call past and future, that is, God's present. It is only by analogy with our own feeble defiance of the bounds of the present that we can think the present, and thus also the presence, of God. The Eternal is not a mere negation of that of which time is our measure; it is the inclusion of that in a real present in which there is neither past nor future. In the sense that it has no beginning or end, no passage from earlier to later, God's present is the everlasting present.

"The only present which we can conceive as really present," says Frank, "is the presence of God. . . . The imperfection and finiteness of man thus manifests itself in his temporal limitation. His apprehension of the present is merely the consciousness of an absence of the present, of transitoriness. From this feeling springs the desire for the unattainable, for true presence, true existence."[1]

The idea of God's present suggests to us our own fulfilment. It is that for which we yearn in our awareness of our own finitude; it is the only remedy for the desperation with which we recognize that each moment of life comes to be only to pass away. The idea of the Eternal present and of our own inclusion within it, the idea that each of our finite presents is included within it, is the only answer to ultimate futility. "I hazard the prophecy," says Whitehead, "that that religion will conquer which can render clear to popular understanding some eternal greatness incarnate in the passage of temporal fact."[2]

No man's experience is long enough or broad enough to show him his place in the life of mankind. History is the "story" in which each of us lives and plays his part. Unless we can see this in its continuity we cannot see ourselves as we are nor can we discover what is our true task in life.

History is not merely the truth about the past. The truth about the past is the material of history, but history is no mere sum of its materials. We know, for example, that Julius Caesar either did or did not cut his face while shaving on his twenty-sixth birthday. This is not history, although indeterminate knowledge of

this kind belongs with the presuppositions of historical knowledge. We could try to find out whether Julius Caesar did or did
not cut his face on that day, but what point would such an inquiry have to induce us to undertake it?

It is not merely any truth which history seeks; nor is it all the
truth, for that is not within our reach. Memory is always selective, even when it is nothing more than the material of fantasy.
A narrative always has a point or else it is meaningless. Suppose
someone says, "I saw a man stop at the corner of Third and Elm
Streets this morning and wait for the traffic light to change. When
it changed from red to green he walked across the street." What
appropriate comment might we make to this except the impolite
"Well, what of it?" On the other hand, if the man who was seen
was wanted by the police then the story may well have some
import.

The existence of no individual person exhausts the significance
of human life. We live in society, and we find much of what
makes our lives significant in our social relationships. We live for
each other when we live at our best, not alone for our contem-
poraries but also for those who have departed and for those who
are yet to come. In so far as we try to advance the things they
cared for, we live for those who helped to make what we have.
We live for those who are not yet born in so far as we try to advance the things they will care about. In so far as we see the meaning of our own lives in relation to the past and future, the very
reason for living takes us far beyond ourselves. This is the condition of all genuine nobility and greatness in human existence.
Without such a perspective, human life is crabbed and mean; creation's most expansive mode of being shrivels into the tiny bit of
space and time occupied by a human body. It denies its own possibilities and plays its nature false. "Just as if the world and its
history had existed merely for our sakes!" exclaims Jacob Burckhardt.

For everyone regards all times as fulfilled in his own, and cannot
see his own as one of many passing waves. . . . But every individual—

we too—exists not for his own sake, but for the sake of all the past and all the future.

In the face of this great, grave whole [he continues] the claims of peoples, times and individuals to happiness and well-being, lasting or fleeting, is of very subordinate importance, for since the life of humanity is one whole, it is only to our frail powers of perception that its fluctuations in time or place are a rise and fall, fortune and misfortune. The truth is that they are governed by a higher necessity.[3]

The significance of the present can be seen only in its continuity with past and future. It is all one; its parts are only episodes, not intelligible in themselves. But we exist actually only in the present: part of our existence was; but when it was, it was present. We are not in past, present and future together. Still, our lives are pointless unless we live for the sake of past and future. We can do this only in part by knowledge. We can know something of the past, and on the basis of this knowledge we can guess at the future. Each finite *now*, taken by itself, is meaningless; its being is in its passing away. To contract our souls into a finite now, even one as long as life itself or of an era, is to lose contact with the meaning of life. Its consequence is either a deadened consciousness which comes with the contraction of perspective or else utter apathy and cynicism. Only by pretending, or by taking refuge in stupidity, can we make sense of devotion and effort which are for the sake only of what comes to be only to pass away. As Albert Schweitzer says, "Only when we are able to attribute a real meaning to the world and to life shall we be able also to give ourselves to such action as will produce results of real value. As long as we look on our existence in the world as meaningless, there is no point whatever in desiring to effect anything in the world."[4]

Does History Have Meaning for Man?

History has no meaning for man unless it is important for him to understand himself in terms of the whole of human life, and to learn to choose and decide in the light of this knowledge. But his knowledge about himself and his kind bears upon his action only if he himself has a definite nature to know and a definite destiny to realize. He need not know just what his destiny is, provided he knows that he has one and that it is one which fits his nature and if he knows what he must do to reach it. If man's knowledge about himself is to be relevant to his action and choice his true destiny must lie to some degree within his own control and yet he must not be able to control it completely or arbitrarily. If man's knowledge is to guide him, including the kind of knowledge he has in his discovery of religious truth, then his destiny must depend partly but not absolutely on his own free act and choice.

History would have no significance for man if his destiny were determined by a necessity beyond himself, nor would it have significance if his future were a matter of arbitrary choice alone. History has significance only if man's destiny is given to him, a destiny which he himself does not make, and yet is somewhat within his own control. How can it be something he does not make, and yet be within his own control? If history is to have meaning for man it seems that he has to stand in this apparently contradictory relation to his destiny. We can hardly reject history as meaningless, for if we do this with reason it would have to be in some sense a lesson we learn from history; unless we were confronted with a challenge from history the issue would not arise. So we are faced with a problem. But before we try to resolve the apparent conflict we need first to see why history would have no significance if man's choice had nothing to do with his destiny and why history would be irrelevant if man's destiny were of his own making.

HISTORY AND FATE

If man's destiny were determined by something out of his control, his destiny would be nothing but fate. Caught in a fate beyond his reach, there would be nothing he could do to influence his destiny. Even his knowledge that he was caught in fate could provide no way for him to influence his destiny; for even his knowing would be a part of the process by which his fate controlled him, and he would know only what he was fated to know —and this for fate's purpose, not for his.

The Stoics tried to find a moral significance in man's voluntary subjection of himself to necessity and fate. Since he cannot change his fate the only thing man can do is to control what is within his power, that is, his attitude toward his fate. So this becomes the content of the good life, to acquiesce in necessity. In the final injunction in *The Manual of Epictetus* there are two quotations, the first from Cleanthes and the second from Euripedes, in which this conception of Man's good is quite explicit:

> Lead me, O Zeus, and lead me, Destiny,
> Whither ordained is by your decree.
> I'll follow, doubting not, or if with will
> Recreant I falter, I shall follow still.

and,

> Who rightly with necessity complies
> In things divine we count him skilled and wise.[5]

The Stoics never answered the question of how man can control his own attitude and be free to acquiesce or not, if all is governed by necessity. If it is good for man to acquiesce, then that must be a part of his destiny; so if his destiny is determined by necessity then it is out of his power whether he will acquiesce or not acquiesce. On the other hand, if it is in his power to accept or to reject, then to the extent that his destiny includes his moral worth it is not entirely the work of necessity.

A fated history is a contradiction, for in a fated history nothing can happen. So when past and future are contemplated as related to the present by an all-inclusive necessity, it is inevitable that they should be seen as endless repetition. For in what other way can we think of a passage of time which excludes novelty? Only if each passage in time is an episode in an endless repetition can it be understood as entirely within the grip of necessity. Novelty and necessity are mutually exclusive; even in science the uniqueness of the individual existent must be ignored just to the extent that we understand the individual in terms of natural law. Once we admit real change, once we recognize that something has happened which has never happened before as precisely the same event, we deny uniformity. If we insist on the retention of uniformity, as we must if we are to think in terms of necessity, then the passage of time can be understood only as unending recurrence.

We must go further, and recognize that any conception of existence which looks upon the natural world as self-contained and self-explanatory has to conclude that everything happens by necessity. It must deny absolutely the very possibility of novelty and real change, or else accept the alternative of unintelligibility. Thus classical atomism reduced all change to the motions of atoms in empty space and then had to deny that change of place could make any difference to an atom. Atoms form groups, and these groups break up as others are formed; but in all this grouping and regrouping the constituent atoms remain ever the same, unaffected by their shifting space relations with each other.

Only a world of nature which is dependent on and sustained by a real existent which is not itself a part of nature can show genuine novelty. For no natural order can produce the novel from itself. From itself alone it can bring forth nothing but new arrangements of what had already been there, and even these must have been present in potentiality before they were actual. In the entire history of thought there have been few more intellectually pathetic episodes than the attempts to assert a theory of emergent evolution within the framework of philosophical naturalism. The evidence seems to support the truth of the theory of emergent evolution, but such a process is intelligible only in a world which depends on something beyond itself for its own existence. The natural order can only receive the novel from a source beyond itself. Even man, as free, owes his freedom to the presence in him of something which is not itself a product of nature alone.

Thus the very idea of history, as a record of genuine change and of unique events, requires that the natural be seen in relation to the supernatural. *History is the daughter of theism.* Even for the Greeks, as far as they were from an adequate theistic conception, Clio was the daughter of Zeus.

Professor John Baillie brings this out with unusual force and clarity:

> Only twice in the history of thought has the idea arisen that history might be tracing another pattern than the circular one, and in both these cases it was the same general pattern that was proposed, namely, that of a non-recurrent movement towards the ultimate triumph of good. This is the conception which unites the religion of the Magi with that of the Hebrews and which differentiates them from all other religions and philosophies save those which have drawn some degree of inspiration from them—Mithraism from the one, Christianity and Islam and Western thought in general from the other.[6]

Professor Baillie comments that

> it is only among the Hebrews that we find any conception of history as a significant process. Nowhere else, if we except the Zend-Avesta, is the sequence of historical events conceived as leading anywhere or as accomplishing anything. The wheel of occurrences rotates eternally on its own axis, and in doing so achieves nothing and advances nothing.[7]

After pointing out the difference between this and Eastern thought, for which history is *maya*, illusion, and Greek thought, for which only the changelessly eternal is real, Professor Baillie goes on to say:

> Thus the essence of that discovery of history which the Western world owes to the Old Testament really lies in its differentiation of history from nature. Nature, as we now understand it, is the realm of uniformity, being governed by general laws that keep producing identical and invariable results, while history is the realm of significant change productive of genuine individuality and genuine novelty.[8]

But the differentiation of history from nature, of which Professor Baillie speaks, is not so complete as he suggests. The idea that science deals with absolute uniformities is Greek; it is not the idea of science which has proved so fruitful in the modern era. Modern science became possible with the recognition that the test of truth requires that we examine the individual instances of our general laws. We cannot formulate laws of nature *a priori*. The long controversy between those who would reduce physics to mathematics and those who insisted upon an irreducible empirical element in physics concerned this very issue. With the conviction that the very things which natural science studies are, as existent entities, unique individuals, and that they and the whole world of nature are in evolution, the victory has gone to those who require the perceptual test of truth in scientific inquiry. Mathematics has not lost its importance in being denied a place among the sciences of nature; for it is more than a science of nature, it is a science of the possible.

According to our modern conception, our scientific knowledge of nature is able to attain to that degree of universality and necessity which it possesses only by means of abstraction. It has to ignore the individuality of the individual and to forget that the processes it studies are not really recurrent but are themselves parts of a history. Nature has its cycles, but it has no circles. Cycles can be seen as circles only if we look at them from a perspective which ignores or obscures their forward stretch. It is for this reason that the natural sciences, and especially those which make extensive use of mathematics, are most fruitful when they direct their attention to those things in which uniformity and similarity are more significant than difference and individuality.

DESTINY WITHOUT NECESSITY

If man were able to fix his destiny by his own arbitrary choice, history would be irrelevant. His only destiny would be what he chose, and it would make no difference what he chose. The fact of his choice, and this fact alone, would make his condition appropriate to his nature; for the only nature he would have would be his lack of any determining factors to influence his action. There would be no determinate human nature, there would be nothing definite and fixed in man or in the conditions under which he attained his ends. There would be nothing to which his choice would have to conform if it were to be right. Every choice would be right by virtue solely of the fact that it was made.

This reminds us somewhat of the conception of God which is held by those who consider the divine intellect as subject to the divine will, so that ultimate good is determined by groundless will. William of Occam, for example, held that what God wills is good solely because He wills it rather than that God wills the good because it is good. As some of his followers saw, this means that nothing is evil in itself but that evil is made what it is because of the divine command.[9] The difficulties of such a view when applied to God become insuperable when the attempt is made to apply them to man.

All truth about the past loses its meaning if man's destiny is only his arbitrary choice. Theories which deny truth, such as Marxism and the Fascist ideologies and pragmatism, also deny the significance of genuine knowledge of the past. They describe the past in whatever guise is useful to their present purpose. So history becomes a deliberately contrived myth. When tales and legends of the past are considered significant only for patriotic edification, for example, the question of whether or not they are true tends to be ignored. Their purpose is to create certain desired attitudes in the popular mind, and those who raise the question of truth are likely to be branded as enemies.

When past and future lose their significance, the present stands alone. All the meaning of an act is in its own now; the present, cut off from past and future, must have all its meaning in itself. Some phases of contemporary existentialism show us the final outcome of this. The present act, senseless, utterly arbitrary, absurd, is the whole meaning of existence.[10] The self-sufficiency of the present act is absolute and yet it consists solely of its being what it is. With this, intelligibility has reached its breaking-point, and with it goes the significance of the theory itself. For what difference does it make what is in the present, if the present is for itself alone? So what difference does it make what we think about existence, if the thought about it is only an arbitrary present act with no meaning beyond itself?

DESTINY WITH NECESSITY AND FREEDOM

If human history is to have meaning for us then our destiny must be both a matter of necessity and of choice. It can be both, and without contradiction, if our own choice and decision can determine the outcome of our lives without destroying necessity. How can these be reconciled?

We are subject to the necessities of our nature and of our world. Although our nature includes the power to choose, to act or to refrain, we are not free from limitation. On the contrary, it is only because of the necessities in things that we are able to use our power of choice for our own purposes. When we decide upon an end, we choose the means which we think will enable us to reach that end. If things did not have definite natures of their own, and if they were not confined in their action to their natures, our attempt to make a choice of means would be useless. We choose a material to fashion what we desire, and we choose the material because of its properties. If it had no definite and stable properties we could not use it. Soft wax will not make a lever, nor do we set sail in a sieve. Only in so far as there is necessity in the relation of means and ends can we choose effectively what means we shall use to gain our ends. The necessity in the relation of means to ends is the kind of necessity in which the acts and functions of a thing are determined by *what it is.*

But what about the ends we seek? If there is a destiny for me is it an end I cannot refuse? In other words, does destiny fix my end? If so, it would seem that I cannot go wrong in the ends I reach: whatever happens, it is what destiny has decreed for me.

So, on such a view, even to fail to see what is my true destiny would be a part of my destiny. Thus we are back again to the view that destiny is fate. Even so, we must not forget that we do have a definite nature; for to evade fate at this price is to lose everything.

Perhaps, however, we can make our destiny in the sense that we choose as we please from the alternatives we recognize as possible. The fact that we have a definite nature only limits the range of possibilities open to us; it does not restrict us to any one of those possibilities. The possible is our only limitation, and within its range one choice is as good as another. What the pragmatist or instrumentalist calls our "felt needs" (but which might be called, more accurately, our "feelings of need") are our only guides. This view is defended by instrumentalists in opposition to the idea that there are certain alternatives which are the right ones and which ought to be chosen, that man really does have a destiny and that his attainment of it or his failure are the marks of his success or failure as a man. Yet even if our actual desires were our only guides, we still should assume that it is good to satisfy our desires and this could not refer merely to the fact that we do desire. It refers to the relation between desire and fact, between anticipation and realization. It assumes that we are beings who *ought* to satisfy our desires, and with this the supposedly repudiated doctrine that man's good is determined by his nature and consists of what will complete that nature returns again.

As we have already seen, unless there is something which a man is not but which he recognizes he ought to be then judgments of right and wrong, desirable and undesirable, good and evil, reduce to statements of fact only. To say that something is right or good would mean only that it is approved; to say that something is desirable would mean only that it is desired. To say that it is right to do what we approve, if "to be right" means "to be approved," would mean only that we approve our doing what we approve. Suppose we do not approve? Well, what of it? We simply do not, and that is all.

Let us try the other supposition, that there is something right for us to do and that when we fail to do it we do wrong. Then suppose we refuse to do what is right. What of that? The answer is that when we refuse to do right we fail, as men. Our action is what ought not to have occurred. But if right and wrong are reduced to fact alone, there can be no failure. Every act is what it is. To assert success or failure presupposes a norm by which we not only recognize *what* a thing *is* but also *what* it *ought to be*.

My nature does determine what is truly good for me. But the nature which I have is one which enables me to determine by my own choice, to some degree and within limits, what I shall be. The laws of our nature are like the laws of Bridge or of Chess; they do not specify what plays or moves we shall make in the game, but tell us what plays or moves shall not be made. I cannot choose and achieve any end contrary to my nature, for to say I can would be to say I can do what it is not my nature to be able to do. But there are alternative ends within my reach which differ in the completeness and success in which they realize my potentialities. I can choose to be less than my nature makes it possible for me to be. This still is in accordance with my nature, for it is a part of my nature to be able to make such choices. Necessity limits the alternatives, and necessity ties together the means and the ends. But I choose from among the ends with freedom, and I am able also to choose a means in spite of the fact that I do not desire the consequences which are bound to follow upon it. I can choose in ignorance and I can choose in defiance of what I know. Nature does not limit my action to the range of my knowledge. By virtue of my nature, my knowledge follows upon my action, and only after I have come to know the things which I learn from experience can I guide action by knowledge.

Although I choose with freedom, my choices are not indifferent. They are right choices or wrong choices. They are right choices when they are choices I ought to make, when they are choices of the good. Where what I choose is good, it is good not because I choose it or desire it but because it satisfies a genuine need. A genuine need, as distinguished from the mere idea of a need, is a lack. It is the absence of something without which I am not what I ought to be. My nature, so long as the need is unsatisfied, is incomplete. So freedom opens the door to failure as well as to success. In order to have a destiny I do not have to determine it for myself. It may be something offered me which would be beyond my own power to bring into being. Yet it is within my power to accept or to refuse it.

History and Progress

We think of progress as improvement, change for the better, closer and closer approximation to a goal. But the only progress which is valuable in itself is that which occurs in the individual human soul, for it is not society or civilization but the individual which has real existence. As Albert Schweitzer says, "The difficult problems with which we have to deal, even those which lie entirely in the material and economic sphere, are in the last resort only to be solved by an inner change of character. The wisest reforms in organization can only carry them a little nearer solution, never to the goal."[11] Progress of civilization is the improvement of the instruments of life and the elimination of hindrances to the development of the individual. The political state, for example, cannot bring positive intrinsic good into being; its function in the promotion of the good is, in Bosanquet's words, to provide the "hindrance of hindrances" to the best life and to the common good.[12]

The striking progress of recent times is the development of technology, based on the rapid increase and diffusion of scientific knowledge. But if we try to treat of advances in technology as valuable in themselves we only create confusion. Technology is significant because of its release of power and because of the ends for which that power is used. Considered in itself, without reference to the ends it serves, it is as much a danger as a benefit. Not only does it provide increased facilities for destruction, but its

475

own advance exacts a high price in terms of the increased sub-ordination of the individual to the technical process itself. The area of individual action and initiative decreases and the impersonal application of controls increases. What a noble destiny to find the meaning of life in the production figures of a factory or the balance sheet of a corporation!

We all must devote time and thought to things trivial in themselves, to the many things we have to do merely to maintain ourselves and our communities. The organization of work saves time and energy. But we benefit from such saving only as it overbalances the time and energy required to organize that work and to maintain the organization. When organization and system cost more than they save, they hinder us. A life devoted to trivialities becomes no less trivial by the mere multiplication and complication of those trivialities. Rather it becomes more trivial, in so far as triviality is a relation of the importance of an act to the difficulty of performing it.

The trivial cannot be eliminated, but it can be kept in perspective. Unless there is a perspective of genuine and intrinsic value there is little in life that we can justify. Unless we can see our drudgery as a contribution to something much more important than what it costs us, we can make our work tolerable only by numbing our consciousness and inhibiting our powers of insight and judgment. Unless we can see ourselves, with all our weaknesses and faults, as a contribution to more than we are in ourselves our only progress will be in disillusionment. If this does not merely weaken our energy, it turns our thought and ingenuity against ourselves to make a mockery of all we are and all we do. To mock ourselves becomes the meaning of our life, and we devote our gifts and efforts to showing that there is nothing worth the devotion.

Men have tried to avoid this degradation of themselves by inventing value schemes to give meaning to life. They have sought conquest and the power and glory of domination over others, as if these were cosmic values. There is only a difference of degree between this and the attitude of one for whom, at the moment at least, the sun has hesitated and the galaxies of space are poised for the outcome of a war or a political campaign or a football game or the turn of a roulette wheel. The prestige of position and wealth, the possession of titles and honors, the admiration of those who cannot possibly know him whom they admire— these are taken to be the ends which give meaning to life. Yet we know that they are nothing in themselves. They are passing things, meaningless in themselves and falsifications of value. They are in themselves of no more point that the drying of a drop of water in the sunshine. Their supposed importance is nothing but empty myth, civilized man's counterpart of primitive man's superstitions.

If we are to find progress in history we need fixed points of reference and absolute values. For only in such terms can we recognize an apparent progress as a genuine one. A theistic philosophy gives us fixed points of reference and absolute values, and it is difficult—now that we have reached this point in our study—to see any promising alternatives. Even so, the progress open to man is in the increasing scope and depth of knowledge, the increase in the effectiveness of action, the growth of love and concern for others which our changing society makes possible to the individual. Nothing which can happen in society will relieve the individual of his responsibility for using the available instruments for his own enlightenment, for the enrichment of his life, and for the fuller appreciation and realization of truth and beauty and goodness. But these values are not merely for our own private satisfaction. The greater our appreciation of them the more intensely we feel the need to make them available to others. It is our good to bring good to those we love; and so far as we truly love ourselves we love all men we know, for we are of one flesh and one kind. "We as individuals are spiritual," Father D'Arcy reminds us, "and a spiritual being is not enclosed in a narrow individualism. Our nature shouts out to us at every turn that we are more ourselves the more we go out in sympathy and service, and our mind is so constituted as to be at its best when it is in some sense everything."[13]

To see ourselves and our lives as contributions to more than we ourselves are is not to see ourselves as mere means to ends. It is rather to see ourselves in true perspective as joined with others in the great work of existence. We are ends in ourselves, and yet our end is to advance mankind toward its true destiny. But does not this make us all mere means to some over-riding historical process or to Humanity, considered as something which has its own real existence? No, the only ends in themselves are individual beings. We are ends in ourselves, and so are those others with whom we are united in our common enterprise. This means that it is intrinsically good, and not merely instrumentally good, that we realize our true nature and do our part in man's work. We find our good in the good of others, but the good we find in the good of others is truly *our* good. If a religion is to teach that man is but an instrument for the realization of the will of God, it must also teach that it is God's will that no man shall be an instrument for any will but that man's own. In so far as any man sees and truly comprehends his destiny as a servant of God he sees that he serves God as His son, and this becomes his own freely chosen end.

By losing ourselves in love and devotion we find ourselves. The great danger is that we give ourselves not to others as people but to others in the abstract. We give to movements and campaigns and causes; our relation with those we help is entirely indirect and impersonal. Merely to serve is not enough, except for an instrument—a mere means to an end. To serve another so that the service for the other is an end in itself and good in itself is possible only in one way, and that is to serve in love. (Likewise, the act done in hate is an end in itself and evil.) In the language of religion we say that each of us exists for the glory of God. If it is true that a man exists for the glory of God, he exists for nothing but the glory of God; but his only true glorification of God, Who is Self-Existence, is to bring his highest potentialities into actual existence. If God is love, then only in devotion can man's life be lived in its true nature.

God's Purpose and Man's Freedom

When we see our world as God's creation we see history as the account of the way in which God's purpose is realized in the world. Or, to use a different figure, history is the account of the realization of those potentialities which the world was created to realize. Whatever happens, it is something which leads toward creation's goal. This does not mean that whatever is is right, as we commonly understand such an assertion. It means rather that what ought to be is what shall be, one way or another. This is no automatic mechanical necessity; it is rather that everything works for good, the union of being and goodness. All acts have their consequences; we can avoid one set of consequences of action only by another act. It is because the other act has its consequences also, and because now the result is the consequence of the two acts, that we do not stand helpless before the unending processes set in motion by one act. The die is not cast once and for all; there is room for other plays. Yet whatever the plays we make, the final end will be the end appropriate to our nature and to the way in which we have used our powers.

The end appropriate to our nature is the end we choose, for it is our nature to choose. Many seem not to choose; they are passive in life, and merely accept the roles and places assigned to them by others. Are they not human, too? To say they are not because they fail to choose is to forget that a supposed failure to choose is itself a choice, and for a voluntary agent to acquiesce in things as they are is that agent's own act. In any choice-situation there is always, among the alternatives, that one of refusal to act.

Whatever our act may be, it is an act which expresses our nature. Our acts are the mode of existence which we, as selves, enjoy. We cannot escape the consequences of our nature. The outcome of any act of which we are capable is an outcome which fits our nature and the nature of the things we act upon. It fits our nature to fail when we attempt what we are not capable of achieving, and yet it also fits our nature to attempt it. To speak in religious terms, it is God's will for us to fail when we attempt what we cannot accomplish. If it is not His will for us to fail then He will give us the power to accomplish it; but even so, He cannot give us any power it is not in our nature to receive and to exercise. It is fitting that we should fail to maintain peace between nations, for example, when we attempt to do so by acts which are not appropriate to the nature of political societies and their relations with each other. It would be Heaven's scandal for men to achieve real and lasting peace with each other by shutting their eyes to fact and by using methods which take no true account of what men are and of the issues which set them against each other. Those who pray for miracles here do not know what they ask. Miracles may happen, but not to negate the nature of existence. The miraculous, understood religiously and distinguished from the magical, is the fulfilment of what is in nature but not contained by it.

To the extent that we do not make ourselves and our world we do not make our destiny. Even within the range of our own power to act and to determine our action by our own decision, we have to act under conditions we do not determine. Our range of effective choice falls within the range of what is possible for us to choose, and this itself is not a matter to be determined by our choice. History is the working out in time and nature of a destiny which comes from outside time and nature. If the end of history were an event in time and immanent in nature, it would be immanent necessity and not history. Every event would be the one and only possible event at that time and place. Nothing would be hazarded; all would be pre-determined. On the other hand, the final end of history cannot itself be within history. Make history the final court of appeal and she will forever reserve her verdict.

But if we have a destiny we do not make ourselves, and if our free choices, no matter what they may be, are the means by which our destiny is realized, in what way do we differ from the puppets of fate? The difference lies in this, *that in each of us there is the power to determine what shall be his own position with respect to human destiny.* How shall I relate myself to man's destiny?

Let us look at an analogy. Suppose we have reason to anticipate that in a certain thickly populated area traffic will increase
much more rapidly than adequate roads can be built, and that
along with this will come increased power and speed of motor ve-
hicles. We may expect a considerable increase in accidents. Given
the conditions, and assuming that no measures are taken to control the consequences, more people are going to be killed and in-
jured. You or I can do little to change this situation, and yet we
are not helpless before it. For we can do much to change our own
action in the light of what we anticipate. We can operate our own
motor cars with special care and vigilance, and thus—to a degree—
control the effect upon ourselves of this situation which is not of
our making and not subject to our will.

I cannot stop a flood, but if I anticipate its coming I may save
myself from it. I do not control the fluctuations of the market, but
I may buy and sell for myself in the light of my knowledge of the
factors which do influence prices. The fact that there is destiny
does not mean that I am helpless. I cannot change human destiny,
for I cannot make man over or create a new world. But I can,
within limits, make myself over and I can accept a new relation
of myself to the world. If I am receptive to the gifts which God
offers me, I may find my true end in this destiny which I do not
control. I cannot help but feel it is better for me to contribute in
this way my own part to the working out of human destiny than
that I serve only as an obstacle against which it shows its irresistible
power.

When we see history as a record of man's attempts to fulfil his
own ends, we can see history only as the record of failure. For
the ends man has fulfilled are not, in the main, those at which he
aimed. As Columbus aimed at the Indies and discovered America,
so man seldom has it in his nature to achieve the ends he sets for
himself. He demands more of himself than he can do; so, relative
to his own standards, he dooms himself to failure. He cannot anticipate the conditions under which he will have to act, and his
course of action is deflected by those conditions.

This is what the Greeks understood as fate, the inevitable failure and destruction which man brings upon himself when he allows himself to be guided by *hybris*, the wanton assertion of his own will. This he does when he tries to make himself important and to create his own destiny. For his true importance is given to him, not made by him to be; and his destiny is for him to find, not to create. Later religious thought added to the Greek idea the recognition that man's effort to control his own destiny is inevitable, and they called it original sin.

THE DRAMA OF HUMAN HISTORY

We can understand better the alternative conceptions of history and destiny if we use the figure of a stage. For a mechanistic and naturalistic determinism, the players are puppets who perform the actions and give the speeches of the one and only possible play. The play is the thing, the players are mere devices by which it works out its immanent necessity. They contribute nothing to the play or to its performance. They are only manipulated. Since the actual play is the only possible play, no author is needed. Since the actions of the puppets are predetermined, no director is needed. But if the play is the only possible play, and if all the action is predetermined, the impenetrable mystery is why the play should be performed. Nothing really happens in it; all is foreordained. The supposed action is only illusion, and the illusion is the illusion experienced by a participant in the illusion, that is, by an illusory participant. What this conception misses is the understanding that if the puppets exist as individual realities then their actual performance, whatever it may be, cannot be the one and only possible series of actions.

As a parallel of relativism, we imagine that each player makes up his play as he goes along, and so it follows that each player plays in a different play. No author or director is needed because no play is being staged. Even the stage is, for each player, what he imagines it to be; so no actual stage is needed, and no real properties. In fact, each player's play needs nothing more than that player's imagination. Since he is himself a character in his play, he is himself only an imaginary character. From this nothing real survives.

The contrast of these opposites helps make plain the true nature of human history. We all belong to the cast and we all play upon the stage of nature. We all play the same play, some of us in some scenes, others in other scenes. The play we perform is not the only possible play, nor is our stage the only possible stage. Our play is fitted to our stage and to ourselves. Each of us has a part to play, and we know our parts more or less adequately. Each of us plays his part in his own way, with his own interpretation of it and of the play. We have to learn our parts as we play them, and we have to assist each other. We have to decide our actions as we play, and many of us misunderstand what the play is about. Some are bewildered, and do only what others with more assurance tell them to do. Those who have very definite ideas of what it is about often argue, and even fight with each other, over their differences, while some who are even more knowing recognize these conflicts as parts of the action of the play. Yet there is a theme and an outcome, and we get hints of it—partly from our missteps and miscues and their consequences, and some think partly from the Author's own suggestions which He whispers in our ears. This description may sound more like a rehearsal than a performance, and there are those who so interpret it.

In our efforts to perform our parts, how can we tell what is a mistake unless we know what the play is about? How can we tell where we go wrong, where we defy our true destiny, unless we know the will of God? Without knowing the script, however, we may still be able to tell when we are and when we are not playing our parts, provided we know something of what the results will be when our parts are played as they should be played. This is what religion tries to tell us. But by our own knowledge we may be sure that the play is not properly given unless the actors work together in harmony and unless the range and content of their performance makes the fullest use of their knowledge and understanding and appreciation and creative imagination and initiative and will. The basis of our confidence in this is, first, that if this is not true then we are cast for parts which do not fit our nature or do not need all our capacities. Secondly, we are sure that the play makes sense, whether we understand it or not; and if it does make sense, then our parts, whatever they may be—if we exist in order to play them—will demand all of what we can put into them. In this way a man finds his vocation, his work and his service.

This means that we know we are doing the will of God, although we may know little more than this of what God's will is, when we act in such a way as to make fullest use of the whole range of our capacities. This includes, of course, the kind of use of our capacities which keeps the subordinate in subordination and which places in control of our action that part of our nature which is fully capable of directing the other parts. Whatever else God's will for us may be, it is something which requires this of us, if existence makes sense. In any action in which we act contrary to the true make-up of our nature, in which the subordinate tries to guide its superior or in which contrary purposes tear us apart without bringing a new and more significant unity of action, we may be sure we are acting against the will of God. Beyond this only faith can take us; but even beyond this the results of action still have to be tested by this criterion.

Still we must not forget that to act contrary to the best that is within our power, and so to fail to realize the highest of our possibilities, is also to act according to our nature. For this, too, lies within the range of the choices we can make because of what we are. If we make the wrong choice, our failure is God's will. It is not His will, however, that we make the wrong choice. Why, then, does He not see that we make the right choice? The answer is that it is God's will that *we* shall make our own choices. He does not will that we make the wrong choice, but He does will that if we do make the wrong choice we shall incur the consequences of our own free act. If we will the means of failure, it is well for us to fail; not to fail would be to sacrifice our power to choose the means for some particular end. Any means would be as effective as any other. This would be truly a denial of our nature.

Where knowing makes a difference and we neglect to know, the result is our own choice. Where reflection makes a difference and we fail to reflect, the result is our own choice. But, we may protest, we did not know that knowing, or thinking, makes a difference to our action. Is this true? If so, we do not know ourselves; we are not conscious of what we do; we are irresponsible, and our claim to be treated as responsible agents is only so much noise.

"To make the fullest use of the whole range of our capacities"— what does this mean? For one thing, it does not mean perpetual busy-ness; nor does it mean tension and anxiety lest we are not doing all we can. There is only one way in which we can try to use our capacities in their full range without dissipating our energies in inner conflict. That method is one of unification of effort and purpose under a single guiding principle. For the theist, for whom God is no mere theory or abstraction or postulate, that principle is to imitate, so far as he can in his contingent nature, the nature of God. To do this is to live in such a way that existence and value come together. In so far as the God-like values are realized they have the power to order the life and activities of him who realizes them. They have power over the lower values and over that part of man's nature which can wreck his life when it usurps the place of control.

What are these values? This is the question which a religion answers specifically, and it is on this question that the most serious differences among religions arise—providing we include as a part of this problem the question of what validates a religion's identification of the values it proclaims as primary. In the Judaeo-Christian tradition the answer is plain. We find it in the Law and the Prophets, particularly in the writings of the Second Isaiah and in Amos and Micah. We find it in the Gospels and in the Epistles on which the Christian Church was founded: Love and devotion, humility, sincerity, submission in the service of others, the constant awareness of our dependence on God, gratitude for our blessings, sorrow and repentence for the evil we do, and joy and satisfaction in our existence as children of God.

The Christian faith goes much further than these generalities will take us by themselves. They are negative conditions which set limits to the area of choice within which man must look for his destiny, if our argument is sound. For the Christian faith, however, the positive meaning of history is shown in specific events and in a particular Person. Not by abstract virtues does redemption come, but by a Person. In Reinhold Niebuhr's words:

> The Christian faith begins with, and is founded upon, the affirmation that the life, death, and resurrection of Christ represent an event in history, in and through which a disclosure of the whole meaning of history occurs. . . . The interpretation of history in the light of this event creates a structure of meaning in which the history of a particular nation, as the center of the whole of history is unequivocally transcended. This "second covenant" between God and His people is not between God and any particular people but with all those of any nation who are "called," that is, who are able to apprehend by faith that this person, drama and event of history discloses the power and the love which is the source and the end of the whole historical drama.[14]

We do not arrive at the Christian view of history by way of philosophy. We arrive, if we do, by the way of faith. It is our sense of the supreme importance of this event that convinces us, although our conviction may be strengthened by the effect it has had in history. We could not infer it, as a conclusion, from any analysis of the nature of history. But once it is made known to us, and comprehended in its significance, it provides the answer to our deepest questions. If not this, we have to find our answer in some other event or set of events if it is true that history is the account of real and unique happenings in time. So philosophy, again, has to wait for its answers upon the revelation of the nature of existence in fact and deed. To find that this is the case may, in truth, be philosophy's greatest gift to us. Whether the Christian view is true, for example, depends on whether the fact on which it takes its ultimate stand, and by which its relevance to real existence is shown, is truly fact. This is not a question for philosophy to answer; philosophy can help us here only by clarifying the criteria by which we distinguish fact from fiction and by showing us the place which knowledge of fact has in answering our questions.

CHAPTER 28

The Problem of Evil

THE PROBLEM

PERHAPS the most frequent charge against theistic philosophy is the inability to cope successfully with the problem of evil. Theism, it is said, is faced with a dilemma: Either God is responsible for evil, or God is finite. If we acknowledge that this world contains evil and insist also that it is God's creation, we say that God creates something that is evil. This is to say that God is the author of evil. On the other hand, if we deny that God is the author of evil, we deny that the world is His creation. We say that there is something in existence which is beyond His power, and so we say that He is finite.

To many this problem has seemed insoluble. Either God is infinite but evil, or He is good but finite. Some have suggested that God must work with a "given," an ultimate surd in existence which limits the range and effectiveness of His activity.[1] Others have been inclined to deny that what seems evil is genuinely evil, but rather is good in disguise. If the supposed dilemma were sound then there would be a real conflict between the infinity of God and the existence of evil, and one of these alternatives would have to be chosen. If neither is acceptable then the problem remains unsolved, or the dilemma itself is defective. We shall try to show that the dilemma is defective, and our first task will be to inquire into the reasons for insisting that evil exists.

DOES EVIL EXIST?

The solution of our problem, we may be told, is simply to deny that anything is really evil. What seems evil is either not really

evil or else it does not really exist. It may be true that much of
what seems evil to some is not really evil, but most of us would
agree also that much which seems good is really evil. We are particularly sensitive to the attempt to deny or belittle the importance of moral evil. To say that the things people do to each
other in hate and malice and in their enjoyment of cruelty are not
evil is to turn the drama of human existence into a farce. It is to
insist that the impact of those things which bring suffering and
despair is nothing but the noise a clown makes as he taps us play-
fully with his slapstick.

Irritated by the crying of his baby son, a father crunches out
the infant life with foot and fist and club. Is this only a bit of
clowning? Or what about the incident recently reported in the
press in which a father, holding his child by the feet, swung the little one's head against the sidewalk? Is this a scene from a farce,
and shall we sometime see the joke? If the father tells us, with
rueful grin, that he did not intend to go so far, what shall we
say? Shall we say, "Oh, well, accidents happen. Children also are
run down by automobiles, they are drowned, and they fall out
of windows"?

The mistress of a Nazi death camp is reported to have had
lamp-shades made of human skin, skin taken from victims of Hit-
ler's production-line of cadavers. Perhaps in imagination we can
see those lamps lighting up a scene of merriment, perhaps we
can see a guest trace with his fingers the delicate lacery of the
tight-stretched skin circling the light, and perhaps we can hear
him chuckle to himself in appreciation of his hostess' sly and play-
ful tricks.

Men and women study the art of torture, not merely to learn
how to inflict the maximum pain with the least dulling of the victim's consciousness. They study this not only to be able to inflict
pain with skill and effectiveness, but in order to use that skill to
rob men and women of their manhood and womanhood. Pain and
the threat of pain are not enough; they must be the means to something worse, the means by which their victims are forced to deny
their own integrity, to see their human dignity destroyed, to see

themselves slowly twisted into acquiescent puppets. In some areas of modern life this has become one of the new technologies, and it is not too fantastic to anticipate the day when respected universities will offer courses in methods of torture and techniques of destroying the human will. And why not, if what seems evil is only good in disguise?

But even if these things are evil, perhaps they are the exceptional evils. We console ourselves with the thought that, after all, people capable of such horrors must by psychopathic. They should not be so much condemned as understood and pitied and treated for their illnesses. Evil is a sickness; its prevention is a problem of hygiene and its cure a problem of therapy.

At the very moment when we feel so superior in the differences which seem to separate us from those despised caricatures of humanity we may be reminded, if we are fortunate, that all humanity is of one kind. The most fantastic abnormality is the expression of impulses and attitudes which we all share. "There but for the grace of God go I" need be no mere ejaculation of self-satisfaction; it can be, and ought to be, a most profound expression of personal debt and of compassion. For what would I be now if I had this other's abilities and opportunities, his obstacles and frustrations, his deadened perceptions and blunted sympathies? The sot and the thief and the murderer and the pervert I can despise only as I forget that their motives are the same as my own, that their nature is my nature, and that our differences are not in our own distinctive original worthiness but in circumstances. In their place I see myself, for one piece of ore is made into steel and another like the first goes out with the slag.

It is the destiny of some to exhibit in their persons the depths of degradation into which human nature can sink and with which it has a natural affinity. Thus they reveal to us what is hidden within ourselves and so is involved in our very being. To these our brothers we should be eternally grateful. They show us what is in ourselves, and by that revelation they may save us from their own failure. They are, in a sense, a sacrifice for us.

Even if it is our good fortune to learn of an evil from its manifestation in others, and so perhaps to avoid its blackest depths, the evil in ourselves of which we learn is no less evil. My own impulses of hate and malice are still desires for the injury and destruction of those to whom I owe the works of love. That I can control these impulses, even that I can learn from them something of myself and even that I may be given through them a new perspective which saps their strength, does not make them the less evil. At my very best I succeed only in avoiding greater evil. Evil is not turned into good, and although he who is evil may become good his goodness will not cancel the evil which he was. We may speak of the "transmutation" of evil into good, but transmutation is not negation. The end does not justify the means, nor does the arrival at a destination undo the journey to it.

The victims of tyranny, in Nazi and Soviet slave-labor battalions and torture-chambers and death-camps, remind us of the depths of human cruelty which seethe beneath the thin smooth surface of civilized society. The sadist, as much as the hero, shows us the possibilities of our own nature. Our problem is to bring ourselves to see these things within ourselves. We see them in others, but we overlook in ourselves what we so severely condemn in others. What do we think of our own lynch mobs and race riots? We who are so quick to feel sympathy for the victims of disaster show little evidence of uneasy conscience for the mass slaughter which hastened perhaps by a few days the surrender of the Japanese. Our pride in our strength to destroy, and the dependence of our national policy upon the threat of force, is the measure of our vulnerability. For this apparent strength is truly weakness, just to the extent that our threat to use it is the principle of our policy; since to use it is to bring our own destruction upon us. So long as we believe in nothing but force, and have no confidence in right and justice, and in the capacity even of those we distrust and hate to be moved by the good, our cause is lost.

It would seem that we cannot escape our problem by denying evil. For evil is no mere illusion, nor is it only good misunderstood. It is rather inherent, as evil, in finite existence. We have sound reason, as we shall see, to acknowledge that it is good that there is a finite world. But the good has its price.

How Does Evil Exist?

We understand evil, in general, as the contrary of good. It is that which destroys the good or interferes in some way with it. To say that evil exists is to say that there are some things which are not as they should be, that some things ought to be other than what they are. As we have already seen, a changing thing realizes its potentialities in time. Its good is the most complete and integrated realization of the possibilities open to it. For a thing to be less than it can be is a loss to existence. As we have seen, also, the more of the range of real existence a thing shows in its own nature and the more it brings into its own existence the nature of other things, the higher is its value—for the more fully it reflects in itself the self-existent.[2] Among all the things we know in the world of nature those which stand out as of highest value are human selves. The higher a thing is in the value scale the greater is the evil of its destruction.

This conception of evil regards it as essentially negative. We can say that evil is the negation of good in a sense in which we cannot say that good is the negation of evil. For evil is a lack, not the intrusion of some new positive quality or being into a situation. Yet this does not mean that evil is mere illusion or unreality. Things which are defective do exist, and their existence is positive and actual. It is only when we consider the defect or lack by itself, in abstraction from the reality of which it is a defect, that we have evil as negation. This means that evil as such, considered apart from the reality to which it pertains, is only an abstraction. Evil action occurs, evil things exist, but evil as such is nothing real. It is only because of what is not evil in an evil thing that we can call it evil at all, for unless it is something actual in itself and has potentialities which properly belong to it there is no sense in which we can say that it *is* something which can lack. Only if I am a writer can my writing be poor, and only if I do play golf can my golf game be in need of improvement. Only if a thing *is* something can it *be* something which falls short of what it ought to be. A man who prostitutes his natural gifts must have natural gifts to prostitute; it is their prostitution, not their possession, that is evil.

With this consideration in mind, we are ready to try to determine what it is in which evil consists. All natural beings maintain their own existence, in some respect and to some degree, at the expense of the existence of other things. Either they destroy other things in order to keep existing themselves or else their own existence prevents the realization of other possibilities. The growth of an oak tree in this particular spot excludes the growth of a maple tree at the same place and during the same time. This is a necessary consequence of the spatio-temporal character of the natural order, a consequence of nature's distinctive finitude. It is as if the very principle of finite existence were sacrifice. And the principle is exemplified even more strikingly in the economy of the animal world, where life preys on life.

We no longer say, however, that the animals of one species exist in order that they may be killed and eaten by the animals of another species. Cats catch and eat mice, but the fulfilment of a mouse's nature is not to be caught and eaten by a cat. The mouse exists to be a mouse; its life is the realization of its own nature. If a mouse is caught by a cat its life is interrupted by a destroyer which is as external and foreign to it as is the lightning bolt which strikes a man dead. The loss of any creature is an evil just in so far as the existence of that creature is a good. To say that nature requires such loss is not to deny the fact of the loss; it is only to acknowledge the necessity of evil.

The destruction of one thing may contribute to or be essential to the existence of another thing. But even if the good more than balances the evil it does not cancel the evil. Evil may be justifiable, but to justify evil makes it no less evil. Forgetfulness of this principle is perhaps the chief cause of the failure which so persistently dogs man's efforts to make over the world and society to suit his own purposes. The solution of one problem creates many more new ones, and each success is gained at the cost of many failures. Our refusal to recognize evil for what it is and to reconcile ourselves to its necessity is responsible for our unrealistic approach to so many of our problems. When we fail to respect the dignity of existence, when we think we can manipulate the real world as we do our dream world, existence destroys the dream. When in industry, for example, we use men as if they were mere things we find that human nature takes its revenge. When we think we can abolish evil we forget our finitude, and in doing this we deny our own nature. This does not mean that we should not attack evils and attempt to right wrongs; it means rather that we need to realize that the issue is never the simple choice between good and evil, but rather between one evil and another.

We are tempted to consider human problems as if they were mechanical problems. They are dislocations, or they are only occasions for replacing broken parts. Such a defect may be "fixed up" once and for all, as a mechanic fixes an automobile—or until some other part of the machine breaks. But human problems are not of this kind. When one part goes wrong other parts are affected. The relations among people are dynamic processes, and the substitution of one person for another may modify the whole process. It is a delusion to believe that conflict among people can be ended, that there is some magic formula or social system which will solve all problems. Such a belief is like the belief in perpetual motion, or like the attempt to abolish death. As friction is inherent in motion, as death is inherent in life, so conflict is inherent in society, and the remedy for one conflict becomes the occasion for others.

Natural and Moral Evil

Our discussion of how evil exists has concerned, in the main, what may be called natural evil. There is, however, another dimension of evil, that of moral evil. Moral evil comes to pass by the purpose and intention of a moral agent. No moral evil is a necessary evil, even though it may be necessary that some moral evil occur. For moral evil is the result of a free act, and no free act is necessitated. The foundation of morality is man's felt obligation to do what he believes is right and to refrain from what he believes is wrong, to seek what he believes is good and to avoid what he believes is evil.

Contained in this are both the absoluteness and the relativity of morality. Moral judgments are relative and fallible just to the extent that the distinction between good and evil, between right and wrong, is not correctly understood. We may be mistaken in what we take to be good and in what we take to be evil. But we cannot escape the moral absolute which is found in our unconditional obligation to act in accordance with our judgment of what is good. That a man cannot be wrong in his recognition that he ought to do what is good and right, although he may be wrong in what he thinks is good and right, is the reflection in human consciousness of the very principle of being itself in so far as being is its own act, that is, in so far as being is free. That we are also obligated to seek true judgments of good and evil, and not to be satisfied with superficial impressions or with accepted social attitudes, is obvious on its face. For to recognize a duty to do the right includes a recognition of a duty to do what we can to avoid error in our judgments of right and wrong. To assert the former and to deny the latter is to found the principle of value upon our own impressions and preferences of the moment.

The higher religions generally distinguish a certain level of moral evil as sin, usually described in religious terms as rebellion against God. The concept of sin can best be understood, perhaps, as moral evil committed in full awareness of what it is. It is evil done deliberately as evil. It is knowingly to take evil as good. Says H. H. Farmer:

> That sin is thus at its heart and centre insincerity most sensitive natures have felt. It is going against the light, such light as one has, not in the sense of snuffing it out as a man might a candle-flame be-

tween his fingers, for that no one can do, but in the sense of screen-
ing it under a veil of excuse and subterfuge. It is "holding down the
truth in unrighteousness."

The result of sin is corruption. When we tamper with the truth
we become

> less and less capable of discerning what the will of God is, or even
> that there is a will of God at all. . . . Insincerity swiftly becomes a
> habit, continually creating fresh opportunity and occasion for its
> exercise; until it ends by being almost a necessity, for the longer
> this way is persisted in, the more the monitions of God—if indeed
> they can break through the increasing dimness and insensitivity of
> the soul—lose their quality of being an invitation to blessedness and
> become instead a condemnation threatening the whole structure of
> the life in a way too disturbing to be faced.[3]

In St. Augustine we find the same conception of the consequence of sin:

> For this is the penalty of sin truly just, that one lose what he
> would not use rightly, when he could so have used it without diffi-
> culty, if he would. That is, that he who knowingly does wrong,
> loses the clear knowledge of what is right. And he who would not
> do right when he could, loses the unimpeded power of doing what
> he has the will to do, when he does will it.[4]

The possibility of sin depends on the awareness of good, and
the deepest depths of sin are possible only for those who have the
highest and purest awareness of God as the source of good. It
seems to be this which St. Paul had in mind when he said that
"through the law comes knowledge of sin";[5] "sin indeed was in
the world before the law was given, but sin is not counted where
there is no law";[6] "law came in, to increase the trespass";[7] "for
the law brings wrath, but where there is no law there is no trans-
gression."[8] "What then shall we say?" Paul asks. "That the law
is sin? By no means! Yet, if it had not been for the law, I should
not have known sin."[9]

Moral evil which does not reach the level of sin is perhaps the evil we do thoughtlessly and carelessly. We know better but we do not think. Or our own desires are so strong and so close to us that we forget about the rights and interests of others. If, in our act, we had reflected on what we knew, or if we had remembered the rights and interests of others as we pressed on to satisfy our own desires, moral evil would have been sin. So the more aware we are of what is right, the more persistently our attention is held upon the way of life which reflects the presence of God in ourselves, the greater is our offence. The height of good and the depth of evil are correlative; to be capable of the one is to be capable of the other. To avoid the risk of evil we must cut away the possibility of good, and this is to stultify ourselves. It is not innocence we want, but strength.

The Inevitability of Evil

Although no morally evil act is itself necessary yet it may be necessary that evil should occur in a world of free but finite agents. A man's life is a battleground of conflicting desires, and yet every desire is good and its satisfaction is good. The evil that man does is evil not because it satisfies a desire but because of the price he has to pay for that satisfaction. So it is that so often from the first buds of our freedom we brew a poison to destroy the plant. The inevitability of moral error is plain when it dawns on us that the ability to choose rightly can be developed only by choosing wrongly and by learning from our mistakes. Only as we catch ourselves acting from motives which, in our more clear-minded moments, we despise and abhor can we learn to bring the motivation of our action to some extent within our conscious control.

Moral strength is no gift, although gifts of family and community may make it easier for us to develop morally. But what moral strength we are to have we must acquire in act. We are finite, and we live in time, and in so far as we are in any sense responsible for what we shall be it is necessary for us to achieve strength of character, the power to do as we will to do, through the pain and anguish of failure. For when first we glimpse the possibilities open to us we are yet unable to govern our acts in accordance with what we see. Our awareness runs ahead of our power. We see in others, perhaps, what we should like to be ourselves, but the seeing no more brings us to our goal than a road sign propels the motorist toward his destination.

Nowhere do we find a more realistic awareness of the value situation in nature and in human life than in the dominant religious traditions of our culture. Theology's doctrine of original sin—whatever else it may mean—is clear recognition of this situation. In Greek tragedy, in Hebrew prophecy and poetry, and in the Christian conception of salvation by sacrifice we have the most profound reaches of human understanding. Their moral realism lies primarily in their recognition that evil is no illusion, that it is no mere obstacle which man has only to push away or surmount, but that it is of the very tissue of finite existence.

Evil and the Infinity of God

We need now to consider whether the fact of evil compels us to revise our idea of God. Although we have already seen the reasons for asserting the infinity of God,[10] we may have come face to face here with facts which require us to reappraise the claim that God is infinite. This issue is of utmost importance, for the concept of a finite God seems to strike at the heart of the philosophical case for theism. A God dependent in any way upon something other than Himself is not self-existent. With the denial of self-existence goes the intellectual foundation for the claim that we can know that God exists, for the proof of God's existence is that finite existence implies self-existence. We have not argued that since the world exists it follows merely that there must exist some being powerful enough to have made the world. Such an argument takes us nowhere. It is unsound for the reason that inference to any existence but self-existence requires direct confirmation in experience. We can go from the world to God in knowledge, as distinguished from mere speculation or imaginative construction or guessing, only by virtue of our recognition of the contingency of the world and our discovery that the fact of contingent existence implies a self-existent creator.

It is in the very contingency of our world, and in our experience of it as contingent, that we find the evidence of the self-existent God. To grasp fully the fact of the contingency of things we need to see its two sides. Contingent things are dependent for their existence upon something not contingent, but this dependence—considered merely as such in abstraction—is no proof of self-existent being. Before it can be seen as proof we have to see directly that these contingent things do themselves really exist. It is in *their existence* that they manifest the need for a self-existent. It is in this sense that we can say, with Maritain: "It suffices for things to exist for God to become inevitable. Accord to a point of moss, to the smallest ant, the value of their ontological reality, and we cannot escape any longer from the terrifying hands which made us all."[11] Whatever may be our conclusions about the problem of evil, we must deal with it without compromising the existence of God.

As we have already seen[12] the infinity of God does not mean that all is realized in God. The potentialities of finite existence are not potentialities which pertain to God. Self-existence is complete actuality, without anything potential, but God's complete actuality excludes potentiality from God only and not from other things. God cannot become that which is not God; nor, unless God were finite, could He become at all.

To say that either God is finite or else He is responsible for evil is to assume that an infinite God would be capable of evil. Or, to put the same thing in a different way, it is to assume that the inability to do evil constitutes a limitation upon God. In so far as we understand evil as a lack, or a falling short, of *what is* with respect to *what it ought to be*, the inability to do evil is not a limitation upon God but the very mark of His self-existence and freedom from contingency.

Unfortunately there is a certain ambiguity in the idea of infinity. With the early Greek philosophers the infinite was the

indefinite, the indeterminate, and so was an expression of imperfection. Yet it is an easy transition from the idea of the indefinite to the boundless and the immeasurable and the inexhaustible. Associated with this is the notion of a positive perfection or completeness as that which has no limitation, and so the meanings of "infinite" and "complete" and "self-contained" begin to over-lap. With this has come the tendency to interpret infinity in terms of all-inclusiveness, as "that from which nothing can be excluded." This is plainly a confusion of the positively infinite, as that which is dependent on nothing beyond itself, with the negatively infinite, as that which is indeterminate or indefinite.

It should be plain that God's infinity is a positive infinity. As positive, God's infinity is not an indeterminate all-inclusiveness. On the contrary, as absolutely determinate existence, God is the very opposite of the indeterminate and the indefinite. We may go so far, perhaps, as to say that any ascription to God of a quantitative infinity can be, at best, only a figure of speech or a mode of eulogistic reference. In religious language we may speak of God as "boundless," but God's boundlessness is not that of the indeterminate. God is truly boundless, and has no limits, in the sense that He is not a being to which limits apply. Limits pertain to that of which there can be more or less, or to that of which we can say it is of this or that nature. Limits pertain to God only as, for example, size and weight pertain to thought.

To deny infinity of God in the positive sense is to deny the existence of God. The notion of a finite God comes close to contradiction in so far as "God" is used in the meaning it has for traditional theism. We should speak rather of a "finite god." There are examples enough of this idea in the mythologies and polytheisms of human history.

We must not forget, in this context, that evil is no illusion. This means we shall have to explore further the problem of reconciling the fact of evil with the existence of God. Since moral evil presents the most formidable challenge to theism, and since the possibility of moral evil presupposes freedom, we shall consider our problem first in connection with human freedom.

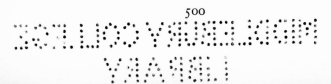

HUMAN FREEDOM AND GOD

Once we see that God's infinity is a positive infinity we need be puzzled no longer by the supposed conflict between God's omnipotence and human freedom. The problem, as it is commonly put, is the supposed dilemma in which we are faced with the alternatives of a human freedom which obstructs the purposes of God, on the one hand, and correct choices which are not free on the other. As John Wild states the dilemma: "Either we are free and sometimes choose wrongly, in which case the divine purpose is frustrated, or we are always made to choose in the proper way, in which case we are not really free."[13]

The fallacy is in the statement of the supposed consequent of the first alternative. There is no sound reason to believe that our wrong choices frustrate the divine purpose. To draw such a conclusion from our freedom is to deny to God the power to create free agents and to use their mistakes in the fulfilment of His purpose. Even a human agent is capable of setting goals which require the free action of others for their realization and which use the mistakes of others as means to those ends.

A father decides, for example, to teach his young son to ride a bicycle. It is unlikely that the boy will learn without several times falling, and some of the falls may be painful. The father could prevent the falls by holding the bicycle, but he refuses to do so. For what is his purpose? Is it merely to give the lad a ride or is it to help him to learn how to manage the thing for himself?

Teaching is seldom possible unless the learner makes mistakes and unless the teacher is willing to let him make mistakes. If the learner performs without a mistake, he does not need to be taught. Unless he makes mistakes neither he nor his teacher knows what instruction he needs. The most benevolent teacher of the human race of which we can conceive could not, consistently with that benevolence, prevent man from making mistakes or protect him from the consequences of those mistakes. If God works in history it surely is not in order to make man less than his capacities promise; it is rather to lead him to fulfil those capacities to the utmost.

We mock ourselves and we mock God when we pray to Him for strength and expect therefore to be sheltered from danger. If we pray for strength, and if we mean what we ask, then we pray for the kind of trial and danger which will enlarge and sharpen our abilities.

There is no reason why the realization of God's purpose should not make use of the free acts and free choices of men. He may well have purposes which can be carried out only by those free agents who have been tried by defeat and failure and, like Moses, have come through the trial strengthened and tempered. Man is a finite creature, and yet he reflects in his nature something of the divine creativity. His knowledge is limited, his motives are impure, and his strength is unequal to his purposes. Yet he has the gift of freedom, and this is the only condition by which he can have any knowledge, no matter how weak; freedom is the only condition under which man can act by conscious motive, no matter how mean his motive may be; it is the only condition under which he can formulate purposes for himself, no matter how far removed they are from his powers of accomplishment. Is it better for man, although finite, to be capable of some knowledge and of growth in knowledge than to be capable of no knowledge at all? Is it better for man, although animal, to be an animal which bears the image of God than to be only a beast? The very capacity for morally responsible action exposes man to the danger of moral evil. But which is higher morally, the virtue of mere innocence or the conquest of evil in oneself?

In Professor Wild's words, the supposed dilemma we have been discussing makes the mistake of failing to recognize that free choice itself is "a value falling within the scope of the divine purpose." It treats free choice

> only as a disruptive factor which might upset the well-laid plans of a human artisan, with only limited time and power at his disposal. Such anthropomorphism, however, is open to serious suspicion. It is quite clear that we are not dealing with a human economic or engineering enterprise, but rather with an agency of an entirely different order, having unlimited time and power at its disposal. The

very fact that man has emerged at the culmination of the evolutionary process shows that voluntary action, the free choice of good, is a major concern of this agency. Furthermore we can understand why this is so, for we ourselves in our rational moments set a very high value on freely chosen acts of sacrifice and devotion.[14]

Human freedom is no restriction upon divine power. On the contrary, if God had to negate man's freedom and force him to choose in the proper way, then His omnipotence truly would be compromised. As Archbishop Temple says, "If God exercised compulsion by forcing obedience or by remaking the character of a self against its will, He would have abandoned omnipotence in the act which should assert it, for the will that was overridden would remain outside His control."[15]

Perhaps the basic error in the notion that there is an inconsistency in asserting both human freedom and divine omnipotence is the idea that God's power is a kind of compulsion, exerted upon and against other things. It should be plain to us, even from our own limited experience, that external coercion is the very feeblest of all forces when used against another's will. You may force another to act in a certain way, but you cannot by force bring him to desire to do what you have determined he shall do, or to mean what you compel him to say. The stronger his will the further does your compulsion alienate him from your purposes. You may break his will, but then his acquiescence is not truly his act. If God is truly omnipotent He does not force man's will; rather He enlists it. Even when man's will remains defiant, God turns that defiance to His own purpose.

Perhaps one of the tragic errors of theological thinking—tragic in the misconceptions it has engendered and in the false problems it has created—is the idea that God's sovereign power is expressed in force and compulsion. As Whitehead puts it, Plato considered the creation of the world to be "the victory of persuasion over force."[16] Elsewhere Whitehead cites this doctrine as one of religion's most important intellectual discoveries.[17] Theology, which owes so much to Plato, has often forgotten this lesson. For if we consider the power of God as an inescapable force acting on man from outside his nature, we cannot escape the conclusions of a mechanistic predestination theory—that man is a mere puppet. But when we see the power of God as persuasive power we can understand something of how God can effect His purposes by using, instead of negating, man's freedom.[18]

EVIL AND GOD'S GOODNESS

We have now to consider the question of whether the fact that evil occurs does in any way compromise the goodness of God. The argument that it does compromise God's goodness is based on the contention that a perfectly good God would not create or permit the existence of a world which contains evil. God is not compelled to create, but acts in perfect freedom. He knows, in His omniscience, that the world will contain evil. If then, He knowingly creates something evil, if it is by His act of creation that the existence of evil becomes possible, then we must conclude that it is His will that evil shall exist. Since an agent who deliberately wills the existence of evil must himself be evil, it follows that if God is omniscient and omnipotent He is evil.

In our discussion of this we shall overlook, for the moment, the obvious fact that these statements about God are not true univocally. It may well be that the most serious difficulty in this whole matter is that the very statement of the problem refers to God as acting under the limitations of time. When we say that God knows the world will contain evil we seem to transfer to Him the time reference of our own knowledge. *We* may know or judge concerning the future, but there is no future for God. The future He knows is our future, not His. Just as the author of a novel or a play may see the time period of the action as a whole, so the time period of the natural order is seen as a whole by God. It is only by some such analogy that we can have any idea of God's relation to nature. In using such an analogy we must remember, of course, that the author of a novel or play exists and acts in his own time, in nature's time; in this respect the analogy does not hold of God.

The supposed conflict between God's goodness and omniscience may be quite plausible, and so it has been to many. Its plausibility, however, is the result of an unrecognized confusion. *It is one thing to say that evil exists, that evil deeds are done, but it is quite another thing to say that it is evil that evil exists.* Even if the second were true it would be a different truth from the first. Our contention here, however, is that although the first is true the second is not. It is true that evil exists, but it is not evil that evil exists. In the words of St. Augustine, "Although, therefore, evil, in so far as it is evil, is not a good; yet the fact that evil as well as good exists, is a good."[19] Just as it is *true* that there is *falsehood* so it is *good* that there is *evil*.

This, too, is open to misunderstanding, and we must be sure that our distinction is correctly drawn. In the first place, to say that it is good that evil exists does not mean that the evil which exists is good. Nor does it mean that things are intrinsically evil but good in relation to other things. In the sense that, and to the extent that a thing is evil, it is not good; if good and evil are merely relative, the problem is artificial.

It is good that evil is because there is good which is worth the price of the evil which has to be paid for it. The good is good not *because* of the evil involved in its attainment, but *in spite of* it. As St. Thomas Aquinas says, in comment upon the statement just quoted from St. Augustine:

> Evil is not of itself ordered to good, but accidentally. For it is outside the intention of the sinner that any good should follow from his sin; as it was outside the intention of tyrants that the patience of the martyrs should shine forth from all their persecutions. It cannot therefore be said that such an ordering to good is implied in the statement that it is a good that evil should be or be done, since nothing is judged by that which pertains to it accidentally, but by that which belongs to it essentially.[20]

St. Thomas explains the relation of evil to God's will in this way:

> Now the evil that accompanies one good is the privation of another good. Never therefore would evil be sought after, not even

accidentally, unless the good that accompanies the evil were more desired than the good of which the evil is the privation. Now God wills no good more than He wills His own goodness; yet He wills one good more than another. Hence He in no way wills the evil of sin, which is the privation of right order towards the divine good. The evil of natural defect, or of punishment, He does will, by willing the good to which such evils are attached. Thus, in willing justice He wills punishment; and in willing the preservation of the order of nature, He wills some things to be naturally corrupted.[21]

The real question here can be put quite directly: Is it good that the world exists? If we insist that it is evil for evil to occur then we must answer that it is not good that the world exists. Those who take such a position are forced to the inevitable conclusion that if God is good the world does not really exist. If we say, however, that it is good that the world exists then we have committed ourselves to the position that it is good that evil shall be. For the only world which can exist must be finite, and so the things of which it is composed must be incomplete and must involve mutual opposition. The higher the level of being a finite thing reaches, the more his actions express his own will and the greater the possible conflict between himself and others.

In order to help clarify the question let us look at some apparently parallel instances. I may say, for example, that certain mistakes were made. It may be an unfortunate thing that these mistakes were made. On the other hand, there are many situations in which it is good that mistakes should be made. As we have already seen, it is a good thing for a learner to make mistakes, for otherwise he would never learn. He learns by making mistakes, by discovering what his mistakes are, and by discovering what caused them and by trying to control those causes more completely. Although the learner does make mistakes it is not a mistake for him to make mistakes.

Let us look at another example which comes closer to our problem. The killing and maiming of thousands of people each year in automobile accidents is an evil. It is one of the tragedies of modern life. There are few families in this country which have not been touched by it. Yet do we believe that it is evil that this slaughter and maiming shall occur? If we did, the means of its control surely would have been applied long ago. We could have outlawed the automobile, or required effective and rigid examinations for licenses to drive, or have enforced the laws against careless and improper operation of automobiles so that the use of the automobile would not be undertaken lightly by anyone. Yet the fact is that we do not attempt to control any but the flagrant abuses and misuses, and the reason is that we value our freedom to use even so dangerous a thing as more important than the prevention of the deaths and injuries which result from its use.

In many areas of life the price we pay for some of the things we prize most is the price of permitting evil to occur. Those who are so quick to say that pain is evil would not likely wish for the abolition of pain so long as we have to depend on the experience of pain to know that something is wrong with our bodies. The forms of cancer most difficult to control are those which are painless in their early stages. By the time pain's signal has become imperative it is too late. It is significant that most of those who are ill or maimed prefer to live with whatever pain they may have to endure, provided it is endurable, than to get rid of the pain at the expense of life itself. It is seldom because they fear death that they prefer pain to its extinction in death, for most of these face death, when it comes, calmly and with serenity.

But are these parallels and instances convincing? Do they not, on the contrary, actually underline the fact of evil? Would it not be a better world if man suffered no illness or pain, if death and disease did not exist, if ill-will and evil intentions never were formed, if desire—itself always good—were never thwarted? If such would be a better world it would not be this world. Why, then, was not a different world created? Why did God create this world which we have, a world of pain and suffering and hate and cruelty?

THE JUSTIFICATION OF EVIL

A world free of evil would have to be a world which contained nothing capable of evil. A world without natural evil would be a world without the use of one thing by another for its existence; and this, it seems, would be a world without change. Considering the problem, however, primarily with respect to moral evil, we can imagine this condition fulfilled in two different ways. A world may contain nothing capable of moral evil because there is nothing in it capable of acting on its own initiative. Such a world would contain nothing which had reached the stage where morally responsible action is possible. The beings existing in such a world would be neither morally good nor morally evil; they would be unmoral. The other sense in which we may conceive something incapable of moral evil is in the sense that it is perfectly good. A world which contained moral agents all of whom were incapable of doing wrong, or were able to refrain from doing wrong and did so refrain, would be a world free of evil. These are the two alternatives to the contention, which we are here defending, that a world which contains free agents is a world which contains evil but that the existence of such a world is good.

It seems quite plain that a world in which free agents are included is in some significant sense a higher existence than one in which free choice would be impossible. The theistic solution of the problem of evil, as against those who see the very possibility of evil as something itself evil, can be summed up in this: *Not even God can love a puppet.* It goes without saying that no puppet, however complicated may be the motions through which it is put, can love.

A being which can make decisions for itself, and so to some degree control its own acts—and thus its own nature, is a higher being than one which is what it is and does what it does solely under the control of external causes. Choice may have evil results, for he who chooses may choose wrongly. But it may be better for him to make the choice, even if it be the wrong choice, to suffer the consequences and to accept responsibility for the suffering of others who are hurt by his action, than to refuse to exercise his power of choice. If, where it is his place to choose, a man refuses to choose, he denies his nature as a man. He is, in effect, trying to be less than what, by his nature, he is in fact. And since he refuses to choose by his own choice, his attempt to deny his nature fails, and the very attempt is itself an affirmation in deed of what he would deny. This does not mean that the evil consequences of a wrong choice are not really evil. On the contrary, even though it is better to choose, where choice is what a man needs to face, than to shirk that function, and though it is better to choose wrongly than to evade the responsibility of choosing, yet the evil which a choice brings is no less evil by virtue of the fact that to make the choice was good.

What of the other alternative? Is it not conceivable that a world might exist which would contain agents capable of free choice yet who would always choose correctly? Is there not even a chance, on statistical grounds alone, that all actual choices would happen to be correct? If so, then no matter how slight the probability, the possibility of such a world would be assured, and we should be faced with the question of why such a world was not created instead of the world which does actually exist.

The answer is that a world of free agents who manage never to choose wrongly is not a possibility. Whatever a created world would be, it would have to be finite, and the beings who would inhabit it would have to be finite. Unless such beings were omniscient they would be subject to error. To deny this is to say that they would be incapable of imagining or contemplating anything beyond the reach of their certain knowledge. They could not thus live and act under the limitations of time, and so they simply would not be making choices at all. Finitude means contingency, and no contingent existent can be fully self-determining. Every finite being is, as such, exposed to causes beyond itself. Thus it is incapable of making sure that its choices will eventuate as it intends.

But would not even our world, filled with evil motives as it is, be a better world if those evil motives were successfully controlled and never issued into evil action? The answer is that evil suppressed is beyond the reach of good. Evil motives which do not show themselves in action, or are in no way expressed, cannot be changed into good motives. Such a world would not only contain evil, but its evil would be incorrigible. A world of corrigible evil seems better than one of incorrigible evil.

Evil, says Jacob Burckhardt,

> is the one condition of selfless good. It would be a horrible sight if, as a result of the consistent reward of good and punishment of evil on this earth, all men were to behave well with an ulterior motive, for they would continue to be evil men and to nourish evil in their hearts. The time might come when men would pray Heaven for a little impunity for evildoers, simply in order that they might show their real nature once more. There is enough hypocrisy in the world as it is.[22]

In order to will we have to desire, and it is the very essence of desire to be limitless. No desire ever limits itself. If it is kept within bounds some other desire must effectively oppose it. Only when we desire the good as we know and understand it rationally is the operation of desire in full accord with our nature. But our real good is almost always more remote than the things which directly and immediately stimulate appetite and desire. The immediate attraction is so much stronger in its power to elicit action than the remote good; only habit and discipline enable us to resist the one for the sake of the other. The power to will a goal and to push ourselves straight to it in spite of the enticements of impulse and wish is won only by the practice of denial. Even the most effectively disciplined will may go wrong unless that will is guided by sure knowledge. Here is the final tie with finitude, for our knowledge is never sufficient to guarantee the success of our choices. Our action anticipates the future, and so it projects us into the unknown. The light of knowledge is very dim when it is turned toward the future.

The very conditions of growth, by means of which we learn to act with confidence and decision, require us to place greater importance upon ourselves and our interests than they deserve. Those same conditions develop in us also that kind of self-assurance which can hardly exist without turning into self-will and pride. It is as if we had to defy God, and set ourselves in His place, before we can discover what our own role in life truly is and in order to acquire the power to act with genuine freedom.

Still, are not the mistakes we make honest mistakes, the result of ignorance? We are forced to choose, but we do not have knowledge adequate to guide our choices. Surely to go wrong here is no moral wrong.

This may be true of certain stages of moral development, but it is only part of the story. As a person grows in moral sensitivity he becomes more fully aware of the moral implications of his need to act in ignorance. When we act in good will we do not presume to interfere in the lives of other people. We do not make decisions for another person, and decide his future with no consideration of his own wishes and plans. We hesitate even to advise another about any choice of importance. Who, for example, would presume to advise a friend about his marriage, or try to influence him in any personal decision of moment? Yet we are forced to do these very things indirectly in our relationships with others. In business, in government, in all aspects of an organized and institutional society, we have to make decisions which affect other people in the most intimate areas of their lives, and we have to do these things in ignorance of what is desirable or undesirable for them as persons. We act in terms of our own interests, or of the interests of the organization we represent. The welfare of those who are affected by our decisions is subordinate to the policy of a business corporation, or a university, or a political organization.

We cannot make an omelet without breaking eggs. This is true, but its truth does not cancel the wrong; it only points up the fact that the human situation involves us in acts which hurt and destroy. We can thicken our skin, but this does not change the fact. Any exercise of power over another, direct or indirect, differs from murder only in degree. It may be spiritual rather than physical murder, but every invasion of another's life, every limitation we impose upon his power to make his own decisions for himself, is the destruction of a bit of his person. When we pick people up and lay them down to suit our purposes, or to suit any purposes but their own, we make them to that extent less than persons. They become things. It is not too much to say that, in one way or another, all moral evil comes down to this. It is all the same in principle—it is to use as mere means to ends what are properly ends in themselves. The more clearly aware we are of what we are, and so the more reverence we have for all levels of existence, the more conscious we are of the wrong we do.

There is a remedy for this. It is to deaden our sensibilities and inhibit our awareness of all but the immediate and obvious. But this remedy requires that we become less than what we are. To take this way is to sink back into the animal nature out of which we have partially emerged. Which would be the better world? Is it one in which evil is not done deliberately and consciously, and so is not moral evil, because those who act are not aware of what they do and so are not capable of moral evil? Or is the higher world one in which finite agents are sensitive and aware of the evil they do, are aware of the fact that their actions do harm others and recognize their inability to act otherwise as persons, and so see the necessity of evil, and yet are aware that the evil they do is no less evil by the fact that it is inescapable? If the latter is not the higher world, then the themes of great poetry and tragedy are false and the most moving heroism is folly.

Awareness of moral evil is the first step in the direction of moral regeneration. If we have to hurt others it is better for us to know the truth than to delude ourselves with the belief that we do no wrong. But to know the truth is, in this case, more than an intellectual act, for the more fully we know the truth the more keenly we feel the wrong we do. In the wrong we have to do our only salvation would be to feel the hurt more than do the victims of our act. We could set things right only if we could expand our awareness and our feelings to include all the consequences of our act, and only if we could include them in a way that would take the evil to ourselves and so lift it from those who suffer.

We cannot do this. At best we can only desire with all our hearts to be able to do this. At best we can see the evil of the world with that helpless longing to take it on ourselves that a mother feels when she sees her child in agony. Can we escape the thought that only the God who created the world can take its pain and evil to Himself, and in taking it to Himself can lift the burden from us?

Unless the cosmic drama is a farce, God's nature is found in the achievement of value through pain and suffering and sacrifice. Again we ask: has man ever learned anything more important than the things he has learned in defeat and failure? Even the capacity for happiness itself depends on the depth of experience. As Gibran says, "The deeper that sorrow carves into your being, the more joy you can contain."[23] The most poignant sorrow and the most intense suffering of which man is capable is not what he feels when he loses those he loves; it is what he feels in his most clear-sighted moments of awareness of the wrong he has done. Losses by accident and by natural causes may leave us bereft and poor; but these things are done to us, not by us. The harm we do by our own free action, especially the wrong we do in awareness of its wrongfulness, is evil which need not have been. It is evil which has taken place by our own deliberate choice. Even when we act with our eyes open, and choose the lesser evil, the evil we do choose we recognize as evil. It is small comfort for one who is an author of evil to know that it might have been worse. Good and evil cannot be understood in terms of a profit and loss account. Yet the agony we feel in the face of the wrong we do is the condition of our salvation.

How does suffering bring salvation? For one thing, by making us know and understand.

> Guide of mortal man to wisdom,
> he who has ordained the law,
> knowledge won through suffering.
> Drop, drop—in our sleep, upon the heart
> sorrow falls, memory's pain,

and to us, though against our very will,
even in our own despite,
comes wisdom
by the awful grace of God.[24]

and

The scales of God
weigh to all
justice: those that suffer learn.[25]

It is no mere intellectual awareness that suffering brings. It is rather the experience of feeling within ourselves the surging pulse of being itself. The final lesson is that no price is too great for existence, and the higher the level of finite existence the greater the price. Those who have learned this, and who live by what they have learned, have found the meaning of life which high religion opens to all who seek it and are willing to pay for it. Whitehead reminds us:

The kingdom of heaven is not the isolation of good from evil. It is the overcoming of evil by good. . . .
God has in his nature the knowledge of evil, of pain, and of degradation, but it is there as overcome with what is good. Every fact is what it is, a fact of pleasure, of joy, of pain, or of suffering. In its union with God that fact is not a total loss, but on its finer side is an element to be woven immortally into the rhythm of mortal things. Its very evil becomes a stepping stone in the all-embracing ideals of God.[26]

CHAPTER 29

Human Blessedness

THE IDEA OF IMMORTALITY

A s LONG as man has been aware of himself he seems to have craved and sought to reach beyond the physical limits of his existence. Out of this have come various ideas of a future life and immortality, and the idea of immortality has developed into one of the central themes of the higher religions. It is usually in terms of some idea of immortality that a religion expresses its ultimate hopes for man. In our concluding chapter we shall consider the significance of this idea for a philosophy of religion.

The idea of immortality and the idea of a future life are not the same. One may involve the other, as is true in many religious beliefs, but they have no necessary connection. It is obvious, for example, that we can imagine a future life of limited duration. When a religious idea of a future life begins to show the possibility of such limitation the tendency is simply to deny that the limit is actual and to conceive of a future which is endless. But an immortality which is only an endless continuation is quite unsatisfying; it seems to be nothing more than an indefinite extension of mortal existence, with all the seeds of death which such existence contains. It is as if man should keep his mortal nature, but with death suspended; and so he would be a creature who ought to die but cannot.

A mere future life, as such, is of little if any religious significance. The poverty and tawdry trivialities of the so-called "Spiritualisms" which attempt to make contact with "the other world" illustrate the religious insignificance of a mere future life. "That the belief in a future life sprang from the mere desire to prolong this life and to enjoy fuller material good is probably not true of any religion," says Principal Oman.

> The belief was man's earliest victory over evanescence: and it does not appear to have been by any kind of reasoning, but by a direct sense of something abiding in himself and something of enduring quality in what he held to be sacred, which subordinated the immediate to the enduring.[1]

Revulsion against such a bleak prospect as a mere indefinite continuation of life may lead to the opposite extreme, where a sharp contrast is drawn between time and eternity. Immortality then comes to be understood as a mode of being which is the negation of time along with space. This leads to the loss of individuality, and to the conception of immortality as an absorption of the finite in the infinite.

The two opposing attitudes may be summed up perhaps in this way: Those who have no conception of what life and existence mean except in their experience of living through a finite time-span are limited, in their idea of an eternal life, to the notion of a time without end. As Oman suggests, this likely is not what the religious idea of immortality begins with. We may say rather it is what is left of a conception of immortality when the religious content is lost or ignored. At the other extreme we have those for whom the idea of immortality seems entirely incapable of expression in terms of a future life, since a life which is future is still a temporal life. They are seeking release not from the present only, but from time itself, and from all the marks of finitude which differentiate one thing from another. For them the essence of immortality is for the finite to be swallowed up in the infinite.

Both of these extreme views are unsatisfactory. For reasons we have already discussed,[2] it is a mistake to try to understand the temporal and the eternal merely as the negation each of the other. Unless the temporal is in some significant respect included within the eternal it cannot find there its own fruition and completion. On the other hand, to identify human blessedness with the mere endless prolongation of what has begun in this life is itself quite pointless, for the significance of an endless prolongation depends entirely upon what is prolonged. If we have nothing in this life which is of eternal value, no mere extension of this life into the future will give value to it. Whatever future life we may look forward to, with the hope which is the gift of faith, its blessedness will be linked with our experience in this life. If we know no present blessedness we can give no meaning to the idea of a future blessedness. But so far as we have tasted the quality of blessedness now the future is already captured in the present. If we are to develop any conception of the ultimate fulfilment of our life we are going to have to see *this* life in its proper relation to the ultimate principle of existence, that is, in its relation to God.[3]

Man's ability to transcend, in the content of his awareness, the immediate moment in which that awareness occurs as an event in time has led him to try to transcend the limits of life itself. Through all the differences in men's ideas of immortality there seems to run one common theme, sometimes explicit and sometimes unexpressed. This common theme is the conviction that the ultimate significance of man's life is something which cannot be erased from existence by the fact of his physical mortality. From this grows the conviction that once man makes effective contact with God, his very existence acquires a new dimension which establishes a foundation for his life in the eternal. Whatever happens to him, nothing can touch this; and if nothing can touch this, all is well.

LEVELS OF LIFE

Life can be lived at different levels. The vegetable can only vegetate. The animal can live at the animal level and, under conditions of hibernation or sleep, its life is little more than a high order of vegetating. Man lives at the human level, but he easily drops to the animal level and he can continue to exist at a level of vegetation. It is easy for man to act like an animal; it is more difficult for him to drop to the lower level unless he is ill or drugged. When he vegetates the complex organization which makes him capable of animal functions does little more than sustain basic life processes. When man lives as an animal the distinctively human in him is dormant, or else it only supports and reinforces the animal functions.

If God is present to man, and if God's presence makes any difference to him, then man is more than a child of nature. The practical consequence of theism is to confront man with a new level of life, a level which he can reach only by response to God's presence within him. This new level of life is not merely more of what he has at other levels, nor is it still the same only in greater complexity. The other levels of life may be considered a preparation for this, but when this new level is reached the whole self is reconstituted. Its point of reference is different, and the functions of the lower levels are seen in a new light. This is not the negation of the natural in man, but its transformation. As sounds, which are relatively meaningless physical events when found separately, may be transformed into music under the guidance of the composer's score, so the events which belong to the natural history of human life may take on a meaning they never could have had by themselves.

Man reaches this new level of life when he finds how to live his life in nature by the model of eternity. He lives in time so long as he remains a part of nature, but this does not require that he live in time for ends which are also in time. In so far as he sees beyond the limits of time he can live for ends which are themselves beyond time. The interests and the goals which belong to him as a part of nature are not simply abandoned, for man cannot divest himself of his physical and animal nature. But temporal interests and goals are not any longer valued by him for their own sake; they are transformed by the new perspective.

When we live merely as natural facts we find our purposes embedded in the life processes and in the social community which supports those life processes. Our physical and psychological needs are the determining factors in all that we do. They provide the basis of our value judgments, they are the justification of our choices and our decisions. We anticipate the future, but we do so in terms of anticipated needs. All of life revolves around this relation of means to ends, where nature fixes the ends and intelligence is only a tool by which we try to reach those goals. In a philosophy such as Dewey's instrumentalism we have here the whole of life. The stronger and more pressing needs are the need for food, for protection against pain and discomfort, and for sexual satisfaction. Then come the needs for status and respect, and the need to control the future so that basic needs will be satisfied. At man's highest reach, according to this conception, there is the need to exercise and develop the powers with which we are endowed by nature. Some who hold to a naturalistic philosophy would include the power to know and understand, to love, and to appreciate.

The difficulty which a naturalism encounters is the fact that the latter group of needs cannot be satisfied at the level of nature alone; their very existence is evidence of the presence to us of something divine. In fact the very organization of the human person makes it impossible for the lower processes to operate effectively except under the influence of the higher. Food and shelter perhaps come the nearest to providing satisfaction at the physical level alone. But we can hardly keep even these most basic functions at the animal level. Food satisfies not physical hunger alone, but our ways of taking food satisfy social and aesthetic hunger as well. Shelter becomes more than mere protection against heat and cold and wet; it is turned into a medium of aesthetic and religious expression. At the religious level food is the means of a sacrament and architecture the symbol of God's presence in the world.

Even sexual satisfaction, which is little if anything more than relief of tension at the animal level, may be unattainable to man unless there are bonds of love and personal commitments to be expressed in it. Most religions, in one way or another, have taken the sexual out of itself and devoted it to God. In barbarism the sex act may be performed as an act of worship; in higher religions the sexual may be a gift to God in self-denial and sublimation. All of these basic satisfactions, the satisfaction of what psychologists call "organic" or "primary" drives, the spiritual nature of man transforms into something higher than the satisfaction of isolated drives or segmental needs, into the satisfaction of a self.

When we look at man's social needs, such as the need for status and respect, we see even more plainly the impossibility of adequate satisfaction on the level of nature alone. There are few sights more pathetic than a person's attempt to satisfy his need for worth by the use of things and events in time. The savage decorates his body to make it more than a mere body, but if his attempt is successful at all it is only by virtue of the symbolism of the decoration. When we seek the respect and admiration of others we ask for something as ephemeral as our own private moments of self-congratulation.

Those who look for the meaning of existence in what is popularly called "success" are the victims of one of life's most ironic deceptions. A man wants love, so he tries to buy it. He wants admiration and respect, so he seeks for power in order to enforce it. He wants peace and leisure, so he entangles himself in a web of operations and activities which he can escape only by narcosis —and his only peace comes when he is not aware of it and cannot enjoy it. In a man whose purpose in life is to accumulate wealth or win prestige the feeling of insecurity must be near to psychopathic intensity. "There is a sickness that infects all tyrants," says Aeschylus, "they cannot trust their friends."[4] As with tyrants, so with him who seeks and finds this kind of success. Its formula is simple and easy; its consequences are devastating: Mix hatred with fear to drive the mind in desperation for something it does not want; then trade love for prestige and value for power.

We are aware of our wants in the form of desires. When a life is lived in time for the sake only of what exists in time, complete satisfaction of desire is impossible. One desire follows another: as each is satisfied, or leaves us without being satisfied, another takes its place. Some may be long-term desires, others brief and trivial. But in either case, as soon as we reach one goal another looms ahead. Satisfaction begins to die as it comes to be—and so it goes until life ceases. The past is gone, and we cannot return to it; so far as we find our good in the temporal, we lose it forever. "And tomorrow, what shall tomorrow bring to the overprudent dog burying bones in the trackless sand as he follows the pilgrims to the holy city?"[5]

In its evanescence, satisfaction is its own negation. Our greatest achievements, as well as our most trivial, are victims of time. How insignificant are the differences among the works of man! A castle in the sand lasts for a few minutes; a castle built of stone and iron lasts a few centuries. In nature's span the difference between a few minutes and a few centuries is almost as nothing. But nature's span itself seems to point to its own end, when all will be cold and dead and motionless in final equilibrium.

> What does a man gain by all the toil at which he
>   toils under the sun?
> A generation goes, and a generation comes,
>   but the earth remains for ever.
> The sun rises and the sun goes down,
>   and hastens to the place where it rises.
> The wind blows to the south,
>   and goes round to the north;
> round and round goes the wind,
>   and on its circuits the wind returns.
> All streams run to the sea,
>   but the sea is not full;
> to the place where the streams flow,
>   there they flow again.
> All things are full of weariness;
>   a man cannot utter it;
> the eye is not satisfied with seeing,
>   nor the ear filled with hearing.
> What has been is what will be,
>   and what has been done is what will be done;
>   and there is nothing new under the sun.
> Is there a thing of which it is said,
>   "See, this is new"?
> It has been already,
>   in the ages before us.

There is no remembrance of former things,
nor will there be any remembrance
of later things yet to happen
among those who come after.[6]

The power to know and understand, to love and appreciate, cannot be exercised with complete satisfaction upon the things of nature. Only when we know the eternal and only when we love that which transcends time do we fulfil our proper role. Yet we can know the eternal only as we find it in time, and what we find in time can content us only as we find in it what time does not possess.

The life we live in time is good, for in seeking and attaining the ends which life sets for us we give real existence to our nature. But the good which belongs to life in nature alone is one we can experience only in the passing feeling of pleasure and gratification. Its value touches us only as we pass. We have a brief glimpse of the beauty of a rose or a sunset. We hear music, then it is gone; the only way we can find it is to hear it again, by ear or in imagery. Even our acts of love, in which we find our greatest satisfaction, are past as they are completed. We can revive our awareness of them in memory, but the memory of the act is another event. Only as we understand that the object of our love is not used up in time can we find in it lasting value.

God, as self-existent, cannot exist in time. Yet God is not completely cut off from the temporal, for if God creates the world which exists in time we can scarcely admit an absolute mutual exclusion of the temporal and the eternal. God is like a mind and will which embraces all of time and acts in all of time without traversing time from moment to moment.

If our argument is sound we may be confident that somehow the temporal is contained within the eternal. But *how* the eternal includes the temporal we do not know. As we try to search this out our analogies weaken. Yet it is not unreasonable that this should be a mystery. We have no trouble recognizing the gap between a child's idea of an adult's awareness and the adult's awareness itself. But, as we have noted before, this difference must be small indeed compared with the difference between man's awareness and God's. Present and future can be present to a finite mind, which is itself caught in time, only in memory and imagination; but all time is present to God. So it is no mystery that this is a mystery; it could lose its mystery for us only if we could lose our finiteness. Still, the fact that the temporal is included within the eternal, even though we do not know how, has important implications for the concept of immortality.

THE PRESENCE OF GOD IN MAN

Perhaps we can get a glimpse of the meaning of immortality, as it may be understood in the context of a theistic philosophy, if we consider the two aspects of man's relation to God. These are the presence of God in man and the presence of man to God. If we are to have the slightest notion of what it may mean for us to be present to God in a life which transcends the physical limits of this life, we must first become aware of the presence of God in us in the life we live now.

We may begin with one of the plainest facts of our experience. This is the fact that although the awareness of each of us is private yet we are able to communicate with each other, to feel with each other, and to understand each other. All our dealings one with another and all our thoughts about each other rest on the assumption that whatever one of us experiences any other of us would experience under the same conditions and with the same equipment and past experience. Our relations with each other thus presuppose that, in a very real sense, it is the same consciousness that is within each of us. My own experience is not only this one self's experience; it is the experience of other selves as well in so far as it is their kind of experience. This leads us to guess that although our experience is private in each of us, yet it is also the experience of a single self and that the mind that is in each of us is one mind.

The same awareness is in all of us even if it is not in us that it is aware of being the same. It is one mind present in our many selves. We may differ among ourselves about what is true and what is false, about what is good and what is evil. But we do not differ in our original response to what we take to be truth and goodness. We cannot believe what we judge to be false, and we cannot approve what we judge to be evil. It is no objection to say that we so often deceive ourselves; the very point is that we *have to* deceive ourselves before we can believe what otherwise we should recognize to be false and approve what we should judge evil.

"We cannot believe what we judge to be false, and we cannot approve what we judge to be evil." But have we said anything when we have said this? "To believe" and "to judge to be true" seem the same, as do "to approve" and "to judge to be good." And so they would be if belief and approval were only acts of intellect. But the intellectual act of belief is always becoming something more; it never remains a merely intellectual act, if it remains at all. To believe that something is true becomes a belief *in* something just to the extent that it concerns the whole self, and intellectual approval becomes acceptance for oneself. There is an original orientation of the self toward truth and toward good which can be lost only by corruption and abuse. There is in us an original union of our own being with value; this is no mere passive conjunction but is the source of all in us that is creative and urgent. It is the presence of God in us.

As we noted earlier, Professor A. Campbell Garnett sees the presence of God in us as the "will to the greatest good."[7] The plausibility of this is plain when we ask how the will to pursue the greatest good, the willingness to sacrifice our own separate and immediate interests to a good which is not our own alone, could arise in separate and self-enclosed individuals. For when we will the good we will it as the good, for its own sake and not for the sake of anything else; and there is one thing a self-enclosed individual would be incapable of—to act in love of another.

What is the will to pursue the greatest good? Will is motive and purpose fused together in act. It requires first of all a desire for the greatest good. The only effective desire for the good is love for him whose good I desire. For I am a self, and as a self I can desire only because I love, and I can love nothing but a person. Desire for a thing is always for the sake of a person, if not for the sake of another then for myself.

There are two ultimate goals in life for a person: power and devotion; the desire to use and the desire to be used for the good; the desire to destroy others in order to exalt myself, and the desire to spend myself in the lives of others. If love is sincere it seeks the guidance of truth; it desires the true good, not merely an apparent good. The key to life is understanding, for understanding is the link of love with truth.

We are often tempted to deal with others in fear or anger, in triumph and disdain, or with contempt and pride. Our only thought is whether *we* approve or disapprove, accept or reject. If we are to show the presence of God in us, our effort must be to understand—as we are understood by Him. This means to appreciate, to have compassion, and to act under the guidance of knowledge and love. It is not for us to judge; it is for us only to understand and to act on our understanding—to link together love and truth. In so far as we understand we show the presence of God in ourselves. We escape frustration, and its offspring—hate; we escape jealousy and envy, and all those corrosive emotions which, when we direct them upon another, turn back upon ourselves and eat away at our own souls.

The presence of God in us has been called the Comforter. What does it mean to be comforted? It does not mean to be pitied, or merely pacified. It is rather to be made to understand the truth in such a way that we are reconciled to it. If truth does not bring reconciliation, we have not really seen it for what it is. Our salvation is to get rid of self-deception and to see ourselves exactly as we are. But we cannot do this of ourselves. It is only as we are shown what the Spirit of Truth sees us to be that we can see ourselves as we are. And only in the assurance that He who sees us as we really are does surely love us can we accept the truth about ourselves and find reconciliation in it. When love and truth compel me, then in those moments of transparent honesty I know God as He is in me.

THE PRESENCE OF MAN TO GOD

Concerning this there are only a few things we can say. That we are present to God is implicit in any genuine theism. If we are present to God we thereby are loosed from the bonds of time and we participate in the life eternal. God is in us that we may come to be in God.

Perhaps we may see something of our relation to God if we look at the relation of an idea to the rest of the content of a human mind. A single idea is part of the unity of a human consciousness. From the standpoint of the idea, however, its position in the whole of that consciousness is not apparent. So if a human consciousness belongs to the life of God its place in the divine unity is not apparent from its own perspective. The hope of immortality is the hope that we may come to see ourselves, to some extent, from God's perspective.[8]

So far as we discover God's knowledge of ourselves we stand in His presence. What does this mean in practice? It means to see ourselves, as far as we can, by the standard of absolute truth and absolute value. Even if we cannot grasp absolute truth and absolute value in their absoluteness, yet we may have a partial grasp of what in itself is not partial but complete. This means, for one thing, to see ourselves now in the light of our fullest possible awareness of all we have been and have done. In so far as we can imagine the physical limitations of memory and attention lifted we can imagine an awareness inclusive in its present of all its past. We can imagine an understanding in which all the implications of what we know are before our awareness. Of course if we cannot endure the awareness of what we have been and have done, and if our knowledge is composed entirely of the trivial and superficial, and if our evaluations are false, then to see ourselves as we are would be most painful, and this is the pain we suffer when we discover God's knowledge of ourselves. Even so, we may repudiate what pains us in ourselves by seeking forgiveness. To seek forgiveness is to seek our transformation in the light of the true and the good; and to seek is to find. For it is the sincere motive which determines the ultimate quality of a self, and the practice of sincerity in the examination of motives is the way to salvation.

Judging from the meager fragments which penetrate the thick resistance of our insensibility in the music we hear and in some of the persons we love, existence must blaze with beauty and loveliness. What can be compared with the prospect of appreciation and understanding which must seem, in comparison with what is available to us now, almost limitless? Can any hope compare with the hope of a life in which we are no longer bound by the physical limitations upon our awareness, where we no longer wait in anxiety for what the future will bring, where we are no longer at the mercy of every chance mishap, where our existence blooms into an actuality so full that the potential is no longer the darkness of the unknown?

"To realize the life eternal under the conditions of terrestial existence," Bowman says,

> is to realize that the life and death of the body are minor episodes in an experience which defines itself as the knowledge of God. . . . Upon the knowledge of God he concentrates all the powers of his nature, cognitive and active alike. As for life and death, he leaves these to a power beyond his own. And thus religion, which begins in a preoccupation with life, ends in a complete indifference to death.[9]

If this is our hope, what evidence have we of its soundness? The answer is that here we have gone beyond evidence, for this is truly a hope and not knowledge. But if God is self-existence, and if we have seen even dimly something of what is implied in God's self-existence and in the relation of His creation to Himself, then our hope is not entirely groundless. What our life ultimately may be, we do not know. But can it be *less* than this?

To live in this hope is to seek in every moment of our temporal life to understand each thing and to interpret each situation in the light of all we know and of all we appreciate. It is to remember constantly that in this we do reach out, in our limited and feeble way, toward God's own awareness. As we try to see ourselves and our concerns from God's perspective we discover something of God and of His presence in us. But more than this, we present ourselves to Him and so participate in the true worship of Him. The better I see God the further from Him I see myself to be, unless my awareness of God is not only His presence in me but my presence to Him and the sacrifice of my own perspective for His.

If man is made in the image of God his true blessedness is to fulfil the promise of his creation. It is for him to be bound to all things by love and truth. As he is so bound, he sees all things as they work together for good, and so he finds a true home for himself in real existence. If hate and falsehood are in his soul they separate him from real existence and drive him in hopeless search for what is worthless. Love and truth go together; neither survives its separation from the other. For in separation love is false and truth has lost its meaning. Whatever form it may take, the practice of high religion in the worship of the God Who Is opens our minds and hearts to His presence and makes us try to see ourselves—in deed and thought—as He sees us. Religious faith is first and foremost the confidence that if we seek Him we shall find Him, and that to see ourselves as He sees us is to make ourselves ready to stand in His presence.

In Conclusion

We have come to the end of a long reflection on the final themes of life and existence. We have tried to follow the argument where it would take us, and we have tried to do this so far as possible without preconceptions or premature finalities. The argument has turned out to be a statement of the case for theism as a philosophy. The statement is not final, nor would we claim it to be free of error and misunderstanding. Theism has its difficulties, perhaps, as a philosophy. Yet its difficulties seem fewer and less serious than those of other philosophies. If we can say of the truth that it is at least this, we leave the way open for advance in understanding.

The enemies of theism may assert the same claim of truth, but the advantage of theism is that it includes so much more, and its foundation in experience and reason is so much broader, than is the case with its rivals. As a philosophy theism differs from them in this important respect: It has room for everything that exists and it finds a place in existence for everything. It proceeds by affirmation, not negation. It does not have to dismiss as nonexistent whatever it does not understand, for its criterion of existence is not found in human understanding. In knowing the existence of that Being whose nature it cannot comprehend, theism alone renders intelligible the fact that we are confronted by mystery.

No one knows better than the theist how his best efforts can resolve only a little of what Morris Cohen called "the abysmal mystery of existence." But the theist does see the mystery, and he attacks it with his best intelligence. Positivism and naturalism, which today are among the more vocal of the anti-theistic philosophies, do not even see the mystery. Because they do not see it they cannot even consider the greatest themes of human thought and experience. The themes of life and death, of God and the world, of good and evil are the themes of great art and great literature. They are the issues for which men bleed and die. In its preoccupation with these, theism directs our thought to the very center of our existence. But positivism and naturalism cannot think on such things; for them the ultimate preoccupations of a life lived at maximum intensity are things which are mentioned only to be dismissed.

Theism, as a philosophy, begins and ends with a sense of our own finiteness. The nineteenth century positivist, on the contrary, was sure of everything. What he knew was certain, and what he did not know he was sure could not be known. Such cocky arrogance was made possible only by his ability to ignore the difficulties involved in any ultimate questioning. It never occurred to

Mill or Comte, nor has it occurred to their twentieth century off-spring, ever to stare at such a problem as that raised by Leibniz's question: Why is there something rather than nothing?

Shall we purchase clarity and finality at the cost of significance and relevance? Can we be satisfied to deal with the difficult problems only by turning our heads and passing by on the other side? Or by drawing arbitrary boundary lines and declaring meaningless all that falls outside those lines? If the world is what the positivist or the naturalist says it is, how can we take that world—and our life in it—seriously? But if existence is what the theist sees it to be, there is enough—and more—to fill all eternity.

Notes

Notes

CHAPTER I. RELIGION

1. *Endymion,* in *The Novels and Tales of Benjamin Disraeli* (The Bradenham Edition, Alfred A. Knopf, Inc., n. d.), Volume XII, p. 371.

2. "Strictly Personal" by Sydney J. Harris in the *Chicago Daily News,* July 31, 1952.

3. From *Puritanism and Democracy,* Copyright 1945 by Ralph Barton Perry. Published by The Vanguard Press, Inc., pp. 257–258.

4. Perry, *op. cit.,* p. 258.

5. Perry, *loc. cit.*

6. *The Individual and His Religion* by Gordon W. Allport (New York: The Macmillan Company, 1930), p. 56.

7. Allport, *op. cit.,* p. 25.

8. Allport, *op. cit.,* p. 26.

9. *Religion in the Making* by Alfred North Whitehead (New York: The Macmillan Company, 1926), p. 16.

10. Whitehead, *loc. cit.*

11. Allport, *op. cit.,* p. 22.

12. Allport, *op. cit.,* p. 23.

13. Allport, *op. cit.,* p. 142.

14. *Art* by Clive Bell (New York: Frederick A. Stokes Company, Fifth Edition, n. d.; London: Chatto and Windus, Ltd.), pp. 91–92.

15. *Time: The Refreshing River* by Joseph Needham (London: George Allen and Unwin, 1948; New York: The Macmillan Company), p. 57.

16. Professor Allport denies that such movements as Humanism, Communism, and Nazism are religions capable of satisfying the mature mind. *Op. cit.,* pp. 68–69. They still may be classed among the religions, however inadequate they may be as such, provided we use the word "religion" in the inclusive sense suggested in our present discussion.

17. "Crusades," by Ernest Barker, in the *Encyclopaedia Britannica* (1948), Volume VI, p. 772.

18. *Feuer und Blut* by Ernst Jünger, quoted from *European Witness* by Stephen Spender (Reynal and Hitchcock, 1946; New York: Harcourt, Brace and Company, Inc.), p. 206.

19. *The Heart of Emerson's Journals* edited by Bliss Perry (Boston: Houghton Mifflin Company, 1926), entry for June 13, 1852, pp. 259–260.

20. This contrast is noted in *Three Greek Plays* by Edith Hamilton (New York: W. W. Norton and Company, Inc., 1937), p. 23.

21. "Natural Pride and Natural Shame" by Arnold Isenberg, in *Philosophy and Phenomenological Research*, Volume X, p. 6.

22. "Proverbs of Hell" in *The Poetry and Prose of William Blake* (London: The Nonesuch Press, 1935; New York: Random House, Inc.), pp. 192–193.

23. *I Corinthians* (Revised Standard Version. New York: Thomas Nelson and Sons, 1946. Used by permission of The National Council of the Churches of Christ in the U.S.A.), Chapter 14, verse 20.

24. This will be discussed further in later chapters. See especially Chapter XXV, "The Reality of Value."

CHAPTER II. THE PHILOSOPHY OF RELIGION

1. *The Individual and His Religion* by Gordon W. Allport (New York: The Macmillan Company, 1930), p. 52. We shall consider this further in Chapter X, "Traditional and Modern Ideas of Man."

2. *The Dilemma of Religious Knowledge* by Charles A. Bennett (New Haven: Yale University Press, 1931), p. 120.

3. *The University and the Modern World* by Arnold S. Nash (New York: The Macmillan Company, 1944), p. 290.

4. "A Religion for Now," by Nathan M. Pusey, in *Harper's* for December 1953 (New York: Harper and Brothers), pp. 20–21.

5. *The Religious Revolt against Reason* by L. Harold DeWolf (New York: Harper and Brothers, 1949), p. 145.

6. *Beyond Realism and Idealism* by Wilbur Marshall Urban (London: George Allen and Unwin, 1949; New York: The Macmillan Company), p. 246. See also pp. 134–135. The same problem is discussed in *The Intelligible World* and in *Language and Reality*, both by the same author.

7. See the discussion of revelation and reason in Chapter XXIV, "The Revelation of God."

8. *Solitude and Society* by Nicolas Berdyaev (London: Geoffrey Bles, 1938), p. 18.

9. See Chapter VIII, "Religious Truth," and Chapter IX, "The Test of Religious Truth."

10. Berdyaev, *op. cit.*, p. 20.

11. Bennett, *op. cit.*, p. 17.

CHAPTER III. SENSORY KNOWLEDGE

1. *Existence and Analogy* by E. L. Mascall (New York: Longmans, Green and Company, Inc., 1949), p. 55.
2. *Op cit.*, p. 56, n. 1.
3. *Philosophical Aspects of Modern Science* by C. E. M. Joad (London: George Allen and Unwin, 1948; New York: The Macmillan Company), p. 81.
4. Joad, *op. cit.*, pp. 106-107.
5. See *Introduction to Realistic Philosophy* by John Wild (New York: Harper and Brothers, 1948), Chapter 18.

CHAPTER IV. RATIONAL KNOWLEDGE

1. *A Mathematician's Apology*, by G. H. Hardy (Cambridge University Press, 1940), p. 70.
2. *A Preface to Logic*, by Morris R. Cohen (New York: Henry Holt and Company, 1944), p. 42.
3. "Reply to Criticisms," by Bertrand Russell. *The Philosophy of Bertrand Russell* edited by Paul Arthur Schilpp (The Library of Living Philosophers, 1946. Third edition, The Tudor Publishing Company, New York, 1951), pp. 683-684.
4. *Intentional Logic* by Henry Babcock Veatch (New Haven: Yale University Press, 1952), p. 88.
5. *Introduction to Realistic Philosophy* by John Wild (New York: Harper and Brothers, 1948), p. 451.
6. Wild, *op. cit.*, pp. 451-452.

CHAPTER V. FAITH AND KNOWLEDGE

1. *The Mind and Heart of Love* by M. C. D'Arcy (New York: Henry Holt and Company, 1947), p. 168.
2. On the doctrine of the two-fold truth see *Christian Knowledge of God* by James Harry Cotton (New York: The Macmillan Company, 1951), pp. 10-11.
3. Cotton, *op. cit.*, p. 9.
4. D'Arcy, *op. cit.*, p. 167.
5. "A Religion for Now," by Nathan M. Pusey, in *Harper's* for December 1953 (New York: Harper and Brothers), p. 22.

6. "The Integrity of Pascal," by Charles Morgan in *Reflections in a Mirror*, First Series (New York: The Macmillan Company, 1945), p. 24.

7. Morgan, *op. cit.*, pp. 23–24.

8. *The Nature and Destiny of Man* by Reinhold Niebuhr (New York: Charles Scribner's Sons, 1943), Volume I. *Human Nature*, pp. 165–166.

9. "Moral and Religious Aphorisms," by Benjamin Whichcote. *The Cambridge Platonists* edited by E. T. Campagnac (Oxford: Clarendon Press, 1901), p. 67.

10. "The Inner Light" by Brand Blanshard, in *The Harvard Divinity School Bulletin* (Cambridge: Harvard University Press), Volume XLIII (1946), p. 63.

CHAPTER VI. THE NATURE OF TRUTH

1. *Sociology* by Kimball Young (New York: American Book Company, 1942), p. 498.

2. *Op. cit.*, p. 502.

3. *Op. cit.*, p. 503.

4. For a penetrating and illuminating discussion of Leibniz's conception of the relation of the actual and the possible, see "Decision and Existence" by Newton P. Stallknecht, in *The Review of Metaphysics*, Volume VI, pp. 31–44.

5. *The Republic of Plato* translated by F. M. Cornford (New York: Oxford University Press, Inc., 1945), p. 74.

6. *Metaphysics*, 993a 30–b 7. *The Basic Works of Aristotle* edited by Richard McKeon (New York: Random House, Inc., 1941), p. 712.

7. Aristotle, *op. cit.*, 1011b 26. *The Basic Works of Aristotle*, p. 749. See also Plato's *Sophist*, 262E–263D; translated in *Plato's Theory of Knowledge* by F. M. Cornford (Routledge and Kegan Paul, 1935), pp. 309–317.

8. We do not have to grant that our knowledge is relative and subjective. The point we are concerned with here is that even if we do go so far as to grant this, still "the relation of knowledge and object cannot be relative also."

9. *Philosophical Understanding and Religious Truth* by Erich Frank (New York: Oxford University Press, Inc., 1945), pp. 99–100.

10. The theory that thought creates its objects, or that the objects we know are ideas, will be considered in connection with our discussion of subjectivism in Chapter XVIII.

CHAPTER VII. PERSPECTIVES AND DIMENSIONS OF TRUTH

1. "An Examination of Critical Realism," by John Wild, in *Philosophy and Phenomenological Research*, Volume XIV, p. 154.
2. *Introduction to Realistic Philosophy* by John Wild (New York: Harper and Brothers, 1948), p. 501.
3. *Intentional Logic* by Henry Babcock Veatch (New Haven: Yale University Press, 1952), pp. 94–95.
4. *An Introduction to Logic* by H. W. B. Joseph (Oxford: Clarendon Press, Second Edition Revised, 1916), p. 149.
5. Joseph, *op. cit.*, p. 146.
6. *Basic Logic* by Raymond J. McCall (New York: Barnes and Noble, Inc., 1952), p. 30.
7. See McCall, *op. cit.*, pp. 31–32, for a concise summary of the supposition of terms.
8. See Veatch, *op. cit.*, pp. 193 *et seq.* See also p. 415, n. 17. Professor Veatch is not responsible for the application we have made here of his doctrine of designation.
9. Veatch, *op. cit.*, p. 195.
10. See the discussion in Chapter II of the unique position of philosophy as a mode of inquiry.

CHAPTER VIII. RELIGIOUS TRUTH

1. "What Is the Method of Naturalism?" by Thelma Z. Lavine. *Journal of Philosophy*, Volume 50, p. 159.
2. This will be discussed further in Chapter X, "Traditional and Modern Ideas of Man."
3. *An Interpretation of Christian Ethics* by Reinhold Niebuhr (New York: Harper and Brothers, 1935), p. 12.
4. *Reality* by B. H. Streeter (New York: The Macmillan Company, 1927), p. 46.
5. Streeter, *op. cit.*, p. 47.
6. "Creative Imagination," by Charles Morgan, in *Reflections in a Mirror*, Second Series (New York: The Macmillan Company, 1947), p. 91. This, the author says, is quoted from "an early book of mine."
7. On truth and symbol in religion see *My Host the World* by George Santayana (New York: Charles Scribner's Sons, 1953), p. 40.
8. *Liberty, Equality, Fraternity* by James Fitzjames Stephen (New York: Henry Holt and Company, 1882), pp. 297–298.

9. Some examples of Bertrand Russell's opinions may be found in his *Unpopular Essays.*

10. For an example of Dewey's usual attitude toward religion see his essay in *Naturalism and the Human Spirit,* edited by Yervant H. Krikorian.

CHAPTER IX. THE TEST OF RELIGIOUS TRUTH

Note: All references to the Bible are to the Revised Standard Version, published by Thomas Nelson and Sons, New York, 1946 (The New Testament) and 1952 (The Old Testament). Quotations are used by permission of the copyright owners, The National Council of the Churches of Christ in the U.S.A.

1. *Micah,* Chapter 6, verses 6–8.

2. *Matthew,* Chapter 5, verses 3–12.

3. *Colossians,* Chapter 3, verses 12–15. See also *II Corinthians,* Chapter 6, verses 4–7.

4. *I Corinthians,* Chapter 13.

5. *Galatians,* Chapter 5, verses 19–21.

6. See *II Corinthians,* Chapter 3, verse 5.

7. *Galatians,* Chapter 5, verses 22–23.

8. *Galatians,* Chapter 5, verses 25–26.

9. The doctrine of analogy will be discussed in Chapter XXIII, "Knowledge by Analogy."

10. *Romans,* Chapter 1, verse 20.

11. *A Preface to Morals* by Walter Lippmann (New York: The Macmillian Company, 1929), p. 8.

CHAPTER X. TRADITIONAL AND MODERN
IDEAS OF MAN

1. *Studies in the Philosophy of Religion* by Archibald Allan Bowman (London: Macmillan and Company, Ltd., 1938), Volume II, pp. 39–40. Used by permission of Mrs. A. A. Bowman, Macmillan and Company, Ltd., London, and St. Martin's Press, New York.

2. *Op. cit.,* Volume II, p. 40.

3. *Loc. cit.*

4. *Op. cit.,* Volume II, pp. 40–41.

5. *Op. cit.,* Volume II, p. 42.

6. *On the Soul* by Aristotle, 411a 8. *Basic Works of Aristotle* edited by Richard McKeon (New York: Random House, Inc., 1941), p. 553.

7. Bowman, *op. cit.*, Volume II, p. 43.

8. See *I Kings*, Chapter 19.

9. Bowman, *op. cit.*, Volume II, pp. 44–45.

10. Bowman, *op. cit.*, Volume II, p. 45.

11. Bowman, *op. cit.*, Volume II, p. 57.

12. *Science and the Modern World* by Alfred North Whitehead (New York: The Macmillan Company, 1926), pp. 18–19.

13. Whitehead, *op. cit.*, pp. 23–24.

14. Whitehead, *op. cit.*, pp. 75–76.

15. Bowman, *op. cit.*, Volume II, p. 52.

16. *Philosophical Understanding and Religious Truth* by Erich Frank (New York: Oxford University Press, Inc., 1945), pp. 4–5.

17. Frank, *op. cit.*, p. 6.

18. See Santayana's comment on this in *Winds of Doctrine* (New York: Charles Scribner's Sons, 1940), pp. 25–26.

19. Frank, *op. cit.*, p. 17.

20. *Beethoven, His Spiritual Development* by J. W. N. Sullivan (The New American Library, 1949; quoted by permission of Alfred A. Knopf, Inc.), p. 18. See also *The Limitations of Science* by the same author.

21. Whitehead, *op. cit.*, p. 80.

22. Whitehead, *op. cit.*, p. 265.

23. Whitehead, *loc. cit.*

CHAPTER XI. MAN'S EXISTENCE

1. *Prolegomena to Ethics* by Thomas Hill Green (Oxford: Clarendon Press, Fifth Edition, 1906), p. 21.

2. *Op. cit.*, p. 23. To recognize the force of Green's argument here does not commit us to the philosophical idealism which appears at a later stage of his argument; for one of the essential premises of his idealism is his theory of sensation, a theory that does not concern us here.

3. *Op. cit.*, p. 14.

4. "The Present Relevance of Catholic Theology" by John Wild, in *Christianity and Reason* edited by Edward D. Myers (New York: Oxford University Press, Inc., 1951), p. 27.

5. *The Liberal Tradition* by William Aylott Orton (New Haven: Yale University Press, 1945), p. 209.

6. *A Modern Introduction to Ethics* by Lucius Garvin (Boston: Houghton Mifflin Company, 1953), p. 96.

7. The distinction between real and logical relations will be discussed in greater detail in Chapter XIV, "Pantheism," and in Chapter XXIII, "Knowledge by Analogy."

8. Orton, *op. cit.*, p. 51.

9. See *Studies in the Philosophy of Religion* by Archibald Allan Bowman (London: Macmillan and Company, Ltd., 1938), Volume II, p. 330.

10. See Chapter I of *Philosophical Understanding and Religious Truth* by Erich Frank. This chapter should be read in its entirety.

11. *Three Greek Plays* by Edith Hamilton (New York: W. W. Norton and Company, Inc., 1937), p. 153.

CHAPTER XII. MAN AS PERSON

1. See *Christian Knowledge of God* by James Harry Cotton (New York: The Macmillan Company, 1951), pp. 97–98.

2. *The Mind and Heart of Love* by M. C. D'Arcy (New York: Henry Holt and Company, 1947), pp. 156–157.

3. *The Meaning of Treason* by Rebecca West (New York: The Viking Press, Inc., 1947), p. 143.

4. "On Being Born Now" by Charles Morgan, in *Reflections in a Mirror*, First Series (New York: The Macmillan Company, 1945), p. 9.

5. *The Dilemma of Religious Knowledge* by Charles A. Bennett (New Haven: Yale University Press, 1931), pp. 118–119.

6. Bennett, *op. cit.*, p. 119.

7. *Job* (Revised Standard Version. New York: Thomas Nelson and Sons, 1952. Used by permission of The National Council of the Churches of Christ in the U.S.A.), Chapter 42, verses 5–6.

8. *Dogmatism and Tolerance* by Étienne Gilson (New Brunswick: Rutgers University Press, 1952), p. 11.

9. This is Edith Hamilton's rendering of *Nicomachean Ethics* 1177b 26 in her *Witness to the Truth* (New York: W. W. Norton and Company, Inc., 1948), pp. 38–39. See also *The Basic Works of Aristotle* edited by Richard McKeon (New York: Random House, Inc., 1941), p. 1105.

10. *I Corinthians* (Revised Standard Version), Chapter 2, verses 10–12.

11. *God in Us* by A. Campbell Garnett (Chicago: Willett, Clark and Company, 1945; New York: Harper and Brothers), p. 43.

12. *Nature, Man and God* by William Temple (London: Macmillan and Company, Ltd., 1951), p. 266. Used by permission of Mrs.

William Temple, Macmillan and Company, Ltd., London, and St. Martin's Press, Inc., New York.

13. *The Revelation of Deity* by J. E. Turner (New York: The Macmillan Company, 1931), pp. 181–182.

14. On this see Temple, *op. cit.*, p. 411.

15. See *Philosophical Understanding and Religious Truth* by Erich Frank, pp. 41–43, for an important comment on the relation of subjective faith to objective knowledge. For a summary of the views of some contemporary theologians who attack reason in the interests of faith see Cotton, *op. cit.*, pp. 5–8. For an extensive and yet non-technical study of this problem as it appears in contemporary religious thought see L. Harold DeWolf's *The Religious Revolt against Reason.*

CHAPTER XIII. THE IDEA OF GOD AND NATURALISM

1. *Timaeus* 29D–30C. Translated by Francis M. Cornford in *Plato's Cosmology* (New York: The Humanities Press, 1948), pp. 33–34. There will be further comment on this later in the chapter.

2. That is, the Sun is not the same thing as the existence it gives to the things we see.

3. *The Republic of Plato*, vi, 508–509. Francis M. Cornford's translation (New York: Oxford University Press, Inc., 1945), p. 220.

4. "Naturalism and Religion" by Sterling P. Lamprecht, in *Naturalism and the Human Spirit* edited by Yervant H. Krikorian (New York: Columbia University Press, 1944), p. 18.

5. *A Common Faith* by John Dewey (New Haven: Yale University Press, 1934), p. 42.

6. Dewey, *op. cit.*, p. 50.

7. Dewey, *op. cit.*, p. 42.

8. Dewey, *loc. cit.*

9. Dewey, *op. cit.*, p. 43.

10. Dewey, *op. cit.*, p. 50.

11. Dewey, *op. cit.*, p. 43.

12. Dewey, *op. cit.*, pp. 47–48.

13. Dewey, *op. cit.*, p. 42.

14. Dewey, *op. cit.*, pp. 53–54.

15. Dewey, *op. cit.*, pp. 51–52.

16. *The Individual and His Religion* by Gordon W. Allport (New York: The Macmillan Company, 1930), p. 68.

17. A view somewhat like Dewey's is that of Henry Nelson Wie-

man, who finds God in the "creative event" in nature and history. See his *Source of Human Good*. Professor Cotton comments that "Wieman writes with a much clearer appreciation of the inner meaning of Christian experience than does Dewey, who has the air of a novice when he writes about religion." *Christian Knowledge of God* by James Harry Cotton (New York: The Macmillan Company, 1951), p. 59.

18. *The Dilemma of Religious Knowledge* by Charles A. Bennett (New Haven: Yale University Press, 1931), p. 49.

19. *Liberty, Equality, Fraternity* by James Fitzjames Stephen (New York: Henry Holt and Company, 1882), p. 291.

CHAPTER XIV. PANTHEISM

1. "Pantheism" by A. E. Garvie, in *Encyclopaedia of Religion and Ethics* edited by James Hastings (New York: Charles Scribner's Sons, 1917), Volume IX, p. 609.

2. *The Natural and the Supernatural* by John Oman (Cambridge: At the University Press, 1931), p. 369.

3. Oman, *op. cit.*, p. 368.

4. Garvie, *loc. cit.*

5. Oman, *op. cit.*, p. 369.

6. Oman, *op. cit.*, pp. 410–411.

7. The reference here is to the Upanishads, where the name of the One is Brahma.

8. Oman, *op. cit.*, p. 416.

9. Oman, *op. cit.*, p. 417. See also *Revelation and Response* by Edgar P. Dickie, pp. 232–233.

10. Garvie, *loc. cit.*

11. *Religion in Human Experience* by John R. Everett (New York: Henry Holt and Company, 1950), pp. 124–125.

12. See above, pp.

13. Any adequate discussion of Spinoza's philosophy must take account of this problem, in connection especially with the relation of "modes" to the "attributes" and "substance," and the problem of the plurality of the attributes. See Edward Caird's *The Critical Philosophy of Immanuel Kant*, Volume I, Chapter III; *A Study of the Ethics of Spinoza* by H. H. Joachim; *Philosophy of Spinoza* by Richard McKeon; and *The Philosophy of Spinoza* by H. A. Wolfson.

14. See *Intentional Logic* by Henry Babcock Veatch, especially pp. 22–27.

CHAPTER XV. DEISM AND THEISM

1. *He Who Is* by E. L. Mascall (New York: Longmans, Green and Company, Inc., 1948), p. 127.

2. *Op. cit.*, p. 128.

3. *Dryden* edited by W. D. Christie (Oxford: Clarendon Press, 1901), p. 132, lines 44-61.

4. *The Natural and the Supernatural* by John Oman (Cambridge: At the University Press, 1931), pp. 25-26.

5. *God and Philosophy* by Étienne Gilson (New Haven: Yale University Press, 1941), p. 104.

6. Nominalism is the view that all real existence is reducible to a plurality of units (or particulars) which have nothing in common with each other and which are thus impervious to rational thought and knowledge.

7. *The Revelation of Deity* by J. E. Turner (New York: The Macmillan Company, 1951), p. 19.

8. Nicolaus Cusanus shows in his doctrine of the "coincidence of contradictories" the consequence of denying the intelligibility of real existence. For his application of this doctrine to God see *The Vision of God* by Nicolaus Cusanus, translated by Emma Gurney-Salter (London: J. M. Dent and Sons, Ltd., 1928), especially pp. 43-44.

9. From *Religion as Experience and Truth* by Warren Nelson Nevius, pp. 313-314. Copyright 1941 by The Westminster Press. Used by permission.

10. On analogy see especially *Existence and Analogy* by E. L. Mascall, Chapter V, and *He Who Is*, Chapter VIII. Our discussion of analogy at this point is of necessity incomplete; yet it is necessary to introduce here the distinction between univocal, equivocal, and analogous concepts if we are to understand the significant distinctions between pantheism, deism, and theism. Since the distinctions between univocal, equivocal, and analogous concepts pertain to our way of knowing God it will be advisable to postpone further discussion of them until later. The whole of Chapter XXIII, "Knowledge by Analogy" is devoted to this problem.

CHAPTER XVI. PROOF IN PHILOSOPHY

1. Chapter II, "The Philosophy of Religion." See section on "The Unique Position of Philosophy as a Mode of Inquiry."

2. *Il Saggiatore* by Galileo Galilei, translated and quoted by Edwin Arthur Burtt in *The Metaphysical Foundations of Modern Physical Science* (New York: The Humanities Press, Inc., 1925), p. 75.

3. *Beyond Realism and Idealism* by Wilbur Marshall Urban (London: George Allen and Unwin, 1949; New York: The Macmillan Company), p. 123.

4. A careful study of Plato's method of dialectic will be found in *Plato's Early Dialectic* by Richard Robinson (Cornell University Press, 1941. New Edition, Oxford: The Clarendon Press, 1953). Robinson argues that not only was the word "dialectic" invented by Socrates or Plato but that the method itself was discovered by Plato. He rejects the view that dialectic goes back to Zeno. See pages 95–96.

5. Robinson, *op. cit.*, pp. 233–234.

6. Robinson, *op. cit.*, p. 179. See also F. M. Cornford's explanation in *The Republic of Plato*, pp. 223, 250–251.

7. *The Republic of Plato*, Francis M. Cornford's translation (New York: Oxford University Press, Inc., 1945), p. 226.

8. See the discussion of rational insight, above, Chapter IV, "Rational Knowledge."

9. See Wilbur Marshall Urban's discussion of the principle of self-refutation in *The Intelligible World*, pp. 42–46. Note especially the part which concerns the relation of dialectic and formal logic, p. 45. See also his *Beyond Realism and Idealism*, pp. 125–132.

CHAPTER XVII. GOD IN IDEA AND GOD IN EXISTENCE

1. *Proslogium*, Chapter II. In *St. Anselm: Proslogium; Monologium; An Appendix in Behalf of the Fool by Gaunilon; and Cur Deus Homo*, translated by Sidney Norton Deane (La Salle: Open Court Publishing Company, 1910), pp. 7–8.

2. See above, Chapter VII, "Perspectives and Dimensions of Truth," especially the section on the extension, supposition, and designation of terms.

3. *Being and Some Philosophers* by Étienne Gilson (Toronto: Pontifical Institute of Mediaeval Studies, 1949), p. 3.

4. Gilson, *op. cit.*, p. 4.

5. On this see *Immanuel Kant's Critique of Pure Reason* translated by Norman Kemp Smith, pp. 505–506.

6. See Kant, *op. cit.*, pp. 504–505.

7. *Meditations on the First Philosophy*, III. *Of God: that he exists*. In *A Discourse on Method, etc.* by René Descartes, translated by John

Veitch (Everyman's Library edition. New York: E. P. Dutton and Company, Inc., 1927), p. 104. The square brackets indicate additions to the original of the revised French translation.

8. *The Spirit of Mediaeval Philosophy* by Étienne Gilson (New York: Charles Scribner's Sons, 1940), p. 60.

CHAPTER XVIII. THE EXISTENCE OF THE WORLD

1. Chapter XIV, "Pantheism."

2. *Benjamin Franklin and Jonathan Edwards; Selections from Their Writings* edited with an Introduction by Carl Van Doren (New York: Charles Scribner's Sons, 1920), p. 222.

3. *Intentional Logic* by Henry Babcock Veatch (New Haven: Yale University Press, 1952), p. 104. Professor Veatch speaks here of the "analogy" of being rather than of the "realm" of being. The doctrine of analogy will be considered below, in Chapter XXIII, "Knowledge by Analogy."

4. "Phenomenology and Metaphysics" by John Wild, in *The Return to Reason*, edited by John Wild (Chicago: Henry Regnery Company, 1953), p. 41. See also "Realism and Phenomenology" by Harmon M. Chapman, *op. cit.*, p. 26.

5. *Timaeus* 52C. In *Plato's Cosmology* by Francis M. Cornford (New York: The Humanities Press, Inc., 1948), pp. 192–193. In his discussion of this passage Cornford calls attention also to Plato's statement in the *Sophist* (240B) that "image" *(eidolon)* is defined as "that which has some sort of existence, but not real being." *Op. cit.*, p. 194.

6. *A Treatise Concerning the Principles of Human Knowledge*, Part I, Section VI. In *A New Theory of Vision and Other Select Philosophical Writings* by George Berkeley, Bishop of Cloyne (Everyman's Library edition. New York: E. P. Dutton and Company, Inc., 1910), pp. 115–116.

7. Generally speaking, ideas are regarded by subjectivists as "states of mind," and as "mental acts" by realists.

8. *Experience and Prediction* by Hans Reichenbach (Chicago: The University of Chicago Press, 1938), p. 164.

9. "An Examination of Critical Realism" by John Wild, in *Philosophy and Phenomenological Research*, Volume XIV, pp. 159–160.

10. Chapman, *op. cit.*, p. 12.

11. Chapman, *op. cit.*, pp. 23–24.

12. This phrase is borrowed from Samuel Alexander who says, referring to Locke's theory of ideas, that Locke assigned "to ideas a

twilight existence between the things they represent and the mind which understands them." *Locke* by Samuel Alexander (Archibald Constable and Company, 1908), p. 32.

13. *Philosophical Aspects of Modern Science* by C. E. M. Joad (London: George Allen and Unwin, 1948; New York: The Macmillan Company), pp. 115–116.

CHAPTER XIX. THE CONTINGENCY OF THE WORLD

1. "An Examination of Critical Realism" by John Wild, in *Philosophy and Phenomenological Research*, Volume XIV, p. 155.

2. See Chapter III, "Sensory Knowledge," with special attention to the section on sense perception and modern science.

3. *The Dialogues of Alfred North Whitehead* as recorded by Lucien Price (Boston: Little, Brown and Company, 1954), pp. 213–214.

4. Whitehead, *op. cit.*, p. 330.

5. See *Introduction to Realistic Philosophy* by John Wild (New York: Harper and Brothers, 1948), p. 343.

6. *The Meaning of Philosophy* by Joseph Gerard Brennan (New York: Harper and Brothers, 1953), pp. 267–268.

7. Brennan, *op. cit.*, p. 267.

CHAPTER XX. THE CAUSE OF NATURE

1. "Naturalism and Religion" by Sterling P. Lamprecht, in *Naturalism and the Human Spirit* edited by Yervant H. Kirkorian (New York: Columbia University Press, 1944), p. 34.

2. *Op. cit.*, p. 35.

3. *Loc. cit.*

4. From *Causality and Implication* by D. J. B. Hawkins, published by Sheed and Ward, Inc., New York (1937), p. 88.

5. Hawkins, *op. cit.*, p. 99.

6. *Being and Some Philosophers* by Étienne Gilson (Toronto: Pontifical Institute of Mediaeval Studies, 1949), p. 100.

7. *He Who Is* by E. L. Mascall (New York: Longmans, Green and Company, Inc., 1948), p. 45.

8. *Existence and Analogy* by E. L. Mascall (New York: Longmans, Green and Company, Inc., 1949), p. 9.

9. *The Meaning of Philosophy* by Joseph Gerard Brennan (New York: Harper and Brothers, 1953), p. 267.

10. *Immanuel Kant's Critique of Pure Reason* translated by Norman Kemp Smith (London: Macmillan and Company, Ltd., 1929), pp. 509–510.

11. Gilson, *op. cit.*, p. 183.

12. Gilson, *op. cit.*, p. 40.

13. See Kant's "Table of Categories," *op. cit.*, p. 113.

CHAPTER XXI. THE EXISTENCE OF GOD

1. See Chapter XIII, "The Idea of God and Naturalism."

2. Chapter XV. "Deism and Theism."

3. Chapter XV. See the section, "Theism and the Analogy of Being."

4. *Mysticism and Logic* by Bertrand Russell (New York: W. W. Norton and Company, Inc., 1929), p. 129. Leibniz makes a comment, which may be something of a surprise to some, that the continuous "cannot be composed of points." See *Leibniz* by H. W. Carr (Boston: Little, Brown and Company, 1929), p. 78. Thus you may *assign* as many points as you please to a line, but there are no points on a line.

5. Chapter XIX, "The Contingency of the World." See the section on the contingency of the world as a whole.

6. Quoted in *The Unity of Philosophical Experience* by Étienne Gilson (New York: Charles Scribner's Sons, 1941), p. 43.

7. *Process and Reality* by Alfred North Whitehead (New York: The Macmillan Company, 1929), p. 500.

8. On the theistic interpretation of God as personal, see *Religion as Experience and Truth* by Warren Nelson Nevius, pp. 313–319.

9. From *Causality and Implication* by D. J. B. Hawkins, published by Sheed and Ward, Inc., New York (1937), p. 104.

10. *The Motion of the Heart and Blood* by William Harvey (Chicago: Henry Regnery Company, 1949), p. 105. See *Science and the Modern World*, pp. 90–91, where Whitehead points out that Marpertuis' discovery of the theorem of least action was the result of inquiry motivated by a theological belief.

CHAPTER XXII. THE LIKENESS OF GOD

1. Chapter XVIII, "The Existence of the World."

2. See Chapter III, "Sensory Knowledge," and Chapter IV, "Rational Knowledge."

3. *Existence and Analogy* by E. L. Mascall (New York: Longmans, Green and Company, Inc., 1949), p. 118.

4. See *Being and Some Philosophers* by Étienne Gilson, p. 207; and *Intentional Logic* by Henry Babcock Veatch, p. 88.

5. *God and Philosophy* by Étienne Gilson (New Haven: Yale University Press, 1941), p. 103.

6. Mascall, *op. cit.*, p. 81.

7. From "A Second Childhood." Reprinted by permission of Dodd, Mead and Company from *Collected Poems of G. K. Chesterton.* Copyright 1932 by Dodd, Mead and Company, Inc. Page 76.

8. Mascall, *op. cit.*, p. 85. See also p. 122.

9. *Process and Reality* by Alfred North Whitehead (New York: The Macmillan Company, 1929), p. 531.

10. *The Individual and His Religion* by Gordon W. Allport (New York: The Macmillan Company, 1930), p. 10.

11. Mascall, *op. cit.*, pp. 123–124.

CHAPTER XXIII. KNOWLEDGE BY ANALOGY

1. *Intentional Logic* by Henry Babcock Veatch (New Haven: Yale University Press, 1952), p. 84.

2. *Existence and Analogy* by E. L. Mascall (New York: Longmans, Green and Company, Inc., 1949), p. 48.

3. Veatch, *loc. cit.*

4. Veatch, *op. cit.*, p. 155.

5. Chapter XV, "Deism and Theism," section on the relation of theism to pantheism and deism.

6. See Mascall, *op. cit.*, pp. 109–110.

7. On the "transcendentals" see Mascall, *op. cit.*, pp. 98–100; *Introduction to Realistic Philosophy* by John Wild, pp. 7–8, 18, 26, 476–477. An extensive elementary exposition will be found in *The Philosophy of Being* by Henri Renard, pp. 163–187.

8. Mascall, *op. cit.*, p. 120.

CHAPTER XXIV. THE REVELATION OF GOD

1. "Revelation" by M. Kahler, in *The New Schaff-Herzog Encyclopedia of Religious Knowledge* (New York: Funk and Wagnalls Company, 1911), Volume X, p. 3.

2. *Nature, Man and God* by William Temple (London: Macmillan and Company, Ltd., 1951), p. 306. Used by permission of Mrs. Wil-

liam Temple, Macmillan and Company, Ltd., London, and St. Martin's Press, Inc., New York.

3. Temple, *op. cit.*, p. 312.

4. Temple, *op. cit.*, pp. 315.

5. *Nein!* by Karl Barth. Translated and quoted by James Harry Cotton in his *Christian Knowledge of God* (New York: The Macmillan Company, 1951), p. 77. Translated also by Peter Fraenkel in *Natural Theology* (London: Geoffrey Bles, Ltd., The Centenary Press, 1946).

6. *Credo* by Karl Barth (London: Hodder and Stoughton, 1936), p. 183.

7. Barth, *Credo*, p. 184.

8. Barth, *Credo*, p. 185.

9. Barth, *Credo*, pp. 185–186.

10. See Temple's answer to Barth, *op. cit.*, p. 396.

11. *Essay concerning Human Understanding* by John Locke, edited by A. C. Fraser (Oxford: Clarendon Press, 1894), Book IV, Chapter XIX, Section 14, in Volume II, pp. 438–439.

12. Chapter VII, "Perspectives and Dimensions of Truth."

13. See "True" and "Truth" in *The Oxford English Dictionary* (Oxford: Clarendon Press, 1933), Volume XI.

14. See Chapter III, "Sensory Knowledge," and Chapter XVIII, "The Existence of the World."

15. Letter of March 25, 1775, quoted in *George Washington, A Biography* by Douglas Southall Freeman (New York: Charles Scribner's Sons, 1951), Volume III, p. 407.

16. Freeman, *loc. cit.*

17. Temple, *op. cit.*, pp. 321–322.

CHAPTER XXV. THE REALITY OF VALUE

1. *Saint Thomas and the Problem of Evil* by Jacques Maritain (Milwaukee: Marquette University Press, 1942), p. 38.

2. *Beyond Realism and Idealism* by Wilbur Marshall Urban (London: George Allen and Unwin, 1949; New York: The Macmillan Company), p. 248.

3. *Science and the Modern World* by Alfred North Whitehead (New York: The Macmillan Company, 1926), pp. 71–72.

4. Whitehead, *op. cit.*, pp. 72–73.

5. Whitehead, *op. cit.*, p. 73.

6. Whitehead, *op. cit.*, pp. 76–80.

7. *Experience and Nature* by John Dewey (LaSalle: Open Court Publishing Company, 1925), p. 399.

8. "Social Science and the Humanists" by Bernard Rosenberg, in *The American Scholar*, Volume 22, pp. 206–207.

9. See Chapter XIV, "Pantheism."

10. "Creative Imagination" by Charles Morgan, in *Reflections in a Mirror*, Second Series (New York: The Macmillan Company, 1947), p. 95.

11. *Rasselas*, Chapter XLVIII, in Samuel Johnson's *Works* (New York: George Dearborn, 1835), Volume I, p. 489.

12. Cf. Plato's Demiurge in the *Timaeus*. See also *Introduction to the Philosophy of Religion* by Peter Anthony Bertocci, pp. 408–418; *The Problem of God* by Edgar S. Brightman, Chapters V, VII; and *A Philosophy of Religion* by Edgar S. Brightman, Chapters VIII–X.

13. *L' Idée de création* by A. D. Sertillanges, quoted by E. L. Mascall in *Existence and Analogy* (New York: Longmans, Green and Company, Inc., 1949), p. 147.

14. *Ex pede Herculem*, sermon at Paul's Cross, November 21, 1624, by Robert Sanderson. Quoted by E. L. Mascall in *He Who Is* (New York: Longmans, Green and Company, Inc., 1948), p. 63, n. 2.

15. This argument was brought into prominence by Kant, and has been stressed by the idealists. See *Moral Values and the Idea of God* by W. R. Sorley, pp. 331–332, for a discussion of the relation of the moral and cosmological arguments.

16. *Christian Knowledge of God* by James Harry Cotton (New York: The Macmillan Company, 1951), pp. 69–70.

CHAPTER XXVI. CREATION AND TIME

1. See above, Chapter XIII, "The Idea of God and Naturalism," the section on "Intelligibility and Unity."

2. *Timaeus*, 30A. *Plato's Cosmology* by F. M. Cornford (New York: The Humanities Press, 1948), p. 33.

3. *Philosophical Understanding and Religious Truth* by Erich Frank (New York: Oxford University Press, Inc., 1945), p. 75, n. 10.

4. "Creation" by J. Strachan, in *Encyclopaedia of Religion and Ethics* edited by James Hastings (New York: Charles Scribner's Sons, 1912), Volume IV, p. 229. See also *Studies in Christian Philosophy* by W. R. Matthews (London: Macmillan and Company, Ltd., 1941), p. 194: "The explicit affirmation of an absolute creation is not to be found in the Old Testament."

5. "Genesis: Exegesis" by Cuthbert A. Simpson, in *The Interpreter's Bible* (New York: Abingdon, 1952), Volume I, pp. 467–468.

6. See *Philo* by Harry Austryn Wolfson (Cambridge: Harvard University Press, 1948), Volume I, pp. 303–310. Wolfson himself says, concerning the Genesis story, "that there is no suggestion in it of creation out of nothing" (p. 302). Nevius states that "the dogma of creation *ex nihilo* is probably first met with in Christian theology, where it represents the repudiation of dualism, on the one hand, and of all forms of emanation theory on the other. It was not a Greek conception, nor is it affirmed altogether beyond equivocation even in the Old Testament." From *Religion as Experience and Truth* by Warren Nelson Nevius (The Westminster Press, 1941), p. 321. Copyright 1941 by The Westminster Press. Used by permission.

7. One of the most explicit expressions of this is found in the philosophy of Malebranche.

8. *Religion in the Making* by Alfred North Whitehead (New York: The Macmillan Company, 1926), p. 153. Compare Whitehead's later development of his distinction between the "primordial" and "consequent" natures of God in *Process and Reality*, pp. 519–533.

9. See Chapter XXV, especially the sections on "The Infinity of God" and "The Analogy of Perfection."

10. "Nature, Mind and Death" by Raphael Demos, in *The Review of Metaphysics*, Volume VI, p. 574.

11. See Chapter VII, the section on "The Extension, Supposition, and Designation of Terms."

12. *Introduction to Realistic Philosophy* by John Wild (New York: Harper and Brothers, 1948), p. 384.

13. *Existence and Analogy* by E. L. Mascall (New York: Longmans, Green and Company, Inc., 1949), p. 125.

14. For a careful analysis of the implications of this experiment and its possible interpretations, see *Scientific Thought* by C. D. Broad, pp. 119–154.

15. Wild, *op. cit.*, p. 343.

16. This may recall our earlier argument that the contingency of the world is implied by its temporal character, and that the mark of contingency is change. See Chapter XIX, "The Contingency of the World."

17. Frank, *op. cit.*, p. 59.

18. *Confessions*, Book XI, Section 26. Translation used in "Theories of Time in Ancient Philosophy" by Catherine Rau, *Philosophical Review*, Volume 62 (October 1953), p. 523. See also "Greek and Christian Views of Time" by Robert E. Cushman, *The Journal of Religion*,

Volume 33, pp. 254–265; and "Time and Eternity in Biblical Thought" by Eric C. Rust, in *Theology Today*, Volume 10, pp. 327–356.

19. *He Who Is* by E. L. Mascall (New York: Longmans, Green and Company, Inc., 1948), p. 119.

CHAPTER XXVII. HISTORY AND HUMAN DESTINY

1. *Philosophical Understanding and Religious Truth* by Erich Frank (New York: Oxford University Press, Inc., 1945), pp. 70–71.

2. *Adventures of Ideas* by Alfred North Whitehead (New York: The Macmillan Company, 1933), p. 41.

3. *Force and Freedom* by Jacob Burckhardt (New York: Pantheon Books, Inc., 1943), pp. 358–359.

4. *The Decay and Restoration of Civilization*, Part I of *The Philosophy of Civilization* (London: A. and C. Black, 1923; New York: The Macmillan Company), Preface, p. x.

5. *The Stoic and Epicurean Philosophers* edited by Whitney J. Oates (New York: Random House, Inc., 1940), p. 483.

6. *The Belief in Progress* by John Baillie (New York: Charles Scribner's Sons, 1951), pp. 57–58.

7. Baillie, *op. cit.*, p. 65.

8. Baillie, *op. cit.*, p. 66. See also the very important discussion of this point by Frank, *op. cit.*, pp. 68–70.

9. For a summary of the mediaeval controversy concerning which is prior, will or intellect, see W. Windelband, *A History of Philosophy*, pp. 328–337.

10. See, for example, the writings of Jean-Paul Sartre.

11. Schweitzer, *op. cit.*, p. 60.

12. See *Philosophical Theory of the State* by Bernard Bosanquet, pp. 177–187.

13. *The Mind and Heart of Love* by M. C. D'Arcy (New York: Henry Holt and Company, 1947), p. 91.

14. *Faith and History* by Reinhold Niebuhr (New York: Charles Scribner's Sons, 1949), pp. 26–27.

CHAPTER XXVIII. THE PROBLEM OF EVIL

1. The formless matter which Plato's Demiurge uses is an instance of such a conception. A recent example of the recognition of a primitive irrational "given" in existence which limits the Creator's activity

is found in the writings of Edgar S. Brightman, especially his *Philosophy of Religion*. A sympathetic discussion of Brightman's position will be found in *Introduction to the Philosophy of Religion* by Peter Anthony Bertocci, especially pp. 430–440.

2. See Chapter XXV, "The Reality of Value."

3. *The World and God* by H. H. Farmer (New York: Harper and Brothers, 1935), pp. 193–195.

4. *The Free Choice of the Will* by Saint Augustine; Latin Text with English Translation by Francis E. Tourscher (Philadelphia: The Peter Reilly Company, 1937), Book III, Chapter 18, pp. 361–363.

5. *Romans* (Revised Standard Version. New York: Thomas Nelson and Sons, 1946. Used by permission of The National Council of the Churches of Christ in the U.S.A.), Chapter 3, verse 20.

6. *Romans*, Chapter 5, verse 13.

7. *Romans*, Chapter 5, verse 20.

8. *Romans*, Chapter 4, verse 15.

9. *Romans*, Chapter 7, verse 7.

10. See Chapter XXV, "The Reality of Value."

11. *The Degrees of Knowledge* by Jacques Maritain (New York: Charles Scribner's Sons, 1938), p. 132.

12. Chapter XXV, "The Reality of Value." See the section on the infinity of God.

13. *Introduction to Realistic Philosophy* by John Wild (New York: Harper and Brothers, 1948), p. 385.

14. Wild, *loc. cit.*

15. *Nature, Man and God* by William Temple (London: Macmillan and Company, Ltd., 1951), p. 399. Used by permission of Mrs. William Temple, Macmillan and Company, Ltd., London, and St. Martin's Press, Inc., New York.

16. *Adventures of Ideas* by Alfred North Whitehead (New York: The Macmillan Company, 1933), p. 105.

17. See reference to this in "The General Practitioner and the Specialist" by Charles P. Curtis, in *Conference on the Profession of Law and Legal Education* (The Law School, The University of Chicago Conference Series, Number 11), p. 6.

18. See Temple, *op. cit.*, pp. 399–400.

19. *The Enchiridion*, Chapter XCVI. *Basic Writings of Saint Augustine* edited by Whitney J. Oates (New York: Random House, Inc., 1948), Volume I, p. 713.

20. *Summa Theologica*, I, Q. 19, Art. 9. *Basic Writings of Saint Thomas Aquinas* edited by Anton C. Pegis (New York: Random House, Inc., 1945), Volume I, p. 210.

21. Thomas, *op. cit.*, pp. 209–210.

22. *Force and Freedom* by Jacob Burckhardt (New York: Pantheon Books, Inc., 1943), p. 363.

23. Reprinted from *The Prophet* by Kahlil Gibran with permission of the publisher, Alfred A. Knopf, Inc. Copyright 1923 by Kahlil Gibran; renewal copyright 1951 by Administrators C. T. A. of Kahlil Gibran Estate, and Mary G. Gibran. Page 35.

24. *Agamemnon*, translated by Edith Hamilton in *Three Greek Plays* (New York: W. W. Norton and Company, Inc., 1937), pp. 169–170.

25. Aeschylus, *op. cit.*, p. 173.

26. *Religion in the Making*, by Alfred North Whitehead (New York: The Macmillan Company, 1926), p. 155.

CHAPTER XXIX. HUMAN BLESSEDNESS

1. *The Natural and the Supernatural* by John Oman (Cambridge: At the University Press, 1931), p. 461.

2. See Chapter XXVI, "Creation and Time," especially the section, "God and Time."

3. *Op. cit.*, pp. 462–463.

4. *Prometheus Bound*, translated by Edith Hamilton in *Three Greek Plays* (New York: W. W. Norton and Company, Inc., 1937), p. 105.

5. Reprinted from *The Prophet* by Kahlil Gibran with permission of the publisher, Alfred A. Knopf, Inc. Copyright 1923 by Kahlil Gibran; renewal copyright 1951 by Administrators C. T. A. of Kahlil Gibran Estate, and Mary G. Gibran. Page 23.

6. *Ecclesiastes* (Revised Standard Version. New York: Thomas Nelson and Sons, 1952. Used by permission of The National Council of the Churches of Christ in the U.S.A.), Chapter 1, verses 3–11.

7. *God in Us* by A. Campbell Garnett (Chicago: Willett, Clark and Company, 1945; New York: Harper and Brothers), p. 43. See above, Chapter XII, "Man As Person."

8. See *Studies in the Philosophy of Religion* by Archibald Allan Bowman (London: Macmillan and Company, Ltd., 1938), Volume II, pp. 429–430.

9. Bowman, *op. cit.*, p. 431. Used by permission of Mrs. A. A. Bowman, Macmillan and Company, Ltd., London, and St. Martin's Press, New York.

Questions and Topics for Study

Questions and Topics for Study

CHAPTER ONE

To the Student: The purpose of these questions and topics is to give you a number of suggestions and starting points for your own further reading and reflection. The questions are not intended to provide a check on your reading of this text; they are not school-boy exercises. On the other hand, your success and satisfaction in working with these problems will give you some indication of your understanding of the discussion in the text. They may lead you to re-read some parts of the chapter. The purpose of these questions and topics is to lead your thinking into important issues; so few, if any, have "right answers." The significant answer is a careful consideration of the problem, an understanding and exploration of the alternative positions which may be taken with respect to it, and a tentative decision concerning your own position based on the fullest possible awareness of the reasons and influences which have led you to your conclusion. The value of these questions and topics will be increased if you put in writing some of the results of your thinking and reading. Your instructor may ask you from time to time to develop your ideas on some of these or related topics into a formal paper.

These questions and topics may provide useful points of departure for discussions in class. Where they bring out different points of view the attempt to uncover the tacit assumptions and to pursue the implications of conflicting positions can contribute greatly to an understanding of the issues.

The first item in many sets of questions and topics is a list of terms which refer to the basic concepts involved in the subject matter of the chapter. Careful consideration of the meanings of these terms will be most helpful, and you will find it profitable to look them up in some of the better reference works. Some terms will appear in more than one list, and this will help you note the progress you are making in your understanding of the concepts to which they refer.

The following reference works are suggested:

Encyclopaedia Britannica
The New International Encyclopaedia
Encyclopaedia of Religion and Ethics, edited by James Hastings.

The New Schaff-Herzog Encyclopedia of Religious Knowledge
The Interpreter's Bible
The Catholic Encyclopedia
The Universal Jewish Encyclopedia
The Oxford English Dictionary

1. *Terms:* Religion; reason; value; God; attitude; person; humanism; atheism; nihilism; monotheism; dogma.

2. How do religious beliefs differ from ethical or moral beliefs? What, if anything, do they have in common? Is it possible to have the one without the other?

3. How do religious beliefs differ from scientific beliefs? Do you feel that there are any significant conflicts between religious and scientific beliefs? If so, do you think reconciliation is possible? If not, how do you account for the fact that many people who have expert knowledge in these fields are not disturbed by the supposed conflicts?

4. Look up information about a religion with which you are unfamiliar, and try to identify the values which are regarded as highest in that religion. Compare it in this respect with a religion with which you are already familiar.

5. If we try to understand religious differences as differences in final evaluations we find that many of the conflicts between religions seem to be quite trivial. Think of some examples of this. Why is it that if these are trivial so far as value differences are concerned some of them have received so much emphasis?

6. Read again the brief quotation from Barker (p. 17), and think of some parallels.

7. Compare some familiar religious attitudes which express the spirit of Sophocles' saying with some which reflect Euripides' view (p. 20).

8. Illustrate Allport's distinction between mature and immature religion.

READING SUGGESTIONS

Gordon W. Allport, *The Individual and His Religion.* New York: The Macmillan Company, 1930.

Archibald Allan Bowman, *Studies in the Philosophy of Religion,* Volume I. London: Macmillan and Company, Ltd., 1938.

J. W. Bowman, *The Religion of Maturity.* New York: Abingdon Press, 1948.

John R. Everett, *Religion in Human Experience.* New York: Henry Holt and Company, Inc., 1950.

Horace T. Houf, *What Religion Is and Does*. New York: Harper and
Brothers, 1935.

John B. Noss, *Man's Religion*. New York: The Macmillan Company,
1949.

James Bissett Pratt, *Eternal Values in Religion*. New York: The Macmillan Company, 1950.

CHAPTER TWO

1. *Terms:* Self; integration of self; truth; theology; apologetics;
philosophy; science; premise; presupposition; assumption; postulate;
conclusion; symbol; meaning; skepticism; agnosticism; logical identity
and noncontradiction; concept.

2. Illustrate the difference between a rational proof of the truth of
a belief and a rational justification for holding a belief and acting on it
even though it is not known to be true. (It will be of some advantage
to look for illustrations in other areas of belief and action besides
religion.)

3. What are some important differences between religious attitudes
and (a) economic activities and attitudes, (b) educational policies,
(c) political policies? Do you regard any of these as serious conflicts?

4. Compare the part which religion plays in these two different
ways of life: (a) A life lived in separate compartments, and (b) the
life lived by a highly integrated personality.

5. Do you think a person's religion may be so completely integrated
into the whole range of his activities and interests that he engages in
no exclusively religious activity at all? Consider a parallel situation
with respect to a person's education, or his friendships.

6. Find out some of the chief theological issues between two differ-
ent religious groups, such as: Jewish and Christian; Protestant and
Roman Catholic; Roman Catholic and Greek Catholic (Orthodox
Church); Presbyterian and Methodist; Congregational and Protestant
Episcopal; Congregational and Unitarian; Christian and Moslem; Mos-
lem and Jewish.

7. Can you find in the field of political thinking and action any parallel with the dependence of theology on faith?

8. Look up some of the arguments used in apologetics. Which of
these arguments assume the truth of the theology they are intended to
defend? Which belong properly to a philosophy of religion? Are
there any which do not fall in either of these groups?

9. *Explain and examine:* Philosophy always buries its undertakers.

10. The relation of the basic assumptions of philosophy to the necessary conditions of meaningful assertion.

11. *Examine:* There is philosophy of religion but there is no such thing as religious philosophy.

READING SUGGESTIONS

Charles A. Bennett, *The Dilemma of Religious Knowledge.* New Haven: Yale University Press, 1931.

Nicolas Berdyaev, *Solitude and Society.* London: Geoffrey Bles, Ltd., 1938.

L. Harold DeWolf, *The Religious Revolt Against Reason.* New York: Harper and Brothers, 1949.

A. Campbell Garnett, *A Realistic Philosophy of Religion.* Chicago: Willett, Clark and Company, 1942.

Immanuel Kant, *Religion within the Limits of Reason Alone.* La Salle: Open Court Publishing Company, 1934.

David Elton Trueblood, *The Logic of Belief.* New York: Harper and Brothers, 1942.

Wilbur Marshall Urban, *Beyond Realism and Idealism.* New York: The Macmillan Company, 1949.

Wilbur Marshall Urban, *The Intelligible World.* New York: The Macmillan Company, 1929.

CHAPTER THREE

1. *Terms:* Belief; knowledge; evidence; implication; proof; sensation; sense perception; atom (Greek philosophy); atom (contemporary physics).

2. Give some examples of beliefs which are neither matters of knowledge nor of faith. Can you explain why you have these beliefs?

3. How might you qualify any statement you make so that its truth or falsity would depend on nothing but your own sincerity?

4. Consider the statement: "The sun will rise again." Do you know this to be true? If so, what evidence have you, and how do you know your evidence is sound? If you do not know this to be true, do you believe it? If so, why? If not, what is your view concerning it?

5. How would you refute the theory that knowledge is impossible, and belief alone is within our power?

6. Compare the kind of evidence used in physical science with the kind of evidence used in history. Compare these with the kind of

evidence admitted in a court of law. In each case what are the safe-guards against error?

7. Give some examples, from any area of controversy (such as politics), of thinking which makes the mistake of substituting "nothing but" for "both and."

8. If we had in our minds copies of things outside our minds, would the presence of these copies be enough to provide knowledge of the things they copied? (Think of some parallels in other situations where there is the relation of original and copy.)

9. To the naked eye a drop of human blood seems uniformly red in color, but the same blood viewed through a microscope is a yellowish fluid with red spots scattered through it. Which is the true percept?

10. What doubtful assumption is involved in the question asked in 8?

11. Is any knowledge possible without any reference whatever to perception?

READING SUGGESTIONS

M. C. D'Arcy, *The Nature of Belief*. New York: Sheed and Ward, Inc., 1931.

C. E. M. Joad, *Philosophical Aspects of Modern Science*. New York: The Macmillan Company, 1948.

John Laird, *Knowledge, Belief, and Opinion*. New York: The Century Company, 1930.

E. L. Mascall, *Existence and Analogy*. New York: Longmans, Green and Company, Inc., 1949.

F. R. Tennant, *The Nature of Belief*. London: Geoffrey Bles, Ltd., 1943.

John Wild, *Introduction to Realistic Philosophy*. New York: Harper and Brothers, 1948.

CHAPTER FOUR

1. *Terms:* Reason; logical relation; universal predication; logical intention; actual and possible; practical reason.

2. Illustrate the distinction between rational insight into possibility and rational insight into existence. Which kind of knowledge have we in physics' laws of motion?

3. How do we know that "mathematical reality" is "built" in such a way that 317 is a prime?

4. Suppose it is true that "if wishes were horses beggars would ride." Does this tell us anything about real existence? If so, what? If not, then what do we mean by saying it is true?

5. The main steps from Descartes' rationalism to Hume's skepticism.

6. The distinction between knowledge and true belief.

7. Find out what you can about Kant's theory of practical reason and compare it with the concept developed in this chapter.

8. What are some of the working assumptions you make in the things you do from day to day? Does the fact that they are successful in practice demonstrate that they are true?

READING SUGGESTIONS

Harold A. Bosley, *The Quest for Religious Certainty*. Chicago: Willett, Clark and Company, 1939.

L. Harold DeWolf, *The Religious Revolt Against Reason*. New York: Harper and Brothers, 1949.

Henry Babcock Veatch, *Intentional Logic*. New Haven: Yale University Press, 1952.

John Wild, *Introduction to Realistic Philosophy*. New York: Harper and Brothers, 1948.

CHAPTER FIVE

1. *Terms:* Faith; fanaticism; value.

2. The place of intellectual assent in faith, and the influence of intellectual doubt on faith.

3. Explain and illustrate the statement that "in action I may discover grounds for belief which are not available to me in mere reflection and abstract thought." Do not confine your illustrations to religious belief.

4. "The weakest faith can stand so long as it is sure it is right." If it is sure it is right then is it not a strong rather than a weak faith? Just what do "strong" and "weak" mean in this connection?

5. Give examples of some kinds of inquiry which a man might make concerning a friend and which, if discovered by that friend, would destroy their personal relationship. Are there kinds of inquiry which might be dangerous to religious faith? The problem here is to see how far the parallel extends between faith in the personal relationships of men and women and religious faith.

READING SUGGESTIONS

Henri Bergson, *The Two Sources of Morality and Religion*. New York: Henry Holt and Company, Inc., 1935.

James Harry Cotton, *Christian Knowledge of God*. New York: The Macmillan Company, 1951.

M. C. D'Arcy, *The Mind and Heart of Love*. New York: Henry Holt and Company, Inc., 1947.

Richard Kroner, *The Primacy of Faith*. New York: The Macmillan Company, 1943.

John Henry Newman, *The Grammar of Assent*. New York: Longmans, Green and Company, Inc., 1947.

Rudolf Otto, *The Idea of the Holy*. New York: Oxford University Press, Inc., 1926.

James B. Pratt, *Eternal Values in Religion*. New York: The Macmillan Company, 1950.

F. R. Tennant, *The Nature of Belief*. London: Geoffrey Bles, Ltd., 1943.

CHAPTER SIX

1. *Terms:* True and false; credible; mores; cynicism; relevance; cognitive truth.

2. Can you justify the assertion that "we are made for truth"? Or is this sheer assumption?

3. Give some examples of things that are taught because it is considered desirable that people shall believe them rather than because they are true. Look for examples not only in formal education but also in politics, business, and the practice of the professions. Under what conditions, if any, do you consider this practice of influencing belief independently of considerations of truth to be desirable?

4. Is there any conflict between the doctrine of the primacy of truth in religion and William James' doctrine of "the will to believe"?

5. Some deny that error has any rights and insist that those who have the truth are justified, in theory at least, in the use of compulsion to force the acceptance of truth and to prevent the teaching of contrary doctrines. Examine this position, and compare it with our own theories and practices concerning differences in political beliefs (for example, our policy with respect to so-called "subversive" doctrines).

6. Consider the relation of credibility to knowledge in (a) religion, and (b) in science.

7. Could life in the most pleasant dream world you can imagine be

preferable to a life in the real world even if that real life is one of suffering and frustration? (This question leads in the direction of a problem to be considered later, whether values pertain at all to non-actual possibilities.)

8. Is the quotation from Plato a statement of the facts, or is it a statement of what ought to be our attitude?

9. The distinction between true *knowledge* and true *being*. (In preparation for this look up some of Aristotle's statements of this distinction.)

10. Compare and examine the following: (a) Our ideas are pictures of things. (b) Our ideas are nothing but pictures of things.

11. Give examples of your own of the confusion of *difference* with *conflict*.

12. How can we have the whole truth without having all the truth?

READING SUGGESTIONS

James Harry Cotton, *Christian Knowledge of God*. New York: The Macmillan Company, 1951.

Erich Frank, *Philosophical Understanding and Religious Truth*. New York: Oxford University Press, Inc., 1945.

John Macmurray, *Reason and Emotion*. London: Faber and Faber, 1935.

Edward D. Myers (Editor), *Christianity and Reason*. New York: Oxford University Press, Inc., 1951.

Newton P. Stallknecht, "Decision and Existence." *The Review of Metaphysics*, Volume VI, pp. 31–44.

Henry N. Wieman, *The Wrestle of Religion with Truth*. New York: The Macmillan Company, 1927.

CHAPTER SEVEN

1. *Terms:* Truth; perspectives of truth; relative and absolute truth; essence; essential truth; existential truth; extension, supposition, and designation of terms.

2. Show how different versions of the same occurrence can be given the appearance of mutual conflict merely by the selection of material to be included, without any outright falsification of specific details. (This might be approached by quoting statements out of context from the same author; then try selecting adjectives for their suggestion of approval or disapproval.)

3. *Explain and illustrate:* "No perspective gives all truth yet any

perspective may give some truth." What is the bearing of this on bigotry and fanaticism?

4. In which of the following is the *primary meaning* essential and in which is it existential?

    (a) Love is blind.

    (b) There is a city larger than Chicago.

    (c) New York is larger than Chicago.

    (d) There is a number larger than any number which can be specified.

    (e) If the heart stops more than a few minutes, death ensues.

5. Consider the extension, supposition, and designation of terms used in the following propositions:

    (a) The City of Brotherly Love is in Pennsylvania. (City; City of Brotherly Love.)

    (b) French and Spanish are closely related to Latin.

    (c) Maple trees in this latitude drop their leaves in late October or early November.

    (d) Two is the square root of four.

6. Consider Descartes' argument by which he proposed to establish with certainty the fact of existence: "I think, therefore I am." Does this demonstrate existence or does it assume existence?

7. Apply the distinction between essential and existential truth to one of the Psalms, or to Milton's *Paradise Lost*. Can you find anything which has existential truth without essential truth?

READING SUGGESTIONS

Raymond J. McCall, *Basic Logic*. New York: Barnes and Noble, Inc., 1952.

Henry Babcock Veatch, *Intentional Logic*. New Haven: Yale University Press, 1952.

John Wild, "An Examination of Critical Realism." *Philosophy and Phenomenological Research*, Volume XIV.

John Wild, *Introduction to Realistic Philosophy*. New York: Harper and Brothers, 1948.

CHAPTER EIGHT

1. *Terms:* Naturalism; positivism; myth; ritual; liturgy; art; music; poetry.

2. Illustrate the distinction between rational proof and rational justification. In what sense, if any, is rational justification a kind of proof?

Would you appeal to proof or justification if questions were raised about the methods of proof?

3. Which of the following are proper matters for proof, which for rational justification, and which for neither?

    (a) Something exists.

    (b) There is no largest number.

    (c) All material bodies gravitate.

    (d) All men are capable of speech.

4. The importance of attitudes (a) in scientific investigation, (b) in relations with a friend, and (c) in selling refrigerators. Is there any sense in which we may call an attitude true or false?

5. *Explain and illustrate:* "It is proper to the nature of some truth that it should come to man more directly, and with greater effect, in act and deed than in formulas and statements of general principles." How is this related to the adage that "actions speak louder than words"?

6. The place of emotion in aesthetic experience.

7. *Examine:* Religious truth is poetic truth.

8. What is the "lie" to which Santayana refers?

9. In what fields (give a few examples) is competence to judge largely a matter of theoretical knowledge and technical information? What are some fields which require personal experience and participation in the activity itself before one is competent to judge?

READING SUGGESTIONS

Edwyn Bevan, *Symbolism and Belief*. London: George Allen and Unwin, 1938.

Ernst Cassirer, *Language and Myth*. New York: Harper and Brothers, 1946.

James Harry Cotton, *Christian Knowledge of God*. New York: The Macmillan Company, 1951.

Erich Frank, *Philosophical Understanding and Religious Truth*. New York: Oxford University Press, Inc., 1945.

Edith Hamilton, *Witness to the Truth*. New York: W. W. Norton and Company, Inc., 1948.

John Macmurray, *The Structure of Religious Experience*. New Haven: Yale University Press, 1936.

Edward D. Myers (Editor), *Christianity and Reason*. New York: Oxford University Press, Inc., 1951.

Josiah Royce, *The Sources of Religious Insight*. New York: Charles Scribner's Sons, 1912.

George F. Thomas, "The Meaning of Truth." *The Christian Scholar*, Volume XXXVI, pp. 172–175.

CHAPTER NINE

1. *Terms:* Attitude; analogy; radical doubt; secularism.

2. How explain the fact that in some societies the mentally disordered have been treated with special respect? What connection has this with the discussion of the criteria of religious truth?

3. Explain and examine the following statement, and illustrate its application: "The test of a religious feeling or emotion is the attitude it evokes."

4. Compare the attitudes commended in the Sermon on the Mount, and by Paul, with those popularly considered today to be essential for "success" in life.

5. What does the phrase, "an act of God," mean in law? Try to uncover the basic ideas from which this concept arises.

6. Under what conditions are we warranted in reasoning from effect to cause? Illustrate the dangers inherent in the careless use of such inference, and show how it may be safeguarded in actual practice. (Those who have some acquaintance with elementary logic may find some suggestions in the relations of antecedent and consequent of hypothetical propositions.)

7. Compare the use of reason in philosophy with its use in theology.

8. The chief causes of contemporary secularism.

9. Do we find radical doubt in any area of thought or action besides religion?

READING SUGGESTIONS

Archibald Allan Bowman, *Studies in the Philosophy of Religion*, Volume II. London: Macmillan and Company, Ltd., 1938.

Richard Kroner, *The Religious Function of Imagination.* New Haven: Yale University Press, 1941.

John Macmurray, *Reason and Emotion.* London: Faber and Faber, 1935.

John Oman, *The Natural and the Supernatural.* Cambridge: At the University Press, 1931.

William Temple, *Nature, Man and God.* London: Macmillan and Company, Ltd., 1951.

D. Elton Trueblood, *The Trustworthiness of Religious Experience.* London: George Allen and Unwin, 1939.

CHAPTER TEN

1. *Terms:* Animism; theism; supernatural; idol; anthropomorphism; scientism; obscurantism.

2. What brought about the secularization of modern culture? Consider and compare the influences of intellectual, technological, economic, and political factors.

3. Explain the meaning of the statement that the concept of the secular is a religious concept. Is atheism also a religious concept?

4. What were the attitudes of the early Greek philosophers toward the divinities of the popular religion of their time?

5. Comment on the statement: "The discovery of God's *supernatural* character invests the natural with a certain independence." What bearing has this same principle on man's freedom?

6. Are anthropomorphic and theistic ideas of God mutually exclusive?

7. The contributions of medieval theology to modern science.

8. Consider some of Whitehead's illustrations (in *Science and the Modern World*) of the anti-rationalism of science. How do you account for this?

9. Why is it impossible, by the use of scientific method, to establish the truth of the belief in an order of nature?

10. Give examples of scientific discoveries which were happy accidents, and of those which depended on the extensive prior formulation of theoretical possibilities.

11. How do the traditional and the modern idea of man agree concerning (a) his subordinate position, and (b) his supremacy in nature? How do they disagree on the same points?

12. *Explain, illustrate and examine:* The weakness of the modern view of man is the strength of the traditional view, and the strength of the modern is the weakness of the traditional.

13. Examine Comte's theory of the relation of philosophy and the sciences.

14. What evidence is there for the value of scientific inquiry?

15. *Examine:* The strength of scientific method is derived from its limitations.

READING SUGGESTIONS

Archibald Allan Bowman, *Studies in the Philosophy of Religion,* Volume II. London: Macmillan and Company, Ltd., 1938.

Hubert S. Box, *God and the Modern Mind*. London: Society for the Promotion of Christian Knowledge, 1937.

Robert L. Calhoun, *What Is Man?* New York: Association Press, 1939.

Erich Frank, *Philosophical Understanding and Religious Truth*. New York: Oxford University Press, Inc., 1945.

James Bissett Pratt, *Naturalism*. Yale University Press, 1939.

Robert Shafer, *Christianity and Naturalism*. New Haven: Yale University Press, 1926.

CHAPTER ELEVEN

1. *Terms:* Noetic existence; determinism; behaviorism; person; occasion, in distinction from cause; cause and reason.

2. Does the conclusion of the following argument necessarily follow from the premises? Can the truth of the premises be plausibly challenged? "If consciousness of change does not change, and if everything in nature does change, then consciousness of change cannot be a part of nature."

3. Suppose someone were to insist that you are deluded and should be placed in a hospital for mental cases. Suppose also that were you to protest that you are in your right mind he would insist that your belief that you are in your right mind is itself a characteristic symptom of the mental disease he says you have. How would you reply? What bearing has this on the question of the relation of freedom to the possibility of knowing?

4. The difference between the awareness of an object and a response to a stimulus.

5. *Examine:* "If a man can lie, then he is free." Consider carefully what it means to "lie," especially what is included in lying besides telling a falsehood.

6. Illustrate the difference between what we are aware of and the awareness of it. Show how the same distinction applies to our awareness of our awareness of something.

7. Illustrate the confusion between real causes and reasons.

8. *Examine:* What a man thinks helps to determine what he does.

9. Look up the word "define," then show how man's discovery of his limits is a way of "defining" himself in act.

10. What is the significance of the fact that man is a tool-making animal? In considering this, pay careful attention to the difference between *making* tools and merely *using* tools.

READING SUGGESTIONS

Nicolas Berdyaev, *Freedom and the Spirit*. London: Geoffrey Bles, Ltd., 1935.

Archibald Allan Bowman, *Studies in the Philosophy of Religion*, 2 volumes. London: Macmillan and Company, Ltd., 1938.

Thomas Hill Green, *Prolegomena to Ethics*. Oxford: Clarendon Press, Fifth Edition, 1906.

William Ernest Hocking, *Human Nature and Its Remaking*. New Haven: Yale University Press, 1923.

William Ernest Hocking, *What Man Can Make of Man*. New York: Harper and Brothers, 1942.

Karl Löwith, "Man between Infinities." *Measure*, Volume I.

William Aylott Orton, *The Liberal Tradition*. New Haven: Yale University Press, 1945.

Paul Weiss, *Man's Freedom*. New Haven: Yale University Press, 1950.

CHAPTER TWELVE

1. *Terms:* Person; self; moral standard or criterion; obligation.

2. Compare the following with respect to what they reveal concerning the person performing or participating in them: (a) handwriting, (b) speech, (c) a musical performance, (d) a musical composition, (e) a card game, (f) an argument or dispute, (g) living with another as a college roommate, (h) living with another as a member of the same family.

3. Would a child become a person if he met with no personal response? Would he become conscious of himself as a self if he were not treated as a self?

4. What are some of the differences between the standards by which a child may judge himself and the standards by which a mature person will judge himself? Granted that the child's judgments are largely false, what significance have they for his moral development and his development as a person?

5. Try to formulate for yourself just what you mean when you admit that you *ought* to do something. What kind of compulsion are you admitting, and why do you recognize it as applicable to yourself?

6. *Examine:* Unless the standard by which we differentiate good and evil is founded in real being, the distinction between good and evil deserves not the slightest respect.

7. What would life be like in a community where no one recognized or accepted any moral obligations? (Make your answer specific and descriptive.)

8. Consider, in the light of the discussion of this chapter, the relation of morality and religion.

9. Compare Garnett's conception of God in us with the popular notion of conscience.

10. Psychologists and psychiatrists seem to assume that people ought to be happy and well adjusted. Can they justify the assumption by psychology alone? Physicians assume that it is better for people to be healthy than to be unhealthy. Does medical evidence have any bearing on this?

11. *Explain and examine:* Religion offers not a principle but a person as its answer to the problem of the good.

12. The importance for religious faith of the philosophical problem of the existence of God. Compare, for example, the views of St. Augustine, St. Thomas Aquinas, Duns Scotus, Luther, Calvin, Kierkegaard, Barth, Reinhold Niebuhr, Étienne Gilson, and others.

READING SUGGESTIONS

Charles A. Bennett, *The Dilemma of Religious Knowledge.* New Haven: Yale University Press, 1931.

James Harry Cotton, *Christian Knowledge of God.* New York: The Macmillan Company, 1951.

M. C. D'Arcy, *The Mind and Heart of Love.* New York: Henry Holt and Company, Inc., 1947.

L. Harold DeWolf, *The Religious Revolt against Reason.* New York: Harper and Brothers, 1949.

Erich Frank, *Philosophical Understanding and Religious Truth.* New York: Oxford University Press, Inc., 1945.

A. Campbell Garnett, *God in Us.* New York: Harper and Brothers, 1945.

Étienne Gilson, *Dogmatism and Tolerance.* New Brunswick: Rutgers University Press, 1952.

Jacques Maritain, "Christian Humanism." *Fortune,* April 1952.

Jacques Maritain, *Ransoming the Time.* New York: Charles Scribner's Sons, 1941.

William Temple, *Nature, Man and God.* London: Macmillan and Company, Ltd., 1951.

Eliseo Vivas, *The Moral Life and the Ethical Life.* Chicago: The University of Chicago Press, 1950.

Franz Werfel, *Between Heaven and Earth*. New York: Philosophical Library, 1944.

CHAPTER THIRTEEN

1. *Terms:* God; naturalism; humanism (as religion).

2. Look up some of the ceremonies of a primitive religion. Describe them and try to explain just what their performance is intended to accomplish and what is the theory, or conception of existence, on which they rest. Try to decide whether the ceremonies you describe include anything specifically religious or whether they are only the attempt to enlist the forces behind nature to work for man.

3. Differentiate religion and magic.

4. The relation between man's self-awareness and the fact that he is religious. Would you expect to find that the more intimately conscious of himself man becomes the more important religion is to him? Consider carefully what kind of "consciousness of himself" is relevant here. In connection with this question consider also the way in which devotional exercises, for example in Judaism and Christianity, enhance self-awareness.

5. *Examine:* A vivid religious awareness releases a person from care and anxiety, for such a person does not deceive himself that destiny waits on his decisions.

6. How can we avoid an infinite regress in our attempt to explain things? For example, suppose we explain nature in terms of atomic structures and space-time fields, how do we explain the fact that nature is of this sort and not another, etc.?

7. When Plato says that the Good is "beyond being" does he mean that it is not real? If he does, how can it be the source of what exists? If not, does he mean it is in some sense "more" than being?

8. What do you think is Dewey's purpose in *A Common Faith?* Just how might one go about making use of the idea of God which he here recommends?

9. What does Dewey mean by "spiritual content"?

10. Is there any inconsistency between Bennett's comment that "man is one of the poorest substitutes for God that ingenuity can propose" and the religious conception of the presence of God in man?

READING SUGGESTIONS

Charles A. Bennett, *The Dilemma of Religious Knowledge*. New Haven: Yale University Press, 1934.

John Dewey, *A Common Faith*. New Haven: Yale University Press, 1934.

D. Luther Evans, "Two Intellectually Respectable Conceptions of God." *Philosophy and Phenomenological Research*, Volume X.

William Ernest Hocking, *The Meaning of God in Human Experience*. New Haven: Yale University Press, 1912.

William Ernest Hocking, *Science and the Idea of God*. Chapel Hill: University of North Carolina Press, 1944.

Yervant H. Krikorian (Editor), *Naturalism and the Human Spirit*. New York: Columbia University Press, 1944.

Corliss Lamont, *Humanism as a Philosophy*. New York: Philosophical Library, 1949.

Oliver Martin, "An Examination of Contemporary Naturalism and Materialism." *Return to Reason*, edited by John Wild. Chicago: Henry Regnery Company, 1953.

James Bissett Pratt, *Naturalism*. New Haven: Yale University Press, 1939.

A. Seth Pringle-Pattison, *The Idea of God*. New York: Oxford University Press, 1920.

Robert Shafer, *Christianity and Naturalism*. New Haven: Yale University Press, 1926.

CHAPTER FOURTEEN

1. *Terms:* Pantheism; pancosmism or cosmic pantheism; acosmic pantheism; mysticism; magic; polytheism; creation; emanation; identity.

2. Oman contends that cosmic pantheism tends to turn into acosmic pantheism. Would it be plausible to argue, for similar reasons, that the worship of nature is likely to lead to the denial of the reality of nature? That the worship of man would endanger our recognition of what man really is? That the worship of the state would obscure our understanding of the true character of the state?

3. Compare these two statements: "Each of these two things is real," and "Each of these two things is reality." Does the difference between these two statements have any bearing on the soundness of the argument for pantheism?

4. How do you think a dualist might reply to a pantheist's criticism of his position?

5. Why does pantheism, which is opposed to dualism in theory, tend to become dualistic in practice?

6. What would you expect to be the attitude of a pantheistic religion toward asceticism?

7. How would the doctrine of the supposition of terms (discussed in Chapter VII) apply in the case of monism's fallacy?

READING SUGGESTIONS

John R. Everett, *Religion in Human Experience*. New York: Henry Holt and Company, Inc., 1950.

Étienne Gilson, *God and Philosophy*. New Haven: Yale University Press, 1941.

Aldous Huxley, *The Perennial Philosophy*. New York: Harper and Brothers, 1945.

William Ralph Inge, *Mysticism in Religion*. Chicago: The University of Chicago Press, 1948.

William Ralph Inge, *The Philosophy of Plotinus*, 2 volumes. London: Longmans, Green and Company, 1918.

CHAPTER FIFTEEN

1. *Terms:* Deism; theism; univocal, equivocal, and analogical concepts; universals and particulars.

2. The relation of eighteenth century deism to early modern scientific thought.

3. In what ways, if any, do you think that contemporary conventional religion reflects deistic ideas?

4. Compare the pseudo-rationalistic deism of the eighteenth century with anti-rationalistic deism.

5. What keeps anti-rationalistic deism and acosmic pantheism apart? If the anti-rationalistic deist were to deny the reality of the world would he find himself in the position of acosmic pantheism?

6. *Examine:* He who conceives God as unintelligible will find the consequence of this conception in the paralysis of his own will.

7. What assumption common to pantheism and deism does theism deny?

8. Compare univocal, equivocal, and analogous interpretations of the idea of God as Father.

9. The agreements and disagreements of theism and naturalism.

READING SUGGESTIONS

Étienne Gilson, *God and Philosophy*. New Haven: Yale University Press, 1941.

D. J. B. Hawkins, *The Essentials of Theism*. New York: Sheed and Ward, Inc., 1950.

Warren Nelson Nevius, *Religion as Experience and Truth*. Philadelphia: The Westminster Press, 1941.

John Oman, *The Natural and the Supernatural*. Cambridge: At the University Press, 1931.

F. R. Tennant, *Philosophical Theology*, 2 volumes. Cambridge: At the University Press, 1928, 1930.

CHAPTER SIXTEEN

1. *Terms:* Irrationalism; proof; premise; conclusion; valid; true; hypothesis; metaphysics; epistemology; intelligible; dialectic; anhypotheton.

2. Formulate statements expressing the attitudes of agnosticism, fideism, aestheticism, and positivism.

3. Compare theistic and atheistic existentialism; for example, the existentialism of Marcel with that of Sartre.

4. Explain and illustrate the nature of proof beyond reasonable doubt. How is it understood in law? Compare it with proof beyond all possible doubt. What constitutes the reasonableness in reasonable doubt?

5. Point out and illustrate the difference between what makes an argument plausible and what makes it sound.

6. Formulate careful statements of some of your strongest beliefs. In each case try to find your reasons for holding the belief. Then examine the relation of reasons and belief to see if it is possible for you to deny the belief and still assert the reasons without inconsistency.

7. What should we expect to accomplish by a proof of the existence of God?

8. Can there be a scientific proof of the soundness of sense perception?

9. Explain why philosophy is the only kind of inquiry which can examine its own assumptions.

10. Illustrate the method of self-refutation.

11. What is the significant difference between philosophy and the natural sciences which makes dialectic the appropriate method for philosophy but not for the sciences?

READING SUGGESTIONS

Mortimer J. Adler, *Dialectic*. New York: Harcourt, Brace and Company, Inc., 1927.

Harmon M. Chapman, "Realism and Phenomenology." *Return to Reason*, edited by John Wild. Chicago: Henry Regnery Company, 1953.

Richard Robinson, *Plato's Early Dialectic*. Oxford: The Clarendon Press, 1953.

William Marshall Urban, *Beyond Realism and Idealism*. New York: The Macmillan Company, 1949.

William Marshall Urban, *The Intelligible World*. New York: The Macmillan Company, 1929.

John Wild, "Phenomenology and Metaphysics." *Return to Reason*, edited by John Wild. Chicago: Henry Regnery Company, 1953.

John Wild, *Introduction to Realistic Philosophy*. New York: Harper and Brothers, 1948.

CHAPTER SEVENTEEN

1. *Terms:* Ontological, cosmological, teleological, and moral arguments; concept; logical judgment or proposition; existential neutrality; perfection; abstraction.

2. What is the difference between Anselm's argument and such an argument as the following? "I have an idea of an island somewhere in the ocean, an island which no one has ever seen but which is more excellent than all other countries. This island therefore must exist, for if it did not then I could think of a place still more excellent." (On this see Gaunilon's reply to Anselm in behalf of the fool.)

3. Try to define "existence." What difficulties do you encounter, and what do you think is the source of these difficulties?

4. In order to think the existence of something we conceive we have to add something to the concept. What do we add?

5. Explain and illustrate the statement that unless our concepts are existentially neutral it is impossible for the existence of something to be both affirmed and denied. Point out some of the practical consequences of this.

6. If lack of existence cannot be a defect, does it follow that no mere possibility is either good or evil? Is there any meaning in the statement, then, that this is the best (or worst) of all possible worlds?

7. If to say that an idea is true means that it is a copy of something real, then what does it mean to attribute truth to the idea that our ideas copy reality?

8. Compare (a) the difference between a hundred possible dollars and a hundred real dollars with (b) the difference between a hundred counterfeit dollars and a hundred real dollars.

READING SUGGESTIONS

Saint Anselm, *Proslogium*. In *Proslogium; Monologium; An Appendix in Behalf of the Fool by Gaunilon; and Cur Deus Homo*. La Salle: Open Court Publishing Company, 1910.

Peter A. Bertocci, *The Empirical Argument for God*. Cambridge: Harvard University Press, 1938.

James Harry Cotton, *Christian Knowledge of God*. New York: The Macmillan Company, 1951.

René Descartes, *Meditations on the First Philosophy*. In *A Discourse on Method*, etc., by René Descartes. Everyman's Library. New York: E. P. Dutton and Company, Inc., 1927.

A. Campbell Garnett, *A Realistic Philosophy of Religion*. Chicago: Willett, Clark and Company, 1942.

Étienne Gilson, *Being and Some Philosophers*. Toronto: Pontifical Institute of Mediaeval Studies, 1949.

Immanuel Kant, *Critique of Pure Reason*. Translation by Norman Kemp Smith. London: Macmillan and Company, Ltd., 1929.

CHAPTER EIGHTEEN

1. *Terms:* Acosmism; illusion; subjectivism; phenomenalism; abstraction; idea.

2. What is the *real existent* in each of the following? The President of the United States; the Presidency of the United States; the Constitution of the United States; the American Revolution; the human race; Lil Abner and Dogpatch.

3. What does Berkeley mean by "the absurdity of abstraction"? What were his reasons for insisting that "an existence independent of a spirit" is an abstraction?

4. Distinguish and illustrate the difference between the following: (a) We cannot be aware of anything except by the use of ideas. (b) We are aware only of ideas. If (b) is false does it follow that (a) is false?

5. Does the process of learning (for example, the learning of a foreign language) support the contention that our awareness of our own mental processes is an indispensable condition of knowledge?

6. Why is the denial of the capacity of any one basic mental process to provide knowledge a denial in principle of the cognitive significance of all mental acts?

7. Logic's law of the excluded middle states that any proposition

577

or judgment is either true or false, that there is no middle ground or third alternative between truth and falsity. With this in mind, examine the following: Phenomenalism could be true only if the law of the excluded middle were false.

READING SUGGESTIONS

Hubert S. Box, *The World and God*. London: Society for Promoting Christian Knowledge, 1934.

Edwin Arthur Burtt, *The Metaphysical Foundations of Modern Physical Science*. New York: Harcourt, Brace and Company, Inc., 1925.

Harmon M. Chapman, "Realism and Phenomenology." *Return to Reason*, edited by John Wild. Chicago: Henry Regnery Company, 1953.

Morris R. Cohen, *A Preface to Logic*. New York: Henry Holt and Company, Inc., 1944.

C. E. M. Joad, *Philosophical Aspects of Modern Science*. New York: The Macmillan Company, 1948.

John Macmurray, *Idealism against Religion*. London: The Lindsay Press, 1944.

Paul Weiss, *Reality*. Princeton: Princeton University Press, 1938.

Alfred North Whitehead, *Science and the Modern World*. New York: The Macmillan Company, 1926.

John Wild, "An Examination of Critical Realism." *Philosophy and Phenomenological Research*, Volume XIV.

John Wild, "Phenomenology and Metaphysics." *Return to Reason*, edited by John Wild. Chicago: Henry Regnery Company, 1953.

CHAPTER NINETEEN

1. *Terms:* Contingent; change; potential; time.

2. Show how our earlier distinction (Chapter VI) between "the whole truth" and "all the truth" applies to sense perception.

3. In which of the following is the identity one which *excludes* change and difference, and in which is it an identity which *includes* change and difference?

    (a) The sum of two and two, and the sum of three and one.

    (b) A human life in infancy, and the same life in maturity.

    (c) The first and last scenes of a dramatic performance.

    (d) The color of a leaf, and the color the leaf is perceived to have.

4. Why do we refer to a football game as *one* game? Why is not each quarter a game? Or each down? Or each play? Is this merely a matter of verbal convention, or does it concern the way in which the game itself exists?

5. Suppose someone were to say, "Granted that anything that exists in time changes, yet there still may be things in nature that do not exist in time." Can this be defended? Can it be answered?

6. (a) *Examine*: To deny potentiality is to deny continuity in time.

(b) Is it true that since they both exclude potentiality, God and a triangle also exclude continuity? (In considering this question distinguish carefully between continuity in the nature of a thing, as in the continuous line that forms a side of a triangle, and the continuity of the existence of something.)

7. (a) *Examine:* In so far as the cause of change lies within the thing that changes, the change is not real but only apparent.

(b) In what way, if any, does this apply to the changes that occur in a person as the result of his own free acts?

8. *Examine:* There cannot be an infinite number of existing entities. (Consider carefully the meaning of "an infinite number.")

9. Does the fact that the world as a whole includes past and future as well as present imply its contingency?

READING SUGGESTIONS

Étienne Gilson, *Being and Some Philosophers*. Toronto: Pontifical Institute of Mediaeval Studies, 1949.

Étienne Gilson, *The Philosophy of St. Thomas Aquinas*. Cambridge: W. Heffer and Sons, Ltd., 1929.

Charles Hartshorne, *Man's Vision of God*. New York: Harper and Brothers, 1941.

Jacques Maritain, *The Degrees of Knowledge*. New York: Charles Scribner's Sons, 1938.

E. L. Mascall, *Existence and Analogy*. New York: Longmans, Green and Company, Inc., 1949.

E. L. Mascall, *He Who Is*. New York: Longmans, Green and Company, 1948.

John Wild, *Introduction to Realistic Philosophy*. New York: Harper and Brothers, 1948.

CHAPTER TWENTY

1. *Terms:* Cause; sensation; perception.

2. *Examine:* A philosophy which ignores or denies causality is enabled to do so only by its failure to distinguish existence from essence.

3. What bearing has the fact that a thing can act only in accordance with its own nature on the contention that no contingent thing can be a cause of existence?

4. Which of the following statements, if any, are incompatible with which? Which do you think are true and which are open to question? Why?

(a) Since we have no sense organs sensitive to causation, as we do have for light and sound, it follows that we do not perceive causes. (Be sure to take account of the ambiguity of this statement.)

(b) We perceive causes but we do not sense them.

(c) We perceive causes but we do not perceive causality.

(d) We perceive things, but we do not perceive them as causes; we think them as causes.

5. (a) If a thing exists in time does it follow that it is in process of change?

(b) If a thing is in process of change does it follow that it is subject to the action of causes?

6. (a) Compare: (1) It is intelligible that this person is the kind of person he is. (2) It is intelligible that this person is.

(b) Can you justify (1) with no reference whatever to (2)?

7. Why can there be no scientific proof of the truth of the causal principle? Does this in any way make its truth doubtful?

8. What is the connection between the principle that a thing can act only in accordance with its own nature and the conclusion that the cause of the world must be self-existent?

9. Show why the idea of God as self-caused makes essence prior to existence, while the idea of God as self-existent makes existence prior to essence. (The "priority" referred to in this question is logical priority, not temporal priority.)

10. Is it a self-contradiction to assert of anything that it is "self-caused"? Compare "self-caused" and "square circle."

11. Compare the distinction between a natural, or contingent, cause and a first cause with the distinction between:

(a) The actions and episodes of the plot of a novel, and the author's composition of the novel.

(b) The relations of specific numerical values and operations within a number system, and the structure of the system itself.

(c) The acts and transactions in which a business corporation engages, and the political and legal system which makes possible the existence of the corporation.

READING SUGGESTIONS

See the references to Gilson and to Mascall for Chapter Nineteen.
D. J. B. Hawkins, *Causality and Implication*. New York: Sheed and Ward, Inc., 1937.
David Hume, *Dialogues Concerning Natural Religion*. Second Edition with Supplement. New York: Social Science Publishers, 1948.

CHAPTER TWENTY-ONE

1. *Terms:* Unity; omniscience; instant; moment; immanent; personal; world order; purpose; anthropomorphism.

2. Compare the argument for the unity and oneness of God with the pantheist's argument for the identity of God and the world (Chapter XIV). If the one is sound why not the other?

3. Show that once we assert the unity of knowledge and being in God we assert that God is omniscient.

4. What do we find in a novel or a play which shows something of the author's own attitudes and judgments? Can the immanence of God be thought by analogy with this?

5. *Examine:* The only alternative to the conception of the world order as the expression of purpose is some form of absolute determinism.

6. *Examine:* In any contingent world, order and value can come together only by virtue of the relation of means and end; consequently, any *existing* contingent world must be a purposive order.

READING SUGGESTIONS

See the references to Gilson and to Mascall for Chapter Nineteen.
G. Dawes Hicks, *The Philosophical Basis of Theism*. London: George Allen and Unwin, Ltd., 1937.
Warren Nelson Nevius, *Religion as Experience and Truth*. Philadelphia: The Westminster Press, 1941.
George Santayana, *The Idea of Christ in the Gospels or God in Man*. New York: Charles Scribner's Sons, 1946.
F. R. Tennant, *Philosophical Theology*, 2 volumes. Cambridge: At the University Press, 1928, 1930.

CHAPTER TWENTY-TWO

1. What connection do you see between the way in which we

think existence and the fact that creative activity in the arts and literature is the work of imagination rather than reason?

2. What are the significant differences between the behavior of a person "not in command of his faculties" (i.e., intoxicated or dazed or drugged) from genuine personal action?

3. Illustrate the difference between imaginative and rational knowledge of another self.

4. In what ways does the writing of a biography require imagination? How does this differ from writing fiction?

5. How is our awareness of the uniqueness of an existing thing an awareness of the likeness of God?

6. Is it because of its contingency, or in spite of it, that contingent existence shows us the likeness of God as self-existence?

READING SUGGESTIONS

See references to Mascall for Chapter Nineteen.

John Baillie, *Our Knowledge of God*. New York: Oxford University Press, Inc., Fourth Impression, 1946.

C. S. Lewis, *Beyond Personality*. New York: The Macmillan Company, 1945.

Richard Kroner, *The Religious Function of Imagination*. New Haven: Yale University Press, 1941.

Paul Weiss, "The Meaning of Existence." *Philosophy and Phenomenological Research*, Volume I, pp. 191–198.

CHAPTER TWENTY-THREE

1. *Terms:* Abstraction; concept; judgment; intention; univocal attribution; equivocal attribution; attribution by analogy; the transcendentals.

2. Compare logical abstraction and real abstraction.

3. How can concepts be "ordered to existence" and yet be "existentially neutral"?

4. If it is true that the essence conceived does not control its own use in judgment what does control the use of concepts?

5. What is the difference between metaphor and analogy? Compare the use of analogy in philosophy with the use of metaphor in poetry.

6. Compare analogy and similarity.

7. Logic textbooks often discuss analogy as a variety of fallacious

argument. What is the difference between what they call "analogy" and the kind of analogy that concerns us here?

8. What conditions must be fulfilled before we can justly claim to have genuine knowledge of God by analogy? How does the satisfaction of these conditions protect analogy from the charge that it is nothing more than figurative language or myth?

READING SUGGESTIONS

See references to Mascall for Chapter Nineteen.

Austin Farrer, *Finite and Infinite*. Westminster: Dacre Press, 1943.

R. L. Patterson, *The Conception of God in the Philosophy of Aquinas*. London: George Allen and Unwin, Ltd., 1933.

Henri Renard, *The Philosophy of Being*. Milwaukee: The Bruce Publishing Company, 1943.

Henry Babcock Veatch, *Intentional Logic*. New Haven: Yale University Press, 1952.

CHAPTER TWENTY-FOUR

1. What do you understand by Temple's phrase, "the coincidence of event and appreciation"? Read the context of the phrase in Temple's discussion and point out what differentiates revelation, as he understands it, from scientific discovery.

2. Distinguish revelation and rational knowledge. Does the fact that they are different mean that revelation is irrational?

3. If revelation cannot authenticate itself but depends for this on reason does it follow that reason is a higher way of knowing than revelation? Develop an analogous comparison of mathematics and sense perception.

4. Examine the view that revelation may be used to fill the gaps in our rational and scientific knowledge. What misunderstanding of revelation does this involve?

5. If revelation is truth in being and if there are degrees of revelation, it would seem to follow that there are degrees of truth. But this, in turn, seems to be in conflict with the law of the excluded middle, which requires that a proposition be either true or false and excludes all middle ground. (Consider this question in the light of the distinction between essential and existential truth.)

6. What is wrong with the attempt to find God in the ideal? In what way do you think such an attempt may be at the bottom of much religious sentimentalism?

7. If asked, "What does it mean to exist?" we can answer only by pointing to instances of existence. What instances do you think would answer this question most completely and satisfactorily?

READING SUGGESTIONS

J. Baillie and H. Martin (Editors), *Revelation*. London: Faber and Faber, 1937.

James Harry Cotton, *Christian Knowledge of God*. New York: The Macmillan Company, 1951.

Étienne Gilson, *Reason and Revelation in the Middle Ages*. New York: Charles Scribner's Sons, 1939.

W. M. Horton, "The Validity of the Concept of Revelation in an Empirical Age." *The Process of Religion*, edited by Miles H. Krumbine. New York: The Macmillan Company, 1933.

William Ralph Inge, *Mysticism in Religion*. Chicago: The University of Chicago Press, 1948.

Richard Kroner, *The Religious Function of Imagination*. New Haven: Yale University Press, 1941.

John Y. MacKinnon, *The Protestant Doctrine of Revelation*. Toronto: The Ryerson Press, 1946.

Dorothy L. Sayers, *The Mind of the Maker*. New York: Harcourt, Brace and Company, 1941.

A. E. Taylor, *The Faith of a Moralist*, 2 volumes. London: Macmillan and Company, Ltd., 1930.

William Temple, *Nature, Man and God*. London: Macmillan and Company, Ltd., 1951.

CHAPTER TWENTY-FIVE

1. *Terms:* Value; ethics; positivism; nihilism; hedonism; substance.

2. Why is it impossible to establish any real difference between good and evil by reference to an ideal standard alone?

3. Does it follow from the ineffectiveness of ideal standards that ethics cannot be both entirely secular and true of real existence?

4. Show how philosophical materialism commits the fallacy of simple location in time.

5. If values are real how do they exist?

6. Give examples of the way in which we distinguish between higher and lower values.

7. In the attempt to think the perfection of God, what do you consider the most satisfactory basis of analogy?

8. *Examine:* The significant differences between religions are the analogies by means of which they think God. Compare some different religions in this respect. (To find the analogies look for the things they hold sacred.)

9. Why is the moral argument for the existence of God inadequate as a proof?

READING SUGGESTIONS

Samuel Alexander, *Space, Time and Deity*, 2 volumes. London: Macmillan and Company, Ltd., 1920.

Henri Bergson, *The Two Sources of Morality and Religion*. New York: Henry Holt and Company, Inc., 1935.

Peter A. Bertocci, *Introduction to the Philosophy of Religion*. New York: Prentice-Hall, Inc., 1951.

Edgar S. Brightman, *The Problem of God*. New York: Abingdon Press, 1930.

James Harry Cotton, *Christian Knowledge of God*. New York: The Macmillan Company, 1951.

Wolfgang Köhler, *The Place of Value in a World of Facts*. New York: Liveright, 1938.

John Laird, *The Idea of Value*. Cambridge: At the University Press, 1929.

Jacques Maritain, *Saint Thomas and the Problem of Evil*. Milwaukee: Marquette University Press, 1942.

W. R. Sorley, *Moral Values and the Idea of God*. Cambridge: At the University Press, 1919.

Eliseo Vivas, *The Moral Life and the Ethical Life*. Chicago: The University of Chicago Press, 1950.

Alfred North Whitehead, *Science and the Modern World*. New York: The Macmillan Company, 1926.

CHAPTER TWENTY-SIX

1. Distinguish the creative part from the fabrication in producing a play, building a house, manufacturing an automobile.

2. How can real possibilities *be* and yet not be actual?

3. Compare the creation and emanation theories with respect to their ideas of the relation of God and the world.

4. Compare the omnipresence and the omnipotence of God with the relation of an author to the events of the world.

6. *Examine:* The doctrine of creation and the theory of evolution

can be in conflict only where there is misunderstanding of the nature of time.

7. Compare *creation in time* with *time in creation*.

READING SUGGESTIONS

Saint Thomas Aquinas, *On the Power of God*. Westminster: The Newman Press, 1952.

Archibald Allan Bowman, *A Sacramental Universe*. Princeton: Princeton University Press, 1939.

Erich Frank, *Philosophical Understanding and Religious Truth*. New York: Oxford University Press, Inc., 1945.

Étienne Gilson, *The Spirit of Mediaeval Philosophy*. New York: Charles Scribner's Sons, 1940.

Charles Hartshorne, *Man's Vision of God*. New York: Harper and Brothers, 1941.

Louise Robinson Heath, *The Concept of Time*. Chicago: The University of Chicago Press, 1936.

John Laird, *Theism and Cosmology*. London: George Allen and Unwin, Ltd., 1940.

Paul Weiss, *Reality*. Princeton: Princeton University Press, 1938.

Alfred North Whitehead, *Process and Reality*. New York: The Macmillan Company, 1929.

Alfred North Whitehead, *Religion in the Making*. New York: The Macmillan Company, 1926.

CHAPTER TWENTY-SEVEN

1. *Terms:* History; destiny; fate; progress; predestination.

2. How can a knowing process which is now taking place give us an awareness of events in the past?

3. *Examine:* A fated history is a contradiction.

4. Are there any significant differences between the concepts of fate and of predestination?

5. *Explain and examine:* History is the daughter of theism.

6. What is the relation between the reality of progress and the reality of value? Can you deny the latter and affirm the former?

7. Show why it is that if man has a destiny he must be free but his freedom must be limited and conditional.

8. In what way might the different ideas of man's destiny, or lack of it, affect his motives and actions? Would some such ideas energize

his efforts while others would tend to make him passive and resigned to whatever comes?

9. What should the petition, "Thy will be done," mean to a theist?

READING SUGGESTIONS

William Foxwell Albright, *From the Stone Age to Christianity, Monotheism and the Historical Process*. Baltimore: The Johns Hopkins Press, 1940.

Basic Writings of Saint Augustine. Two volumes. Edited by Whitney J. Oates. New York: Random House, Inc., 1948.

John Baillie, *The Belief in Progress*. New York: Charles Scribner's Sons, 1951.

Jacob Burckhardt, *Force and Freedom*. New York: Pantheon Books, Inc., 1943.

Erich Frank, *Philosophical Understanding and Religious Truth*. New York: Oxford University Press, Inc., 1945.

W. R. Matthews, *The Purpose of God*. New York: Charles Scribner's Sons, 1936.

Reinhold Niebuhr, *Faith and History*. New York: Charles Scribner's Sons, 1949.

Reinhold Niebuhr, *The Nature and Destiny of Man: II. Human Destiny*. New York: Charles Scribner's Sons, 1943.

Leslie Paul, *The Annihilation of Man*. New York: Harcourt, Brace and Company, Inc., 1945.

H. Wheeler Robinson, *Redemption and Revelation in the Actuality of History*. New York: Harper and Brothers, 1942.

Albert Schweitzer, *The Decay and Restoration of Civilization*. (Part I of *The Philosophy of Civilization*.) New York: The Macmillan Company, 1949.

Marie Collins Swabey, *The Judgment of History*. New York: Philosophical Library, 1954.

F. R. Tennant, *Philosophical Theology*. Two volumes. Cambridge: At the University Press, 1928, 1930.

Arnold J. Toynbee, *Civilization on Trial*. New York: Oxford University Press, Inc., 1948.

Arnold J. Toynbee, *A Study of History*. New York: Oxford University Press, 1946.

CHAPTER TWENTY-EIGHT

1. Distinguish natural evil and moral evil; moral evil and sin.

2. How are we indebted to those who show us what man is at his worst? Is there any way we can pay this debt?

3. Distinguish the positive and negative aspects of evil, and illustrate the difference.

4. Is evil justified by its inevitability?

5. Compare the view that the existence of a finite world shows that God is capable of evil with the view that the existence of the world shows God's goodness.

6. What is the relation between the doctrine of a finite God and the failure to distinguish between positive and negative infinity?

7. In what sense is it good that there is evil? If it is good that there is evil, is not the evil only apparent?

8. Are pain and suffering evil?

READING SUGGESTIONS

Nels F. S. Ferré, *Evil and the Christian Faith.* New York: Harper and Brothers, 1947.

Jacques Maritain, *Saint Thomas and the Problem of Evil.* Milwaukee: Marquette University Press, 1942.

W. R. Matthews, *God in Christian Thought and Experience.* London: James Nisbet and Company, Ltd., 1930.

Reinhold Niebuhr, *The Children of Light and the Children of Darkness.* New York: Charles Scribner's Sons, 1944.

Reinhold Niebuhr, *An Interpretation of Christian Ethics.* New York: Harper and Brothers, 1935.

Hastings Rashdall, *The Theory of Good and Evil.* Two volumes. Oxford: At the Clarendon Press, 1907.

William Temple, *Nature, Man and God.* London: Macmillan and Company, Ltd., 1951.

Mary Frances Thelen, *Man As Sinner.* New York: Columbia University Press, 1946.

Radoslav Tsanoff, *The Nature of Evil.* New York: The Macmillan Company, 1931.

Paul Weiss, *Man's Freedom.* New Haven: Yale University Press, 1950.

John Wild, *Introduction to Realistic Philosophy.* New York: Harper and Brothers, 1948.

CHAPTER TWENTY-NINE

1. Compare *everlasting* and *immortal; immortal* and *timeless.*

2. What is suggested to you concerning the meaning of immortality by the fact that we do not live wholly in the present?

3. What do you think is the significance of the fact that we who live in time seem not to be able to find the fulfilment of our nature in time? Compare the view that this is evidence that man is a failure as a product of evolution with the view that this means we are made for eternity. Might both of these interpretations be true?

4. In what sense does the absolute privacy and inaccessibility of the internal experience of each self suggest the presence of God in each of us?

5. Develop your own interpretation of the statement that understanding is the link of love with truth.

6. If to be known by God is to participate in the life eternal is there any way in which we can practice for eternity now?

7. What is human blessedness?

READING SUGGESTIONS

J. Seelye Bixler, *Immortality and the Present Mood.* Cambridge: Harvard University Press, 1931.

Archibald Allan Bowman, *Studies in the Philosophy of Religion.* Two volumes. London: Macmillan and Company, Ltd., 1938.

A. Campbell Garnett, *God in Us.* New York: Harper and Brothers, 1945.

William Ernest Hocking, *Thoughts on Death and Life.* New York: Harper and Brothers, 1937.

John Oman, *The Natural and the Supernatural.* Cambridge: At the University Press, 1931.

Josiah Royce, *The Conception of Immortality.* Boston: Houghton Mifflin Company, 1900.

A. E. Taylor, *The Faith of a Moralist.* Two volumes. London: Macmillan and Company, Ltd., 1930.

Radoslav A. Tsanoff, *The Problem of Immortality.* New York: The Macmillan Company, 1924.

Radoslav A. Tsanoff, *Religious Crossroads.* New York: E. P. Dutton and Company, 1942.

Paul Weiss, *Man's Freedom.* New Haven: Yale University Press, 1950.

Alfred North Whitehead, *Essays in Science and Philosophy.* New York: Philosophical Library, 1948.

Index

Index

Abstraction, 6, 376–81
Acosmism, 288–90
Actual (*See* Potential and Actual)
Adams, J. C., 265
Aeschylus, 81, 513–14, 520
Agnosticism, 259
Allport, Gordon W., 8, 9, 10–11, 12, 24, 224–25, 372–73
Amos, 485
Analogy, 141–42, 250–53, 375–91; of perfection, 428–31
Anselm, 274–84
Apologetics, 30
Appearance and Reality, 105–107
Argument and Conviction, 26–27
Aristotle, 67, 86, 93, 95, 96, 110, 167, 203, 271, 320
Art, 128–30
Astronomy, 171–72
Atheism, 12–16
Atomism, Greek, 55, 58
Augustine, 458, 496, 505

Baal, Religion of, 16–17
Baillie, John, 469–70
Barker, Ernest, 17
Barth, Karl, 83, 394–95
Behaviorism, 179
Belief, 13, 91, 92; and knowledge, 43–48; and faith, 73–76, 118–19
Bell, Clive, 13

Bennett, Charles A., 26, 39–40, 201, 226
Berdyaev, Nicolas, 38, 39
Berkeley, George, 290–93, 300
Bible, The, 397; The Old Testament, 16, 437, 469
Blake, William, 22
Blanshard, Brand, 83–84
Bosanquet, Bernard, 475
Bowman, A. A., 158, 159–61, 163–64, 527
Brahma, 229
Brennan, J. G., 318, 320, 337
Broad, C. D., 179
Brunner, Emil, 84
Bruno, Giordano, 168
Burckhardt, Jacob, 464–65, 510

Catherine of Genoa, 9
Causality, 326–27; and the natural sciences, 332–34; and mathematics, 333–34
Cause, 65, 328–32; and occasion, 181–85; and the Cause of Nature, 327, 334–36, 336–40
Change, 307–12, 326–27
Chapman, Harmon M., 296, 301
Chesterton, Gilbert, 372
Christ, 486
Christian (*See* Hebrew-Christian); theism, 447

Christianity, 135, 138, 140, 432, 469, 485–86

Christians, 14, 22

Cohen, Morris R., 62, 529

Communism, Marxist (*See also* Marxism), 246

Comte, Auguste, 13, 171, 220, 226, 530

Concepts, 38, 65, 69; univocal, equivocal, and analogical, 247–53, 381–82; and existence, 275–78, 362; how they can be used to think about God, 375–76; and judgments, 376–81

Conflict and Difference, 96–98, 107–108

Contingency, 303–22, 499; of the world order, 351–53; as showing the likeness of God, 374

Copernican Cosmology, 168

Cosmological Argument (*See also* God), 273

Cotton, James Harry, 77, 432

Creation, 230–31, 435–36, 437–39, 439–42, 452–55; and time, 346–48, 435–59

Credibility and Truth, 91

D'Arcy, M. C., 78, 191, 477–78

Death, 527

Deism, 241–47; relation to pantheism and theism, 247–51, 253–54, 345–46; as an equivocal concept of God, 249–50

Demos, Raphael, 443–44

Descartes, René, 66, 106; argument for the existence of God, 280–84

Destiny, 27, 29; history and human, 460–87; and freedom, 470–75

Determinism, 179

Dewey, John, 135–36, 519; conception of God, 220–26; on value, 419

DeWolf, L. Harold, 33

Dialectic, 268–72, 306–307

Difference (*See* Conflict and Difference)

Disraeli, Benjamin, 3

Divine, Father, 396–97

Dogma, 20–21

Doubt, 49, 150–53; and faith, 75, 78

Dryden, John, 243

Ecclesiastes, 521–22

Edwards, Jonathan, 288

Emanation, 230–31, 236–37

Emerson, Ralph Waldo, 18

Essence, 109; existence and, 251–53, 275–78, 363–68, 376–81; concepts and, 275–78, 363–68

Euripides, 20

Everett, John R., 230

Evidence, 44–50

Evil, 19, 488–14; and existence, 427–28, 488–94; natural and moral, 494–97; the inevitability of, 497–98; and the infinity of God, 498–500; and God's goodness, 504–507; the justification of, 507–14

Evolution, Creation and, 449, 451–52

Existence: knowledge of, 4; intelligibility of, 33–35; and

Existence—*cont.*
value, 86, 411–15; demonstration of, 114–15; and essence, 251–53, 363–68, 376–81; concepts and, 275–78, 363–68; of God, 341–58; of the world order, 356–58; how we think, 363–68; and time, 415–18; evil as the negation of, 427–28
Existentialism, 110, 260

Faith, 27–31, 73–79, 80, 82, 86; and reason, 37, 82–83; childish, 38; compared with belief and knowledge, 43, 73–76, 79–85, 118, 207–208; as a basis of action, 71, 79–85; guidance of, 85–86
Fanaticism, 79
Farmer, H. H., 495–96
Fascism, 471
Fate: history and, 466–70; Greek idea of, 481–82
Forms as Objects of Rational Insight, 61, 64–66
Francis of Assisi, 174
Frank, Erich, 96, 136, 165–66, 167, 170, 187, 437, 451, 463
Freedom, 178–80, 193–94; and determinism, 181–85; God and human, 458–59, 479–82, 501–504; and destiny, 472–75
Freeman, D. S., 405–406
Freud, Sigmund, 135

Galileo, Galilei, 168, 266–67, 400
Galle, Johann, 265
Garnett, A. Campbell, 204, 524
Garvie, A. E., 227–29

Garvin, Lucius, 181
Gibran, Kahlil, 513, 521
Gilson, Étienne, 66, 203, 244, 277, 283–84, 330, 339, 348, 364–65
God, 9, 11–15, 22, 27, 75, 82–83, 86, 116, 193, 200–207, 211–19, 250–51, 409, 446; religion as contact with, 127–28; problem of the existence of, 140–49, 150–53, 207–208; and nature, 160–61, 445–47; naturalism's idea of, 219–26; as Humanity, 220, 226; Dewey's conception of, 220–26; pantheistic idea of, 227–34, 249; Spinoza's conception of, 234–35; deistic idea of, 241–51; kinds of proofs of, 273; Anselm on, 274–80; ontological argument for, 274–80; Descartes on, 280–84; and conceptual thought, 282–283, 361–74; from the existence of the world to the existence of, 284–85, 287–358; not self-caused, 336–40; the unity of, 342–45; the immanence of, 345–50; and purpose, 351, 356–58; our knowledge about, 361–63, 370–74; knowledge by analogy, 375–91; revelation of, 392–410; the infinity of, 426–28; moral argument for, 431–32; as creator, 435–59; and miracle, 454–55; and time, 455–59, 463–64, 522; in history and human destiny, 460–67; and human freedom, 479–82, 501–504; presence in man, 523–26; presence of man to, 526–28

Good (*See also* Value), 19, 196–200; as transcendental, 387–88; the standard of, 425–26

Greek: and Hebrew concepts of creation, 437–39; thought, 469; concept of fate, 481–82; philosophy and infinity, 499–500

Green, Thomas Hill, 176–77

Hamilton, Edith, 189
Hardy, G. H., 62
Harris, Sydney, 5
Hartshorne, Charles, 136
Harvey, William, 357
Hawkins, D. J. B., 329–30, 351
Hebrew-Christian: ideas of man, 167–70; concept of creation, 230–31, 437–39; idea of miracle, 454–55; tradition, 485
Hebrews, The, 16, 373, 469
Hegel, G. F. W., 97, 236, 237
History, 27, 265, 460–87; the continuity of, 462–65; and fate, 466–70; and nature, 469–70; and progress, 475–78; the drama of, 482–87; Christian view of, 486–87
Hocking, W. E., 136
Humanism, 13, 142, 224–26
Hume, David, 66, 136, 162, 298, 300
Huxley, Julian, 13

Identity, Logical, 33, 61–62, 95, 237–40; knowledge requires, 384–85
Immanence of God, 345–50
Immortality, 515–17, 523
Implication, 44–45

Infinitesimals, 347–48
Infinite Series, 320–21
Infinity: of God, 426–28, 498–500; positive and negative, 500
Intelligibility: and unity, 216–19; and acosmic pantheism, 234–35; philosophy and the principle of, 33–35, 267–68
Irrationalism, 260
Isaiah, 81, 485
Isenberg, Arnold, 21
Islam, 16, 469

James, William, 174
Jesus, 13
Joad, C. E. M., 55, 57, 302
Job, 201, 373
Johnson, Samuel, 427
Joseph, H. W. B., 111
Judaism (*See also* Hebrew-Christian, Hebrews, The) 16, 135, 138
Judgments, The Relation of Concepts and, 376–81
Jünger, Ernst, 17

Kahler, M., 393
Kant, Immanuel, 273, 287, 338–40
Kierkegaard, S., 83
Knowledge: of existence, 4, 47, 275–78, 363–68; and belief, 43–48, 67; in relation to necessary and certain truth, 45, 66; rational and scientific, 45, 172–73; as founded on sense perception, 50–55, 67–68, 106; as founded on rational insight, 61–67; conditional character of, 66; as founded on practical

Knowledge—*cont.*
reason, 69–72; and faith, 73–79, 207–208; involves perspective, 105–106; and freedom, 178–80; not a cause, 184–85; of causes, our, 328–32; of the nature of God, the problem of our, 361–63, 370–74; of other selves, 368–70; requires identity, 384–85; by analogy, negative and positive, 389–91
Kruger, S. J. P., 174

Lamprecht, Sterling P., 219, 324–25
Lavine, Thelma Z., 119
Leibniz, G. W., 92
Leverrier, U. J. J., 265
Lippmann, Walter, 152
Locke, John, 299–300, 397–98
Logic, 32, 237–40
Logical Relations: as known by rational insight, 61; knowledge of as knowledge of being, 61–64
Logical Terms, 110–14
Love, 18; in the religion of Israel, 17
Lucretius, 136

Machiavelli, N., 9
Maimonides, M., 348
Man, 27, 28; traditional and modern ideas of, 157–58, 164–74; dual existence of, 175–78; freedom of, 178–80, 479–82; and his discovery of himself, 185–96; the moral nature of, 196–200; a religious answer to

Man—*cont.*
the problem of, 200–207; and his need of the idea of God, 212–16; as the image of God, 409; presence of God in, 523–26; presence of to God, 526–28
Maritain, Jacques, 411–12
Marxism, 13–14, 134, 142, 471
Mascall, E. L., 52, 241–42, 333, 334, 362–63, 372, 374, 377, 390, 429, 430, 447, 458–59
Mathematics, 62; relation to existence, 64; and causality, 333–34
McCall, R. J., 112
Meaning, 6; and intelligibility, 33–35; of logical terms, 111
Micah, 139, 485
Michelson-Morley Experiment, 60
Mill, John Stuart, 530
Milton, John, 81
Miracles, 454–55
Mithraism, 469
Monism, The Fallacy of, 237–40
Monotheism: development from polytheism to, 215–16; pantheism, deism, and theism as forms of, 218–19
Moral, 7; nature of man, the, 196–200; argument for the existence of God, the, 273, 431–32; and natural evil, 494–97
Mores and Religion, The, 91–92
Morgan, Charles, 79, 128, 197, 423
Moses, 81, 340
Murry, J. M., 13
Music, 18, 65

Mysticism and Theism, 229–31
Myth, 126–27, 217, 461; time and religious, 448

Nash, Arnold S., 29
Naturalism, 119–20, 324–25, 519; its confusion of essence and existence, 185; and its idea of God, 219–26; and theism, 253–54, 529–30
Nature: worship of, 13; God and, 160–61, 334–40, 435–59; distinguished from history, 469–70
Necessity (*See* Fate): destiny with freedom and, 472–75
Needham, Joseph, 13
Neo-Platonism (*See* Pantheism; Plotinus), 236–37
Nevius, W. N., 247–48
Newton, Isaac, 448–50
Niebuhr, Reinhold, 82, 126, 486
Nihilism, 15
Non-contradiction, Logical Principle of, 33

Obscurantism, 174
Occasion: distinction from cause, 181–85
Oman, John, 228–29, 243–44, 516
Ontological Argument, 273, 274–78; criticism of, 278–80; Kant's reduction of the cosmological to the, 339–40
Orton, W. A., 179, 186

Pantheism: cosmic and acosmic, 227–30, 237–40; distinguished from theism, 229–31; the argument for acosmic, 231–34; de-

Pantheism—*cont.*
struction of thought in acosmic, 234–35; the dilemma of, 235–37; relation to deism and theism, 247–51, 253–54; as a univocal concept of God, 249
Parmenides, 131, 269
Pascal, Blaise, 79
Paul, 23, 139–40, 142–43, 203–204, 496
Perception, Sense: and hallucination, 47, 52–53; as a foundation of knowledge, 50–55, 293–301; and sensation, 51; tests of, 51–55; as a source of error, 53; and modern science, 55–60; as test of truth in empirical science, 263, 304–305, 358
Perfection, The Analogy of, 428–31
Perry, Ralph Barton, 7–8
Person: the discovery of man as, 190–96; God as, 206–207
Perspectives of Truth, 102–105
Phenomenalism, 301–303
Philo, 437, 439
Philosophy, 4, 28, 31–35, 63–64, 264; of religion, 24–40, 394–95; and theology, 31–32; and the sciences, 32, 173, 263–68; and religion, 38–40, 118–21; and its premises, 263–68; and the method of dialectic, 268–72
Physics, 55–60, 171–72, 448–50; distinguished from philosophy, 56–60; provides no distinction between the real and the unreal, 60, 267

Plato, 67, 92, 131, 212, 217–18, 231, 268–71, 290, 324–25, 335, 337, 374, 424, 437, 445, 503

Platonic-Aristotelian Metaphysics, 167

Pleasure, 18, 22

Plotinus, 230, 337

Polytheism, 215–16

Positivism, 119–20, 260, 529–30

Possibility and Mathematics, 62

Potential and Actual, 307–18, 335–36, 411–32; in creation, 442–45

Pragmatism, 471, 473

Price, Lucien, 308–309

Progress, History and, 475–78

Proof, 44–45, 48–50, 259–63; and rational justification of belief, 120; in philosophy, 263–72; of the existence of God, steps of the argument, 285–86

Psychoanalysis, 205–206

Psychology, 171

Ptolemaic Astronomy, 167

Puritan, 7

Purpose, and action, 7; the world order and, 356–58

Pusey, Nathan M., 29, 78–79

Rational Insight: as a foundation of knowledge, 61–67; as the culmination of dialectic, 270

Rational System in Theology, 27–28

Rationalization, 30

Realism: and subjectivism, 291–301, 303–304; and phenomenalism, 302, 303

Reality, Appearance and, 105–107

Reason, 4–5, 45, 61–67, 172–73; in theology, 27–31; and meaning, 33–35; and faith, 37, 82–83; relation to sense, 67–68; practical, 69–72; in things, 71; revelation and, 394–98

Reichenbach, Hans, 293

Religion, 3–23; as escape, 10–11; and culture, 16; conflict between different kinds of, 17; cheapness in, 18; true and false, 19–23; primitive, 19; test of truth in, 20, 37, 133–40, 145–49; authority in, 20, 133–36, 396–98; philosophy of, 24–40, 394–95; truth of, 24–40, 118–53; and science, 24, 101, 104, 125, 173–74, 451–52; metaphysical pretensions of, 26; and theology, 27–31; as contact with reality, 36, 39–40, 96, 108–10, 113–17, 118–36, 138, 140–53, 398–403; difference between philosophy and, 38–40; and the problem of truth, 89–93; and the mores, 91–92; and myth, 126–27, 448; what it tells us, 130–33

Religious: and the secular, the, 158–64; answer to the problem of man, a, 200–207

Revelation, 392–410; and reason, 394–98; truth as, 400–403; degrees of, 403–10

Robinson, Richard, 269

Rosenberg, Bernard, 419

Russell, Bertrand, 63–64, 135–36, 347–48

Sanderson, Robert, 430
Satanism, 19
Schopenhauer, Arthur, 287
Schweitzer, Albert, 465
Science: and religion, 24, 101, 104, 125, 173–74, 451–52; sense perception and modern, 55–60, 358; as the product of the secular standpoint, 161; made possible by medieval theology, 161–62; as fundamentally anti-rationalistic, 162; as resting on faith, 162–63; incompleteness of, 172–73; philosophy and, 32, 173, 263–68; causality and, 332–34; laws of, as aspects of the world order, 354; and evidence of purpose in nature, 357–58; and its test of truth, 263, 304–305, 358, 470
Scientism, 174
Secular: modern life as, 24; the religious and the, 25, 158–64
Self, 25, 175–208; transformation by religion, 39; our knowledge of another, 368–70
Sense (See Perception, Sense): relation to reason, 67–68
Sertillanges, A. D., 429
Simpson, Cuthbert A., 438
Sin, 495–497; original, 482, 498
Sincerity and Truth, 90
Skepticism, 33, 66, 106, 150–53
Sociology, 171
Socrates, 13, 67, 268, 270
Sophists, The, 271

Sophocles, 20
Spencer, Herbert, 287
Spinoza, 212, 234–35, 236
Stephen, James Fitzjames, 131, 226
Strachan, J., 437–38
Streeter, B. H., 126–27
Subjectivism, 50, 57, 106, 201, 290–301; and phenomenalism, 302, 303; and realism, 291–301, 303–304
Sullivan, J. W. N., 173
Supernatural, The, 454
Supposition, 444; compared with extension and designation, 110–14

Teleological Argument, 273
Temple, William, 206–207, 393–94, 410, 503
Thales, 160
Theism, 152–53, 341–42, 447; and mysticism, 229–31; pantheism, deism, and, 229–31, 247–51, 253–54; and the analogy of being, 250–53; opposition to naturalism, 253–54, 529–30; its adequacy as a philosophy, 529–30
Theology, 27–31, 265; as aware of its assumptions, 28; distinguished from philosophy, 31–32
Thomas Aquinas, 271, 505–506
Thompson, Francis, 201
Time, 309–312, 346–48; existence and, 415–18; creation and, 346–48, 435–59; God and, 455–59, 522; and the eternal, 463

Tragedy, 81, 189, 498, 513–14
Transcendentals, The, 385–88
Truth, 5, 8, 13, 90, 93–96; religion and, 20, 89–93, 119–30, 133–49; unity of, 36, 96–97, 104–105; relation to belief, 43; doctrine of double, 76; and credibility, 86, 91; the whole truth and all the truth, 98–101; perspectives of, 102–105; versions of, 103–105; dimensions of, 107–109; existential and essential, 96, 108–110, 113–17, 120–21, 124, 138, 140–44, 398–400; religious and aesthetic, 128–30; test of, in the sciences, 55–60, 170–74, 263, 304–305, 358, 470; as a transcendental, 387–88; as revelation, 400–403
Turner, J. E., 207, 245–46

Universals, Platonic, 68
Unity: and intelligibility, 216–19; of God, 342–45
Urban, Wilbur Marshall, 35, 268–69, 412

Value, 8–10, 12–16, 23, 85–86, 116, 411–32, 504–14, 523–28; God and, 15–16, 426; differences in religions, 16–23, 38; as the primary concern of faith, 73; and existence, harmony of,

Value—cont.
86, 411–32; as revelation of God, 400–10; the reality of, 411–32; existence and, 411–15; the nature of, 418–23; and feeling, 419; and potentiality, 423–24
Veatch, Henry Babcock, 66, 288, 377, 378, 379
Vishnu, 230

Washington, George, 405–406
Wesley, John, 174
West, Rebecca, 193
Whichcote, Benjamin, 83
Whitehead, Alfred North, 9–10, 136, 161–62, 173–74, 302, 308–309, 348, 372, 416–17, 441–42, 463, 503, 514
Wild, John, 68, 107, 109, 178, 289, 295–96, 304, 447, 451, 501, 502–503
Will and Faith, 74
William of Occam, 471
Wilson, J. M., 13
World, The, 27; denial of the existence of, 287–302; contingency of, 303–22; order, 351–58

Young, Kimball, 91–92

Zeno of Elea, 269, 321